CHINA AND RUSSIA

CHINA AND RUSSIA

FOUR CENTURIES OF CONFLICT AND CONCORD

PHILIP SNOW

YALE UNIVERSITY PRESS
NEW HAVEN AND LONDON

For information about this and other Yale University Press publications, please contact:
U.S. Office: sales.press@yale.edu   yalebooks.com
Europe Office: sales@yaleup.co.uk   yalebooks.co.uk

Set in Minion Pro Regular by IDSUK (DataConnection) Ltd
Printed in Great Britain by TJ Books, Padstow, Cornwall

Library of Congress Control Number: 2022948973

ISBN 978-0-300-16665-1

A catalogue record for this book is available from the British Library.

10 9 8 7 6 5 4 3 2 1

FSC www.fsc.org MIX Paper from responsible sources FSC® C013056

For my children
Renata, Alexander and Isabella
and for my son-in-law
Pierce

CONTENTS

ILLUSTRATIONS AND MAPS

PLATES

MAPS

NOTE ON NAMES AND ROMANISATION

My object throughout has been to use those forms of Chinese and Russian names I felt would be most familiar to the ordinary Western reader.

PERSONAL NAMES

For Chinese names I have used the now standard *pinyin* system of romanisation, except in cases such as Sun Yat-sen and Chiang Kai-shek where a traditional spelling has been long established. Having made an exception in Chiang Kai-shek's case it seemed logical to make another one for his son Chiang Ching-kuo.

For Russian names I have followed the conventional US Library of Congress system, with some modifications where another form is in general use. I prefer Yuri to Iurii, Trotsky to Trotskii, Yeltsin to Eltsin. As in the Chinese case I have preserved one or two old spellings which have been hallowed by time, e.g. Tchaikovsky, Chaliapin.

PLACE NAMES

My preference has been to use those Chinese and Russian names that were current in the West *in the period under discussion*. For the greater part of the four centuries covered by this book the northern Chinese capital was known to the Western world as 'Peking' – until the summer of 1979, when the Chinese authorities decreed that it should from now on be universally rendered 'Beijing'. This was entirely logical in the sense that 'Beijing' is the correct pronunciation of the name in Mandarin Chinese. However to refer to 'Beijing' in a seventeenth- or nineteenth-century context, as many Western writers now do, seems to me to introduce a grating note of modernity: I have consequently retained 'Peking' for the first seven chapters of the book, switching over to 'Beijing' only in the final, contemporary chapter where the new form was wholly appropriate. I have used the same principle in naming the southern Chinese capital and the major city of Guangdong province, referring to these respectively as 'Nanking' and 'Canton' for the first seven chapters, as 'Nanjing' and 'Guangzhou' only in the eighth. In discussing the 1950s I have referred to the Nationalist-held islands in the Taiwan Straits by the names which were widely current for them at that time, 'Quemoy' and 'Matsu', rather than by the now standard but unfamiliar forms of Jinmen and Mazu.

In the Russian case similarly I have referred to the sometime capital as St Petersburg in Chapters 2 and 3, as Leningrad in Chapters 4 to 7 (the Soviet period) and as St Petersburg again in the post-Soviet Chapter 8.

Absolute consistency is impossible. I have for example ignored names that were current for some of these cities for relatively short periods, such as 'Petrograd' in Russia from 1914 to 1924 and 'Beiping' or 'Peip'ing' in China from 1928 to 1949, since to introduce these could only make for confusion. Certain other Chinese cities which I have alluded to by their modern *pinyin* names such as Tianjin and Xiamen could arguably have been left in their old spellings of 'Tientsin' and 'Amoy', but this seemed to me less essential than in the cases of Peking, Nanking and Canton. I only hope I have done enough to guide the reader and make the atmosphere of these chapters more authentic than it might otherwise be.

ACKNOWLEDGEMENTS

I very much doubt that I have remembered the names of all the people who helped me during the long gestation of this book. My most basic debt has to be to Professor Mark Elvin, under whose guidance I started to structure my inchoate thoughts about Sino-Russian relations long ago in the mid-1970s and to develop an outline chronology. In 2003 Professor Elizabeth Wishnick gave an inspiring talk on the subject during a visit to Hong Kong and unwittingly persuaded me that the time was approaching when I should have a shot at a Sino-Russian book. During the years of research I received welcome encouragement from Professor Odd Arne Westad, who helped me to arrange a useful visit to Moscow in the autumn of 2013 and enriched my work periodically with helpful insights and pieces of information. I was grateful too for the constant enthusiasm of Professor Robin Milner-Gulland, who first drew my attention to the Sino-Russian pidgin language that evolved at various times on the border between the two countries and to the Chinese-style buildings that were put up in St Petersburg during the reign of Catherine the Great.

Over the years a succession of friends and well-wishers provided me with important books, articles and document references, sometimes at my request and sometimes unsolicited and out of the blue. I remember with especial gratitude Fr Dionisy Pozdnyaev and Ms Irina Ustyugova, Professor Priscilla Roberts and Professor Victor Zatsepine, my friend and teacher Mr Tang Tien-chung and my old friend Robert Lloyd George. Professor Robert

Bickers of Bristol University alerted me to some illuminating studies in the Sino-Russian field which had been published by his former students. Professor Peter Cunich and his colleagues at the University of Hong Kong kindly accorded me the status of an Honorary Research Associate of their History Department, which enabled me to make full use of the university libraries and to attend some rewarding conferences and seminars. In Beijing I was also able to benefit from the insights of Melinda Liu, the veteran bureau chief of *Newsweek* magazine.

I am grateful as well to a number of friends who helped me gain access to various places and institutions which might otherwise have been beyond my reach. In Beijing Adam Williams and Hong Ying played a part in arranging for me to embark on a stint in the Foreign Ministry archives, and in Shanghai I was guided by Professor Zhang Zhiyun (Chihyun Chang) in approaching the Municipal Archives there. Back in 2006 Alan Babington-Smith negotiated for me a wide-ranging exploration of Heilongjiang province. I very much appreciated the help I received from the archivists in both the Chinese and Russian Foreign Ministries as well as the staff of the Moscow Historical Library.

Having said all this I must emphasise that my book is essentially a work of synthesis: covering four hundred years it could scarcely be anything else. A glance at the notes and bibliography will indicate how much I owe to the generations of scholars, Chinese, Russian and Western, who had dug deep in the different chronological slices of my four centuries long before I appeared on the scene. I can only repeat with even more insistence than usual the conventional statement that any errors of fact or interpretation in the book are entirely my own.

Throughout all these years I have counted myself extraordinarily lucky to be in the hands of Yale University Press. First Robert Baldock and more recently his successor Heather McCallum have shown the utmost patience and kindliness to an author who doesn't do speed, and I have never for one moment had the sense of a pistol pointed at my back. Rachael Lonsdale and Frazer Martin have steered me deftly through the production process, and Katie Urquhart has pointed the way to promising illustrations and helped me to make a sensible choice. Martin Brown has drawn half a dozen intricate maps, and Lucy Buchan, Meg Pettit and Michelle Tilling have directed my work on the proofs and the index. Warmest thanks to them all.

Special mention must be made here of the contribution of two very dear friends. Linden Lawson, who played a vital part in the production of both my two previous books, kindly agreed to undertake the copy-editing of this one. Minutely attentive to detail yet always sensitive to my style and idiosyncrasies, her work was quite simply beyond praise. She even recruited her son Laurence Mitchell, a graduate in Russian and German, to double-check the Russian titles in my bibliography. Dr Jannie Roed provided the tireless logistical back-up without which the book could never have been assembled in its final shape. I would also like to offer some particular words of gratitude to Dr Sarah Borwein, Ms Sara Chung, Ms Judith Gould, Dr Rebecca Lau and Dr Kenneth Ng. I frequently mentioned my book to them, and I'm sure that none of them thought I would ever complete it. Yet I have completed it, and the fact that I've done so is in no small part due to them.

Acknowledgements of this kind always seem to close with the author's expression of thanks to his or her family for their tolerance of the months and years of disruption the book has inflicted on family life. I can only echo this, and with the most heartfelt remorse: I am only too conscious of the many hours spent mulling over Sino-Russian matters which might have been spent with my wife and three children. But that isn't the half of it. The completion of my text still left me with a mass of ancillary tasks so enormous, and so complex from a technical point of view, that I couldn't possibly have dealt with them on my own. But this was where the family stepped in. My amazing daughter Renata somehow found time in the midst of a highly pressurised job to track down missing references for me, burrowing almost as deep into the sources as I had done myself and making a number of well-judged criticisms of my notes. Renata is living proof that to be a fine veterinary surgeon is not incompatible with also being a first-rate history scholar. My son-in-law Pierce took time off from a demanding schedule at Harvard Law School to check some of the more elusive references for me, a practice he continued after his return to Hong Kong. My wonderful wife Amanda has almost exhausted my range of superlatives. Not content with having read and commented on each of my chapters as I completed them, she plunged with titanic energy into the ancillary work. Nothing has been beyond her, from typing out quick-fire notes in three languages to converting my scrawls into legible sketch maps, to assembling presentations of images for my plate section and ensuring that even the most impossible-looking assignments could be broken down into manageable chunks. Yes, I completed the book, all right; but without the devoted work of Amanda, Renata and Pierce on the ancillary operations it could never have seen the light of day. Of the two younger children my son Alexander broadened my perspective with his shrewd observations about world affairs, while my daughter Isabella typed almost the whole of my index with the most marvellous speed and precision.

INTRODUCTION

Ever since they emerged from the rubble of the Second World War Western societies have looked with apprehension on either Russia, or China, or both. During the 1950s they were alarmed by the grand alliance between the two Communist giants – the greatest challenge to Western supremacy, in the judgement of one scholar, since the Ottoman armies sat at the gates of Vienna.[1] That alliance collapsed amid acrimony, but Western apprehension continued, with the main focus of dread shifting periodically from one to the other of the two former allies. For a few years following the Cuban Missile Crisis of 1962 the Soviet Union was viewed with a degree of indulgence as China plunged into the xenophobic frenzy of the Cultural Revolution. An optimist, it was said, was someone who learnt Russian; a pessimist someone who learnt Chinese. The Soviet Union's stock then plummeted with the invasion of Czechoslovakia in 1968, while in the early 1970s after the advent of 'ping-pong diplomacy' the West embarked on the long love affair with the People's China which lasted essentially up to the Tiananmen crackdown of 1989. The Soviet Union was now restored to relative favour after the coming of Gorbachev, and following his replacement by Yeltsin hopes remained high that the new, post-Soviet Russia would pursue a generally pro-Western course. Instead the new Russia chose to make common cause with its old Chinese enemy, quietly building up year by year a political, military and economic partnership which has long since outlasted the much vaunted alliance of the 1950s. The West was initially slow to react to this new phenomenon, but by the early 2010s Russia and China were habitually bracketed as the awkward squad in international diplomacy, and by the early 2020s the two powers – Russia still bristling with its Soviet nuclear arsenal, China incomparably richer than it had been half a century earlier and possessed of its own ever more high-tech armed forces and missiles – now posed a challenge that made comparisons with the Ottoman empire seem a distinct understatement. The two powers have now come to be perceived as a kind of Eurasian Mordor, not merely confronting the West on land and at sea, in Ukraine or the Taiwan Straits, but threatening the internal security of Western countries through infiltration and the latest techniques of espionage and cyberwarfare. Demonisation, however, is not in itself a constructive response to the threat, and the close embrace between China and Russia calls for a rather deeper analysis.

Over the years I have glimpsed some of the inner workings of these two great countries from an admittedly privileged vantage point. As a boy in the 1960s and early 1970s I accompanied my parents, the novelists C.P. Snow and Pamela Hansford Johnson, on visits they made to Russia as guests of the Soviet Writers' Union. This was not an exercise in 'fellow-travelling' but reflected a deep conviction of my parents that in the conditions of the Cold War it was vital to maintain some kind of a dialogue, to persuade each side that not everyone on the other side had horns and tails. In the course of these visits we met a wide range of Soviet literary figures, Sholokhov, Simonov, Tvardovsky, Yevtushenko, Aksyonov, to name just a few, from hardliners to liberals and eventual dissidents. We met one or two individuals we guessed to have murky pasts, and others who were good people by any standards. We found much common ground, and sometimes also fought our own corner in ding-dong arguments. Through these visits I also had the opportunity to travel to far-flung parts of the country, including Central Asia, Siberia and the Soviet Far East. I was sufficiently enthused by my experiences to embark on a Russian language course back at school in England. In the meantime however my attention was caught by that other great pariah nation, the People's Republic of China, which was just coming out of the shadows at the end of the Cultural Revolution and was evidently destined to play an increasing part in all of our lives. In my second year at Oxford, in 1972, I launched into a degree course in classical and modern Chinese, and for three years following my graduation, in 1976–9, I worked for the Sino-British Trade Council, escorting Chinese technical study groups around the United Kingdom and British trade missions venturing into remote parts of China. It was a wonderful opportunity to observe this immense land emerging from isolation and taking the first steps on its road to power and wealth. I remember the contrast between the nominal heads of the Chinese groups, Communist Party appointees to a man (no women!), monolingual and lacking any obvious knowledge of the technologies their delegations had come to research, and the veteran scientists who accompanied them, educated as often as not in the West before 1949, typically English-speaking and relaxed and sophisticated in their world view. I remember arriving by train one night with a British Rail mission in the obscure north-western city of Baoji to find the streets packed with thousands of people eager to observe the arrival of the first Europeans most of them had ever seen.

Given this background it was perhaps inevitable that my attention would focus at some point on the interaction between the two peoples. In 1973–4, in the midst of my Oxford Chinese course, I spent some months at a language centre at Nanyang University in Singapore with a view to improving my spoken Mandarin. At this centre I encountered a team of a dozen or so young Russians who were also there to learn Mandarin because in the current climate of extreme Sino-Soviet hostility they had no prospect whatever of admission to Beijing. This encounter left me curious about the whole history of contact between the two powers, and on my return to Oxford I got permission to take as part of my Final exams, under the supervision of Professor Mark Elvin, a paper of my own devising on 'Sino-Russian Relations from 1644 to the Present'. It was a first step towards an eventual book.

Conditions for researching a book about Sino-Russian relations at this time were far from ideal. The Sino-Soviet feud dragged on into the 1980s, and it was all too easy to get caught in the crossfire. On one occasion in 1980 when a Soviet correspondent came calling on my father in London I was injudicious enough to allude to some 'Chinese friends' of mine. I still remember the answering hiss of '*Your friends . . .!*'. Two years later I was in Zimbabwe researching a book about Chinese relations with Africa, and was given dinner by a husband and wife couple who ran the local branch of Xinhua, the New China News Agency. In the course of a relaxed conversation I talked quite freely about myself, my Chinese studies and the visits

I had made with my parents to the USSR. My last trip there, I recalled, had taken place in 1971. '*And when did you say you started learning Chinese?*' 'In 1972.' A pregnant pause. Happily this exchange took place shortly after Brezhnev's speech in Tashkent, when Chinese wariness of the Soviet Union had begun to abate slightly, and any dark suspicions the Xinhua couple may have harboured had no repercussions for me. At the start of the 1990s I began to think seriously about writing a Sino-Russian book, but the timing still seemed wrong. With the Soviet Union newly defunct and replaced by a shambolic new Russia the way ahead seemed too murky to attempt such an exercise. By the late 2000s, with the new Sino-Russian partnership moving steadily forward along broadly predictable lines, the time seemed at last to have come.

Soon after settling into my research I was told that no fewer than 1,200 books on Sino-Russian relations were to be found in the US Library of Congress. This was not, on the face of it, an encouraging revelation; but as I burrowed deeper into my sources a new perspective began to take shape. The subject can be divided into a number of chronological segments (eight by my reckoning), and each of these segments has been exhaustively studied by a legion of capable Chinese, Russian and Western scholars. What has been largely missing, in the English-language studies at any rate, has been an attempt to take a panoramic view of the entire four centuries of Sino-Russian contact and to tease out any patterns which might emerge from that vista. Two exceptions have been *China and Russia: The Great Game*, by a former US Foreign Service officer named O. Edmund Clubb, and *Sino-Russian Relations: A Short History*, by Rosemary Quested. But these works were published respectively in 1971 and 1984, and are long out of date. There seemed to me to be scope for an updated historical narrative, addressed primarily though not exclusively to the general reader, which would help to uncover the complexities underlying the current one-dimensional image of a Eurasian Mordor. The present book is the outcome of that calculation.

At the most obvious level I have sought to trace the shifts in the balance of Sino-Russian power. Which country has had the upper hand, when, and why? What political, economic and technological factors have led to these changes? Has conflict or cooperation been the dominant state of affairs?

What role has been played by third parties in pushing the two powers together or prising them apart? To what extent has Russia been able to steal a march on the West in its dealings with China, and how far has this been the result of sheer physical closeness? Why have the two countries tussled incessantly for control of the borderland regions between them yet have never taken the plunge into full-scale war? How far has ideology served to unite the two peoples and how far has it been trumped by the forces of nationalism? Which of the two states has typically shown itself more afraid of the other? Beyond these macro-questions I have also tried to examine the human fundamentals. How have Chinese and Russians surmounted the language barrier, and what part has been played in this process by intermediaries? What effort has each country made at different periods to build up a specialist knowledge of the other side? Does an unbridgeable gulf separate Orthodox Christian Russians and Chinese with their heritage of Confucian thought, or have there been signs of a mutual attraction among intellectuals and artists or in the domain of popular culture? What personal ties have been forged in the process of doing business or making revolution? Have the periodic displays of racial hostility been more or less characteristic than the occurrences of romance and intermarriage?

One final question which cries out for an answer is, naturally, how long will the current Sino-Russian partnership last? At the end of this book I have sketched out a number of possible scenarios; but the prospects are opaque, much depends on the rapidly changing Ukraine crisis and it would be a fool's game to venture any definite prediction. Insofar as this quasi-alliance presents a menacing face to the West it is only natural for Westerners to hope for a loosening of the current close ties. But no person of goodwill can surely wish to see these two peoples at each other's throats as they were in the near-Armageddon of 1969. Is it too much to hope for a placid relationship among all the key players which would enable us to join forces in combating the larger dangers which threaten our planet as a whole?

Philip Snow
Hong Kong
October 2022

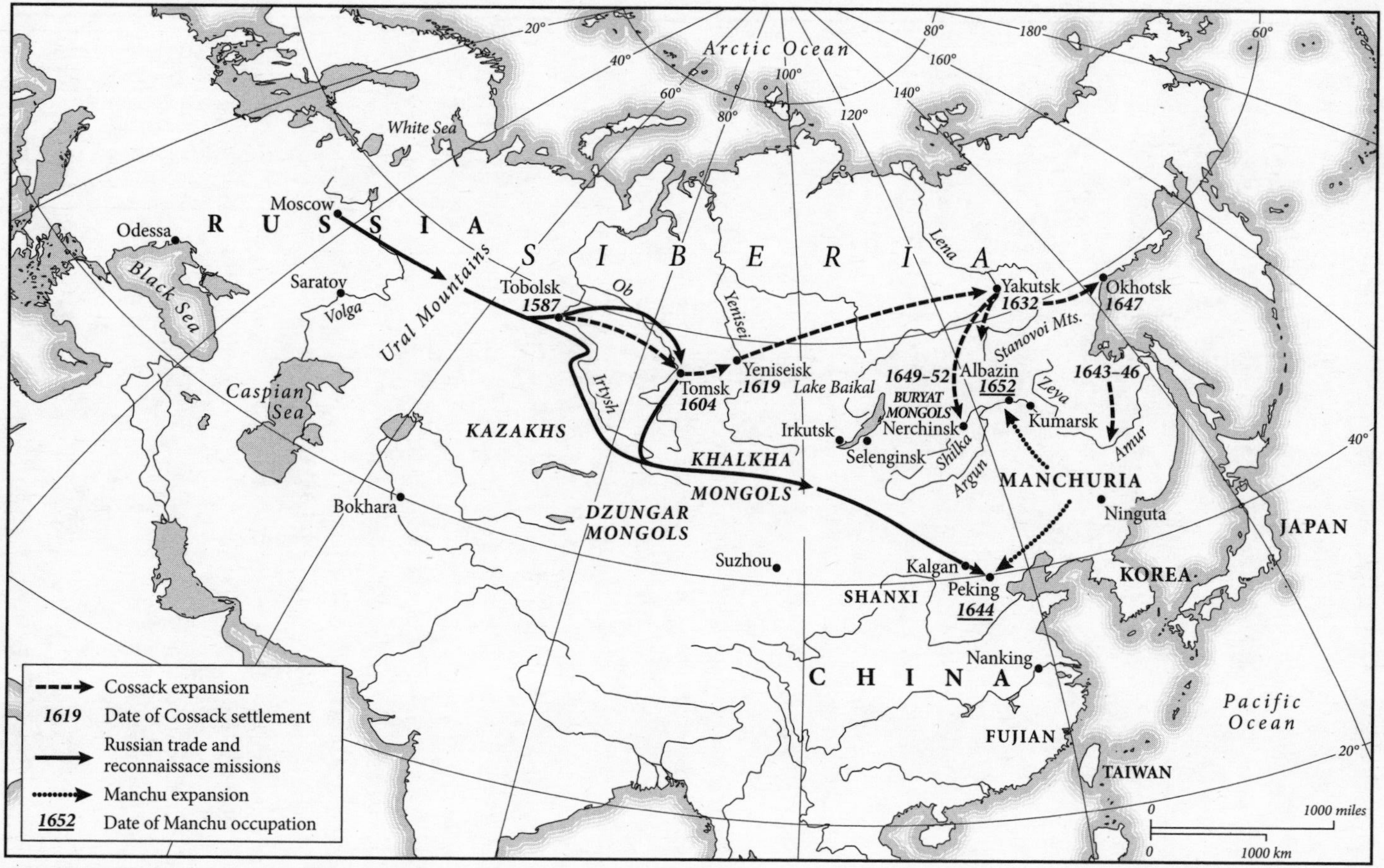

Map 1. Mid-seventeenth century: Collision course.

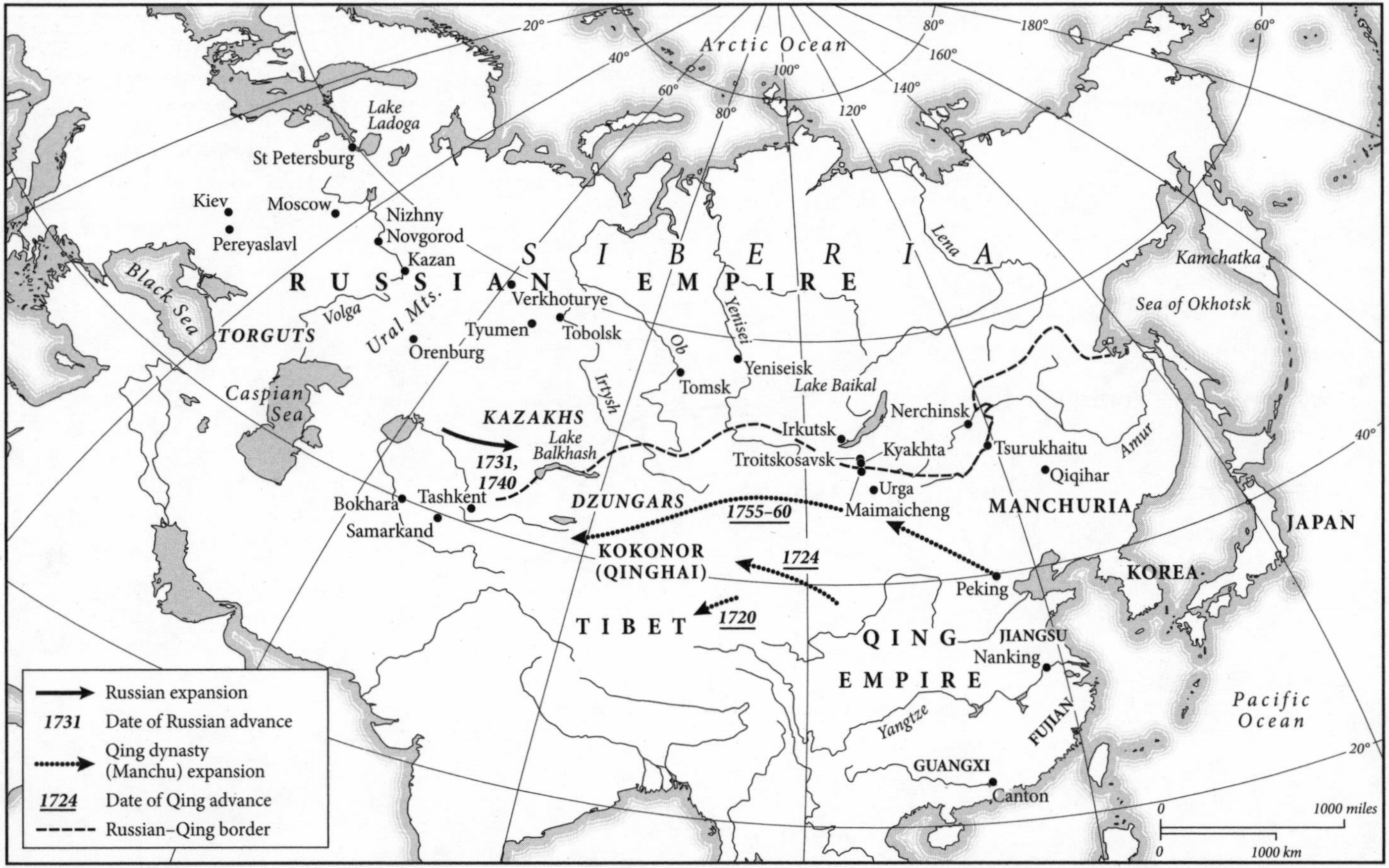

Map 2. Mid-eighteenth century: Russia and China 'moved towards each other until they divided all the territory between them'.

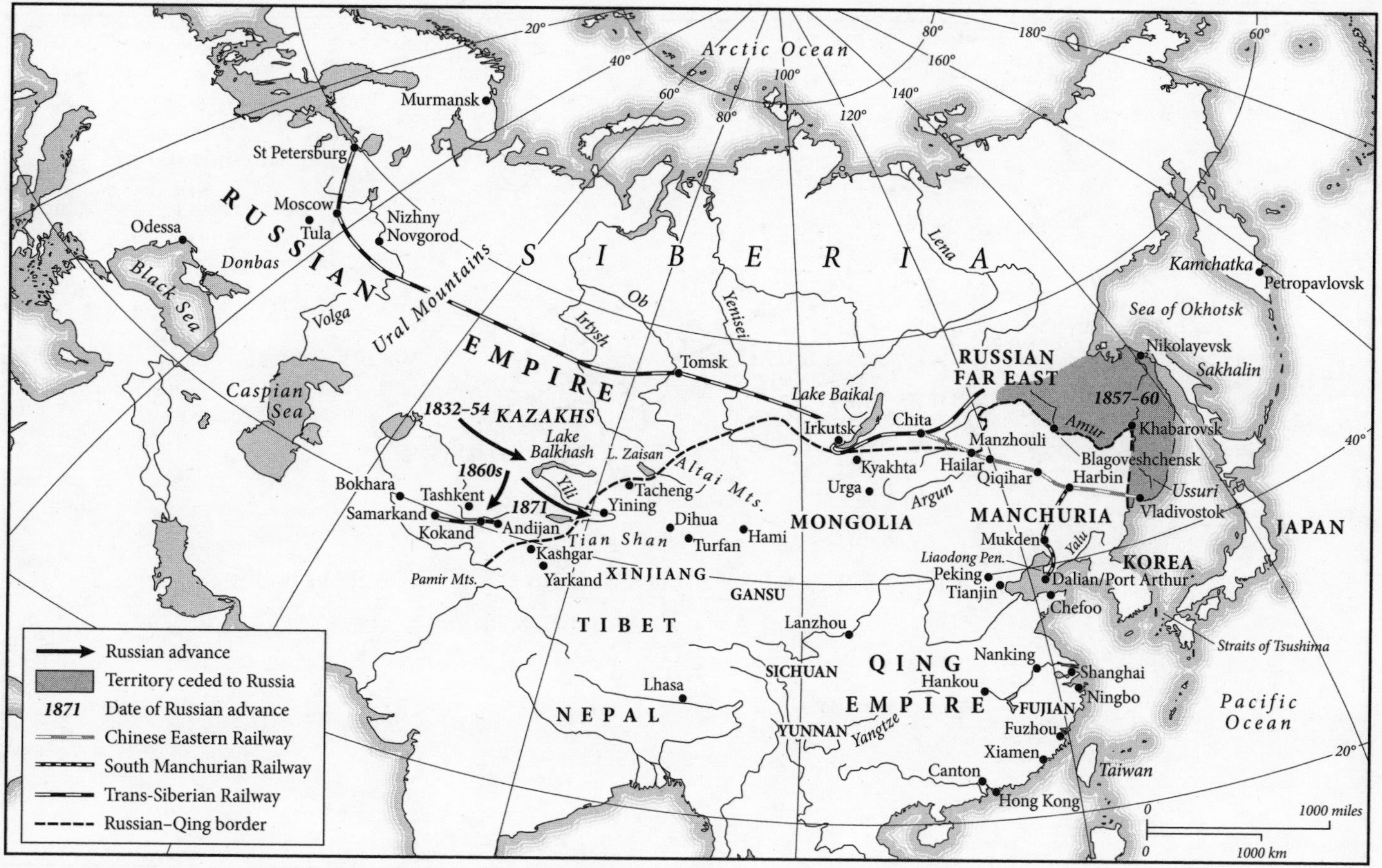

Map 3. Late nineteenth century: Russia breaks the bounds.

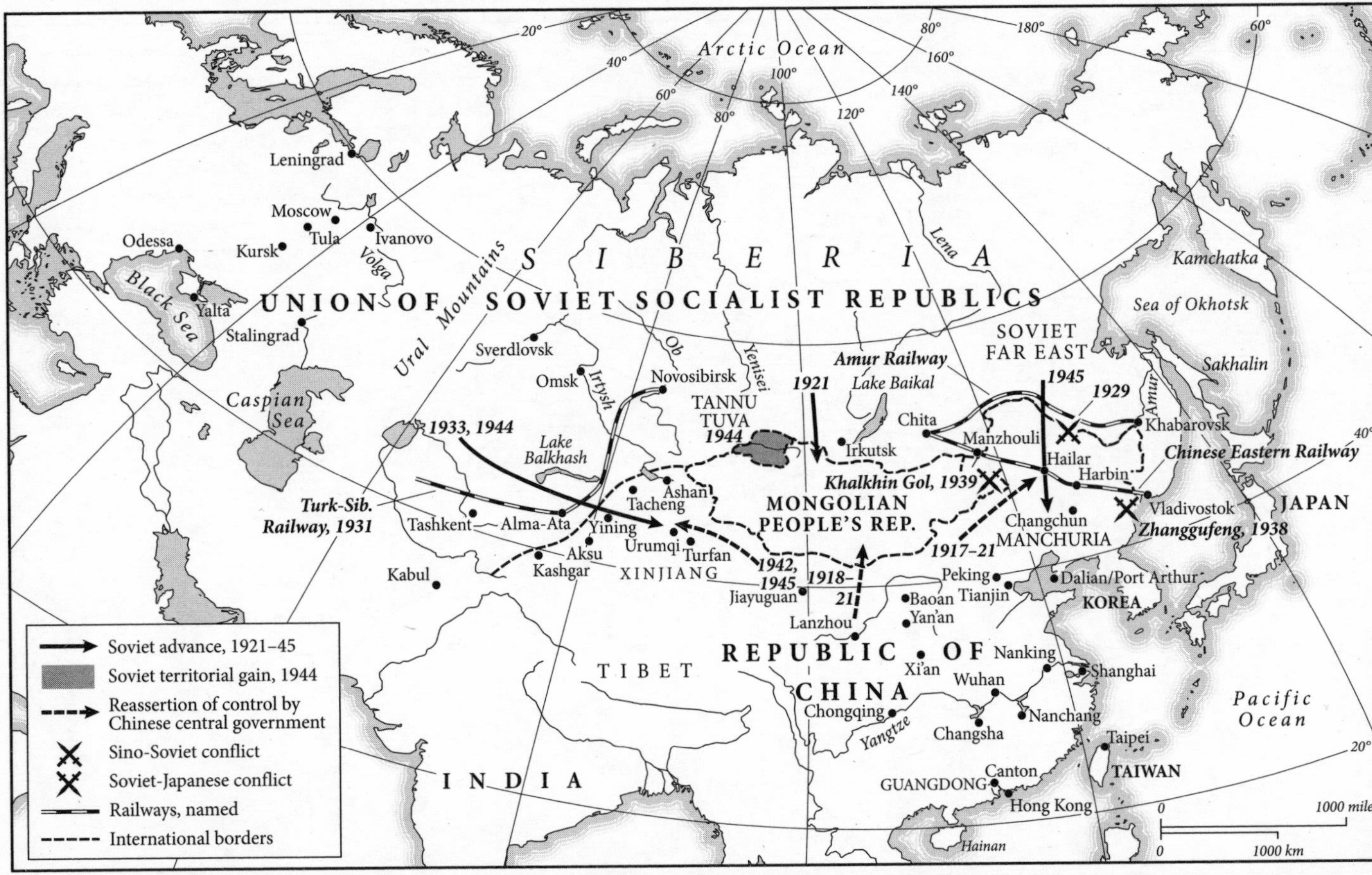

Map 4. Early to mid-twentieth century: War, revolution and the Sino-Soviet border.

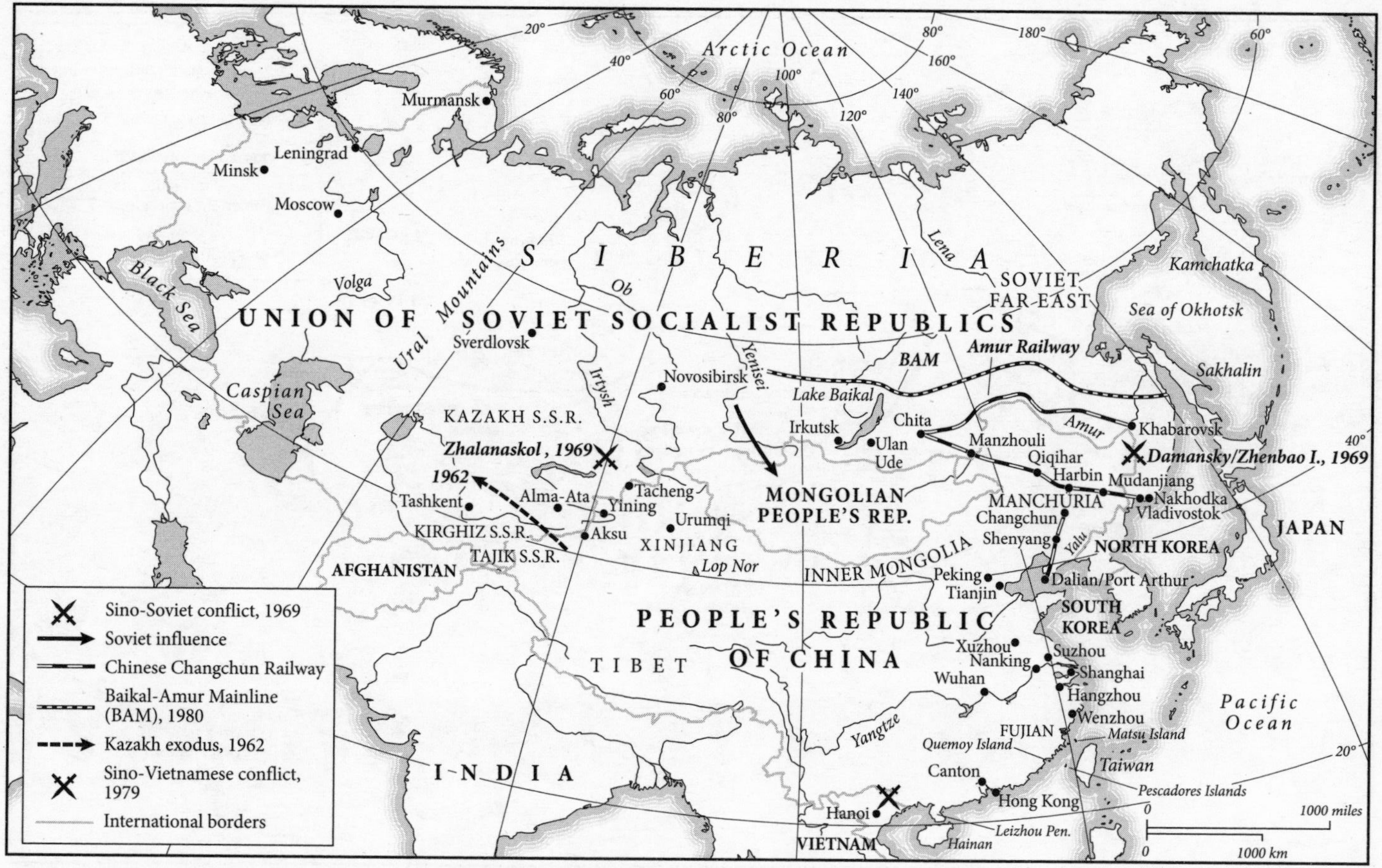

Map 5. Mid- to late twentieth century: From allies to enemies.

Map 6. Early twenty-first century: The Eurasian bloc.

CHAPTER 1

WORLDS IN COLLISION

In 1553 the explorer Richard Chancellor struggled ashore on the coast of the White Sea to make the first English landfall on Russian soil.[1] Invited to Moscow by Tsar Ivan the Terrible, he successfully opened a Russian market for English woollen cloth, and made his name as the pioneer of Anglo-Russian relations. But Russia had not in fact been the original object of Chancellor's journey. His main purpose had been to discover a North-east Passage that would provide access to the fabled riches of China. English interest had been piqued by the publication respectively in 1544 and 1549 in Denmark and Germany of two maps purporting to show the River Ob, westernmost of the great Siberian rivers, flowing out of a 'Lake Cathay'.[2] During a second visit to Russia in 1555, as representative of a newly formed Muscovy Company, Chancellor spent time closeted with the tsar in an effort to find out the details of this northern route; while a volume that appeared in the same year in England was entitled hopefully *On the North-east Frostie Seas and the Kingdoms Lying that Way*.[3] Chancellor's talks led to nothing, but the English kept up the pressure.[4] During the early years of the seventeenth century the merchant John Merrick, established by the Muscovy Company as their permanent agent in Moscow, bombarded the tsarist court with repeated requests for an English expedition to cross Russian territory in search of both the river and the supposed Chinese lake. In 1608 he submitted a first letter to this effect from King James I's government to the tsar, Vasily Shuisky. In 1612 he offered to mediate, in exchange for the hoped-for permission, in the current war between Russia and Sweden. And in 1617, 'bitterly acknowledging' his lack of progress so far,[5] he sweetened his proposal by tabling it in the form of a joint venture in which the English side would cover the costs.

The Muscovy that was being besieged by these English petitions was still a fairly rudimentary state. In 1460 it had emerged from nearly two hundred years of Mongol domination.[6] The rule of the Mongol Golden Horde had bequeathed to the Russians a legacy in the form of a few techniques of administration, a certain amount of vocabulary (including the words for treasury, money and customs) and the wearing of Central Asian skullcaps and kaftans, but also a psychological scarring and a deep horror of invasion from the east. Agriculture was poor. Law and scholarship were undeveloped. Bureaucracy was basic, with a crude foreign ministry, the *Posolsky prikaz*, emerging only in the mid-sixteenth century. And by the time Merrick started to press his demands the country was being convulsed by the mixture of civil conflict and Polish and Swedish invasion remembered as the Time of Troubles. Still, the Russians were already showing some evidence of their future vigour. By the late fifteenth century they were beginning to push their frontiers eastwards, largely, it seems, to fend off the prospect of any further Mongol assaults. In 1483 and 1499 their reconnaissances had reached as far as the Ob – hence the awareness of that river which had filtered through to the Danish and German cartographers. A century later the Cossacks, a caste of fugitive peasants and freebooters who made their homes on the frontiers and served as the spearhead of the Russian advance, were establishing their first permanent footholds in Siberia, drawn by the lure of the 'soft gold', the fur of the sables, martens, arctic foxes and other creatures that teemed in the Siberian forests. In 1579 the Cossack Yermak Timofeevich, sponsored by the Stroganov brothers, merchants who in turn had the tacit consent of Tsar Ivan the Terrible, crossed the Ural mountains with an armed band, and in 1582 he attacked and eliminated the neighbouring Tatar kingdom of Sibir. Over the next quarter-century the Cossacks went on to found the two major townships of western Siberia – Tobolsk in 1587 and Tomsk in 1604.

But where China was concerned, the Russian endeavour seemed oddly sluggish by comparison with that of the English and other western Europeans. At the height of the Eurasian empire which the Mongols created in the thirteenth century, in the Great Khan's capital of Karakorum, Russian goldsmiths had rubbed shoulders with Chinese artisans. A fourteenth-century Russian chronicler referred to China as another country subdued by the Mongols, and Russian linguistic borrowings from the Mongols included their name for China, *Kitai*.[7] Archaeologists have discovered near the town of Saratov on the Volga evidence for at least some degree of indirect trading in the form of a flowered brocade Chinese gown and a quantity of decorated Chinese bronze mirrors from the time of the Golden Horde.[8] But little if any of this early contact seems to have lingered in the collective memory of post-Mongol Russia. Popular knowledge of China appears to have been limited to a vague notion of a distant Oriental realm. A fairy tale entitled *Ivan Bogatyr, the Peasant's Son* tells of a youth who rides 'to the land of Kitai' in thirty days and thirty nights. There he meets the three daughters of the Chinese 'tsar', Duaza, Spasa and Laota, and falls in love with the youngest, Laota. He defends China from the attacks of the marauding army of Polkan, and eventually wins both the hand of Laota and the Chinese throne.[9] Any interest in trading with China seems to have been of a distinctly passive kind. Occasional Russian traders made their way to the markets of Samarkand and other cities of Central Asia, where they haggled alongside their Chinese counterparts; but none of them was apparently tempted to follow the Chinese to their point of origin. In 1466–72 a particularly enterprising merchant named Afanasy Nikitin penetrated as far as India, but contented himself with referring in his account of the journey to a country called China which could be reached from India by land in six months and by sea in four days (*sic*). 'There they make porcelain, and their goods are all very cheap.'[10] In 1582, the year Yermak conquered Sibir, Ivan the Terrible planned to move matters forward by sending a group to Siberia to investigate the possible opening of a trade route to China; but the project was abandoned when Ivan died in March 1584.

Merrick's pressures, however, spurred the Moscow government into belated action. Sluggish though they had been up till now, the Russians were quite clear that they didn't want interlopers from England monopolising their transit trade and possibly even threatening their precarious settlements in western Siberia. Already in 1608, in the thick of the Time of Troubles, Tsar Vasily Shuisky reacted to Merrick's first overture by instructing the governor of the new township of Tomsk to send out a reconnaissance mission to gather information on China for Russia's benefit from the nearest

Mongol chief. No longer a united empire, the Mongols were divided into two main warring branches, the Dzungars and the Khalkhas, and the Russian mission was directed to a Khalkha ruler, the Altyn Khan ('Golden Prince'), who at this time held sway in north-western Mongolia. The Russian mission arrived to discover that the Altyn Khan had been put to flight by his Dzungar enemies, and the expedition was given up. By 1616 the Time of Troubles was over, the Russian throne was occupied by the youthful Tsar Michael, first sovereign of the Romanov dynasty, and Moscow was ready for a more determined reconnaissance. Two fresh deputations were now sent off, this time from Tobolsk. A mission to the Dzungars came back with reports of a land to the east with 'stone-built walls' and a city it took ten days to ride round, full of temples and a mighty ringing of bells. Corn grew plentifully, and the people possessed an abundance of satins and velvets, gold and silver. Their domain was protected by muskets and cannon and frequented by big sailing ships.[11] Emissaries to the Altyn Khan were told similarly of a land with a 'brick wall' around it, and given Chinese silk and a first taste of tea.[12] The Altyn Khan was delighted to offer his Russian neighbours access to the China trade in return for supplies of firearms and furs, and he even sent two envoys back with the reconnaissance party to Moscow, where in 1617 Merrick, newly returned from fulfilling his promise to fix up a peace settlement between Russia and Sweden, was amazed and no doubt disconcerted to run into them at a banquet given by the tsar.

The Council of Boyars advising Tsar Michael now felt in a position to see off the English challenge. They kept a long-standing promise to hold a negotiation with Merrick about his China scheme, but their answer was a definitive no. They were not prepared to allow English traders to search for the Ob, not even in the context of a joint Anglo-Russian endeavour, though they did kindly offer to ask their Siberian governors to collect information about the river on Merrick's behalf. They tried their best to persuade Merrick of the impossibility of going to China. In any case, they observed, there was no point in going there since the country was a poor one. It was, furthermore, surrounded by a brick wall, 'and therefore it can be known that the place is not large.'[13]

In the meantime they hurriedly set about launching a China expedition of their own.

On 9 May 1618, a twelve-man exploratory party set out from Tomsk under the leadership of Ivan Petlin ('Ivashko', as he is often referred to in the casual style of the period), a Cossack who served as a government clerk and seems to have had some knowledge of the Mongolian language. Escorted by two Buddhist lamas supplied to them by the Altyn Khan, Petlin's group made their way on horseback across the Mongolian steppe until they encountered 'a wall built of stone about fifteen *sazhens* high'. They followed this wall for ten days before turning south, and eventually arrived in Peking in early September. The report written by Petlin after his return to Russia was suffused with awe at the glimpse of another civilisation more advanced and prosperous than his own. Coming from a land where the buildings were almost all wooden, he was fascinated above all by the Chinese use of masonry, and his record was full of allusions to Chinese stone and brick. Peking, for example, had 'streets paved with grey stone' and 'stone shops' with 'brick dwellings over the shops'; and the other cities he passed were all 'stone-walled'. He was not quite prepared to concede explicitly the superiority of Chinese cities to Russian ones, but he observed that the border town of Kalgan was 'good, a fine affair, and the towers are as high as those of Moscow'. Chinese markets were bursting not merely with velvets, damasks and silks, but with melons and watermelons, cucumbers, garlic, radishes, onions, turnips, cabbages, parsnips, horseradish, rhubarb 'and other fruits and vegetables such as we know not'; and when you walked along the shop rows in Huailai you smelt 'a fragrance of cooking that seems to have come from Heaven'. The inhabitants came and went in crowds, 'like flies going to and fro', but the people of both sexes in China were 'clean'. Petlin's chief reservation related to the temples, to his Orthodox Christian eyes crammed with idols – 'as in Mongolia', he lamented, 'they frighten you!'. But he was also struck to note that the Chinese 'let anyone in to look at the temples'. Petlin's group were received by officials of the reigning Ming dynasty and installed in a cavernous hostel which the Ming government used to accommodate foreign missions.[14]

Ming China, like Muscovy, had emerged from the shadow of Mongol power. The rule of the Yuan (Mongol) dynasty over China from 1279 to 1368 had been nearly a century shorter than the Golden Horde's overlordship of Russia, and partly for this reason the Chinese seem to have been somewhat less traumatised in the long run than the Russians were by the 'Mongol yoke'. But the Ming proved quite as fearful of a northern as the Russians were of an eastern attack. In 1420 they transferred the capital from Nanking in the south to Peking, the old Mongol capital of Khanbalik, in order to be close to the northern frontier; and they looked on the various peoples to the north of them without distinction as unreasoning beasts. In their earlier decades they had shown immense energy, pushing the overthrown Mongols all the way back to their homeland and sending their fleet far and wide across the oceans: by the time Petlin arrived, however, they had settled into a long-term decline. The Wanli emperor was a monarch so indolent that in the last thirty years he had received his grand secretaries exactly five times, had performed no public ceremonies and hadn't even turned out for his own mother's funeral.[15] Petlin gleaned in the course of his stay that in China the people were 'timid'. They were 'good at doing business but afraid of fighting battles',[16] even though they were obliged to fight battles occasionally against a new coalition of tribes that had gathered on their north-eastern border – the Manchus.

Unlike the Russians, the Ming court possessed in their archives a short but clear record of Sino-Russian encounters in the Mongol heyday. In their history of the Yuan dynasty, compiled according to custom by the dynasty following, a series of entries for the early 1330s refer to a people called the *Woluosi* who formed a regiment of the imperial guard at Khanbalik and were renowned for their loyalty. In 1330 they were granted a parcel of land to the north of the capital where they could hunt and grow crops. In 1331 600 new troops were added to the Woluosi regiment, and in 1332 further groups of 1,000 and 1,500 Woluosi were presented to the khan by his vassal lords and were allotted clothing and corn.[17] The generally accepted explanation of Woluosi as meaning 'Rus' is supported by a fourteenth-century map in which a land of *Eluosi* is located on the north-western fringe of the Mongol empire.[18] As with the Russians, however, so with the Chinese: there is little sign that any public memory of these early encounters survived when contact was renewed in the seventeenth century. The Woluosi imperial guards disappear from the record, either swallowed up in the Chinese population or carried north by their retreating Mongol masters. In 1537–8 a Portuguese, Mendes Pinto, who claimed to have travelled in China, reported seeing Russian servants employed by Mongols in the northern province of Shanxi.[19]

Four days into their sojourn Petlin and his party were visited in their hostel by officials of the Board of Rites, the Ming government organ responsible for ceremonial matters. Petlin hoped for an audience with the emperor, but unfortunately failed to pass the first test of Chinese protocol. He brought no presents and no diplomatic credentials. The Ming officials coaxed him to produce 'some trifle', but he had brought nothing whatsoever so nothing could be done.[20] The officials, however, did let the party stay for a month, and made some attempt to reply to the questions which Petlin put to them. No, they knew nothing of a River Ob, but they did know of foreign people who came to their empire by sea – a perhaps unwelcome disclosure for the Russians of the competition that would be likely to threaten them from maritime trading powers such as Portugal and Holland.[21] And they issued Petlin with a letter for Tsar Michael from the emperor; a letter no doubt written on behalf of Wanli, rather than composed personally by that imperial dropout. The letter expressed no particular appetite for more contact ('our sovereign sends no envoys to you because your sovereign has all sorts of things and ours has them too'), and certainly no desire to take the initiative ('by my custom, O Tsar, I neither leave my own kingdom nor allow my ambassadors and merchants to do so'). Michael was nonetheless invited to 'bring the best you have, and I in return will make you presents of good silk-stuffs'.[22] The problem was that the letter was written in Chinese. When Petlin arrived in Moscow to report to the government he discovered that no one was able to decipher the communication; and in Moscow it languished for the next several decades. It is possibly no coincidence that 'a Chinese document' (*kitaiskaya gramota*) is the Russian expression for double-Dutch.[23]

And there, for the moment, Russian government activity ground to a halt. In 1620, soon after Petlin's return, the authorities issued an edict decreeing that no one should engage in any further dealings with China, or with the Altyn Khan for that matter, without their consent. It seems likely that they simply failed to see any commercial advantage in taking matters further. The distances involved were immense. To get from Moscow to Peking entailed a journey of nearly 5,000 miles across trackless forest, grassland and desert. In reaching Peking in five months Petlin had made remarkably good time; but then he had started from Tomsk, already halfway there, and had not been encumbered by any baggage. A fully equipped expedition from Moscow to Peking was going to take something more like a year and a half. In view of the language barrier, any contact that could be arranged was bound to be wholly dependent on middlemen, which at this stage meant either the Dzungar or Khalkha Mongols; and the Mongols were as likely to rob Russian travellers as to escort or interpret for them. Even if the language barrier could be surmounted any dialogue would be hard to maintain: the time lag was so great that any message sent from one side to the other was liable to be outstripped by events on the ground. As the years passed, too, word seeped through of growing turmoil in both Mongolia and China. In 1635 a venturesome boyar of Tomsk sought permission to go to Peking, but was promptly slapped down.

In the meantime, however, the pace was being set by the Cossack frontiersmen. Pushing ahead at a staggering rate from western into eastern Siberia, taking boats eastwards along the tributaries of the great northward-flowing rivers, negotiating portages from one tributary to another, putting up wooden stockades (*ostrog*s) at strategic river junctions or in mountain passes, raising tribute in furs (*yasak*) from the Tungus forest tribes and moving on when the fur supplies were exhausted,[24] they organised a long string of rudimentary bases and ran affairs as they saw fit until officials from Moscow could move in to enforce control and levy tithes on their furs. It is impossible not to be reminded of the pioneers of the American West two centuries later. By 1619 the Cossacks had founded Yeniseisk, on the River Yenisei; by 1632 Yakutsk, on the River Lena; and by 1647 they had reached Okhotsk on the Pacific, giving Russia an outlet on that distant ocean before it had got through to either the Baltic or the Black Sea. In advancing first to Yeniseisk and then to Yakutsk they had, however, executed a curious veering to the north. A more obvious route would have led them south-east around the southern fringe of Lake Baikal; but it seems they met a degree of resistance from the Buryat Mongol tribes in that area, and the northern forest peoples were easier to deal with. The result was that in reaching Yakutsk, where they made their headquarters for eastern Siberia, they had landed themselves in a region of sub-arctic tundra where food was scarce. By the early 1640s the settlers in Yakutsk were listening to tales spread by the local Tungus of *another* river, southwards across the mountains, where corn was abundant and silver, copper and lead could be had. In June 1643 a Cossack named Vasily Poyarkov set out from Yakutsk with a band of 150 men, and by autumn he had reached the River Amur, where he found broad valleys, fertile fields and large quantities of sables and fish. Like Brigham Young he determined that this was the place, proclaiming triumphantly that 'the warriors of the Sovereign will not go hungry in this land'.[25] Unfortunately, he spoke too soon. Brutalised possibly by years of intense cold and scarcity, the Cossacks treated the local Daur and Dyucher villagers with exceptional violence, alienating the very people who might have supplied them with food. By the winter they were in the grip of a severe famine, in the course of which they are said to have killed and eaten about fifty Dyuchers.[26] Poyarkov continued his reconnaissance in 1644–5, pressing on all the way to the mouth of the Amur – the only Siberian river that flows east to the Pacific. In June 1645 he limped back to Yakutsk, having lost 130 of his 150 men to disease, cold and malnutrition but confident nonetheless that Russia would be able to occupy the entire Amur basin with no more than 300 well-armed troops. His mission was taken up by a wealthy resident of Yakutsk, Yerofei Khabarov, who in 1649 led a first serious Russian effort at settling the Amur. In 1650 Khabarov moved into a village belonging to the Daur prince Albaza at the confluence of the Amur's two main tributaries, evicted Albaza and his people and set up an advance base that he called Albazin. Khabarov, like Poyarkov, applied his own drastic techniques to impose Russian rule. 'With God's help', he reported of a conflict the following year, 'we cut them all down, head by head . . . big and little we killed 661.'[27] Western readers should not feel too smug at this chronicle of Cossack ferocity – after all, the pioneers of the Old West weren't entirely gentle in their treatment of the Native Americans.

But at this point the Cossacks ran up against a problem which the pioneers of the Old West would never experience. They found their path blocked by another power more formidable than their own. Even before Poyarkov set off on his reconnaissance trip he had learnt from the Tungus that the silver and other minerals to be found along the Amur were brought there from a wealthy land to the south of the river by 'great ships with many masts and guns'.[28] Confronted in 1650 by Khabarov's demand for immediate payment of *yasak*, the Daur villagers told him, 'We give *yasak* to the Bogdoi Khan ['Sacred Lord']: what is your claim to *yasak* over us?'[29]

The Cossacks were about to collide with the northernmost outposts of the newly formed Manchu empire. In 1644, as Poyarkov made his way down the Amur, the Manchus had finally burst from their forests south-west into China and captured Peking. The enfeebled regime of the Ming had already been brought down by domestic rebellion, and the Manchus were quick to replace it with their own Qing dynasty. Unlike their Ming predecessors, the new Manchu rulers of China were not battle-shy. They deployed a highly mobile cavalry force and possessed guns and cannon. And they were aiming to dominate not merely China but also the empty lands to their immediate north. Their original base had been limited to the central and southern parts of geographical Manchuria, but they were beginning to push into northern Manchuria, which included the valley of the Amur.

At this juncture there was, as it happened, no outside authority in control of the valley. The Chinese had, however, made their presence felt there sporadically for a good many centuries. One of the great naval squadrons that the Ming had sent out in their early, vigorous period had made landfall in 1413 at the mouth of the Black Dragon River (Heilongjiang), as the Chinese called the Amur, and had put up there a Temple of Eternal Harmony.[30] The Cossacks themselves had caught sight of a bell and some stone monuments left behind by the Ming at this period, though they were inclined to attribute such relics to a visit by Alexander the Great.[31] The early Ming rulers had also drawn the Tungus tribes of the region into their tribute-paying network, and it was this tribute relationship that the Manchus now proposed to restore. Already in the 1630s, before they embarked on the conquest of China, they had received recognition of their suzerainty from a number of tribes, in particular the Daurs, the Dyuchers and the Maoming'an.

Faced with a choice between the Qing dynasty, who at least sweetened their demands for tribute by conferring titles and gifts of brocade, and the Cossacks, who simply grabbed it, the Tungus chiefs were inclined to side with the devil they knew. By 1651 they were calling for Qing protection. The Qing learnt that their north-eastern border was being disturbed by intruders, whose name was, presumably on account of their reported cannibalism, transcribed in the Chinese records as *Luocha*, i.e. *Raksha*, the Sanskrit term used by Buddhists for flesh-eating demons. The dynasty took urgent steps to consolidate their still flimsy power in the area. A fortress was built at Ninguta, a Qing outpost 240 miles to the south of the river, and an initial force of 1,000 troops was sent there. In June 1651 the collision at last took place when Khabarov, battling the Daurs, was confronted by a party of fifty Manchu horsemen who had been ordered to gather tribute from them. The Qing party cautiously opted to sit the battle out. On the following day they sent envoys who talked at great length to the Cossacks, presumably in an effort to persuade them to withdraw. None of the Cossacks, however, understood a word of Manchu, and the meeting broke up amid mutual incomprehension.

The Qing now resorted to sterner tactics. Early in the morning of 26 March 1652, Russia and China came to blows for the first time as a force of 600 Manchu troops under General Haisai, supported by 1,500 Daurs and Dyuchers and equipped with six cannon, thirty arquebuses and twelve clay gunpowder shells, stormed the Cossack stockade of Achansk. Heavily outnumbered, the Cossacks beat off their assailants with the help of one large bronze cannon and a certain amount of sheer grit ('We will never give ourselves alive into the hands of the Bogdoi people!').[32] Considerably shaken by the setback, the Qing court began to deploy a wide range of resources. They requested the vassal king of Korea to send musketeers to reinforce the Ninguta garrison. They adopted a scorched earth policy, instructing the Daurs and Dyuchers to abandon their fields and move south to deny the Russians access to their crops. Little by little the superior Qing numbers and tactics began to tell. In June 1654 Khabarov's successor, Onufri Stepanov, head of a now sharply reduced band of 500 men, was ambushed and forced to retreat by a larger Qing host. During the following winter the Cossacks scored one more success, beating off a 10,000-strong Qing army from the stockade of Kumarsk; but from then on it was downhill all the way. 'The Bogdoi forces', Stepanov lamented, 'are hard by us, and we have nothing with which to stand and fight the Bogdoi, not the least gunpowder or lead.'[33] On 30 June 1658 another Qing general, Sarhuda, wiped out the bulk of Stepanov's remaining 200–300 men near the confluence of the Amur with a southward-flowing tributary, the Sungari. Stepanov himself was stabbed to death and his body flung in the river.[34] During the following year the Qing forces destroyed the Cossack forward base at Albazin, and in August 1660 the Qing displayed their prowess on the waterways when two of their warships cornered a Russian boat. 'More than sixty of the bandits were beheaded and numerous others were drowned.'[35] The Russians had for the moment been cleared out wholesale from the Amur basin.

Each of the combatants seems to have been aware of having come up against an opponent of unexpected toughness. During the first engagement at Achansk, Haisai's troops were under orders not to kill the Cossacks but to try to take them alive – presumably to find out more about them. The Qing authorities are said to have been impressed by the valour of 'that tribe who use the dog sleds',[36] and the transfer south of the Daurs and Dyuchers may have been motivated in part by fear of the influence which the Cossacks might be able to wield over them.[37] But it was the Russians who showed the clearer signs of shock. They simply didn't have the troops. Frantsbekov, the governor of Yakutsk, talked of sending 6,000 men to the region, but no such force was available in the whole of Siberia. The Moscow government planned to dispatch a 3,000-strong army, but no concrete action was taken. Instead, instructions were issued to the Amur Cossacks urging them to desist from raiding and robbing the indigenous Tungus tribes, and warning them to avoid further conflict with the Qing.

This Russian restraint, however, wasn't simply dictated by a sense of weakness. The fact was that Moscow had bigger fish to fry. The court had got wind, through the usual Mongol intermediaries, of the fall of the Ming dynasty, the accession of the Qing and the return of stability to Mongolia and China. The door was open for trade, and the Russian government, for a range of broad economic reasons, now wanted trade badly. By the mid-seventeenth century the demand for Siberian furs on the western European markets was starting to fall as rival fur supplies were imported from North America. A glut of furs was accumulating in the treasury, which the government needed to exchange for gold, silver and other forms of ready cash that would help them sustain the current wars against Poland and Sweden; and China looked like an obvious substitute market. A lively private traffic had already grown up at Tobolsk in western Siberia, where another set of middlemen, Central Asians whom the Russians called generically 'Bokharans' after the town of Bokhara, arrived regularly with Chinese goods they had brought across the deserts of Turkestan to exchange for Siberian furs. Many of these goods were luxury silks, but there were also some textiles designed to appeal to quite ordinary people. Settlers in Siberia were in frequent need of clothing as well as food. Around 1649 the first bales appeared in Tobolsk of *kitaika* ('Chinese' or nankeen), a cheap, strong cotton cloth which the settlers wore over fur coats and their women sewed into men's shirts and pinafores.[38] In addition there were some niche items of medical interest. One example was rhubarb, and in particular its ungulate or horsehoof-shaped variety grown near the town of Suzhou in north-western China,[39] which first appeared on the Tobolsk market in 1649. Valued throughout seventeenth-century Europe for its supposed effectiveness as a purgative in treating diseases of the liver, spleen, kidney and general frenzy ('Rhubarb! O for rhubarb / To purge this choler!' cries Duke Ferdinand in *The Duchess of*

Malfi),[40] it could be re-exported at great profit to Russia's western neighbours. Another example was tea, first recorded in the Tobolsk customs registers in 1654, which the Russians at this time regarded purely as a tonic, referring to tea leaves as 'grass'.[41] The Russian state had perceived they could buy up the more valuable Chinese products at Tobolsk and pass them on to the treasury. Or better still, they could follow the trade to its source. In 1652 an embassy from the Dzungar Mongols arrived in Moscow bearing gifts in the form of Chinese silks, satins – and rhubarb. A 'Bokharan' merchant named Seitkul Ablin who came with the embassy supplied 'interesting information' about China trade prospects, and the envoys reported the willingness of their princess, Gundja, to let Russian traders through her lands.[42]

The reigning Tsar, Alexei, who had succeeded his father Michael in 1645, decided therefore to resume Russia's drive for the Eastern trade in a fairly big way. Command of the drive was entrusted to a certain Fyodor Isakovich Baikov, a boyar's son from Tobolsk, illiterate possibly but competent, who had been employed in a series of middle-ranking provincial posts. In 1653 Baikov was sent to Tobolsk at the head of a state caravan, equipped by the treasury with a hefty investment of 50,000 roubles to buy Chinese goods as well as Siberian produce for resale in China. He did vigorous business, obtaining Chinese fabrics and rhubarb for dispatch to the treasury as well as a quantity of Siberian furs. Early in 1654 the scope of the mission was expanded. Baikov was now to proceed to Peking as the head of a formal embassy, not a reconnaissance mission as Petlin's had been; and, unlike Petlin, he was to carry a letter of accreditation and gifts for the emperor. The main task of his embassy was to be nothing less than establishing permanent diplomatic and commercial relations with China. In addition, he was to collect some commercial intelligence on topics ranging from trade routes, tariffs and the ability of the Chinese market to absorb Russian goods to the availability of vegetables – the latter perhaps with a view to improving the diet of the hungry Cossacks in Yakutsk. Finally, he was to form some idea of Qing military strength. (Information-gathering seems to have been in the air at this time – 1654 was also the year in which Tsar Alexei organised Russia's first specialist intelligence agency.)[43] On 20 March Baikov sent off an advance party headed by the 'Bokharan' merchant Seitkul Ablin to Peking to herald his arrival. Later in the year he set out from Tobolsk with a thirty-strong suite, and in March 1656, after a journey of nineteen months, he arrived at Peking.

The result was a head-on collision over protocol. The new Manchu rulers in Peking had inherited the traditional Chinese view in which China was the centre of the world to which barbarian vassals came bearing tribute. They had somewhat refined the tribute system of their Ming predecessors: north-western peoples, including both Mongols and Russians, were handled by a new body called the *Lifanyuan* ('Court for Managing Barbarians') to distinguish them from the peoples to the east and south, who remained under the jurisdiction of the old Board of Rites. But the posture of Chinese supremacy was unaltered. Newcomers as they were, not yet in control of the southern half of the country, the Qing had at all costs to make it clear to the Chinese bureaucracy and public that they were upholding the country's pre-eminence in every respect. China, however, was not the only state to be protocol-conscious. Seventeenth-century envoys everywhere were acutely sensitive to matters of status.[44] Baikov was under explicit instructions to do nothing that would detract from his sovereign's dignity, and his entourage would have been watching to see that he didn't put a foot wrong. Trouble began before he had even entered the capital. The Lifanyuan officials who met him required him to get off his horse and bow down symbolically at the doors of the temple that stood by the city gates. But Baikov had been ordered not to bow to anyone or anything but the emperor, and in particular not to bow before any *threshold*.[45] The officials then proffered a cup of tea, prepared in Manchu or Tibetan style with butter and milk, which had supposedly been sent in token of welcome by the Shunzhi emperor himself. But Baikov was observing the Orthodox Lenten fast. Prodded by the officials ('At least accept it!'), he took the cup but handed it straight back to them.[46] Matters quickly went from bad to worse. Baikov insisted on presenting his letter and gifts to Shunzhi in person rather than submitting them first to official scrutiny according to the rules of the tributary process. Nor would he go to the Lifanyuan offices to practise performing the ritual kowtow to the emperor, but was only prepared to bow to him standing in Russian style. 'Your Empire is great,' he said stoutly, 'but ours is not small either';[47] and he puffed the importance of Alexei, whose letter proclaimed his descent from Caesar Augustus and Grand Prince Rurik.

Matters were further confused by the fact that, presumably owing to the language barrier, the Qing court had interpreted Seitkul Ablin's advance party as the official embassy. The seasoned Central Asian merchant had made no trouble about kowtowing, and the Qing were initially hard pressed to work out who Baikov was and why he was behaving so differently. Faced with his insistence on presenting his gifts and letters in person they said tartly, 'That is your master's way; not ours; and one Emperor does not dictate to another'; and as Baikov continued to drag his feet they became truculent. On the second day they removed his gifts forcibly, though not without giving him a receipt. Baikov and his group were put up in the dilapidated Ming hostel where Petlin had stayed, and after a few weeks of relative freedom were effectively imprisoned there. By August the confrontation had grown so acute that the officials even tried threatening the Russian envoy with execution; but still Baikov held out. 'Though the Emperor should order me to be torn limb from limb, yet will I not go to the Ministry [Lifanyuan] before I have seen his eyes, nor give up to you the Tsar's gracious letter.' In the end Baikov's gifts were returned, his letter was neither accepted nor answered, and on 4 September he was expelled from the capital, 'by no means politely'. A few days out of Peking Baikov apparently got cold feet (what would the tsar think?) and sent a courier back to the capital offering to fulfil the Lifanyuan's demands. The Qing officials sent a messenger to investigate, only to find that Baikov had already moved on – an act they regarded as a further token of disrespect. They concluded that he 'had not the slightest inkling how to show respect to a sovereign', and indeed that he 'could not be in his right mind'.[48]

Empty-handed, and without even a concrete negotiation to show for his pains, Baikov had failed miserably in the substantive part of his mission. But what he lacked in diplomacy he made up for in observation. In the report he composed (or possibly dictated) for his government he supplied a full range of political and commercial intelligence. Like all Russians at this period he viewed China through a Mongolian prism, muddling up the Manchus with the Mongols, calling Peking by its old Mongol name of Khanbalik and the Qing sovereign by the Mongolian title of Bogdoi Khan, in its Russian form Bogdykhan ('Sacred Lord').[49] In refusing to fall on his knees before the gates of Peking on the grounds that this would mean bowing down to a threshold, he was gratuitously objecting to a custom that was in fact Mongolian and not Chinese.[50] But he had grasped the essential distinction between the Manchus, who had taken Peking just a dozen years before, and the 'old Chinese', the Ming remnants who continued to hold out in the south;[51] and he brought the no doubt reassuring news that the soldiers on guard in the gateways of northern Chinese cities had iron muskets and small iron cannon but no heavy artillery. His commercial intelligence was unexpectedly down-beat. He found no market in Peking for Russian goods other than ermine and arctic fox pelts, gave long lists of silks, precious metals and jewels, fruit and vegetables, but was unable to say for certain where they had come from.[52] His gloom was, however, belied to some extent by the trade he succeeded in doing in the weeks before his group were confined to the hostel: he returned to Tobolsk in 1658 with a handsome profit and goods worth a total of 1,668 roubles.[53] It was also belied by his comments on the splendour and sophistication of China. Like Petlin, he was awed by the abundance of stone. The main thoroughfares of Peking, he remarked, were paved with natural granite 'so that there is no mud in the streets', and pipes were provided to carry off the rainwater. The rivers were spanned by 'rich and quaint bridges' of natural stone, and the five marble bridges that led to the Forbidden City were 'admirably made'. The cities were equipped with stone bath houses, and the people were 'well grown and clean'. Only the diet was a problem. The Chinese, he lamented, ate 'all sorts of abominable food . . . they eat dogs, and sell boiled dog-meat in the shops; and they eat all sorts of things that have died'.[54]

If the Russian focus was commercial, that of the Qing was strategic and defensive. Above all the Qing were preoccupied by the continuing threat on their north-eastern border. In the course of the 1660s the Cossacks began once again 'appearing and disappearing' in the Amur valley.[55] A vagabond Pole named Nikifor Chernigowski, who was wanted for murder in his home town of Ilimsk, moved in with a band of followers and refounded the old forward base at Albazin. A Chinese exile in the region who witnessed as a child the arrival of these intruders in 1668–9 described them as having high noses, red hair and fierce temperaments. They were, he said, expert in fire-arms and possessed in particular a 'watermelon cannon' which could measure the distance of the enemy to such effect that anyone touched by the explosion would be mortally wounded; and the Manchus were 'all afraid of this cannon'.[56] More ominous still was a stirring of disaffection among the hitherto docile border tribes. In 1667 a chief of the Evenki people named Gantimur who had fought for the Qing in the previous campaigns on the river shifted his allegiance in the opposite direction from usual. Dissatisfied with a title the Qing had bestowed on him, he went over to the Russians, who in due course baptised and ennobled him as Prince Pavel Gantimurov.

These trends were of visceral concern to the court in Peking. If the Cossacks moved any further southwards they would encroach on the dynasty's sacred homeland in central and southern Manchuria, which had been largely denuded of people since the Manchus poured out of it on their way to the conquest of China in 1644. The defection of Gantimur might give a lead to the other tribes on the border, deprive the court of their customary tribute and unravel the whole spider's web of tributary arrangements which enabled the Qing to sustain their claim to the Amur. Over the following years the return of Gantimur would become the perennial Chinese demand, the perennial sore point which the recovery of Taiwan has been for the government of China in our own time. Compared with such issues as these, trade was a secondary matter. Furs from Siberia were indeed quite appreciated by the Manchu nobility and the wealthy Chinese: centuries of intensive hunting had taken their toll and few fur-bearing animals remained in north China to provide warm clothes for the winter. But, in the traditional Confucian outlook which the Qing had inherited from their Chinese predecessors, trade was a despised occupation, and not one which should be allowed to take precedence over matters of state.

Into this worrying picture stepped a pockmarked young man of outstanding ability who had succeeded to the Qing throne in 1661 as the Kangxi emperor. On attaining his majority seven years later, Kangxi determined to tackle the Russian problem root and branch. To begin with he had to solve a conundrum: what, if any, was the connection between the Luocha marauders on the *north-eastern* frontier and Baikov's people, the Eluosi as the Chinese records called them, who arrived from the *west* seeking trade? Baikov in 1656 had disclaimed any knowledge of the Luocha and their activities. But the conduct of his entourage had shown at least some resemblance to Luocha behaviour: one additional reason why Baikov's party had been confined to the old Ming hostel in Peking had been that his Cossack attendants had roamed the city walls beating up the Manchu guards, and had 'forced their way into the brothels' and 'provoked noise and scandals'.[57] To disentangle this question Kangxi decided in 1669 to make an approach to Nerchinsk, a town north-west of Albazin which the Cossacks had founded sixteen years before on the River Shilka, a tributary of the Amur, and which had since emerged as their headquarters for the region. A local chief named Sharanda was directed to go to Nerchinsk on the pretext of trading and gather the necessary intelligence through talks with the settlers. In addition he was to deliver a message from Kangxi in person, complaining politely about the new Cossack raids being launched from Albazin and submitting a first request for the rendition of Gantimur.

Sharanda performed his duties efficiently. By the spring of 1670 Kangxi knew for sure that the Luocha and the Eluosi were identical, with all that implied about the dimensions and possible power of Russia. In May his deputation came back to Peking with a Cossack called Ignaty Milovanov, who in turn brought a written reply for Kangxi from Daniil Arshinsky, the governor of Nerchinsk. Arshinsky and his Cossacks still seem to have laboured under the impression that the Sacred Lord in Peking was a minor feudal prince, and his letter contained the remarkable proposal that the *emperor of China* should pay tribute to the *tsar*! This appalling solecism, unique perhaps in Chinese history, didn't have the repercussions that might have been expected. One explanation put forward has been that the message was not understood, and perhaps not even read out (Milovanov was certainly illiterate). It seems equally possible, though, that the Lifanyuan officials escorting Milovanov got the message all right, but opted to turn a blind eye. For the resourceful Kangxi had perceived that the discovery of one single, immense Russian state offered him a possibility of linkage: that the trade desired by the Eluosi could be used as a bargaining chip to secure the withdrawal of the Luocha from the Amur. The lowly Milovanov was treated to lavish hospitality. The Qing officials who talked to him even stressed the advantages of trade between Russia and China, and the demand for Siberian furs which had eluded Baikov was suddenly present in abundance. 'The Chinese', Milovanov happily conveyed to his chief in Nerchinsk, 'asked them many times for young sables and summer-killed black ones, and sable-bellies and ermines, and squirrels and white arctic foxes.'[58] In August 1670 Milovanov was sent back to Nerchinsk with a further letter from Kangxi requesting the necessary quid pro quo – that Gantimur be extradited and that the tsar's government restrain their subjects on the Amur. The message was repeated in 1671.

The Moscow government were only too pleased to take advantage of the apparent invitation to trade. In 1670–1 the treasury had been further depleted by the cost of suppressing the great Cossack rising led by Stenka Razin, while the western European market had contracted still further with the outbreak of the Third Anglo-Dutch War. And in the meantime, even in the absence of a diplomatic relationship, Russian trade with China had begun to acquire a momentum of its own. The bustling Central Asian merchant Seitkul Ablin had continued to organise caravans of Russian treasury goods to sell in Peking. In 1662 he returned to Moscow with Chinese goods worth 1,969 roubles, including 352 precious stones. In 1668 he came back with a profit of 300 per cent, and in 1672 he achieved a return of 18,700 roubles on an initial investment of 4,500.[59] Much of this business consisted of the familiar exchange of Siberian furs for Chinese textiles; put another way, of Russian raw materials for the sophisticated products of Chinese industry. But the niche items were starting to make modest headway as well. In 1665 a consignment of tea leaves brought back as a present for Tsar Alexei cured him of an upset stomach, and by 1674 small amounts of Chinese tea were beginning to appear in the Moscow shops.

Private Russian trade was increasingly lively. Despite the continued exertions of Central Asians like Ablin, Russian merchants were more and more tending to deal directly with their Chinese counterparts. By the end of the 1660s Russian subjects in quest of Chinese goods were going from Tobolsk to the annual trade fair at Lake Yamysh, close by Turkestan, and even on into China, rather than waiting for Central Asians to come to them. The 'Bokharan' and Tatar middlemen were getting squeezed out of the market, and by the mid-1670s it appears they were doing all in their power to obstruct the new direct trade. In a trend less agreeable to the Kremlin, these private merchants were also starting to nip at the heels of the state. In 1674 a private caravan organised by the great Moscow merchant house of Filatiev travelled all the way to Peking, incidentally opening up a new trade route that approached the Qing capital from the north-west across the Mongolian steppe rather than from the west across the deserts of Turkestan. The Russian court had no wish to see private entrepreneurs encroaching on their profits. As early as 1656 they had declared a state monopoly on the traffic in ungulate rhubarb. In 1671 private merchants diverted a shipment of sables intended for the town of Yeniseisk to exchange for Chinese products in the Daur lands, thus sharply diminishing the town's revenue; and in the following year a first decree ordered the confiscation of goods from private Russian merchants trading with China.

Galvanised by these various factors, the Russian government returned to the charge. In 1673 they began to fit out an embassy more ambitious than anything conceived of before. The party was to consist of 150 men, including a geographer, a cartographer, a herbalist and other experts, and its task was to negotiate a complete opening of the Chinese market. Russian merchants were to obtain the right to trade in all parts of China. The Qing for their part were to send a trade mission to Russia each year bringing gold and silver ingots, precious stones, silks and herbal medicines with a view to exporting an annual total of 4,000 *pood*s of silver and precious stones of all kinds in exchange for Russian wares.[60] As a bonus, Tsar Alexei sought access to Chinese technology in the form of some stonemasons who could build him the wonderful bridges Baikov had described. In pursuit of these objects the embassy was to be headed by a man capable (as Baikov had not been) of holding his own intellectually with the Qing officials. And not only with the Qing. During his months in Peking, Baikov had encountered a number of Jesuit missionaries from the western European countries. Attached to the Chinese court since the early years of the century, these Jesuits had secured a position at the elbow first of the Ming and more recently of the Qing emperors. In one of the most spirited cultural transfers in history they had acquainted the court with mathematics, astronomy and other branches of western science; and they had also played a leading part in the introduction to China of western armaments, from arquebuses to cannon. Knowing no Latin, Baikov had been unable to converse with these western clergymen, but he had formed an impression of their goodwill. The thought was that by dispatching an ambassador who could communicate with them in Latin the Russian government might be able to secure more effective intermediaries than the Mongols on whom they had had to rely till now. A suitable envoy presented himself in the shape of Nikolai Gavrilovich Spathar Milescu.[61]

Milescu was about as much of a contrast to the all-Russian Baikov as could reasonably be imagined. A Moldavian born in the Peloponnese, he had been educated in the school of the Greek Patriarch of Constantinople and was steeped in the learning of the long-defunct Byzantine empire. He had a knowledge of numerous languages, including Greek (both ancient and modern), Latin, Turkish and Arabic, and was 'well conversant in philosophy and controversy'.[62] As a young man he had secured a post as adviser to the prince of his native Moldavia, but had been caught attempting to seize the throne for himself, and in true Byzantine fashion had his nose slit. Evidently disliking the epithet 'chicken-nosed', he had moved on to Brandenburg, where he underwent a seventeenth-century equivalent of plastic surgery, and was able to pursue a career as a diplomat at the courts of Brandenburg-Prussia, Sweden and France. In between times he managed to produce a number of written works, among them a Romanian translation of the Bible. He was, in short, a cosmopolitan intellectual, a representative of the highest of seventeenth-century high culture. He was also conceited, disputatious and fond of intrigue. Returning to Constantinople, he obtained an introduction to the Russian court from Dositheos, Patriarch of Jerusalem, and in March 1671 left for Moscow, where by December he had been awarded a permanent job as translator in the proto-foreign ministry, the *Posolsky prikaz*.[63] Following his selection as head of the new Russian embassy he embarked on some serious homework, mulling over the records of previous missions, and in February 1675 he set out from Moscow with copies of all the previous letters the court had received from Peking. These included the baffling Ming document which Petlin had brought back with him fifty-six years before, and which Milescu was finally able to decipher with the help of a Chinese he found in Tobolsk. Milescu also held exhaustive talks in the west Siberian capital with Yuri Krijanić, a Croat Roman Catholic monk who had been exiled there by Tsar Alexei but was nonetheless filled with pan-Slavic enthusiasm and had become a keen advocate of the China trade. After four weeks in Tobolsk Milescu's delegation resumed their journey, and in January 1676 they arrived at the River Naun in the Qing frontier zone, approaching China from yet another direction – from the north-east by way of Nerchinsk and the disputed Amur.

There followed what seems at first glance a repeat of the protocol confrontation of twenty years earlier, only even more tiresome and more drawn-out. On one side stood Milescu, a foreigner less than five years in the Muscovite service, almost certainly feeling the need to be more Russian than the Russians, to defend his master's dignity even more stubbornly than Baikov had done, and equipped, as Baikov had not been, with a battery of arguments he had picked up in Europe, the new teachings of Grotius on international law, the post-Westphalian principles of the *ius gentium naturale* and the legal equality of sovereigns. Facing him stood the official sent from Peking to act as his escort, Mala, vice-president of the Board of Rites, who had gradually been emerging since 1669 as the Qing dynasty's first Russia Hand. 'An experienced man and a clever one', as Milescu acknowledged, 'learned according to their ideas and possessed of many Oriental languages',[64] his task was to uphold the hierarchical Chinese concept of the emperor in Peking as a universal ruler to whom all other sovereigns were subordinate. The wrangling began in late February, before the two men had even met, over the question of which of them was to call on the other. Milescu sent word that he wouldn't go to meet Mala and Mala must call on him. Mala suggested they meet at a house halfway between their encampments; Milescu refused. Mala suggested they meet at a tent set up in the open; Milescu refused again. Mala suggested that Milescu should perhaps suggest something. Milescu proposed that they should set off for Peking at the same time, and Mala should call on him at the first halting-place. Mala counterproposed that they should converge on a tent set up in a distant field, where two chairs and a table would be prepared for them; but Milescu refused once more. Mala suggested converging on a village house with wide doors which they could enter simultaneously, but Milescu declined even that. After several days during which Milescu's own Russian suite began to show signs of restlessness ('Your Majesty's people', he told the tsar, 'begged me to give way, as time was passing'), Mala finally agreed that the two men should meet in a tent at a place of Milescu's choosing. Milescu would enter the tent first and seat himself, and Mala would arrive with a chair 'on hearing from him'.[65]

Tied up with all this was Milescu's predictable unwillingness to submit his credentials for Mala's inspection. He wasn't prepared to show Mala so much as the seal of Alexei's letter, or to give him the least idea of its contents: the letter was to be presented by him to Kangxi, and to Kangxi alone. Mala pointed out – not unreasonably, if he had been aware of Arshinsky's demand for Chinese tribute – that he needed to make sure the letter contained nothing offensive to the emperor, and warned that if Milescu persisted in behaving like Baikov he would 'go back as Baikov did'. The dispute carried on all the way to Peking, where the party arrived on 16 May, and for over two weeks after that. Milescu wanted to know why the Qing ruler should be prepared to receive an ambassador in person, 'yet refuse to receive his credentials, which are the more honourable of the two'. Mala fell back on the adamantine posture of Chinese tradition: 'As when the hair on a man's head grows thin or grey, nothing can alter it, so with their customs, which could not be changed just to please the Tsar.' In the end a solution was reached under which the tsar's letter and gifts were brought to the gates of the Imperial Palace, placed on a table covered with silk of imperial yellow and picked up by a senior counsellor on the emperor's behalf. Even before this issue was settled, on 30 May, Mala had brought up the subject of the kowtow, which gave rise to 'a violent quarrel'. On 15 June Milescu finally agreed to perform the 'three bows and nine prostrations' in the distant presence of the emperor; but he did so in a most perfunctory manner, 'bending neither low nor slowly', as though deliberately setting out to make a mockery of the rite.[66]

The climactic showdown came in August, when Milescu was asked to accept the emperor's gifts for the tsar and the embassy kneeling in a muddy courtyard in the rain. The ambassador flatly refused to go through with this ritual, as entailing disgrace for the tsar, with the result that his whole entourage were obliged to remain standing in the courtyard for six hours until nightfall, without food or drink. A further attempt was made to enforce the ceremonial three days later, and this time we hear that some of the Russians 'wanted to fall on their knees' when the gifts were finally doled out in a contemptuous manner to the still-standing delegation. On 29 August Milescu again refused to kneel to receive Kangxi's return letter to the tsar, and his entourage fairly boiled over: we can almost hear them muttering, '*Oh, for God's sake . . .!*' At this point the presiding official of the Lifanyuan took the remarkable step of appealing to the entourage over Milescu's head, asking if *they* would receive the emperor's letter with honour. All of them shouted 'We will!', and some declared to Milescu, 'If you, Sir, will not take the letter, we will – whatever its contents!' The Qing court were now thoroughly angered by Milescu's obstinacy. The emperor's letter was withheld, and on 1 September Milescu was dispatched from Peking, as Baikov had been, amid thinly veiled acrimony.[67]

Once again, in the course of these months the Qing reinforced their rhetorical pressure with a certain amount of practical arm-twisting. Milescu's contingent, like Baikov's, were confined 'as if in prison' to the old Ming hostel, with its run-down and partly ruined buildings. They 'were not allowed even to look beyond the barred gates', their food supply was restricted, and Mala made it clear that they wouldn't be freed until they gave up the tsar's letter for the scrutiny of the Lifanyuan. A number of Chinese merchants were allowed in, under strict surveillance, to trade with the embassy; but there was no sign on this occasion of the golden prospects the Qing had dangled before Milovanov six years before. Milescu complained that his people were only able to dispose of a few fox bellies, and that 'the offers were so low that no business could be done'.[68]

On closer inspection, however, the attitude of the Qing to Milescu looks by no means the same as their unyielding rejection of Baikov's mission. What impresses is not their stubbornness but their repeated attempts to show flexibility. During the tussle on the border, after all, it was Mala who made the great bulk of the proposals for compromise, and Mala who ultimately fell in with Milescu's solution of meeting in a tent at a place of Milescu's choosing at which the Russian envoy would take his seat first. During the arguments over the presentation of gifts and credentials, Mala framed his case in a kind of intelligent relativism on the lines of 'when in Rome do as the Romans do'. He observed, for example, that whereas in Russia the custom was to take off one's hat when bowing to the tsar, in China it would be unthinkable to bow to the emperor *without* wearing one's hat. Milescu should therefore do as the Lifanyuan asked; but Mala guaranteed that if Qing envoys ever came to Moscow, they would comply with whatever ceremonial would be in force there. After the argument moved to Peking, Kangxi ordered Mala and his colleagues to trawl through the old Chinese records to see if any precedent could be found for the emperor's receiving an envoy's credentials in person, and was said to be 'most inclined to do so'. The arrangement eventually made for Milescu to place his letter and gifts on a table for collection by the Qing grandee represented a very considerable wrenching of Chinese court procedure. Even during the final collision in August, the Lifanyuan officials went out of their way to justify their demands for Milescu to kneel with a clarification the Russians might find acceptable. '*We are well aware*', said Mala, 'that your master is no subject of the Emperor; but time out of mind our custom has been to speak and to write in that fashion.'[69]

Protocol had in fact been trumped for the Manchu court by the larger strategic imperative. Imbued with what one historian has labelled 'barbarian pragmatism',[70] Kangxi and his ministers were intent on securing their northeastern frontier even if that meant unobtrusively bending one or two of the old rules of Chinese etiquette. Over the last few years the position of the Qing regime had been drastically weakened. At the end of 1673, one of the three Chinese generals who had subdued southern China on behalf of the Qing fifteen years before and the sons of the two others rose up in rebellion against their Manchu overlords. With the southern provinces engulfed in this 'War of the Three Feudatories' and the very survival of the dynasty in question, it had become more important than ever to neutralise the menace in the north-east. After allowing Milescu a slight edge in the initial protocol tussle, Mala had therefore lost no time in raising the basic Qing grievances, in particular the outrages committed by the Amur settlers, who had been beating up local tribespeople and grabbing their sable skins. 'That is the nice sort of person your Cossack is!', he remarked sardonically. 'There is no one like him on this earth!'[71] The discussion continued in Peking through the Lifanyuan, with Kangxi conveying his annoyance that the tsar had failed to reply to the letters he sent in 1670 and 1671 regarding the surrender of Gantimur. Neither the emperor nor Mala could believe that the Russians weren't even capable of reading a letter written in Manchu.[72]

The Russians had scented Qing vulnerability. Already on his way to the border Milescu had learnt from a series of Mongol informants that the Chinese in the south had twice defeated the Manchus, and that the dynasty was on the road to collapse. This message was powerfully reinforced in Peking by the Jesuits, whom Kangxi had himself prodded forward in the hope that they might be able to break the deadlock over presenting credentials. Led by the Fleming Ferdinand Verbiest, astronomer, engineer and confidant of the emperor, the Jesuits settled down to converse with Milescu in Latin. And the Jesuits unexpectedly sold the Qing down the river. They began by avowing that they would be delighted to do what they could for the Russians, since they didn't love the Manchus as they had done the Ming. They gave Milescu a detailed account of the dynasty's military and financial weakness. They explained that the Qing saw some advantage in talking to the Russians, insofar as any sign of Russian backing for them might alarm the Three Feudatories, but at the same time were mortally afraid of the Russian advance to their border. And they warned Milescu that Kangxi had every intention of making war in due course on the Cossacks in Nerchinsk and Albazin if Gantimur were not returned.

Various explanations have been put forward for the astonishing behaviour of Verbiest and his colleagues. It seems likely that they really did judge the Qing to be doomed, and were putting their money on a Ming restoration. They may well have harboured feelings of genuine loyalty to the Ming, plus resentment at the rough handling some of them had received in the first years of Manchu power. They are known to have entertained hopes of a '*via Moscovitica*' – of securing the tsar's permission for their order to travel from Rome to Peking overland via Moscow and thereby escape the dangers of the long ocean voyage. At all events it seems clear that the cumulative effect of this intelligence was to embolden Milescu considerably. During the talks in Peking he made a point of observing to Mala, '*We are well aware that you have enemies as well as friends*.'[73] He refused to respond to the Qing demands for the evacuation of the Amur and the rendition of Gantimur, on which matters in any case he had no instructions from Moscow. And it was this, much more than the trouble he gave over protocol, that made his mission capsize. In place of Kangxi's letter he was dismissed from Peking with an oral instruction. Russian merchants would only be permitted to trade with China on three conditions. The Cossacks must give up their harassment on the Amur. Gantimur must be extradited. And (perhaps as an afterthought) the next Russian ambassador must be 'a most reasonable man'.[74]

So it all ended in stalemate. The Russians were no closer to getting the business they wanted. For a time, it seems that Milescu's mind ran along the alternative track of military conquest. He had learnt, he told the tsar, from a Russian merchant lately in Peking that 2,000 troops would suffice to take over the whole of north China up to the Great Wall. And if the Qing dynasty toppled, what might not be possible? Independent south China had at some point got mixed up in the Russian mind with the mythical kingdom of Nikan, the dominion of Prester John, the supposed Christian ruler in the depths of the Orient; and it may be that Milescu had come to cherish the personal fantasy of an alliance with the '*Nikantsy*' that would take the Turks in the rear and restore Christian rule in Constantinople. Other thinkers in Russia, however, had by this time developed a healthy respect for the military power of the Qing. Back in Tobolsk in 1675 the Croat publicist Krijanić had warned Milescu of the risk of a two-front war, urging that Russia should not get bogged down in a 'stupid' conflict with the Qing that would lay her open to invasion by the Germans and Turks in the west.[75] In any case the acquisition of empty lands couldn't really compete with the appeal of developing trade with an advanced and sophisticated empire. On his return to Moscow Milescu composed both a lengthy report for the government and a *Description of the Chinese State* in which, perhaps rather surprisingly after his haughty behaviour, he matched or exceeded Russia's earlier envoys in his admiration of all he had seen. Like Petlin and Baikov he lavished praise upon Chinese stone architecture, pointing out that he had seen no fires in the course of his stay in Peking on account of the glazed tile roofs. Unlike Petlin he didn't restrain himself in comparing the buildings to Moscow's, stating frankly that one of the walls in Peking was 'higher than the Kremlin'. Unlike Baikov he found Chinese food 'good and varied', noting in addition that Chinese doctors with their herbal remedies treated all kinds of diseases better and faster than their European counterparts. He was struck by the intensive cultivation of land, and by the complexity of the Qing administrative system, with 'so many noblemen and officials of so many different ranks that it is hard for one man to understand them all'. And, first and foremost, he marvelled at the material abundance, judging there to be more wealth in China alone than in all other countries put together. The Chinese, he believed, could 'dress the people of the whole world in cotton clothes', as well as possessing countless mineral ores and an abundance of gold. 'China in the world', he concluded, was 'like a precious stone set in a ring'.[76] In spite of the adverse trading climate Milescu was able to negotiate the purchase of a magnificent ruby as a gift for Tsar Alexei. And in the meantime the trade between private merchants continued to flourish regardless of the nominal prohibition imposed by the Qing. In 1677 the Moscow authorities felt obliged to take a further step to head off private competition, decreeing that only individuals bearing permits from the tsar could travel to China. Far from official eyes trade was beginning to gather momentum in the disputed borderlands. By 1680 Chinese merchants were starting to offer their wares inside Russian territory, and by 1684 Siberian traders in the lands of the Daurs were reported exchanging their furs for Chinese cloth. The vision of a permanent trade agreement to unlock this huge potential continued to beckon.

The Qing for their part were no closer to achieving their object of defusing the border threat. They too had shown signs of a growing respect for the strength of their neighbours. During Milescu's stay in Peking, Kangxi twice invited groups of sturdy Cossacks in the Russian contingent to take part in exhibitions of swimming and diving, and was impressed by the ease with which they outperformed their Manchu competitors. The Qing courtiers wanted to buy the long muskets carried by Milescu's attendants, and showed a particular interest in Milescu's own Turkish sword of top-quality steel.

After Milescu's departure Verbiest and his colleagues presented Kangxi with a map of Russia, as if to remind him of the immensity of the neighbouring country. As the Jesuits had warned Milescu, Kangxi did indeed intend to wipe out the Cossack settlements in the Amur valley as soon as he was strong enough to do so. He knew that the garrisons there were not sizeable, and that the main Russian forces were far away on the other side of the Urals. But the Manchus themselves had only a limited knowledge of the Manchurian frontier territories they meant to absorb. As late as 1677 they were still engaged in the exploration of Changbaishan, the Long White mountains on the edge of Korea. And above all, Kangxi couldn't act while his authority was still being challenged by the Chinese rebel armies in the south.

Early in the new decade all this suddenly changed. In 1681 the Qing finally crushed the revolt of the Three Feudatories, and in 1683 they overcame the last remnants of Ming resistance on the island of Taiwan. Kangxi's hands were now free. On 16 September 1682 he issued an edict commanding an intelligence party to probe Cossack strength in the Amur settlements on the pretext of hunting deer. The party were to 'survey carefully the distance of the roads' to Albazin and to 'examine carefully the strategic points of their dwellings'.[77] This intelligence drive was accompanied by a major logistical effort overseen in great detail by the emperor himself. Kangxi gave elaborate orders about the establishment of military colonies at Ninguta and a string of other outposts which the Qing had by this time established to the south of the Amur. Twelve thousand *piculs* of grain, he instructed, should be levied from the Kherchin tribe to support the Qing forces for a total of three years,[78] and the newly arrived troops should immediately set about tilling the soil. Cattle and sheep should be taken from the Solun tribe to deny the Russians the ability to provision any local people who might side with them. Other imperial orders concerned the size of the staff to be installed in a newly organised network of postal stations and the number of warships and supply boats which would need to be built to enable the Qing to exploit the Manchurian waterways. Five hundred ethnic Chinese troops under Marquis Lin Xingzhu were to be brought up from the recent theatre of conflict in the south-eastern province of Fujian: these troops would be excellent for boarding enemy vessels, in that they bore rattan shields which they held over their heads to protect them from bullets and arrows while they laid about them with their huge swords. Marquis Lin, Kangxi added thoughtfully, was however a southerner who couldn't stand the cold, so he couldn't be expected to stay for too long.[79]

In the midst of these preparations Kangxi didn't overlook the possibility of a peaceful outcome. 'The use of force', he reminded his ministers in January 1683, 'is after all not a good thing.'[80] Although this sounds in part like a stereotyped utterance of the benevolent Confucian ruler, there are also indications that the emperor was taking a long-term view. Kangxi seems to have grasped clearly that Russia was a neighbour for the long term, and that even if the Amur could be cleared of Cossack settlers as he intended, this would not in itself represent a lasting solution. 'If we advance and they retreat and we retreat and they advance there will be no end to the conflict and the border peoples will not be at peace.'[81] Qing preparations were therefore interspersed in the early 1680s with repeated messages sent to the Russian authorities both in Moscow and on the Amur urging them to pull right back to Yakutsk without fighting and collect their sables there.

We may notice in passing the growing role played in these Qing operations by stray individuals from the Russians' own side. From as early as the 1650s we find a handful of Russian deserters turning up in the Manchu camp. One of the first such defectors was a certain Ruslanov, who crossed over in 1653. A Crimean Tatar by origin, he had been forcibly converted to Christianity by the Russian troops who made war on the Crimean khanate, and evidently nursed an ethnic grievance against his Muscovite overlords. As open fighting resumed in the early 1680s, fair numbers were captured in Manchu excursions and brought to Peking. In September 1683, for example, a total of thirty-one Russians were caught near Nerchinsk and sent to the capital on Mala's instructions; and by the end of the year they were joined by around thirty others who had been captured by the Qing general Sabsu at the confluence of the Amur with its tributary the Zeya, where they were trying to found a new settlement. This last group included an Orthodox priest, Father Maxim Leontiev. Kangxi issued orders that the POWs should be treated well, given plentiful food and drink and fur hats and gowns for the winter. We cannot tell what impelled them to work with the Qing, but it seems possible that any allegiance they felt to distant Moscow was eclipsed by the immediate attraction of a higher standard of living.[82] Organised into a company under Ruslanov (by now a long-term Peking resident), they were soon being used to help implement Kangxi's various tactics to gain the

Amur. On one occasion we find the emperor ordering that the Luocha officer Ivan was to ride to Albazin, 'where he will order [the garrison] to surrender and at the same time find out their actual condition and report back to us'.[83] Cossack defectors were also now used to surmount the language barrier by providing Russian translations of the letters Kangxi sent to both Moscow and the Amur settlements.

In spite of the help of these Russian auxiliaries, the Qing received no constructive response to their overtures. Moscow was too far away to reply in a timely fashion, Nerchinsk and Albazin showed no interest and a conflict seemed inevitable. On a suggestion from Mala rapidly endorsed by Kangxi, General Sabsu moved up near Albazin in the summer of 1684 and seized the harvest in an attempt to destroy the economic basis of the Cossack forward post. In March 1685 a second Qing general, Duke Pengcun, appeared in front of Albazin with 15,000 troops, 100 cannon forged under Verbiest's supervision and fifty heavy siege engines.[84]

The Russians were wholly incapable of matching the Qing in numbers, logistics or intelligence work. In 1682, when Kangxi's campaign was initiated, the governor of Nerchinsk had written to the Siberian Department in Moscow that the combined strength of the garrisons in the Amur settlements came to precisely 202, and that 'even in Nerchinsk we live in great fear'.[85] The following year Moscow ordered the Siberian garrisons to mobilise an additional 1,000 men; but only 600 could eventually be levied because of the 'scarcity of population', and these reinforcements mutinied on their way east and threatened to throw their commander and officers into a river. By 1685 the Russian strength in Albazin had finally been brought up to around 1,000, with 300 muskets and one large cannon mounted at each of the landward-facing gates of this riverside fort. Qing informants continued to report with some awe on the Russians' equipment, talking of 'firearms so extraordinarily good that they can hit the target at every shot' and of cannon that were so explosive that no one dared face them.[86] But the three great cannon appear to have had at their disposal just four cannon balls. And in spite of having taken some Qing prisoners who might have supplied them with useful intelligence, the Albazin defenders had available not a single man who could speak Manchu. Yet, regardless of their disadvantages, the Cossacks were grimly determined to stand their ground. When Duke Pengcun, after holding back for three months, read out to the garrison

Kangxi's final edict calling on them to surrender, their commander, Alexei Tolbuzin, is said to have answered 'insolently and cheekily'. We may guess he replied with something along the lines of the *mot de Cambronne*.[87]

On 23 June Duke Pengcun attacked Albazin with a force of 3,000. The Cossacks fought bravely and threw back the initial assault. Their artillerymen, however, had incompetently been allowed out of the town at this critical juncture, so that no one was available to fire the big guns. On 25 June a party of reinforcements tried to enter the town by raft from the Amur side, but at this point the Qing brought their naval arm into play. The marines from Fujian attacked the rafts in their Roman-style *testudo* formation, holding their rattan shields over their heads to ward off the Cossack bullets. The Russians are said to have shouted in fright, 'Behold the big-capped Tartars!';[88] some of them fell in the river and over thirty were killed. In the meantime, the Qing bombarded the town with incendiary devices in the form of cannon shot and flaming arrows. By 26 June it was clear that resistance was useless, and an exhausted Tolbuzin asked for terms.

Taking his usual long-sighted view, Kangxi had determined to treat the defeated Cossacks with magnanimity. Instructions had been issued in advance that any surrendering Russians should not be killed but allowed to withdraw to Nerchinsk if they so desired. Around 600 of the survivors led by Tolbuzin accepted this offer and were permitted to set off on the journey complete with their horses, provisions and even their weaponry (apart from their guns). A minority, however – estimates vary from twenty-five to forty-five – elected to give themselves up to the conquerors and were carried off to Peking. Less consideration was shown to the town of Albazin, which was destroyed for a second time.

In November 1685 the court in Moscow belatedly received two letters in Latin which Kangxi, courtesy of the Jesuits, had sent earlier in the year demanding the Russian withdrawal from Albazin, plus a report from Vlasov, the governor of Nerchinsk, conveying that Albazin had subsequently been taken by storm. A decision was quickly reached that the Amur valley was indefensible and should be given up in exchange for trade. On 10 December the court designated two couriers, Nikifor Venyukov and Ivan Favorov, who had taken part in Milescu's abortive mission and were thus in some sense China Hands, to proceed to Peking and inform the Qing government that a new ambassador had been appointed and was on his way to discuss the border question. On 28 December the choice of ambassador was declared to be Fyodor Golovin, a nobleman who along with his father had served as an aide to both Tsar Alexei and his successor Fyodor, and as such was the most prestigious envoy Moscow had yet sent.

But the court hadn't reckoned with the pace of events on the ground. Governor Vlasov was determined to recover Albazin, and so were the Cossack refugees who had joined him in Nerchinsk; and while Moscow's new policy crawled slowly east in the saddlebags of the couriers, the Amur valley settlers were free to pursue their own agenda. In mid-July, just five days after Tolbuzin and his followers arrived in Nerchinsk, the governor sent off a seventy-man scouting party down the Shilka tributary to the Amur and the site of Albazin. These scouts were able to establish, from a solitary Chinese they found squatting among the ruins, that the Qing army had withdrawn to quell a disturbance further south, and by late August the settlers were moving indomitably back. By the end of 1685 Albazin had been rebuilt with an extra-strong wall made up of two rows of logs separated by densely packed earth, and was garrisoned once again, as though nothing had happened, by Tolbuzin and a force of 1,000. When the news reached Kangxi, he decided that the Russians in Albazin would have to be suppressed before they could 'multiply and store more grain'.[89] A fresh army of 2,000 men was assembled, and by July 1686 the outpost was once more under siege. After a series of unsuccessful onslaughts, and a systematic bombardment during which Tolbuzin was killed, the Qing force settled down to starve the defenders out. Desperate Cossacks began to slip into the surrounding forests in search of game, firewood and pine needles and bark, which they boiled into a decoction for treating scurvy. By December, 100 of the garrison troops had been killed making sorties, over 500 had died of scurvy and only 150 were left alive.[90]

At the end of October 1686, after a relatively brisk journey of ten months, Venyukov and Favorov finally arrived in Peking to announce the appointment of Ambassador Golovin. Kangxi was clearly delighted to glimpse a possibility of the harmonious outcome he preferred. The two couriers were well received and even shown the imperial collection of gerfalcons.[91] With a chivalry worthy of Saladin, the emperor directed his troops to relax the siege by pulling back some distance from the beleaguered fort and sent two doctors up from Peking to go into Albazin and treat the sick Russians, as well as the afflicted and hungry on their own side. But the Cossack spirit remained unbroken. Suspecting a ruse to spy out his defences, Tolbuzin's successor, an engineer named Afanasy Beiton, rejected the offer of medical treatment. Venyukov and Favorov were unwilling to send the garrison instructions to submit on behalf of the Manchu authorities, and the siege went on. At the end of March 1687 Beiton caused a large Easter pie to be baked and delivered to the Qing headquarters as evidence that the garrison were still doing fine. But by midsummer their numbers were down to a mere sixty-six.[92] Luckily for the survivors, Kangxi had received further word (slightly premature) of Golovin's approach, and on 19 August he gave a command for the siege to be raised altogether.

The stage was now set for a decisive resolution of the Amur issue. Kangxi seems to have felt from the outset that the novel problem of an organised state on China's northern fringes would have to be dealt with in a novel way. Once again breaking sharply with precedent, he accepted on 29 October a proposal from Golovin's advancing embassy that the talks should be held at Selenginsk, a fort which the Russians had founded in 1666 to the south-east of Lake Baikal, close to the lands of the Khalkha Mongols. Any agreement, in other words, would be reached right outside Chinese territory and well away from the scrutiny of the Chinese bureaucracy in Peking. Led by the emperor's uncle, Prince Songgotu, the Qing delegation was to be overwhelmingly Manchu, and only two ethnic Chinese officials of relatively low rank were included. The interpreting was once again to be entrusted to two of the Jesuits, the Frenchman Jean-François Gerbillon and the Portuguese Tomas Pereira. At the same time considerable effort was made to ensure the safety of the party and to put maximum pressure on their Russian interlocutors. Songgotu was to be escorted by a fully fledged army of 6,000 men, and full use was apparently to be made of the Khalkha nomads. Caught between two expanding empires, the Russian to the north and the Qing to the south, the Khalkhas had already made up their minds to throw in their lot with the Qing. The Russians, they felt, were too different from themselves culturally, and unlikely to protect their newly espoused Buddhist faith. Finding out in the winter of 1687–8 that Golovin's party amounted to no more than 1,500 men, the Khalkhas promptly mobilised a force of 4,000 and laid siege to them in Selenginsk. Equipped with Qing rifles and cannon, the Khalkhas may also have been encouraged by the Qing government to launch their attack with a view to softening up the Russians in advance of the forthcoming talks. As Songgotu's huge delegation set off across the Gobi desert to their rendezvous in May 1688, the Qing unmistakably held the whip hand.

Seven weeks into their journey, however, the unexpected occurred. The delegation found their road blocked on the way through Mongolia by several thousands of Khalkhas fleeing in chaos with their children and their tents. In the midst of their effort to storm Selenginsk the Khalkhas themselves had been subjected to an all-out attack by their western neighbours, the Dzungars. Back in 1670 the Dzungars had thrown up a new prince named Galdan, a young man of some military skill and distinct imperial ambitions. During the following decade he had steadily extended his power over the oases of eastern Turkestan (the modern region of Xinjiang). Now he was setting out at the head of a 30,000-strong army to unify the Mongol tribes and lead Mongolia back to the vanished glories of Genghis Khan. With this horde lying ahead any further progress by Songgotu towards Selenginsk was out of the question, and after a swift exchange of couriers an edict arrived from Kangxi directing that the delegation should be recalled. This news was greeted with huge relief by the delegation members, who had been suffering horribly on the trek across the Gobi from heat, thirst, brackish water, black gnats in their drinking vessels, paths 'as winding as a sheep's intestines', a constant lack of grass for the horses and a worsening shortage of grain.[93] One of the two Chinese officials to take part in the expedition recorded in his journal that 'if the edict had arrived a few days later we would all have become ghosts in a foreign land'.[94]

The irruption of a third force in the form of Galdan and the Dzungars dramatically altered the strategic equation from the Qing point of view. The Russian threat had been chronic; that of the Dzungars was immediate and acute. The Dzungars, like the Manchus, aspired to control Central Asia, and they lay right across the path of potential Manchu expansion in Mongolia and Turkestan. Occupying as they did the north-western region from which invaders of China had traditionally come, there was, furthermore, nothing obvious to stop them contending with the Manchus for possession of the Celestial Empire itself. The Qing objective could no longer simply be to roll back the Cossack settlers from the Amur valley: urgent action was called for to head off the appalling scenario of a Russian–Dzungar alliance. And this was liable to entail a more flexible stance in negotiating with the Russians than Kangxi may originally have had in mind.

When a messenger from Golovin arrived in Peking in the winter of 1688–9 to discuss a new rendezvous in Russian-held territory, the emperor, then, was only too happy to cooperate. In 1689, as Pereira wryly recorded, 'we were to be fortunate enough to enjoy the same recreational trip'.[95] The route chosen this time, however, lay mercifully to the east of the Gobi. Kangxi had settled for the talks to be held at Nerchinsk, the long-standing Cossack headquarters on the banks of the River Shilka. In late July Prince Songgotu advanced to the rendezvous even more strongly supported than he had been the previous year, with a retinue of 12,000 men, 15,000 horses and 4,000 camels. Partly apprehensive of a possible Russian attack, the Qing envoys were also aware that a show of potential force might 'help the negotiation'.[96] The Russians, who arrived some days later, numbered only 1,450, little over a tenth of Songgotu's contingent.[97] But they did have a sturdy negotiator in Golovin, 'a short, corpulent man but of a good presence and easy carriage',[98] who was backed up by Vlasov, the hawkish governor of Nerchinsk. As well as the usual Mongol interpreters they had brought along a Latin speaker in the person of Andrei Bielobotski, a Polish graduate of the University of Krakow. And they were under some pressure from Moscow to achieve a respectable outcome: Sophia Miloslavskaya, who was acting as regent for the two young tsars, Ivan V and Peter, had seen her army defeated by the Tatars in a Crimean campaign in 1688, and was badly in need of a diplomatic success to enable her to hold on to power.

The formal negotiations began on 22 August 1689, on the open ground outside Nerchinsk. The Russian ambassadors rode up in Oriental splendour, dressed in cloth of gold and black sable furs. Coming into their side of the open pavilion set up for the meeting, they seated themselves in chairs of state on a portion of ground spread with Turkey carpets, at a table covered with Persian fabrics of gold and silk and equipped with a pile of papers, an inkstand and a clock. Outside the pavilion their soldiers paraded with drums, fifes and bagpipes (the last a contribution of Scottish mercenaries). The Manchu grandees by contrast came forward in studied simplicity. They discarded their usual regalia apart from the large silk umbrellas traditionally carried before them, and sat down in their half of the tent on a plain bench covered with cushions of cloth. They appear to have been put out by the magnificence of their Russian counterparts and concerned not to be drawn into an embarrassing competition with them; but perhaps we may also suspect a quietly confident knowledge of where the real power lay. Both sides promptly set out their claims to the Amur region, neither outstandingly persuasive to a twenty-first-century eye. The Russians based their claim on the argument that the region belonged to no one at the time they arrived, the Qing on the tributary relationships they had established with the Daur and Maoming'an tribes. Songgotu made an opening bid for the whole stretch of eastern Siberia as far as Lake Baikal, subsequently allowing that the borderline might be drawn at Nerchinsk. Golovin replied sarcastically, 'I am very grateful to you and I thank you very much for letting me stay here tonight.'[99] He doggedly pressed for a border along the Amur. By the evening of 23 August the Qing envoys were already making a show of having their tents packed up, and on 24 August the Qing army commander, Langtan, decided the time had come to 'give the Russians a fright'.[100] In the course of the night around 3,000 troops of the 12,000-strong Qing force encamped on the far side of the Shilka, crossed the river and 'filled the hills' overlooking Nerchinsk.[101] Similar operations took place at Albazin. Golovin and his embassy were under siege.

All now depended on the interpreters. The Mongols brought by Golovin had quickly been dropped as incompetent. The Qing had their Russian deserters but had elected not to use them, no doubt because the Russian side viewed them as traitors. The talks were accordingly left in the exclusive hands of the Latin speakers – the Frenchman, the Portuguese and the Pole. During the last days of August Gerbillon, Pereira and Bielobotski scurried incessantly between the two camps, with the two Jesuits seemingly playing the key role in formulating proposals. We may note that the Jesuits in Peking had by this time shifted from the stealthily pro-Russian posture they had adopted at the time of Milescu's mission to one of neutrality. Pereira later recalled that he had not shown partiality towards the Orthodox Christian Russians at the expense of the Qing because 'schismatics and pagans, in the eyes of the Lord, are equal'.[102] A more compelling reason may be that the Jesuits had by now realised the Qing rulers of China were there to stay. Pereira, by his own account, 'yelled' at the Qing delegates that they had to appreciate the Muscovites 'were human beings endowed with reason and were not wild beasts';[103] but at the same time he made it clear to Golovin that Albazin at least was a non-negotiable Qing demand and must be given up. Golovin answered coldly, 'We concede nothing because you ask too much.'[104] But the pressure was mounting. On 28 August the Qing forces were joined by a cavalry squadron of 2,000 Buryat Mongols from the Lake Baikal area who had risen up in revolt against Russia's subjugation of their tribe some forty years earlier – a reminder, presumably, that Golovin couldn't even count on security in his rear. Gerbillon and Pereira came up with a compromise border to be drawn at the River Gorbitsa, which flowed into the Shilka to form the Amur at a point halfway between Nerchinsk and Albazin. Golovin saw that his position was hopeless, and a final settlement was rapidly hammered out. By the night of 6 September festive lanterns were burning in the Manchu camp.

On 7 September 1689 the first treaty between China and Russia was concluded – in Latin. Russian and Manchu versions were also prepared (not Chinese), but the Latin text was the definitive one. On the face of it the Qing had won the encounter hands down. Neither side was entirely clear about the geography, but the Russians were firmly obliged to withdraw to the west of the Gorbitsa and the north of the Stanovoi mountains, leaving the whole Amur basin in Manchu hands. Albazin was to be demolished once and for all. One clause also provided for the mutual repatriation of fugitives, protecting the Qing from any further defection of border tribes. On his return to Moscow Golovin was blamed for the loss of Albazin, though it is hard to see what he could possibly have done to retain it.[105] The Treaty of Nerchinsk came to be regarded by Russians as an unfair agreement extracted from them under duress. The Amur valley entered their consciousness as an idyllic lost realm they must one day recover. The two-year siege of Albazin was recalled like the Alamo – as a heroic last stand in the face of overwhelming odds.

In reality, though, the Russians had not done so badly. The Treaty of Nerchinsk had been not merely the first between China and Russia, but the first concluded on approximately equal terms between China and any European or indeed any foreign state. There had been no disputes over protocol. The ambassadors had taken their seats in the tent simultaneously, 'with the greatest equality', as Gerbillon put it.[106] The language of the treaty was free of any kind of traditional Chinese condescension, though the event was recorded by officials back in Peking in the usual haughty terms. (Was it sheer chance that the Qing envoys made no attempt to produce a Chinese version of the original document?) The substantive concessions made by Songgotu and his colleagues were as striking as the ceremonial ones. The Qing not merely abandoned the wilder ideas they had recently voiced of confining the Russians to Yakutsk or Lake Baikal; they even permitted them to keep Nerchinsk. The Russians were compelled to hand over Albazin, but the Qing undertook not to settle there and to leave that area as a buffer zone. The Russians were even allowed to keep Gantimur. Pereira had thoughtfully inserted a clause letting bygones be bygones, so that only fugitives crossing the border after the treaty came into force would be liable for repatriation. Most important of all, the Russians had secured the commercial opening they had pursued intermittently ever since the early years of the century. From now on any Russian subjects holding proper passports could cross the border to trade; as could any Chinese who might wish to travel in the opposite direction. After a tortoise-like start, groping their way through a fog of misunderstandings, the Russians had finally made the most of their growing geographical closeness and won access for their merchants to the Chinese capital a clear century before any other European power tried to achieve that objective.

Cannon were fired; oaths were taken. Under instructions from Kangxi, the Manchu envoys were even prepared to swear on a crucifix as the Russians had done, but their oath was to be couched in Roman Catholic form and the Russians themselves objected on theological grounds. The day ended with much celebration. The Russians contributed sweets and a loaf of white sugar from Madeira. 'The Muscovites also', Pereira recorded, 'had wine made of grapes and of grain, which however our ambassadors did not like as it was too strong.'[107]

On his way home, in Irkutsk in March 1690, Golovin received an envoy sent by Galdan of the Dzungars with a belated proposal for a Russo-Dzungar axis. The Dzungar chief urged that the Amur was really Mongolian territory, and that China had no business to be in the region at all. Nor, for that matter, had the Russians; but Galdan was prepared to waive his claim to these lands if the Russians would carry on building towns there as a defensive barrier against the Qing. At the same time, he proposed an offensive alliance against the Qing and the Khalkhas. Right through the summer he went on repeating his proposal through agents dispatched as far west as Tobolsk. The ink had at this point barely dried on the Nerchinsk agreement, and the Qing were still edgy. When news reached Kangxi in late June of the Dzungar approach to Golovin, he sent word through a Russian courier still in Peking that if Russia supplied troops to Galdan it would constitute a violation of the treaty and would lead to war.[108] The emperor was fretting needlessly. Golovin and his colleagues were tempted by Galdan's overtures, but their answer was thanks but no thanks. The treaty was a done deal, and Galdan could be given no help without fresh instructions from Moscow. The fact was that the lure of the China market outweighed any possible inducements Galdan had to offer. In the same way, from Kangxi's point of view the Russians, once relocated to the far side of the new north-eastern frontier, were bound to appear less alarming strategically than Galdan's whirling horsemen to the north-west. The two sedentary powers were perhaps also influenced to some degree in their choices by their shared past experience of Mongol invasion. The written record gives no clues on this last point: we can only conjecture. But whatever their calculations, it seems clear they preferred to work with each other.

CHAPTER 2

THE GREAT EQUILIBRIUM

THE CARAVAN AGE (1689–1728)

The Treaty of Nerchinsk ushered in a thirty-year flurry of Russian trade. In March 1692 the young tsar Peter the Great, sole effective ruler in Moscow since the overthrow of his half-sister, the regent Sophia,[1] sent a first state-sponsored caravan to Peking to explore the prospects for enriching the treasury through the development of a regular traffic with Kangxi's domains. The government invested 42,000 roubles' worth of export furs in the venture, and Eleazar Isbrandt Ides, a Danish merchant long resident in Moscow, was 'pitch'd upon', in the charming phrase of a contemporary English translation of his journal, to serve as the caravan leader.[2] The visit began affably, with Isbrandt lavishing hospitality on the official in charge of the Manchu border outpost of Qiqihar: 'I entertained him in the European manner, and put a glass of good sack briskly about, causing the trumpets and other music to play, all of which wonderfully pleased this gentleman, so that he and his company returned home pretty mellow'.[3] And the business was a triumphant success. The government made a 48 per cent profit on their investment, and the decision was taken to organise a state caravan trade on a permanent basis. Between 1696 and 1719 a total of nine state caravans made the long trek on horseback and camelback across the Eurasian landmass to Peking,[4] headed in each case by a seasoned merchant like Isbrandt who acted as the government's agent and negotiator. Some of these expeditions were strikingly large. In 1698, for instance, a caravan led by the merchant

Spiridon Lyangusov comprised 478 men including servants and Cossack escorts, and in 1703 Ivan Savadeev is said by one source to have brought a contingent of no fewer than 830.[5] Some of the caravan heads (from 1710 they were dignified with the title of 'commissars') made the journey two or three times, and established a niche for themselves as Russia's first China Hands.

In exchange for their furs the state caravans brought back from Peking quantities of both silver and gold with a view to building up the country's monetary reserves – the policy of mercantilism which Peter had absorbed in the course of his study visits to England and Holland. In addition they brought a variety of luxuries for the Russian court. Attention focused especially on the fine Chinese silk known as *kamka*, which was widely worn in upper-class circles and which Peter used for his flags and battle standards. After the capital was moved from Moscow in 1712 to the newly built city of St Petersburg the tsar decreed, seemingly in another mercantilist effort, that his army and naval officers should be paid in *kamka* rather than coin, and in 1717 he insisted that they were to wear 'no spun and drawn gold and silver . . . but only Chinese silks from Siberia'.[6] The attraction of Chinese medicine persisted. Isbrandt's party was accompanied by a German apothecary whose task was to seek out rhizomes, herbs and seeds for medicinal use, and jars of these items were ferried back to the Grand Pharmacy in Moscow. Peter placed a personal order for a set of the celebrated purple clay tea ware from Yixing in Jiangsu Province, and in 1715 he arranged for a Chinese porcelain stove to be made in Peking to his specifications. In spite of all this consumption most of the caravans managed to bring in a healthy revenue for the treasury. In 1707 a caravan led by Pyotr Khudyakov sold 180,000 roubles' worth of furs for 270,000 roubles' worth of assorted Chinese goods – a cool 150 per cent profit.[7]

Private trade continued to snap at the heels of Russian government business. The ink was scarcely dry on the Treaty of Nerchinsk before the agents of two prominent Moscow firms were scurrying home with goods they had bought from the Qing delegation.[8] On his way out to Peking Isbrandt passed a returning Russian caravan of 150 merchants and 300 camels. Private merchants were given full scope to take part in the early state caravans: the 42,000 roubles invested by the state in Isbrandt's expedition compared with 114,000 roubles' worth of export produce contributed by private interests. Isbrandt himself had a major stake in the success of the venture: threatened by bankruptcy, he had sought his appointment as caravan leader in the hope of recouping his fortunes, and the personal profit he made in Peking did indeed enable him to pay off his debts. Private merchants, in contrast to the state, continued to focus mainly on supplying the basic needs of the Russian and especially the Siberian population through the import of cheap cottons and grain. 'Brick' tea, made by pressing the dust of the tea leaves into the shape of tiles, was sold to the Buryat Mongols of Siberia, and Chinese tobacco balls had by 1700 acquired a large Siberian market. While the state profited amply from the duties they levied on these private goods at Nerchinsk and again at Verkhoturye, on the border between Siberia and European Russia, the competition from private trade soon became a major nuisance from the government's point of view. The merchants in charge of the state caravans had a habit of selling their own goods first before they attended to the government cargoes. In 1698 Peter reissued the long-standing ban on private import of highly prized goods like gold, silver and rhubarb, and extended it to new items such as *kamka* and the ever more popular Chinese tobacco. The results were unimpressive. In 1702 the value of private imports from China dwarfed the government's revenues by 566,000 to 47,000 roubles, and in 1706 a complete state monopoly was imposed on traffic with China, with private participation in the caravan trade forbidden on pain of death. Even this didn't quell the ravenous hunger for the China market. Several private merchants continued to bring caravans to Peking with bogus credentials, and by the mid-1720s the Qing bureaucracy had recorded visits to their capital of some fifty Russian 'embassies' – many more than the Russian government had ever been aware of. In the meantime a lively smuggling trade had grown up on the newly drawn frontier in Manchuria. In 1716 a Qing report noted,

> Annually towards the end of autumn sixty or seventy or occasionally a hundred Russians, sleeping in tents, wearing woollen coats and caps, come to the west bank of the Gorbitsa River to trade . . . They buy low-grade silks, cotton, tobacco, ginger, pepper and sugar, and sell horses, oxen, furs, wool, glass and swords.[9]

State or private, in Peking or on the border, the import trade from China was now to all intents and purposes in the hands of Russians alone. By the beginning of the eighteenth century the 'Bokharan' middlemen had virtually disappeared from the scene. Customs records reveal that in 1703 Central Asian traders brought only three batches of Chinese goods to Tobolsk while Russian traders brought twenty; and European Russian firms were in any case tending to move their activities at Tobolsk all the way to the border at Nerchinsk. And at Peking or on the border these traders were starting to come into contact with every stratum of Chinese society.

For a good many years Kangxi and his court took a largely benevolent view of this Muscovite traffic. Some effort, to be sure, was made to keep the influx of Russian traders within reasonable bounds. In 1694, following Isbrandt's visit, the Qing authorities ruled that a caravan should be received in the capital no more than once every three years. No more than 200 men, not including the merchants, were to take part in each caravan, and each caravan's stay in Peking was to be confined to a maximum of eighty days. To keep a fairly close eye on their dealings the caravan staff were to be housed in the familiar Ming hostel, now known as the Russia House, whenever the Russians were in residence (when the Koreans arrived it became the Korea House[10]), and any traffic in contraband goods was severely punished. But no drastic action was taken when the number of caravan personnel shot up way beyond the official limit, or when the caravans started coming once every two years instead of every three. And the detailed arrangements for looking after the caravan staff were distinctly hospitable. Russian goods were to be allowed into China free of duty, and warehouses and food were to be laid on free of charge. The Qing government advanced loans to distressed Russian merchants, and supervised the repayment of debts by Chinese traders who typically bought their furs from the Russians on credit. The authorities even paid the caravans' expenses for their journey back to Russia, and provided escorts to ensure that the returning caravans didn't get robbed on their way to the Russian frontier. Some of this treatment reflected the traditional protocol for entertaining what the dynasty persisted in regarding as tribute missions; but certain aspects, notably the arrangements for the return journey, were privileges never previously bestowed by a Chinese court on any visitors from abroad.

Kangxi indeed proved remarkably magnanimous to the Russians in general. Especial favour was shown to the small community of Russian deserters in Peking, which had lately been boosted by the thirty-odd prisoners taken on the fall of Albazin in 1685. Known from now on in Russia as the *Albazintsy*, these expatriates were allotted their own quarter in the north-east corner of the capital. Impressed by his glimpses of Cossack strength and valour, the emperor formed them (like that hazy band of Russians attached to the Mongol khans in Peking four centuries earlier) into a unit of the imperial guard, the Eighth Company of the Bordered Yellow Banner,[11] and supplied them with government housing, clothes, rice rations, a financial subsidy and plots of arable land. Partly to ensure their allegiance and hive them off to some extent from the Chinese subject population, the Albazintsy were encouraged to follow their own Orthodox Christian religion, and Kangxi assigned for their worship a disused temple of Guan Yu, the god of war. The expatriates were allowed to install an icon of St Nicholas the Miracle-Worker which they had brought from Albazin, the captured priest Father Maxim Leontiev performed divine service and in 1696 the makeshift chapel was consecrated as the St Nicholas Church. At the same time the Albazintsy were granted permission to take local wives. According to some sources these women were widows of executed convicts, doled out to the Russians by the Board of Punishments because no one else would be willing to marry the red-haired barbarians; though later generations of Albazintsy protested indignantly that their forefathers married respectable Manchu and Mongol ladies. Whatever the truth it seems clear that the Albazintsy merged quite smoothly into Peking society. The Qing authorities referred to them as 'our Russians'. The Albazintsy soon carved themselves out a role as intermediaries servicing the Russian caravan trade. With the knowledge they quickly acquired of the Manchu and Chinese languages they acted as translators and brokers, introducing the merchants to their Chinese counterparts, showing the sights of Peking to their compatriots, feasting with them in the city's eating houses and meeting their spiritual needs in the St Nicholas Church.

Part of the aim of the Qing was to draw on these local contacts to build up their still feeble knowledge of the shadowy neighbour to the north. Certainly by 1708 and perhaps by as early as 1690 the Lifanyuan had established a Russian Language School designed to train young Manchus in batches of twenty-four at a time to work for the government as translators and experts on Russian affairs. The Albazintsy were swiftly co-opted as teachers, supplemented within a few years by merchants drafted in from visiting caravans. By the early eighteenth century the Qing had succeeded in forming a small corps of reasonably competent Russianists. One of these was a Manchu named Maci. Initially put in charge of the Russian Eighth Company of guardsmen, he emerged as a leading Qing bureaucrat supervising the caravan trade and rose up in due course to the exalted rank of grand secretary. Another leading expert, one Tulisen, took the Qing quest for knowledge of Russia into Russia itself.

The flow of contact between Russia and China had continued up to this point to be strictly one-way. Russian deputations made the great trek to the Chinese empire but never vice versa. In June 1712, however, a Qing embassy including Tulisen set out from Peking in the company of a returning Russian caravan and its 'commissar', Khudyakov. The ostensible aim of the embassy was to escort home the nephew of a chief of the Torguts, a far-flung Mongol tribe who were living under Russian protection by the lower reaches of the Volga. But the visit entailed cutting through a great swathe of Siberian territory, and at least part of the purpose was to hold talks with the Russians and develop a closer acquaintance with the tsar's domains. Tulisen and his colleagues were even instructed to be ready for an invitation to the Russian capital if Peter took it upon himself to issue one. The journey was long and at times wearisome, with five months spent at Selenginsk waiting for permission from the tsar to proceed to the next stage and another four months at Irkutsk waiting for the ice to melt on the rivers; but it gave Tulisen ample chance to collect information which he later shaped into the first published Chinese description of Russia. Tulisen was of course conscious of Russia's status as an emerging power. The Russian state had originally, he reported, been 'a poor insignificant spot called Kiev in the vicinity of the north-western ocean', but for the last three centuries its 'strength and revenues had been constantly increasing'. Unlike the early Russian descriptions of China, however, his account displayed little sign of awe. The Russian empire, he agreed, was very extensive and densely forested, but the habitations were 'only thinly scattered' – 200 to 300 households at Selenginsk, 800 at Irkutsk, 1,000 at Yeniseisk, garrisoned respectively by just 200, 500 and 800 troops. The people were engaged in simple occupations, fishing for omul in Lake Baikal and sterlet on the rivers and producing a certain amount of fine hempen cloth. By comparison with the Chinese they were rather poor boatmen, with a tendency to hug the riverbanks. Their social life was engaging, but a trifle unsophisticated. Tulisen wrote of joyous festivals at which men drank and grew merry to the sound of the balalaika ('different kinds of guitars with metal wires'). The women, he observed with a hint of disapproval, vied with each other in ornamenting their persons, 'gadding about everywhere according to their pleasure' and sometimes 'assembling to sing on the public roads', while the children sold raspberries at the way stations. People made crockery out of the white and shining bones of a huge animal which 'burrowed into the earth' – in other words, of mammoths disinterred from the Siberian permafrost. Some of the keenest interest displayed by this Manchu envoy was inspired by his geographical surroundings. He was naturally impressed by the northern latitude, where in summer 'at the hour of greatest darkness, though the sun is down, there is still light enough to play at cards'. And he wrote with real pleasure of the beauty of some of the scenery. On the River Ob, for example,

> Upon the surface, and near the banks . . . we saw vast numbers of white moths; some flying among the trees, others seemingly floating on the water. They appeared like the catkins of willow trees, when they are wafted by the wind; or the blossoms of the poplar, when they lie on the ground.[12]

In the autumn of 1713 the party crossed the Urals. 'Close to our road on both sides', Tulisen rhapsodised, 'the surface was like a piece of rich embroidery spread out before us, so variegated was it with wild flowers of all descriptions.' Some four weeks later they arrived at the town of Kaigorod. 'Here', noted Tulisen, 'the great roads branch off to Moscow and Kazan, the former to the north-west and the latter to the south-west.' The group had become the first Chinese embassy to set foot in Europe.[13]

The half-expected invitation from Peter didn't in fact materialise, largely because the tsar was preoccupied with his Great Northern War against Sweden; a preoccupation confirmed by the clusters of Swedish POWs who greeted the Qing party at various points on their route. Tulisen and his colleagues consequently took the south-western road to Kazan and the Volga and discharged their official mission to the khan of the Torguts before travelling home by the way they had come. They were, however, left in no doubt, either on the outward or return trip, of the warmth of their welcome. 'Our treatment and reception', wrote Tulisen, 'was extremely respectful and attentive throughout.' At Udinsk, Irkutsk and Yeniseisk they were greeted with guards of honour, drums and trumpets and musket and cannon salutes, and the local dignitaries came forward to offer them food. At Tobolsk, the Siberian capital, they were received cordially by the governor-general, Prince Matvei Gagarin, and questioned with the keenest interest about the workings of the Chinese administrative machine. Gagarin and his aides were particularly fascinated by the different ranks of ministers and high officials in the Qing government, wanting to know how the Qing posts corresponded to those of the various high officials attending on Peter; and it is tempting to speculate that the details provided by Tulisen and his group may have fed to some small degree into the meritocratic Table of Ranks which Peter introduced into the Russian administration in 1722. Gagarin and his officials were also full of praise for the stability of Qing China by comparison with the continual warfare in which Russia indulged: China indeed, said Gagarin, was 'at present the only empire which enjoys any peace or tranquillity'. Tulisen returned home satisfied that the Russians had achieved a sound appreciation of 'the many excellent virtues of our empire'.[14]

THE RUSSIANS TEST THE LIMITS (1689–1728)

To the Russians it must have seemed that the sky was the limit. Peter's ambitions especially were whetted, in these early years of the Enlightenment, by the advice he received from the German philosopher and mathematician Gottfried Wilhelm Leibniz. Leibniz was enthralled by the role which Russia looked like playing as a bridge between the civilisations of China and the west, and in 1713 he wrote urging the tsar to establish the closest possible exchange between them in goods, information and the arts. The restless and inquisitive Peter was only too happy to respond to his call, and in the following years we find Russia persistently testing the bounds of the possible as it tried to achieve the next obvious goal in the relationship – a permanent presence in Peking.

One promising route to this goal, as the Jesuits had shown, was that of religion. In 1693 the merchant Isbrandt had brought with him to Peking a request from the tsar that a parcel of land should be granted there to the Russian government for the erection of an Orthodox church. The function of this church would be to meet the needs of the caravan traders – not the Albazintsy, whom official Russia continued to regard as 'traitors and scoundrels'.[15] Within a few years, however, traders who had attended the little

Church of St Nicholas and clergy in Russia who had entered into correspondence with the expatriates started to paint a sad picture of the Albazintsy plight. Father Maxim Leontiev was growing old and blind. The community were swiftly 'going native' as their menfolk, including Father Maxim, shaved their foreheads and grew pigtails in the Chinese style and wore Chinese clothes while their 'corrupt pagan wives' brought idols and superstition into the household.[16] A young mixed-race generation were growing up who were losing their Orthodox faith and even their command of the Russian language (hence the need felt to supplement Albazintsy teachers with visiting merchants at the Qing Russian Language School). Here surely was a spiritual challenge which Holy Russia could not ignore. And it raised, furthermore, the prospect of a broader evangelism on which the Russian Church had already made a start among the Tatars and the Tungus tribes of Siberia. In 1695 the metropolitan of Tobolsk wrote to Father Maxim, 'Your captivity is not without use for the inhabitants of China, insofar as the light of the truth of Christian Orthodoxy is being opened to them by you', and directed the old priest to include in his liturgy a prayer that Kangxi might 'be united with Your Holy and Apostolic Church, so that he might receive Your Heavenly Kingdom'.[17] And in June 1700 Peter himself issued a decree that a 'good and learned man' should be sent out to 'lead the people of China and Siberia immured in the blindness of idolatry into the knowledge and service of the true living God'.[18]

But Peter also saw a possible angle beyond mere evangelism. From an early stage he had shown signs of realising that Peking might provide a useful base for acquiring various kinds of China-related knowledge. The Isbrandt caravan of 1692–4 had included a specialist group sent to study the Chinese technique of inoculation for smallpox and the quarantine system for smallpox which had been introduced by the Qing regime. The evangelical mission which was taking shape in the tsar's mind was also to include a distinctly modern-sounding contingent of language students whose task would be to acquire, on the spot, a command of the Manchu, Mongolian and Chinese tongues and a grasp of local customs and culture.

Finally Peter dropped a hint of an underlying motive. The evangelism, he instructed a counsellor, was not to be overdone. The mission was to proceed cautiously and avoid angering either the Qing government or the Jesuits on to whose turf the Russians must inevitably tread. The implication was clear that the tsar envisaged the mission at least in part as a diplomatic entity which would promote trade, collect information, bring the two countries closer together and beat the Jesuits at their own game of combining religious activity with the accumulation of secular influence.

Requests to dispatch a band of Russian missionaries to the Chinese capital were consequently submitted through the medium of the caravan merchants in 1704 and again in 1712. By the second of these dates the time was propitious. The aged Father Maxim had finally died, leaving the Albazintsy in obvious need of a priest to maintain their religious observances; and more important, the Qing needed Russian permission to send off their embassy across the length of Siberia to the Volga Torguts. Caravan commissar Khudyakov entered into negotiations with the Qing authorities, and an agreement was reached that in exchange for their Russian transit visa Tulisen and his colleagues would bring back a first Russian Orthodox mission to Peking. The mission was to be headed by Archimandrite Ilarion Lezhaisky, a Little Russian or in modern parlance Ukrainian graduate of the Kiev Ecclesiastical Academy. (Ukrainian Orthodox were favoured because they were felt to be better educated than other Russian subjects and able to hold their own in theological controversy as a result of their constant disputes with the Roman Catholics of the local Uniate Church.) At the end of 1715 Father Ilarion arrived in the Qing capital with an entourage of a priest, a deacon and seven language students.[19] The Russians had succeeded in their first bid to entrench themselves in Peking.

Yet the deep underlying Qing wariness of Russian intentions had not gone away. As early as 1693, amid the warmth and conviviality with which the Isbrandt caravan was received in his capital, Kangxi warned his counsellors that while there were undoubtedly many able men in Russia their nature was 'narrow and obstinate' and their character 'persistent and slow'. All was well with Russia at the moment; but 'We fear . . . that after we have passed through some generations, probably she might cause some trouble in the future.'[20] The Qing still looked on Russia essentially as a strategic threat to be neutralised, and as the years passed Russian conduct began once again to give rise to alarm. The Russian pressure which had been successfully deflected from the north-eastern, Manchurian frontier now showed signs of resuming in the Mongolian steppes to the north. In 1691 Kangxi had received the submission of the entire Khalkha Mongol tribe, thereby bringing his expanding empire up against the Russian outposts to the south-east of Lake Baikal. But the border in this region was wholly undemarcated. Russians were settling thickly in places like Selenginsk and Udinsk which the Qing claimed as theirs, and were also giving shelter periodically to disgruntled Khalkhas who wanted to get away from Qing rule.

A still keener anxiety was provoked by Russian manoeuvres in the far north-west. In June 1696 Kangxi had scored a great victory against his Dzungar challenger Galdan at the Battle of Jaomodo: Galdan had fled into the desert and poisoned himself the following year. But the Dzungars were far from finished. Under Galdan's nephew and successor, Tsewang Araptan, they even showed signs of evolving from mounted nomad warriors into an organised state engaged in mining and agriculture, the building of towns and the promotion of trade: one European traveller noted that they were 'not such savage people as they are generally represented'.[21] Against this background the relationship between Russia, China and Dzungaria began to assume the dimensions of what a later generation would call a 'strategic triangle'. Much of the Qing diplomatic effort in these years was devoted to keeping Russia neutral in the continuing duel with the Dzungars. The embassy to the Torguts, for instance, is generally believed to have had as its secret agenda the recruitment of the remote Mongol tribe for an anti-Dzungar alliance and the Russian government's blessing for that operation. But it was by no means certain along which side of the strategic triangle the Russians were going to squint. In 1712 Peter heard from Governor-General Gagarin reports that gold deposits had been found in Dzungar-controlled eastern Turkestan. For the tsar, with his monetarist outlook ('Gold is the heart of the state', he is quoted as saying[22]), the lure of gold mines was irresistible. An initial expedition of 3,000 troops to look for gold on the upper reaches of the River Irtysh was attacked by the Dzungars: by 1715, however, Peter was starting to contemplate a radical switch from the Qing to the Dzungar side. If Tsewang Araptan could be persuaded to let Russia found settlements and prospect for gold on the upper Irtysh he might even be willing to form an offensive alliance with the Dzungar chieftain against the Qing. By 1717 Gagarin had sent him a draft proposal for such a realignment.

Some further irritation was also aroused in Qing government circles by aspects of the caravan trade. Trade was as ever a minor consideration from the Qing point of view – a carrot to be dangled in front of the Russians or withdrawn if occasion demanded. By the second decade of the eighteenth century, however, unauthorised Russian traders were pouring in to do business at Urga, the chief Khalkha settlement, which further heightened Qing fears for their grip on Mongolia. The Qing rulers were also now coming round to the view that too many Russian caravans were turning up in Peking; and there was mounting dissatisfaction with the conduct of the caravan crews. As a Russian source put it,

> The Russian in China remained a Russian: his broad, wild nature made itself felt even here. Drunkenness, uproar, fights, violence on the part not only of the Russian merchants but of the caravan escorts, the commissars and the other servants aroused . . . the complaints of the Chinese.[23]

Many Russians traded illegally with Qing officials, and some brutality was shown by the commissars to Chinese debtors who were handed over to them.

For all these reasons Qing answers to Russian requests to expand the official relationship beyond the Nerchinsk framework were apt to be negative. Isbrandt's petition to have a church built for the use of the caravan teams was rebuffed with the observation that churches in China could be put up only for permanent residents. The first attempt by a caravan leader in 1704 to win consent for the sending of an Orthodox mission was likewise turned down (some of the Russians blamed this on the intrigues of the Jesuits). And in the late 1710s the Russian behaviour in Mongolia and Turkestan plus the minor commercial annoyances led the Qing to strike back with the economic sanctions that were their most potent weapon. In June 1719 the Qing court refused to grant the latest state caravan permission to cross the border. The Lifanyuan wrote to Gagarin that the trade with Russia was unnecessary, unprofitable and had to be stopped.

The Russian government were far from happy with the condition of trade themselves. By the mid-1710s the market in Peking for Siberian furs was well and truly glutted, largely owing to the incessant coming and going of illegal private caravans. Local demand was plummeting, and by 1716 the prices of Russian goods are said to have been no more than 60 per cent of their level in 1693. This downward trend had been one further reason for Peter to dally with the thought of transferring his diplomatic affections to the rising Dzungar state. But at the same time the government couldn't accept the abrupt closing off of the China market that had proved to be such a nourishing source of revenue. Accordingly in 1719 a full-blooded embassy was sent off to Peking, for the first time since Nerchinsk, on a trouble-shooting venture commanded by the tsar's special envoy, a guards officer named Lev Izmailov.

Izmailov's embassy also went, however, with the unmistakable purpose of upping the ante. One of its tasks was to secure the continuance, on a more elevated footing, of the fledgling Russian Orthodox Mission. Father Ilarion's sojourn had been a short one. After a wild attempt to make converts by doling out sables and fox furs to any Manchu officials who called on him he had used up his resources and taken to heavy drinking; and in late 1719 he died on his way back from a journey outside the capital to get treatment for rheumatism at some nearby hot springs. Peter now envisaged replacing him with a much grander figure, a bishop who would be enthroned in Peking as the head of a formal diocese of the Orthodox Church. A second Ukrainian, Innocent Kulchitsky, was hastily consecrated Bishop of Pereyaslavl and attached to Izmailov's embassy in Irkutsk. Izmailov was further directed to obtain for Russia a commercial position in the Qing realm as yet undreamt of by any other European power: a free-trade zone encompassing the whole of both empires, extra-territorial rights for all Russian subjects in Chinese territory and the appointment to Peking of a consul in the shape of a Swedish engineer named Lorents Lange. Of obscure antecedents, Lange was most likely brought to Russia as one of the many Swedish POWs who had been taken in the Great Northern War. By 1715 he had found a niche in the government's service, and had accompanied Father Ilarion to Peking where he had negotiated the manufacture of Peter's Chinese porcelain stove. Now he was back in Peking as Izmailov's assistant.

In pursuit of these goals Peter had no intention of getting held up by the old tiresome squabbles over protocol. Conscious that trouble had even arisen on the otherwise smooth Isbrandt visit, when a letter he sent for Kangxi was refused by the Lifanyuan on the grounds that his name and titles had been placed before the Qing emperor's, the tsar now composed a new message putting Kangxi firmly in first place, acclaimed him as 'Emperor of the Great Asiatic Nation, the Most Absolute Monarch, the Very Bogdoi and Chinese Khan', dropped all enumeration of his own lengthy titles and signed himself humbly, 'Your Majesty's good friend, Peter'.[24] Izmailov was under instructions to comply with all the requirements of Chinese ceremonial, including the kowtow. Like Milescu before him the envoy seems to have felt the need to put up a show of resistance, giving, in the words of a Jesuit onlooker, 'unequivocal signs of resentment by certain motions of his mouth, and by turning his head aside, which under the circumstances was very unseemly'.[25] But he did as he was told.

The ageing emperor had also grown ever more flexible in pursuit of his own agenda. On his first meeting with Izmailov in January 1721, calmly ignoring the rules for presenting credentials which had tormented the seventeenth-century delegations from Moscow, he took Peter's letter personally from the envoy's hands with the staggering comment that because he regarded the Russian ruler as a friend and neighbour equal to himself he had 'abandoned the customs of the past'. He inquired in a fatherly manner about Peter's welfare, voicing concern that the tsar was making too many ocean voyages, and offered Izmailov with his own hands a gold cup of 'warm tarassum' (a sweet, grain-based liquor, perhaps rice wine) to make the envoy feel comfortable on a cold winter's day. He tried to play down mounting tensions by stressing the futility of any possible Sino-Russian conflict. If the Qing tried to conquer Russia, he noted, their armies would freeze, and if the Russians tried to conquer China their armies would perish of heat prostration. In any case, 'we both have enough territory to live by ourselves'.[26]

On the substantive issues, however, Kangxi and his government gave almost no ground at all. In spite of Russian efforts to conceal Bishop Innocent's high ecclesiastical rank, to avoid referring to him as bishop-designate of Peking or bishop of anywhere within easy reach of the Chinese frontier, the Qing court had somehow detected that this new head of mission was to be sent to them as representative of a foreign authority planning to impose its will on the Chinese populace. It was an issue which had already brought them into conflict with the Roman Catholic missions when the Vatican tried to claim Chinese allegiance. Bishop Innocent was consequently denied permission to enter the Qing empire side by side with Izmailov, and was left hovering in the Siberian borderlands. He was still there in the autumn of 1722, sending aggrieved messages to his Church superiors. The foxes had holes, he sighed biblically, and the birds of heaven had nests, but he, Innocent, had nowhere to lay his head.[27]

Peter's commercial demands received similar treatment. His requests for free trade and for extra-territorial privileges for Russian subjects in China were flatly dismissed. The state caravan which had been denied entry was finally let through to Peking, but it might as well not have come. The Lifanyuan insisted that the best-quality sables and other furs should be set aside as gifts for the emperor, in effect converting this trading venture into the very different status of a tribute mission. And at the same time the Qing court released a total of 20,000 Amur sables from the imperial stores in a deliberate ploy to undercut the caravan's business.

Kangxi did consent, in the face of some keen disapproval from his ministers, to let Lorents Lange stay on in Peking after the rest of the embassy left for home. But the Qing never viewed Lange as a consul in the European sense, stationed in a foreign capital as a long-term representative of his country's interests. So far as they were concerned he was there on a strictly temporary basis, giving a helping hand to the caravan team. Unable to get his credentials accepted, he spent the bulk of his time trying to collect the debts owed by Chinese merchants to the caravan traders; and his board and lodging were scarcely those of a diplomat. On his first day alone in the Russia House in March 1721 he saw 'a man who had the appearance of a poor beggar' who arrived with 'some poor starved fowls, and salted cabbage' and 'some pots of a Chinese beverage' and dumped them in the courtyard before making off. This represented his rations from the Lifanyuan.[28] The old hostel was now in the final stage of dilapidation. On 1 May, the worthy Swede recorded in his journal, a mighty wind got up: 'All the wall of one side of my bedchamber fell, about midnight, into the courtyard, which made me very apprehensive for what remained.'[29]

It was all, of course, pressure, designed to secure the curtailment of what the Qing saw as Russian misbehaviour in the strategically critical border zones. During the months Lange spent in Peking the news seeping through to the Qing court made tensions still worse. In the north 700 disaffected Khalkha Mongols had crossed over to take refuge in Russian-held territory. To the west, where the duel between the Qing and Dzungar powers was intensifying (in 1720 Qing forces had taken control of Tibet to repel a Dzungar expansion into that vast area), the dreaded Russo-Dzungar axis showed signs of taking shape. In September 1721 Peter received an emissary from Tsewang Araptan and offered him a defensive alliance in return for free passage of Russian prospectors to his gold-bearing lands, and two months later a Captain Ivan Unkovsky set off from St Petersburg in the company of the returning envoy, with a brief to receive the submission of the Dzungar leader and negotiate an agreement for military and economic assistance to him. By May 1722 the old emperor in Peking seems at last to have come to the end of his patience with his northern neighbours. He was tired, he conveyed to the Russian 'consul' by way of the Lifanyuan, of 'receiving the law in his own country from foreigners of whom his subjects reaped no benefit'.[30] All trade with Russia was to cease until the frontier problems were settled and the Mongolian fugitives were handed back. The caravan must go home – in Kangxi's opinion it would be a long time before another one was allowed into the empire – and Lange must go with it. It was a total diplomatic rupture, and Lange didn't fail to let fall a dark hint of the possible consequences. He pointed out to the Lifanyuan that the tsar was about to bring his war with Sweden to a close, and there was nothing to stop him 'turning his arms to this side' if the Qing 'exercised his patience too much'.[31] Lange left for home in July with his consular venture in tatters; and by the time the old emperor died in December it looked as though the exertions of more than thirty years had been wasted and the Sino-Russian relationship was back to square one.

Very quickly, however, the two sides were pushed back together by the logic of their agendas. Kangxi's son and successor, Yongzheng, was bent on renewing his father's drive to expand and consolidate the Qing empire. In 1723 he began to advance his troops westwards into Kokonor (present-day Qinghai Province), a buffer region whose princes were apt to ally with the Dzungars and which had therefore to be brought within the Qing orbit. It was the first step towards an eventual attack on the Dzungar state itself. With these objects in mind it made no sense for Yongzheng to have a hostile Russia on his northern flank. In July 1724 he dispatched two senior officials to the Mongolian border zone to proclaim his peaceful intentions and to ask when the Russians proposed to send a new embassy to the Qing court.

The Russians too lost little time in grasping the need for a rapprochement. Peter was not in the end prepared to pursue his Dzungar flirtation beyond certain limits. In the course of 1722 Tsewang Araptan confirmed to Unkovsky that he was indeed willing to render allegiance to the tsar; but he wanted in exchange a Russian army of 20,000 men to be used against the Manchu forces, and Peter with his memories of the Amur war was not disposed to get into another collision with the Qing. He was ready to try to persuade the Qing emperor not to attack the Dzungars, and if, and only if, he failed in that effort he would help the Dzungars defend themselves – but that was the most he would do. Unkovsky stayed by the side of the Dzungar chief until 1724, but without coming to any agreement. After Peter died in January 1725 his widow and successor Catherine I and her advisers were still less inclined to give up the rich trading connection that had been forged in Peking for a mess of Central Asian pottage. Within a few months, as though in response to the inquiry made by Yongzheng's officials the previous summer, they had fitted out a new embassy headed by the imposing figure of Count Sava Vladislavich Raguzinsky, a nobleman of Bosnian Serb extraction who had built up a track record as a merchant in Constantinople before migrating into the Russian service. Sava's basic assignment was to get the caravan trade reinstated at all costs, and not to break off the negotiations until he had done so. At the same time he was authorised, like Izmailov before him, to up the ante and reach for the moon. In addition to getting the ban on the caravans lifted he was to demand Russian access to the southern Chinese port of Canton. The Russians had noticed the influx of Portuguese, Dutch and British merchants to that distant centre and were keen to get in on the act. If necessary they would be happy to make their approach to Canton along China's inland waterways. Sava was also to resume the quest for a Russian government-sponsored church to be built in Peking and for Bishop Innocent, still by his own glum account 'standing on the border, neither on one side nor the other',[32] to be admitted to China as head of a reorganised mission. At the end of October 1726 Sava entered Peking accompanied by the tireless Lange and a retinue of 120 men.

The talks began tensely. As at Nerchinsk, the Qing showed themselves quite prepared to display their superior military power and twist Russian arms. Sava and his party were sealed off in the Russia House by a contingent of 750 Qing troops. From time to time, when discussions grew difficult, they were denied food and given nothing to drink but brackish water. One half of them, Sava included, fell ill and had to be treated by three of the emperor's doctors. Sava for his part responded with more sabre-rattling hints about Russian arms shifting from Europe to Asia. In spite of all this the will to make progress was strong enough on both sides that by March 1727, after five months of exhausting dialogue, some general principles had been agreed. But the major question of the Mongolian border remained unsettled.

At this point the decision was made to transfer the talks to the border region itself. One source suggests that Sava had grown desperate for a change of venue ('Your Majesty, you cured me of illness; now cure me of grief'[33]), but the decision more likely reflects a sensible judgement by Yongzheng that the border could best be worked out on the spot. On 23 June Qing and Russian frontier commissions met for the first time by the River Bura, near the Russian outpost of Selenginsk. Some aggravation was now caused by the chairman of the Qing commission, Lungkodo, the emperor's uncle, who adopted a hardline approach, offering no concessions and even demanding that the Russians should hand Nerchinsk back. But the Russians manoeuvred adroitly, exhibiting for the first time an ability to distinguish between the Qing Russia Hands who were likely to show them some sympathy and the irredeemable hawks and to play off the former against the latter. Sava is said to have sent to Peking two separate bribes in the form of furs – 100 roubles' worth for a French Jesuit, Father Dominique Parrenin, to secure the good offices of Grand Secretary Maci, the former head of the Albazintsy Eighth Company, and 1,000 roubles' worth to Maci, to smooth the negotiations and get Lungkodo recalled. Lange meantime nobbled Tulisen, the former envoy who had crossed Siberia and was now serving as vice-chairman of the Qing frontier commission, and urged on him the dangers which might result from Lungkodo's obstinacy. Lungkodo was duly brought back to Peking and replaced by Tulisen as the commission chairman, the talks moved forward without further difficulty and on 20 August 1727 Russian and Qing signatures were affixed to a Treaty of the Bura which largely confirmed the de facto frontier. Survey commissions were organised and in the following months demarcated some 2,600 miles of border between Siberia and Mongolia with conical markers of earth or stone.

The diplomacy now shifted back to Peking, where on 14 June 1728, after a total of forty-eight rounds of talks, Sava and his Qing counterparts signed a wide-ranging document that became known to posterity as the Treaty of Kyakhta. The Treaty of Kyakhta embodied the same basic concepts as the Treaty of Nerchinsk, but was worked out in much greater detail, laying down rules and creating institutions. Once again the Qing rulers contrived to secure all their principal aims. The Bura agreement was built in as Article 3 of the Treaty, giving them the clear-cut border they wanted, and detailed steps were prescribed for the rendition and punishment of any deserters, bandits or cattle rustlers who crossed the border from either side, up to and including the death penalty – Qing subjects were to be strangled by their own authorities and Russian subjects hanged. A clause providing for 'eternal peace' between the two empires carried the implication that Russian military aid would be withheld from the Dzungars. The caravan trade would be restored, but on the basis of a strict return to the 1694 regulations: one caravan every three years, no more than 200 persons per caravan and a maximum stay in the Qing capital of eighty days. The illicit Russian traders at Urga were to be evicted, and private border trade was to be limited to two places – a newly founded settlement near Selenginsk called Kyakhta (hence the name of the Treaty) and Tsurukhaitu, an outpost on the Manchurian part of the frontier by the River Argun. The various extra demands that the Russians had tried their luck with were swept to one side. Free trade and Russian consuls were once more refused by the Qing officials on the grounds that if they were permitted 'it will be your China, your agents and free merchants will breed throughout all of China'.[34] There could be no question of Russian access to Canton. The journey there was long and perilous, and besides Canton was reserved for those maritime trading powers that were not China's neighbours. And nor under any circumstances could a Russian bishop be received in Peking. A letter sent to the Lifanyuan by the governor-general of Siberia had unfortunately referred to Innocent Kulchitsky as a 'religious person and grand gentleman',[35] reigniting Qing fears of a high-ranking prelate whose evangelical goals might extend well beyond the small Albazintsy community. Poor Bishop Innocent was once and for all denied entry to the Qing empire, though he managed to carve himself out a new vocation as apostle to the Siberian Tungus tribes. Decades after his death his remains were said to be untouched by decay and he was canonised, somewhat ironically, as an Orthodox patron saint of China.

In spite of all these rejections the Russians had also emerged from the diplomatic tussle surprisingly well. In their eagerness for a settlement the Qing court had once more proved willing to negotiate a treaty on a more or less equal footing. On the protocol side Sava, like Izmailov, had been allowed to present his credentials direct to the emperor, holding the papers above his head on a small tray covered with imperial yellow cloth; and to avoid future awkwardness about titles and forms of address it was ruled that from now on correspondence should no longer be between the two sovereigns but between the Russian Senate and the Lifanyuan.[36] Concretely the Russian government had secured the resumption of their cherished state caravan trade. They didn't mind the removal of the Russian traders at Urga who had been causing them extreme annoyance insofar as they sold top-grade sables to the Chinese there and thus ate away at the state revenues.[37] Above all they had won the acceptance of a permanent Orthodox mission in Peking, consisting of three priests (of relatively low rank) and six language students to be replaced by a new team every ten years, with a church to be built for them at Qing expense. Apparently fearful of the spiritual corrosion which the Albazintsy had suffered as a result of 'going native', they also obtained a provision that all further intermarriage between Russian and Qing subjects should be banned. Buddhist lamas were to be forbidden from migrating to Russia and spreading their own religion at Orthodox expense.

The treaty was a fair example of the restraint which was starting to typify the relations between the two immense neighbours. The only alternative, as Sava later observed, was war – but as he also remarked, 'this would not be an easy undertaking'.[38] Instead China and Russia had opted for a solid compromise. The uncontrolled rush of encounters that had taken place in the post-Nerchinsk decades had been replaced by a new formula, acceptable to both sides, of *direct but limited contact*; and the faltering diplomatic machinery had been adjusted to bring about a more perfect balance.

A WORKABLE COMPROMISE (1728–57)

During the two tranquil decades that followed trade between the two empires gradually began to assume the form it would keep for the next 100 years. The state caravan traffic resumed straight away, with caravans coming and going at regular intervals under the competent direction of Lange. The Qing court had developed a high regard for Russia's Swedish factotum: 'all was confusion', they commented, 'before Lange came'.[39] Nervous possibly of some further attempt by the Swede to stay put as a resident consul, they were not best pleased with the six months he spent in the capital looking after the first post-treaty caravan of 1728: 'Did he think to die in Peking, that he lived here so long?'[40] But they were perfectly happy for him to appear intermittently with the caravans in the role of commercial agent. The Russian government seem to have relaunched the caravan trade with high hopes, probably aiming to secure large amounts of gold and silver that would enable them to withdraw much of the debased coinage they had circulated in the years before 1730. The trouble was that the caravans failed to pay their way. Large sums of treasury money went into fitting them out for the long, dangerous journey across Eurasia: 44,000 roubles, for instance, were spent on the first of the post-treaty caravans and for the second, in 1731, 33,000 roubles went into equipping the caravan retinue alone.[41] But the Peking market was once again glutted with furs from Siberia, and business was dismal. The first post-treaty caravan, which sold only half of its pelts in terms of value, is said to have been 'probably a financial failure', and the next two, which arrived in Peking in 1731 and 1735, apparently made only 'modest profits'.[42] By the end of the decade the trade was becoming too expensive for the treasury to support. As early as 1730 Sava had suggested that the state fur trade might be better managed by a shareholding enterprise on the lines of the British East India Company, and in 1737 Lange seconded his suggestion, urging for good measure that the proposed enterprise should be open to participation by foreign capital. The proposal foundered for lack of takers. Some Qing officials were also unhappy with the caravan system, partly because of the outflow of bullion and partly because they regarded the Russian presence in Peking as a security risk.

The future instead proved to lie with the private trade that had been hived away on the border. Sava himself had founded the trading post of Kyakhta, named after a river which flowed through the sandy steppe to the south of the Russian border fortress of Troitskosavsk.[43] The beginnings were humble, a cluster of thirty-two huts with a marketplace in the middle. Government expectations of trade there were low, and in 1728 Lange simply used the place as a dumping ground for the goods that his caravan had failed to sell in Peking. With state monopolies on the sale of Siberian furs still in force, and reinforced by edicts in 1731 and 1734, Kyakhta soon turned into a centre for illicit traffic, contributing to the renewed glut of furs on the Peking market. Lange complained that the purchase of Chinese cottons and silks by the border traders was causing 'not a little disarray in the sale of crown goods'.[44] Merchants from the Chinese interior were put off by the extra expense of taking their trade to the edge of Siberia instead of transacting it at Urga as they had done in the past, and in 1737 Lange reported that while an adequate number of Russian traders were coming to Kyakhta the number of Chinese there was still very small. In around 1740, however, a sea change appears to have come over Russian thinking, as the authorities finally started to grasp the overwhelming advantage in dealing with China of private trade in general and the Kyakhta trade in particular. Trade at Kyakhta, they began to appreciate, was quick, cheap and flexible, and highly sensitive to changes in demand. It could operate every year, not just every three years, and all year round, if more vigorously in some seasons than others. Russian merchants could get there without necessarily travelling far, and could store their wares safely on Russian soil. The Chinese merchandise bought at Kyakhta could meet the needs of Siberian settlers, hard to supply from European Russia but easily provisioned from the south. And above all the Kyakhta trade promised to yield a plentiful inflow of customs revenue. In September 1740 the Russian Senate acknowledged that the various state monopolies were harmful to private trade, and over the following years they were steadily lifted.[45] By 1743 the Siberian Office was actively encouraging Russian merchants to move to Kyakhta along with their families. The results were dramatic. In the course of the 1740s the Kyakhta trade became worth an annual total of up to 600,000 roubles, far outstripping the value of the caravan business; by the 1750s the total had risen to 900,000.[46] And this traffic in turn was yielding between 157,000 and 230,000 roubles in customs receipts.[47] Russian merchants on the border were doing handsomely, and the Kyakhta settlement began to acquire the sobriquet of the Sandy Venice.

The Kyakhta trade also had increasing merits from the point of view of the Qing. It relieved them of the burden of looking after the Russian state caravans, and it kept the sometimes rowdy Russian traders at a safe distance from the capital. Most important, it was a barter business, with brick tea and bales of cotton the units of value, and thus avoided the outflow of bullion to the Russian side. By the 1740s, consequently, Chinese merchants were coming to Kyakhta in growing numbers and expanding their own small settlement, 500 to 800 feet to the south of the Russian, which they called by the prosaic name of Maimaicheng – Trade Town. The Chinese soon showed themselves both better organised and better disciplined than their Russian counterparts. As in Canton they formed themselves into a *hang*, or trade association, under the direction of a Manchu official, the *zarguchei*. They were required to observe absolute secrecy and absolute unanimity in pricing their goods, and the amount they sold was restricted to enable them to maintain high and fixed prices and to acquire Russian wares at a steady profit. The Russian merchants, to whom it had never occurred to do business in concert, were inclined to regard all this as sharp practice.

The trade nonetheless went ahead with surprising placidity. Now and again there were small incidents in the form of cattle-rustling or border raids. In 1742 some Russians were reported to have crossed the frontier in search of fuel, and in 1744 two drunken Russians killed two Chinese traders in a squabble over vodka, leading the Qing authorities to close down the market for seventeen days. But there was no major conflict, and when disputes arose no resorting to force. Social contact was limited. Mongolian continued to be used as the lingua franca, and while some Chinese picked up a smattering of Russian this is said to have grated on Russian ears. No Russians appear to have learnt Chinese, and the Chinese took care not to help them to do so in case they became able to listen in on Chinese business conversations. Chinese women were banned from Trade Town, to discourage their menfolk from staying there permanently and perhaps absorbing dangerous foreign concepts and customs. But human nature will have its way, and in 1753 some Chinese were reported by the aggrieved Qing authorities to have crossed into the Sandy Venice and engaged in 'obscene, indecent and infamous affairs' with women on the Russian side.[48]

In the meantime the Orthodox Mission were putting down roots in Peking. Under the terms of the Treaty of Kyakhta the old Ming hostel became the Russia House permanently, and by 1735 it had even undergone some repairs. The new church provided for under the treaty was completed close by the Russia House in 1732, and consecrated in 1736 as the Church of the Purification. It was built in the Chinese style, with a sloping roof edged with bricks shaped like flowers and windows made of paper, and Chinese artists were brought in to paint the icons. The old Albazintsy Church of St Nicholas, which had been felled by an earthquake in September 1730, was rebuilt with equal speed and reconsecrated as the Church of the Assumption. Together the two Russian bases began to be referred to as parts of a single complex – the North House founded by the Albazintsy and the South House (the Russia House) the main centre of operations where Russian visitors stayed.

Aside from these building activities it is a little hard to make out what the Mission actually did. Nominally it retained an evangelical function. At the end of 1734 the missionaries were enjoined by their religious superiors to 'summon the Chinese to piety and to the knowledge of the holy and glorious God'.[49] But these inroads were minimal. In 1731 Archimandrite Antony Platkovsky, who had arrived in Peking in the aftermath of the treaty to head the Second Mission, reported uninspiringly that the number of converts was down on the previous year but that he had recently baptised nine Chinese and had hopes of baptising eight more.[50] It seems likely that after the Qing rejection of Bishop Innocent the Russians were anxious not to upset the authorities by embarking on any kind of spiritual offensive, and the instruction of 1734 did indeed carry the rider that the missionaries should summon the Chinese to piety '*so far as opportunity allows*'.[51] The priests were undoubtedly meant to reclaim for the Church the deracinated Albazintsy, but there is little sign that they even did much about this. One Mission historian retails a dismal sketch from the period of a typical specimen of these descendants of Siberian Cossacks who continued to serve in the Qing emperor's guard:

> Extravagant, taken up with himself and his status, coarse, uneducated, *superstitious*, treacherous, cunning, not knowing what to do with the free time and the intolerable boredom that hung over him, constantly mooching about the streets, inns and theatres, sometimes smoking opium, getting into gambling and other criminal activity, *sick in both spirit and body*, he soon found himself hopelessly in debt to the money-lenders in the capital, ultimately becoming the talk of the town.[52]

By the 1740s we find allusions to 'the few baptised Albazintsy left in Peking'.[53]

But the Orthodox Church had never in fact been cut out for intensive evangelism in the style of its Roman Catholic and Protestant rivals. From its earliest days in Byzantium its interests had been closely bound up with the state, and the offshoots of the Byzantine Church which sprang up in Russia and other emerging countries of eastern and south-eastern Europe were unfailingly national Churches devoted to the service of their local princes. In Russia this tendency was underlined by the actions of Peter the Great, who in 1721 abolished the old Moscow Patriarchate and replaced it with a Holy Synod composed of a mixture of clergy and laymen chosen by the tsar and guided by a set of Spiritual Regulations that reinforced the submission of Church to state. In the eyes of St Petersburg the Russia House in Peking was an 'ambassadorial court' (*posol'sky dvor*). The Mission fell under the supervision of Lange and the other caravan commissars, and their principal tasks were to represent the Russian government's interests and to gather intelligence.

The problem was that the Mission were *scruffy*. Eighteenth-century Russian clergymen were not in general men of high calibre or advanced education. The handful who sought to go to China were attracted purely by the hope of financial rewards and possible preferment. Once they got to Peking for their ten-year stints they were quickly demoralised by the isolation, the 'heavy air' and high mortality rate, the absence of women and the erratic arrival of subsidies from the motherland. They went around drunk and dirty and uncomfortable in their compulsory Chinese dress. Deeply inward-looking, they couldn't or wouldn't learn Manchu or Chinese, and all they wanted was to go home. Archimandrite Antony was a case in point. Described to begin with in one report as a 'sober and not unintelligent man',[54] this prelate had intrigued for years to replace Bishop Innocent as head of the Second Mission, even on one occasion getting the bishop drunk in order to damage his reputation with Count Sava Vladislavich. But no sooner had Antony got his way than he regretted it. On the very day of his arrival in Peking, 16 June 1729, he begged the Lifanyuan to let him return, and in each of the following years he is said to have badgered them further, demanding for instance a sum of 20,000 roubles, a diamond ring and a gold crozier 'without which it is impossible for an Archimandrite to live'.[55] In June 1731 he got into a brawl with a drunken priest named Ivan Filimonov, who spat in his eye, threw a brick at his right shoulder and 'practically stabbed him to death'.[56] Another Second Mission cleric, Hierodeacon Joasaph, is said in a state of tipsiness in September 1730 to have clambered into the Forbidden City and 'made a din in the chambers', accosting a bevy of Qing ministers.[57] The Third Mission were no great improvement. The head of this mission, Archimandrite Ilarion Trusov, is said at various times to have reeled drunkenly around the Church of the Purification and the grounds of the Russia House dressed up in women's clothes.[58] One western scholar sums up trenchantly that 'in spite of strong charges to the contrary, not all of the Russians in Peking were dissolute, licentious, lazy, rude, perverted, dishonest, or deceitful, only most of them'.[59]

Any initial respect the Qing court may have felt for these Russian 'lamas', as they called them, was swiftly corroded by these manifestations. 'Bored' by Father Antony's persistent approaches, the Lifanyuan are said on one occasion in 1731 to have thrown him out of their offices by the scruff of his neck.[60] After the brawl between Antony and the priest Filimonov the Lifanyuan had the priest imprisoned and then deported to Russia. The head of the Lifanyuan questioned Lange about the incident, remarking that he was 'ashamed even to mention such a matter'.[61] Antony, as the head of the mission, was left alone for the moment, but his 'devotion to spirits' grew worse with the years and in 1737 Lange found it judicious to have him flogged and sent off in chains to St Petersburg. The cross-dressing antics of Father Ilarion aroused the mirth of Chinese onlookers, and the head of the Fifth Mission recalled from the 1750s how 'the Chinese, seeing the foreigners, even wearing their kind of clothes, would swear, laugh, and spit'.[62] Not surprisingly under such circumstances there is no evidence to suggest that these successive ecclesiastics made any contacts or wielded any diplomatic influence at a high level in the Qing court, while their refusal to tackle the local languages made them unfit for any kind of intelligence work. Their activities seem to have been confined in the main to conducting divine services for the caravan traders.

The language students were a different matter. These were young men of real education, some of them graduates of the prestigious Slavonic-Greek-Latin Academy in Moscow. While they too were known to divert themselves with drinking and card games, they seem to have been distinctly better behaved than their clerical colleagues and quite often complained about the priests' misdemeanours. As early as 1730 one student is said to have made overtures to the Jesuits in the hope that they could get Father Antony deported from China, and ten years later two others returned to the Russian capital protesting that Father Ilarion Trusov's way of life was 'embarrassing the Chinese'.[63] These students after all had something concrete to be getting on with in the form of their languages. In 1728, in conformity with the treaty, the Lifanyuan had set up in the South House a Russian School in which the students were given instruction by local teachers in both Chinese and Manchu.[64] Most of the lessons appear to have been of the dry, rote-learning sort used in China to inculcate the Confucian classics, but the Qing authorities did also cater for special requests, appointing Mongolian doctors to teach the students medicine and monks to instruct them in the Buddhist scriptures. Within a few years one or two of the students were making real progress, in particular a young man of Buryat Mongol extraction called

Ilarion Rossokhin. The Qing were sufficiently impressed by Rossokhin's performance that in 1735 they co-opted him to translate documents for the Lifanyuan. The risk from the Qing point of view was of course that the students might acquire more information than they were meant to from living in China and (in Rossokhin's case) working in the depths of the Chinese bureaucracy. Already in 1733 Lange had forwarded to the Russian cabinet a fine map of China which Rossokhin had compiled, and in 1737 a Manchu censor named Heqing sounded the alarm. The Russian students, he demanded, should not be allowed to go anywhere outside Peking that would enable them to glean the secrets of the Chinese interior, and 'maps, atlases and other contraband' should not be sold to them.[65] In 1746 two students are said to have provided a returning caravan commissar with some 'quite important secret intelligence' which 'would be highly advantageous to the Russian Empire'.[66]

Rossokhin however had also embarked on a quest for knowledge of a more disinterested kind. He had learnt to appreciate Chinese culture. In 1740 he returned to St Petersburg with a collection of 100 volumes in Chinese, Manchu and Mongolian. Appointed initially to the Board of Foreign Affairs to continue his work as a translator of diplomatic correspondence, he was shortly seconded 'for the translation and teaching of the Chinese and Manchu languages' to the Imperial Russian Academy of Sciences founded by Peter in 1724,[67] and over the next two decades he busied himself with the translation of over thirty books. Some of these books, perhaps suitably, were primers intended for the instruction of small children, such as the sixth-century *Thousand Character Text*, which was the main reading textbook in traditional China, and the thirteenth-century *Three Character Classic*, which was designed to instil the basic ideas of Confucianism; but he had also tackled the great multi-volume historical work of the Song dynasty, *The Comprehensive Mirror for Aid in Government*. In 1757 he was reinforced by Alexei Leontiev, another gifted graduate of the Russian School in Peking, with whom he set about the translation of a monumental Qing work entitled *Detailed Description of the Origin and Condition of the Manchu People and of the Forces Comprising the Eight Banners*. Rossokhin was a pure translator: he engaged in no analysis and produced no original compositions. Most of his work was unpublished, and he doesn't seem to have been greatly appreciated by his colleagues. He died in 1761 obscure and in debt. But he had laid the foundations of Russian Sinology.

The Qing for their part carried on taking an outward-looking approach to their northern neighbour. As usual they were guided by strategic concerns. To make war on the Dzungars they had to be sure of Russian neutrality, and to win Russian neutrality they had to be flexible. And Yongzheng, it turned out, was prepared to go even further in flouting protocol for strategic advantage than his father Kangxi. In 1729, with the Treaty of Kyakhta safely concluded, he felt able to announce the opening of a major new Dzungar campaign. But to make assurance doubly sure, to make certain of Russian acquiescence, he took at the same time the remarkable step of dispatching an embassy to congratulate the new tsar, Peter II, on his accession to the Russian throne following the death of his mother Catherine. It was nothing less than the first Chinese embassy to a European court. The embassy was headed by Tuoshi, vice-president of the Lifanyuan, and he brought with him an entourage of thirty-five people. Some months into their journey Tuoshi and his party learnt – a further reminder of these immense distances – that Peter II had died in his turn and been succeeded by his cousin, Anna Ivanovna. But they proceeded unfazed with their expedition, all the way to Moscow, which they reached in January 1731. There they declaimed fulsome greetings to the new tsaritsa and presented her with the eighteen lacquer chests of gifts intended for Peter II, gifts that included a fine array of jewelled swords in gold scabbards. As Mala had promised would happen six decades before, they complied meekly with the requirements of Russian ceremonial, though accounts differ as to whether they genuflected to Anna, or knelt, or performed the whole Chinese kowtow. And Tuoshi declared frankly that while it was Chinese custom for envoys to issue an imperial edict to states they visited, '*since our country and Russia are equals* it is not appropriate to issue an edict to you'.[68]

On their way home to Peking Tuoshi's party encountered a second, twenty-strong Qing embassy on its way out to Russia headed by Dexin, a sub-chancellor of the Grand Secretariat. Yongzheng had decided to send off a back-up delegation to compensate for any possible defects in the previous one by bearing greetings specifically addressed to the 'All-illuminating, Most Powerful, Great Sovereign Empress, Autocratrix of All the Russias'.[69] Arriving in St Petersburg in April 1732, Dexin and his party repeated the last year's obeisances and presented Anna with nineteen more lacquer chests, this time containing gifts a little more tailored to feminine tastes such as jewellery boxes and bags of perfume.

Both of these embassies were received by the Russians with even more splendour than the welcome accorded to Tulisen and his colleagues in the Siberian towns. Tuoshi's group were escorted into Moscow in nine sedan chairs to the sound of four military bands and a thirty-one-gun salute, and Dexin found the streets of St Petersburg lined with three infantry regiments and was greeted with a roll of drums and another thirty-one-gun salute from the Admiralty cannon. Both embassies were treated to lavish banquets and were also given a good look at the sights. On 6 June 1732 Dexin's group in St Petersburg were taken on a tour of the new Imperial Academy of Sciences, where they were shown, among other curiosities, a rather basic 'Chinese Museum' explaining the essence of the Chinese language and Chinese literature and a printing press which ran off a sheet of headed paper in Chinese for the benefit of Yongzheng. Dexin's party were also given tours of the Kronstadt naval base, and of some new textile mills that had sprung up in Moscow. Finally both embassies were received by the Empress Anna for private audiences. The discussions are said to have been amiable, though Dexin may have startled his hostess somewhat with the observation that the eyes of the Princess Elizabeth were too big for her face.[70]

These conversations gave the two envoys the opportunity to bring up the real motive underlying their visits. Tuoshi and Dexin were hoping to reach an agreement with Anna that if the new Dzungar chief, Galdan Tsereng, and his people were put to flight by the Qing in the coming campaign and took refuge in Russia the Russian government would extradite them. The Qing court were prepared to compensate the Russians with a portion of the territory that was seized from the beaten Dzungars, and even invited Russia to take an active part in the military operations. To the Russians, always cautious, this looked like upsetting the delicate balance of the strategic triangle. Anna and her ministers were prepared to discuss the extradition of Dzungar fugitives, and allowed that they would be an interested party if Dzungaria were to be carved up. They would not, however, help the Qing militarily, and nor would they permit a further Qing overture to the Volga Torguts, whom the Manchu rulers were once again hoping to recruit for their cause. Still, they had confirmed their neutrality in the coming conflict, and that was enough.

If the Qing had made the effort to keep up their Russian contacts at this level they might have been able to monitor the steady emergence of a formidable power. The Kronstadt naval base shown to Dexin, for instance, was one of the first fruits of the drive for modern armed forces that had been set in motion by Peter the Great. Already under Peter some Russians had begun to remark on the contrast between Russian military technology and that of the Qing. In 1715 Prince Gagarin had commented to Tulisen and his fellow envoys on the equipment of their entourage, 'We Russians used also formerly to fight with bows and arrows; but ever since the accession of the present Tsar we have laid these weapons aside entirely.'[71] In 1720 John Bell, a Scottish physician who accompanied Izmailov's embassy to Peking, had confided to his diary, 'I know of but one nation who could attempt the conquest of China with any probability of success, and that is Russia.'[72] In the years after Peter's death Russian military preparations continued to forge ahead with the founding of army and navy cadet corps and schools of military engineering and navigation, and by 1741 tsarist technicians had succeeded in producing a quick-firing gun.

In the same way the new Moscow mills seen by Dexin betokened growing Russian ambition in the economic sphere. Peter had called in entrepreneurs to build Russia's first industries – textile mills to make uniforms and ordnance factories to turn out arms. By the time of the tsar's death in 1725 around 200 such plants had come into being. Peter also intended that Russia should replace Chinese silk imports by launching a silk-weaving industry of its own which would meet the demands of the upper classes and in due course enable the country to export silk fabrics to western Europe. By the end of his reign a substantial cottage industry was already in existence, and in 1734 a factory owner named Alexei Milyutin who set off for Peking with a state caravan was given permission to buy around 700 *pood*s of raw silk for use in his mills. Women in Tomsk and Tyumen began to process Chinese silk into sashes and girdles, and by 1749 production had risen sufficiently that the empire no longer needed to import foreign silks. A similar import substitution campaign was developed to cut out the expenditure on another luxury item – Chinese porcelain. In 1736–7 a Siberian merchant, Osip Myasnikov, travelled out to Peking in a caravan with a brief from the Senate to ferret out the secrets of Chinese porcelain manufacture. Myasnikov made little progress, but the Russian government weren't disposed to give up. The next caravan brought with it a silversmith from Kyakhta who approached the master of a porcelain workshop twenty miles from Peking and bribed him to the tune of 1,000 *tael*s (Chinese ounces) of silver to disclose the workshop's process for casting hollow porcelain idols. An attempt was then made to replicate the production of Chinese porcelain with Russian raw materials near St Petersburg at the imperial country retreat of Tsarskoe Selo.

But the Qing failed to keep up with these changes. Following the early death of the Yongzheng emperor in 1735 his son and successor, Qianlong, found no further occasion to launch any grand diplomatic initiative in Russia's direction. Nor did Qianlong's court show any desire to copy the Russian experiment by sending students to St Petersburg to study the language and culture of the partner country on the spot. By the 1730s a few individual Chinese were beginning to turn up in European Russia. In the course of that decade we encounter the saga of a person known to the Russians as Fyodor Dzhog. Dzhog was originally a Qing agent with the double-barrelled Chinese surname of Zhuge.[73] He had been sent on a mission of espionage to Dzungaria, where the locals had captured him and handed him over to a Russian army officer. Brought first to Tobolsk and then to Moscow, he arrived in 1736 in St Petersburg, where he was baptised and enlisted in the Russian military service. In 1738 he was hired to give Alexei Leontiev and another prospective language student a basic grounding in Manchu and Chinese before they set off for Peking. Rewarded for his efforts with fifty roubles and a promotion to ensign but still, it appears, not entirely trusted, he was sent off to serve in the garrison of the remote Arctic port of Archangel, about as far from the Chinese border as it was possible to get, where he died in 1751. Dzhog appears to have shown the way to several other interpreters, who in turn formed the nucleus of two Chinese trading communities that began to take shape in Moscow and St Petersburg. But no new awareness of Russia seems to have filtered back from these stray individuals to the court in Peking.

MID-CENTURY CRISIS (1757–64)

In the middle of the century the generally smooth flow of interaction was disrupted by a sudden crisis. Essentially what had happened was that Russia and China had embarked on a process by which, as one Russian author later put it, they 'moved towards each other until they divided all the territory between them'.[74] In 1731 and 1740 Russian forces moving into the steppes to the south of Siberia had received the submission respectively of the Lesser and Middle Hordes of the Kazakh nomads, bringing them close up to the Dzungar domains.[75] Yongzheng's army had received a bloody nose in the attempt it made early in the 1730s to conquer Dzungaria, but after a twenty-year pause for breath the Qing were ready to resume their assault on the now fragmenting Dzungar state. In 1755 Qianlong sent his forces off in a campaign directed at nothing less than the extirpation of the Dzungar people – the emperor is even said to have called it 'the final solution'.[76] Between 500,000 and 600,000 Dzungars were hunted down and killed, and the very name 'Dzungar' was prohibited. By 1759 the Qing had taken over the whole of eastern Turkestan, a region they shortly renamed Xinjiang, the New Frontier.[77] They were now poised for an even more far-flung expedition against the western Turkestan khanates of Tashkent and Samarkand. They had received the submission of one Kazakh chieftain and were reaching out to others, and they even showed signs of excluding Russian trade from the area. The Central Asian peoples between the two empires were steadily getting squashed. The tectonic plates were beginning to grind together.

From now on we need to think of the Russo-Chinese borderlands as an immense triptych on which an incessant struggle for influence between the two imperial powers would be displayed – Xinjiang with its deserts, Mongolia with its grasslands and Manchuria with its forests and rivers. Trouble erupted successively over each of them.

The Qing rulers had not had an altogether easy time in their conquest of Xinjiang. Late in 1756 their second-in-command there, a western Mongol chief named Amursana, had turned on his Qing masters and raised a Dzungar rebellion which obliged Qianlong's forces to conquer the region all over again. In July 1757 the beaten Amursana fled through the Kazakh lands to Siberia and sought refuge there. He was moved to Tobolsk, where he died of smallpox the following autumn. In the meantime however the episode had raised once again the question of extradition, expressly required under the terms of the Treaty of Kyakhta. The Russians were initially reluctant to admit that Amursana had fled to their territory. They maintained he had drowned while attempting to cross the River Irtysh, which the Qing troops spent a futile month dredging. The emperor in Peking didn't believe for a moment that Amursana was dead. In his judgement the traitor had 'wagged his tail and sought pity' from the Russians,[78] who in turn meant to use him as a puppet to extend their influence into Turkestan. In February 1758 the Russian government finally acknowledged that Amursana had died in their territory; but this only led to further aggravation. The Qing now wanted to lay their hands on the traitor's remains so that they could exhibit them in appropriate parts of the empire. 'Obviously', wrote the Lifanyuan, 'his body has become putrid but his bones cannot have decomposed.'[79] Regarding this demand for a dead man's bones as 'superfluous',[80] the Russian court twice refused to return Amursana's body. The most they would do was to allow Qing representatives to view the corpse at Kyakhta. Qianlong was enraged.

In Mongolia meanwhile the Khalkhas had been seething at the demands for forced labour which were made on them by their Qing overlords and the exploitation they suffered from Chinese merchants. Sizeable bands of them had been fleeing across the border to Russia for a good many years. In July 1756, in a move carefully coordinated with Amursana, they had risen in revolt under the leadership of a general called Chingunjav and had appealed to the Russians for military backing. The Russian court were attracted by this opportunity of extending their influence, and in October they authorised their representatives in Selenginsk to maintain contact with Chingunjav and discuss a possible transfer of allegiance by the Khalkhas as a whole.

Where Manchuria was concerned the Russians had by this time begun to grow restive at their decades-long exclusion from the Amur. From the early 1750s Russian expeditions were once again nosing around the headwaters of the great Far Eastern river. The governor of Siberia wrote to the Empress Elizabeth stressing the importance of the Amur as a route to the Northern Pacific region (the Sea of Okhotsk, the Kamchatka peninsula, the Aleutian Islands) where Russia now hoped to replenish its dwindling fur stocks, and an adviser to the court at St Petersburg urged that the Treaty of Nerchinsk should be revised and the Amur restored as the frontier. In 1757 Elizabeth sent a courtier, V.F. Bratishchev, to Peking to hold talks about the various border issues and win the right for Russian vessels to navigate the Amur. The idea was to offer the Qing Russian cooperation in returning the corpse of Amursana and the Khalkha defectors from Mongolia as a quid pro quo for the desired navigation and territorial concessions in the north-east. In a rare attempt to carry out their intended diplomatic function the Orthodox Mission, in the person of Archimandrite Ambrose Yumatov, tried to intercede with the Qing ministers in Bratishchev's interests, hoping to win their compliance with gifts and feasts. Goaded still further by this importunity, the Qing made it clear that access to the Amur wasn't even negotiable.

Over the next seven years the two empires appeared to be teetering on the verge of war. In February 1758 Qianlong remarked to his Grand Council that if the Russians failed to produce Amursana's remains it would not be too late to raise a punitive army. Russians were banned from coming to trade in the newly acquired Xinjiang, no more Russian students were admitted to Peking and by the autumn of 1759 it looked as though the whole structure of quasi-diplomatic relations was breaking down. Qianlong ordered the Russia House to be sealed off, and Father Ambrose's Fifth Mission within it; and decrees were affixed to the gates threatening any Chinese who presumed to enter with capital punishment. By 1762 Qing troops were patrolling the Siberian frontier on a regular basis.

Even more ominous signs were apparent in Russia. In April 1758 in St Petersburg the Empress Elizabeth held a secret military conference, and a dragoon regiment was moved east from the Orenburg Line of forts facing the Kazakh lands to the Siberian Line opposite Mongolia. In 1761, reflecting the expansionist mood of the time, Mikhail Lomonosov, the polymath founder of Moscow University, wrote an ode to the new Tsar Peter III expressing the hope that a route to the East would open before him

> So that the Chinese, Indians and Japanese
> May become subject to Your Land,[81]

and in 1762 the German princess Sophia von Anhalt-Zerbst, after overthrowing her husband Peter and seizing the reins of power as Catherine II, proclaimed her intention of punishing the Qing for their obstinacy in words which were turned into verse by her court poet Gavril Derzhavin:

> We will gain access to the centre of the world,
> We will gather gold from the Ganges,
> *We will suppress the arrogance of China*
> Like a cedar establishing our root.[82]

But it was all so much huffing and puffing. From the outset the practical measures the Russians took showed a consistent restraint. In 1757 when

Amursana, newly arrived in Siberia, offered to accept Russian suzerainty, Elizabeth made it clear that she would only protect him if he settled down quietly among the Volga Torguts. In spite of their initial reluctance to yield the dead rebel's remains the Senate resolved in July 1758 that 'Amursana's bones, contemptible things in themselves, are not worth the dissolution of the friendship between the two empires';[83] and the remains were eventually handed over in the 1760s. On the Mongolian question the Russian government were even more obviously letting 'I dare not' wait upon 'I would'. They didn't immediately grant either military or economic help to Chingunjav's rebellion, and by the time they began to take an active interest the Qing armies had already put it down. Within two months of her accession, in August 1762, the young Catherine the Great had already revised her idea of a punitive expedition and proposed instead to send an envoy to China to preserve the border trade and avoid a plunge into war.

The truth was that the Russian garrison force in Siberia was still far too weak to embark on any conflict with the Qing. In 1755 it consisted of precisely one regiment and a grenadier cavalry squad. Officials in Siberia reckoned that 35,000 troops would be needed to safeguard the territory east of Lake Baikal, but even a force of that size would have been puny by comparison with the tens of thousands of Manchu and Mongol soldiers the Qing were able to field. Worse still, the border tensions with China had broken out at exactly the time Russia became embroiled in the Seven Years War in Europe, confronting the Russians once again with the dreadful prospect of a war on two fronts. It followed that such military preparations as the Russians did launch weren't triumphalist, but defensive and frantic. 'Desperate' attempts are said to have been made to shore up the defences of eastern Siberia against the expected Qing onslaught.[84] The Siberian authorities pleaded for urgent reinforcements, but all that could be spared in the end were 1,000 Cossacks assigned to Kyakhta and Nerchinsk and a few thousand conscripts from the Tungus tribes. In 1761 the governor of Siberia and the commandant of Selenginsk even petitioned for Kyakhta to be *moved further back*. In October 1764 Catherine called a conference of her seven top ministers to discuss what to do about China. The Seven Years War was now over, and the threat of a two-front collision with both Prussia and China had disappeared. But the idea of attacking the Qing to regain the Amur was dismissed, and the military steps proposed were entirely defensive. Catherine and her advisers did not want to risk sacrificing the lucrative Kyakhta trade for the hypothetical profits which might accrue from the Amur and the Sea of Okhotsk.

In any case there had been no compelling evidence at any point in these years that the Qing wanted a fight. Even while citing the option of punitive measures in 1758 Qianlong reminded the Grand Council they shouldn't necessarily assume that the Russians were lying or would fail to return Amursana's body. While they strengthened their military presence to the south of Siberia the Qing took no steps to build up an offensive force there, and Russian intelligence sources repeatedly pointed out the absence of warlike preparations. In 1763 Qianlong turned aside from the attempted conquest of Tashkent and Samarkand, signalling in effect that the great Qing expansion was over, and in 1765 he indicated his readiness to drop the Amursana quarrel. To judge from a comment he made that same year he had no further worries about anything Russia might do. Referring to the 1750s he said, 'Since the Russians did not move in the past they will certainly not cause trouble now.'[85]

A SHIFT IN THE BALANCE (1764–*c.* 1815)

Equilibrium had been preserved. Following the mid-century crisis, however, significant changes began to make themselves felt in the Sino-Russian balance. The most obvious change was in Qing attitudes. Now that the Dzungars had been eliminated the Manchu rulers of China no longer had any strategic need for Russian support or neutrality, and their attitude to the Russians quickly reverted to one of haughty disdain. As early as 1758 Qianlong had decided that 'if we treat them with courtesy they become more arrogant; if we awe them with power they naturally fear us.'[86] From the time of Catherine the Great's accession in 1762 Qing correspondence with Russia began to exhibit an increasingly insolent tone. When the Russian Senate sent a letter in 1764 pointing out that their empire spanned half the globe and should not be referred to in the same breath as the petty khanates of Central Asia, the Lifanyuan replied with a hoot of derision: 'This is truly ridiculous! How can any sovereign now be compared with our all-powerful sovereign the Emperor, let alone the sovereign of Russia who is a woman?'[87] After a few more messages of this kind Catherine not surprisingly declined to allow any further response. The Qing now no longer showed interest in any high-level diplomatic exchange with St Petersburg. When the courier Catherine had sent off to Peking to preserve the peace proposed the dispatch of a formal Russian envoy the idea was brushed aside as 'not in the least necessary'.[88]

In the same year, 1764, Qianlong decided to resume the old practice of taking in Russian deserters, in flagrant contravention of the Treaty of Kyakhta. By the end of the decade around sixty Russians had been given shelter on the Qing side of the border. Then in January 1771 a contingent of up to 170,000 of the Volga Torguts, aggrieved at Russian demands for military service and growing Russian encroachment on both their autonomy and their grazing lands, decamped from the Volga and began to migrate back eastwards in the direction of Xinjiang. So far as Qianlong was concerned the Torguts didn't count as deserters but were merely making their way back to the original home they had left in the seventeenth century; and he was happy to settle them in the pastures of northern Xinjiang which had been left empty by the destruction of the Dzungars. He ignored Russian pressure to hand back the Torgut 'rogues and traitors',[89] and dismissed the concerns of his courtiers who fretted that his defiance of Russian wishes might lead to war.[90] A number of Russian cavalrymen who had been chasing the Torguts were even taken prisoner and conveyed to the far southern provinces of Fujian and Guangdong where they were put to work as soldiers, or slaves of soldiers, in the local Manchu banner forces. In 1773 one such slave named Fyodor and two other Russians who had escaped from captivity in Fujian were caught and executed, and in 1776 one Ivan, a sixty-six-year-old soldier with the Bordered White Banner in Guangdong, was also reported to have made a getaway. Qianlong inquired peevishly, 'Since Ivan could not speak Chinese and his countenance is different, how could he have escaped?'[91]

Finally the Qing began to suspend the Kyakhta trade, capriciously and incessantly, for periods ranging from a few weeks to a matter of years. The trade was closed down in 1764–8, in 1775, in 1778–80 and in 1785–92. Sometimes the grounds given were commercial. The Qing court complained frequently of the Russian practice of levying duties at the border, which they maintained was prohibited under the terms of the Treaty of Kyakhta. More often, however, the cause for suppression was non-economic, some local Russian misdemeanour which had annoyed the authorities – the removal or shifting of border markers, personal clashes between Russian and Chinese merchants, or, in the case of the final seven-year shutdown, the robbing by Buryat Mongols subject to St Petersburg of a Chinese trader from Urga. The Qing didn't encourage Chinese merchants to trade at the border, and had little interest in the border traffic as such.

From their point of view the trade was little more than a lever which they could manipulate to keep the border peaceful, and they looked down on the Russians who seemed to have, as one official wrote scornfully, 'no other idea than trade'.[92] The final shutdown was accompanied in 1789 by a full-scale ban on the export of rhubarb to Russia, apparently meant in part to quash Catherine's claims to imperial status and put the Russian ruler in her place. The Qing had convinced themselves that the Russians couldn't live without rhubarb, and they extended the ban to include even rhubarb traded from the south China ports or across the Xinjiang frontier to western Turkestan – anywhere that rhubarb from the empire might be resold and find its way into Russian hands. By the time Qianlong lifted the Kyakhta suspension in 1792 his edict to Russia had shed any trace of the flexibility, the acceptance of Russia as an equal partner implicit in the earlier Qing agreements and had reverted to the traditional Chinese language of sovereign to vassal:

> The trade at Kyakhta is of absolutely no benefit to us, but because the Great Emperor loves all human beings and sympathises with your poor and miserable people, and because your Senate has appealed to His Imperial Majesty, He has deigned to approve its petition. If you do not respect this friendly relationship you must never dream of being allowed to trade again.[93]

The impression all this gave of vast Qing supremacy was, however, misleading. In reality the balance was starting to tilt, quietly but perceptibly, in the other direction. Qianlong himself remarked that the Manchu empire was 'like the sun at midday',[94] as though sensing there was nowhere to go but down; and the Qing arrogance masked a spreading debility. Hard-working and dutiful, Qianlong lacked the deep intelligence of his grandfather Kangxi. As he grew old he became more and more narrow-minded and apt to be swayed by favourites. The Manchus as a whole were becoming increasingly Sinicised. At the beginning of the eighteenth century, we are told, senior Qing officials understood no Chinese; 100 years later the bulk of them understood no Manchu.[95] Culturally they were evolving from a hardy body of warrior horsemen into a sedentary ruling caste, displaying the traditional Chinese disdain for the military profession and losing, perhaps, the last traces of their 'barbarian pragmatism'. From the mid-eighteenth century the imperial bureaucracy seem to have grown less and less reform-minded and ever more disposed to condone the pervasive corruption embodied, for instance, in the emperor's favourite Heshen, who salted away millions in the final years of the reign. From the 1770s the empire was convulsed by a series of peasant rebellions caused in part by the mounting pressure of population on the land. The campaigns launched to stamp out these uprisings didn't say much for the progress of Qing military technology: in an operation conducted from 1771 to 1776 against peasants in the south-western province of Sichuan the Qing cannon are said to have been liable to explode after two to three days of heavy firing. Excursions launched into Burma in the 1760s and Vietnam in the late 1780s showed a declining level of generalship.

The same slow corrosion can be seen in different aspects of the dynasty's dealings with the Russian empire. In each of the great border zones which the early Qing had occupied next to Russia we find symptoms of imperial overstretch. During the last decades of the century no military inspections were carried out to the north of the Amur, and the Qing presence there is said to have been 'light and weak'.[96] The Mongolian frontier was likewise neglected, and in 1791 an attempt by the Qing to push their pickets forward to the formal boundary line at Kyakhta was not followed through. The last recorded Qing survey of the Xinjiang border took place in the 1780s, and by 1800 the dynasty had abandoned their earlier efforts to win the allegiance of the Kazakh tribes. In the realm of trade it appears that by the end of the century the cartel system under which the Chinese merchants of Trade Town had combined under Manchu direction to keep up a steady flow of profits from their sales at Kyakhta had fallen into disuse. Actual Qing knowledge of Russia stagnated or even shrank. With no more Qing embassies to Moscow or St Petersburg there was no chance of any description of Russia appearing to give the Chinese public an update on Tulisen's book. In 1787 Qianlong remarked approvingly to his Grand Council on the condition of Tibet, 'which has long been incorporated into Qing territory and *should not be compared with Russia which is still savage and to be tamed*'.[97] The early Qing drive to learn Russian had flagged, and the low rank accorded to graduates of the Russian Language School didn't encourage new pupils. In 1791

Qianlong issued an edict regarding a magistrate named Yuan Chengning, who was familiar with Russia and had 'carefully and properly translated' all documents relating to Russian affairs. 'We should keep Yuan Chengning in Peking so that whenever we are confronted with this kind of affair he can be our expert.'[98] The implication was that there was nobody else.

Russia by contrast was going from strength to strength. While the Qing struggled with their exploding cannon the Russians had continued to upgrade their armaments, with the development in 1757 of a *licorne* or field gun. By 1782 Russia possessed an army of 435,000 troops, over twice what it had been in Peter's time, seasoned in conflict with Ottoman Turkey and shortly to be further seasoned in Suvorov's campaigns against revolutionary France. Russia's headache where the Qing were concerned, as we have noticed, was how to deploy adequate armed forces in distant Siberia; but measures were gradually being taken to cope with this challenge. Steady efforts were made to encourage the settlement of Siberia, where the adult male population had risen from 169,000 in 1719 to 410,000 by 1792. And a first step had been taken to tackle the problem of distance with the start in the 1760s of work on the Great Road from Moscow to Irkutsk.

Russia was also progressively narrowing the economic gulf between it and the Qing. The last of the state caravans had made its unsatisfactory way to Peking in 1755. On her accession in 1762 Catherine the Great accepted the cumulative logic of all the previous decades and privatised the entire China trade. The last of the old state monopolies was abolished, and ordinary Russian merchants were given permission to do business with China as they pleased. At the grand China strategy conference which was convened by Catherine in October 1764 the proposal was made that a single, disciplined 'company' of Russian merchants should be formed at Kyakhta to put a stop to competitive bidding for sales and end the Chinese domination of the Kyakhta market: the Russians, in other words, were grasping the merits of the Chinese cartel system just as the Chinese themselves were about to forsake it. The result of all these measures was that Russia's Kyakhta trade surged, from an annual value of 837,000 roubles in 1755 to 6 million roubles at the start of the 1780s, and was now bringing in a major proportion of treasury revenues through the collection of customs dues. Russian exports to the Qing still consisted overwhelmingly of furs – 85 per cent of the total in the 1780s and 50 per cent as late as 1800. But Russia was by this time producing significant quantities of manufactures, including fine leatherware ('Russia leather'), ironware and glass; and some of these manufactured goods had begun to creep in. Russian merchants continued to make handsome profits from the import of cheap Chinese cottons: between 1768 and 1785 over 300,000 bales of *kitaika* and 150,000 to 300,000 bales of coarse woven *daba* were shipped in through Kyakhta each year. But on top of this, by the final decades of the century the Kyakhta traders were exploiting an immense new Russian addiction to tea, known to the Russians as *chai* from the northern Chinese word *cha* (the English 'tea' and French '*thé*' were derived from a dialect of the south-eastern tea-growing province of Fujian). No longer just a tonic for the nobility, Chinese black and especially green tea had become the indispensable beverage for Russians of every social class. Between 1750 and 1781 imports of tea through Kyakhta almost doubled, from an annual quantity of 210,000 kg to 400,000 kg; and the demand was sufficiently great that when the Qing government closed down the Kyakhta trade for the long interruption of 1785–92 Russian merchants hurried to ship tea in through England instead.

And while Qing knowledge of Russia contracted to vanishing point the Russian language students in Peking were performing with ever-growing efficiency the intelligence function intended for them. By the late eighteenth century Qing vigilance over the Mission, as over so much else, had perceptibly slackened. Students could now leave the Russia House, roam around Peking as they pleased and even make excursions outside the capital to the hot springs and the canal port of Tongzhou where trading vessels arrived from the south. Manchu and Chinese visitors were allowed access to the Mission headquarters, where the students were able to win their friendship 'through kindness or gifts'.[99] The Sixth Mission students were consequently able to put together a 'journal of the secret activities and changes which took place in the Great Qing State from 1772 to 1782'.[100] Apparently sensing an opportunity, the Board of Foreign Affairs issued instructions to the head of the next, Seventh, Mission, Archimandrite Joachim Shishkovsky, to gather information on 'whatever events taking place in the Empire might affect the Qing government's thinking or behaviour' and relay this secretly to St Petersburg.[101] One of the Seventh Mission students, Ivan Orlov, accordingly drew on his dealings with both Manchus and Chinese to compile a *New and Detailed Historical and Geographical Description of the Chinese Empire*. The

Board of Foreign Affairs had by now fully grasped the importance of language proficiency, and in May 1798 they established in St Petersburg a new school for training translators of Manchu, Chinese and other Oriental languages.

This growth in tsarist power and wealth and omniscience wasn't reflected in any immediate falling-off of respect for the Chinese empire. On the contrary, it was at this precise period that Russian admiration of China soared to its zenith. For many years Russian knowledge of China, like Russian knowledge of much else in the eighteenth century, was acquired overwhelmingly via the maritime powers of western Europe – through accounts written by Jesuits, through the travelogues published by western writers, through the musings of various leaders of the western Enlightenment. We have already noticed the prod which Leibniz gave to Peter the Great to turn Russia into a bridge between western and Chinese civilisation. As so often the Russians were a little slow to pick up western fashion, but from the middle of the century the western craze for Chinese culture and chinoiserie was taking a spectacular hold on the Russian upper classes – ironically at just the point when the craze was abating in western Europe itself and admiration was starting to give way to contempt. The leading part in this vogue for things Chinese (*kitaishchina*, as the Russians called it) was played by none other than Catherine the Great. Although harbouring an 'old grudge' for the lack of respect which Qianlong had shown her in his court's official correspondence,[102] Catherine also nurtured, on the other side of her mind, what one might call a cutesy image of the Qing emperor and his exotic realm. Writing to the French author and diplomat the Prince de Ligne she referred to Qianlong as 'my nice and ceremonious neighbour with the tiny eyes',[103] and even wrote a piece of doggerel about him:

Le roi de la Chi-i-i-ne
Quand il a bien bu-u-u-u-u
Fait une plaisante mi-i-i-ne

('When China's emperor gets tight
His face becomes a funny sight').[104]

The tsaritsa developed a passion for all the aesthetic features of the Celestial Empire that had enchanted her western counterparts. In the course of the

1760s she commissioned the Neapolitan architect Rinaldi to work Chinese décor into the Oranienbaum Palace at St Petersburg, and in the following decade she had him design at Tsarskoe Selo an entire Chinese Palace including a Blue Drawing Room with walls lined with Chinese silk showing scenes of Chinese life and statues of a Chinese Man and a Chinese Woman. The park outside was adorned with her 'Grand Caprice', a monumental arch surmounted by a Chinese Kiosk or pagoda in the style of Fujian Province; a group of bridges decorated with Chinese dragons and Chinese figures holding lanterns; and a Creaking Pavilion in Chinese style whose floor-boards were deliberately constructed to make an evocative noise. In 1777 work began on a Chinese Theatre where two years later an Italian comic opera, *The Chinese Idol*, was performed. 'Here a theatre, there a swing,' exulted the poet Derzhavin, 'Behold, an Eastern pleasure dome!'[105] In the grounds of the Alexandrovsky Palace she built for her grandson Catherine commissioned a whole Chinese Village consisting of nine or ten small houses with curved roofs surrounding a pagoda. The nobility joined their sovereign in the scramble for chinoiserie. The Fountain House put up by the Sheremetiev family in St Petersburg had a Chinese Pavilion in the garden, and other families packed their mansions with Chinese paintings, lacquered tables and screens, stone lions in the gateways and gilded and coloured dragons spouting water at the intersections of the garden paths.

Western taste also ignited the Russian craving for Chinese porcelain. After the effort to copy Chinese techniques at the source proved abortive, the first porcelain factories in Russia were built using processes developed in Sweden and Saxony. But Russian admiration was no less sincere for being second-hand. In a poem written in 1752 Lomonosov acclaimed 'the ingenious Chinese', who had

> Transformed into porcelain with their artistry
> The heavy immensity of the fruit of emptied hills.[106]

Catherine personally imported china, and Derzhavin in 1780 extolled the 'precious Chinese porcelain' which was displayed at luxurious banquets in St Petersburg.[107] The big Russian samovar, first manufactured in 1778 to accommodate the surging demand for tea, was typically surmounted by a *chainik* or Chinese teapot which it heated as the water boiled. In an early chapter of *War and Peace* set in 1805 Tolstoy had a certain Dr Lorrain, summoned to attend the dying Count Bezukhov, sip tea from 'a delicate Chinese handleless cup'.[108]

Chinese literature started to seep into the tsarist empire through the same western channels. In 1759 the playwright A.P. Sumarokov translated a German version of Voltaire's play *L'Orphelin de la Chine*, which had itself been based on a Chinese play from the fourteenth century, *The Orphan of the House of Zhao*. In the course of a correspondence she conducted with Voltaire Catherine was apprised of Qianlong's gift for poetry, and wrote acknowledging her envy of the Qing emperor's literary skills. Voltaire gallantly and no doubt judiciously answered that Catherine was the foremost person in the universe not excluding Qianlong, 'even though he is a poet'.[109]

And literature led naturally into the realm of ideas. From Voltaire and the other savants of the Enlightenment Catherine imbibed the basics of the Confucian philosophy and with them the concept of China as an enlightened monarchy founded on reason. Not content with merely grasping these notions, she even took active steps to disseminate them in her own domain. In 1781 she published a *Russian Primer for the Instruction of Youth* in which Confucius was listed along with Plato and Aristotle as an authority to be followed. A French physician attending her son Paul wrote for his edification *The Great Yu and Confucius: A Chinese History*, and in 1783 Catherine composed for her grandsons *The Tale of Prince Fevei*, a description of how an imaginary Chinese ruler in Siberia raised his son to be a noble and benevolent man. With a view to strengthening her administration and increasing the honesty of the average Russian the tsaritsa enrolled Lomonosov in a project for compiling a Russian edition of the Qing Criminal Code; and for good measure she issued in 1786 a Statute of National Schools which prescribed the teaching of Chinese to Russian children in regions adjoining the Qing empire. Another of her court poets, Maria Shishkova, summed up the tsaritsa's endeavours gushingly, 'On the Northern Throne we see Confucius'.[110]

Even Catherine's opponents found it suitable to couch their attacks on the sovereign in this western-stimulated Confucian discourse. In 1770 the dissident editor Nikolai Novikov published a translation of advice given by a Chinese sage as to how a truly enlightened ruler should behave, along with a translation of the will of the Emperor Yongzheng strongly hinting that the tsaritsa ought to abdicate in favour of Grand Duke Paul. In 1779 the playwright Denis Fonvizin translated a French version of Confucius's *Great Learning* explaining the duty of an enlightened ruler to be benign. The translation was seen as a hit at Catherine's ruthless suppression of the peasant revolt led by Yemelian Pugachev five years earlier, and the Tsaritsa unsurprisingly censored it.

Not all of this Sinological knowledge came through western Europe. A small but increasing trickle continued to be supplied by former students of the Orthodox Mission in Peking. In 1784, for instance, Alexei Leontiev finally completed the seventeen-volume *Detailed Description of the Origins and Condition of the Manchu People* which he had begun to translate with Rossokhin twenty-seven years before. Leontiev was also the translator of the collection of Qing laws which Catherine assigned to Lomonosov to edit and the moral treatise and will of Yongzheng which Catherine's critic Novikov published for his own subversive purposes. Most of Leontiev's energies, like Rossokhin's, went into translating Chinese writings of a philosophical nature; but the scope of activity was beginning to widen. Leontiev also provided the Russian public with accounts of the Chinese tea and silk industries, a description of Chinese chess, a first Russian version of Tulisen's Siberian memoir and a translation of forty-six short Chinese poems; and another ex-student, Anton Vladykin, produced the first Russian translation of a Chinese novel, *The Tale of Jin, Yun and Qiao*.

The Russians weren't altogether unconscious of the decline of Qing power and energy by comparison with their own. In the 1770s John Bell's account of his journey to Peking with Izmailov fifty years earlier was published belatedly in Russian translation, and his assessment that Russia alone among all other countries might have the potential to conquer the Chinese empire excited some interest. And by the final decade of the century we come across one clear dissentient from the general chorus of esteem for the Qing. Archimandrite Sophronius Gribovsky, the head of the Eighth Orthodox Mission, composed in the 1790s a *Report on China* which substantially tore apart the rose-tinted St Petersburg image of Qianlong's realm. 'The praises attributed by Europeans to the present Manchu government', he declared tartly, did 'not deserve the slightest credence.' Qianlong himself was 'extremely rapacious', had twice pardoned a provincial governor in return for bribes and had set 'a fatal example of avarice to his ministers'. The 'extortion, grave contempt and unbearable slavery' to which the Chinese populace were subjected by their Manchu overlords had aroused considerable resistance; and the Qing army had proved ineffective in their attempts to put down the rebels in the western provinces. Sophronius further lashed out at the various other shortcomings of life in China, from the 'stupid rites of the Chinese, dictated by their empty theory' to the poverty of the people and the environmental ghastliness of the Chinese capital. When the canals in Peking were opened in March the smell was sometimes 'so overwhelming one can hardly go out on the street'. 'Thus,' he summed up, 'if this nation is examined very thoroughly, in all fairness it can be said to be in great need and distress.'[111] Sophronius however seems to have been a voice in the wilderness, and there is no sign his report had any impact or aroused in the Russian authorities any urge to dismantle the status quo.

That impetus, once again, was provided by the west. In 1793 George, Earl Macartney arrived in Peking at the head of a 100-strong British delegation, resplendent with valets and guards and enriched with a sprinkling of artists and scientists. Macartney's arrival reflected a British awareness, and envy, of the advantageous position that Russia appeared to enjoy in the Qing capital through the presence of the Orthodox missionaries. The British, he intimated, wished to establish a trading company in Peking 'after the example of the Russians'.[112] Macartney's embassy was not a success. The British came up against the same protocol hurdles the Russians had contrived to negotiate a century earlier, offending the Qing court through their blunt refusal to kowtow. They notoriously failed to impress their Qing hosts with a display of scientific gadgetry, telescopes, clocks, barometers and so forth, partly, we may conjecture, because the court had already been presented with similar gadgets by Izmailov and Sava in the 1720s. Qianlong rebuffed their demand for a commercial presence in his capital by clearing up their apparent misconception that the Orthodox Mission was a trading enterprise. Decades before, he agreed, Russian merchants had indeed been admitted to Peking to trade; 'but this was only for a time, until a place had been appointed for them at Kyakhta'.[113] The British already had scope to trade in the south, at Canton: why, then, did they need a trading company in Peking as well? Macartney's venture was nonetheless disquieting to the Russians insofar as it represented a first British effort to gatecrash the sphere of commercial influence they had built for themselves in north China. Worse was to follow.

During the last few decades, as the fur stocks in Siberia grew ever more depleted, Russian trappers had moved their activities further and further across the northern Pacific as far as Alaska, and in July 1799 the Russian American Company was set up to exploit the resources of their new North American settlements. But in the newly globalised world of the late eighteenth century competition was moving in fast. Merchantmen from both Britain and the infant United States were transporting furs rapidly from north-western America to Canton, where they sold them at substantially lower prices than the Russians could manage at Kyakhta. By 1799 their incursions were making a 'major impact'.[114] With furs still Russia's dominant export, urgent action was needed if the westerners weren't to kill off the Kyakhta trade altogether.

In 1803, then, Tsar Alexander I, who had succeeded to the Russian throne after the murder of his deranged father Paul, launched an imposing new embassy to Peking under the leadership of Count Yuri Golovkin. A British account of Macartney's expedition had been published in Russia in 1796, and the embassy was clearly intended to outdo its British predecessor in both size and magnificence. Golovkin set off with a retinue of 242 embassy members and something like the same number of service personnel. Russia's new-found intellectual appetite for knowledge of China was manifest in the inclusion of twelve eminent scholars and scientists, among them Count Potocki, a Polish historian and ethnographer, Julius Klaproth, a German philologist, a zoologist and a botanist; and an artist named Shchukin was assigned both to paint Chinese scenes and to study Chinese painting techniques. The demands to be presented to the Qing government amounted to nothing less than a complete overturning of the old Kyakhta system of direct but limited contact. Golovkin was to request the right for Russian merchants to trade across the entire land border, from Yili and Tacheng in Xinjiang all the way to Manchuria. Permission should be accorded for Russian vessels to navigate the Amur, to enable them to supply the new outposts in the northern Pacific and Alaska. And most important of all, Russian merchants should be allowed to trade by sea from Kamchatka and Alaska to Canton and if possible Nanking in the Yangtze valley, which was seen as an important source of cottons. To press this last demand further Russia was to make an attempt (hard enough in these pre-telegraphic days) at a pincer movement. A naval squadron commanded by Admiral Ivan Kruzenstern, which was sent off in the same year on a round-the-world voyage to exhibit Russia's new maritime prowess, was to arrive simultaneously in Canton and begin trading there.

This démarche ended in a still bigger fiasco than Macartney's had done. In January 1806 Golovkin and his suite arrived at Urga in Mongolia – to a hopeless reception. The decline of the Qing's Russian Language School was at once illustrated by a bevy of Manchu students who had been sent to act as interpreters, but who proved unable to understand a word that the Russian envoys were saying or to say anything coherent in Russian themselves. As for the documents they produced, the philologist Klaproth huffed that they had 'failed to observe the simplest rules of grammar . . . in the very first lines of their translation'.[115] More ominously it turned out that the Qing had reverted to the protocol rigidities of the past. Undermined by incessant domestic turmoil, the new Manchu ruler, Jiaqing, who had taken full power on the death of his father Qianlong in 1799,[116] seems to have wished at all costs to avoid a repetition of Macartney's humiliating refusal to pay his father the traditional honours. The chief Qing officials in Urga directed Golovkin to 'practise' kowtowing by crouching on all fours, with his credentials reposing on a pillow on his back, before a yellow draped table with smoking incense which had been set up to symbolise the new emperor. Golovkin for his part had been instructed, like all of the recent ambassadors from St Petersburg, to kowtow to the emperor if necessary for the greater good of the Russian state. But, 'vain and haughty', we are told, as well as 'highly charming and able' when he wanted to be,[117] and conscious perhaps of the huge growth in his country's relative power, he was not prepared to submit to this unexpected indignity. He expostulated that he was ready to kowtow to Jiaqing in person, but not to 'a yellow dyed snippet of cotton'.[118] The Qing officials struck back with a petulance they had not displayed since the seventeenth century, throwing the chests of gifts which the Russians had delivered to them on the ground in front of Golovkin's lodgings; and brought down at the first fence, before even reaching Peking, the whole grandiose Russian cavalcade had to head back home, 'cold and hungry'.[119]

In December 1805, meanwhile, Kruzenstern with commendable timing had arrived in Canton with his two ships, the *Nadezhda* and the *Neva*. They were the first Russian vessels to enter a Chinese port. The superintendent of maritime customs, a certain Yanfeng, was baffled as to the origin of

Kruzenstern and his lieutenant, Lisyansky, but found them 'respectful and submissive'.[120] A local Chinese merchant insured their ships for them, and they began to unload their furs from North America and to take on board an initial consignment of tea. But for the Russians to do business alongside the British and other westerners at Canton went against the whole Qing foreign policy, which was grounded in security concerns. By keeping the foreigners cooped into airtight compartments the dynasty hoped to prevent any single foreign power from gaining excessive advantages at their expense. If the Russians were allowed to trade at Canton they would master the sea route along the entire Chinese coast; and if they got to know the coastline they would acquire undesirable knowledge of the turmoil in the inland provinces.[121] The result was that Peking cracked down hard. The viceroy of Guangdong and Guangxi arrived in Canton and repeated the familiar mantra which the Qing had addressed decades earlier to Count Sava Vladislavich and more recently to Macartney. Russian traders belonged in the north, on the land border, westerners in the south at Canton, and those limits were not to be transgressed. To drive the point home the two Russian ships were detained briefly on suspicion of carrying contraband rhubarb before being freed with instructions to sail away and never come back; while the unfortunate Yanfeng was relieved of his office and sent off to labour on a public works project. Kruzenstern, hitting an altogether new note of superiority, grumbled that 'if our ships had been detained for more than one day we would have been plunged into the atrocities of thoroughgoing savages'.[122] The admiral seems to have shared the view of Father Sophronius that Qing tranquillity and power were just a façade. He left warning darkly that if the Qing government refused to grant Russia trading privileges at Canton 'force will be met with force'.[123]

During the years that followed this setback we find Russia starting to probe in the Qing borderlands, generally with a view to commercial penetration but sometimes with a hint of expansionist aims. On his way home in 1806, still smarting no doubt from his rejection at Urga, Golovkin detached a staff officer, one Colonel d'Auvray, to reconnoitre Qing military strength in Manchuria and prepare for a 'secret expedition' into Russia's lost territory to the north of the Amur, and in 1815 a purported religious schismatic named Gurii Vasiliev crossed illegally into the region, creeping back like a cat in 1816 and 1822.[124] In 1811 Putintsev, a Russian interpreter, entered the fertile valley of Yili in Xinjiang in a secret commercial reconnaissance; some Russian merchants arrived two years later, and by the 1820s an illicit trade had begun to grow up on the Xinjiang border. In 1813–14 successive contingents totalling some 500 men poured past the Qing border posts in Xinjiang near the northern settlement of Tacheng in hot pursuit of a Kazakh chief who had kidnapped a number of their local allies. No comparable incursions were made on the central, Mongolian section of the frontier; but a Russian officer crossing Mongolia in late 1820 noted with interest local Khalkha resentment of Manchu haughtiness and Chinese greed, reporting at the same time that the Khalkhas had 'conceived a high idea of our power, and on every opportunity manifest their regard for Russia.'[125] Russian aspirations were even discernible as far afield as Tibet. One of the minor demands that Golovkin had hoped to submit in Peking had been for Russian 'supervisors' to accompany groups of Torguts still living on the lower Volga on their periodic Buddhist pilgrimages to Lhasa, and a British veterinarian who travelled from India to Tibet in 1808 in search of horses was surprised to be greeted in one village by a terrier and a pug which the villagers said they had acquired from Russian traders.[126] The court's focus on China was growing increasingly sharp. In a decree of 1818 the Russian government spelt out more clearly than ever before that the main function of the Orthodox Mission in Peking should not be religious: rather they were to pursue a systematic study of China's economy and culture and keep the Senate informed of important political events. They were also directed to win the favour of senior Qing personnel. And in 1819 a specialist Asiatic Department was set up for the first time in the Foreign Ministry.

In spite of all this no further Russian effort was made to shatter the long preserved equilibrium. Following the Golovkin fiasco the Russians strengthened their forts in Siberia, but at a time of confrontation with Napoleon's France they had no wish to initiate a conflict in the East. In 1807 Alexander I's foreign minister, Count Ya. Budberg, wrote to I.B. Pestel, the governor-general of Siberia, underlining the government's wish to maintain harmonious relations with the Qing. It was possible, he pointed out, that the Qing were afraid of reprisals for the rebuff they had dealt to Golovkin, and in this case measures should be taken to overcome their mistrust. In 1810 N.I. Treskin, the governor of Irkutsk, was authorised to hold talks at Kyakhta with the two senior Qing officials in Mongolia, making 'systematic efforts to conform with Chinese etiquette' and proposing the dispatch of a new Qing embassy to St Petersburg.[127] Russian respect for Qing power was still too great, and the status quo too attractive, to warrant going beyond the occasional frontier probe. The theory was that the mutually lucrative trade at Kyakhta would help keep the peace and obviate the need which would otherwise arise to maintain a far larger army on the Chinese border. In April 1833 K.K. Rodofinkin, the head of the new Asiatic Department, summed up that the chief Russian aim with regard to the Chinese empire was to preserve and accelerate the existing friendly ties and develop trade further – for the benefit, he observed, of Russian native industry.

The Qing also reacted to the stand-off with Golovkin by boosting their border defences. But in spite of their arrogant posturing they too remained wedded, for practical purposes, to the comfortable status quo. On taking power in 1799 Jiaqing had drawn the attention of his Grand Council to the venerable nature of the relationship: 'Our reigning dynasty has been friendly with Russia for more than a hundred years.'[128] Savages though the Russians might be, they were a familiar part of the scenery, and there was nothing to be gained by provoking them. One story goes that in 1806 Napoleon made an overture to the Qing court suggesting that the Qing should assist his strategic designs by attacking Russia in the East. The Qing refused, stating tersely that 'it was better to live at peace with Russia.'[129] The idea mooted by Governor Treskin in 1810 that the Qing should send a new embassy to St Petersburg was brushed aside as 'an annoying request', since it had 'never been the Chinese custom' to send envoys to foreign countries (the Qing rulers appear to have been unaware by this time that the Tuoshi and Dexin embassies of the early 1730s had ever taken place);[130] but the Qing officials dispatched to hold talks with him were encouraged to be cooperative, and it was intimated that if another Russian ambassador came through Urga he would not be required to kowtow. Qing responses to the Russian border probes were restrained to the point of timidity. When the tsar's hot-pursuit squads passed by the Qing border posts into Xinjiang in 1813–14 the fugitive Kazakh chief was instructed to comply with Russian demands, seemingly out of fear that the Russian troops might push deeper into the empire's interior at a time when Jiaqing's throne had been placed in immediate danger by the major revolt of the anti-Manchu Eight Trigrams sect. The persistent infiltrations of the Amur region seem effectively to have been ignored. A ragged-looking Russian named Pyotr who was picked up in a rowing boat on the Amur in 1819 claiming to be a runaway serf was simply issued with a new suit of clothes and sent home. When Georgi Timkovsky, the Russian officer who had been crossing Mongolia, reached Peking with his party at the end of 1820 he was assured that the Qing government 'without being guided by preceding examples would be always ready to assent to all the just requests of the Russians'.[131]

AN ERA OF GOOD FEELINGS (*c.* 1815–*c.* 1845)

The period from the mid-1810s to the mid-1820s in the United States has been called an Era of Good Feelings; and the same label can reasonably be applied to the atmosphere which set in between Russia and China at approximately the same time and which endured for the next three decades. The Sandy Venice of Kyakhta was now in its glory. The trade suspensions of the late eighteenth century were a thing of the past. The volume of business increased steadily at a rate of some 20 per cent to 25 per cent every five years, and a Russian saying ran, '*One Kyakhta is worth three provinces*'.[132] The structure of the trade, to be sure, had changed out of all recognition since the Kyakhta entrepôt was founded in 1728. Russian exports were no longer dominated by furs, since fur stocks were becoming exhausted even in Russian North America, and as sable, ermine and Arctic fox disappeared from the market the Russian traders had little to offer but cheap squirrel pelts. By the mid-1820s furs were down to 47 per cent of the total value of exports; by the late 1830s, to just 28 per cent. Instead Russia was now developing a major new market for Rodofinkin's 'native industry'. By the early nineteenth century Russian manufactured goods such as leather and ironware accounted for some 15 per cent of the total trade. In 1807 we find an early reference to Chinese imports of Russian textile wares, woollen cloth to begin with but by the 1830s increasingly cotton fabrics which the Russians had started to turn out, replacing their own previous imports of cheap Chinese cottons. Chinese exports to Russia now consisted overwhelmingly of tea, which from the 1820s onwards hovered consistently around 90 per cent of the total value of Qing merchandise. Trade had metamorphosed, in other words, from an exchange of Russian raw materials for Chinese manufactures to an exchange of Russian manufactures for one single semi-processed Chinese commodity. But the new trading structure brought immense profits for both sides.

Merchants from northern Chinese regions which didn't themselves produce tea, and in particular from the nearby northern province of Shanxi, went down to invest in the processing enterprises in the tea-growing south, and transported the processed tea back along a 'Tea Road' by way of Kalgan to Kyakhta to sell it to Russian wholesalers. And these wholesalers then shipped the tea off to Russia to market in towns like Irkutsk and at the thriving new trade fair at Nizhny Novgorod.

From its ramshackle origins Kyakhta had evolved into the largest town on the border, an emporium of spectacular wealth. Up to sixty Russian merchants now lived there in splendid mansions designed by western European architects; tea was graded and sewn into sacks in a grand neoclassical packing house; and a cathedral partly designed by an Italian architect had doors of solid silver embedded with diamonds, rubies and emeralds and was said to hold more treasures than any other church in Siberia. The Russian merchants socialised in a clubhouse and organised literary evenings and charity balls, and the exiled artist Nikolai Bestuzhev was invited to the Sandy Venice to paint portraits of the leading tea barons and their wives. The Chinese settlement, Trade Town, now contained around 100 permanent shops, reinforced by 1830 with a regular summer influx of some 700 merchants from interior provinces like Shanxi. The physical backdrop may not have been quite as magnificent as the township that was being created on the Russian side. One of Golovkin's lieutenants who stepped into Trade Town in 1805 found the houses low, the roofs 'beetling' and the streets 'like Odessa in winter in the rain'.[133] From the 1820s, however, European visitors frequently gasped at the sudden 'exhibition of gaudy finery', at the 'clean houses' and at the 'luxurious and dissolute manners'.[134] Entertainments were colourful, and in 1829 a 'company of players' were observed complete with drums, gongs, cymbals and female impersonators.[135]

Sandy Venice and Trade Town were still kept apart by a wooden barricade, and the inhabitants on both sides were supposed to return to their own quarters by nightfall. But much of the old wariness was by this time dispelled, and we find repeated descriptions of cheerful commingling. In 1820, for instance, on the name day of Tsar Alexander I, the Manchu *zarguchei* and the leading Chinese merchants were invited over from Trade Town for a reception on the Russian side. Toasts were drunk to the health of Alexander and Jiaqing, and to eternal Sino-Russian friendship, and a mood of 'joy and frankness' prevailed. Ten years later, at a similar festivity, the Russian host told the *zarguchei* that he could 'turn water into wine'. He took two glasses of soda water and poured some white wine into them, creating a sort of ersatz champagne. Entering into the spirit of the occasion, the *zarguchei* responded that he could 'turn wine into nothing': he took one of the glasses and tossed it off.[136] The Russians had made some attempt to cater for the tastes of their visitors by serving them dried fruit and jam instead of the traditional *zakuski* (cold appetisers), and had even laid on some music to keep them entertained. The guests from Trade Town are said to have listened to the Russian part of the concert with 'great indifference'; but when a chorus of trebles attempted a native Chinese song they were moved to tears.[137] Some friendly hobnobbing also took place from one day to another. The Russian director of the Kyakhta customs house is said to have gained the affections of the local Qing officers by 'making them acquainted with Champagne wine'.[138] By the 1830s Chinese traders were coming over daily to the Sandy Venice to call on their Russian counterparts 'from idleness and boredom'.[139] Russians who visited Trade Town became sufficiently familiar with the local temples that they could distinguish the different Chinese 'idols', and were intrigued by the picturesque Chinese opera shows. At a less refined level they also seem to have been tempted by the Chinese equivalent of dirty postcards. Some Trade Town shopkeepers sold pornographic scrolls, paintings and teacups – the obscener the picture, the higher the price.

Even the old language barrier had been effectively, if bizarrely, surmounted. The Chinese at the border had always had trouble with Russian words, with their fiendish inflections and their traffic jams of consonants – they could manage *baran* ('ram') and *kon'* ('horse') but not *verblyud* ('camel'). From 1820, however, we begin to hear reports of a Russian-Chinese pidgin comparable to the pidgin English used to communicate with British traders at Canton. Grammar was drastically simplified, pronunciation was mangled. Russian *tebe kakoi tovar nadobno*? ('What goods do you need?') became *ti chekai duval nadu*?; *tsenu govori* ('State your price') turned into *tsaina gaovuli*. But it seems to have worked. By 1829 Chinese merchants in Trade Town were confidently pressing their Russian visitors to *pi khai* ('drink tea').

Other transmissions that cannot be dated seem also to have taken place across the wooden barricade of Kyakhta. In both Russian and Chinese, for example, we find an identical saying, 'God is high and the emperor is far away' (*Bog vysoko i tsar' daleko*; *Tian gao, huangdi yuan*), used to lament, or perhaps sometimes justify, the corruption of local officials. This adage must clearly have crossed at some point from one side to the other. On balance it seems likely that the Chinese version was the original one: it is said to have been formulated in the eastern province of Zhejiang during the Yuan (Mongol) dynasty of the thirteenth and fourteenth centuries, and is even embedded in a poem. The Russian version by contrast is first reported from Kamchatka in the early 1820s and from Siberia in the early 1840s, most likely diffused by traders who had been in contact with Chinese merchants at Kyakhta. Both Russians and Chinese consume meat-filled dumplings, known respectively to the two peoples as *pelmeni* and *jiaozi*. Once again the evidence tends to point to a Chinese origin, since *pelmeni* are specifically a Siberian dish while *jiaozi* and their southern cousins *hundun* (*wonton*) are prepared the entire length of China. It is even possible that the word *pelmeni* may derive from a Chinese dialect term for dumplings, *baomian* ('wrapped flour').[140] Whatever the answer the salient point is that at Sandy Venice and Trade Town ordinary Russians and Chinese were beginning to make a perceptible impact on each other.

In the meantime the passion for all things Chinese which had gripped intellectuals in Russia in the late eighteenth century was revived unexpectedly by the blazing enthusiasm of a single eccentric monk. Born in 1777 to the family of a sacristan from the Chuvash minority on the middle Volga, Nikita Bichurin took the first steps into a church career by enrolling at the Ecclesiastical Academy of Kazan, where he attracted attention through his brilliant mastery of Latin, Greek and French. In 1799 he took his monastic vows, choosing the misleadingly effete-sounding name of Hyacinth, and in 1802 he was raised to the rank of archimandrite and sent to Irkutsk to serve as the prior of the Voznesensky Monastery and rector of the local seminary. It soon became apparent that religion was not altogether Father Hyacinth's natural calling. In 1805 he was stripped of his archimandrite's rank and 'scandalously discharged' from his posts for failing to control his seminarians and for keeping a serf girl as a 'servant'. At this juncture however he was rescued by the appearance of Count Golovkin, passing through Irkutsk on his ill-fated embassy to Peking. The count was impressed by Hyacinth's learning and recruited him to take the place of a dull-witted and semiliterate hedge-priest, Apollos, who had been travelling out with the embassy as the designated head of the new Ninth Orthodox Mission. Golovkin's debacle and general Manchu obstructiveness kept the mission in Irkutsk for eighteen more months,[141] but in January 1808 Father Hyacinth and his retinue finally arrived in the Qing capital. In the course of his journey Hyacinth had taken the opportunity to get to grips with the Mongolian language, and after reaching Peking he became the first head of mission, so far as we know, to embark on the study of Manchu and Chinese, prodding the rest of his clergy as well as the usual language students to follow suit. He was also the first head of mission not to wish to go home at the earliest opportunity, and in 1816 he appealed unsuccessfully to the Holy Synod to let him stay on in Peking for a second ten-year term to enable him to deepen his knowledge of Chinese. He loved wearing his Chinese gown, and roaming the streets, and chatting to passing citizens. When he reluctantly set off for home in 1821 he took with him fifteen camel-loads of Chinese books.

Unfortunately Father Hyacinth's zeal for Oriental studies wasn't matched by much practical competence or even interest in the day-to-day running of his Mission. When Napoleon's invasion of Russia in 1812 distracted the tsar's government from the Mission's affairs the Mission abruptly found themselves cut off from their regular source of maintenance and plunged into debt. Hyacinth's solution was simply to sell off or pawn Church property – the land, the sacred vessels, the clock in the bell-tower. He apparently let out one of the Russia House buildings as a gambling den. He is even said to have given up the somewhat basic task of conducting church services. The result was that he arrived back in St Petersburg in January 1822 to a distinctly frosty reception. Charged with neglecting his missionary duties, going to public places in improper (presumably Chinese) garb and frequenting Chinese theatres and taverns, he was rusticated to the Valaam Monastery on an island in the north-west of Lake Ladoga, close to Finland, where he languished for the next three years. Once again, however, he was saved by his reputation as a towering intellect. After the intervention of a scholarly-minded diplomat, Baron Pavel Schilling von Kanstadt,[142] he was brought back to St Petersburg in 1826 and attached as a translator to the Foreign Ministry's new Asiatic Department. From this point on he began to produce a cascade of Sinological books and articles, in quantity tantamount to the work of a whole generation, of a range possibly unequalled until the advent of Dr Joseph Needham in the mid-twentieth century. His hundred-odd major translations and studies dealt variously with Chinese history, geography, philosophy, morals, religion, society, literature, painting, linguistics, food, medicine, chronology, coinage, law, statistics, regional government, the Yellow River embankments and the peripheral regions of Mongolia, Xinjiang and Tibet; all of this not including a Chinese grammar and a nine-volume Russian–Chinese dictionary. He wrote his compositions so quickly, we are told, that the government censors hardly had time to finish one volume before he presented them with the next. Like Joseph Needham he 'praised everything Chinese to the skies',[143] arguing, for example, that Chinese laws had 'passed through the furnace of experience for forty centuries and were moulded so near the true beginnings of administration that even the most educated state can learn something from them'. In more detached moments he acknowledged that there was 'both much good and bad' in the Chinese people, but was adamant that 'the good outweighs the bad'. He took up the cudgels against the negative image of China that was now being widely disseminated in the west, 'exposing' the Roman Catholic missionaries for 'intentionally showing China only from the bad side' and for depicting it as a barbaric and ignorant country.[144]

By the late 1820s Father Hyacinth had become a celebrity lionised in the salons of St Petersburg. With a faint whiff of brimstone about him (there was a touch of Rasputin there as well as of Needham) this tall, gaunt, swarthy figure with his deep-socketed eyes overhung by thick, black brows, his black hair streaked with grey and his long grey beard, who wore a cassock but didn't behave like a monk, stirred an agreeable frisson in the tsarist *beau monde*. He had a taste for champagne and cigars. He was rumoured to be an atheist who had admired Voltaire in his seminarian days, who rated Christ no higher than Confucius and doubted the immortality of the soul. The society dandies, we hear, 'loved his chatter because he knew an endless number of scandalous stories and scabrous anecdotes about Chinese women'.[145] But at the same time he managed to infect some of the leading literary figures of the day with his passion for China, and his works are said to have met with the 'broad approval of advanced Russian opinion'.[146]

One of his converts was Alexander Pushkin. In his early years the great poet had wandered in the gardens of Tsarskoe Selo, overgrown and neglected since Catherine's time, and had been haunted by the melancholy of the abandoned Chinese-style pavilions. The 'deserted shelter of love' he described in 'Inscription in a Summer House' (1816) is thought to have been inspired by Catherine's Grand Caprice with its Chinese Kiosk, and in his narrative poem *Ruslan and Ludmila* (1820), the heroine, abducted by a wizard, is shown roaming forlornly through the wizard's garden where

> The cooling airs of May run throbbing
> Along the wonder-stricken ground;
> In shades of trembling foliage sobbing
> The Chinese nightingale is found.[147]

Reading Voltaire's *L'Orphelin de la Chine* Pushkin had wanted to write a Chinese play of his own to 'annoy the shade' of his French predecessor.[148] And now, in 1828, probably at the house of the historian Karamzin, he met Father Hyacinth for the first time and his stray Chinese fancies were given direction. By the end of the year he was proclaiming:

> Let me go, I am ready, friends,
> Wherever you wish to go
> I will follow you closely, go with you
> To the foot of the distant Great Wall.[149]

This verse was probably written on the rebound – the poet had just had his first proposal of marriage rejected by his beloved Natalia Goncharova. In 1830, however, Pushkin made a serious attempt to get to China, applying Tsar Nicholas I for permission to join Baron von Schilling and Father Hyacinth on an embassy-cum-scientific expedition which was to travel to Peking by way of Kyakhta. The notoriously repressive monarch, who was suspicious of Pushkin's dissident leanings and sympathy for the foiled Decembrist uprising at the outset of his reign, refused to let the poet travel to China or anywhere else. Pushkin nevertheless maintained both a close friendship with Father Hyacinth and an interest in China, publishing the monk's articles in the two journals he edited, *Northern Flowers* and the *Literary Gazette*.

Father Hyacinth also frequented the salon of Prince Vladimir Odoevsky, a man of letters who rapidly came to share his Chinese enthusiasm. In 1838 Odoevsky composed a curiously modern-sounding science-fiction story, *The Year 4338*, in which Russia and China join forces in the far distant future to prevent the Earth colliding with Halley's Comet. Russia is by this time the benign centre of world civilisation. China has undergone a 'deathly stagnation', but has revived since the thirty-ninth century thanks to the leadership of its great ruler Khin-Gin. Now Russia has taught China the art of travelling in 'galvanic flying machines', and China in turn will help Russia by sharing the cost of the apparatus which will be used to divert the comet away from the Earth.[150]

The Qing showed no immediate sign of responding to this Russian interest. Under Hyacinth's lackadaisical supervision the Ninth Mission in Peking was as scruffy as any of its predecessors, and Hyacinth's ability to converse with the Qing officials didn't make up for that. On one occasion both Hyacinth and the entire Mission staff were hauled up before the Lifanyuan for unspecified dissipation, and the Lifanyuan are said to have lodged a written complaint with the governor of Irkutsk. A turning-point came, however, with the arrival of the Tenth Mission at the beginning of 1821. This new Mission were charged with effecting the instructions issued by their government three years earlier, and in particular with doing whatever it took to win the approval of the local bigwigs. The new head of mission, Archimandrite Peter Kamensky, was an accomplished scholar who had served a previous stint in Peking in the 1790s. Like Father Hyacinth he got his clergy studying Chinese along with the language students, noting that 'Peking is a wonderful school for learned missionaries, but an agonising captivity for the ignoramus',[151] and like Father Hyacinth he assembled a formidable collection of Chinese books. Unlike Father Hyacinth, however, he was mild, devout and morally irreproachable. If Hyacinth had been a weird mixture of Rasputin and Joseph Needham, Father Peter was the Mission's Dr Arnold. He defended his clergy's study of Chinese on the additional grounds that by keeping them occupied it would maintain their 'Christian morality and physical health',[152] and took prompt steps to smarten up the Russia House both materially and in respect of its inmates. By 1826 he had had both the old Church of the Assumption and the Church of the Purification substantially rebuilt, and had bought back two houses which were sold off by Father Hyacinth a decade earlier; while under his guidance the Mission appear to have behaved vastly better than any mission before. Father Peter had with him a team of far higher calibre than any of their predecessors, with experts in medicine, law, agriculture and economics, and at least one or two of them went to great trouble to make themselves useful in practical ways to the local community. Stepping into Peking in 1821 in the midst of a cholera epidemic, Dr Osip Voitsekhovsky, the Mission's first medical man, a graduate of the St Petersburg Institute of Surgeons, set about deploying his skills in the teeth of deep Chinese suspicion of foreign remedies. Testing the waters initially through the treatment of a seventy-year-old Muslim from Xinjiang, outside the Chinese mainstream, he gradually extended his practice to serve poor Chinese who had failed to respond to their country's indigenous medicine. And after some years of these efforts, in 1829, he successfully cured the tumour afflicting a certain Prince Li, relative of none other than the reigning Daoguang emperor.[153]

The upshot was that for the first time in the Mission's long history the Russians began to win the respect of their hosts. The mature, dignified Father Peter became known as Pa Lao ('Peter the Old'), a Chinese form of address expressing the highest veneration. Heads began to turn in Voitsekhovsky's direction after he successfully treated Chinese whom the Peking doctors had written off as hopeless cases, and he was soon being consulted by both senior Manchu officials and wealthy Chinese. After the cure of Prince Li he became a sensation. On 14 November 1829 he was solemnly presented with a board of honour bearing the inscription 'Wonderful Healing Like Chang Sang' – an allusion to a celebrated Chinese physician of ancient times. The Russian medical effort continued triumphantly into the Eleventh Mission of the 1830s. Voitsekhovsky's successor, Porfiry Kirilov, pressed ahead with the earlier doctor's work among the Chinese poor. Writing in July 1832 from a village outside Peking he reported, 'The people have apparently forgotten that I am a foreigner.'[154] And he too attracted the upper classes in ever-growing numbers. The new head of mission, Father Benjamin Morachevich, observed that important people had for the first time stopped running away from the Russians and had 'even begun to seek our acquaintance',[155] and by the mid-1830s 'the first ministers and princes of China' were beating a path to the Russia House.[156] Dr Kirilov was even given access to the women's quarters of Chinese households which were by long tradition forbidden to males, and one princess rewarded him for her cure with an enormous and valuable root of ginseng. In 1836 he received two boards of honour commending the 'Beneficial Conduct of One Arrived from a Foreign State'.

One attraction led to another. The Eleventh Mission also included a certain Legashev, a painter from the St Petersburg Academy of Fine Arts who had been sent to Peking to depict local life. The Qing upper classes began to be intrigued by his work, and especially by his portraiture (never a strong Chinese suit). On the eve of the Chinese New Year in 1832 the Manchu supervisor of the Russia House, Wensan, paid a call on Legashev and asked the artist to paint portraits of him and his father. A further stampede ensued, and by the end of the decade Legashev had been requested to paint portraits of 'all the Peking notables'.[157]

Two major changes had, in other words, taken place as a result of the reforms introduced by Father Peter and his successors and the exertions of their small teams of professionals. The Qing had begun for the first time to look up to Russian scientific and artistic attainments instead of vice versa. And the Mission had finally broken through to the local elite.

The Russians by now occupied a supremely advantageous position in China by comparison with their western rivals. Right through the eighteenth century the Mission had still been obliged to share their foothold in Peking with the Jesuits and other clergy from the Roman Catholic world. But the Catholics' star was falling as the Qing government grew ever more suspicious of their evangelical aims. In 1805 the court banned the printing of Christian-related books, and in 1815 those Chinese who had accepted the Catholic faith were forced to renounce it. The Russian Mission, by contrast, continued to show a sublime lack of interest in winning converts among the Chinese or even among the surviving Albazintsy (by 1821 their Albazintsy congregation had dwindled to precisely three – an old man called Alexei and his two youthful relatives), and this suited the Qing government to perfection. The Lifanyuan even informed the Tenth Mission that they would like the Russian clergy and students to take over from the Jesuits in the latters' long-standing role of court astronomers. In 1825 the last Catholic missions in China were closed, and for the next thirty years the Russian contingents enjoyed the distinction of being the only Europeans whatsoever allowed to live in Peking. By the following decade we find them more at home there than ever before. In June 1836 Dr Kirilov described in a letter how he and a companion had gone for a ramble in the Peking suburbs: he had sat on a rock beside a stream and had drunk sweet tea while his friend munched a street snack in the form of a piece of fried fish.

One result of this Russian monopoly was a sharp advance in the Sinological field. In 1837, by decree of the tsar, the first chair of Chinese in Russia was established at the University of Kazan. The instruction there was to be based on Father Hyacinth's grammar, and teaching of Chinese in Russia would from now on be standardised rather than drawing on the random efforts of a few individual China Hands. The first professor appointed was Father Daniel Sivillov, a former Tenth Mission member who brought with him a large collection of Chinese materials; the second was Dr Voitsekhovsky. In terms of formal institutions the Russians were no more than level pegging with western Europe: Paris and Naples already had Chinese professorships, and the British installed their first chair of Chinese at University College London in the same year the chair at Kazan was created, 1837. In terms of content, however, it seems likely that Chinese studies in Russia were at this point appreciably in advance of anything in the west. The Russians certainly thought so. Father Hyacinth was disdainful of the work of western European scholars who, in the words of the Chinese proverb, 'called an ass a horse, a goat a cow',[158] and his colleagues berated those western Sinologists who pontificated about China without ever having been there as 'empty drums'.[159] One tsarist official proclaimed in 1841 that the University of Kazan taught Oriental languages in 'a depth and variety unsurpassed by any other institution of higher learning in all of Europe'.[160] But some western authorities also seemed to take the same view. The books and articles which Father Hyacinth went on churning out from his cell in the Alexander Nevsky Monastery were acclaimed by academic circles in both France and Germany. One work reviewed in *The Chinese Repository*, a journal published in Canton by American Protestant missionaries, paid tribute to the huge amount of Chinese literature 'that comes to us by way of St Petersburg'.[161] The sheer quantity of texts the Russians were able to extract from Peking was undoubtedly staggering. In 1845 Nicholas I personally sponsored a request to the Qing government to supply ancient Chinese books with particular reference to the Buddhist scriptures. The Daoguang emperor approved the request, and the tsar was duly presented with 800 volumes of classics from Peking's Lama Temple.

More immediately useful, from the point of view of the chiefs in St Petersburg, was the favour of high Qing officials which the Mission had won through the dignified conduct of Father Peter Kamensky and the calibre of the new specialist teams. At long last they were able to use the Mission effectively as a source of high-grade intelligence. By the early 1830s Father Benjamin of the Eleventh Mission was making a regular habit of reading the Peking newspapers. The Russia House could find out about the latest trends and proposals at the Qing court, its attitude to their country and dealings with the western powers, and could relay all this data in timely fashion to the authorities at home.

Western governments were frantic with envy. Sir John Bowring, a British official and future governor of Hong Kong, who arrived in the East in the late 1840s, is said to have complained, quite unjustly, of these privileged rivals that 'there had never been an example of even one person sent to their Peking Mission who could explain himself in a [European] language other than his native Russian; and this was precisely with the object of averting the communication to Europe of the information they had received in Peking'.[162] The Mission themselves felt this envy was not wholly warranted. They did not, as the westerners fancied, exert a 'great influence' on Qing government policy; they didn't, or couldn't, intrigue at the court. Life in Peking was scarcely idyllic: they were starved of European company, and frequently cursed the supposed good fortune of their residence there. But the fact remained that they had at last secured in the Qing capital what Russian governments ever since Peter the Great's time had coveted – an inside track.

CHAPTER 3

THE TSARIST SUPREMACY

THE OLD ORDER IN QUESTION (1840–54)

Events in the early 1840s brutally undercut Russia's cherished advantage in the China trade. In pursuit of their urge to sell opium the British bombarded the Chinese coast, blasted the Qing war junks out of the water and in 1842 secured through the Treaty of Nanking the possession of Hong Kong Island in perpetuity and the right for their merchants to do business in the 'treaty ports' of Canton, Xiamen, Fuzhou, Ningbo and Shanghai. France and the United States followed suit with similar treaties in 1844. The western maritime powers could now transport goods between China and Europe more quickly and cheaply than the Russians could by the overland route through Kyakhta. The Russian government were alarmed for their revenues. Urgent instructions were sent to the priests of the Twelfth Orthodox Mission to brief the tsarist authorities on Chinese market conditions; and the reports that came back presented a depressing picture of western encroachment. In 1846 the head of mission, Archimandrite Polycarp Tugarinov, described the advent 'in astonishing proportions' of western goods in Peking. Prices of western cottons were steadily falling, 'so you can guess how readily they must be bought here – quite unlike our cloth'.[1] One year later these western European goods were still selling prolifically. 'We could see even English cloth among them, large amounts of it and of a very high quality too.'[2] Polycarp's successor, Archimandrite Palladius Kafarov, who became head of the new Thirteenth Mission in 1850, took up the story in even gloomier tones. Shops selling Russian wares in Peking, he declared, were now 'almost deserted', while light blue British cottons were pouring in.[3] The British were also trying out various other industrial products, from gold and silver watches to, astoundingly, porcelain. In March 1851 Russian cotton cloths were still lying unsold. Some Chinese merchants were starting to dislike the sheen of Russian cottons, which they viewed as a sign of flimsiness by comparison with the sturdier British light blues.

These snippets from the Mission were fully borne out by official statistics. By as early as 1844 Britain accounted for 68 per cent of China's imports, as against Russia's 19 per cent, and 60 per cent of China's exports, as against Russia's 16 per cent.[4] Russia's exports through Kyakhta dwindled from 8 million roubles' worth in 1840 to 5 million roubles by 1849.[5] The Sandy Venice was visibly no longer adequate to cope on its own with the pressure of western competition, or to satisfy the mounting Russian and more especially Siberian appetite for trade with the East. New outlets were needed to offset the western advance.

The Opium War of 1839–42 had disclosed for the first time the military weakness of Qing China in the face of the outside world. Father Peter Kamensky, the former Tenth Mission chief, summarised the outcome of the war with the comment, 'Legions of Chinese troops scatter at the neighing of a northern horse.'[6] The priests in Peking were as adept in ferreting out political as commercial intelligence, and by the late 1840s it was clear to them that the Opium War had been merely a foretaste of greater upheavals to come. In March 1846 Father Polycarp advised the Asiatic Department of the Russian Foreign Ministry that China was starving, because the British had drained away all the country's silver in exchange for their opium and the government were on the brink of bankruptcy. He foresaw that a peasant rising would shortly break out and engulf the whole empire. Five years later, in March 1851, Father Palladius supplied one of the first intimations of the immense convulsion of the Taiping rebellion which was taking shape under the leadership of the self-proclaimed 'younger brother of Jesus Christ'. 'Remarkable events', he declared, were unfolding in the depths of south China where 'new social ideas' were gaining ground. China, it seemed, was moving forward into a new era, different from the past but 'without a real future'.[7]

With Qing prestige tottering the prevalent western disdain for China and its people was starting belatedly to win a widespread adherence in Russia as well. Nikolai Lyubimov, the deputy head of the Foreign Ministry's Asiatic Department, wondered whether China was capable of renewal, and marvelled that it had endured for so many centuries, 'almost without a religion, without pure morality, without anything that makes a nation strong and hardy and gives it a long existence'.[8] In the St Petersburg journals the eminent critic V.G. Belinsky assailed Father Hyacinth for 'prettifying' a country he felt to be 'rotting in moral stagnation',[9] while the sardonic Polish Orientalist Osip Senkowski derided Hyacinth and his followers for being in denial of the abject collapse of Qing forces before British arms and poured scorn on Hyacinth's admiring editions of Chinese texts which would 'undoubtedly have brought to a rapture the entire Peking Department of the Ten Thousand Ceremonies'.[10] Even in the Peking Mission the younger priests were exhibiting a distinct absence of veneration towards Chinese culture. One Twelfth Mission member, Gurii Karpov, recalled, 'There was so little wisdom in China that two or three years would be enough for a Russian to grasp it to perfection.'[11]

As this sense of Chinese worthlessness grew, the renewed western competition began once again to prod a phlegmatic Russia into action, and this time with far-reaching results. During the 1840s the tentative border probings of earlier decades intensified sharply. In 1844 Alexander von Middendorff, a professor of German extraction who had been sent with an expedition to study the Siberian permafrost in the neighbourhood of Yakutsk, took the unauthorised step of dispatching a reconnaissance team into the Amur basin. He returned to Europe proclaiming the importance for Russia of taking back the Amur. The Qing, he maintained, had no documentary proof of their right to the territory, and more to the point, there was no sign of any Qing garrison or administration there. The following year Tsar Nicholas I personally sent a Lieutenant Alexander Gavrilov on a ship of the Russian American Company to nose around the Amur estuary. The crew were supplied with Virginia tobacco and given instructions that if confronted by any Qing outpost they were to pass themselves off as Americans. On China's western flank, meanwhile, the Foreign Ministry official Lyubimov dressed himself in Central Asian garb to comply with the practice imposed locally upon merchants from Russia and journeyed to the Xinjiang border towns of Yili and Tacheng to discuss the scope for expanding Russian trade. In Tacheng he went so far as to inquire whether Russian merchants in future could come to do business in their own national dress. (The answer was no.)

In September 1847 the pace quickened further with the appointment of Major-General Nikolai Muraviev to the new post of governor-general of Eastern Siberia. Still youthful at thirty-eight, with an imposing military record followed by a stint as governor of the province of Tula, Muraviev is said to have been a mercurial character. 'At moments of rage he was terrible, and ready, it seemed, to bury a man alive; but in another hour he had turned into a kindly and sympathetic father-commander, dealing placidly with the person who had just provoked that storm of rage within him.'[12] Remarkably progressive with regard to domestic affairs, he had called publicly for the abolition of serfdom and supported the institution of an independent judiciary and a free press; and the tsar referred to him darkly as a 'liberal' and a 'democrat'. But he was also a fervent expansionist, placing himself at the head of a group of like-minded '*Amurtsy*' who favoured an all-out advance into the former Cossack domains. In 1849 he gave his formal backing to the venture of a young naval officer named Gennady Nevelskoi. In another reconnaissance launched without a formal nod from St Petersburg Nevelskoi sailed a troopship to the mouth of the Amur, establishing clearly for the first time that the river was navigable from the sea and once again finding no sign of Qing authority and nothing more than a hazy awareness of Qing suzerainty on the part of the local Gilyak tribe. One year later, in August 1850, Nevelskoi took a momentous step forward, raising the Russian flag at a point on the estuary he named Nikolaevsk in honour of the tsar and planting a settlement there. In a letter to his sovereign Muraviev neatly summed up the situation to date:

> Our destiny is down the Amur and into the Pacific. The English, by forcing trade concessions from China, are drying up our overland trade, and the merchants of Kyakhta will starve. Our settlements on the Pacific must be fostered.[13]

Over in the west Major E.P. Kovalevsky, another adherent of Muraviev's 'forward school', was busy conducting the latest in a series of Russian attempts to win official Qing permission to trade in Xinjiang. In August 1851 he succeeded in concluding an agreement with the military governor of Yili. Under the terms of this Treaty of Yili Russia was accorded the right to establish consulates in Yili and Tacheng, conduct duty-free trade there and establish 'trade circles' in which Russian merchants could build homes and warehouses, graze their livestock and bury their dead free of Qing authority and subject only to Russian consular jurisdiction. The effect was that Russia had created two new 'treaty ports' on China's land frontier to offset the western ones on the coast. The commercial benefits were modest, but the treaty was nonetheless a striking new departure. It was the first time an agreement had been extracted by the Russians from an unenthusiastic China under pressure. In the talks leading up to the old treaties of Nerchinsk and Kyakhta, we remember, the Qing had been able to deploy their superior military strength to hasten Russian compliance. This time the boot was on the other foot. The governor-general of Western Siberia, Prince Gorchakov, is said to have alerted all his troops near the Xinjiang frontier to ensure that the Qing negotiators conceded more readily.

Advances on the land frontier didn't reduce Russian interest in gaining a foothold on the Chinese coast. In the summer of 1848, and again in 1850, the *Prince Menshikov*, a ship of the Russian American Company, put in at the new treaty port of Shanghai in the hope of being allowed to trade. It was followed in May 1853 by the *Pallas*, a frigate commanded by Count Yefim Putyatin, who had been tasked with attempting the development of sea trade with China alongside his main assignment, the opening up of Japan.

This abrupt Russian shift from a passive to an expansionist posture didn't by any means go unchallenged at home. Fear of Qing military might was still strong among a group of veteran tsarist diplomats headed by Count Karl von Nesselrode, foreign minister since 1815. In the mid-1840s Nesselrode expressed deep unease at the lunge made by Middendorff's expedition into the Amur valley, and in 1850 he argued before a committee set up to discuss the Amur question that the region should on no account be occupied in order to avoid 'extreme danger' from China.[14] When news came through of Nevelskoi's unauthorised foundation of the outpost of Nikolaevsk the foreign minister voiced his outrage at this 'impudent deed' and demanded that the officer be stripped of his rank and reduced to the status of an ordinary seaman.[15] The conservative holdouts were only quelled in January 1851 when the committee, following a démarche by Muraviev, decided to strengthen the Nerchinsk outpost, and the tsar proclaimed that 'where the Russian flag has been hoisted it must not be lowered'.[16]

Hand in hand with fear went continued respect. Impressed by Father Hyacinth's glowing descriptions of Chinese high culture, many educated

Russians still questioned the increasing tendency to run China down. Sergei Georgievsky, for instance, a young Sinologist of the Hyacinth school, condemned the Russian public for sympathising with articles that portrayed the Qing empire as a stagnant morass. He voiced his admiration for Chinese achievements, and like Prince Odoevsky the science fiction writer looked forward to a time when a Sino-Russian alliance would dominate the world. This disagreement in turn fed into the great debate of the period over Russia's own identity, the dispute between 'Westernisers' and 'Slavophiles'. For Westernisers such as the philosopher Pyotr Chaadaev and the dissident man of letters Alexander Herzen, who wished Russia to follow the path of the free, dynamic societies of western Europe, China was a symbol of the Asiatic autocracy and backwardness they wanted their country to escape. For Slavophiles, on the other hand, who preferred to view Russia as a unique society distinct from those of Europe, China was a reminder that a stable and creative civilisation was possible outside the European tradition.

The effect of these conflicting elements in the Russian outlook was that the shift to expansionist policies in the 1840s and 1850s was offset by behaviour of a strangely avuncular kind. When the British began their assault on Qing China in 1840 Tsar Nicholas, in an uncharacteristic display of enlightenment, signalled his support for the Qing cause by issuing a decree that forbade Russian subjects to export opium to the Chinese empire. Ten years later, as the scale of the Taiping rebellion in southern China grew obvious, the would-be empire-builder Muraviev wrote to St Petersburg urging that Russia should back the Qing government against this pseudo-Christian insurgency, and that the tsar should make a declaration of friendship to the new emperor Xianfeng and offer him shelter inside Russian territory if the rebellion forced him to flee from Peking. Russia, in other words, was to be presented to the Qing as a benevolent patron even as plans were afoot to establish Russian footholds on Qing soil and to prise away chunks of Qing land. The thinking behind these manoeuvres is not far to seek. Since Russian opium exports to China were minimal a ban on opium sales was a cost-free way for the tsar's government to win credit in Peking at the expense of the western powers. As for the Taiping revolt, there were solid commercial reasons for Russia to take the Qing side. Father Palladius noted that the rebellion posed a threat to Russia's already disturbed China trade insofar as it had broken out 'in the very places from which caravans set out every year with brick tea for Siberia'.[17]

At the same time we should not overlook a degree of real sympathy in Russian intellectual circles for the Chinese predicament. Secretary to Putyatin during his call at Shanghai in May 1853 was Ivan Goncharov, the satirical novelist who a few years later won fame with his creation of the apathetic Russian noble Oblomov, 'the superfluous man'. Watching the 'civilising' descent of the British on Shanghai Goncharov remarked in his journal that he 'didn't know who should be civilising whom'. The Chinese were paying for the opium they imported with their 'tea, silk, metals, medicines, dyestuffs, sweat, blood, energy, brains, lives'. The attitude of the British towards the Chinese in Shanghai was in general 'either imperious and rude, or cold and disdainful'. Goncharov and his companions noted how British officers treated Chinese who were blocking their path, pulling them to one side by their pigtails or striking them with their walking sticks. 'They don't regard the natives as people, but as some kind of draught animals.'[18]

The Qing response to the incipient change of tack by St Petersburg was correspondingly mixed. The tsar's ban on opium exports undoubtedly won some goodwill in Qing government circles. Among those officials impressed by the Russian move was Lin Zexu, the imperial commissioner who in 1839 famously seized and destroyed the opium stocks of the British merchants in Canton. Having studied his maps Lin proposed, in conjunction with his assistant, the scholar Wei Yuan, that the Russians should be encouraged to join up with the still unsubdued Gurkhas of Nepal and relieve Britain's pressure on the Chinese coast with a grand offensive against British India. In 1850, when Russia sought talks with the Qing authorities over the question of gaining formal access to Yili and Tacheng, a Mongolian member of the Grand Council, Saishanga, was credited by Father Palladius with having played a key role in persuading his colleagues to negotiate. Russians still generally fell into the category of foreigners whom later generations of Chinese diplomats would describe as 'old friends', and indeed the Lifanyuan observed to the Russian Senate in a letter of 1853 that the two empires had 'enjoyed a continuous friendship of two hundred years, which may be called a long time'.[19]

Doubts were, however, beginning to creep in. One of the first Qing officials to sound the alarm was none other than ex-commissioner Lin Zexu. Sent off to the far western frontier in 1842 to be governor of Yili, a form of punishment for his having brought down on the Qing the calamity of the

Opium War, Lin came round to the view that Russia was in fact the most serious threat to the dynasty. He tried to build Yili into a base of resistance to Russian attack, and warned his younger colleagues that the tsarist empire would become the greatest source of trouble for China within their lifetimes. After Kovalevsky's success in securing a permanent Russian presence in Yili and Tacheng a bureaucrat named Shengbao observed gloomily to Emperor Xianfeng that the Russians 'sought trade through force and their intentions were avaricious'.[20] Now that they had been given permission to settle merchants in the two Xinjiang towns they would 'first feel gratitude, then regard it as their right and finally become more and more insatiable'.[21] Direst forebodings of all were expressed by a Mongol prince, Delekedorji, who served as the dynasty's chief official in Urga. In 1852 he reported that the Russians had stationed troops among the Buryat Mongols on the other side of the border, and that large contingents were being transferred to the East. He even voiced concern about the activities of the Orthodox Mission. 'The correspondence coming in to the lamas [i.e. Russian priests] in Peking is twice what it was before, and I am afraid the lamas may be leaking some information.'[22] This chorus of doom-mongers seems to have roused the authorities to a modicum of obstruction. The Xinjiang negotiators managed to stop Kovalevsky acquiring a third Russian base in the southern town of Kashgar, arguing that they wouldn't be able to protect the tsar's merchants from the fierce local Muslim tribes. The Lifanyuan wrote to the Russian Senate that while the right to trade at Yili and Tacheng had been granted to Russia as a special favour, access to Shanghai was another matter altogether. If Russian merchants came to trade in Shanghai their expenses would in any case soar and their profits would be reduced. But the Qing court were still on a low alert with regard to the Russians, and the zealous Delekedorji was discreetly counselled not to bother the emperor so often.[23]

AN AVUNCULAR CONQUEST (1854–60)

For some time now the Russians had feared that the sudden intrusion of British naval power into Pacific waters might prove a strategic as well as a commercial threat to their interests in the Far East. In 1848 an Englishman by the name of Austen had been found by a party of Russian scouts on the lower Amur trying to sail up the river on a raft. Austen was clearly not just there to enjoy the jolly boating weather or the hay harvest breeze, and

Muraviev promptly had him arrested and sent to St Petersburg. Muraviev was convinced that a British fleet might at any time seize the mouth of the River Amur and the island of Sakhalin opposite it, with dire consequences for Russian security. 'Whoever shall control the mouth of the Amur', he declared portentously, 'shall control Siberia.'[24] Writing to Nicholas I in 1850 he outlined the still grimmer prospect that the rise of British sea power in the region might enable Britain to gain political sway over China, creating potentially a second Indian empire on the tsar's eastern flank. Within a few years Muraviev's nightmares began to look like being realised. In March 1854 the Crimean War broke out in Europe between Britain, France and Ottoman Turkey on the one hand and Russia on the other. Sir John Bowring, the governor of the new British colony of Hong Kong, sent a naval force out to harry the Russians in the Pacific, and in August a joint Anglo-French squadron made an initial attempt to force their way up the Amur. Failing to find the estuary, they instead lunged across the Sea of Okhotsk to attack the Russian naval base of Petropavlovsk on the Kamchatka peninsula.

If Muraviev had needed any further excuse for an all-out thrust into China's north-eastern borderlands, here it was in abundance. In May 1854, after sending a notification to the Qing court but without waiting for a reply to it, he set off from Nerchinsk down the Amur in the first of a series of what the Russians called 'flotillas' – a squadron consisting of twenty-nine rafts, eighteen launches, thirteen barges, five lighters, five whalers and (hint of a new age) a steamship, and carrying 800 officers and soldiers, a team of engineers and an expert topographer. The main task of the squadron was to reinforce the Russian outposts at the mouth of the River Amur and establish a line of communications with Kamchatka, which they reached just in time to repel a 1,000-strong Anglo-French landing party at Petropavlovsk. Muraviev did however take the opportunity to assert Russian claims to Amuria by founding two new settlements on the north bank of the river – at Ust-Zeisk, facing the main Qing garrison at Aigun, and at Khabarovsk, named after Khabarov, the old Cossack pioneer, at the confluence of the Amur with the northward-flowing River Ussuri. By June 1855 a second flotilla was on its way, comprising ten large ships and ninety other vessels, and this time the objective was unmistakably one of colonisation. With the eager support of the new tsar, Alexander II, the Russians were aiming at the seizure, or as they saw it the recovery, of the entire vast wilderness to the north of the river where Cossacks had roamed in the years before the Treaty of Nerchinsk. This second flotilla brought with it some 7,000 to 8,000 men and women, including peasants destined for settlement and an escort of 2,500 troops. With the Crimean War brought to a close by the Treaty of Paris in 1856 the pressing strategic case for a drive down the Amur no longer existed; but the sting of defeat in that conflict only increased Russian yearning for a compensating success in the East. Already at the start of the war the historian Mikhail Pogodin had appealed to Russia to switch its attention to Asia and concentrate on establishing its supremacy over its non-European neighbours: '*Let Japheth tower over his brothers*.'[25] In May 1856 a further 1,660 troops were dispatched down the river, and in 1857 a Cossack post called Albazin was set up on the site of the seventeenth-century fort. One year later, in 1858, Muraviev embarked on a culminating expedition with three large ships and 200 settler families. Meeting the Qing military governor Yishan at Aigun on 26 May, the tsarist proconsul called for a new treaty allotting to the Russian empire all the lands to the north of the Amur and all the lands to the east of the Ussuri as far as the Pacific. Muraviev is said to have opened the negotiations in a tone of 'blustery bonhomie',[26] but when the Qing official demurred at the Russian requests he erupted in a tantrum – calculated no doubt to intimidate the opposition, though it also tallies with what we know of his volatile character. Gone, at any rate, was the politeness of yesteryear. Giving Governor Yishan twenty-four hours to accept his demands Muraviev stamped off to his vessel, 'glaring angrily' at the Manchu crowd.[27] All through the night the lights blazed on Muraviev's flagship, while the Russian gunboats kept up a mock cannonade. Cowed by this demonstration, Yishan caved in and undertook to behave in future 'so that the general would not be angry';[28] and on 28 May a Treaty of Aigun was concluded according to which the Amur was to be recognised as the border and its north bank was once again to become Russian territory. The Ussuri region to the east would be held jointly by the two empires pending final determination, and Russia would be the sole outside power to have access to the Amur and the other Manchurian rivers. The outpost of Ust-Zeisk was renamed Blagoveshchensk ('Glad Tidings') in honour of the Russian breakthrough, and Muraviev was ennobled as Count Muraviev-Amursky ('Muraviev of the Amur').

Russian expansion was meanwhile being pushed ahead further south by a second tsarist empire-builder. We have already met Vice-Admiral Count

Yefim Putyatin, commander of the frigate *Pallas* which called at Shanghai in the spring of 1853. In February 1857 this tough naval officer, 'a cold, impassive man of about fifty',[29] was directed to proceed to Peking at the head of an embassy to hammer out an agreement with the Qing court themselves. Opportunity beckoned. As if the Taiping rebellion were not enough to contend with, the wretched Qing dynasty had been locked since the previous year in a second Opium War with Britain and France, and their vulnerability was more apparent than ever. Arriving at Kyakhta, Putyatin applied for permission to travel via Urga to the Qing capital in the traditional fashion. When no reply was forthcoming he sent a curt note to Peking stating that 'Everyone knows it does not take more than 25 days for documents to pass between the Lifanyuan and Urga',[30] and warning that if he had heard nothing further by 23 May he would enter China anyhow by way of the Amur. His deadline ignored, he accordingly set off with Muraviev's latest flotilla along the Amur to Nikolaevsk, where he embarked on the steamship *Amerika* and journeyed round the Korean peninsula to the north China coast, resubmitting his request to Peking from the unexpected proximity of Tianjin on the Gulf of Beizhili. Further attempts to win access to the capital turned out equally useless, leading one downcast member of Putyatin's entourage to remark in September that the waters where they had been anchored should be renamed the Gulf of *Pechali* ('Gulf of Sorrow' in Russian). The admiral now shifted tactics by making a show of collusion with those very western countries with which Russia had been at war only eighteen months earlier. Buzzing around the China coast like a sort of mosquito, he put in first at Shanghai, where he expressed himself in favour of 'combined action' by the western powers, and then at Hong Kong, where an Anglo-French expedition under Lord Elgin was assembling to sail up north and enforce Qing acceptance of western commercial demands. By April 1858 Putyatin was back in Tianjin as one of a quartet of British, French, Russian and United States representatives, each poised to besiege the Qing government with their own set of terms. Weeks of negotiations ensued, with their full quota of diplomatic longueurs: the American envoy, William Reed, recalled how Putyatin spent one typical evening aboard Reed's ship in the 'Gulf of Sorrow', reading a newspaper 'with his spectacles far down on his nose and twirling his long moustaches'.[31] Allied pressure, however, was relentless, stepped up on 20 May when British and French forces stormed the Dagu coastal forts. On 13 June, a clear fortnight ahead of the rest of the quartet, Putyatin managed to conclude a Treaty of Tianjin extracting a new set of concessions from the prostrate Qing. The China coast was at long last prised open. The five coastal treaty ports were to be opened to Russian trade, plus two additional ones on the islands of Taiwan and Hainan. Russia was to be permitted to station consuls in each of these places, and Russian merchants there were to enjoy extra-territorial rights. Various old restrictions on Russian overland trade were abolished – on the number of traders who could be admitted in a party, on the quantity of goods they could bring. A most favoured nation (MFN) clause guaranteed that any fresh concessions which might be obtained by the rival western powers would automatically be extended to Russia as well. Finally, a first step was taken towards securing a formal Russian diplomatic presence in the Qing capital. Future official contacts, it was agreed, should take place between the Russian Foreign Ministry and the Qing Grand Council, rather than between the Senate and the demeaningly lowly Lifanyuan. And Putyatin contrived to arrange that the escort arriving with the new Fourteenth Orthodox Mission should be allowed to remain in Peking as a secular head of mission and a 'political agent' responsible for securing the ratification of the two new treaties of Aigun and Tianjin.

Over the following two years the gains achieved by Muraviev and Putyatin were cemented through the efforts of the most formidable tsarist fixer of all. Seemingly disillusioned with their first 'political agent', a Manchu language interpreter used by Muraviev at Aigun who had turned out to be lazy and (it was hinted) inclined to succumb to the joys of Peking's taverns and brothels, the Russian government decided at the beginning of 1859 to replace him with a diplomatic whizz-kid. Known in his childhood as Bright Sun, Major-General Nikolai Pavlovich Ignatiev had risen in an astonishingly short time to a leading position in tsarist government circles. Following service in the Crimean War he had been attached as a military agent to the Russian embassy in London, where he employed a local mapmaker to provide him with charts of British ports and railway lines and was described by the foreign secretary, Lord Clarendon, in a letter to the prime minister, Lord John Russell, as 'a very clever, wily fellow'.[32] Now, at the age of just twenty-eight, he was hurried back from a posting in Central Asia and reassigned to Peking with the rank of ambassador, to enhance his status with the Qing bureaucracy and also no doubt to offset any scorn they might feel at his conspicuous youth. In March 1859 he set off for Eastern Siberia in a whirl of energy, bounding from floe to floe, we are told, across the cracking ice of the Ob and Yenisei rivers. From Kyakhta he strode across the Qing frontier to the sound of a cannon salute, accompanied by almost the entire population of the Sandy Venice – we can almost see the last barriers of the old trading system uprooted and thrown to one side. Reaching Peking at the end of June, he took up his new post with the same confident brashness, commanding the Mission members to abandon the Chinese dress that had been imposed on them for about one and a half centuries and revert to European clothes. None of this vigour appears to have made any instant impression on his Qing interlocutors, who had refused to ratify the treaty signed by their man at Aigun and now flatly rejected a draft convention in which Ignatiev hoped to incorporate the provisions of both Aigun and Tianjin. After many months without progress Bright Sun duly switched, like Putyatin before him, to a technique of cosying up to the western powers. At the end of May 1860 he withdrew to Shanghai, where the British and French were mustering a fresh expedition to break China open for good. He soon established 'cordial' relations with Lord Elgin and his French counterpart, Baron Gros, and in late September, when the Allies had once again taken the Dagu forts and were moving inland, he was at their side actively encouraging the advance on Peking. He even supplied Elgin with a plan of the capital showing 'every street and house of importance',[33] which had been compiled by the diligent intelligence gatherers of the Orthodox Mission. When the Allied troops entered Peking on 1 October Ignatiev was once again present, and on 14 November, after the western powers had concluded their business with the Qing government, he secured the signature of Prince Gong, the senior Manchu official still left in the capital, on a climactic summary of Russia's demands. This Supplementary Treaty of Peking stated baldly that the rules once laid down at Nerchinsk and Kyakhta were no longer applicable. It reasserted the articles signed at Tianjin (hence the term 'supplementary'), with their concession to Russia of their coastal ports and their MFN clause. It reaffirmed the allotment to Russia of the eastern part of what is now Kazakhstan, from Lake Zaisan to the southern spurs of the Altai mountains. Russian merchants were to be granted permission to trade at Urga in Mongolia and at the entrepôt of Kashgar in southern Xinjiang (the objective denied them in 1851), and Russian consulates were to be opened in both these centres. To all intents and purposes Russia had swept the board. On 22 November Ignatiev was borne out of Peking in triumph, in a palanquin carried by sixteen litter-bearers, for all the world like a senior member of the Qing imperial house.

It was a drastic, a staggering breakthrough. Between them these three tsarist officers, the terrible troika of Muraviev, Putyatin and Ignatiev, had prised away from the Qing empire the entire vast expanse then known as Outer Manchuria, an area of around a million square kilometres or approximately the size of France and Germany put together. A Treaty of Tacheng signed in 1864 to finalise the details of the Kazakh cession added a further 500,000 square kilometres to Russian ownership. Far away in London, as the news came through, Lord Clarendon wrote bemusedly to Lord John Russell of Russia's 'gigantic prospects on the Amoor and in the country they are filching from China'.[34] By the end of 1860 Russian settlers had founded a city on the coast of their new Maritime Province beyond the Ussuri, changing the name of the site from the humble Chinese Haishenwei ('Sea-Slug Cliffs') to Vladivostok – 'Ruler of the East'.

On closer inspection, however, the arresting feature is not so much the scale of the takeover as the near-total bloodlessness with which it was carried out. While the British and French three times stormed the Dagu forts before Tianjin, while they forced their way into Peking and burnt down the Yuanmingyuan, the old Summer Palace, the Russians quietly snaffled their winnings without major violence and with negligible losses to either the Qing or themselves. The sole Russian casualty reported during these years of advance in Manchuria was a trader named Chebotarev, who in 1859 in the town of Sanxing crept into the house of a local resident 'to play around with Mrs Wang Gao' and was hacked to death with an axe by an angry neighbour.[35] On one occasion at the start of 1860 we read of a squad of Russian cavalry burning down a Qing outpost to the north of the Amur and driving the local Qing officers and soldiers across the river; and it is difficult to believe that no Manchu or Chinese bones were broken in the course of this operation. But there were no battles, no sieges, no large-scale wreckings.

Russia had no intention of turning the Chinese empire upside down. By the mid-1850s the tsarist authorities were quite clear that their strategy had to be to preserve the Qing dynasty from the double menace of the Taiping and the west. In 1854, in a policy statement drafted as his first great flotilla prepared to sail down the Amur, Muraviev recorded the view of his government that the dynasty's survival was '*the only outcome likely to be favourable to us*'.[36] Instructions issued to Ignatiev during his 1859–60 sojourn in the Qing capital explained clearly why. 'It would be extremely disadvantageous', the envoy was told, 'to replace the Manchu dynasty with an ethnic Chinese dynasty.'[37] Such a dynasty would be likely to move its capital from Peking to the south, and in that event it would be 'bound to shake off Russian influence and fall under the control of the maritime powers, especially Britain.'[38] Russia was, certainly, to take the chance to build itself spheres of influence in the non-Chinese parts of the fraying Qing empire, and specifically in the border regions of Manchuria, Mongolia and Xinjiang. But it should in the meantime do all in its power short of armed intervention to maintain the political status quo that had served it so well in the past.

The result of this thinking was an approach quite distinct from that of the western powers, and appreciably subtler. The avuncular posture we saw taking shape in the 1840s had by this time been developed into something like an art form. The thrust down the Amur, for example, was justified to the Qing court as a measure taken to ensure the security of both Russia and China: Muraviev even wrote to the Xianfeng emperor that his men had suffered heavy losses fighting the British on behalf of both empires in the Eastern Sea. The Treaty of Aigun was presented as being drawn up for the joint benefit of Russian and Chinese subjects and for their protection from foreigners.[39] From his post in the Russia House Archimandrite Palladius embroidered this theme by echoing the allusions the Qing liked to make to the antiquity of Sino-Russian relations. In August 1854 he observed to Qing notables that Russia and China had been friends for so long there could be 'no room for the slightest doubt' of Muraviev's benevolent intentions.[40] 'Our country', he pointed out to Xianfeng three years later, 'is an old friend of yours; our two countries have always lived in peace and helped each other.'[41] By late 1859 the quick-witted Ignatiev had taken up the same concept, observing that Britain had already fought China on three occasions while Russia had never waged war on China at all.

Thanks to the long years of contact the Russians were manifestly more sensitive than their western rivals to traditional Chinese courtesies. In 1857–8 the language used in Putyatin's communications to the Qing representatives at Tianjin was still couched in something approaching the old phraseology of tribute-bearing vassals. 'I have already', he pleaded to them, 'sent a Note to your capital requesting to be informed if the Great Qing Emperor assents to the two items I asked to be memorialised on my behalf.'[42] Putyatin had also a keen appreciation of the importance of gift-giving. In late 1857 after he left Tianjin for the first time a Qing official advised Xianfeng that the Russian had 'brought from his country several kinds of presents of local produce: he strongly desired that our commissioners should take these back with them, and he conveyed to the commissioners several pieces of woollen cloth.'[43] When the talks with the four foreign envoys wound up at Tianjin in July 1858 Putyatin was ready with eight gifts each for the chief Qing negotiators, including clocks, paintings and woollen fabrics, while Elgin gave them no presents whatever and Reed, the United States envoy, could produce nothing better than a drab-looking, if potentially useful, Chinese translation of an American medical work.

The Russians also kept a keen lookout, as their Western counterparts appear not to have done, for individual bureaucrats who might be inclined to give help to their cause. In May 1856 Palladius wrote to Muraviev drawing attention once more to the Mongolian councillor Saishanga, who in his view had proved well disposed during the Xinjiang negotiations of five years before. 'He is one of the few statesmen here who understands the importance of an alliance with a neighbouring Power, or to use my previous expression follows a Northern policy.'[44] Help could of course be accelerated by a few deft inducements. In June 1860 Ignatiev bribed a certain Pan Zhihe to carry a message in invisible ink from Tianjin to the Russia House in the capital, and his embassy were said to have 'scattered money like dirt to win people over'.[45]

These miscellaneous tactics in turn formed part of a complex manoeuvre in which Russian diplomats sought to present themselves as benign mediators between the Qing and the west. While aligning himself with the Allied envoys in Tianjin in 1858 and urging Lord Elgin to follow a policy of 'firmness and threats' towards China,[46] Putyatin simultaneously conveyed to the Manchu negotiators his willingness to help them fend off western pressure. By May he was busy advising them to reject British demands for a permanent diplomatic presence in Peking and for the freedom to travel and trade in the Chinese interior, as well as a number of similar requests from the French. He even apparently urged them to renew their opposition to the opium trade. These consultancy services, however, carried a hefty quid pro quo in the form of Qing acquiescence in Russian demands – to include not merely Russia's Tianjin treaty with its provisions for access to coastal trade and for MFN status but also the absorption of the Amur territories, which were referred to only obliquely in the Tianjin document but were to be handed over in a separate, secret protocol behind the backs of the British and French. Directed by St Petersburg to attempt a similar intermediary role to that of Putyatin, Ignatiev in 1860 embarked on an even more intricate double game. After linking up with the Allied forces in Shanghai he made his separate way to Tianjin, which he reached at the end of August as the Anglo-French troops headed inland in their advance on the capital. From Tianjin he addressed a letter to the Xianfeng emperor, assuring him that the tsar 'desires that your country should reap benefits and also wishes to avoid your bringing disaster upon yourselves'.[47] In an accompanying note Father Gurii, the senior priest of the Fourteenth Mission who had succeeded Palladius as Russia's clerical man on the spot in Peking, pointed out to the emperor on Ignatiev's behalf that the Russians felt 'disturbed' by the advance of the Allied forces and 'would like to help your country come to a settlement'.[48] Catching up with the Allied troops in September, Ignatiev accompanied them as far as the walls of Peking, while his priests scurried to and fro unmolested between the Russia House and the Anglo-French camp. On 16 October he entered Peking ahead of the Allied expedition and plunged into talks with Prince Gong and the rump Manchu government, agreeing to give them the benefit of his diplomatic services on condition that his demands for Russia were met. After the Anglo-French forces moved into the capital two days later and showed no sign of leaving he further agreed to procure their departure; and after they eventually pulled out on 6 November he garnered his pay-off in the form of the Supplementary Treaty of Peking. Both the two Russian ambassadors claimed credit for Allied concessions that either got retracted afterwards or had little or nothing to do with them. Putyatin declared he had managed to convince Elgin to drop two disputed demands in the British Tianjin treaty. Ignatiev maintained he had persuaded the British to reduce their demand for a war indemnity by a million *taels*, and insisted to Gong that the withdrawal of Allied troops from Peking was entirely due to his efforts (in fact they had been held up by a technical hitch). But, pressing their services and playing hard to get as occasion demanded, the two envoys may have helped to spare the Qing harsher treatment than they got. Ignatiev in particular seems to have made a major attempt to restrain the triumphant Allies. He is thought to have played a large part in dissuading the British and French from following up the burning of the old Summer Palace with a devastating sack of the whole of Peking. When Lord Elgin mulled over the thought of installing a Taiping emperor at the rebel centre of Nanking he argued strongly against such a drastic intervention and may even have been responsible for prolonging the life of the dynasty for another fifty years.

Finally Russia proposed to combine its good offices with a distinctly modern-sounding programme of military aid. In February 1857 Major E.P. Kovalevsky, who since negotiating the Treaty of Yili had risen to head the Asiatic Department of the Russian Foreign Ministry, requested Archimandrite Palladius to inform the Qing court that his government were ready to give them 'both moral and to some extent material help', the latter consisting of weapons and artillery shells 'for internal use', i.e. against the Taiping.[49] Arriving in Tianjin four months later Putyatin expounded to the Qing authorities the dismal vulnerability of their regime to the simultaneous threat from the west. 'In your country', he observed, 'it is the autumn of many things. The Treasury is depleted, and everyone knows it.'[50] Above all the authorities seemed

> totally unaware how the foreign countries are developing their vehicles and ships. Not only can they set out to distant lands, they can capture the strongest places. Although your troops are extremely valiant their uniforms and weapons are very unsuited to [meeting an attack from] the Western Ocean . . . Because you have no understanding of the recent improvements in military technology you will have no way of resisting the attack they are preparing to launch on you with their land and naval forces . . . [You] have not paid attention to the discovery of new kinds of destructive weapons.[51]

The Qing consequently needed a mentor. They had so far 'lacked any model of a foreign people from whom they can learn'; but before long they 'would have to trust us'.[52] By April 1858 Putyatin had put together a tentative aid package. He ordered the archimandrite to offer the court 20,000 repeating rifles and twenty cannon plus a team of five military instructors and 300,000 *taels* of silver – all of this, naturally, to be supplied in return for the Qing accepting the Russian frontier demands. The Russians also sought permission to inspect the Qing gun emplacements in the capital and point out how they might be repaired and strengthened. By the spring of 1859 a large part of the promised consignment was on its way to the Russo-Chinese border, including 10,000 of the 20,000 rifles, 1.6 million bullets and fifty instead of the original twenty cannon. At this point Ignatiev, who had taken over command of the operation, appears to have had an attack of cold feet. The Qing were now toughening up and refusing to ratify the previous year's treaties: was it wise to equip them with all this additional firepower? Putyatin's training programme, he ruled, could go ahead as envisaged; but the arms were to be held back at Verkhneudinsk for diversion to Muraviev, and no cannon whatever were to be supplied to the dynasty unless they were needed for coastal defence. By November 1860, however, with the British and French in Peking and the Qing on the verge of disintegration, the old Russian fear had abated and the military aid scheme was put forward once more. Ignatiev now proposed to make the dynasty a 'farewell present' of guns which could be shipped to south China to help suppress the Taiping.[53] Russia would also send officers to instruct the Qing in the manufacture of guns, mortars, torpedoes and land mines; but in order to escape the attention of Britain and France any such training would have to take place at some remote spot to the north or west of the capital. Although the instructions from St Petersburg clearly laid down that direct force was not to be used to prop up the Qing dynasty, the promises made by both envoys seem once or twice to have edged beyond that constraint. Putyatin is said to have offered to help 'destroy the British and French' if his demands were accepted. In conjunction with his 'farewell present' Ignatiev apparently offered to send a naval contingent of 300 to 400 men to sail up the Yangtze and wipe out the Taiping insurgents at their Nanking base.

All of this generosity must once again be seen in the cold-blooded context of tsarist strategic and commercial designs. We may, however, notice in passing the outlook of Father Palladius, who served the Russian expansion so faithfully as both intelligence agent and diplomatic go-between but who seems nonetheless to have felt a genuine sympathy for China's plight. On one occasion in May 1858 when Putyatin was striking a hard-to-get attitude Palladius urged the ambassador to resume his mediation between the Qing and the western powers. He is also said to have extracted a promise from Putyatin that after the latter's return to St Petersburg he would urge the government to negotiate with the western Allies to reduce the war indemnity they had imposed upon China and to arrange a convention committing all parties to refrain from any further attacks on the desperate Celestial Empire.

For at least one Manchu border official the Russian transition from sleepy neighbour to predator came as a shock. Poor Yige, the first Qing commander at Aigun to be confronted by one of Muraviev's flotillas, recalled how the experience

> threw me into a fever: my head whirled, my eyes darkened, my heart palpitated, my ears were deafened and I would have fallen unconscious if I had not been supported by my servants.[54]

The authorities in Peking, however, got their bearings quite rapidly, and we can follow their reactions through the stream of correspondence between Xianfeng and his functionaries.

They were not for a moment fooled by the Russian attempt to play the honest broker. From the young emperor, worn out by debauchery in his late twenties but still capable of cynical if unconstructive observations, down to the Mongol Delekedorji, now no longer a prophet of doom on the fringe but a spokesman for the Qing consensus, the word that incessantly crops up for the Russians is 'crafty'. Their hearts were 'unfathomable'. Putyatin was 'exceptionally crafty' and Ignatiev 'inscrutable'.[55] 'All the barbarians', thought Prince Gong, 'have the nature of brute beasts. The British are the most unruly, but the Russians are the most cunning.'[56] Qing responses to each new avuncular gambit the Russians deployed were shot through with suspicion. Right at the outset in 1854 Xianfeng judged that Muraviev's ships must have 'some treacherous plan besides intending to fight the English',[57] and ordered defensive measures to be taken in the coastal ports. By the autumn of 1857, when Putyatin was knocking at the gates of Tianjin, it was already clear to his Qing interlocutors that the Russian 'was hoping to mediate from a position of neutrality in order to obtain concessions',[58] and the following spring, when he turned up there again with the Allied envoys, the commissioners sent from Peking agreed that he wished 'to make use of the British and French to facilitate his private interests'.[59] When Ignatiev moved down from Peking to

Shanghai at the end of May 1860 the verdict was that he was egging the British and French on to storm the Dagu forts, and when he in turn offered in August to mediate with the western Allies in the letter transmitted by Father Gurii Prince Gong advised the emperor that Russia 'may have ulterior motives, and therefore it is not desirable to receive Gurii's letter'.[60] Two months later, when the Anglo-French forces were encamped in Peking and Prince Gong had found it expedient to accept Ignatiev's services, he explained to Xianfeng he was well aware that the Russians had been at the back of the western invasion. If Ignatiev were not permitted to mediate, however, he would certainly 'get up to worse tricks'; and 'he who tied the bell on the tiger should be allowed to take it off again'.[61]

The Qing response to the Russian military aid project was correspondingly wary. The initial reply to Putyatin's offer of guns was a resolute no. In particular the dynasty were dead against taking Russian instructors: Xianfeng ordered Delekedorji to inform the ambassador that China had never 'borrowed troops from other countries'.[62] After the offer was brought up again in the autumn of 1860 Prince Gong drew attention to one or two other disturbing features of the tsarist package: the Russians were, for example, demanding as part of their training scheme to open up mines and factories on Chinese soil. Gong also thought that Ignatiev's offer of arms to help fight the Taiping was 'very deceitful and should be given no credence',[63] and a colleague, Yuan Jiasan, put forward some detailed arguments for turning the offer down. 'If the Russians collude with the rebels', he asked, 'how shall we be able to restrain them?'[64] On the other hand, if the Russians helped wipe out the Taiping as promised they would 'get even more arrogant, their covetousness even more rampant'.[65]

The court's sceptical attitude was accompanied for the first time by clear signs of anti-Russian feeling among the general public. Far off to the west, at Tacheng, trouble had started in 1853 when Chinese labourers moved in to work a gold deposit in a disputed area on the Russian-Xinjiang border. In April 1855 a force of 200 tsarist troops cleared the gold miners out, killing several in the process, and in July, finding the site reoccupied, the troops shot more miners and smoked them out of the shafts. The following month the Chinese struck back. A band of 500–600 evicted miners descended on the Russian 'trade circle', pillaging and burning the Russian houses and godowns and putting the Russian merchants to flight. In the spring of 1859 an eruption took place in Peking itself, possibly caused by news of the previous year's humiliating treaties but more likely provoked by the 'unseemly behaviour' of the first Russian 'political agent', Pyotr Perovsky, and the excesses of his Cossack escort, who were said to have got drunk and 'dragged women out of their conveyances'.[66] Perovsky found himself pelted with stones at the Chongwen Gate, and some members of the Fourteenth Mission riding back through the streets to the Russia House had stones thrown at them similarly by soldiers or idlers from the top of the city walls. Ignatiev's cavalier order to the Mission to switch from Chinese to European dress appears to have made an already bad situation still worse. On 8 July Ignatiev announced in a letter to his father,

> No Russians visit any Chinese, and no Chinese visit any Russians . . . All the Chinese are hostile to us . . . Now even in the shops the Chinese do not want to sell anything to the Russians, and we have to buy stores through the servants (mostly Albazintsy) and a few permanent suppliers to the Mission.[67]

Yet for all this the Russians were never regarded in quite the same light as their western competitors. The importance the Qing attached to the antiquity of relations was very real. The Russians had been slotted in comfortably since the early years of the dynasty among the various northern peoples who traded with China in conventional fashion under the auspices of the Lifanyuan; the British and French were extraterrestrials. In the spring of 1858 Xianfeng directed his officials in Tianjin that Putyatin should be received 'properly'. 'China', he pointed out, 'has been on good terms with the Russian barbarians for over a hundred years and there is no ill-will between us as there is between us and the British and French. Consequently there must be a certain difference in the way we treat them.'[68] One Western scholar has noted that in Chinese documents during these years the character for 'Russia' was never written with the 'mouth' radical – the insulting prefix routinely attached to the characters for 'Britain' and 'France'.[69] As tsarist pressure intensified, Qing use of the 'old friends' theme began to assume a positively plaintive tone. In May 1859 the Grand Council complained to Perovsky that 'in the Kangxi reign they fired a cannon and swore to Heaven that the Sino-Russian frontier had been fixed on the Xing'an range: this frontier should accordingly have been maintained according to the old regulations'.[70] As regards the new Russian claim to the Ussuri region and the misdemeanours committed by Chebotarev and other Russian merchants in the town of Sanxing, the Lifanyuan lamented to the Russian Senate, 'Your country has hitherto lived in harmony and without enmity with China, and you should not act wildly and irrationally in this way.'[71]

In addition the Russians were clearly the lesser of the two evils. The threat posed by Russia was one of encroachment in the remote border wilderness, while the Anglo-French forces aimed straight at the empire's heart. If the Qing were clear-eyed about the underlying motives of the men from St Petersburg, there were at least moments when the tsarist avuncular posture seemed preferable to the naked force of the west, when they clutched in spite of themselves at the straw of Russian intercession. After the British and French stormed the Dagu forts in May 1858 Tan Tingxiang, the governor of the surrounding Zhili Province, was so frightened that he repeatedly begged for Putyatin's good offices. Suchanga, the head of the Lifanyuan, made three separate visits to plead with Palladius at the Russia House in Peking, promising that the Qing would do everything Putyatin asked if only he would step in, and imploring the priest, 'in a passionate and sincere unprepared speech',[72] to mediate with the mediator. Issuing long-distance edicts from his hideaway in Jehol in October 1860, Xianfeng ordered Prince Gong to allow Ignatiev to enter Peking ahead of the Allies and agreed to the Russian envoy's being used as a go-between. The crisis was so acute that Ignatiev 'must not be resisted if there is an opportunity which can be seized'.[73] The same frantic hopes seem to have gripped the Chinese public as well. Travelling towards Tianjin on his own in the wake of the Allied forces, Ignatiev was hailed by the local villagers as a possible protector, and when he got to Tianjin he was treated by the city merchants to a welcoming feast.

And whatever the Russians' intentions the advantages of drawing on their military assistance could not be ignored. Since the seventeenth century, as we have noticed, Qing weaponry hadn't merely stagnated but even regressed: the garrison encountered by Muraviev at Aigun in the 1850s were armed predominantly with bows and arrows. And again since the seventeenth century, Chinese observers had been consistently impressed by the effectiveness of Russian firepower. At the end of June 1858 the Qing commissioners at Tianjin proposed that Putyatin's arms offer should, after all, be accepted. Xianfeng endorsed the proposal, even conceding, after a brief hesitation, that a few Russian officers might be let in to give instruction in the use of rifles and cannon and to repair the mouldering gun emplacements on the Peking walls. A full-blown military alliance still wasn't altogether discounted in some Manchu dreams. In February 1860 the military governor of Yili, a certain Zhalafengtai, brought up once again the old project first floated by Lin Zexu and Wei Yuan twenty years earlier for using the Russians in a diversionary role. He suggested a joint Russian–Gurkha attack upon British India, with the Russians striking this time, a trifle implausibly, with a naval force from the south-east. The Qing would play their part by advancing upon the British Raj from Yunnan and Tibet. Back in the realm of reality Prince Gong indicated in late November that he was inclined to accept Ignatiev's renewed offer of arms and instruction, though it would be better to have the training administered at Kyakhta, on the Russian side of the border. Zeng Guofan, for some years now the main Qing commander against the Taiping, was well disposed to begin with to Ignatiev's proposal that a Russian naval squadron should be dispatched to the Yangtze to take on the rebels. Kangxi, after all, he recalled, had made use of Dutch warships to impose Qing control over Taiwan in 1683. Such an intervention might also help to put the west in its place. 'The Russians', he asserted, 'are more powerful than the British and French: they have fought with the British barbarians, and the British are afraid of them.' His caveat was that the number of Russian warships and troops would have to be strictly limited.[74]

THE ABOLITION OF DISTANCE (1860–97)

In 1860 the old institutional barriers were demolished for good. Over the following decades the direct but limited contact which had typified the Sino-Russian encounter since the Treaty of Kyakhta was replaced by a new kind of interaction, at close quarters, in less predictable contexts, on a far larger canvas. For the Russians it was a time for taking advantage of the benefits conferred on them by the treaties of 1857–60 or inherited by them thanks to their MFN clause from the treaties obtained by the western powers. In 1861 the tsar's government were able at last to establish a formal diplomatic legation in Peking. By the autumn of that year the first Russian minister, L.F. Ballyuzek, was passing through Urga en route to the capital with a large retinue, and his couriers were rushing ceaselessly to and from Peking making full use of new access granted them to the Qing postal system on business that was perpetually 'urgent'. On their arrival in Peking the legation were installed in the former South House of the Orthodox Mission, which immediately gave them the biggest compound in the new Legation Quarter.

Relegated to the original seventeenth-century North House, the Mission were rapidly stripped of their old diplomatic and intelligence functions. In a decree of November 1863 Alexander II announced their removal from the jurisdiction of the Foreign Ministry and handed them over 'to the full disposal of the ecclesiastical branch'.[75] But this didn't mean they relapsed into idleness. They continued to keep up their high standard of Sinological studies: Father Palladius, for instance, back in Peking for a second stint as head of mission, devised the system still in use today for transcribing Chinese into the Cyrillic alphabet, compiled a celebrated Russian–Chinese dictionary and wrote extensively about the practice in China of both Buddhism and Islam. And in addition they showed for the first time a tentative interest in evangelising the ordinary Chinese public, rather than confining their spiritual services to the tiny contingent of Albazintsy. Father Gurii of the Fourteenth Mission settled down to produce a Chinese translation of the New Testament, declaring proudly that his work would be 'a fine robe of Chinese satin when we sew on to it a shred of coarse red Russian cloth'.[76] Other translations were made of prayer books, psalters, canticles and theological tracts. On the initiative of Father Flavian, head of the Sixteenth Mission, a young man named Ji Chong was given the baptismal name of Mitrofan and ordained in 1882 as the first Chinese Orthodox priest. And with the advent of Mitrofan Ji services even began to be conducted in Chinese, it having at last been appreciated that the Old Church Slavonic used in the liturgy was incomprehensible even to the Albazintsy, let alone to the average Chinese citizen.

Russian merchants lost no time in making use of the access now granted them to China's coastal and river ports. Already in 1861 a private Russian vessel made its way to the Yangtze port of Hankou, the centre of the Chinese tea trade. Mutual incomprehension was almost total, but the Russians apparently managed to take on a cargo of tea as intended before sailing off. No longer content with a simple exchange of merchandise, some tsarist entrepreneurs now set out to control the whole process of tea production. Under a Statute of Overland Trade agreed with the Qing government in 1862 they obtained the right to buy tea leaves directly from the growers in the southern Chinese provinces and to process the tea themselves rather than buying the already processed bricks from a Chinese warehouse, thus reducing both the number of middlemen involved in the transaction and the cost price of the finished tea. In 1863–4 a trader named Litvinov and an entrepreneurial nobleman named Mikhail Batuev arrived in Hankou, and in the course of the following decade they built three tea-processing factories at Yangloudong outside the city, finally moving them into Hankou itself in 1874. They installed in these factories advanced technology in the form of steam engines and hydraulic presses to manufacture the tea bricks, which improved both the quality of the product and the speed of production, incidentally giving Hankou a first taste of modern European industry. From Hankou they were able to ship the processed tea in their own vessels down the Yangtze and up the coast to Tianjin, which they were now permitted to use as their principal entrepôt for the onward shipment to Kyakhta. Once again this enabled them to cut out the middlemen, the Shanxi merchants who had for decades brought tea overland from Hankou to the Sandy Venice, and a further agreement secured from the Qing in 1869 laid down that they wouldn't have to pay tax in Tianjin if the goods they brought there were only in transit and if they had already paid tax on the goods in another port. The actual volume of the tea trade didn't appreciably grow in the late nineteenth century, but Russia's share of the market crept up as the British increasingly shifted their tea-purchasing to their possessions in India and Ceylon. By 1895 49 per cent of all Chinese tea was exported to the Russian empire.[77] In both Hankou and Tianjin small Russian communities started to take shape around the great tea-trading firms. In 1876 a first Russian Orthodox church was put up in Hankou with funds provided by the tea merchants, and a Church of St Alexander Nevsky followed in 1885.

Into the Chinese interior, with or without Qing permission, there poured at the same time an assortment of Russian explorers – botanists and zoologists, geologists and cartographers, commercial prospectors and just plain travellers. Between 1867 and 1885 Nikolai Przhevalsky, discoverer of the eponymous wild horse, led no fewer than four expeditions into the wilder parts of the Chinese empire, concentrating especially on the peripheral regions of Xinjiang, Mongolia and Tibet. In 1874 Pyotr Piassetsky set off from St Petersburg with two associates to study the 'tea route' which led from Hankou to the north-west as far as Lake Zaisan in Russian Kazakhstan.

A medical man by profession, Piassetsky also took the opportunity to compile information on sanitary conditions and medicine in China. Five years later a botanist named Albert Regel who had slipped into Xinjiang past the Qing border guards made an unforeseen contribution to European knowledge of the Silk Road by stumbling on the remains of the old Uighur capital of Karakhodja, and in the 1890s a Baltic German called Emil Bretschneider took advantage of his post in the Russian legation to make an exhaustive study of Chinese flora.

Finally Russian power was surging up at new points around China's perimeter. The last major nomad contingent in Central Asia, the Great Horde of the Kazakhs, had finally submitted to the tsar in 1844. During the 1860s tsarist armies established control of the khanates of western Turkestan, occupying in the process the last major portion of land which divided them from Qing territory. Tashkent fell in 1865; Samarkand in 1868; Bokhara and Kokand retained only a nominal independence. The tsar's forces were brushing against the western fringes of Chinese-ruled Xinjiang.

All of this was made possible by the triumphant advance of Russian communications. In the decades after 1860 the vast distances which had separated the nerve centres of the two empires were all but abolished. We have already noticed the presence of a steamship in Muraviev's 1850s flotillas along the Amur. From 1869 Russian steamers were able to take advantage of the newly opened Suez Canal to ship cargoes of tea from Shanghai to the Black Sea port of Odessa, and in 1880 a Russian Volunteer Fleet established a regular Vladivostok–Odessa service which within a few years featured stops to pick up Chinese cargoes in both Shanghai and Canton. The old overland slog along the Siberian rivers and post roads was becoming redundant as the journey time between China and European Russia was cut from months to a matter of weeks. It was the beginning of the end for Kyakhta, which already by 1870 had declined from a great trading centre to a mere transit stop. But it meant that the Russians could once again transport goods between China and Europe as quickly and cheaply as their western competitors.

The dissident Alexander Herzen had described Tsar Nicholas I as 'Genghis Khan with a telegraph'. By the beginning of the 1870s the telegraph network which had begun to be set up in European Russia under Nicholas had been extended to China as well. One line ran from Vladivostok by way of Japan to Shanghai, and two further undersea cables were laid from

Vladivostok to British Hong Kong. Telegraph lines also followed the advance of the Russian armies into the khanates of western Turkestan. By the mid-1870s the telegraph had got as far as Tashkent, and twenty years later it had crept further eastwards as far as Irkeshtam on the Xinjiang border. The advent of the telegraph enabled the tsarist authorities to make decisions on China policy in real time rather than lagging months behind local events as they had had to do since the seventeenth century. It also reduced the ability of mavericks such as Middendorff and Nevelskoi in the late 1840s to take the initiative on the spot without consulting their chiefs in St Petersburg.

Last and perhaps most important was the impact of the Railway Age. During the 1880s Russian businessmen and industrialists started to press for the building of a Trans-Siberian Railway to galvanise the still fragile economies of both Siberia and the newly acquired lands of the Russian Far East. Such a railway would hasten the flow of goods across Russia to compete with the British and other maritime powers in East Asian markets and allow Russian merchants to step up their exports to Qing China of cotton and woollen fabrics and metalware. It would further accelerate the tea trade, perhaps even taking the place of the new steamship route. It would boost colonisation of the Russian Far East in the same way the Pacific Railway had hastened the settlement of the American West. From a strategic angle it would also help Russia solve the abiding problem of its military weakness beyond Lake Baikal by enabling it to shift large armies and supplies to East Asia in case of emergency. The leading backer of the venture, Count Sergei Witte, summed up the advantages neatly by urging that *Russian power in the East would increase in proportion as the distance diminished.*[78] In March 1891 Tsar Alexander III gave his approval to the Trans-Siberian project, and by the middle of the decade the railway had pushed eastwards as far as Irkutsk. Passing some twenty miles to the west of Kyakhta it drove a final nail in the coffin of the Sandy Venice, as the tea cargoes were rerouted and the last of the merchants abandoned their mansions and club houses. Hundreds of miles to the south, in Russian Turkestan, another, shorter railway advanced from Samarkand to the neighbourhood of the Xinjiang frontier at Andijan. As the railways rolled eastwards the time taken to travel between the heartlands of the two empires began to be cut down still further, from six weeks to more like two.

For China the years after 1860 were a time of regrouping, of searching for new ways to contain the incursion of the foreign powers. The composition of the Qing regime had undergone a significant change. The effete Manchu military caste had been severely depleted during the wars against the Taiping and the Anglo-French alliance: ethnic Chinese officials, some of them men of considerable vigour, were starting to predominate at the upper levels of the administration. Much of their energy focused on the attempt to build a modern army and navy in what became known as the Era of Arsenals. But they also made a major new effort to upgrade Qing knowledge of the outside world – tsarist Russia included. In March 1861 the Lifanyuan, go-between for so long in the notional tributary relationship between the Russians and the Qing, was transformed into the Russia Bureau of a new, streamlined Office of General Management, the *Zongli Yamen*, which was designed to perform the functions of a modern Foreign Ministry; and in 1862, the hopelessly incompetent Russian Language School was incorporated into a new School of Foreign Languages, the *Tongwenguan*, with Russian tuition to be provided to a new generation of diplomats by a former member of the Orthodox Mission, one A.F. Popov. Within a few years the Qing too had started to work, in their own way, on the abolition of distance. In February 1866 the Zongli Yamen dispatched an envoy in the mildly implausible form of Bin Chun, head of the Department of Imperial Herds, who was to lead the first official Qing delegation to St Petersburg since the early 1730s. Bin Chun's reconnaissance was soon followed by the arrival in 1869 of a study group sent to research current systems of government in Europe and America under the auspices of Anson Burlingame, a former United States minister to Peking, and including six students from the new School of Foreign Languages; and in 1878 a permanent Chinese embassy was established for the first time in the tsarist capital. In 1887 a further delegation was directed by the Zongli Yamen to make a tour of Russia in order

> to see with their own eyes all the mountains and rivers and strategic points, their political advantages and disadvantages, the surplus or deficit in their treasury, the strength or weakness of their armed forces, the abundance or paucity of their produce, the density or sparseness of their populations, the beauties or defects of their customs.[79]

Intelligence-gathering was a game that two could play.

At the same time the Qing were employing some cunning new stratagems to push back the Russian tide. From the seventeenth century onwards ethnic Chinese had been officially forbidden to migrate to the dynasty's sacred homeland of Manchuria. In October 1859, however, as tsarist diplomacy amputated the outermost swathes of that homeland, two of Xianfeng's officials advised him that the only way to check further Russian expansion was to open the empty north-east to settlement by impoverished immigrants from China proper. The emperor's reaction was negative; but from the 1860s the regency guiding his successor, the child ruler Tongzhi, were gradually lifting the restrictions on Chinese entry into Manchuria, and in 1878 the edict prohibiting Chinese settlement there was formally repealed. Immigrants from the south duly moved in to farm and herd livestock in ever-growing numbers, and in 1880 a Russian traveller to the region was struck to observe that most of the population were now Chinese, not Manchu.

Nor did the pushback stop at the new Amur frontier. The Qing had by no means resigned themselves to the loss of the Outer Manchurian wilderness. They continued to use the old Chinese names for their former outposts: Vladivostok, for instance, remained 'Haishenwei' in their documents, and Khabarovsk remained 'Boli'. In both the treaties of Aigun and Peking they made a point of retaining jurisdiction over a handful of villages on the north bank of the Amur, later known as the Sixty-Four Settlements, where the Manchu inhabitants were to be allowed to continue their hunting and trapping without being subject either to Russian taxes or Russian military service. It was a ploy adopted more than once by the Qing at this period, a way of keeping a stake in the lost dominions, a tactic reminiscent of the Chinese board game *weiqi* (the Japanese *go*) in which the player sets out to create defensible nuclei in the middle of the opponent's counters, to be enlarged later at the opponent's expense.[80] In addition a good many of the new Chinese arrivals in Manchuria were pushing further northwards of their own accord. Eager to build the economies of the newly annexed Amur and Maritime provinces, the tsarist authorities to begin with encouraged immigration of any kind, whether Russian or foreign. No restrictions were imposed on entry, and settlers were offered both land and a twenty-year tax holiday. Enterprising Qing subjects were quick to respond. Right from the start of the 1860s Chinese traders from Aigun were crossing the Amur and opening new shops in Blagoveshchensk on the opposite bank, and other Chinese migrants were soon slipping into both provinces to engage in fishing, hunting and the gathering of ginseng roots. Not all of the migrants' activities fell within the law. In the second half of the decade we begin to get news of the Chinese bandits known as the *honghuzi* or Red Beards. It would seem that this label had originally been attached to Cossack freebooters in the seventeenth century, but in the course of the decades had somehow been transferred to apply to Chinese marauders instead. (One visitor remarked in bewilderment that 'not one of them has a red beard, or any other kind of a beard.'[81]) By 1867 the Red Beards were engaged in illicit gold-panning on the north bank of the Amur, and the following year they poured into the Maritime Province in a gold rush directed at Askold Island. At this stage there are said to have been around 10,600 Chinese and Manchus in the two Russian provinces, and by 1881 15,000 Chinese were recorded in the Maritime Province alone.

Russian attitudes to the great eastern neighbour weren't changed overnight by these multiplying proximities. Back in European Russia the old respect for the Celestial Empire continued to linger on. Bin Chun's pioneer delegation of 1866 were received in St Petersburg with marked hospitality. They were granted the honour of an audience with Crown Prince Alexander, and were assigned thoughtfully to the day-to-day care of one of the government's principal China Hands. A former member of the Thirteenth Orthodox Mission, Konstantin Skachkov had lived in Peking for eight years under the Chinese name Kong Qi before serving as the Russian consul in Tacheng and more recently as a translator for the Foreign Ministry's Asiatic Department. He did his utmost to make Bin Chun's group feel at home, inviting them to his mansion, serving them tea, noodles and dumplings ('You should enjoy this because it's the same as in China'[82]), and showing them his collection of Chinese paintings, poems and books. On another occasion he gave them a taste of European culture with a tour of the Hermitage art treasures at the Winter Palace. Receiving the Burlingame delegation in 1869–70 the government went one better, arranging an interview with Tsar Alexander II himself; and 'brilliant remarks', according to one Chinese report, were addressed to them by a prominent scholar, Vasily Pavlovich Vasiliev.[83] This courtesy to Chinese visitors was shown consistently during the following decades, and not all of it was necessarily scripted. Wang Zhichun, a special envoy sent by the Qing court to St Petersburg in early 1895 to convey their condolences on the death of Tsar Alexander III and congratulations on the accession of Nicholas II, was struck to observe that during a tour which his party were given of one of the city's museums, 'when a group of Russian ladies and gentlemen who were sketching saw the Chinese arrive they all got up respectfully'.[84]

Quite a few Russian intellectuals were still disinclined to subscribe to the concept of terminal Chinese stagnation. Vasiliev, whom we have just met, was one of the leading dissenters. After a stint with the Twelfth Mission in the 1840s he had been appointed to the chair of Chinese that was established at the University of St Petersburg in 1854, and he remained for the rest of the century the dominant presence in Russian Sinology. While conceding the current supremacy of European science and technology and the obvious indications that the Qing had decayed, he reminded his public that no one had a monopoly of brainpower and 'man, wherever he may live, remains man'.[85] He saw no reason why, given access to European knowhow, China might not eventually manage to catch up with or even overtake Europe. Russia, he believed, would in due course play its part in this transformation, and 'one day we will truthfully be able to say, *Ex Oriente lux*'.[86]

Vasiliev's convictions were carried a good deal further by a less qualified but vastly more celebrated Sinophile. Count Leo Tolstoy had begun his career as a student in the Oriental faculty of the University of Kazan, and though his focus had been on Arabic and the Turkic and Tatar languages rather than on Chinese, he had not been long in showing distinct signs of sympathy for China's situation. By 1857 he had 'read about the repulsive dealings of the British with China and had argued about this with an elderly Englishman',[87] and in 1862, in an article entitled 'Progress and the Definition of Education', he recalled the Second Opium War and the way in which the three great powers (including Russia as well as Britain and France) had 'with complete sincerity . . . introduced their belief in progress to China with powder and shot'.[88] In the late 1870s, during a spiritual crisis which followed the publication of *War and Peace* and *Anna Karenina*, the great novelist began to steep himself in ancient Chinese philosophy. Above all he was fascinated by the Daoist teaching, with its message that 'toughness and strength are the companions of death' and its concept of triumphant inaction (*wuwei*).[89] He had already been groping his way towards a similar outlook with his description in *War and Peace* of the Russian people's victory over Napoleon in 1812 despite their apparent defencelessness and the absence of any head-on engagement after the Battle of Borodino. Now he developed *wuwei* into his own doctrine of *neprotivlenie*, or non-violent resistance to evil, hailing the Daoist Way as a higher principle signifying love and virtue and saluting Laozi, the supposed author of the Daoist classic, the *Daodejing*, as a 'huge influence' on his own moral condition. He was enthralled by what he saw as Laozi's appeal 'to live not for the body, but for the spirit', and maintained that the essence of Laozi's creed was 'the same as the essence of Christianity'.[90] For Tolstoy, unlike Catherine the Great and the other Russian enthusiasts of a century earlier, the system and harmony of the Confucian state took second place to this, and it was only in 1884 that he began to pay detailed attention to the works of Confucius and his follower, Mencius. Nonetheless he described the Confucian philosophers also as having exerted a 'very great influence' upon his thought.[91] He was attracted by Confucius's aversion to war, and by Mencius as a figure pointing the way to moral self-perfection. After his first day perusing the sayings of Mencius he jotted down in his diary, 'Very important and good. Mencius taught how to recover, to find one's lost heart. Lovely.'[92] Of the society shaped by Confucian ideas he observed, 'The Chinese are the most peaceful people in the world. They seek nothing from each other, nor do they engage in war. This is because the Chinese are tillers of the soil. The ruler himself begins the ploughing.'[93] Tolstoy even burrowed into the works of a relatively obscure early Chinese sage, Mozi, delighting in his 'utilitarian, democratic' principle of 'universal love'. Unable to read Chinese himself, though he spoke of wanting to learn it, the writer painstakingly vetted Russian translations of the Chinese classics by comparing them with their counterparts in western European languages, and by 1893 was working on his own Russian version of the *Daodejing*. It was his aim to compile a book about Chinese philosophy, introducing to the Russian public such major issues of early Chinese speculation as whether human beings are naturally good or evil and whether they should strive to be individualistic or loving. Tolstoy's mental picture of an idyllic, contemplative, agrarian China was undoubtedly a long way from late Qing reality. But he stood out from his contemporaries in viewing China implicitly neither as a degenerate relic nor even, like Vasiliev, as a potential equal but as a civilisation superior to anything Europe might have to offer.

As the Russians drove deeper into inner China, however, familiarity seems increasingly to have bred a degree of contempt. Przhevalsky, for example, appears to have been one of that familiar type of outdoorsy explorer who is lost in admiration for the rugged nomad, the Mongol or Kazakh herdsman, but has little if any sympathy for the settled farmer or city dweller. The Chinese in his opinion were 'a treacherous and cowardly set of thieves' who only respected force. 'Decrepit mentally and morally', they were incapable of staging a national revival.[94] As Russia modernised, too, the material conditions in major Chinese centres no longer excited admiration. Unlike earlier Russian visitors Przhevalsky found Peking an 'unpleasant' city, where 'cesspits and crowds of naked beggars' constituted 'a necessary component of the very best streets'.[95] And the food was 'disgusting'.[96] Something of the same jaded attitude may be found in the writings of a lady named Alexandra Potanina, who travelled with her husband in Sichuan Province in the early 1890s. While conceding that the villagers 'behaved respectfully' and 'always treated us well', she too complained of the 'inexpressibly dirty and narrow streets'.[97] And in spite of the beauty of certain individual places she found that the country presented a 'terribly boring appearance'.[98]

In the new Amur and Maritime provinces the tsarist authorities started to speak with disdain of the *Manzy*, a term probably first applied to the Manchus but later transferred to the growing numbers of Chinese immigrants. In 1868 the illegal gold-mining activities of the Red Beards were curbed in a brief 'Manza War', as Russian troops and gunboats moved in to drive out the intruders, and in the following year an Ussuri Cossack Battalion was formed to defend the easternmost segment of the new frontier. The 1870s and 1880s were punctuated by a series of 'hot pursuit' episodes as the Cossacks chased bands of marauding Red Beards back into Qing territory. In the course of these decades the original Russian settlers put down in the region by Muraviev's flotillas were gradually reinforced by an influx of peasants from European Russia and Siberia who were transplanted to the Far East as part of a state-sponsored migration programme. The idea was that these new arrivals would grow food to support the tsarist military forces holding the line against the Manza menace.[99]

On the Chinese side the late Qing envoys who were received with such courtesy in St Petersburg showed a new respect for Russian power and progress that sometimes bordered on awe. Bin Chun, for example, is said to have been almost paralysed by his presentation in 1866 to Crown Prince Alexander. 'As white as a sheet', the head of the Department of Imperial

Herds advanced towards the tsar's heir 'with very slow, timid steps', and his replies to the crown prince's questions were 'scarcely audible'.[100] At the Hermitage he paid no attention to the works of the European masters, 'staring only at the pictures of naked women's figures',[101] but was astounded to find it was possible to go sightseeing in an imperial palace in the emperor's absence; and at the Peterhof Palace he was 'so enchanted by the fountains that he forgot his Chinese haughtiness and admired them, sometimes hopping about like a child'.[102] Wang Zhichun, special envoy in 1895, was markedly more sophisticated, but he too was impressed in one way or another by the sights he was shown. A tour of a ship model workshop revealed to him 'the source of Russia's military strength',[103] and the glimpse of a newly built iron-clad confirmed in his mind the need for the Qing government to imitate Russia's construction of warships. For good measure he called, just two centuries after Tsar Alexei had sought Chinese stonemasons to build bridges in Russia, for a copying of Russian bridge designs. Taken round the Imperial Mint, he envisaged tens of thousands of Russian workers busy with the production of coins – and guns. 'How', he inquired in his journal, 'can China strengthen itself if it puts aside railways and manufacturing?'[104] On a lighter note he recorded his appreciation of the Winter Palace ('like a square piece of jade'), and of a performance of Tchaikovsky's ballet *Swan Lake* – 'a beautiful spectacle', the plot 'a bit like the tales of Chinese storytellers'.[105]

Back at home, on the other hand, the dominant Qing response to the new Russian inroads was predictably bitter. Grumbling started almost as soon as the Russians began to take advantage of the new treaty terms. In 1861 a report to the throne from the Urga officials described the new Russian minister, Ballyuzek, as 'arrogant and rude'. There were rumours his entourage might include (horrors) two women, who could on no account be permitted to enter Peking; 'but they are all wearing men's clothes so it is impossible to be sure'.[106] The demands of the tsarist couriers were placing an intolerable strain on both the personnel and the livestock deployed by the Qing postal system: 'Are the Russians unaware', the officials wailed, 'of the fatigue of the postal staff?'[107] The small Russian communities growing up in the new treaty ports quickly found themselves on the receiving end of the xenophobia directed by the Chinese public at all Europeans. The wife of the Russian vice-consul in Hankou wrote that a European going down the city streets must have eyes in the back of his head, 'otherwise he will be subjected to various kinds of unpleasantness'.[108] He should try not to get too indignant at the incessant use of the term 'foreign devil', since the person concerned 'might not have any other expression'.[109] In May 1870 a tea merchant called Protopopov, his wife and a colleague were dragged out of their sedan chairs on a Tianjin street and slashed to death with watermelon knives by two Chinese who had mistaken them for French people in the course of a backlash against the French Catholic missions.

Even out in the East, though, it wasn't a straightforward picture of mutual aversion. Russian and Chinese settlers who converged from the 1860s onwards in the Amur river basin found themselves driven together by the sheer ferocity of their environment. In this remote and unwelcoming region of dense forests and swamplands, bitter winters and primitive communications, there grew up over the decades a distinctive society, based on the tacit assumption that everyone should help their neighbour survive without regard to ethnicity. Indigenous hunters of the Goldi and Oroqen tribes helped Russian and Chinese newcomers to exploit the furs, ginseng and other products of the surrounding *taiga*, and they in turn helped each other, mingling with a freedom they couldn't have had closer to the centres of Qing and tsarist power.[110] Cossack immigrants hired Chinese peasants to till their fields, and Chinese traders supplied Russian villagers with food plus a millet-based spirit called *khanshin* they brought up from Manchuria in return for consignments of contraband gold.[111] Neither settler community paid much attention to the imperial governments in St Petersburg and Peking, or to the new international border which those two governments had drawn along the Amur and its tributary, the River Argun. For their part, the imperial governments had little hope of controlling the incessant two-way flood of illegal immigrants and smuggled goods – not surprisingly, given the vast distances, with sentry posts on both sides a day's ride apart and the border between those sentry posts demarcated only by small cairns of stones.[112] Decisions handed down from the imperial capitals were apt to be disregarded by local officials, who likewise found their instructions sidestepped by unofficial interests.[113]

One brief episode actually saw Russian and Chinese pioneers joining hands in defiance of their metropolitan masters. In the spring of 1883 a local trapper of the Oroqen tribe stumbled upon gold deposits while visiting the grave of his mother in a remote Manchurian valley near Mohe, on the extreme northern tip of Qing territory. News quickly spread of the 'Amur California', and Chinese freebooters began to pour on to the site behind the backs of their government. These prospectors were followed in turn by Russian adventurers from the other side of the border, and by 1884 a mixed encampment had arisen consisting of around 3,000 Russians and other Europeans and 6,000 Chinese. One source suggests that there may have been some initial fisticuffs when the Chinese majority were first confronted by Russian competition; but within a few months the Zheltuga Gold Mine, as the Russians called it, had been organised into a stable, self-governing community, with an elected president, public meetings convened to take major decisions, taxes to be paid into a common treasury and a rough-and-ready law code prescribing penalties for murder and for 'the falsification of gold-bearing sand'. The Russians exerted effective hegemony, but protected their Chinese counterparts with a system of fortifications and guards and paid high wages to any Chinese labourers they hired. The Chinese on their side took part in the election of Zheltuga's first president and accepted Russian leadership as their best hope of defence if the Qing government chose to crack down on this unauthorised venture. The two contingents seemingly lived and worked apart, but in peace. By 1885 Zheltuga had developed into a flourishing township complete with eighteen hotels and taverns, 160 shops, seven public baths, two jewellers' establishments, a church, a theatre, a hospital, a billiard saloon and a photographer's studio; but at this point the wrath of the Qing administration started to make itself felt. Protests were lodged with the nearest tsarist officials, who felt obliged to cut off supplies from Amur Province to Zheltuga and order their subjects out, and by the beginning of 1886 Manchu forces were mustering for an assault. The Chinese miners appealed to their remaining Russian colleagues to save them from certain death, and at least 500 Russians and 500 Chinese were said to be ready to make a joint stand in defence of their settlement. At the end of January the Qing forces moved in. They massacred their own citizens, hanging their severed heads by the pigtails on a row of wooden posts erected along the Amur, but the remaining Russians were tactfully allowed to make a getaway, with a few Chinese drifters in tow. These survivors passed on their story, and decades later the memory lingered of the mutual tolerance that had prevailed between the two peoples in the short-lived 'Zheltuga Republic'.[114]

The basic policy question confronting the tsarist regime at this period was whether to content themselves with digesting the gains they had made or to seek to press their advantage in China still further. From 1860 their path to significant further expansion was blocked by the rivalry of the other European powers, and especially Britain. In January 1862, for example, the Qing government abruptly withdrew their officers from the military training programme the Russians had organised for them at Kyakhta under pressure from the new British legation. In the course of a day-long discussion the British minister, Sir Thomas Wade, also alerted the Qing court to the danger of letting Russian forces conquer Taiping-held cities on their behalf. Wiping out the Taiping, he insisted, was a task to be accomplished by China alone. In the event the destruction of the Taiping rebels was completed in 1864 by the Qing commander Zeng Guofan, with some help from the British in the shape of General Charles ('Chinese') Gordon. By the 1870s Russia's European rivals had been joined by the new Asian power of Japan, which had designs of its own on China's eastern seaboard and was also anxious to check any further extension of Russian influence. As early as 1873 the Japanese legation in Peking voiced concern at the danger of Russia's expanding its presence from the Amur to Japan's own northern fringes. Rather than locking horns with these adversaries the tsarist rulers preferred to maintain their established avuncular posture, differentiating themselves from their rivals by the moderation of their dealings with China. As their small merchant colonies grew up in Hankou and Tianjin the Russians, unlike their rivals, didn't race to secure extra-territorial concessions with their provocative trappings of prisons, law courts, police forces and troops. Unlike their Roman Catholic and Protestant counterparts the Orthodox priests didn't hurry to take advantage of the new treaties to set up mission stations in the depths of the Chinese provinces: the single such step they took in these decades was the establishment in 1861 of a church dedicated to St Innocent of Irkutsk and a school for seven children in the village of Dongding'an near Peking, where some of the inhabitants seem to have had Albazintsy roots. When the Russian tea merchant and his party were mistakenly slaughtered alongside French Catholic missionaries in Tianjin in 1870 the tsarist government distanced themselves from the French clamour for vengeance. Instead the Russian consul, Konstantin Skachkov, the same China-friendly Skachkov who had hosted Bin Chun in St Petersburg four years earlier, paid a quiet call on Li Hongzhang, the governor-general of Zhili Province, and actually asked for the execution of the culprits to be delayed. Skachkov's immediate concern is said to have been to avoid jeopardising the Russian tea trade in this major entrepôt; but his restraint also made a favourable impression on Li, a military protégé of Zeng Guofan now well on his way up the bureaucratic ladder, and on the Chinese public in general.

One or two voices were indeed being raised to demand a shift to a more drastic approach. Continuing disappointment in Europe once again impelled some Russians to look for compensation in the East. In January 1881, after the gains made by tsarist armies in the recent war against Turkey had been pared down by the western powers at the Congress of Berlin, Fyodor Dostoevsky urged the readers of his *Writer's Diary* to redirect their attention to Asia. 'In Europe', he declared, 'we were hangers-on and slaves, while in Asia we shall be the masters. In Europe we were Tartars, while in Asia we can be Europeans.'[115] More concretely Przhevalsky called for Russia to go to war with the Qing and put an end to 'two hundred years of ingratiating'.[116] In reports to the Ministry of War in St Petersburg he made various recommendations in detail for the seizure of China's outermost territories, including a number of possible invasion routes. But the one attempt that was made in these years to abandon the old subtle policy and seize a fresh slice of Qing land culminated in a near-disaster.

During the 1860s, at exactly the time the tsar's armies were completing their conquest of western Turkestan, rebellion flared in Xinjiang, on the other side of the border, among the Turkic and Muslim peoples whom the Qing had subdued 100 years before. Leadership of the anti-Qing movement was seized by Yaqub Beg, an adventurer from the western khanate of Kokand who had arrived in the region at the invitation of a local chieftain in 1865. Raising troops and mopping up competitors in successive oases of the old Silk Road, Yaqub rapidly built up his power, and by the end of the decade he had overrun almost the whole of Xinjiang, arrogating to himself the title of Champion Father (*Athalik Ghazi*). By the first months of 1871 he looked set to complete his campaign through absorbing the Yili valley on the Russian frontier, where Qing control had already been shaken off for the best part of five years. And this prospect caught the attention of the Russian authorities from two points of view. From the defensive angle Yili was of major strategic importance, something close to a tsarist equivalent of the Khyber Pass, an avenue of approach through whose gorges in the Tian Shan mountains Mongol invaders had ridden in centuries past to attack Central Asia and points further west. To make matters more ominous Yaqub had in recent years been accepting money and rifles from Russia's British adversaries. Two envoys from British India had been sent to Yaqub's headquarters to size him up as a protégé able to stem the tide of Russian empire-building, and the danger clearly existed that Britain, spotting a breakthrough in the 'Great Game', might sponsor the Champion Father in a *jihad* to advance through the passes and drive the Russians out of their newly captured Central Asian possessions. From the acquisitive angle Yili, where Russian traders had been active since the start of the century, was a juicy sliver of territory that had come up for grabs. The first area west of the Great Wall to be capable of supporting a large population, it served as the granary for a considerable part of western China, and its latent mineral wealth had attracted the interest of Russian geologists. Guided by these various calculations a Russian army under Major-General G.A. Kolpakovsky marched in and took over Yili in July 1871, before Yaqub could get there. The official Russian posture was once more avuncular: Russia's role was to be to 'look after' Yili for the Qing government and return it to them as soon as they were in a position to reclaim it. Different views, however, were held by Kolpakovsky, who is said to have issued a proclamation soon after his arrival in Yili declaring that he was annexing the district for good.[117] And with no likely chance of the Qing ever mustering the strength to retrieve this most distant of all their possessions the Russians soon embarked on a wide-ranging colonisation drive. Taxes were levied on the local Turkic populace to support the new rulers. An Orthodox church was erected and its congregation placed under the diocese of Tomsk. Land belonging to former Qing military colonists was leased out to Russian settlers, and doctors, engineers, teachers, agronomists and above all merchants were encouraged to move in. In 1872 Russia even negotiated a trade agreement with the Champion Father, offering full recognition of his conquests in exchange for a market for Russian goods.

Halfway through the decade, however, the unexpected began to take place. Fortified by the efforts made during the Era of Arsenals, the Qing staged a comeback. General Zuo Zongtang, yet another of the tough new commanders to have emerged from the struggle against the Taiping, ground his way across western China at the head of a massive army. By the end of 1876 he had taken Dihua (modern Urumqi), the principal town of Xinjiang, and in March 1877 he smashed Yaqub's forces in a battle at the Turfan oasis.

A few weeks later the Champion Father was dead (poisoned by his own hand, or possibly murdered), and by 1878 the greater part of Xinjiang was back in Qing hands. Coming down once again on the side of their fellow empire at the expense of the rebels in the middle, the Russians had helped Zuo's reconquest through the supply of around 1,000 tons of Siberian grain. But as the obligation loomed up of returning Yili to the Qing in accordance with their government's promise, neither Kolpakovsky and the military nor the civil officials in St Petersburg felt inclined to do any such thing. The Qing court sent off to negotiate the return of Yili a Manchu functionary named Chonghou who has some claim to rank as the most egregious bungler in the annals of diplomacy. Arriving in St Petersburg early in 1879, he embarked on the talks with no knowledge of either the country he was dealing with or the disputed territory he was supposed to discuss; and the Russians proceeded to kill him with kindness. The Foreign Ministry organised a 'caressing' reception, housing him in a nobleman's mansion on the south bank of the Neva, laying on the whole package of banquets, theatrical spectacles and sightseeing tours and collecting him from his residence in an imperial carriage drawn by six horses.[118] The treatment worked wonders. Sent to extract concessions, Chonghou ended up making them. In a treaty signed on 2 October at the tsar's summer palace of Livadia in the Crimea the envoy handed over to Russia the entire western portion of Yili containing both the richest land and the critical Muzart and Tekes Passes, and agreed for good measure that China would pay the Russians an indemnity of 5 million roubles for the costs of their occupation and award them a string of new consulates with the accompanying trade privileges in Xinjiang and Mongolia and the right to navigate the River Sungari in the Manchurian hinterland. He had in fact settled for terms, as one scholar has noted, as harsh as any imposed on a defeated army. In recent years an attempt has been made by some scholars to rehabilitate Chonghou as an experienced and competent diplomat. But it is probably safer to go by the verdict of the Russian negotiator, N.K. Giers, head of the Foreign Ministry's Asiatic Department, who described the Qing envoy as 'a pleasant man, but not prudent'.[119]

The Qing court exploded. 'Chonghou must die!' shrieked the all-powerful Empress Dowager Cixi. On his return to Peking the wretched envoy was stripped of his rank and flung into prison awaiting decapitation. The Treaty of Livadia was denounced, and the dynasty, boosted by the victory over Yaqub Beg and other Muslim insurgents, got ready for all-out war with Russia on every front. General Zuo Zongtang offered to march on St Petersburg with 2,000 men to dictate a new treaty, and in May 1880 he set off for Hami in eastern Xinjiang, accompanied by his coffin to indicate his determination to fight to the death. Zuo's hard line was supported by virtually all of the top Qing officials, with the notable exception of Li Hongzhang, who from his vantage point as the man in charge of Qing naval defences stressed that Japan was the real danger and advocated a policy of peace and friendship with the tsar. Zuo and his fellow hawks were undoubtedly better informed about the Russian empire than the previous generation of Qing ministers. They knew, for instance, that Russia had exhausted itself in the recent war against Turkey, with a national debt the equivalent of 52 million *taels*, and was in no real state for a new campaign in the East. They had even grasped that the tsarist regime was threatened by internal unrest. In strictly military terms, though, this exhibition of Qing bellicosity was of course absurd. Russian military technology was still way ahead of anything the Qing could come up with (their Manchurian defences continued to be manned by Solun tribesmen with bows and arrows), and the Russians also enjoyed the advantage conferred by the telegraph: the high command could convey orders instantly to their troops on the Xinjiang border, while the Qing court were unable to transmit a decree to the border and receive a reply in less than three months. The British felt obliged to restrain the Qing hotheads from an adventure which might throw their dominions wide open to a Russian advance. Right at the start of the uproar Queen Victoria had stepped in with a personal plea to the Qing to release the unfortunate Chonghou, letting it be known that 'the Queen was much shocked';[120] and in the summer of 1880 'Chinese' Gordon was diverted from an assignment in India to throw his support behind Li Hongzhang. Gordon was not a man for polite circumlocution. Appearing before the Grand Council to head off the cries for a frontal assault against the Russian army, he called for an English-Chinese dictionary and jabbed his finger at the word *Idiocy*.[121]

The Russians were also rolling up their sleeves. A fleet of twenty-three warships under Admiral S.S. Lesovsky staged a demonstration off the Chinese coast, and voices were raised urging Russia to 'protect its rights and dignity'.[122] But the truth was that in spite of their military advantages the Russians were more afraid of fighting China than the Chinese were of fighting them. The country's economic predicament was all too obvious. In the Foreign Ministry Giers's sidekick A.G. Zhomini remarked to his boss that the need which had seemingly arisen to give the Qing a good beating was 'rather hard on our poor finances'.[123] Logistical calculations were equally gloomy. Russia remained as unable as ever to field a significant army in the Far East until a Siberian railway had been built. In the course of 1879–80 all that the General Staff had been able to send to the East was a small force of 5,000 troops to take on the nightmare host of 180,000 which they imagined Zuo Zongtang to have at his disposal. And even if they managed to rout the Qing there remained the dread that a mightier native regime might replace the Qing dynasty and 'put us face to face with a fearful unknown'.[124]

The only way forward was clearly a renegotiation. At the end of July 1880 the Qing ambassador to London, Marquess Zeng Jize, son of the general who had crushed the Taiping, was dispatched to St Petersburg to reopen the Yili question. The Russian delegates were initially truculent ('How is it possible to negotiate with a people who cut off the heads of their ambassadors?'[125]), but following Chonghou's release in August they started to thaw. Zeng quickly turned out to be an altogether different proposition from his hapless predecessor. He was, noted the Russian Foreign Ministry men, 'very well informed', 'very adroit' and he 'reasoned very tightly'.[126] Giers declared that in all of his forty-two years of diplomacy he had never come across any interlocutor, either European, American or Asian, who was equal to Zeng. Well aware of Russia's travails, the Qing envoy shrewdly 'played dead', dragging out the talks into the winter and thereby staving off the threat of a naval attack from Lesovsky in Vladivostok until the ice had melted in six months' time. Little by little he wore the tsarist diplomats down. By October Zhomini was moaning, 'This cursed affair is giving us insomnia!',[127] and by early November he was driven to confess ruefully, 'We have made the mistake of absorbing immense territories with an appetite which bears little relation to our digestive capacity.'[128] The upshot was the signing, on 24 February 1881, of a new agreement – the Treaty of St Petersburg. Under this agreement the Russian government gave up most of the territorial gains they had wrested from Chonghou. Most of Yili, including the strategic passes, reverted to Qing hands apart from an area on the western bank of the River Khorgos. The economic price was still stiff: the Qing were obliged to consent to the opening of seven new consulates and 'trade circles', and the indemnity payable to

Russia for the occupation of Yili was actually raised from 5 million to 9 million roubles. Nonetheless the outcome was hailed as a diplomatic triumph by both the Qing court and the wider world. The British foreign secretary, Lord Dufferin, crowed to his ambassador in St Petersburg that 'China has compelled Russia to do what she has never done before – disgorge territory that she has once absorbed.'[129]

Once bitten, twice shy. Thwarted in their attempt to detach a significant portion of Xinjiang territory the tsarist government reverted to their old avuncular stance. In 1891–2 troops were briefly dispatched to secure Russia's border in the Pamir mountains south-west of the region, the last tiny piece of the Xinjiang frontier (and indeed of the whole Sino-Russian borderland) where a demarcation hadn't yet taken place; but there was no further thought of territorial conquest, with its attendant trouble and expense. Instead Russian efforts were focused on peaceful commercial penetration. With western Turkestan added to the empire, and linked to European Russia by an ever-growing network of railways and roads, Xinjiang was now economically closer to St Petersburg than it was to Peking. Ease of transportation reduced the cost of Russian exports, and the tax-free status accorded to the special 'trade circles' further helped Russian merchants to significantly undercut their local competitors. Between 1850 and 1893 Russian exports to Xinjiang are said to have risen by 680 per cent, from 211,500 to 3,063,000 roubles,[130] and cheap Russian manufactures such as cotton fabrics and leatherware were rapidly filling the Xinjiang bazaars. Xinjiang in turn supplied Russia with livestock, hides and other raw materials. By the 1890s Xinjiang traded almost exclusively with Russia, and the Russian rouble was starting to drive out Chinese silver as the regular currency of the region. Domination of this kind proved only a shade less effective than outright conquest would have been. Bestriding the scene in the southern outpost of Kashgar from 1882 onwards was the tsarist consul, Nikolai Petrovsky, an unequivocal bully (even his Russian staff were afraid of him) who made his way around town escorted by an armed guard of uniformed Cossacks and had no hesitation in browbeating the local Qing intendant, the *daotai*. If the *daotai* proved obdurate, Petrovsky would threaten him with a whipping; if the *daotai*'s officials voiced even the mildest opposition to Russian wishes, Petrovsky would swear at them. By 1890 he had become for all practical purposes the ruler of Kashgar. Local people whose knowledge stretched back to the Mongol conquests of earlier centuries referred to him as 'the new Jagatai Khan'.[131] Russian consuls in the other Xinjiang towns appear to have taken their cue from Petrovsky's behaviour. The consul installed in Dihua in 1896 is said to have treated the Qing officials with minimum courtesy, 'leaping around' when challenged and threatening to call in the Russian army to back him up.[132] Other consuls interfered in local government, applying pressure to secure the dismissal of difficult bureaucrats and the appointment of malleable ones. Some of them sought to tilt Xinjiang demographically in Russia's direction by settling Russians surreptitiously in the region and by inducing Uighurs, Kazakhs and other Qing subjects to take Russian citizenship. What was developing, in other words, was a new phase in the relationship in which tsarist functionaries were starting to manage Chinese organisations and domestic affairs.

The Russians also did their best to ensure that no competitor power threatened their commercial monopoly. In 1890 the British deployed a young interpreter named George Macartney in Kashgar as an unofficial representative, to keep an eye on Petrovsky's activities and generally to maintain a British foothold there. The Russians weren't always overtly hostile to this British rival, and Petrovsky from time to time displayed an urbane, charming and even hospitable manner to this fellow European in the back of beyond. But it was made very clear to Macartney that the rights conceded by the Qing in Xinjiang were for Russia alone and there was no room in the region for any third party. Macartney persistently hoped that the British government would win the consent of the Qing to have his status upgraded to that of a consul. In August 1897, however, a tsarist diplomat told him, 'You will never have a consulate in Kashgar or even Yarkand. If the Chinese make you such a concession your Salisbury will hear such a noise from the other end of China that he will soon forget it.'[133]

In the meantime in Manchuria a fresh chance had arisen for Russia to play the avuncular card. At the beginning of August 1894 the Japanese launched a military assault on Qing China, overwhelming the Qing forces both on land and at sea, and by the Treaty of Shimonoseki in April 1895 they secured for themselves, along with other territorial booty, the Liaodong peninsula of southern Manchuria with its port of Dalian and its naval base of Lushun. Indirectly the Japanese coup was a blow struck at Russia as well. The Trans-Siberian Railway had by now reached as far as Lake Baikal, and the Japanese were anxious to lay the foundations of their planned empire on the Asian mainland before the railway reached the Pacific and enabled the tsarist authorities to deploy for the first time a significant military force in the Russian Far East.

Japan's onslaught clearly dictated a show of Russian solidarity with the humiliated Qing. In St Petersburg Count Sergei Witte, the brains behind the Trans-Siberian project who had now become minister of finance, played vigorously on the old tsarist themes. It was in Russia's interests, he urged his fellow ministers, to preserve the Qing empire and stop it being eviscerated by rival foreign powers; and 'a strong but passive China' was greatly to be preferred as a neighbour to a predatory Japan.[134] Witte's position was backed, in more abstract terms, by Count Esper Ukhtomsky, a self-proclaimed Buddhist and admirer of things Oriental who also happened to be a press baron, diplomat and adviser to the young Tsar Nicholas II. Ukhtomsky firmly believed that Russia belonged in Asia, not Europe, and that Russia and China as traditional autocracies were natural allies against the constitutional systems espoused by the west (and just lately Japan). He saw a role for Russia as an 'elder brother' of the Chinese and protector of their Manchu overlords. Spurred on by this mixture of pragmatism and romanticism, the tsarist authorities quickly assumed their traditional mantle of China's protector. Receiving the Qing envoy Wang Zhichun in early 1895 the young tsar set the tone by informing him, 'We must do our utmost to help each other.'[135] Days after the Treaty of Shimonoseki was imposed on the Qing in April the Russian government mobilised their ally France and their neighbour Germany to join them in a Triple Intervention, a diplomatic démarche which successfully 'advised' Japan to disgorge the Liaodong peninsula. Two months later, in June, Witte and his colleagues put together a consortium of (mostly French) banks to float a 400-million-franc loan guaranteed by St Petersburg that would help the Qing pay off the huge war indemnity the Japanese had inflicted on them. And one year after that Russia placed itself fairly and squarely in the Chinese corner. In May 1896, when the veteran Qing statesman Li Hongzhang arrived in Russia to attend Nicholas II's coronation, he spent the first few weeks of his visit closeted with Witte negotiating a defensive alliance against Japan. The talks had their moments of cultural puzzlement (Witte recalled that when he asked Li whether he would like to smoke, the latter 'emitted a sound not unlike the neighing of a horse' as he called for his hubble-bubble to be brought up to him[136]), but concluded satisfactorily with the signing on 3 June of a Secret Treaty of Alliance under which Russia and China were to support each other in the event of any further Japanese aggression and Russia would have the use of the Qing ports in wartime. In the long sequence of Russian attempts to differentiate themselves from the other foreign powers in relation to China this was indeed a remarkable moment. It is difficult to imagine any of the other great powers of the period stooping to an alliance with the despised Manchu empire, and suggests that Russia was still inclined, in a way its competitors weren't, to look upon China as in some sense an equal. These avuncular measures were rounded off with another aid package, broader in scope than the previous one concocted in 1857–60. There was the same military component. By 1897 a Colonel Voronov had been dispatched with a party of military instructors to Zhili Province to train the Qing cavalry. But in addition a number of engineers, technicians and other civilian experts were sent off to work in various parts of the Qing dominions, from Manchuria to Xinjiang. In the course of a visit to China that May Prince Ukhtomsky donated a sum of 1,200 roubles towards the establishment of a Russian Language School in Tianjin. And Chinese students were received for the first time at the University of St Petersburg.

But when Nicholas II said that Russia and China should help each other he meant very definitely that China should help Russia too. In his role as finance minister Witte harboured another plan, for a huge economic penetration of the Manchurian provinces. Xinjiang apart, Russian exports to China had continued to fall in the decades since the western nations had elbowed their way into the treaty ports, from a total value of 7,127,000 roubles in 1850 to a mere 4,087,000 roubles in 1893.[137] With its closeness to the Russian border and a market of 9 million potential customers, Manchuria beckoned. Russian backing for China against the Japanese danger came accordingly at a stiff price. In November 1895 the loan floated to help the Qing pay Japan's war indemnity was followed up by the creation of a Russo-Chinese Bank, with an initial capital of 6 million roubles, to compete with the British and other western banks in concluding loan agreements with the Chinese government. One of its purposes would be to fund the advance of Russian communications into the Qing empire through the construction of telegraph lines and more especially railways. In its journey along the new border between the Russian Far East and Manchuria the Amur made a huge loop which seemed liable at first glance to require the Trans-Siberian Railway to execute a long and difficult detour to its final destination on the Pacific. By as early as 1892 Witte had his sights set on building a short cut across northern Manchuria, from the town of Chita in Transbaikalia to Vladivostok. In addition to shortening the route by 350 miles, with the attendant savings of time and cost, this short cut would bring with it immense opportunities to trade with the Manchurian population, and Russia would achieve, in Manchuria as in Xinjiang, a virtual monopoly of the local economy. By August 1895, without waiting for the consent of the Qing government, Russian surveyors were quietly moving in to mark out the prospective line. As winter set in, we are told, their long moustaches 'froze fast to their fur sleeping bags' and 'had to be thawed out with lumps of burning cow or horse dung'.[138] And by May 1896 the building of the short cut had turned into the sine qua non of the Sino-Russian Secret Treaty. In addition to pointing out the strategic merits of the line insofar as it would bring Russian troops to the aid of the Qing more swiftly in the event of a Japanese attack, Witte and his colleagues made it clear to Li Hongzhang that no railway would mean no defensive alliance; and once agreement had been reached on the railway the Qing were obliged to deposit a sum of 5 million *tael*s of silver with the Russo-Chinese Bank as a guarantee of their good faith. These pressures were accompanied by a busy greasing of palms. The tsarist authorities had been insistent that Li Hongzhang should represent China at Nicholas II's coronation rather than the previous special envoy, Wang Zhichun; and while this could readily be justified by Li's far greater eminence, the Russians are also likely to have been guided by a perception that Li was 'their man'. He had shown them goodwill during the Tianjin incident of 1870, and had been the leading dove during the Yili crisis ten years after that. History doesn't record whether any money changed hands on these two occasions, but in 1889, when a clash had developed between Russian and British syndicates over the building of telegraph lines on the northern Qing frontier, Li is said to have been coaxed into taking the Russians' part 'by the attraction of gold bars snugly nestled in silk-lined boxes',[139] and in 1896 the tsarist leaders moved rapidly on the assumption that Li could be bought. Witte conveyed a promise to the Qing statesman that he would receive a sum of 3 million roubles in exchange for expediting the Manchurian short cut, and money was set aside in the Russo-Chinese Bank in what became known to the Russians as the Li Hongzhang Fund. The

Empress Dowager Cixi herself is said by some sources to have received a substantial pay-off. On 28 August 1896 the Qing minister in St Petersburg, Xu Jingcheng, signed an agreement with the Russo-Chinese Bank for the construction and management of the 'Chinese Eastern Railway' (CER).

The creation of these entities was achieved without the dispatch of a single gunboat or squadron of cavalry. But in Manchuria as in Xinjiang it showed what advantages Russia could gain even without the adoption of such crude methods. The Russo-Chinese Bank, for example, had become in a formal sense a joint venture with the enforced Qing investment of 5 million *taels* towards the construction of the CER. But its headquarters was in St Petersburg, its president was Prince Ukhtomsky and five-eighths of its capital was provided by Russia's French allies. The Qing government had no control over its operations. 'At first', Witte recalled, 'the Chinese took some part in the work of the Bank, but their role in it subsequently declined.'[140] Over the following years the bank opened branches in all the main towns of Manchuria. It is said to have accumulated wide powers to coin money, raise taxes and even set up local governments. The CER was a similar story. The Qing minister, Xu Jingcheng, was awarded the nominal presidency of the railway, but the real power lay with his Russian deputy, and day-to-day operations were directed by a Russian chief engineer. Most of the labour employed in constructing the line was made up of Chinese workers, who were favoured by the railway authorities because they could be paid less. Once again we come up against the new phenomenon of Russians managing Chinese. Building the railway entailed the concession to Russia of an extra-territorial zone on either side of the line corresponding to the western settlements in the treaty ports. The zone was protected by a contingent of Russian railway guards over which Witte took personal command. (This force became known unofficially as 'Matilda's Guards', in sardonic honour of Witte's wife.) And the railway was to be operated by the Russian government for a theoretical period of eighty years. By 1897 Witte and his associates were nursing a further scheme for a spur of the CER to be built into southern Manchuria as the next step in the creation of their peaceful 'railway empire'. Like the consular staff in Xinjiang they aimed to secure exclusive Russian access to this region of tsarist economic hegemony. Witte was confident that once the CER was completed 'no other line or branch would be built in north China without Russia's consent'.[141]

The immediate Qing reaction to Russia's moves was nothing short of euphoric. In the light of the Triple Intervention of 1895 senior officials agreed that the tsarist empire looked to be China's most promising ally. News of the signing by Li Hongzhang of a defensive alliance with Russia to contain Japan was generally welcomed, and the Russo-Chinese Bank was accorded the Chinese name 'Sino-Russian Bank of the Victory of Righteousness' (*Zhong-E Daosheng Yinhang*). The Qing cavalry commander in northern Zhili rejoiced at the 'model order' imposed on his men by Colonel Voronov and his fellow instructors, and appealed for a prolongation of their stay.[142] Russia's stock remained high in Peking, to all outward appearances, at the time of Prince Ukhtomsky's visit in May 1897. The prince was given a splendid reception, and Dr G.E. Morrison, the redoubtable Australian correspondent of the London *Times*, noted sourly that the Chinese regarded Ukhtomsky as 'the Tsar's brother if not the Tsar himself'.[143]

Under the surface, however, anxiety didn't take long to creep in. As early as December 1895 the Russian minister in Peking reported to his government that the mood of gratitude towards them was 'beginning to weaken and give place to a certain vague feeling of apprehension and distrust',[144] as though the Qing sensed that exorbitant new demands might be in the offing; and as news spread of the content of the Secret Treaty, of the CER agreement and all that it entailed, disenchantment grew fast. The Manchu general Enze, military governor of Heilongjiang Province where the railway was being built, commented of the Russians, 'It seems as if they are patting us on the back and throttling us at the same time.'[145] When Li Hongzhang, who had continued from Russia on a round-the-world tour, arrived back in Peking in October 1896 he was received at the court with hostility and was protected only by the personal intercession of the empress dowager. Even Li had misgivings, in spite of his demonstrable enthusiasm for Russian lucre. Part of the purpose of Prince Ukhtomsky's visit in 1897 was to disburse the first million roubles of the Li Hongzhang Fund, since 'the old man was very tired of waiting'.[146] But when the prince took the opportunity to press for the hoped-for extension of the CER into southern Manchuria 'the old man' pulled him up short. 'We have admitted you to the courtyard, now you wish to get into the rooms where we house our wives and small children.'[147] He warned Russia sternly against making any attempt to 'go south'. In the privacy of his diary Li sighed to himself, '*If Russia did not want to control us in all our home affairs what a strong alliance would be possible between us.*'[148]

In the meantime a new voice was starting to make itself heard, the voice of a rising Chinese political class intent on the reform if not the complete overthrow of the Manchu regime; and this class had no truck with the tsarist alliance at all. Already in 1888, before the first sleeper had been laid for the Trans-Siberian line, the constitutional monarchist Kang Youwei had expressed alarm at Russian railway-building; and in 1894 a reformist official named Chen Zhi condemned Russian 'nibbling and gobbling' on the border.[149] 'Ah, how cruel', lamented Tang Caichang, a political activist, 'is the Russian practice, not to appear suddenly as an oppressor, but first to subvert with bribes!'[150] And the journalist Liang Qichao simply urged advocates of an alliance with the tsarist government, '*Let me remind you of Poland.*'[151]

TOWARDS A 'YELLOW RUSSIA'? (1897–1905)

It was now the high noon of imperialism, as the great powers of Europe and their Asian rival, Japan, in quest of land, trading facilities and access to minerals, circled hungrily above the moribund Qing. In Russia too the pressure to take advantage of Qing weakness started to mount to the point where it became overwhelming. Why not simply march in? One leading advocate of such a course was a certain Pyotr Badmaev, a Buryat Mongol who had converted from Lamaist Buddhism to Russian Orthodoxy and had made a name for himself in the tsarist capital as a practitioner of 'Tibetan' herbal medicine. In 1893 Badmaev submitted a paper to Tsar Alexander III outlining a plan to extend Russian rule through the whole of what he termed the 'Mongol-Tibetan-Chinese Orient'. His idea was that the eastern section of the Trans-Siberian Railway should be diverted through Mongolia to the north-western Chinese city of Lanzhou in Gansu Province and from there carried onwards as far as Tibet. Lanzhou would be turned into a secret base for fomenting a general rising against the Manchu regime. He himself would establish a trading company to provide cover for the operation, and would dispatch a few thousand of his fellow Buryats to fan out through the region in the guise of pedlars and prepare for the rising by distributing trade goods and arms. The tsar could then send an army of 400,000 from Russian Turkestan to assume control of the East. The conquest would be bloodless, since the name of the 'White Tsar' had long been 'engraved on the minds' of the Mongols and Tibetans, while the Chinese 'did not pay attention to who was ruling them'.[152] The level-headed Alexander dismissed the whole project as 'new, unusual and fantastic'.[153] After Alexander's death in 1894, however, Badmaev returned to the charge, urging that if Russia didn't take steps to acquire the wealth of the region the western powers would get in first; and this time he succeeded in winning a hearing. He was appointed adviser on Tibetan affairs to Tsar Nicholas II, and more concretely was endowed with a capital sum of 2 million roubles to set up his proposed trading firm. Some resistance to Badmaev's wild plan was put up by Finance Minister Witte, if we are to believe the account in his memoirs. After initially helping Badmaev to push his ideas Witte had come round to the view that the man was a charlatan in both medicine and geopolitics, whose railway scheme would 'arouse the whole of Europe against us' and might even provoke the great powers into instigating a Qing assault on the Russian Far East.[154] But the peaceable minister of finance was by this time a lonely voice at a hawkish cabinet table. Leading the hawks was the young Tsar Nicholas himself. Viewing China as 'his India', Nicholas seemed to be 'merely possessed', in Witte's sour recollection, 'by an unreasoning desire to seize Far Eastern lands'.[155] Backing the tsar were successive war ministers, and the new foreign minister, Mikhail Muraviev, whose Chinese ambitions would earn him the sobriquet of 'Muraviev-Pekinsky' (Muraviev of Peking), in an echo of his famous namesake, Muraviev of the Amur. The watchword in St Petersburg had become '*We must take*' ('*Nado vzyat*').[156]

The expansionist mood of the time can be detected in other facets of Russian activity. In 1896, for example, an old self-denial was abandoned when the tsarist government finally moved to secure an extra-territorial concession in the tea-trading city of Hankou. A concession in Tianjin followed in 1900. And in the same years the Orthodox Mission began to take the first serious steps to spread the Gospel beyond the bounds of Peking. In 1896 the newly appointed head of the Eighteenth Mission, Father Innocent Figurovsky, an imposing prelate with an 'energetic, authoritative look in his radiant eyes',[157] began his tenure with a series of visits to London, Oxford, Paris and Rome to research the more strenuous form of evangelism practised by his Protestant and Roman Catholic opposite numbers. His object was to resume the attempt to win over the Chinese to Orthodoxy which Peter the Great had briefly embarked on with his appointment of the luckless Bishop Innocent Kulchitsky. Arrived in Peking, Father Innocent found the Mission in a demoralised state. One of his recent predecessors had replied to the question of when the Chinese would become Christian with the brusque answer 'Never!',[158] and the solitary Chinese priest Mitrofan Ji had neglected his flock in the outlying parish of Dongding'an and apparently succumbed to a nervous breakdown. The new head of mission moved vigorously to turn things around, building a new church in Kalgan on the edge of Mongolia and a new church and monastery at Beidaihe on the coast, where Chinese converts were baptised in the sea. Within two years the Chinese Orthodox community had risen to an unprecedented if still microscopic total of 458.

The great break with the past was made finally during the winter of 1897–8. In November 1897 Kaiser Wilhelm II and his ministers seized on the pretext provided by the murder of two German missionaries in the eastern province of Shandong to install their fleet in the attractive anchorage of Jiaozhou Bay. The tsarist government raised no objection (Willy had squared Cousin Nicky already the previous summer), but were gripped by what they now perceived as the overwhelming necessity of following suit. Muraviev-Pekinsky alerted the tsar to the risk that the British might copy the German example by seizing the Qing naval base at Lüshun unless Russian forces pre-empted them, thereby posing a further threat to Russian plans for Manchuria. Even more cogent, however, was the inherent lure of Lüshun as the warm-water port which Russian strategists had for years dreamt of gaining on the Pacific. Muraviev-Pekinsky urged further that the tsarist navy should occupy the trading port of Dalian, which would give Russia an excellent opportunity to develop its merchant fleet. The wheels were rapidly set in motion. When Li Hongzhang approached the Russian minister in Peking with a request for avuncular help against the German intruders on the east coast the response was firmly negative; and on 3 December, on the tsar's direct order, Admiral Fyodor Dubasov led a Russian squadron into Lüshun for the winter without any attempt to obtain Qing permission. In January 1898 a new war minister, General Alexei Kuropatkin, took the next step by proposing that Russia demand the cession of the entire Liaodong peninsula; and in March the tsarist government compelled the Qing to sign an agreement granting Russia the peninsula on the basis of a twenty-five-year lease, plus the right to build the hoped-for spur of the CER southwards to the two Liaodong ports. Mention was made of protecting the dynasty from British encroachment; the usual bribes were dispensed to Li Hongzhang and others; but the clinching argument was naked force in the shape of a fleet within easy reach of Peking. It was a staggering transformation. In the space of a few months the Russian hawks had given up the benevolent posture their country had assumed in its dealings with China ever since Qing power began to crumble in the middle decades of the century. They had dropped the restraint which had so long enabled Russia to distinguish itself from the blunter techniques of the other great powers. Above all, through the seizure of the Liaodong peninsula they had made a mockery of their own benign intervention to retrieve the peninsula for China from the Japanese conquerors less than three years before. Witte at least was appalled. He regarded the takeover of the peninsula as 'an act of unparalleled perfidy' which had 'destroyed all our traditional relations with China and destroyed them forever'.[159] But Witte was quelled by Tsar Nicholas, who advised him 'with obvious embarrassment' that he had decided to occupy Lüshun and Dalian because of Muraviev-Pekinsky's advice about the British threat.[160]

Russia had all of a sudden turned into an active player in the game of imperial carve-up. Tsarist spokesmen started to claim a formal sphere of influence encompassing not only Manchuria but also Zhili, the metropolitan province that included Peking. By the first months of 1899 Russian muscles were even being flexed at Hankou on the Yangtze, where the Cossack troops of the new concession had begun to meddle with the activities of British trading firms. Out on the fringes Russia also claimed a formal sphere of influence in Xinjiang, where Petrovsky remarked ominously to one of the staff of the British diplomatic outpost in Kashgar that it was 'impossible to permit such a nation [as China] to exist as a ruling power any longer'.[161] In Tibet Dr Badmaev was busy fomenting pro-Russian and anti-British feeling with the help of Agvan Dordzhiev, a fellow Buryat who had worked himself into an influential position as tutor and adviser to the Dalai Lama. The British for their part did not take long to react to the challenge. In January 1898 Morrison of *The Times* warned that Russian domination of north China was now far advanced and might indeed prove to be the first step in a tsarist annexation of Asia. Britain, he urged, had to halt the encroachment as quickly as possible through an alliance with Japan. Other

British observers, however, took a more phlegmatic approach. Alfred Hippisley, an official on the staff of the Imperial Chinese Maritime Customs, noted correctly that Russia had 'thrown aside the silken glove',[162] but inclined to the view that a deal could be reached under which Britain would acknowledge Russian supremacy in north China in return for a free hand in the Yangtze valley and the south. And the Russians soon proved amenable to such a bargain. Under the terms of an Anglo-Russian protocol signed behind China's back in April 1899 the tsarist government retreated from one or two of their more alarming pretensions. They abandoned their bid for priority in Zhili Province and disclaimed any wish to pursue railway concessions in the Yangtze valley. In return, however, they secured the unquestioned right to build railways and embed themselves economically throughout the whole of Qing territory to the north of the Great Wall.

The impact upon China was seismic. Through their land grab of 1897–8 the Russians, as Witte had predicted, lost effectively all of the residual goodwill they had enjoyed at the Manchu court. Senior mandarins who had approved of St Petersburg's role in the Triple Intervention of 1895 were now shifting to favour an anti-Russian alliance with Britain and Japan. True, these two powers had also elbowed their way into China; but at least they had not displayed the breathtaking hypocrisy with which the tsarist rulers had rescued the Liaodong peninsula from Japanese occupation only to snatch it back for themselves. Even Li Hongzhang was driven to comment in November 1897 that he was reluctant to make the Russians any more promises in view of their apparent reluctance to help against Germany. During the summer of 1898 power in Peking fell briefly into the hands of the group of reformists who, as we have seen, had their faces set against tsarist Russia from the start. Kang Youwei charged the dynasty with maintaining the secret alliance with the Russians, and Liang Qichao claimed to hear 'the hooves of the Cossack cavalry pounding over East Asia'.[163] Even after the empress dowager crushed the reform movement in September the outcry continued, with street demonstrations supported by the loyalist troops of General Dong Fuxiang, and from October 1898 to March 1899 a detachment of 100 Russian sailors had to be deployed in Peking to protect tsarist interests. In the meantime, Li Hongzhang had been dismissed from his post in the Zongli Yamen and sent off to supervise water conservancy work on the Yellow River. Still licking his wounds, he described the Anglo-Russian agreement of April 1899 as a 'partition of China'.[164]

These immediate ructions had barely subsided when Russia was caught in a wave of pent-up Chinese popular fury against all the foreigners and all their works. Starting off in Shandong, the 'Boxer' rising of fanatical peasants had spread fast across northern China and by late May 1900 had reached the edge of Peking. Much of the Boxer rage was directed against foreign Christian establishments, and the Russian Orthodox Mission was no exception. On 11 June the venerable North House of the Mission which had stood peacefully on its site since the seventeenth century was reduced to 'ruins and smoking wreckage'.[165] Father Innocent and his staff withdrew to the shelter of the Russian legation bearing the Mission treasures, among them the icon of St Nicholas which had been brought to Peking from Albazin in 1685. Sad to relate, it does not seem to have occurred to them either to rescue or to share the peril of their much increased Chinese flock. Boxer revenge was now aimed, with some help from a few spiteful neighbours, at those local citizens who had been won to the Orthodox creed. On the same night the insurgents broke into a house where the Chinese priest Mitrofan Ji had gathered some seventy of his fellow converts and slaughtered the lot of them. Boxer spears pierced Mitrofan's chest 'like a honeycomb';[166] other rebels hacked the shoulders of his eight-year-old son and chopped off the boy's toes. Murder and arson took place throughout the old Russian district. 'You crazy wreckers, what harm have we done you?' cried Viktor Fu.[167] The Boxers promptly killed him and plucked out his heart as a ritual offering to their divinities. Kapitolina Huai apostasised under pressure from her son-in-law, and was rewarded by having her feet cut off. By the end of the rampage the Boxers had massacred a total of 222 converts, or roughly half of the Orthodox Chinese community. Outside the capital Mitrofan's church in Dongding'an village and the two new churches which Father Innocent had put up in Kalgan and Beidaihe were razed to the ground.

Russian residents huddled alongside the other foreign communities in the diplomatic quarter, where the ministers of the powers had joined forces to organise a defence centred on the British legation. By 21 June the stranded foreigners had to contend not only with the Boxers but with the Qing government too, as the empress dowager declared war on the powers and threw in the weight of her troops on the Boxer side. During the siege that ensued Russians played a vigorous part in the collective defence. Russian volunteers did the night rounds of the British legation and manned exposed posts overlooking it on the Tartar Wall. Russian ladies arranged the provisions, sewed sacks out of silken fabrics to be used to make sandbags and looked after the sick and wounded (mostly fellow Russians and Germans) who couldn't speak English. Ominous news periodically seeped in from outside – that the Peking branch of the Russo-Chinese Bank had been showered with bullets and burnt down, that Xu Jingcheng, the token Qing president of the CER, had been executed for his 'services to Russian interests'.[168] Grim though the ordeal must have been both materially and psychologically, it does seem to have had one or two lighter moments. Some Russian sailors built up a vocabulary of Chinese obscenities sufficient to rebut the besiegers' cries of 'Kill the foreign devils!' with an answering 'Kill the turtle eggs!'. Sometimes, we are told, a Russian lady of striking beauty who had been a professional opera singer supplied entertainment to the besieged diplomats in the form of an aria 'as the nocturnal bullets whistled overhead'.[169] And in the end Russian losses were small. Out of a total of sixty-six foreigners who lost their lives in the Siege of the Legations a mere three were Russian. One young CER trainee who had overdone the liquor lurched out of the foreigners' compound towards the Qing barricades and was shot dead at point-blank range, and two other men died of dysentery.

Far more dreadful and damaging, from the Russian perspective, was the backlash in Manchuria. By late June the first Boxers had entered the region, and on 23 June the Qing government ordered the generals in command of the three Manchurian provinces to muster and train them. The repercussions were swift. By the end of the month upwards of thirty Russian railway workers plus a woman and child had gone missing on the western section of the CER. Some of Witte's railway guards were flayed alive, or crucified in a display of anti-Christian fervour; Russian corpses were discovered with crosses carved into their chests. And the Qing had their sights set on wiping out not merely the railway personnel but the railway itself. On 5 July Zengqi, the military governor of the province of Fengtian (modern Liaoning) in southern Manchuria, wrote to his colleague in neighbouring Jilin that the CER was 'a cancer' and must be destroyed.[170] Qing soldiers ripped up the tracks and demolished the bridges along about 130 miles of the railway's advancing southern spur. Finally, on 15 July, a Qing force on the southern bank of the Amur opened fire on some Russians they had spotted swimming on the other side of the river in front of the border town of Blagoveshchensk.

This ferocity quickly engendered reprisals from the Russian side. On 13–14 August a Russian contingent of 4,000 troops broke through the eastern gate of Peking as part of the eight-nation Allied Expeditionary Force which had marched up from Tianjin to lift the by this time fifty-five-day siege. Like the other contingents the Russians were vengeful, and greedy for loot. Dmitri Pokotilov, the manager of the Russo-Chinese Bank, recorded the complaints that had reached him of looting and terrible violence by Russian soldiers, the rumours of rapes. Even the top brass, it seemed, had been egging the soldiery on. General Linevich, the senior commander in the Allied relief force, who on 28 August had the honour of leading the joint victory march through the Imperial City, is said personally to have made off with ten trunks filled with treasure from the Peking palaces. Up in Blagoveshchensk the reaction to the Qing bombardment was hideous panic, as the populace turned on the community of Chinese traders who had lived peacefully among them for years. 'Throw the Chinese across the Amur', directed the commandant, Lieutenant-General K.N. Gribsky.[171] From 17 to 21 July nearly 8,000 Chinese were rounded up with whips and at gunpoint and shoved into the river to make their way to the opposite bank, regardless of whether or not they happened to be able to swim; 3,000–4,000 are reckoned to have been drowned or chopped up on the northern bank of the river with sabres and axes.[172] 'The execution of my orders', confided one appalled Russian officer, 'made me almost sick, for it seemed as though I could have walked across the river on the bodies of the floating dead.'[173] Local troops took advantage of the mayhem to liquidate, for good measure, the Sixty-Four Settlements, the cluster of Manchu and Chinese villages on the Russian side over, which the Qing government had contrived to retain jurisdiction. Another 7,000 people are said to have been massacred in this piece of ethnic cleansing.[174] All in all the outrages committed by both antagonists in the course of this terrible summer marked a sad abandonment of the long Sino-Russian tradition of pragmatic restraint.

The tsarist authorities weren't put off their expansionist course by this descent into horror. Their response on the contrary was to double down. His face 'radiant', War Minister Kuropatkin declared to Witte at the start of the troubles, 'This will give us an opportunity for seizing Manchuria.'[175] The finance minister jibbed to begin with, but as the days passed he shifted his outlook and by 9 July he too was advising Tsar Nicholas that an army of occupation would have to be sent. The railway network had to be protected at all costs. In the third week of July a Russian army of some 100,000 (getting troops to the East was no longer an insurmountable problem) invaded Manchuria at five or six points, from the Amur in the north to the Liaodong peninsula in the south, in the first significant outbreak of fighting between Russia and China for over two hundred years. In the northern theatre, in Heilongjiang, the fighting was bitter. The Qing troops held out stubbornly, and the tsarist forces were commanded by Pavel Rennenkampf, whose ferocity earned him the Chinese name of the Tiger General. 'Here a leg, there an arm,' wrote one Chinese witness. 'The smell of death and putrefaction filled heaven and earth, and wolves and crows gnawed and pecked.'[176] In the south, though, resistance was feebler, and by the end of September the Russians had displaced the Qing military governors and had established a rough-and-ready control of Manchuria with a force that now totalled 173,000 men. Some attempt was made to win Qing consent for this latest incursion through a show of concern for the dynasty's interests elsewhere. Tsarist representatives in Peking urged the need for magnanimous handling of the humbled Qing government, and Russian troops were pointedly withdrawn from the capital several months in advance of the rest of the Allied relief force. In November Vice-Admiral Yevgeny Alexeev, an illegitimate son of Tsar Alexander II who had been made governor-general of Lüshun, signed an agreement with an envoy of Zengqi, the deposed military governor of Fengtian Province, ostensibly giving the Russians Qing permission to station their forces in southern Manchuria. And every care was taken to avoid the dread word 'annexation'. The fact remained that tsarist armies had finally sliced off the first panel of the great triptych of territories that constituted the Sino-Russian borderland.

The Orthodox Church lost little time in resuming their gentler expansion. In January 1902 the Holy Synod in St Petersburg declared China a bishopric, formally endorsing the Mission's return to the grand evangelical hopes of the early eighteenth century; and Father Innocent was appointed Bishop of Pereyaslavl, the same see that had been occupied by his unhappy namesake Innocent Kulchitsky when he sought admission to eighteenth-century China to spread the faith. Returning to Peking in August after a two-year absence, the new Bishop Innocent took rapid action to clear up the wreckage left by the Boxers. A new Monastery of the Assumption was planned on the ruins of the North House, and a Church of All the Holy Martyrs was put up (was there a hint of guilt here?) to house the remains of the 222 Chinese Orthodox converts who had perished at Boxer hands. Finally Bishop Innocent took up with new vigour his drive to install mission stations beyond the bounds of Peking. By 1903 a Chinese deacon named Sergius Chang, son of the martyred Mitrofan Ji, was catechising the villagers of Fengkou, near Hankou in Hubei Province, where he founded a chapel and launched a campaign against opium-smoking.

Russia's continuing thrust into the tottering Chinese empire didn't pass without protest. The Russian literary world had one or two things to say. From October 1900 to February 1901 the ageing Tolstoy busied himself composing an *Address to the Chinese People* couched in language of furious sympathy:

> You have lived your lives apart from the Europeans, requiring nothing of them and asking only that they should leave you in peace. But they, on their own strange excuses, crept in with their goods, their religion, and as soon as they had any pretext have fallen on you like wild beasts, like bandits, and have torn from you what they needed.[177]

Maxim Gorky wrote two letters to Anton Chekhov entreating the playwright to go with him to China and witness the atrocities there. Rather more serious, from the point of view of St Petersburg, was the opposition of the other great powers. By March 1901 the Japanese had promised the Qing government that they would help to secure a Russian withdrawal from Manchuria 'under any circumstances',[178] and in January 1902 Britain and Japan finally came together in the Anglo-Japanese alliance which Morrison of *The Times* had urged so insistently as a bridle on Russia's ambitions just four years before. The British were chiefly alarmed by the spectre of Russian designs on Tibet. Reports from a Japanese agent suggested that the Dalai Lama's Russian Buryat mentor, Agvan Dordzhiev, had induced people there to identify Tsar Nicholas II with a northern messiah of Buddhist legend, that a caravan of Russian weapons had reached the northern plateau of Chang Tang; and rumour had it that the tsar's diplomats in Peking had extorted from the empress dowager a secret treaty ceding to Russia all former Qing rights in the territory. At the end of 1903 the British Indian government sent an expeditionary force under Colonel Francis Younghusband slogging into the

Himalayas to put an end to these machinations. (They arrived in Lhasa to find that the Dalai Lama and Dordzhiev had fled to Mongolia, and no trace of either the arms or the treaty was ever brought to light.)

Tibet was however a sideshow to the tsarist hawks by comparison with the all-important Manchurian conquest. In March 1901 Vice-Admiral Alexeev wrote to Kuropatkin recommending that the occupation of Manchuria should be continued indefinitely. Kuropatkin for his part favoured a Russian withdrawal – as soon as the region had been turned into a friendly buffer state on the lines of Bokhara in Central Asia. Great-power pressure was strong enough that in April 1902 the tsarist government felt obliged to sign an evacuation agreement with their Qing counterparts providing for a staggered troop withdrawal over a period of eighteen months; and a first stage of this pull-out was, indeed, completed the following August. Further withdrawal was, however, delayed. By October 1902 even Witte had come out against any further evacuation. In August 1903 Alexeev was appointed the tsar's viceroy for the Far East, a move that scarcely smacked of retreat, and at the beginning of 1904 a 'well-known officer' in his entourage was quoted as saying that Russia had no intention of leaving Manchuria even at the risk of war with Japan. Talk was rife among the top brass of annexing Manchuria formally and converting it into a 'Yellow Russia' on the tsar's eastern flank. The Russians were creating a colony.

One day in 1897, we are told, a pair of Russian railway engineers on Siberian ponies pitched their tents by an abandoned Chinese distillery on the banks of the River Sungari, at a spot known by the Manchu name of Harbin ('Place for Drying the Nets'). It was the start of a process of breakneck settlement. In March 1898 Harbin was formally established as the headquarters of the CER. Tsarist officers were encouraged to move in with their families, and workers from European Russia poured in to help with the building and running of the railway and generally take advantage of the openings presented by what one Western scholar has described as 'a wild, wooden boom town'.[179] A majority of ethnic Russians were interspersed with members of various smaller groups from the empire of Nicholas II – Poles, Latvians, Ukrainians, Georgians and in particular Jews, many of them in flight from the late tsarist pogroms. After the conquest of 1900 the influx grew still faster, and by 1903 the Russian civilian population of Harbin is said to have climbed to a total of some 30,000. Measures were quickly taken to endow this Russian town with a suitably Russian environment. In October 1899 the first timbers were laid of a wooden church in the style of the late medieval churches of north-western Russia, and by December 1900 work was complete on this Church of St Nicholas, otherwise known as the Pearl of Harbin or more colloquially from its colour as the Chocolate Church. Entertainments mushroomed, both highbrow and lowbrow. There were chamber concerts and plays, the latter slightly marred in the eyes of a British journalist, B.L. Putnam Weale, by the old-fashioned appearance of the actresses: 'straight-fronted corsets and bell-shaped skirts have not progressed as far as Harbin yet'.[180] There were *cafés-chantants* such as the Golden Anchorite, and what Weale referred to mysteriously as 'tingle-tangle shows'.[181] Perhaps inevitably Harbin became known as 'the Moscow of the East'. A similar process of Russification was under way to a lesser extent in the other Manchurian centres. By November 1902 Hailar on the north-western edge of the region had turned into 'a Russian town, with Russian shops, hotels and hospitals'.[182] In Jilin, in the centre, earnest efforts were made to get Chinese schoolboys declaiming the works of Pushkin and Lermontov in place of the sayings of Confucius, and in Mukden, in the south, the announcement was made in November 1901 that Mme Nadezhda Slavyanskaya would be bringing her choir to town for four days of performances. Down in the Liaodong peninsula Dalian had its name changed to Dalny, the Russian for 'distant'; and the Chinese name for the naval base of Lüshun was likewise dropped, though in this case the Russians contented themselves with the European name already bestowed by the British – Port Arthur.

Every possible opportunity was seized by the Russian arrivals to put down economic roots. During the conquest of 1900 tsarist forces had taken control of five major Manchurian gold mines, and with the conquest completed Witte and his colleagues quietly set about extracting concessions from the prostrate Qing for the exploitation of both gold and the region's abundance of other resources, iron, nickel, petroleum, coal and timber. Large-scale enterprises set up to work the gold mines included Countess Apraxin and Co. and Troitsky and Kutuzov Co., names straight from the pages of *War and Peace*, as well as the more prosaically styled Russia Gold Mining Co. A Grand Dukes' Concession for mining and timber-felling covered an area of some 20,000 square miles in Jilin Province, and Messrs Skidelsky and Kowalski between them invested a total of 5 million roubles in timber concessions.[183] In 1900 a

Russian merchant established a Harbin Brewery, and a succession of flour mills and vodka distilleries soon sprang up around the Eastern Moscow to cater for settler tastes. Manchuria also provided the terrain for a huge breakthrough by I. Ya. Churin and Co., a general trading business which had been founded in Irkutsk in 1868. Opening first in Harbin in 1900, Churin's quickly went on to set up further branches in Jilin, Fengtian and Dalny, operating department stores like so many Manchurian Saks or Harrods while at the same time acquiring a lucrative portfolio of warehouses and residential property. In 1903 the CER, Boxer damage repaired, was completed with the arrival of the southern spur at Port Arthur, finally bringing close to fulfilment Witte's dream of penetrating the markets of Manchuria and northern China beyond. Throughout this expansion the Russians were indebted to the good offices of a couple of well-disposed Chinese entrepreneurs. One was Ji Fengtai, a merchant better known by his Russified name of Nikolai Ivanovich Tifontai. Starting off, it is said, as a labourer in Shandong, Tifontai had migrated to the Russian town of Khabarovsk and had there built himself a multi-million-rouble empire as contractor to the tsarist armed forces. In the mid-1890s he had turned his hand to helping Russian business make inroads in the west of Manchuria, and from 1898 on he had busied himself building dockyards in Dalny and harbour fortifications at the Port Arthur naval base. His spoken Russian was excellent, and the Russians in Port Arthur were reported to be 'very proud of him.'[184] Much help was also forthcoming from an affable fixer by the name of Zhou Mian. Originally an official on Li Hongzhang's staff, Zhou had been placed in the mid-1890s in charge of the northernmost Qing gold mine at Mohe, and from 1896 onwards he is said to have 'laid himself out' to be of service to the Russians.[185] In November 1900 he negotiated the agreement between Alexeev and Zengqi that lent a colour of legitimacy to the Russian occupation, and as head of a newly created Department of Foreign Affairs for Heilongjiang Province he arranged to provide Russia with three large timber concessions and ultimately with the right to chop down trees anywhere within 3.5 kilometres of the CER.

Lastly, the newcomers started to grope their way to a long-term relationship with the subjugated Chinese populace. Here and there efforts were made to copy the habits of the British colonial rulers. The authorities in Harbin and Port Arthur imported Sikh watchmen, dressed up for the climate in long Russian boots and embroidered Astrakhan coats. Certain Russian employers were known to address their servants as *boika*, a term borrowed from the British colonial 'boy'. 'In the Orient', mocked one liberal Russian journalist,

> some Russians wholeheartedly follow British etiquette and conduct. They are so thoroughly Anglicised that (like a real British gentleman) they speak English, read *The Times*, play tennis, wear a pith helmet, white shoes and black socks, drink whisky daily and condemn the Chinese. In short, all behave in line with the mission of civilised behaviour in the East.[186]

What struck the British, however, was not the similarity between Russian practice and their own but the sharp difference. Above all British visitors commented on the contrast between their own practised aloofness and an incorrigible Russian tendency to muck in. Russian officers, noted Morrison of *The Times* on a trip to the region in 1902, seemed 'to treat the Chinese with more consideration, friendliness and familiarity than we are accustomed to elsewhere'.[187] Chinese merchants and business agents, even local functionaries were invited to Russian official balls at Port Arthur. Putnam Weale complained that 'the Russian does not know how to treat servants except as family friends'.[188] Chinese domestics were given Russian pet names such as Vanya and Kolya and settled into the household like bit parts in a Chekhov play – with the result, grumbled Weale, that 'they become absolutely spoilt and lose all their Chinese manners'.[189] Russian officers were known to adopt Chinese orphan girls whom they brought up to be nursemaids, and orphan boys whom they took back to Russia and sometimes even provided with a full education. But the real shock came at the foot of the tsarist social ladder, where lower-class Russians were observed 'fraternising with easy freedom' with their Chinese counterparts.[190] In the southern Manchurian port of Niuzhuang, for example, the river police were said to be a 'Russo-Chinese force', and in Dalny the Russians and Chinese were seen to toil side by side 'in the rougher forms of work'.[191] In some places the Russians even seemed content to work under Chinese supervision. On a steamer he took from Japan to Port Arthur in 1903 Putnam Weale found himself waited on by a Chinese chief steward and five Russian under-stewards, one of whom meekly approached his boss for instructions. The journalist 'winced, for it is somehow not right for the white man to be the servant of the yellow'.[192] At Niuzhuang Russian soldiers were found to be on back-slapping terms with local Chinese employees of the CER, and one soldier was even seen giving his loaf of bread to a Chinese beggar. Such easy mingling has been ascribed to the fact that the living standards of lower class Russians in late tsarist times were not so very much higher than those of the mass of Chinese. Even the huts of Chinese peasants, as one general noted, weren't necessarily dirtier than those of their counterparts in the Russian heartland.[193] In the course of this fraternisation Chinese words were absorbed into Russian, and Russian into Chinese. The northern Chinese word for a house, *fangzi*, became Russian *fanza*, a word that survives to this day in Russian dictionaries, and even acquired a diminutive, *fanzochka*. The Russian words *soldat* (soldier), *plat'ye* (dress), *vedro* (bucket) and *kvass* (beer) turned into the new Chinese coinages *saodasi*, *buleyi*, *weidaluo* and *gewasi*. Once again a Sino-Russian pidgin language began to evolve, as it had years before among the frontier traders at Kyakhta. The Chinese expressions *shang hao* (good, literally 'number one'), *bu shang hao* (bad) and *kuaikuaidi* (quickly, hurry) were transmuted into the Russian-sounding pidgin words *shango*, *bushango* and *kakoido*. 'Wait a bit' was expressed by the wonderful compound *chut'-chut' mamandi*, from the Russian *chut'-chut'* (a little) and the Chinese *manmandi* (slowly). To be sure, this new pidgin had an upstairs-downstairs flavour the old one had lacked. Chinese beggars chanted beseechingly to Russian passers-by, '*Bol'shoi kapitan, shango kapitan, kuss-kuss mei you*?' a mixture of Russian, tsarist army slang and Chinese meaning 'Great captain, good captain, can't you spare a penny?'. But the use of this jargon seemed to point to the future emergence of an integrated society.[194]

Many obstacles, however, stood in the path to the desired 'Yellow Russia'. Like the Americans in Iraq a century later the tsarist troops in Manchuria found that overrunning a country was a great deal easier than keeping it pacified in the long term. Regular Qing troops had melted away, but the Heilongjiang force that had fought the hardest continued to hold out on the edge of Mongolia till the spring of 1901. And from 1900 onwards a stubborn guerrilla resistance was kept up by the Red Beard bandits who still haunted the Manchurian forests. Old Russian ladies are said to have frightened their grandchildren with tales of the dreadful *honghuzi*, and the Chinese name even lent itself to two further Russian coinages, *khunkhuzichat'* (to turn Red Beard) and *khunkhuzichestvo* (Red Beard depredation). By August 1901 2,000 Russians had been killed in counter-insurgency operations,[195] and the costs mounted steeply. In Fengtian in the south the challenge of local subversion was still more intractable. Up until 1902 an anti-Russian secret society was active in the province, and Pokotilov of the Russo-Chinese Bank reckoned that it would take a permanent army of 130,000 to hold Fengtian down.[196] The conquest by foreign troops had inevitably given rise to much hatred, and heavy-handed attempts to suppress the ensuing resistance offset any benefit the conquerors might have derived from their sociability or from their individual acts of kindness. Chinese urchins were seen cursing Russian passers-by in the new pidgin tongue. Till at least the beginning of 1903 it remained unsafe for any Russian to venture out at night or to travel around the region without an armed escort.

Even if Manchuria could be pacified there was little likelihood that the Russians would ever be able to administer it by themselves. In Harbin, their own purpose-built city, the 30,000 Russian settlers were outnumbered by a mass of 250,000 Chinese immigrants. In the south of the region the demographic disparity was vastly greater. Kuropatkin, who by February 1903 had come round to supporting the annexation of northern Manchuria, is said to have been just as clear that it would be a futile undertaking to annex the south. Limited numbers aside, the occupiers were hamstrung by a drastic shortage of Chinese-speaking interpreters. By as early as mid-October 1900 Vice-Admiral Alexeev was directing that the day-to-day government of the region should be put back in Qing hands as quickly as possible. The three Manchu military governors were restored to their posts in the provincial capitals of Qiqihar, Jilin and Mukden, attended by three tsarist military commissars, whose status was conceived of as something like that of the British advisers to the Indian princely states but whose practical functions seem to have been confined to exercising a loose supervision over the appointment of the local Manchu top brass. Even then their control was quite tenuous. In Jilin the Qing governor is said to have found ways of manipulating his military commissar, and in Mukden Governor Zengqi, not the most forceful of characters, is nonetheless reported to have kept up a level of obdurate, quiet opposition to Russian decrees. Up until 1902 the Foreign Ministry in St Petersburg maintained a certain V.G. Lyuba as their representative to Manchuria as a whole; but there is little sign that he made any more impact than the provincial advisers. A Russian colleague described him as 'old-fashioned, reminding one of an old butterfly'.[197]

More doubtful still were the prospects for an economic ascendancy. The success of the Russian flour mills in Harbin is said initially to have 'filled the Chinese with envy';[198] but they lost little time in catching up. In 'a sort of counter-invasion' tough Shandong merchants moved into the region, underbidding and undercutting the competition and 'pushing aside the smaller Russian fry'.[199] By 1902 the commercial position of the Russians in Manchuria was judged to be 'precarious'; by 1903 it was 'hopeless'.[200] For every cooperative Tifontai or Zhou Mian the Russian business community were faced with a dozen outright rivals. One hotelier in Harbin complained to Putnam Weale, 'The Chinese have got all the money. We have been spending millions, hundreds of millions, and what have we got for it in return?'[201]

Yellow Russia – or Yellow Peril? From the 1860s onwards Manchuria, as we have seen, had been a springboard for Chinese migrants advancing into Russia's new eastern provinces, and the numbers of migrants had grown exponentially during the last decades of the nineteenth century. In June 1890 Chekhov had written to his friend Alexei Suvorin at the start of a trip to the Far East, 'You begin to encounter Chinese from Irkutsk on.'[202] By 1900 Blagoveshchensk, as we saw, had come to contain some 8,000 Chinese traders and their families, while a total of 36,700 Chinese were reported in Vladivostok, the capital of the Maritime Province. In Khabarovsk more than a third of the inhabitants were by this time Chinese, and in Vladivostok the Chinese community sometimes made up as much as half of the population with the influx of seasonal workers.[203] Many thousands of these migrants were driven out in the backlash that followed the Boxer upheaval, but in 1902 15,000 Chinese were still recorded in Vladivostok as against 11,500 Russian civilians and 13,000 tsarist troops.[204] In the heart of the city, in a district known variously as Semyonovsky Bazaar and Millionka, a prosperous Chinatown had grown up with a Buddhist temple, a club, restaurants and theatres, gambling houses and opium dens; and the police force had felt obliged to create a special Chinese section in order to keep some kind of a grip on community crime. With Russian settlers slow to come out from Europe in spite of all that the government could do to attract them, these Chinese migrants by now played a pivotal role in the local economy. Chinese farmers and market gardeners met the basic settler needs for bread and vegetables: travellers sailing down the Amur remarked on the contrast between the rich Chinese harvests and the 'unkempt fields' of the Cossacks.[205]

Chinese cobblers, dry cleaners and dress designers all did their bit to keep the settlers clothed. Chinese labourers built roads and railways, cut timber, dug wells, mined for coal and iron, put up public buildings and harbour fortifications. Some of the migrants only appeared on a short-term, contractual basis, but others signalled their intention to stay by converting to Orthodoxy and even by marrying Russian wives. And while employers undoubtedly valued this source of cheap and hard-working labour the overall effect was to generate a new Russian fear of a demographic flood. 'The Chinese will take the Amur from us,' Chekhov wrote to Suvorin; 'this is beyond doubt.'[206] In a poem entitled *Pan-Mongolism* that was written in 1894 by the religious philosopher Vladimir Soloviev we find this new demographic fear fused with the persisting strategic dread of a Chinese or Japanese invasion and atavistic memories of the Golden Horde in a single nightmare vision:

From Malayan waters to the Altai
Chieftains from the Eastern isles
At the walls of rebellious China
Gather their hosts.

Like innumerable locusts
And like them insatiable
Protected by occult powers
The tribes head north.

O Russia! Forget your former glory.
The double-headed eagle is smashed
And yellow babes play
With rags remaining from your banners.[207]

Seen in this light, a Russian absorption of Manchuria could only make a dire situation worse. In 1898 War Minister Kuropatkin argued against taking over the region (apart from the Liaodong peninsula) on the grounds that it would result in Russia's existing 'weak colonies' being 'swamped by the flowing tide of yellow'.[208] 'If we abolish the Russo-Chinese border', he pursued two years later, 'and permit the free movement of Chinese into Siberia . . . the Siberian centres would in a short time be Sinicised and the Russians start to be driven beyond the Urals.'[209] The occupation of 1900 was undertaken in part in the hope of creating a buffer zone which could be used to curb any further Chinese infiltration into Russia's Amur and Pacific territories – but the buffer turned out to be more like a funnel. At a meeting held in Khabarovsk in 1903 Russian settlers pressed for a complete ban on Chinese entry into their territories, and 'every speech exhibited utter helplessness in resisting the impending storm'.[210]

Taking into account all these troubles and terrors, it seems likely that the Russian colonial experiment in Manchuria would have had to be given up sooner or later whatever happened. But before the experiment could succumb to its inner contradictions the tsarist rulers had already managed to bring the whole enterprise crashing down on their heads.

Satiety, hubris, destruction, said the ancient Greeks. Not content with Manchuria, the hawks in St Petersburg were starting to look even further afield, to the precariously independent kingdom of Korea. In 1901 a cabal of grand dukes, senior officers and powerful merchants grouped around a mildly unbalanced adventurer, Captain Alexander Bezobrazov, had secured a concession from the court in Seoul entitling them to exploit the rich timber resources on the Korean side of the River Yalu on the Manchuria-Korea border. And this move towards fresh economic and strategic expansion pushed the Japanese over the brink. From Japan's point of view the Russian presence in Manchuria was already bad enough: a grab at Korea, still closer to the Japanese homeland and earmarked as the first target for Japanese empire-building on the Asian continent, was one grab too many. Even as the Russians began to implant their Manchurian colony Japanese intelligence agents were creeping in everywhere, taking advantage of their physical similarity to pose as local Chinese and sometimes even landing jobs with Russian employers. The Russians weren't altogether blind to the danger, and by mid-1903 they had switched the focus of their military operations in the region from quelling local resistance to defending the frontier against Japan. Viceroy Alexeev endeavoured to stand his ground, urging the grand dukes that Russia had to consolidate its grip on Manchuria and there must be no turning back. But in February 1904 the Japanese struck, with a devastating naval attack on the tsarist fleet at Port Arthur. The 'short, victorious war' that had been welcomed by Russia's interior minister as a way to busy giddy minds with foreign quarrels turned out to be one long-drawn-out calamity, as tsarist military might was shattered before the eyes of an astonished world in a series of further Japanese hammer blows, on land at Liaoyang (September 1904) and Mukden (February 1905), and at sea once again in the Straits of Tsushima (May 1905).

Neither Russia nor Japan took the trouble to obtain Qing permission for this war they were fighting over Chinese territory. Both however endeavoured to win the support of the Qing court and the broader Chinese public. The Russians pleaded their cause through a tsarist-sponsored Chinese language newspaper, the *Peking Daily* (*Yandu Ribao*), and the Japanese riposted through the columns of their *Piety Daily* (*Shuntian Ribao*). The Qing government prudently declared their neutrality, informing Alexeev that China proposed 'to look on with her hands in her sleeves' while reminding both combatants that Manchuria was a Chinese possession.[211] But this didn't mean that they didn't have hopes for the outcome. While the sympathies of the Manchu court were reported in spite of everything to be 'still largely with Russia',[212] most of Chinese society seems to have tilted perceptibly to the Japanese side. Yuan Shikai, the powerful governor-general of Zhili Province, who had 50,000 troops on the southern flank of Manchuria, is said to have recommended that the Qing government should declare war on the tsar. Prompted unobtrusively by Morrison of *The Times*, the Chinese press in Peking, Tianjin, Shanghai and Yantai in Shandong embarked on a campaign to discredit the Russo-Chinese Bank, triggering a run on the bank as deposits were withdrawn and Chinese merchants refused to accept the bank's notes. Even before the war started, in 1903, Chinese students in Japan and Shanghai had formed an Anti-Russia Volunteer Corps, who underwent military drills with a view to going to Manchuria and doing battle with the tsarist armies there. The anti-Qing reformist press commented on the initial Russian defeats 'Highly gratifying! Highly gratifying!',[213] and in June 1905 the Qing minister in Korea chortled in a letter to Morrison, 'What a licking the Russians got!'.[214]

In Manchuria itself anti-Russian feeling wasn't sufficiently strong to provoke a wholesale revolt in the Japanese interest. Kuropatkin made a genuine effort to keep the population on side, directing his officers to ensure that requisitions were paid for, that Chinese villagers were treated respectfully and that any troops caught molesting them were severely punished. And not everyone was in a hurry to choose between two alternative sets of foreign invaders. Even so an appreciable number of local Chinese were impelled by resentment of the occupation and by memories of the still recent killings at Blagoveshchensk to assist Japan's advance in one way or another. Chinese interpreters whom the Russians had been driven to hire by their own linguistic inadequacies fed information to the Japanese military. Villagers didn't hand over and sometimes even sheltered Japanese officers who had made their way to the rear of the tsarist armies in Chinese disguise. Above all the soldiers of General Nogi Maresuke were able to draw on the services of the ubiquitous Red Beards. Bands of up to 10,000 *honghuzi* in the pay of Japan and frequently under the command of Japanese officers resumed the harassment of the occupying forces and joined in attacks upon Russian-owned gold and coal mines. At a spot between Port Arthur and the River Yalu they blew up landmines which the Russians had laid to forestall a Japanese descent there, to a loss of some 200 tsarist troops; and in August 1904, with Japanese prodding, they launched attacks on Russian refugees moving into and out of Mukden. After the fall of Liaoyang in September relations between the Russian military and the Chinese population grew markedly worse. Peasants suspected of treachery by the retreating Cossacks were bayonetted or had their huts smashed for firewood; and local people who had aligned themselves with the occupation began to shift their posture as it became obvious that the Japanese would come out on top. Cracks even began to appear in the ranks of Russia's main business partners. Zhou Mian, for example, had issued proclamations at the start of the war enjoining the public to cooperate to the best of their ability with the Russian authorities and the CER. By the autumn of 1904, however, he was passing information to Yuan Shikai, and was even suspected by Russian intelligence of contact with Japan. Thought to have played a role in the murder of Colonel Bogdanov, a tsarist military adviser in the city of Qiqihar, he was dismissed from his post in the Heilongjiang Foreign Affairs Department and eventually made his way out of Manchuria to serve under Yuan. The merchant Tifontai remained loyal – for a price. Occupying the lucrative niche of chief supplier of provisions to the tsarist forces, he offered additionally to recruit for the Russians a special squad of 500 mounted Red Beards whom he would pay out of his own pocket for the first three months. His charge for this service would be 3 million roubles. The Russian commanders are said to have turned down this demand as exorbitant; but Tifontai did apparently form in the end a guerrilla detachment which gathered intelligence and munitions in the Japanese rear.

With or without local backing the Russians were doomed. Already after the fall of Liaoyang Nicholas II had abandoned his grandiose plans for annexing Manchuria. In September 1905 Russian envoys were brought to terms with Japan in the unlikely setting of Portsmouth, New Hampshire, through the good offices of President Theodore Roosevelt. Under the Treaty of Portsmouth the Russians were obliged to transfer to Japan their leasehold on the Liaodong peninsula. All of their property in the south of Manchuria passed into Japanese hands, including the southern spur of the CER from Changchun to Port Arthur which now became known as a separate South Manchurian Railway (SMR). The port of Dalny had its name changed again, to the Japanese Dairen, and southern Manchuria was transformed from a Russian into a Japanese sphere of influence. The dream of a Yellow Russia was shattered, and the memory of the tsarist troops who had died in a gallant but futile attempt to sustain it was preserved only in a Port Arthur cemetery and in the words of a hauntingly melancholy waltz, 'On the Hills of Manchuria'.

ONWARDS AND DOWNWARDS (1905–17)

Following this catastrophe the immediate instinct of the tsarist government was to stop pursuing any active policy in the Far East. Russia, it was felt, should now be shifting its military and financial resources westwards to stifle domestic unrest and to bolster its diplomatic position in Europe. Where China was concerned this entailed giving up the expansionist drive and reverting to the avuncular posture which had served the tsarist rulers so well in previous decades. Nicholas II himself had come round, however reluctantly, to the need for a change of course. 'In China', he affirmed in May 1906, 'we ought not to identify our interests with those of Western Europe: we must endeavour to continue our pre-1898 policy, that is to act pacifically and apart from other countries.'[215] In keeping with this approach Russian diplomats in Peking began to concentrate on rebuilding their old inside track with the Manchu court. The charm offensive was spearheaded by Dmitri Pokotilov, the former Peking manager of the Russo-Chinese Bank who had been appointed Russian minister in Peking in the final months of the Japanese war. Morrison of *The Times* noted that the Chinese liked Pokotilov and 'knew that he understood them'. He had 'the largest knowledge of Chinese gossip and quips and cranks and Chinese games and those little amusements which while away the time at a Chinese dinner'. Morrison acknowledged ruefully that he would have been more comfortable if this skilled China Hand had been appointed minister resident in Paraguay.[216] Dead since 1901, Li Hongzhang was no longer available for tsarist blandishments; but Pokotilov was soon reported to be 'on intimate terms' with Li Lianying, the chief eunuch and favourite of the Empress Dowager.[217]

In the eyes of some Russian observers the two neighbour empires now found themselves substantially in the same boat. Both had been severely weakened by military setbacks; both faced a clear and present danger in the form of Japan, 'the new hordes of Mongols armed by modern technology'.[218] The obvious answer was for them to draw together. One improbable champion of this idea was Dmitri Mendeleev, developer of the Periodic Table of the elements. In his younger days the great chemist had studied Chinese education and agriculture and had steeped himself in the works of Vasiliev and other leading Russian Sinologists. Like Vasiliev he believed that China, technologically backward as it was, would emerge in due course as a leading world power; like Tolstoy he judged that China was in many ways ahead of Europe in spiritual terms. In *Cherished Thoughts*, a book published in 1905, he argued that Russia and China should form 'a peaceful and protective alliance', since 'the closer our alliance with China the less likely will be the triumph of the Japanese fervour'.[219] But this inching towards solidarity of both officials and intellectuals was rapidly swept aside by harder-edged calculations.

The fact was that Russia was down but not out. The Treaty of Portsmouth had still left the tsar the sphere of influence Witte had negotiated in northern Manchuria before the lunge for expansion in 1898. The defeat by Japan doesn't seem to have discouraged Russian settlement in the region, and by 1906 the settler population is said to have 'passed the 100,000 mark'. In particular Russia was still in possession of the CER, that vital, fragile railway which formed the sole link between Siberia and the Far Eastern provinces, had attracted over 440 million roubles in Russian investment capital, and included the CER Railway Zone that accommodated about half of the Russian settler community.[220] Russian officials did now take some measures to make their control of the railway a little more palatable. In 1906 General Dmitri Khorvat, the CER general manager, gave orders to his railway guards and managers to be more polite to the Chinese passengers. But whatever the views of the Qing the tsarist authorities were determined to hold on to the

CER like grim death. In the same year they resumed their purchasing of land in the Railway Zone. A special conference was called in St Petersburg 'for the examination of questions touching upon the function of the CER',[221] with the task of working out legislation to regularise the status of the Railway Zone – at the expense of Qing sovereignty.

Where Japan was concerned an alliance with China to check its advance wasn't necessarily the most attractive way forward. An alternative option presented itself – *if you can't beat 'em, join 'em*. At the end of December 1906 Foreign Minister Alexander Izvolsky took the first step towards a rapprochement with Tokyo, informing the Japanese minister in St Petersburg that if Russia could only be given a solid guarantee of peace with Japan, 'we shall not hesitate to make even more concessions'.[222] The Japanese for their part signalled their readiness to let bygones be bygones, unveiling in Port Arthur a monument to the Russian dead of the late war at a ceremony presided over by General Nogi himself. In May 1907 the Japanese Foreign Ministry advised the tsarist ambassador in Tokyo that his country had no desire to oppose the furtherance of Russian interests in *Mongolia*; and in July the two powers concluded a secret agreement confirming their respective spheres of influence in northern and southern Manchuria and recognising Outer (northern) Mongolia as a special Russian concern. Two years later, in November 1909, Japan raised the stakes sharply, proposing through its minister in St Petersburg a formal alliance before which 'not only China but all the powers would have to bow'.[223] This startling new alignment offered two major benefits from the tsarist point of view. At a time of mounting tension in Europe it would protect the Russians from a deadly Japanese attack in their rear – Japanese forces, the military experts reckoned, could take Vladivostok in a few days and the entire Amur Province in a couple of weeks. And it held out to the tsar and his ministers the prospect of 'returning to the Far East',[224] of resuming their abandoned expansionist project albeit within certain definite limits imposed by Japan. Izvolsky passed on to the tsar his recommendation that Russia and Japan should combine to pursue a joint guardianship over 'Manchuria and ultimately the whole of China';[225] and Nicholas, a hawk once more, concurred that a 'hard and fast agreement with Japan' was just what was needed.[226] Russia was back on the imperial path. A second Russo-Japanese treaty, signed in July 1910, provided for joint action by the two powers to forestall any challenge by foreign (notably United States) business interests to the railway monopolies they enjoyed in Manchuria. A third, in July 1912, marked out fresh spheres of influence in western Manchuria and in Inner (southern) Mongolia. And a fourth and final convention negotiated in July 1916 against the background of the First World War established a fully fledged military alliance between the two powers intended to stop China falling under the influence of any third party that might be hostile to them. This climactic agreement in theory gave Russia Japan's blessing to intervene in any part of the Chinese dominions at a time when the attention of all other foreign powers was distracted by the European war. But in practice the chief benefit for the tsarist regime of the series of deals was the free hand it gave them to operate in their new Mongolian stamping ground.

This central panel of the borderland triptych had been relatively neglected during the years Russia worked to secure its economic and political grip on Xinjiang and Manchuria. Under the Treaty of St Petersburg which wrapped up the Yili crisis in 1881 the tsarist government had been accorded the right to open a string of consulates in Mongolia, and Russian merchants had been permitted to trade there duty-free. But Russians were slow to appear in the region, and it was many years before they posed a significant challenge to the Chinese trading community. By the late 1890s, however, the Mongolian grasslands were starting to be allotted their place in the tsarist programme of expansion. Witte and his planners began to consider the possibility of pushing a railway through Mongolia to Peking. When the British negotiated with Russia the demarcation of the two powers' spheres of influence in the Qing empire in April 1899 the finance minister scrawled on a copy of the British proposals, '*And what about Mongolia?*'.[227] In 1900 the Russo-Chinese Bank provided funds for the creation of Mongolor, a joint stock enterprise designed to exploit the region's colossal resources of gold, iron and other minerals. Operations took time to get going, but by 1906 extraction from a number of Mongolian gold mines was well under way. Russian ascendancy in the region was symbolised by the Green House, the tsarist consulate which sat perched on an eminence in the chief Mongol settlement, Urga, midway between the Chinese and Mongolian quarters of the town.

And just as the old Cossack pioneers of the seventeenth century redirected their advance to the Mongolian steppes after being driven from the Amur basin by the Treaty of Nerchinsk, so Nicholas II and his ministers in turn switched their gaze from Manchuria to Mongolia after their rout in the

Russo-Japanese war. Their overriding thought was strategic. The defeat by Japan had left the tsarist government keenly aware of their strategic vulnerability along the whole length of their Asian frontier. Flanking as it did a vast stretch of central Siberia, Mongolia represented a tempting route for an enemy seeking to cut the all-important Trans-Siberian Railway; unless, that is, it could somehow be converted into a safe buffer area. Looked at from this angle Mongolia offered one or two clear advantages that Manchuria lacked. In the first place Russians seeking to build up a presence there wouldn't be in danger of getting submerged in a sea of Chinese. The Qing government had indeed started to think of filling Mongolia with demographic cement in the same way they had the north-east, and a Colonisation Bureau was set up for that purpose in 1906; but the infiltration procedure was slower than it had been in Manchuria, and on a much smaller scale. Secondly Russia could count on a significant measure of goodwill from the native population. The Khalkha Mongols chafed more than ever at Manchu taxes and the demands of Chinese moneylenders, and looked more than ever to Russia as a source of salvation. Nomads in the west of the region even cherished a myth that the last Dzungar leader, Amursana, was still alive on Russian territory, awaiting the time when he would return, like King Arthur, and call up snowstorms and rainstorms to confound his Qing foes. In August 1911 opportunity knocked at the Russian door. A deputation of princes from Outer Mongolia arrived in St Petersburg to request Russian arms and support in their struggle for independence. The immediate Russian reaction was cautious. The prime minister, Pyotr Stolypin, and his cabinet didn't want to take drastic action that might upset the traditional ties with the Qing they had worked to rebuild over the last few years, and nor did they want to arouse the alarm of their new-found Japanese partners. They were prepared to support a campaign by the Mongol princes to 'preserve their distinctiveness' in the face of Chinese encroachment;[228] but they would not give their backing to a fully fledged breakaway movement, and they would not provide arms.

Opportunity knocked again, and this time more loudly. On 9 October a band of dissident Chinese officers in the Yangtze city of Hankou (in the Russian concession, as it happened) accidentally detonated a bomb in a butcher's shop they were using as headquarters and arsenal for an armed uprising against the Qing. The effect of the accident was to make them bring forward the start of their uprising to the very next day; and the effect of that uprising, spreading fast through the country, was to bring down at long last, after nearly three centuries, the alien Manchu regime. In November the princes of Outer Mongolia seized their chance to declare independence from the emerging Chinese Republic, on the grounds that while they had formed part of a multi-ethnic Qing empire they could scarcely be expected to accept transformation into a mere province of a Chinese national state. The tsarist ministers now found themselves confronted by a whole new scenario. The decrepit Qing empire which they had tried to prop up for the greater part of the time since the late 1850s was now being replaced by a weak and chaotic republican government, and the border zones with their restive minority peoples were up for grabs. The first steps were at once taken to lend support to the Mongol independence campaign. On the orders of the war minister, Vladimir Sukhomlinov, a consignment of 15,000 rifles, 15,000 sabres and 7 million cartridges was dispatched in December from the Irkutsk military district to the Russian consul in Urga for delivery to the Mongol rebel leaders. When the main Qing official in the region, the *amban*, took refuge in the Green House the consul refused to help him reassert his position, and instead packed him off to the old Russian trading post of Kyakhta with an escort of Cossack troops. Some tsarist generals were even said to be licking their lips at the prospect of annexing the entire massive region. As the months passed, however, it became clear that Russia couldn't after all throw its weight behind Mongolian independence in the fullest sense of the word. Foreign Minister Sergei Sazonov was thinking of his country's future relations with China, always ultimately more important in Russian minds than the gains to be had from supporting the minorities in between; and after the Manchurian failure the costs of occupying Mongolia seemed too enormous to contemplate. Instead the tsarist government went for a subtler gambit, presenting themselves as the champions of Mongol autonomy. In November 1912 they concluded with the princes at Urga a Russo-Mongolian agreement committing them to train a Mongol army which could be used to keep out Chinese soldiers and colonists, and a Russo-Mongolian Commercial Treaty granting them the whole gamut of mining, lumbering and fishing rights; explaining, however, to the Chinese minister in St Petersburg that they had no intention of letting Outer Mongolia break off completely from China providing the Chinese respected the deals they had made. One year later, in November 1913, Yuan Shikai, the Qing general who had emerged as the president of the new Chinese Republic, was induced to sign a Sino-Russian Declaration confirming the autonomy of Outer Mongolia under nominal Chinese suzerainty. 'Severe threats and pressures' are said to have been applied to secure this outcome, and Russian recognition of Yuan's presidency was indeed made conditional on his playing along.[229] And in June 1915 the entire arrangement was reaffirmed in a tripartite Chinese-Russian-Mongolian Treaty signed, with a due nod to history, at Kyakhta. Taking advantage of the feebleness of the new republican China, and with the tacit acquiescence of Japan, the tsarist government had once again sawn off a panel of the border triptych; and this time without firing a shot.

During these same years the Orthodox Mission enjoyed a brief golden age as Bishop Innocent's operations reached into the depths of central and southern China. One missionary dispatched to Hubei near the Yangtze found local villagers ready to accept 'with complete credence' the Orthodox Word of God ('but you cannot easily get them to understand what it is all about'[230]), while Pavel Tang, a catechist, embarked on a costly and tiring journey by steamship to his south-eastern posting in Fujian. The diplomat Pokotilov, who is said to have loathed Bishop Innocent, disapproved of this drive to win converts, writing caustically that he had always considered the absence of missionaries to be 'one of the serious advantages' of the Russian position in China.[231] And the Orthodox drive was in any case puny compared with the substantial inroads being made by the Mission's Roman Catholic and Protestant rivals. The Mission were nonetheless able to report, by the end of 1915, a record total of 5,587 Chinese converts in Peking and six provinces in the north and centre of the country – further evidence, in its own small way, of late tsarist bullishness.[232]

Russia's renewed forward movement, however, collided head-on with a new local truculence. The Russian empire's defeat by Japan, the first all-out trouncing of a European by a non-European power, had made a deep impact in China, as it had in many parts of the non-European world. Even the feeble Qing court did their best to exploit the discovery that the tsarist colossus had feet of clay. Already by 1905 they were cautiously trying to reassert their authority over the CER Railway Zone, and the following year they gave voice to strong protests at a first Russian effort to introduce a statute of civil government there. They proclaimed their refusal to recognise any concessions obtained by the tsarist authorities during their occupation of Manchuria, and insisted on the surrender of the Russian stake in Mohe and the other Manchurian gold mines. In 1907 they went so far as to demand the return to Qing jurisdiction of the Sixty-Four Settlements on the Russian side of the border. When the thirty-year-old Treaty of St Petersburg came up for renewal at the beginning of 1911 the Qing Foreign Ministry unexpectedly jibbed, seeking changes intended to claw back the benefits which the old document had conferred on Russian subjects in Xinjiang and Mongolia. The number of Russian consulates, they proposed, should be slashed, and Russian traders deprived of the tax-exempt status and extra-territorial rights they had enjoyed in both regions.

A still sharper backlash was apparent among the Chinese nationalists who opposed the Qing dynasty. Chinese nationalist intellectuals had now come to focus their anger at the foreign domination of their homeland rather specifically at the tsarist empire, which they perceived as a land of darkness – corrupt, despotic and backward into the bargain. Chinese students residing in Tokyo in May 1911 were said to fear Russia more than any other foreign power. This attitude was maintained in full measure by the nationalist insurrection which swept away the Qing rulers the following autumn. The stealthy tsarist detachment of Outer Mongolia was bitterly resented, and outbreaks of Russophobe bile were reported from Chinese communities all over the borderlands. In Xinjiang, for example, by the end of 1912 regular diatribes were being directed at Russia in the Chinese-language press, and the following summer Brigadier Yang Zuanxu, who had led the nationalist rising in Yili, was seizing 'every opportunity to express his anti-Russian sentiments'.[233] The Russian editor of the CER's Chinese-language paper received a barrage of insulting and hostile letters, including four death threats.

Neither the failing Qing Empire nor its chaotic republican successor state were in any position to fend off tsarist pressures by political or military means. But they still had their demographic weapon. From 1905 onwards the Qing government took steps to speed up the influx of Chinese migrants into northern Manchuria as a contribution towards their ultimate goal of reclaiming the CER. And the attempts by the Russians to push forward their influence in China were offset by a countervailing increase in Russian dependence upon the Chinese. A British journalist reporting from Harbin in 1907 expected that the Chinese traders there would before long 'eat up the Russians by subtle economics'.[234] Russians continued to manage the flour mills, but it was the Chinese farmer who made the money on account of the high price of wheat. 'The Chinese thrive everywhere the Russians live,' a correspondent of the English-language *North China Herald* reported in 1913, 'and Harbin is no exception.'[235] And as Manchuria came more and more to depend on Chinese enterprise for its economic output, so the Russian Far East was dependent on Manchuria for the grain, meat and soya beans it consumed and exported, and on Manchurian Chinese labour for much of its infrastructure. By 1910 over 150,000 impoverished Chinese workers were active in the Amur and Maritime provinces, laying out a new railway that would supplement the CER by looping round the Amur on the Russian side of the border and building a commercial port for Vladivostok.[236] With the outbreak of the First World War four years later the desperate tsarist need for manpower to replace the industrial workforce being mobilised for the struggle against Germany and its allies brought Chinese labourers all the way into European Russia. Between 1914 and 1917 an estimated 200,000 Chinese contract workers were imported into Russia to help with the war effort – a figure even higher than the 135,000 who were deployed by the western Allies in France and Belgium.[237] These Chinese reinforcements toiled variously in the coal mines of the Donbass, in the Baku oilfields and the Petrograd steel mills. From Petrograd they constructed a railway north to the shores of the Arctic, where they helped to set up the new port of Murmansk to meet the needs of a putative tsarist naval flotilla. Up to 50,000 were assigned, in defiance of the terms of their contracts, to the Eastern Front, where they were put to work digging trenches and transporting munitions.[238] Some of these labourers went on to take root in the cities of European Russia in much the same way they had done in the Russian Far East. In Murmansk they established themselves in a district that soon became known as 'Shanghai'. And both there and in Moscow they eked out a precarious living as purveyors of moonshine.[239]

The effect was that even now, at a time when Russia's industrial and military superiority remained overwhelming, its underlying dread of China would not go away. In 1909 the plan for a second railway to loop round the Amur as a back-up for the CER was conceived of as providing against an attack by either China or Japan, or still worse, both at once. In February 1911 the tsarist government responded to the Qing demands for revision of the Treaty of St Petersburg in a 'forcible, peremptory and minatory' manner,[240] staging armed demonstrations on the borders of both Xinjiang and Mongolia; but when Morrison of *The Times* made a trip to St Petersburg, and later when he called on the Russian legation in Peking, he found on every side 'an insane fear of the Chinese'.[241] The first secretary of the legation asked whether his visitor was aware that the Qing had mobilised two divisions on the Xinjiang frontier, complete with two Maxim guns. Morrison thought this apprehension excessive, given that he had personally just crossed the frontier at the town of Sharasume and found there a Qing garrison of just 126 scruffy and poorly armed troops: a friend had remarked to him that 'a dozen London washerwomen would account for the lot'.[242] Three or four marauding Red Beards in Heilongjiang, he observed, were blown up by the Russian press into 300 or 400 – this at a time when Russia was believed to have at its disposal 150,000 troops to the east of Lake Baikal. The refusal of Stolypin's cabinet to tangle with the moribund Qing regime over Mongolia in the summer of 1911 may be understood partly in the context of this terrified mindset. Russian ministers also perceived that a more vigorous China was on the way, and they didn't entirely care for the prospect. Foreign Minister Sazonov told Morrison that he wanted to see '*a happy and a contented and a prosperous China – but not a strong China*'.[243] As the new Chinese Republic got unsteadily to its feet tsarist officials watched with alarm the stirrings of a new, revolutionary spirit. Even the priests shared the panic. Bishop Innocent took the view that only the widespread diffusion of Orthodoxy in China could save the Russian empire from 'a new and terrible Mongol invasion';[244] and the head of his mission station in Henan Province wrote nervously of his anticipated converts, 'We shall baptise them with water, and they will baptise us with boiling oil.'[245] When news of Russian mobilisation seeped through to Cossack settlers in Semipalatinsk on the southern fringe of Siberia in July 1914 the assumption was that the tsarist regime had pushed too far in their lunge for Mongolia and that China, not Germany, had declared war.

Chinese economic advance bred the same deep disquiet. In July 1910 the authorities tried to hold back the influx of migrants by banning the use of Chinese labour on state engineering projects in the Russian Far East – unavailingly, as it turned out, since private construction firms were quite happy to take on the Chinese instead. The governor of Amur Province,

Nikolai Gondatti, who saw his task as ensuring that his jurisdiction contained 'lots of Russians and very few yellows',[246] expressed his belief that 'the Chinese suck dry our state and natural resources and bring nothing except harm'.[247] And the peasants in Siberia had their own dark saying: '*When China approaches, drop your ploughs and your harrows*.'[248]

Far away from the stressed borderlands, in St Petersburg, Moscow and the other cities of European Russia, a number of intellectuals continued to regard the Chinese in a positive light. Some of the writers who during the first two decades of the twentieth century made up the so-called Silver Age of Russian literature found in China a focus for their fascination with the mystical and the exotic. At approximately the same time that Arthur Waley in England was embarking on his translations of Tang and Song dynasty poems the Symbolist poet Konstantin Balmont tried his hand at composing verses in Chinese style:

> What can be more beautiful than China?
> Here even a quarrel is picturesque,
> And an instant dream shines like a firefly.
>
> To sit for centuries and drink a fragrant tea
> With a Chinese lady in front of me;
> The whole world is one floral heaven.[249]

In 1910 the great theatre director Vsevolod Meyerhold applied the principles of Chinese drama on the Russian stage for the first time in his production of *A Family of Hidden Secrets*, and in 1913 at the Moscow Free Theatre Alexander Tairov used the forms of classical Chinese opera to stage an American play, *The Yellow Riding Jacket*. In the border regions themselves the relaxed informality with which some Russians dealt with some Chinese during the occupation of Manchuria was still reported in places right up to the First World War. General Khorvat, the manager of the CER, and his wife are said to have built up a personal friendship with Zhao Erxun, the last Qing viceroy of Manchuria. In the autumn of 1911 the Khorvats paid a visit to Viceroy Zhao in Mukden, after which Mme Khorvat stayed on at the viceroy's residence for a further three weeks, with a lack of inhibition probably unique for the wife of a European official in China at the time. Dr Budberg, a Harbin physician, converted to Buddhism and went about in a

Chinese gown. At the foot of the social scale Russian settlers quite often seemed happy to throw in their lot with Chinese migrants, in some cases going all the way to intermarriage. 'The Russian woman', a British visitor to the Maritime Province remarked on the eve of the war, does not object to the Chinese as a husband, and the Russian takes a Chinese wife.'[250]

One or two Chinese managed to carve themselves a professional niche in the distant reaches of European Russia. A young man named Liu Zerong, whose father had been brought out of China in the mid-1890s to demonstrate tea cultivation in the northern Caucasus, grew up in the tsarist empire and studied architectural engineering at the University of St Petersburg before taking a job as a teacher of mathematics in a secondary school. Yang Mingzhai, who had started off in 1901 as a migrant labourer in Vladivostok, had by 1907 moved to Moscow and embarked on an accountancy course. Chinese traders in the Russian Far East and northern Manchuria seem to have made a genuine effort to fit in with their Russian neighbours, adopting Russian or Ukrainian dress and hiring Russian language tutors for their children, with the result that some at least were able to establish themselves on a socially comfortable footing.

Overall, though, the trajectory of relations in the eight decades from 1840 on was unmistakably downwards. At the start of that period the governments of the two powers had looked on each other with genuine, if sometimes wary, respect. By the end of it the official Russian perception of China was characterised by a mixture of arrogance and apprehension, the Chinese perception of Russia by impotent rage. At the grass-roots level we have to weigh the occasional glimpses of friendly hobnobbing in Harbin or Khabarovsk against the dark record of Boxer atrocities and the slaughter at Blagoveshchensk. Against the modest social advancement of a Liu Zerong or a Yang Mingzhai must be set the grim memories of Chinese navvies in the tundra near Murmansk, who recalled 'eating black bread and drinking marsh water that had turned black',[251] and of Chinese lumberjacks in the forests of central Russia who were expected to work without shoes or warm clothing at the onset of winter and who were beaten with leather straps by the tsarist police when they ventured into neighbouring villages to forage for food. Individual contacts had indeed multiplied, and sometimes even prospered, since the mid-nineteenth century; but there isn't much sign that this had led to a broad increase in the understanding of one population by the other. After the relative of a migrant who had died in St Petersburg sent his body off home to be buried in keeping with Chinese custom, packed in salt to make sure that it didn't decompose on the way, Russians all over the empire are said to have taunted Chinese with the question, '*Friend, do you want salt?*'.[252] Chinese are said to have looked down on Russians as 'curious Arctic creatures, covered in long hair and dressed in heavy furs',[253] and referred to them as the *lao maozi*, the Old Hairy Ones. Legend had it that the Russians were particularly impulsive and uncontrolled foreigners, that their sweat even smelt more strongly than the sweat of other Europeans.[254] By the second decade of the twentieth century the prospects for constructive interaction between the two peoples appeared somewhat dismal. But history had a trick up its sleeve.

CHAPTER 4

LIGHTHOUSE OF THE MIND'S SEA

DISCOVERING THE OTHER RUSSIA (1890–1920)

In 1894 a traveller named Konstantin Vyazemsky reported having talked, seemingly at some place in the Russian Far East, with a Chinese who had heard of Tolstoy. This anonymous Chinese even mentioned by name the author's controversial novella published five years previously, *The Kreutzer Sonata*. Many of his compatriots, he declared, were familiar with Tolstoy's works, or were studying Russian in order to keep abreast of Tolstoy's latest writings. Ten years later, in December 1905, a certain Zhang Qingtong, yet another of the handful of educated Chinese who were scattered about in late tsarist Russia, sent a letter to Tolstoy at his country estate of Yasnaya Polyana. Zhang was writing to convey his admiration for 'the great author of the Russian land'. He 'dared to suppose' that if Tolstoy's works were translated into Chinese they would produce 'a great revolution in our attitude to Russia', and announced his intention of translating a selection of them.[1] As evidence of his linguistic skills he enclosed a translation he had made into Russian, with the help of a Russian Sinologist, of a book on modern Chinese history by the reformer Liang Qichao.

These incidents formed part of an unexpected Chinese discovery of Russian literature. There were as yet no facilities for any kind of cultural exploration of Russia in China itself. The School of Foreign Languages which had been set up by the Qing government in 1862 had been concerned solely with the pragmatic training of diplomats and interpreters. But as Chinese students made their way to Japan and other foreign countries they began to encounter translations, in Japanese, German and English, of the Russian nineteenth-century classics which they proceeded to retranslate into Chinese. In 1900 a Chinese version appeared of Krylov's *Fables*, and in 1903 it was followed by a rendering of Pushkin's short story, *The Captain's Daughter*. In 1909 seven translations of Russian tales were included in a pioneering collection of *Stories from Abroad* published in Japan by two brothers: Zhou Shuren, who would later mature into the brilliant Chinese short story writer and essayist Lu Xun, and Zhou Zuoren, who would also become a distinguished man of letters; and by 1911, when the Qing dynasty toppled, Chinese versions had been produced of some twenty short Russian fictional works. Various writers received the attention of the translators, including both Chekhov and Gorky, but it was visibly Tolstoy who made the most powerful impact on the Chinese intellectual world. In August 1908 a group of Shanghai intellectuals joined in cabling congratulations to the Russian literary giant on the completion of his 'eightieth journey around the sun'.[2]

This was more than a matter of cultural taste. In reaching out to Tolstoy and the other great masters the Chinese intelligentsia were making contact for the first time with the Other Russia – the Russia of mavericks and oppositionists who had so often voiced a distant sympathy for China's suffering at the hands of the Manchus and the foreign imperial powers, including the tsarist regime. In reading Tolstoy in particular they learnt for the first time that Russian society was not so different from their own but contained, as theirs did, a downtrodden underclass of peasants and slum dwellers. And they looked, consequently, to this Other Russia for moral support in their efforts to construct a more bearable future. In the letter he wrote to Tolstoy in December 1905 Zhang Qingtong emphasised his perception of Sino-Russian affinity. China and Russia, he noted, were both relatively backward by comparison with the western European countries, and it followed that the 'phenomena of Russian life' must be less alien to China than they were to the west. In particular the 'evolution of the Russian state system', the social upheaval which had broken out in the tsarist empire after the defeat by Japan and had led to some limited reform of the constitution, must be 'reflected to a greater degree in China than in Europe'. The 1905 revolution had shown that the harsher the regime was, the greater must be the demand of the people for an 'upsurge of ideas'.[3] In March 1906 a similar overture was made to Tolstoy by Gu Hongming, a scholar and civil servant of Malayan Chinese origin who was currently employed as director of the Huangpu River Authority in Shanghai. Gu accompanied his greetings with a book entitled *Papers from a Viceroy's Yamen* in which he pleaded 'the cause of good government and true civilisation' and a pamphlet he had written about 'the moral and ethical causes of the Russo–Japanese War'.[4] He set out for Tolstoy's contemplation his proposals for an overhaul of China's social and economic life, including the rapid development of an independent Chinese industry, a modernisation of agriculture, an introduction of the latest breakthroughs in science and technology and a reform of the administration – this last, however, qualified by his staunch allegiance to the Qing monarchical order.

Other Chinese, impelled by their passion to overthrow the Manchus, found in Russia a template for opposition of a more drastic kind. In 1894 Dr Sun Yat-sen, the physician who had emerged as the spearhead of the Chinese nationalist movement, made the acquaintance in London of Felix Volkhovsky, a veteran revolutionary whose anti-tsarist activities dated back to the 1860s and who was currently heading a group of exiles from the newly formed Russian Social Democratic and Labour Party (SDLP). Sun was struck to observe that in both planning and revolutionary spirit Volkhovsky's operation appeared more advanced than his own. In the first years of the new century discontented Chinese were enthralled by the Russian Nihilists and the bomb-throwing exploits they spoke of as their 'propaganda of the deed'. When the tsarist minister of the interior Vyacheslav Plehve was assassinated in 1904 even the moderate Liang Qichao chortled, 'Great is the dagger! Holy the bomb!'[5] A passion developed for stories of Nihilist feats in the form of both translated English accounts of actual incidents and home-grown 'Nihilist novels'. A cult in particular grew up around the figure of Sophia Perovskaya, the woman Nihilist who was sent to the gallows for her part in the murder of Tsar Alexander II in 1881, and her example was invoked by the feminist Qiu Jin, beheaded by the Qing authorities for her involvement in a revolutionary plot. According to one source the Russian Revolution of 1905 helped to inspire the formation in Tokyo that August by Sun and his followers of a new United League (*Tongmenhui*) which brought together for the first time a motley assortment of anti-Qing groups.[6] This claim has been disputed; but it seems at least certain that by March 1907 one of Sun's lieutenants, Huang Xing, was in touch with anti-tsarist exiles in Japan, and a vague agreement was reached that whichever side toppled their monarchy soonest should lend help to the other. In the event the Chinese activists won the race with their 1911 revolution, but were in no state, amid the confusion and power-grabbing of the early republic, to hold out a hand to kindred spirits on the other side of their northern frontier. Instead they went on drinking in the alluring ideas which continued to flow out of the Other Russia. In 1916–20, for instance, a craze reached its peak for the works of the Russian anarchists Mikhail Bakunin and Prince Peter Kropotkin. One teenager with literary aspirations, Li Yaotang, was intoxicated by his reading of Kropotkin's *Appeal to the Young*. Later he would adopt the pen name of Ba Jin, derived from the first syllable of Bakunin's name and the last (in Chinese) of Kropotkin's.

In his responses to Zhang Qingtong and Gu Hongming Tolstoy showed himself still immersed in his dreams of a Chinese utopia. He continued to believe that China's salvation lay in maintaining the peaceful agrarian way of life prescribed in the classics of Confucianism, Daoism and Buddhism. He was firmly against China carrying out any modernisation along western lines, political, industrial or military, which he saw as a recipe for 'malice, irritation and unceasing strife'.[7] At the same time he made a number of encouraging noises from Zhang's and Gu's point of view. He judged that the time had come for the Chinese to 'look for ways of liberating themselves' from the despotic power of the Qing, the depredations of Qing officials and the greed of the European and Japanese predators – always provided they followed his cherished approach of non-violence.[8] Leaders of the active Russian political opposition to tsarism were a good deal less equivocal. When the Qing dynasty was overthrown at the end of 1911 and Sun Yat-sen emerged briefly as president of the Chinese Republic, Pavel Milyukov, the head of the liberal Constitutional Democrats ('Kadets') in the post-1905 Russian parliament, praised Sun's achievement and criticised tsarist encroachments in Manchuria and Mongolia, only to be labelled by his conservative adversaries 'the Chinese representative in the State Duma'.[9] In an article published in July 1912 Vladimir Ilyich Lenin, exiled leader of the hardline Bolshevik faction of the SDLP, conceived the possibility of an alliance between a future socialist Russia and Sun in his capacity as a 'revolutionary democrat'. Writing four months later in his party newspaper, *Pravda*, Lenin added the thought that 'a quarter of the world's population have passed, so to say, from torpor to enlightenment, movement and struggle'.[10]

Here and there some quite ordinary Chinese were beginning to notice the changes in Russia and even to participate in Russian events. From 1906 onwards Chinese labourers were joining in strikes launched by their Russian counterparts working on the Chinese Eastern Railway and other enterprises in Russian-dominated northern Manchuria. In January 1907, for instance, a Bolshevik agitator named Boris Shumyatsky called for strike action to mark the second anniversary of the 'Bloody Sunday' massacre of protesters in St Petersburg that had triggered the anti-tsarist convulsion of 1905. Shumyatsky spoke first to the Russian workforce and then, using the local Sino-Russian patois, to the Chinese, a portion of whom replied in broken Russian, 'Russian Tsar kill Russian workers so we no work.'[11] By 1912 joint cooperatives of Chinese and Russian workers had appeared once again on the upper Amur in a solidarity reminiscent of the short-lived 'Zheltuga Republic' of the 1880s (the participants were even known nostalgically as *Zheltugintsy*). Subversion was also spreading among Chinese who had found occupations in Siberia and the Russian Far East. In 1908 a man named Ren Fuchen, who had been employed as an interpreter for the tsarist forces during the Russo–Japanese war and had later worked as a teacher in a Russian army school, is said to have been the first Chinese to join the Bolshevik Party. Dodging arrest by the tsarist secret police, the Okhrana, Ren was assigned the task of helping Russian Bolsheviks sent to serve prison terms in Siberia to escape across the Manchu frontier. In December 1914, following the large-scale engagement of contract labourers from the new Chinese Republic to bolster the tsarist empire's workforce in the First World War, he was given the further task of fomenting disaffection among a group of 2,000 Chinese toiling on railway and lumbering projects at Perm in the Urals. Whether his activity extended any further than that is unclear, but in 1915–17 Chinese workers undoubtedly rose up in violent protest against their appalling conditions both in the Urals and beyond them, from a railway station north of St Petersburg to a gold mine near Odessa on the Black Sea coast.

In 1917 Russia finally arrived at its watershed, when the tsarist monarchy toppled and was replaced by the liberal-minded Provisional Government, and the latter in turn was replaced eight months later in the seizure of power by Lenin's Bolsheviks. These events found a rapid response among both Chinese in the Russian sphere of Manchuria and the Chinese scattered around Russia proper. 'Inter-ethnic euphoria' was reported when news of the fall of the tsar got through to Harbin.[12] In April Liu Zerong, the young man we last met teaching mathematics in a Petrograd secondary school, joined forces with eight Chinese students to organise a Union of Chinese Citizens in Russia, with the object of looking after the interests of the mass of Chinese contract workers who had been left without jobs or direction by the upheaval. The new union was duly registered with the Provisional Government; but Liu's sympathies seem already to have lain with the emerging Bolsheviks, and his union indeed received a donation of 3,000 roubles from the leading woman Bolshevik, Alexandra Kollontai. By December 1918 the union had mutated into a Union of Chinese Workers, and Liu and his colleagues were reported to be 'working hand in hand' with the new Soviet Russian regime.[13] By May 1920 we find mention of a 'Moscow Central Orgburo [Organisational Bureau] of Chinese Communists',[14] and in August Liu received Lenin's personal blessing for the publication in Russia of a Chinese- language newspaper called *Great Equality*. And in the meantime, as Russia descended into civil war between the Red Army and the loose assortment of tsarist loyalists, constitutional monarchists, liberal republicans and revolutionary sectarians known as the Whites, an estimated total of 40,000 to 50,000 displaced Chinese labourers flocked of their own accord to the Soviet banner. Fighting on all the fronts, in central Russia, the Baltic, the Ukraine and the Caucasus, they were also charged by their Red superiors with a number of special responsibilities, including the defence of the Smolny Institute, the Bolshevik headquarters in Petrograd, and of the Kremlin in Moscow – and the physical safety of Lenin himself. According to one account former Chinese contract workers made up no fewer than seventy of the 200 members of Lenin's bodyguard. Lenin is said to have looked with some favour upon these Chinese adherents; but it also seems clear that the Chinese were viewed as a good bet from the point of view of security insofar as they were unlikely to be connected by any personal ties to unreliable Russians or to entertain any sentimental feelings towards them. In November 1918, we are told, a Red Army commander named Dmitri Oskin formed a special brigade of Chinese to help him take reprisals against a group of deserters in the Tula region, on the grounds that the Chinese would be 'more merciless' than the 'soft-hearted Russians'.[15] By 1919 the new Bolshevik secret police force, the Cheka, had recruited a contingent of 700 Chinese agents who were employed to arrest White troops and carry out executions in cases where the Red rank and file refused to do so.

Some displaced Chinese labourers fought on the White side as well. When Admiral Kolchak, briefly recognised by the various White groups as Supreme Ruler of All the Russias, was shot by the Reds at Omsk in February 1920, the same firing squad dispatched a lieutenant of his named Cheng Tingfan, whose exploits were said to have earned him the epithet of 'the hangman'.[16] Up in the Arctic north a contingent of 219 Chinese, part of the workforce brought there by the Murmansk railway project, attached themselves to a 'Slav British Legion' set up by the Whites to help the expedition which Britain had sent to intervene in the conflict on their behalf. The White leaders, however, made little sustained attempt to recruit Chinese soldiers and instead preferred to strike a xenophobic posture, depicting the Chinese along with the Latvians and other minorities as foreign ogres deployed by the Reds to spy on and brutalise the Russian people. In the Don country controlled by General Anton Denikin the Cossacks are said to have arrested all the Chinese they could find before packing them off to unknown destinations. It is unclear just how many Chinese rallied to the White armies, but their numbers were certainly small compared with the tens of thousands who joined up with the Reds.

This early ripple of Chinese support for the Bolshevik cause should be kept in perspective. Even the more educated of the Chinese flotsam in Russia such as Liu Zerong seem not to have had an in-depth understanding of the new Marxist creed. One circular issued in July 1920 by the new 'Moscow Central Orgburo of Chinese Communists' reads like a curious mish-mash of Marxist and Confucian thinking, with a dash of St Paul's Epistles thrown in for good measure: 'You should not quarrel among yourselves, comrades, you should respect each other; you should not insult or cheat each other but unite strongly, go firmly hand in hand and help each other.'[17] As for the ex-contract labourers, the vast majority of them knew nothing about Communism, or Soviets, or trades unions. The slide into civil war had left them destitute in a strange country thousands of miles from their homeland, unable (for the most part) to speak the local language, without shelter or sustenance and easy prey to the constant outbreaks of typhus and dysentery. Their needs were basic, and the Reds won them over not through ideology but through the provision of food, clothing, accommodation and a degree of respect. Li Fuqing, for example, one of Lenin's bodyguards, was recruited originally with a band of his followers on the

Ukrainian steppe in the spring of 1918 by a Soviet officer who told them that they must enlist with his unit to fight the tsar's forces *in order to stay alive*. Only later, we are told, did Li grasp that the unit was led by the Bolsheviks. Nonetheless the ex-labourers managed to win themselves a reputation for doughtiness that raised hopes for the future. A headquarters which had been created in Moscow in 1918 to form Chinese detachments in Soviet territory had by 1920 been moved east to Irkutsk, where Red officers trained Chinese troops in clandestine warfare in a fort named Kitaiskaya ('Chinese') on the shores of Lake Baikal. Could the October Revolution be poised to sweep south into China? Liu Zerong advised Lenin, 'The situation in China is favourable to us.'[18]

COUNTER-CURRENTS (1917–22)

It was and it wasn't. Seen from the point of view of soft power Russia in its new Soviet guise did indeed have some reason to expect a warm welcome from significant parts of the Chinese public. Seen from the point of view of geostrategy the Bolshevik takeover had led to a dramatic weakening of Russia's position in the East. As the old tsarist empire dissolved into chaos and civil war, Russia had lost, for the moment, the ascendancy over its great Asian neighbour that it had enjoyed since the mid-nineteenth century. China itself was descending the stairway into anarchy, as the weak central government of the early republican period gave way to the 'warlord' era in which local generals built up strongholds in the provinces and jostled each other for power in Peking. But amid their mutual rivalries the warlords did share certain consistent ideas. They disliked Russian domination of either the Red or the White kind; and they saw in the turmoil to their north a unique opportunity to claw back the rights which their country had lost to the tsarist empire over the last few decades.

The clawback started in northern Manchuria. By the autumn of 1917 the Russian guards stationed on the Chinese Eastern Railway had swung four-square behind the Bolsheviks, and on 4 December Lenin gave orders for them to take power in Harbin. On 13 December the current warlord regime in Peking in turn issued instructions for troops to be sent to relieve General Khorvat, the beleaguered tsarist administrator of the CER, suppress the Bolsheviks and 'if circumstances permit assume responsibility for guarding the railway'.[19] Six days later Zhang Zongchang, a minor warlord later known as the Dog Meat General, arrived in Harbin at the head of 4,000 troops, and by 28 December he had disarmed the mutinous Bolsheviks and packed them off in trains to Siberia. It was the first time in history that a large contingent of Europeans had been compelled to submit to a Chinese armed force. General Khorvat was reinstated, but his authority was precarious and from now on Chinese soldiers guarded the line. Emboldened by their success the Peking rulers began to assert themselves on the other side of the Manchurian border. In March 1918, at the request of the local Chinese chamber of commerce, they sent a warship and a merchantman to evacuate Chinese traders from Vladivostok, at that juncture in Bolshevik hands; and the following August they sent a division of 4,000 soldiers to Vladivostok to take part in the Allied intervention on the White side in Siberia and the Russian Far East.

This bid by the Chinese to win back their rights in Manchuria grew steadily more determined as the Russian fighting went on. Ever since 1860 Russian governments had blocked Chinese shipping from navigating the lower Amur. Now, however, in the absence of any effective Russian power, Chinese steamships and even gunboats began to appear on the river. On one occasion in 1919 a Chinese gunboat captain demanded permission from the White commander in Khabarovsk to sail up the Amur as far as its confluence with the River Sungari. The commander, one Ivan Kalmykov, responded with classic tsarist bravado, opening fire with the message 'If you want to pass Khabarovsk, do it along the river bottom.'[20] But this time bravado didn't work. At the end of the year the Reds drove Kalmykov from Khabarovsk; and the Chinese captured and shot him. In March 1920 renewed agitation broke out among the Russian workers on the CER against the administration of General Khorvat, and this time the government in Peking seized the chance to roll back the last traces of tsarist authority in the railway zone. Khorvat was dismissed from his post by the governor of Heilongjiang Province, and the railway was placed in the hands of a mixed Sino-Russian board of directors under ultimate Chinese control. The old tsarist domination of northern Manchuria gave way to the overlordship of Zhang Zuolin, a formidable warlord of Red Beard origins who became known to the world as the Old Marshal. Under Zhang's supervision Russians in Harbin became subject to Chinese law. Russian residents were confined to certain districts and only allowed to move around with the special permission of the Chinese police. Confucian and Buddhist temples sprang up in the midst of Russian churches: Orthodox Street was renamed Culture Street and Nicholas Street Temple Street. The Old Marshal's troops beat up Russian householders to rake in his taxes, and Russians were observed to be taking their hats off to Chinese officers, even to officers in civilian dress. It was, noted *Harper's Magazine* with dismay, 'the only white city in the world ruled by yellows'.[21]

A still more tempting objective was Outer Mongolia, the immense border region which Russia had prised from Chinese control in the last tsarist years. By 1918 the Chinese high commissioner in Urga, Chen Yi, had launched a cautious campaign to win the Mongol princes back to their former allegiance, and by June 1919 he had reached a sixty-four-point agreement with them under which the autonomy Russia had secured for them under the 1915 Second Treaty of Kyakhta would be quietly given up. In October, however, before this agreement could take effect, brusquer action was taken by Xu Shuzheng, another minor warlord attached to the Peking regime who was known as Little Xu to distinguish him from the current head of state, President Xu Shichang. Described by a western observer as 'one of those choice morsels of humanity who had to his credit such actions as having a rival assassinated in his garden after inviting him to lunch',[22] Little Xu had his sights set on establishing himself as 'King of the North-West'. Marching on Urga at the head of three infantry divisions, he proclaimed the formal annulment of the 1915 treaty, putting paid at one stroke to both Mongol autonomy and Russian influence, and proceeded to install a harsh and exploitative Chinese administration. At the Chinese New Year of 1920 the Mongolian notables were compelled to prostrate themselves before a portrait of 'Big Xu', as their forebears had done before the Qing emperor, while Little Xu stood proudly alongside.

In far-off Xinjiang the trade that had underpinned Russian domination for decades collapsed following the eruptions of 1917. Power in the province was now concentrated in the hands of a strong and astute Chinese military governor named Yang Zengxin. Operating for the most part without reference to the Peking warlords, Yang was equally quick to detect in the Russian disintegration an unrivalled chance to assert his authority. During the next three years he gradually sealed off the border with Russia, sending troops to strengthen the border defences at Yili and Tacheng, and eventually issuing a formal ban on entry into Xinjiang through the passes in the Tian Shan mountains. Starting in May 1918 a succession of tsarist troops in their long grey coats, half starved, typhus-ridden, demoralised, straggled into the province in a desperate effort to get away from the encroaching Red Army. Yang had them disarmed and brought under Chinese control. In the meantime the Soviet rulers who had taken over in Russian Turkestan made overtures to Xinjiang for a new trade agreement. Yang decided to cooperate. The collapse of the old tsarist trade had plunged the province into an economic decline, and an upsurge of traffic with British India doesn't seem to have filled the gap adequately. But the trade deal he went on to sign with Soviet emissaries in May 1920 was calculated to keep the new Russian partners firmly in their place. For the first time Russian exports and imports were to be subject to duties levied by the provincial bureaucracy. A customs post was to be established for this purpose at the border station of Khorgos, and any goods crossing the border by other routes were to be treated as contraband. And the right to extra-territorial judgement by their own country's consulates which had been enjoyed by generations of Russian traders was to be brought to an end. In the spring of 1921 Yang went so far as to allow a Red Army unit into his domains to help crush a White Guard band under Lieutenant-General Andrei Bakich that had been giving him trouble, but this was a temporary expedient. Yang had cast himself as a good neighbour to the new Soviet Russia – but an independent one.

The warlords weren't the only obstacles that the new Russia faced. Behind them were a number of powerful foreign backers, united in their resolve to check any seepage of Communism across China's frontiers. The initial Chinese disarming of Bolshevik troops on the CER was carried out at the invitation of British and United States diplomats in Harbin and Peking. Above all the warlords were urged on by Japan. The 'Anhui clique' who were dominant in Peking at this period were beholden to Japanese interests, and so, massively, was the Old Marshal up in Manchuria. While by no means unwilling to make their mark on the international stage, the Peking government were propelled into joining the Siberian intervention by a secret treaty of May 1918 which they signed with Japan against the new Soviet Russia; and the 4,000 Chinese troops sent ('in their crumpled, dirty uniforms they were more like scarecrows', thought one Russian eyewitness[23]) formed a subordinate part of a 70,000-strong Japanese expeditionary force. More perhaps even than the ruling circles of the other great powers, the military and political chiefs in Japan felt threatened by Bolshevism, by the risk that it might spread into their preserve in southern Manchuria or even into their home islands. At the same time the fall of tsarist Russia, and the consequent weakening of the restraints Japan had accepted under the Russo-Japanese pacts of 1907–16, opened the way to huge geopolitical gains. With Imperial Japanese forces advancing as far as Lake Baikal there seemed every chance for Japan to detach the entire eastern portion of Asiatic Russia. Other Japanese strategists mulled over the possibility of creating a buffer state that would include the whole Manchuria–Mongolia border zone. Wedged between Russia and China such a state could be used as a barrier to any Soviet advance in the region as well as a base for attacks upon either neighbouring country. In February–March 1919 two successive congresses were held under Japanese supervision in the towns of Dauria and Chita in Japanese-occupied Siberian territory with the object of fostering a Pan-Mongolian movement linked to Japan by the two peoples' shared Buddhist faith. The Japanese even pressed Yang Zengxin (unsuccessfully) to agree to their stationing troops at Yili and Tacheng to help police the borders of Xinjiang against Red penetration.

Finally the Bolsheviks had to contend with a stubborn White Russian resistance in the Asian theatre of the civil war. Up and down Eastern Siberia White Guard commanders with Japanese backing continued to hold out against the Red Army's advance. In Chita Captain Grigory Semyonov, part Cossack, part Buryat Mongol, ran a sybaritic White government while at the same time encouraging the Pan-Mongolian zealots who had earmarked him as senior adviser to their future state. In Dauria Semyonov's lieutenant, the fearsome Baltic baron Freiherr Roman Nikolai Maximilian von Ungern-Sternberg, nursed a toxic world view that combined anti-Communism, anti-Semitism and fanatical monarchism with an esoteric selection of Buddhist ideas. He was said to keep wolves in his attic to feed on Red prisoners, to take his rest on the neighbouring hillsides amid 'rolling skulls, skeletons and decaying body parts'.[24] In the summer of 1920, as the White position to the east of Lake Baikal began to unravel, these White chieftains began to shift their forces southwards to the relative safety of the Sino-Russian borderlands. The 'Mad Baron' veered south-west into Mongolia at the head of a cavalry division of 2,500 troops together with some sixty Japanese artillery officers and other military men. In October he launched an initial attack upon Urga, and by February 1921 he had evicted the Chinese regime installed by Little Xu and replaced it with his own anti-Bolshevik rule. He celebrated his advent with a slaughter of suspected Red commissars, whom he had exposed on ice, roasted in ovens, torn up by wild beasts and generally subjected to a range of torments inspired by depictions of the Buddhist hell. As his next step he proposed to restore Genghis Khan's legacy, setting up a steppe empire based in Mongolia, presided over by a restored Qing emperor and gathering under its wing Japan, China and all the rest of the principal Asian lands. In the meantime Semyonov was moving the mainstream White forces due south to Manchuria, where in March 1921 the Japanese military brought him together in anti-Soviet fellowship with the Old Marshal, Zhang Zuolin. The stage was set for a future of cross-border harassment.

The White pull-out into China also threatened Soviet prospects there in another, more indirect way. The retreating White military formed only one part of a huge exodus of upper- and middle-class Russians into Chinese territory, an exodus thought to have totalled some 300,000 men, women and children or roughly half the entire population of foreigners living in China at this time. The first wave of 100,000 or so refugees headed overwhelmingly for Harbin and 'the ice floe called Russian Manchuria'.[25] A second, slowly strengthening wave made its way to the Chinese coastal ports, and above all to Shanghai, where an initial 1,000 migrants in the spring of 1918 had increased to 2,000–3,000 by 1920 and roughly 10,000 by the end of 1922.

The refugees in Manchuria did at least have the comfort of being able to huddle together in a Russian milieu. Even after the Chinese administrative takeover in 1920 Harbin remained the only city on Earth where the foreign population was larger than the native one. Some of these refugees actually managed quite well. Persons of substance among them, merchants, bankers and factory owners, seem to have got away with at least part of their wealth, and could go on to spend it at Churin's department store on Russian liquor and delicacies, tobacco and fabrics and shoes. Artists and intellectuals, who included a talented Jewish substratum, brought with them their training in music, dance and drama, and the result was that Harbin for some years 'breathed culture',[26] with its own symphony orchestra and opera house staging works by Glinka, Tchaikovsky and Rimsky-Korsakov. Efforts were made to provide education for refugee children: in October 1920, for instance, the CER founded a new Industrial and Technical School which in due course matured into a Harbin Industrial University. In the background of all this, however, was a larger picture of bleak dispossession. Other accounts speak of ex-tsarist officers sweeping the CER railway cars, emptying the ashtrays and cleaning the passengers' boots, of a gently born Russian lady obliged to breastfeed her baby in a CER carriage in full view of gawping Chinese soldiers.

The refugees who fetched up in Shanghai were uniformly destitute, and the reception awaiting them was vastly worse. In Shanghai was no welcoming Russian environment: the foreign community there were emphatically western, and the handful of Russian officials and merchants from pre-revolutionary times had no wish to make room for these shabby, dejected newcomers whose arrival was liable to reflect unattractively on themselves. A few of the luckier men found jobs of a kind. They served as bodyguards to rich Chinese merchants, perched precariously on the running boards of their bosses' limousines as they shielded them from the danger of kidnapping, or imparted the knowledge of fencing and other military skills, or gave riding lessons to bored Chinese ladies. Others however sank straight to the depths of society, cadging and thieving alongside the Chinese mendicants on the great waterfront known as the Bund. They begged in low voices, shamefacedly, from passing Europeans, 'one hand stretched out, one hand pulling tightly at their filthy collars for fear of the cold wind'.[27] Lacking the organisation of their Chinese counterparts they failed to take the most minimal care of themselves and each other, and winter mornings often found them dead on the pavements. As with the men, so with the women. A lucky few found a niche for themselves as dressmakers or hairdressers, nurses or language teachers. Many others were driven to support themselves and their families through various forms of prostitution. 'Beautiful, haughty, desperate and very, very fascinating',[28] they wound up as the concubines of wealthy Chinese. Or they found work as hostesses, serving up 'pleasure, gin and jazz' at the Del Monte Dance Hall and the Venus Café. They took orders from Chinese employers, and were forced to share their tips with the Chinese staff. Subjected to registration and physical check-ups like the common prostitutes of the streets, they 'looked withered before the age of thirty'.[29]

This massive influx didn't result in a corresponding expansion of Sino-Russian intimacy. Most of the émigrés were introverted, sunk in nostalgia for their lost motherland and with minimal interest in Chinese culture. Few were disposed to surmount the language barrier. 'Even the Chinese we had to deal with spoke Russian,' one lady recalled of her arrival in Harbin in 1918, 'sparing us the need to study Chinese.'[30] Turning inwards like everyone else, the old Russian Orthodox Mission gave up their pre-revolutionary drive to win Chinese converts. In 1919 the last Orthodox Mission station in China was closed, and the priests now switched their focus exclusively to meeting the spiritual and material needs of their stricken compatriots. Churches and charities sprang up in unparalleled numbers, but the Mission was once again what it had been to start with – an enterprise run by Russians for Russians.

What the influx did produce was a sharp change in the way the Russians were perceived by the Chinese around them. Here and there, to be sure, there were signs of a fitful comradeship of the gutters. On the Bund in Shanghai some of the Chinese beggars would pull out their cigarette butts and invite 'Mr Russian' to have a drag.[31] Others, however, are said to have mocked, cuffed and cursed their fellow down-and-outs; and in general the attitude of the Chinese to the 'Russian Tramps', as they called them, was one of deep scorn.[32] There they were, leftover subjects of a once-mighty empire, jobless or reduced to working in a range of degrading capacities *for Chinese pay*. After 1920, when the Peking government withdrew diplomatic recognition from the former tsarist regime and formally abolished their extraterritorial rights, they were, furthermore, stateless, consigned with the mass of the public to the tender mercies of local law courts and prisons. Chinese seldom treated White Russians with the same respect that they did other foreigners. Chinese officials would be rude to or arrest an unidentified westerner, only to apologise on discovering his nationality that they had 'mistaken him for a Russian'.[33] This wasn't especially reassuring to westerners, who saw the White Russians as having subverted the colonial order and let the side down, and repeatedly voiced their conviction that the Russian refugee influx was '*not the least of the causes*' of '*the white man's loss of prestige in the East*'.[34] The White Russian émigrés had, in other words, inadvertently helped to stoke the fires of Chinese nationalism; and this had implications for all Europeans having dealings with China, including the Bolsheviks. The new Soviet Russians were going to have to differentiate themselves in no uncertain terms from both the Whites and the Europeans as a whole if they were to make a positive impact on a China that was increasingly prone to say no.

A NEW KIND OF MISSION (1919–26)

Lenin and his colleagues, however, were afloat on a tide of evangelical fervour. Rather as the early Christians had looked forward to an imminent Second Coming, so the first Soviet leaders expected a rapid breakthrough of socialist revolution worldwide. Bolshevik thinking at this time was largely shaped by the theories of Lenin's lieutenant Leon Trotsky, who argued that the global spreading of revolution was not merely imminent but essential if the new Soviet state was to weather attacks from outside. In March 1919, with their territory still besieged by White forces, the Bolsheviks established the Comintern (Communist International) to push the revolution forward in all directions; and in July, among many overtures of a similar kind, they put forward in the name of Lev Karakhan, deputy commissar for foreign affairs, a manifesto addressed to 'the Chinese People and the Rulers of Northern and Southern China', which did indeed stand out dramatically from any message sent to China by either their tsarist predecessors or the rulers of the other great powers. The 'Karakhan Declaration' repudiated all the 'secret treaties' concluded by tsarist diplomats in recent decades in relation to China, such as the treaty of alliance coaxed out of the Qing in 1896 and the four demarcations of influence signed behind China's back with Japan in 1907–16. Soviet Russia would give up without compensation all the special rights that the tsarist empire had obtained in Manchuria as a result of these treaties, including the CER and its related factory and mining concessions, and would renounce both the old tsarist extra-territorial privileges and the Russian share of the indemnity imposed by the powers upon China after the Boxer Rebellion of 1900. In the same year that the Orthodox Mission had dropped its attempt to evangelise the Chinese population the Bolsheviks had embarked on a mission of their own. 'We bring freedom to the people', the Declaration summed up ringingly, 'from the yoke of the foreign bayonet and the yoke of foreign gold.'[35]

All of this was still talk and no action. By spring 1920, though, the Bolsheviks were increasingly ready to project themselves on the Chinese stage. The Red Army were now visibly getting the upper hand in the Russian Civil War: Kolchak had been captured and shot, the White armies were reeling and their various Allied backers were pulling out their interventionist forces (all but the Japanese, who hung on in the Maritime Province until December 1922). After the topsy-turvy years which had followed the revolutions of 1917 a strong new Russian state was at last emerging. At the same time the hopes which the Bolsheviks had entertained for a socialist breakthrough in the more advanced states to their west had been disappointed. 'Socialist republics' set up in Bavaria and Hungary had been stifled, and a brief lunge by the Red Army into newly independent Poland had resulted in a bloody nose. Just as the old tsarist planners had switched their ambitions to the East after their defeat in the Crimean War, so the Bolsheviks now shifted the focus of their revolutionary ardour from Europe to Asia. The hostile western powers were to be undermined by arousing against them their Asian colonies – or 'semi-colonies', in China's case. 'The shortest route to Paris', Lenin proclaimed, 'is via Peking and Calcutta.'[36] Like Vasiliev, the nineteenth-century Sinologist, the Soviet leaders saw light pouring in from the East, *ex Oriente lux*; and a hotel established in Moscow to house the guests of the Comintern was indeed named the Hotel Lux. Russia's whole centre of gravity appeared to be shifting eastwards. Already in 1918 the capital had been moved back inland to Moscow from Petrograd. Even Russian writers, by no means all of them Bolsheviks, seem to have felt the tug of the country's new eastern calling. Where their forerunners of twenty years earlier had sketched nightmare visions of encroaching Mongol hordes these intellectuals caught up in the revolution began to picture Russia itself as a product of the Asian steppe. 'Yes, we are Scythians!', exulted the poet Alexander Blok. 'Yes, Asiatics, a slant-eyed, greedy tribe!'[37]

In April 1920 a lonely evangelical threesome crept south from the Russian Far East to Peking. They consisted of Grigory Voitinsky, a twenty-seven-year-old agent of the Comintern who had made his name by orchestrating a rising of Bolshevik prisoners against their White captors on the island of Sakhalin; his wife Maria; and as interpreter Yang Mingzhai, the young Chinese migrant whom we last met embarking on an accountancy course in Vladivostok, who had since become a representative of the Chinese serving in the Soviet Red Army and a member of the Bolshevik Party. In the absence of diplomatic relations between the Peking government and the new Soviet Russia the Voitinskys had no formal Chinese hosts to receive them and were, in effect, approaching China from square one – we are back in the days of Ivashko Petlin and his small band of seventeenth-century pioneers. They began by contacting Professor Sergei Polevoi, an expatriate Russian employed as a language teacher at Peking University. Despite his expatriate status Polevoi was known to be sympathetic to the new Soviet order; and he was also in touch with Chinese intellectual and oppositionist circles. Polevoi passed Voitinsky's group on to Li Dazhao, the university librarian, whom he had been supplying with pamphlets from Moscow as well as an English-language edition of Nikolai Bukharin and Yevgeny Preobrazhensky's *The ABC of Communism*. Li in turn forwarded the group to Professor Chen Duxiu, a Shanghai-based educator, philosopher and editor of the progressive journal *New Youth*. To both these two radicals Voitinsky proposed the establishment of a Chinese Communist Party (CCP); and over the following months the groundwork was laid for a major infusion of Soviet influence. By August Voitinsky had formed what he called a Revolutionary Office in Shanghai, under the dual cover of a Sino-Russian press agency and a Foreign Language School at which Mme Voitinsky and Yang gave tuition in Russian to young Chinese whom they meant to dispatch for more profound cultivation in Russia itself. Voitinsky himself served as a conduit for Soviet funds – for a new Socialist Youth League created that autumn, for travel expenses for graduates of the Foreign Language School, for subsidising *New Youth* and more generally for the upkeep of various small Marxist study groups that had sprung up around the country.

By the summer of 1921 Soviet influence was developing into outright control. In early June two new Comintern apostles arrived in Shanghai, a Dutch Jewish activist, Hendricus Sneevliet, commonly known as Maring, who had worked as an agitator in the labour movement in the Dutch East Indies, and Nikolsky (pseudonym of Vladimir Neiman), a taciturn military intelligence man. In July these two operatives convened an assemblage of fifty-three members of six or seven scattered groups of enthusiasts at a Shanghai girls' school unoccupied for the summer holidays to carry out the formal inauguration of the CCP. Two hundred Chinese yuan were disbursed to each province of origin to cover the delegates' costs, with a further fifty yuan thrown in for their return journey. The two Comintern men seem to have played a dominant role in this first CCP congress. According to one source Maring began the proceedings with a speech that lasted several hours: other accounts differ here, but all agree that when an unidentified stranger peered into the conference room the Dutchman, with his underground worker's antennae, sensed the presence of a police spy, 'brought his fist heavily down on the table' and ordered the meeting to adjourn.[38] Under

Maring's auspices the new CCP was endowed with a constitution and statutes on the model of the Bolshevik Party as well as a hierarchical, tightly organised Bolshevik structure consisting of a permanent headquarters, branches and cells. Maring explained that the CCP would become automatically a branch of the Comintern, and required weekly sessions at which Chen Duxiu, the party's newly elected General Secretary, would present him with work reports. This subordination of the CCP to the Comintern was formally endorsed at a second Party congress convened in July 1922, and underpinned by the Soviet grip on the purse-strings. In the autumn and winter of 1921–2, we are told, the Comintern bankrolled the CCP with a total of 16,665 yuan while the CCP themselves came up with less than 1,000; over the following months the Comintern contributed a further 15,000 yuan while the funding raised by the starveling Chinese Communists was precisely nil.[39] By 1922, then, Soviet Russia had succeeded in moulding a Chinese movement in its own image, with a compact if somewhat microscopic membership of roughly 200.

But the Bolsheviks were after bigger game. Their priority in China, we recall, as in Asia in general, was to stir up the populace against the foreign imperial powers that controlled their economy; and there was no way the infant CCP would be capable of doing that. Instead Soviet Russia needed to find a heavyweight local force that would be willing and able to pursue the short-term goal of a *national* revolution. In the same years that they organised the CCP, then, we find the Bolsheviks busy fingering a succession of possible Chinese partners who might be ready to work with them in overthrowing the Peking warlord regime. Rival warlords were by no means excluded. In central China, for instance, there was Wu Peifu, known as the Philosopher General for his supposed Confucian erudition. In August 1922 Adolph Joffe, who had arrived in Peking as a Soviet plenipotentiary, wrote to Wu hailing him as 'the greatest military and political personage in China', and judged him to be both quite bright and well educated, if somewhat vainglorious.[40] Even the Old Marshal up in Manchuria was perceived as a 'practical force' that could not be ignored.[41] And then there was Sun Yat-sen. Sidelined immediately after his short-lived triumph as the hero of the republican uprising of 1911, Sun had withdrawn to Japan only to re-emerge in 1917 as the head of a new Nationalist Party (KMT) presiding over an independent regime in the southern city of Canton. Leaning precariously on the support of a local general, Chen Jiongming, he mulled over a project for an expedition to march north and unify the fractured country by force of arms, and appealed for help to Japan, the United States and any other power that might be disposed to provide it. From 1920 onwards a series of Comintern envoys were holding discussions with Sun, but their initial appraisals of the KMT leader were dubious. Some dismissed him as just another warlord, while others found him wishy-washy, conceding that he had in his 'Three People's Principles' of Nationalism, Democracy and People's Livelihood 'a programme similar to our Social Revolutionaries' while lamenting the 'lack of clarity and contradictory nature of his tactics'.[42] Retreating somewhat from his earlier golden opinion of Sun as a revolutionary leader, Lenin in Moscow is said to have characterised him as 'a man of inimitable – some might say virginal – naïveté'.[43] In any case the consensus was that Sun would require the concrete military backing of the Philosopher General and the Old Marshal before he could be elevated 'to sit on the Peking throne'.[44] Gradually, however, the balance of Soviet judgement began to tilt in Sun's favour. In September 1922 Joffe suggested the time had now come for Russia to give up the old tsarist habit of backing the reactionary regimes that held sway in north China and switch its attention instead to the south, which had always been the home of insurgency. By January 1923 the Comintern had come round to the view that Sun's KMT were 'the only serious national revolutionary group in China',[45] while Joffe, after further talks with the Nationalist chief in Shanghai, had emerged with the firm conviction that Sun was 'our man'.[46] No support, he now urged, should be given to the Philosopher General at Sun's expense, while the Old Marshal was nothing more than 'a Red Beard who has got rich from seizing Manchuria'.[47] On 26 January Joffe and Sun issued a joint communiqué heralding a new era of cooperation between the Soviet Union and the Chinese Nationalist Party.

In March 1923 the Politburo of the Central Committee of the Bolshevik Party duly passed a resolution providing for steps to meet Sun's immediate requests for money and arms. The Nationalist leader was to be sent a sum of 2 million gold roubles, along with 8,000 Japanese rifles, fifteen machine guns, four artillery pieces and two armoured cars.[48] But the Bolsheviks weren't in a hurry to encourage Sun's dreams of a march to the north, and indeed their immediate purpose was to restrain his 'fantastic military plans'.[49] Political work had first to be made, as they put it biblically, 'the head of the corner'.[50] A political adviser had to be dispatched from the Comintern, to work at Sun's elbow and remould his party in the Soviet image in the same way that Maring had already moulded the CCP. At the end of July an appropriate candidate for this assignment was put forward by Joseph Stalin, already a dominant figure in the Moscow leadership and beginning to take a keen interest in Chinese affairs. Stalin's choice fell upon a seasoned revolutionary organiser who went by the name of Mikhail Markovich Borodin. Born Mikhail Gruzenberg in a Byelorussian shtetl in 1884, Borodin had joined up with the Bolsheviks at the age of nineteen, plunging into years of underground work in a number of countries, including the United States (where he taught immigrant children in Chicago and may already have formed a passing acquaintance with Sun) and Britain (where he did time in Barlinnie Prison in Glasgow). Looking like a cartoon Bolshevik, with a thick walrus moustache, a rumpled tunic and baggy trousers, he was by all accounts a man of enormous personality, with formidable charisma and a booming voice. One American reporter described him as 'a large, calm man with the natural dignity of a panther'.[51] On 6 October he arrived in Canton with a team of aides in the guise of a journalist, walking down the gangplank of a small cattle boat with 'the presence of a royal envoy'.[52] Borodin seems initially to have shared his predecessors' reservations about Sun, describing him as 'an enlightened little satrap, to be used but not to be trusted'.[53] But he plunged into his task with huge vigour, and in an astonishingly short time had carved himself a central place in the Canton regime. On 25 October he was formally designated Special Adviser on the reorganisation of the KMT. In November his status was further enhanced when Chen Jiongming, the dodgy neighbouring warlord, decided to turn his guns on his Nationalist protégés. Borodin quickly drew up a plan for repelling the onslaught. Illustrating the Bolshevik thesis that firm political backing was the key to achieving military success, he proposed economic reforms to increase the support for Sun's government and drummed up local sympathy further by staging a series of rallies at which the speakers were encouraged to pour out the hardships of their daily lives – a technique which appears to have prompted the subsequent Chinese revolutionary practice of prompting local people to 'speak their bitterness'.[54] Finally he assembled, with Sun's acquiescence, a band of 540 fighters who helped to put Chen's assault force to flight. In the meantime the Special Adviser was working to turn Sun's ramshackle party into a disciplined organisation on the Soviet model, with a Central Committee ('Central Executive Committee' in this case) whose decisions would be binding on all party members, a Political Bureau to steer the Central Committee's endeavours, lesser bureaux to shape policy towards the cities, the countryside, women, the military and other basic sectors of society and a Propaganda Department to help raise recruits. He himself served ubiquitously at the apex of KMT power, as a member of the Political Bureau, a permanent member of the Political Bureau Standing Committee and a top-ranking adviser to both Sun's Foreign Ministry and Sun himself. In these capacities he took part in debates over all major issues, and is said to have had the last word in whatever decisions resulted from them. In January 1924 he played the key role in organising the first congress of the streamlined Nationalist Party, personally drafting the party's new constitution as well as a manifesto directed against the warlords and the foreign imperial powers. To arouse popular zeal he revamped Sun's Three People's Principles to include such radical themes as the 'equalisation of land rights' and the 'restriction of private capital'.[55] And 'again and again' he asked Sun to give up the illusion that the Nationalists would receive help from any other quarter, whether Britain, the United States or Japan.[56]

Back in late tsarist times we found Russians beginning to manage Chinese, pressuring Qing officials in the Xinjiang government offices or directing coolies on the Manchurian railway sites. Borodin and his team brought in micromanagement and then some. A report sent to Stalin on 8 January 1924 advised him bullishly that Sun had accepted 'all our decisions and advice' and 'in practice does everything we tell him',[57] and five months later Stalin inquired with regard to Canton, 'How are our lads running things there?'[58] One of Borodin's admirers observed that alongside the Special Adviser all of the Nationalist functionaries 'seemed to be, and were, docile puppets'.[59] Where Canton was concerned, at least, Soviet Russia had firmly recaptured the inside track once enjoyed by Orthodox priests and tsarist diplomats at the former Qing court.

In the midst of all this the Chinese Communist Party weren't forgotten. They could help, for example, to mobilise the peasant masses, whom the Comintern seem to have identified rather sooner than the CCP's own city-based intellectuals as a vital auxiliary force in the battles to come. In the judgement of Lenin and his followers, however, an agrarian 'semi-colony' such as China was nowhere near ready for a textbook socialist revolution of the industrial working class. The transformation of China would have to proceed in two stages: the national revolution against the imperial powers led by local middle-class forces, and the socialist revolution against the middle class to be led by the Communists at some unspecified future date. For the moment the task of the Communists was to piggy-back on the national revolution by joining up with the middle class in an 'Anti-Imperialist United Front'. In January 1922 Lenin personally stressed, at a Congress of Peoples of the Far East held in Moscow, that the CCP would have to work with the Chinese Nationalists. The need for such cooperation was further impressed on the CCP by their mentor, Maring; and the following August, at a special conference held on the West Lake in Hangzhou, Maring declared it compulsory for all CCP members to enlist with Sun Yat-sen's party. In July–August 1923, at the same session of the Soviet Politburo at which he proposed the dispatch of Borodin to serve as Sun's political adviser, Stalin narrowed the room for manoeuvre of the Chinese Communists appreciably further. Borodin, he decreed, was to be 'guided by the interests of the national revolutionary movement in China' and was 'not to be diverted by the goal of implanting Communism there'.[60] Borodin himself explained to the CCP following his arrival in China that the proposed revolution would have to be led by the Nationalists. The role of the CCP, for the time being anyway, was '*to do coolie service for the Chinese Nationalist Party*'.[61] In January 1924, at the inaugural Nationalist congress choreographed by Borodin, the Chinese Communists were formally ushered into the ranks of the KMT in this mandatory United Front.

With these foundations established the Bolshevik project for launching a revolution in China could get going in earnest. The first and most pressing task was to set up a military school at which a truly revolutionary army could be moulded for Sun Yat-sen. By early 1924 Borodin was already at work drawing up a curriculum, and in April he cabled to Moscow for a first contingent of Soviet military instructors to be sent to Canton. On 15 June, with the help of 900,000 roubles transferred to Sun's treasury, the Whampoa Military Academy was formally inaugurated on Changzhou Island in the Pearl River opposite the Whampoa docks. Twenty-five Soviet military instructors were by this time installed there, most of them former officers in the Russian Imperial Army who had fought on the Red side during the civil war. Their first leader, a General Pavel Pavlov, was bizarrely drowned in July while crossing from a boat to a steamer on the nearby East River; but by early October he had been replaced with General Vasily Blücher, an officer of German antecedents whose name conjured up visions of Wellington's ally at Waterloo, but who had adopted the *nom de guerre* Galin after his first wife, Galina. The distinctive feature of Whampoa was its political training, designed to produce the Chinese equivalent of Cromwell's 'plain, russet-coated captain that knows what he fights for and loves what he knows'. Thus Sun's lieutenant Chiang Kai-shek served in traditional fashion as commandant of the academy, but a role was created beneath him for a young Communist, Zhou Enlai, who was appointed head of the Political Department. In a report on the academy's activities from December 1924 to July 1925 Blücher announced that 'for the first time in the history of the Chinese army political education has been introduced as part of the curriculum'.[62] But Blücher was also a hard-headed soldier aware, as he put it, that 'the main force deciding the fate of Canton will be military for a long time to come';[63] and the political teach-ins were accompanied by a programme of conventional military training with modern equipment. Blücher arrived in Canton with the batch of 8,000 Japanese rifles which had been promised Sun by the Moscow Politburo early the previous year, and in May 1925 the new National Revolutionary Army (NRA) received a further consignment of 9,000 rifles, 9.5 million cartridges, 100 machine guns and 10,000 hand grenades. In addition the Soviet military chiefs played a micromanaging part as the NRA's strategic advisers. The ill-fated Pavlov inspired in the course of his brief time in charge the formation of a Defence Council under Sun's chairmanship, and drew up a programme for propaganda activity and the arousing of disgruntled peasants behind warlord lines. In December 1924 Blücher set up a Military Council in which, we are told, by the following summer he played the 'decisive role' and delivered reports at each session.[64]

Within months of the setting up of the Whampoa academy the Soviet military intervention in Canton was already beginning to yield some results. On 15 October 1924, with the help of Soviet arms and advisers, Sun's forces took on the Merchant Volunteer Corps, a British-backed group that had risen against the Canton government, and routed them in a single day. Then in February 1925 Chiang Kai-shek, accompanied by Blücher, led the NRA out of Canton in an Eastern Expedition intended to rid Guangdong Province of the persistent nuisance of Chen Jiongming. Once again the Russians appear to have played the lead part in the action. One Soviet official reported that the Red Army men were consistently in the front line, as was Blücher himself – 'contrary', the writer interjected sardonically, 'to the Chinese custom by which the general is supposed to be at least 100 kilometres from the battlefield'.[65] At one point Blücher had even assumed control of an armoured train; and he was said to have been much better informed of the state of play on the battlefield than his nominal superior, Chiang. During a second Eastern Expedition launched the following autumn Chiang himself acknowledged that his Soviet advisers had taken part in the decision-making and direction that led to the NRA's final victory over Chen; and one junior member of the Bolshevik apparatus in China maintained later on that the Nationalist commander did little more than confirm the plans already drawn up by his Soviet mentors. By the last months of 1925 Blücher had set to work drafting a 'Great Military Plan' for the Northern Expedition that would bring Sun's dreams to fulfilment and unify China under Nationalist rule.

The Bolsheviks had in the meantime identified an unusually promising northern Chinese warlord who seemed well positioned to complement their designs in the south. Soviet hopes had been excited by Feng Yuxiang, a burly warrior based in Inner Mongolia and the north-western provinces who had earned himself the sobriquet of the Christian General on account of his celebrated penchant for baptising his regiments with a hosepipe and marching them to the strains of 'Onward Christian Soldiers'. He had named his troops, encouragingly, the National People's Army, and had impressed the Soviet planners with his earthiness and his apparent ability to win the allegiance of ordinary Chinese. In October 1924 he had staged a coup in Peking that evicted the unfriendly warlord regime there and gave him control of the capital for the whole of the following year. And he needed arms to maintain his position against the other big regional barons, the Philosopher General and the Old Marshal. In the spring of 1925 a Soviet military mission led by General A.S. Bubnov, head of the Red Army's political administration, visited Feng at his Inner Mongolian headquarters of Baotou and agreed on a deal under which the Christian General would receive arms and military training in return for accepting political workers from the Nationalists in the south. Soviet aid now unfolded on much the same lines as it had in Canton. Between August 1925 and March 1926 the

Bolsheviks organised a Sun Yat-sen Military Academy on the model of Whampoa in the north-western city of Xi'an. Several dozen Soviet instructors were assigned to the different branches of the National People's Army, and 6 million roubles' worth of weaponry was provided to some 300,000 of the Christian General's men. Plans were mooted to strengthen Feng's cavalry and endow him with an air force. The Moscow Politburo even discussed the possibility of providing the Christian General with ingredients for chemical weapons or enabling him to set up a chemical warfare plant, and instructions were issued to furnish him with a supply of gas masks from the Red Army's reserve. Feng also received from the Soviet Union financial subsidies ranging from $10,000 to $500,000 a month.

All this activity was rounded off by a strenuous effort in Russia itself. As early as February 1921 a Communist University for the Toilers of the East (perhaps we may be permitted to call it by its somewhat incongruous acronym, CUTE) was established in Moscow for the training of Asian revolutionaries, and by the spring it was starting to take in some of those early Chinese Communists who had received Russian language tuition from Mme Voitinsky and Yang Mingzhai in Shanghai. On arrival at the CUTE they were given a grounding in the basics of Marxism and in the theory of world revolution propounded by Lenin and Trotsky. With the civil war still in progress and famine stalking Russia, their living conditions were dismal. They had almost nothing to eat, their coats and boots were Red Army hand-me-downs, their accommodation was primitive, their teachers scarce and their classes rudimentary. But their numbers slowly began to creep up. Chinese attendance at the CUTE rose from thirty-six in 1921 to forty-two in 1922 and ninety in 1924 out of a total of 700-odd students of forty-odd nationalities. By 1925 the increase was sufficiently striking for the idea to take hold in Moscow that there might be a case for creating a special centre of higher education for Chinese alone. The students there would naturally include both Nationalists and Communists, in keeping with the formation of the United Front. On 7 October, accordingly, there was founded with Soviet money a new Sun Yat-sen University for the Toilers of China – 'Sunovka', the Russians called it – with an initial intake of some 340 young people. Borodin in Canton supervised the recruitment of students as counsellor to a three-man selection committee. In November Leon Trotsky appeared in person at the new university and gave an inaugural speech in which he stressed the importance of the Chinese Revolution and warned his fellow Russians rather pointedly to eradicate any racial prejudice left over from tsarist days. 'From now on', he declared, 'any Russian, be he a comrade or a citizen, who greets a Chinese student with an air of contempt, shrugging his shoulders, is not entitled to be either a Russian Communist or a Soviet citizen.'[66] Karl Radek, a Bolshevik of Lithuanian Jewish extraction and disciple of Trotsky, was named as the new university's rector. Under the more benign economic conditions which had followed the end of the civil war and the replacement of War Communism by Lenin's more liberal New Economic Policy (NEP), the Sunovka intake were welcomed into something verging on luxury. We are told the authorities gave them no fewer than five meals a day, stuffing them to the point where they had to appeal for the cancellation of their afternoon tea and their late night snack. The food was delicious, and when they got tired of Russian dishes the management promptly recruited a Chinese chef. The women students were housed in the mansion of a dispossessed nobleman on Petrovka Street; and when complaints were voiced about the segregation of the sexes the authorities thoughtfully provided a 'secret meeting room' for the benefit of married couples. Special performances of plays, concerts and ballets were staged on the campus, and the students were also given free tickets for opera performances in town. In the meantime they were kept busy with Russian lessons and trained in such matters as the infiltration of governments and the fostering of peasant and labour movements.

At the beginning of 1925 the Soviet missionaries found themselves faced with a crisis when it emerged that their protégé Sun was succumbing to cancer of the liver. A Soviet liver specialist was rushed to Peking, where the Nationalist leader had been able to travel thanks to the dominance of the well-disposed Christian General; but Sun was beyond help. 'Why the devil', grumbled Stalin, 'has he taken it into his head to die now?'[67] The obvious danger existed that Soviet influence on the ranks of the KMT would perish when Sun did. But the Soviet team in China were equal to the emergency. By early February Borodin and leading colleagues of his were attached to Sun's retinue, and word was sent to the People's Commissariat of Foreign Affairs (Narkomindel) in Moscow, 'Right now we are struggling to produce a detailed manifesto, something in the nature of a political testament.'[68] After Sun's death on 12 March Borodin gave it out that the Nationalist leader had cried repeatedly in his final moments, '*If only Russia will help!*'[69] Sun's close associate, Wang Jingwei, a matinée idol of seemingly radical views, was summoned by the Russians and told that he was the dead leader's natural successor: in the following months, though, the Nationalist leadership vacuum was filled to a remarkable extent by Borodin himself. On 15 June the Special Adviser attended a meeting of the KMT's Central Executive Committee and decreed the formation of a new, all-powerful Political Bureau. Back in Canton in the autumn he was driven to the bureau's meetings by car amid tightest security, with Mauser-wielding Chinese soldiers on the running-board. Sometimes the meetings were held in Borodin's own residence, and we are told Wang Jingwei meekly followed whatever initiatives Borodin proposed. Some onlookers even referred to the Special Adviser as 'the dictator of Canton'.[70] In the 'Red City', festooned with red flags, around 1,000 Soviet agents were said to be active; and the Soviet grip was spreading from political and military affairs to the fine details of domestic administration. The Kremlin issued credits worth 10 million Chinese yuan to the Canton regime to facilitate the creation of a central bank; and three economists from Leningrad were attached to the central bank, the Finance Ministry and the government generally to sort out the financial and economic system. They were also asked to advise the Ministry of Justice, and to introduce the Central Bureau of Statistics to the basic principles of Soviet accounting. Sociologists, lawyers and even historians followed in their wake.

The Soviet achievement at this point seems all the more extraordinary given the crippling handicaps under which the Bolshevik pioneers had to work. In the first place their knowledge of China was virtually nil. Lenin himself confessed that he knew little of China except that Sun Yat-sen was the leader of the revolution, and Grigory Zinoviev, the head of the Comintern, admitted to being 'very poorly and casually informed' about Chinese affairs.[71] It was the same story with the civilian and military advisers on the ground. China-savvy emissaries in the mould of the old tsarist diplomats Skachkov and Pokotilov were totally lacking. One Soviet military attaché in Peking observed gloomily in the mid-1920s, 'We must remember that we are currently carrying out work in China knowing nothing about China, not knowing the language, having at our disposal only three or four interpreters who *do* know it.'[72] Language in particular was a major constraint. Borodin addressed rallies of Sun's supporters in the impeccable Midwestern English he had picked up in Chicago, helped by a Chinese interpreter and painfully aware that Canton was 'a babel in which one is liable to get completely lost'.[73] Maring likewise harangued the congresses of the CCP in English, and English was the language habitually used to communicate with the leadership of the United Front. Borodin and his colleagues were equally conscious of their ignorance of the Chinese people, of their history, culture, morals and way of life. Communication between Moscow and its agents in China had almost reverted to the fits and starts of the seventeenth century. Instructions from the Kremlin didn't always get through, and nor did the answers from Bolshevik envoys. In January 1923 Adolph Joffe complained bitterly to Lenin at the end of his negotiations with Sun,

> For months we have received nothing from Moscow, neither directives nor orders nor even serious information of a newspaper type. When I endeavoured to send a cable of information to Moscow I was told that it was too expensive and had to be cancelled; any information about China, as a rule, has to go by courier and only by telegraph in exceptional cases. Taking account of the fact that China as a whole is experiencing its own revolution and events here are unfolding at extraordinary speed, thanks to all this *a complete mutual rupture* has been created under which facts communicated by me via courier have been changed and replaced by others by the time you receive them, frequently by facts negating them, and the ideas received by you no longer correspond to events.[74]

Finally, Bolshevik efforts were plagued by a lack of cohesion. In the haphazard conditions of the early Soviet era different entities often pursued the same goals without reference to each other. Crucial intelligence operations were carried out independently by three distinct networks – the Comintern; the state security organ, the Cheka, known from 1922 as the GPU; and the Red Army's military intelligence branch. Chronic in-fighting took place both between and within these establishments, often reflecting disputes at the highest level of the Soviet regime. In May 1924, for example, the Comintern's first apostle to China, Voitinsky, was back on the scene urging the CCP to reverse the decision imposed on them by Maring to submit to the leadership of the Nationalist Party, and by the following year he was at odds with Borodin as well. Certain centralising endeavours were made. In March 1925 a Special Commission was created within the Moscow Politburo to improve the coordination of China policy, and in Canton in the autumn Borodin made a bid to assert his authority over everyone else, even depriving Blücher and the military team of the right to send information by telegraph without going through him. This attempt seems only to have widened the fissures still further, as relations between Borodin and Blücher grew increasingly strained and Voitinsky's associates sniped that the Special Adviser seemed to think of himself as Napoleon. Matters probably weren't improved by the fact that the Russians in Canton were suffering miseries from the humid tropical climate. Borodin was afflicted by both dysentery and malaria, and many other advisers were stricken by ailments that persisted for the rest of their lives.

Yet the Soviet envoys proved adept at making a virtue out of necessity. Wholly unqualified to communicate with ordinary Chinese, Borodin with his fluent English and cosmopolitan background was admirably suited to breaking the ice with Sun Yat-sen and his entourage, with the English-speaking, westernised, Christianised Chinese elite of the treaty ports. Well versed in the Bible, which had been the only reading matter permitted to him in Barlinnie Prison, he appealed to one of Sun's retinue with a skilful blend of Christian and Marxist exegesis, lamenting that 'Jesus's promise to give them a new Jerusalem cleansed of corruption, oppression and inequality perturbed [the Jewish elders] and they returned death for love',[75] while insisting that 'you can only bring in the kingdom of God by force'.[76] In lighter moments he treated the Nationalist inner circle to gramophone records, playing the ballets of Igor Stravinsky and the arias of Fyodor Chaliapin without undue concern for the fact that both these two masters had joined the White emigration. If contact with Moscow was fitful and unreliable, this at least gave Borodin and his colleagues a certain flexibility, enabling them to decide locally on the tactics they judged most appropriate to the needs of the moment. One account by a colleague even captures Borodin on the cusp of on-the-spot decision-making, mulling a gambit with his subordinates in quite an open, consensus-seeking manner: 'Let's accept 20 per cent to 25 per cent of this line and no more. What do you say?'[77]

In addition we must remember that most Soviet Russians at this early period genuinely believed in what they were doing. They believed in the secular religion called Marxism. They wanted to follow the path laid down by Lenin and Trotsky and spread revolution from Russia to other, less fortunate lands. And those of them who came into contact with China or thought about China were swept by a surge of affection for the Chinese people. Alexei Ivanov, an Orientalist trained in the late tsarist years who now held the post of professor at Peking University, was thrilled to observe in the growing disorder around him the ferment of nineteenth-century Russia 'coming to life before his eyes'. In the students on his campus protesting against the warlord regimes he found the same 'admiration of science' as that of their Russian forerunners, the same 'rejection of all authorities, traditions and foundations'. In China he discovered 'a world unknown yet strangely close to us, the Russians, as it is to none of the Europeans'.[78] Vera Vishnyakova, who arrived there in 1925 as part of a team of trainee interpreters from Vladivostok, recalled that 'we were all in love with China, with her rich yet laconic language, her difficult yet descriptive characters, her ancient distinctive culture and history'.[79] She 'loved Peking with all her heart', and 'fell in love' with Canton 'passionately and forever'.[80] Some of these young Russians recorded the deep shock they felt at the hideous poverty. Vishnyakova left a haunting account of a beggar on a Peking street:

> The beggar raised his eyes to me. Keeping them fixed on me, with an effort he placed a trembling hand, dry as a stick, on his son's head. Words cannot convey the meaning in this gesture and that look in which despair and a fatal weariness struggled with hope.[81]

More shocking still was the way other foreigners continued to bully Chinese at every level of society. M.Y. Shass, one of the financial advisers from Leningrad, described seeing a British party getting a wealthy Chinese evicted from the first class saloon of a Yangtze steamer because they couldn't bear to sit at the same table as him; drunken American sailors buying under-age Chinese girls off the river boats; Japanese beating up rickshaw coolies and throwing their vehicles into the water. For these young people imbued with the new spirit of Soviet morality, taking rickshaws drawn by sweating Chinese labourers was an absolute no-no – a taboo which however rebounded on them in Peking when a deputation of rickshawmen arrived to complain that the de facto embargo by Soviet Russians was losing them wages. Quite a number of Russians reached out in friendship to Chinese individuals. Borodin, for example, is appears to have felt deep affection for his interpreter, a young Chinese Communist named Zhang Tailei: he brought Zhang in to live at his house in Canton, and the Borodin family are said to have treated the young man 'like a close relative'.[82] Back in Moscow, meanwhile, where poets still retained the public voice they had lost in the west and gave declamations of their verse to rapturous audiences, Vladimir Mayakovsky delivered in 1924 a verbal broadside directed at the foreign oppressors of the Chinese population:

> In the Embassy quarter they sit like Tsars,
> Spinning intrigues.
> Let's sweep away the web.
> Hands off China!
>
> Coolie, instead of dragging their sacks,
> Driving them in rickshaws,
> Straighten your neck.
> Hands off China![83]

A THREAD OF STRATEGY (1919–26)

Right from the start, however, this crusading benevolence was intertwined with a thread of hard strategy. The Bolshevik move into Asia was certainly launched in part with the high-minded purpose of weakening the imperial powers (Britain and Japan in particular) that were battening on the economies of the colonised and 'semi-colonised' Asian lands. But this also served Moscow's defence needs, insofar as it was those same imperial powers that had intervened on the White side in the civil war and posed a continuing threat to the new Soviet Russia. During the first years this strategic aspect wasn't all that conspicuous in Soviet policy, but its importance was growing. After Lenin died in January 1924 an opposition began to emerge between the doctrine of world revolution championed by Trotsky and the alternative outlook of Stalin, who by the end of that year had begun to propound his conception of 'socialism in one country', implying a narrower focus on strengthening and defending the Soviet state. And this issue became a core part of the struggle which now ensued between Trotsky and Stalin for Lenin's mantle.

Where China was concerned a first sign of strategic as distinct from evangelical thinking was shown in the Soviet readiness to play all of the numerous pieces on the Chinese chessboard. The Karakhan Declaration of

1919, which offered to surrender all the tsarist rights in the country, was addressed sweepingly, we recall, 'to the Chinese People *and the Rulers of Northern and Southern China*' – a formula which didn't even exclude the warlord regime in Peking. A division of labour emerged between the Bolshevik version of a Foreign Ministry, the Narkomindel, headed by Karakhan and his boss, the aristocratic Georgi Chicherin, who were responsible for dealings with the official Chinese government, and the Comintern, who handled contacts with the Nationalists and other revolutionary bodies. From 1920 onwards, even as the Voitinskys and the other Comintern envoys built their grass-roots networks, a series of Narkomindel proxies made their way to Peking to negotiate with the government there. One object of this activity was to forge diplomatic relations with China now that the Peking warlords had withdrawn recognition from the former tsarist regime, thus enabling the besieged Soviet state to break through the *cordon sanitaire* imposed by the powers. Another goal, less explicit, was to stem the tide which had rolled back Russian power in East Asia during the chaotic years after 1917. From the start there had been hidden limits to the tsarist acquisitions which the Bolsheviks were prepared to give up. Even the Karakhan Declaration, for all its spectacular generosity, made no mention of revising the mid-nineteenth-century treaties which had deprived the Qing empire of 'Outer Manchuria' and settled the Sino-Russian border in its current form. Lenin himself declared that Vladivostok was 'our city'.[84] And by 1920, as the tide of civil war swung in the Red Army's favour and Soviet confidence grew, the leaders in the Kremlin were starting to have second thoughts about the Declaration as well, most especially the clause in it which provided for the unconditional yielding of the Chinese Eastern Railway. The CER was perceived as a key strategic asset which could not be allowed to fall into the hands of the Whites or their Japanese backers. It conferred the economic advantage of allowing Russians to transport their goods between Siberia and Manchuria duty-free. And after all it had been built with Russian money. Even Trotsky ranted, 'I absolutely do not understand why resisting imperialism presupposes renouncing our property rights . . . I absolutely do not understand why the Chinese peasant should have the railway at the expense of the Russian peasant.'[85] The result was that Moscow effectively retracted the Declaration in the form in which it had been communicated to China the year before. A whole cluster of explanations were given. One of Karakhan's subordinates had failed to excise a paragraph which Karakhan had already crossed out; the clause about the CER had been inserted by error in the French-language translation; the text had been 'absolutely reworked' by Chinese migrants living in Moscow; the content had been distorted by the White Guards.[86] Moscow was also regretting the loss of the old Russian presence in Outer Mongolia, as the Chinese regime of Little Xu was replaced by the still more disturbing irruption of the 'Mad Baron' Ungern-Sternberg with his Mongol cavalry and his Japanese artillerymen. In October 1920 the Kremlin leadership even wrote to the Peking warlord government urging a joint expedition to put a stop to the Baron, but were rebuffed by the warlords with the haughty assertion that they could handle the intrusion on their own. By June 1921, when the Baron had actually launched an attack on Kyakhta, Lenin and the Politburo weren't prepared to wait any longer, and the decision was made to send in the Red Army. The Baron's forces were routed and he himself was betrayed to the Reds by his own Mongol followers, still proclaiming himself the head of the Asian Cavalry Division as he writhed in the dust and the ants crawled over his body. A force of 10,000 Red Army troops entered Urga, and a new government was installed there of pro-Soviet Mongol revolutionaries. In a comment revealing the fear which had prompted the Bolshevik action Chicherin reported to Lenin on 18 October,

> The [Mongolian] revolutionary government is the ace of spades in our hands. Its creation foils the plan of Japan to set up an anti-revolutionary front stretching from the Pacific Ocean to the Caspian Sea.[87]

In September 1923 a fourth in the series of Narkomindel emissaries arrived in Peking in the person of Karakhan himself. In his reports to Chicherin the author of the idealistic Declaration expressed himself in distinctly hard-headed terms. In November he complained that the Peking government 'consider that we aren't strong enough simply to take what we consider belongs to us by right, and can therefore allow themselves the luxury of scorning the requests and desires of at any rate one Great Power'.[88] The following March, when talks finally got under way, he declared he had been 'quite sharp, even rude' with the Peking regime's negotiator, Wang Zhengting, telling Wang that he 'didn't want to hold a Chinese bazaar'.[89] In the course of the next few weeks Karakhan got what he wanted. Through a treaty concluded on 31 May 1924 diplomatic relations were finally established between the Soviet Union and the Chinese Republic. Karakhan did keep the promises made in his Declaration to give up the old tsarist concessions and extra-territorial rights and the Russian share of the Boxer indemnity, which was to be reapplied to Chinese educational needs. The CER, however, was to be accepted as Soviet property and placed under joint Soviet–Chinese management with an inbuilt Soviet majority of eight votes to seven on the board of directors – provisions confirmed in September in a similar treaty signed with the Old Marshal, Zhang Zuolin, in whose territory the CER lay. Outer Mongolia was to resume the autonomy it had enjoyed under the tripartite treaty of 1915 between China, Mongolia and tsarist Russia. China was to regain its sovereignty over the region but to desist from meddling in Mongolian domestic affairs; Soviet troops would be withdrawn from Mongolia, but only after the White remnants had been completely eliminated and the Mongols were able to fend for themselves. By 1924, in other words, the Soviet leaders had wholly reversed China's short-lived resumption of power in the borderlands. Over, in northern Manchuria, was the brief interlude when the Chinese had supervised the CER through a management made up of pliant White Russians. Soviet gunboats were now deployed, like tsarist gunboats before them, to stop Chinese ships on the River Sungari from navigating the Amur. Over too in Mongolia was the fleeting Chinese restoration under Little Xu. Chinese administrators had not been allowed back to Urga after the Soviet rout of the Mad Baron's forces in 1921. Thanks to the Red Army's presence, upheld in the following years by Narkomindel diplomacy, the late tsarist detachment of Outer Mongolia from Chinese overlordship had been reaffirmed. Soviet counsellors were said to stand at the elbow of each minister in the new Mongolian revolutionary government, and 'their advice was never ignored with impunity'.[90] Moscow had also hived off from the west of Mongolia a slice of land which it turned into the nominally independent Republic of Tannu Tuva, and which specialised in producing colourful postage stamps to the delight of philatelists the world over. Even in Xinjiang, still in the firm grip of Yang Zengxin, the old Russian influence was slowly creeping back, and in 1924 Moscow obtained permission to open five new consulates in the province. While maintaining their posture as liberators the Bolsheviks had quietly substituted a new Soviet ascendancy for the old tsarist one.

The Bolsheviks weren't unaware of the latent contradictions in their China policy. A purist stance was adopted by Adolph Joffe, the Narkomindel envoy who travelled to China in 1922 and courted Sun Yat-sen. Unsettled by the tweaking of the Karakhan Declaration, Joffe warned that 'by becoming the most ordinary imperialists in our foreign policy we would cease being the ferment of the world revolution'.[91] With regard to the CER he pressed for a further adjustment, once more 'handing over our property rights without compensation to the Chinese people'.[92] He lamented the Soviet seizure of Mongolia as 'tactically wrong', on the grounds that 400 million Chinese were more important than 2 million Mongolians and that Mongolia was 'the only card the imperialists hold against us'.[93] Even Chicherin noted ruefully that 'on the one hand we issue declarations of solidarity with the oppressed peoples . . . and on the other hand we pursue [the CER] in the spirit of tsarist satraps'.[94] But Chicherin managed to persuade himself most of the time that the interests of the Soviet state and the Chinese Revolution were one.

CHINA RESPONDS (1919–26)

So how did the Chinese react to the Soviet phenomenon? The attitude of the warlords was relatively simple. Like their forebears they sought weaponry from the ever-abundant Russian arsenal to enable them to smash their rivals. The Old Marshal, Zhang Zuolin, asked Karakhan for the arms and the military training he needed to settle accounts with the scoundrel Wu Peifu. Wu Peifu, the Philosopher General, pressed Karakhan for the weapons to deal with the Red Beard Zhang Zuolin, and for the right to march his troops across Soviet territory to attack Zhang Zuolin in the rear. But the warlords were also consumed with a terror of Communism. As early as September 1920 the Peking government sent a deputation to Moscow led by a Lieutenant-General Zhang Silin to look into the plight of the Chinese expatriate population in Soviet Russia. The Bolsheviks spotted the chance for a diplomatic breakthrough, and Lenin was even induced to give a dinner in the general's honour. But when word of this fraternisation got through to Peking the general was judged to have exceeded his brief and was promptly recalled. In November 1925 a left-leaning commander delivered a speech at a ceremony marking the opening of a Soviet-aided military school in Henan Province which he had been appointed to head. The school was intended to turn out cadets for one of the National People's Armies of the Christian

General, Feng Yuxiang. But when the commander happened to refer to the Soviet Union as China's friend, the provincial governor, a rightist soldier who was also present, had the speech stopped immediately and took over as head of the school himself. The warlords were also by no means immune to the currents of nationalism which were coursing through the bloodstream of republican China. All of the three major chiefs, the Old Marshal, the Philosopher General and the Christian General, voiced their rage at the Soviet detachment of Outer Mongolia, and indeed the Christian General, the most progressive of the trio in Soviet eyes, also turned out to be the most nationalistic. 'Shut up!', he exploded at Karakhan after Mongolia's fate was determined by the Sino-Soviet treaty of 1924. 'You damned Russians, you aggressors!'[95] During his spell of influence over Peking in the following year he inspired the raising of a string of 'injustices' in Sino-Russian relations which the previous Japanese-friendly clique had failed to touch on, including the borders and the wiping out of the Sixty-Four Settlements; and he issued his troops with a 'National Humiliation Map' of China's lost territories, including Transbaikalia and the Amur and Maritime provinces of the Russian Far East. The appetite for Soviet arms, or for Soviet money to buy arms, inevitably led the warlords into a certain amount of mendacity to conceal their underlying anti-Soviet bias. After the Congress of Toilers of the Far East held in Moscow in early 1922 a Soviet official complained that a Chinese woman delegate had 'behaved badly'. She had approached Alexandra Kollontai for funds for a 'Chinese women's movement' only to be unmasked as an agent for Sun Yat-sen's bugbear, the southern general Chen Jiongming.[96] Calling on a Soviet adviser in Tianjin in January 1926, a certain Deng Baoshan 'like most generals straddled his hobby-horse and instead of discussing military matters rendered a discourse about his revolutionary spirit and his concern for the people's welfare'.[97] And the following May the Christian General, who had taken refuge in Moscow after a recent defeat, found it judicious to make a personal donation of 100 roubles for the participants in the British General Strike.

The Nationalists exhibited a more complex response, because the Nationalist Party was a more complex organism. Sun Yat-sen presided over a broad coalition, ranging from the westernised intellectuals of the treaty ports to urban business interests, rural landowners whose sons made up the bulk of his officer corps and the Overseas Chinese communities of South

East Asia that had financed his activities from the earliest days. As Nationalists with a large 'n' these groups tended to esteem Soviet Russia as the one outside power apparently willing to help them in overthrowing the rule of the warlords and unifying the country. They rejoiced in the Karakhan Declaration, and seem not to have paid too much attention to the subsequent Soviet back-pedalling over part of its content. They hailed the Soviet-Chinese agreement of May 1924 as the first 'equal treaty' concluded with China since the Opium Wars. As Nationalists with a large 'n', however, they were also apt to resent the onset of Soviet micromanaging. Nationalist officers were hostile to the mere presence of Soviet advisers beside them, fearing that they would 'lose face' if they were seen to obey the instructions of these foreigners who were nominally under their command. 'Whenever there was a battle to be fought', complained Blücher, 'we were treated with respect and asked for help, but as soon as it was over they adopted their old stance.'[98] ('For it's Boris this an' Boris that . . .', one is tempted to murmur.) Civilian Nationalists didn't like to see their teachings and experience played down by comparison with the new gospel from Moscow. China, not Russia, after all had been first off the mark in overthrowing its monarchy. A Nationalist delegate to the Moscow Congress of Toilers of the Far East maintained that the Bolsheviks were only saying what Sun Yat-sen had been saying for the past twenty years. Where Marxism differed they found it repugnant. Neither the urban middle class nor the rural landowners were happy with the concept of class struggle, and the rural bosses especially were alarmed by Soviet proposals for the redistribution of land. Even the handful of radical Nationalists who made the journey to Russia sometimes showed a certain lack of ideological preparedness. Another delegate bound for the 1922 Congress of Toilers was overheard in Irkutsk singing a racy Chinese ditty entitled 'My Little Darling Is Playing Dominoes'.

So Sun had to tread an extremely fine line. Within weeks of the Bolshevik takeover in 1917 he had sent a cable of greetings to Lenin; and in the following years he was steered in the Soviet direction by his foreign affairs adviser, Eugene Chen, a cosmopolitan Chinese born in Trinidad, and perhaps even more by his wife, Song Qingling, one of the famous Soong sisters, a classic treaty port product who wrote affectionate letters to 'My dear Mr Borodin' expressing anxiety over 'Mr Joffe's health' and her hope of travelling with 'Mr and Mrs Borodin' from Shanghai to Canton.[99] Encouraged by these two comparative radicals, Sun declared that 'the revolution in Russia has engendered great hope among all of mankind'.[100] When an American journalist aimed an anti-Semitic jab at Borodin by asking Sun if he knew the real name (Gruzenberg) of his foreign assistant the Nationalist leader shot back, '*Lafayette*'.[101] But Sun was also well aware that he couldn't afford to antagonise a large part of his support by displaying excessive partiality to the Communist state. The introduction of Lenin's New Economic Policy in the autumn of 1921 allowed him to argue that the most extreme phase of the Bolshevik Revolution was over and that the Russians were set on a similar path to the Economic Construction Programme laid down in his Three People's Principles. But in the communiqué he signed with Joffe in January 1923 proclaiming his new partnership with the Soviet Union he made a point of stressing that 'the Communistic or Soviet system cannot actually be introduced into China';[102] and he further insisted that members of the Chinese Communist Party could only be allowed to join his KMT as individuals under Nationalist direction and not as a bloc. When Borodin's arrival in Canton that autumn gave rise to a deluge of telegrams from panic-stricken men of property warning that the 'sovietisation' of Guangdong Province was imminent and the Overseas Chinese likely to abandon his party en masse, Sun deliberately kept the Special Adviser at arm's length, dodging meetings repeatedly when Borodin sought to present his suggestions for land reform. After Borodin helped him to repel Chen Jiongming's warlord troops he relaxed somewhat, but nonetheless turned down the proposals for land reform when they finally reached him. Eugene Chen was assigned to point out to the Special Adviser that Chinese landowners were hard-working, unlike the idle Russian aristocrats of tsarist times. Over the following year Sun continued to duck and weave, even absenting himself from the hall where Borodin stage-managed the first congress of the revamped KMT in January 1924. Protean as always, he seems never quite to have turned his back on the notion of allying with Japan under the slogan of 'Asia for the Asiatics'; and Japan was his last port of call before he went back to Peking to die at the beginning of 1925.

After Sun's death the division between the left and right wings of the Nationalist Party became starkly obvious. Leading the left were the glamorous Wang Jingwei, hand-picked by the Bolsheviks, and Liao Zhongkai, who sported a hammer and sickle over the door of his office but who was, however, assassinated the following August. On the right a conservative group mustered their forces at a conference held in November in the Western Hills outside Peking, where they called for the dismissal of the over-mighty Borodin and are said to have shown a clear wish to replace their Soviet advisers with Japanese ones. And somewhere in the middle, looming ever larger, was the enigmatic figure of the Nationalist military chief, Chiang Kai-shek. Supportive initially of Sun's opening to the Bolsheviks, Chiang had been sent to Moscow in the autumn of 1923 as the head of a mission assigned to investigate the political and military organisation of the Soviet Red Army. He appears to have been genuinely impressed by the political commissar system and the mobilisation of young Russians into the Communist Youth League (Komsomol), which he described in his diary as a 'number one good policy'.[103] He felt some of the Soviet leaders to be well disposed, in particular Trotsky, whom he 'found the most forthright of them all, both in speech and conduct',[104] and later claimed in his memoirs, perhaps with the benefit of hindsight, to have detected the first signs of conflict between Trotsky's 'internationalist clique' and Stalin's 'domestic organisational clique'.[105] Back in China, as head of the new Whampoa Military Academy, he worked in seeming harmony with the Soviet advisory team, interacting especially well with the no-nonsense Blücher, whom he praised as 'an outstanding Russian general as well as a reasonable man and a good friend',[106] and whom he consulted frequently, 'sitting on the edge of his chair and folding his hands on his knees as a mark of respect'.[107] In December 1925, at the close of the Second Eastern Expedition, he gave a banquet for the advisers in the city of Shantou at which he compared the Soviet-Nationalist partnership to the First World War Allies and likened Borodin to Marshal Foch. He even permitted his teenage son, Chiang Ching-kuo, to travel to Moscow with a group of young KMT members to study at the new Sun Yat-sen University. Small wonder that he became known in western circles in Shanghai as 'the Little Red General' and that many of the Russians, including Borodin, regarded him as a reliable friend.

But as with Sun, so with Chiang there was another side to the picture. Evidence from Chiang's writings, his diaries as well as his memoirs, suggests that he developed in Moscow a deep underlying suspicion of Soviet aims. While still in the Bolshevik capital he cautioned a KMT student against being 'manipulated by outsiders',[108] and he was moved to fury when Trotsky on one occasion implied that Mongolia wasn't in fact part of China. And on his return to Canton he began unobtrusively to sow doubts. In December 1923 he advised Sun Yat-sen that the Russians were working to 'sovietise' his country. In March 1924 he wrote a letter to Liao Zhongkai warning him that only 30 per cent of what the Bolsheviks said could be trusted, that Soviet Russia harboured territorial designs on Manchuria, Mongolia, Xinjiang, Tibet and perhaps China proper and that the Soviet policy of 'world revolution' was merely 'tsarism under another name'.[109] In November he counselled Sun against accepting an invitation transmitted to him by Borodin to visit Moscow, on the grounds that the Bolsheviks would 'spread rumours to confuse the people',[110] and in 1925 he began to expound the idea that Soviet advisers coming to China should promote Sun's Three People's Principles rather than the teachings of Lenin. To advance his career it had made sense for Chiang to hitch his star for a time to the Soviet military mission. To win power over China, however, he needed support from the serried ranks of the city merchants, the landowners and the officer caste. Behind a façade of neutrality the commandant of the Whampoa Military Academy was quietly trending to the right.

Untroubled apparently by these ambivalences, the handful of intellectuals who made up the young Chinese Communist Party looked with rapture on Soviet Russia as a new civilisation based on social justice. Even before the advent of Voitinsky the Peking University scholar Li Dazhao had been urging his students to 'go to the people' like the Russian radicals of the 1870s – to plunge into the countryside and 'spread the principles of humanism and socialism'.[111] At a less rarefied level some of the Chinese labourers stranded in Russia by the upheaval were starting to come back home with positive accounts of what they had experienced in the new Soviet state. By the end of 1920 the first Chinese enthusiasts were beginning to go the other way, braving the widespread famine and the rigours of War Communism to make their pilgrimage to the new proletarian Mecca. A young man named Qu Qiubai who had been posted to Moscow as correspondent of the Peking newspaper *Dawn* told his friends that 'for the sake of a thorough enlightenment I am going to the Land of Hunger'.[112] On arrival he exulted,

> Now I am happy, for I have seen the lighthouse of the mind's sea. Even though it is at present just a single red ray, weak and indistinct, it is possible to see in it the approaching infinite progress.[113]

Some of these earliest visitors, including Qu, either met Lenin or heard him speak, looking upon the director of the revolution 'as one might regard the pure and incorruptible leader of a religious order'.[114] And Qu was also granted an interview with Anatoly Lunacharsky, the Bolshevik leader in charge of the highly relevant subject of education. In the following years growing numbers of young Chinese Communists were sent off, in their coded expression, 'to do business a long way away',[115] embarking on the courses which had been created for them at the CUTE and the Sun Yat-sen University. Some were smuggled directly from Chinese into Soviet territory, while others were diverted on their way back from 'work-study' programmes in France or Germany to complete their political training at one or the other of the Moscow finishing schools. By April 1924 around 9 per cent of the entire CCP membership had spent time there, and by 1925–6 the CCP student body in Moscow was reaching the hundreds. Alumni who would become famous included Liu Shaoqi, who attended the CUTE in 1921–2, and Deng Xiaoping, who in 1926–7 studied successively at both the CUTE and the Sunovka. Zhou Enlai was primarily involved in recruiting students for the CUTE, but he too is said to have received 'instructions' on his way back from western Europe to China in 1924. It is no exaggeration to say that to one degree or another every prominent member of the first generation of Chinese Communist leaders was a product of Soviet tuition.

With one striking exception. Mao Zedong, a young activist from Hunan Province, had observed in an article that 'a little flower of new culture' had 'emerged on the shores of the Arctic Ocean',[116] and had contemplated making the journey to Russia to learn more about it. He had even gone so far as to take Russian language lessons from Professor Polevoi at Peking University. But he proved unable to master the Russian alphabet, let alone the grammar, and is said to have been teased for this by his peers. In the end he abandoned the project, explaining in later years that he 'felt that I did not know enough about my own country, and that my time would be more profitably spent in China'.[117]

Mao apart, the young CCP trainees poured into Moscow and entered into what many clearly found an uplifting experience. They were enthralled by their courses, 'instantly fascinated' by the 'freshness' of dialectical materialism, inspired by the 'first-class professors' who gave them instruction in Leninism and political economy.[118] Military science, taught by a Soviet divisional commander who had spent time in China, was a 'distinguishing feature' of Sun Yat-sen University, and the students recalled with some relish their introduction to the 'military research room' containing sample cannon, rifles, machine guns, hand grenades and howitzers and their regular trips to nearby army garrisons to practise their marksmanship.[119] Less popular was the intensive Russian language tuition which the students had to undergo before their political and military training began. Some of the students were driven half-crazy by the complexities of Russian grammar, so different from that of their own uninflected language, and there were calls for Russian tuition to be made a sideline rather than a sine qua non. But the more generous of them nonetheless paid tribute to the 'professionalism and responsiveness' of their lady instructors.[120]

The trainees took up cheerfully the more colourful trappings of underground work. They adopted the Russian *noms de guerre* dreamt up for them by their Soviet hosts: thus Zhou Enlai was at various times known as 'Moskvin' or 'Strakhov', while Deng Xiaoping became in rapid succession 'Kresov' and 'Dozorov'. A young man named Zhang Wentian assumed the alias of 'Izmailov', though this seems to have been a bit too much of a mouthful for his Chinese comrades, who shortened it to plain 'Lov' or Luo Fu. Many trainees embraced local fashions with vigour. Sun Yat-sen University students wore high-collared 'Lenin jackets' and violet Ukrainian blouses that buttoned up on the left-hand side. Some of the women had their plaits cut off and their hair bobbed in the Soviet style – a piece of radical chic that they brought back to China.

On a personal level the students felt real affection for some of their Soviet supervisors. Karl Radek, the rector of Sunovka, was 'an idol to all',[121] in spite of the fact that he lectured on the Chinese revolutionary movement without having been anywhere near China and in spite of his being the epitome of an absent-minded professor:

> He was very near-sighted and if he did not wear his glasses he couldn't even walk. His hair was often uncombed and his beard untrimmed. He never seemed to change the dark grey suit which he wore every day . . . He always clenched a pipe in his mouth whether there was tobacco in it or not.[122]

But Radek also had 'a smile that completely filled the space between two enormous sideburns'; had 'a warm personality, like that of a common man'.[123]

Personal friendships off campus were hindered by the limited nature of the students' Russian vocabulary, which largely consisted of dry academic and ideological terms. But this visibly didn't prevent a lively interaction arising with Russians of the opposite sex. In the relaxed moral climate of the early Soviet years liaisons between the sexes took root easily: gossip in China is said to have hummed with accounts of the loose life of students in Moscow and the resulting crop of 'little revolutionaries'.[124] Right at the outset the handsome Liu Shaoqi was rumoured to have had an affair with Larisa Reisner, the 'Red Rose of the Revolution', who was also a friend of Lenin and mistress of Radek;[125] and Luo Fu apparently had a son by a woman captain in the Soviet Army. Other young Chinese Communists met their future Soviet girlfriends or wives in a park, or even in the university dining hall. (In this last case, however, the man's fellow students had doubts about his future with his lovely Russian waitress: 'He occasionally turned up with deep scratches on his face, which we took as evidence of connubial incompatibility.')[126]

We should also notice in this context the continuing fascination of Russian letters for the entire Chinese left. By the early 1920s a stream of translations had appeared of the great Russian classics, including some thirty works by Tolstoy and a generous assortment of writings by Turgenev, Lermontov, Gogol, Goncharov, Dostoevsky and Chekhov.[127] In the following years the stream turned into a torrent, with a new interest developing in the bleak, pessimistic writers of the late tsarist Silver Age such as Mikhail Artsybashev and Leonid Andreev. Some of the future Chinese Communists were in the forefront of this translation endeavour. As a new Chinese literature stirred into life against the background of the First World War and the cultural renaissance known as the May Fourth Movement the traces of a strong Russian influence could be clearly discerned. Lu Xun took the title and theme of his first work of fiction – the first modern Chinese short story, published in 1918 – from Gogol's 1834 tale *The Diary of a Madman*, and ascribed the end of his story *Medicine* to the 'sombre chill' of Andreev, whom he regarded as 'mystical and profound'.[128] He also provided some clues as to why Russian literature exerted such a pull on radical-minded Chinese. He drew attention to the humanism of Russian writing, to the quality of 'art for life's sake' that distinguished it from the 'art for art's sake' of the west.[129] Written mostly, as he understood it, for ladies, nineteenth-century English fiction had exuded a 'sweet sweat' which had since been challenged by the 'rank sweat' from Russia.[130] And this literary appeal in turn generated a sense of affinity. In a lecture delivered in 1920 Lu Xun's younger brother Zhou Zuoren deduced from the 'moral commitment' of Russian literature that the Chinese national character 'had more in common with the Russian national character than with the national character of any European people'.[131]

Not all of the Chinese radicals who admired Russian literature were CCP members; but the appeal of Russian letters undoubtedly helped to propel Chinese radicals in the direction of the CCP. Qu Qiubai's journey to Moscow at the end of 1920 was a cultural as much as a political pilgrimage. Besides hearing Lenin orate and talking to Lunacharsky, he found time to stroll with Tolstoy's granddaughter on the estate of the now deceased author at Yasnaya Polyana, and to hear Chaliapin sing settings of Pushkin's poems. In the following years he joined in the translation endeavour, producing Chinese versions of works by Gogol and Tolstoy. Zhang Wentian (Luo Fu) brought out translations of Tolstoy and Turgenev, and in 1923 also published his rendering of a play by Andreev, *The Waltz of the Dogs*.

The Chinese Communists were however suffused with nationalism quite as much as their counterparts in the KMT. For all their zeal for the Soviet experiment and for Russia in general Chen Duxiu and his followers didn't appreciate being told what to do by agents of the Comintern any more than the Nationalists did. They liked their first Comintern mentor, Voitinsky, whom they found tactful and intelligent and who impressed them with his youthful energy and his 'sad, thoughtful eyes'.[132] Maring the Dutchman was another matter. 'An elegant and rather pompous gentleman who dressed in a grey three-piece suit and bow tie', he had the air not so much of a Bolshevik as of a plantation owner in the Dutch East Indies. Rude, arrogant and unwilling to listen to dissenting voices, he would 'persist in his views with such stubbornness that you would think he was prepared to challenge his opponent to a duel'.[133] Borodin was clearly an improvement, but even he is said to have riled the party's district committee in Canton on occasion by both failing to consult them before he made a move and omitting to tell them the full story afterwards.

Complaints were many and various, and the first CCP congresses organised by the Comintern agents were tense affairs. Chinese delegates didn't want to be made subject to the Comintern. 'So we don't need to hold meetings', one angry person expostulated, 'just take orders from the Russians!'[134]

They didn't want to be forced to submit work reports at a time when the Party was still in its infancy and there was nothing to report anyway. Above all they didn't want to be pitchforked, as the Russians insisted, into the KMT, particularly in view of Sun Yat-sen's stipulation that they could only join his party as individual members and not as a bloc. Looking through the pure eyes of fresh converts, they viewed Sun as just another politician and the KMT as a middle-class outfit in cahoots with the warlords and foreign enemies such as the United States and Japan. Why, some of them wondered, should China be reckoned too backward to make the transition to socialist revolution at one bound as Russia had done in October 1917? At the same time they shared with the Nationalists a dissatisfaction with the pragmatic underside of Soviet policy. In December 1923 four disgruntled Chinese students at the CUTE sent a letter to Karakhan in Peking in which they accused the author of the famous Declaration of being 'full of secret plans such as the seizure of the CER and Mongolia' and manipulating the northern warlords – 'the Chinese dogs whom you feed, making use of their rabid barking'.[135]

For the time being, though, the CCP were too weak to do anything but grumble. Professor Chen is said to have yelled at his meetings with Maring, banged his glass on the table and thrown the teacups around with such fury the Dutchman called him 'the volcano'.[136] But Chen was also aware that the CCP was wholly dependent on Soviet money, and that he who pays the piper calls the tune.

THE TENSION MOUNTS (1926–7)

In the course of 1926 the Soviet missionary venture in China advanced to the brink of triumphant success. On 9 July that year Chiang Kai-shek's National Revolutionary Army, 100,000-strong, set out from Canton on the long-awaited Northern Expedition to vanquish the warlords. The expedition marched first into the next-door province of Hunan and then branched into two columns, a left-hand one under a local commander named Tang Shengzhi striking due north to the Yangtze to wrest the contiguous cities of Wuchang, Hankou and Hanyang, collectively known as Wuhan, from the Philosopher General Wu Peifu, and a right-hand one under Chiang himself heading north-east to Nanchang in Jiangxi Province to do battle with Wu's protégé, the 'Nanking Warlord' Sun Chuanfang. The NRA forces were bankrolled by Soviet funds and equipped by the Bolsheviks with an overwhelmingly strong arsenal that included twenty-four aeroplanes, 157 field guns, forty-seven mountain guns, 128 mortars, 295 heavy machine guns, 73,993 rifles, 110,000 hand grenades, 124 million rifle cartridges and 500,000 artillery shells. And General Blücher and his team of military advisers were present in full micromanaging mode. During the run-up to the expedition Blücher held a series of consultations with Chiang on both strategic and tactical matters, advising him, for example, to concentrate on Hunan initially and to maximise the impact of the offensive by getting all his forces assembled on a fixed day for a concerted attack. Once the offensive began Blücher took direct charge, frequently turning up on the battlefield and making reconnaissance flights over warlord positions. Senior Soviet officers were assigned to each of the six NRA army corps, where they helped to draw up plans and coordinate the action of the different combat groups. During the left-hand campaign, which concluded victoriously on 10 October, an expert Soviet artilleryman directed the fire of up to 4,000 shells, while five Soviet pilots dropped bombs from dilapidated aircraft, gave flying instructions to would-be Chinese airmen and at spare moments expressed their commitment in a sad little song, 'Perhaps Tomorrow We'll Be Buried at Wuchang'. Similar hefty back-up was given to Chiang's right-hand campaign. Sometimes Chiang is said to have countersigned Blücher's commands without so much as reading them, and there is still no sign that the Nationalist leader resented his dependence on Soviet military aid. When Nanchang fell in early November a delighted Chiang ordered a dozen splendid gold watches for Blücher and his associates which Soviet morality didn't permit them to accept. On 5 December Blücher made a formal entry into the city on horseback amid cheering crowds. His *nom de guerre*, Galin, became a generic Chinese term for a Soviet adviser, and some enthusiastic KMT partisans are even said to have bestowed it on their children. On the last day of the year Chiang gave a banquet in honour of his lieutenants from Moscow. The interpreter Vera Vishnyakova, who was present, reported that he 'bared his large, horse-like teeth and seemed about to neigh from pleasure that the success of the Northern Expedition had turned into a personal success for him'.[137] The National Revolution to unify China was well under way.

Hopes were even rising that the change of gear from a national to a social revolution which Leninist dogma held out for China at best as a vague future prospect might take place sooner than anyone had foreseen. In January 1926 a second congress of the Nationalist Party, once again organised by Special Adviser Borodin, had been held in Canton. The proceedings were dominated by the Left KMT and the Communists, who between them secured almost all of the main Party posts. Wang Jingwei, the Left KMT leader anointed by the Bolsheviks, took every step in consultation with the Special Adviser, and is said to have struck an even more left- wing pose than the Communists did. From a small coterie of intellectuals the CCP was growing rapidly into a mass movement, its membership on the way up from just under 1,000 in January 1925 to just under 58,000 in the next two years. After the Northern Expedition set out in July CCP agitators advanced in the van of the NRA forces, spreading propaganda in true Bolshevik style and supervising the peasant insurgencies they had helped to arouse against local landowners. In early December Borodin moved up with his Left KMT and CCP entourage from Canton to newly captured Wuhan, where he like Blücher was hailed as a hero by a rapturous crowd of 300,000. On 13 December he established a Provisional Joint Assembly of Party and Government Organisations which was for all practical purposes run by himself. The nominal head of this government, a Left KMT man named Xu Qian, is said to have taken Borodin's orders, and during his periodic illnesses the entire corps of ministers would gather at his bedside. Some of Borodin's directives were in keeping with the accepted goals of the National Revolution: thus, for example, he launched through the press a campaign aimed at Britain which reached its climax early in the New Year when a mob of demonstrators took over the British concession in Hankou. But there were also signs he was shifting towards a more radical course. In his spare time he held long discussions with the westernised KMT types who had travelled with him from Canton, endeavouring to persuade them of the merits of Communism. He addressed himself not merely to long-standing sympathisers like Eugene Chen, foreign minister in the new Wuhan government, and the now widowed Mme Sun Yat-sen but also to so far uncommitted figures such as Mme Sun's younger sister, Song Meiling, the future Mme Chiang Kai-shek (on whom he seems to have developed something of a crush: a fragment of his blotting paper was found to contain the doodle 'Mayling Darling, Darling Mayling'[138]). More substantially he proclaimed 'three great policies' for the new government – unity with the Soviet Union, unity with the CCP and unity with the peasants and workers. And he drew up a plan for 'bolshevising' the NRA officer caste, winning over the lukewarm and executing any diehards who clung to their anti-Communist views.

Beneath this promising surface, however, all the tensions inherent in the Bolsheviks' relations with their Chinese clients were grimly fermenting. Already by the turn of 1925–6 there were indications that the Soviet missionaries were overreaching themselves. Both Blücher and Borodin were away from Canton in the course of that winter, Blücher at home for health reasons, Borodin on his way back for consultations in Moscow, stopping off in Mongolia for a parley with the Soviet Union's promising north-western ally, Christian General Feng. In their absence the reins were held by two men of lesser calibre, N.V. Kuibyshev, aka Kisanka, the acting chief of mission, and V.P. Rogachev, the chief of staff, both of whom showed themselves overconfident in the strength of the Soviet foothold and insensitive in the extreme in their dealings with Chiang Kai-shek and his Nationalist officers. Their reports were full of cocky allusions to the power they and their colleagues wielded in the NRA behind the fig leaf of their advisory role. They treated Chiang condescendingly, ignored him when possible and conferred with the civilian Wang Jingwei over military affairs. They urged Chiang to create a more centralised army structure, reducing the room for manoeuvre of his local generals, and even prodded him to transfer the whole army to Vladivostok, unsurprisingly sparking rumours of a Soviet plan to take over the army and send Chiang to languish somewhere in the wastes of Siberia. Such tactlessness only fuelled Chiang's existing suspicions of Soviet motives, and by the spring it appears that his patience had come to an end. On 8 March he burst out to Wang Jingwei, '*We cannot permit a situation in which the effective leadership of the National Revolution is in the hands of the Russians*.'[139] And on 20 March he took action, through the bizarre method of staging an imaginary coup against himself. Li Zhilong, a CCP member serving as commissar of the warship *Zhongshan*, was directed to bring his vessel up from Canton to the NRA headquarters at Whampoa – which he very properly did, only for Chiang to proclaim his action to be evidence of a Communist plot. In the ensuing crackdown Chiang sent troops to disarm the guards stationed in front of the Soviet advisers' residence and detain around thirty of the Soviet military men. Matters were quickly smoothed over and the advisers released; but the display of Chiang's muscle had been an ominous warning, and the Bolsheviks knew it. Moscow plunged into damage limitation. At

Chiang's insistence Kisanka, Rogachev and eight of their colleagues were whisked back home within days. In late April Borodin returned to Canton bringing clearance for Chiang to embark on his cherished Northern Expedition, on which Moscow had lately been dragging its feet.

But Chiang's patience was fraying with Borodin as well. Among other gripes he objected to Borodin's demand that he speed up land redistribution as part of his Northern campaign. By the autumn he was making no secret of his opinion that 'foreigners were becoming too important in Chinese affairs'.[140] And Borodin no longer concealed his antipathy to the Nationalist leader. By October, apparently on his own private initiative, he was conferring with his fellow advisers about the possibility of replacing Chiang as head of the NRA with Tang Shengzhi, the commander of the left-hand column, who had been making radical noises and had even held a discussion with the CCP. A report filed two months earlier had praised Tang for his 'liveliness' and his 'great determination' – forbidding his entourage to smoke, for example, on the grounds that he didn't smoke himself.[141] There was at least an outside chance that he might be prevailed on to break with the mainstream Nationalist leadership. Encouraged apparently by this assessment, the Special Adviser met up with Tang declaring that he no longer trusted Chiang Kai-shek, but only him, and holding out to the general the prospect that he might soon be 'the greatest figure in China'.[142] And as the NRA basked in their triumph after the fall of Wuhan and Nanchang the friction between Chiang and Borodin flared up into open hostility. At a banquet held by Chiang in Nanchang on 2 December Borodin made a speech slamming the Nationalist chief for levying heavy taxes in the areas under his control, squandering money on his officers and troops and delaying the all-important reforms on the land. The Soviet Union, he noted, held the purse-strings of the Expedition, and had no intention of backing a campaign that was visibly heading the wrong way. The reaction is said to have been 'a stunned hush'.[143] One month later, on 11 January 1927, Chiang was induced to pay a lightning visit to Borodin's new base at Wuhan. The two men found themselves in immediate deadlock. Chiang refused to accept Borodin's regime as the National government, or Wuhan as its capital; and he wasn't prepared to join up, as Borodin expected, with the Wuhan column in a final advance on Peking, but instead planned to move his troops east to the lower Yangtze valley and the fleshpots of Nanking and Shanghai –

literally, in Borodin's eyes, taking the Revolution in the wrong direction. At a dinner that evening the Special Adviser once more harangued Chiang, this time in frankly menacing terms:

> We have a general who pursues his own political line that runs counter to that of the Government and its decisions. He ought to remember that wherever he may hide he will not elude the justice of the people; the strong arm of the people will find and punish him. Comrade Chiang Kai-shek, together with you we have reached the Yangtze, and I hope that we shall continue to go arm in arm.[144]

He is even said to have issued a secret order to have Chiang arrested. Enraged and humiliated, Chiang returned to Nanchang to prepare countermeasures of his own. In the course of February he made two appeals to Moscow demanding that Borodin be recalled and replaced by someone he judged more amenable, such as Radek or Karakhan. And in the following weeks, as he moved into the lower Yangtze, he started to slough off his Soviet aides altogether. On 14 March a reluctant Blücher was shunted back upstream to Hankou. On 27 March the remaining Soviet military advisers followed the NRA into newly captured Nanking, where they were accommodated in Chiang's own headquarters but found that their services were no longer called for. Under constant surveillance, they were denied access to newspapers and any other reports from outside, aware only that 'something was brewing' in Chiang's wing of the building and that 'the very air was permeated with danger'.[145]

Friction was equally growing with the CCP. As their clout and membership grew the Chinese Communists were ever more restive at their enforced alliance with the Nationalist Party. Their desire was to break with the Nationalists and set up revolutionary councils – soviets – in the Bolshevik style as a first step towards seizing power for themselves. After Chiang's show of force in Canton they were also keenly conscious that it could only be a matter of time before the KMT rounded on them in earnest. Some of their Soviet mentors agreed with these views. Voitinsky, for instance, is said on his own authority to have urged the CCP to carry on stirring up peasant unrest against the KMT-leaning landlords. Back in Moscow, however, Stalin clung doggedly to the settled policy of upholding the Nationalists as the engine driving the unification of China, with the Communists patiently waiting their turn in the framework of the United Front; and every signal from Moscow reinforced this approach. In January 1926 the foreign policy boss Chicherin wrote to Karakhan in Peking in connection with the KMT's second congress, expressing alarm at the way the CCP seemed to be systematically taking over the Nationalist Party, even elbowing out the amenable KMT left wing. In October, at Stalin's prompting, the Moscow Politburo issued a directive prohibiting any struggle against the Chinese middle classes, and in December word went out from the Comintern, '*No soviets in Wuhan!*'.[146] Moscow's agents in China might not be best pleased with these orders, but in the last resort they had no choice but to fall in line. For all his manoeuvring against Chiang Kai-shek Borodin never abandoned the dogma of the United Front, dismissing with a 'cold refusal' on the eve of the Northern Expedition a request from the Chinese Communists to supply them with arms designated for the NRA.[147] Even Voitinsky was obliged at the end of the year to spell out Moscow's line to the CCP, to the shock and rage of their leader Chen Duxiu. In late March 1927, when the CCP in Shanghai with the help of Comintern funds organised a workers' uprising to take place on the eve of the entry of NRA forces into the city, the constraints imposed by the Kremlin were still more emphatic. The Chinese Communists were to bury their guns and avoid clashes with the NRA troops and commanders 'at any price'.[148] We are told that when one of the CCP activists in Shanghai saw the cable containing these guidelines he 'indignantly threw it on the floor'.[149]

Stalin remained imperturbable. On 5 April, at a meeting of the Moscow committee of the Bolshevik Party, he painted a rosy picture of events. The CCP, he continued to posit, needed the Nationalist Party, the right wing as well as the left. Whatever the KMT's shortcomings, 'a bad mare was still a mare'.[150] Chiang Kai-shek would cooperate with his partners like an obedient soldier, and could be used and then later on 'tossed away like a squeezed-out lemon'.[151] As the Nationalists marched towards victory against the remaining warlords in the great Expedition, with the CCP, as it seemed, snugly perched on their shoulders, the mood in Moscow was euphoric. Stalin's ally Bukharin hailed 'a turning-point in world history'.[152] Mayakovsky wrote a hymn of praise to the Shanghai workers' rising. Soviet girls blew kisses and flirted and offered themselves in marriage to the Chinese students at Sun Yat-sen University. After four years of effort it looked as though the Soviet missionaries to China were at last within sight of their goals. But catastrophe was already upon them.

SHATTERED HOPES (1927)

The first stirrings of a major backlash against the Soviet presence came, perhaps not surprisingly, from the warlord side. At the end of February 1927 a Soviet vessel, the *Pamyat' Lenina* ('Memory of Lenin') which was carrying Borodin's wife and fellow revolutionary Fanya down the Yangtze from Wuhan to Shanghai, was boarded and taken over by troops of Zhang Zongchang, the Dog Meat General from Shandong Province. Together with a contingent of diplomatic couriers and the forty-seven-strong crew, Mme Borodina was spirited away to Jinan, the Shandong capital, where she was subjected to a curious stick-and-carrot routine, prison and threats of beheading interspersed with banquets at which her captors voiced their respect for her husband's 'refined psychological approach to our people' and asked only that he give up his political activity.[153] She was released in a few months and published a booklet about her experiences entitled, with commendable detachment, *In the Torture Chambers of the Chinese Satraps*.[154] The next episode was a grislier one. On 6 April a force of 500 soldiers and police dispatched by the Old Marshal Zhang Zuolin broke into the Soviet embassy in Peking and seized about twenty diplomats, plus a group of some sixty CCP members who had taken refuge there. Professor Li Dazhao, the sometime librarian of Peking University who had been among the first Chinese intellectuals to draw attention to Marxism, was garrotted, and twenty-four other Chinese were hanged. The raiding party also discovered a stash of documents setting out current Bolshevik plans and progress in China, which they were quick to appropriate for future publicity: 'the din of locks being forced and the revving of lorries could be heard all night long'.[155]

Then on 12 April, just one week after Stalin delivered his optimistic prognosis for the United Front, Chiang Kai-shek turned his newly arrived NRA troops on their Chinese Communist allies in Shanghai. Plans had long since been concerted by Chiang and the Right KMT with local business and gangland interests and through them with the foreigners in the city's concessions. More than 5,000 striking workers and CCP activists were massacred by the NRA and the gangsters between them over the course of three weeks. Some attempt was initially made to draw a distinction between the CCP on the one hand and the Russians on the other, but the reality soon showed through. At a banquet held in Nanking on the evening of 18 April the Soviet military advisers still at Chiang's side were treated, perhaps for the first time, to the frightening spectacle of a complete Chinese loss of self-control. In a diatribe aimed at both the CCP and Borodin Chiang 'began to screech and lapsed into hysteria'.[156] Various of his generals lashed out at their former Soviet patrons in similar tones. 'Almost none of them spoke in their normal voices: they yelled, screamed and shrieked.'[157] The Soviet team thought of pointing out to their hosts that they had, after all, come to China at the KMT's invitation and had played a somewhat critical role in the recent defeat of the warlords; 'but seeing the hysteria of the over-excited generals we decided to walk out'.[158] Calling on Chiang at the end of the month the ranking Soviet officer, Lieutenant-General A.V. Blagodatov, found the Nationalist leader calmer, but no more congenial. Now he 'sprawled in his chair, his hands folded on his chest in imitation of Napoleon and his lower lip protruding in disdain'.[159] On 4 May Chiang delivered a first public tirade against 'Red imperialism'. The door to the Right KMT had slammed shut.

There remained still the Left KMT. In spite of the Shanghai disaster Stalin and his agents in China continued to pin their hopes on a partnership between the Chinese Communists and the progressive Nationalists in Wuhan. On 15 April, three days after the start of the purge in Shanghai, the Wuhan leadership prodded by Borodin obligingly issued an order dismissing Chiang Kai-shek from his post as commander of the NRA; and Borodin set about persuading his colleagues to mobilise a new Eastern Expedition directed at Chiang. In a speech delivered on 13 May at the Sun Yat-sen University Stalin depicted Chiang's coup as 'a partial and temporary setback', and reminded his audience of the role played by the Nationalists in opposing the foreign imperial powers.[160] At the end of the month he cabled Borodin instructions of a quite untypically cavalier kind, effectively urging the Wuhan leaders to spearhead an all-out bid for revolutionary change. Agrarian uprisings were to be launched in every province. An army was to be formed of 20,000 CCP members, and 50,000 peasants in the provinces of Hubei and Hunan were to be organised into a new fighting force. Unreliable generals were to be eliminated or put on trial, and sympathetic ones to be exploited. (As Lenin had promised with reference to the British Labour Party, 'We shall provide them with the support a rope gives to a hanged man.'[161]) And peasants and workers were to be inducted into the KMT Central Committee. The result was yet another calamity. Even before Stalin's telegram the Wuhan ministers had begun to take fright. While talking extravagantly of his hopes to stage an October Revolution in China their flamboyant but slippery leader Wang Jingwei had conferred in mid-April with Chiang in Shanghai on his way back from a protracted absence in Europe. He had noted uncomfortably that westerners were dismissing the Wuhan government as 'Russian', while Chiang and his faction were considered to be authentically Chinese. And neither he nor his associates, middle-class to a man, had any more sympathy for class struggle and the eviction of landowners than their counterparts on the KMT Right. When on 1 June, consequently, a hot-headed Indian agent of the Comintern, M.N. Roy, who had been sent to Wuhan to buttress Borodin, in an act of extraordinary crassness showed Wang Jingwei Stalin's cable, the Left KMT chief exploded, storming into the office of the Special Adviser and announcing that he had been 'double-crossed'.[162] Even the friendly Wuhan foreign minister, Eugene Chen, is said to have exhibited 'dismay and displeasure'.[163] And the Left KMT, like the Right, duly turned on the Bolsheviks and their CCP protégés. In the course of June the ministers assembled at Wang's house and decided to 'de-Borodinise' Wuhan, and on 14 July they resolved formally that the Special Adviser should be packed off home to the Soviet Union. Ties with the Chinese Communists were severed the following day.

No more joy was forthcoming meanwhile from the supposed revolutionary generals. On 21 May a local commander in Changsha, the Hunan capital, turned his troops bloodily on the trades unions and peasant associations that had been set up in the province by the CCP. When Borodin and five of his colleagues set off for Changsha to investigate the killings they received a cable from the commander threatening to shoot them on the spot; whereupon they beat a hasty retreat. A week later Tang Shengzhi, once billed as the champion of the anti-Chiang forces, justified the doubts voiced over his reliability by the more cautious Russians by declaring that he was anti-Communist and that his support for Borodin had ceased. And in a final blow Feng Yuxiang, the 'Centre of the North-West', the one warlord in whom the Russians had made a major investment, whom they had hosted in Moscow, whom they had even induced to ally himself with the Left KMT, suddenly swivelled and put the knife in his Soviet sponsors. Holding talks first with Wang, then with Chiang, the Christian General cabled in late June to the Wuhan government that they should rid themselves of their Communists and send Borodin back home. By this juncture the Bolsheviks in Wuhan were at risk of their lives. An attempt was apparently made to poison Blücher and his officers at a feast held to celebrate the latest victories of the NRA troops, who had now penetrated as far as the North China Plain. Blücher recovered from his dosage, but a cipher expert named Zotov succumbed.

In the thick of all this, finally, making every possible use of the anti-Soviet backlash, were the exiled White Russians. Just as Chinese had fought on both sides in the Russian Civil War, so Russians fought on both sides in this conflict in China. Upwards of 4,000 White troops had taken service with the Dog Meat General and the other northern warlords, and as the backlash gathered strength these contingents were only too happy to get in a blow at their Bolshevik foes. White Guards in the uniform of Chinese officers were prominent in the party that boarded the *Pamyat' Lenina* to effect the abduction of Borodin's wife. On the day that the Old Marshal's soldiers broke into the Soviet embassy in Peking, armed White troops acting seemingly in conjunction with them surrounded and raided the Bolsheviks' Shanghai consulate; and as events in Shanghai neared their climax the Whites showed themselves easily the most stubborn opponents of the revolutionary cause. To begin with they pitted themselves against both the Communist-led insurgents and Chiang Kai-shek's National Revolutionary Army, with a crack force under General K.P. Nechaev machine-gunning savagely at the city's North Station from the shelter of a makeshift armoured train. Later, after the NRA had turned their guns on the Communists, they joined hands with Chiang's troops and had the satisfaction of taking part in the anti-Bolshevik crackdown. As the Nationalists linked up with the British and other authorities in the foreign concessions some Whites seized the chance to pursue their vendetta there too. Inside the British-dominated International Settlement 150 of them were formed into a first Russian regiment of the Shanghai Volunteer Corps, while others gained admission to the counter-intelligence section of the Shanghai Municipal Police.

So the Soviet mission unravelled. On 27 July Borodin set off from Wuhan with a small entourage on the first leg of a long journey home. Deeply despondent, but voluble as ever, he observed to a foreign reporter that the

Revolution had been brought up short at the Yangtze. 'If a diver were sent down to the bottom of this yellow stream he would rise again with an armful of shattered hopes.'[164] As the main target of Nationalist fury he took the overland route back to Moscow, keeping well away from Chiang's strongholds in the coastal cities. Hauling their vehicles painfully through the sands of the Gobi, singing mournful snatches around their camp fires, the Special Adviser and his team were eventually able to cross on to Soviet soil and link up with the Trans-Siberian Railway. Limping into the capital in early September Borodin delivered himself of a parting shot at the likes of Christian General Feng: 'When the next Chinese general comes to Moscow and shouts "Hail to the World Revolution!" better send at once for the GPU. All they ever want is rifles.'[165]

Most of the other Soviet advisers and their wives made their way more sedately by steamer down the Yangtze to Nanking and Shanghai. Arriving in Shanghai, however, they were frequently greeted by an unpleasant surprise as their vessels were boarded by Nationalist or British policemen. Sometimes the police were accompanied by a blond young Russian with 'shifty eyes and a pale face' who went by the name of Eugene Pick.[166] On Borodin's payroll two years before, he had since gone over to the White side, and now specialised in ferreting out Bolsheviks and their secrets. One group of Soviet officers found themselves taken to a KMT police headquarters where they were herded into an interrogation chamber full of pulleys, rods and other discouraging instruments and had manacles clamped on their wrists and legs. Gasping in the stifling heat they embarked on a hunger strike, while executioners came in and out busy with the beheading of their CCP comrades. In the end their release was secured by a second group from Canton, who interceded directly with Chiang and enabled them to catch an onward connection to Vladivostok. The other leading Bolshevik personage, Blücher, was spared these indignities. 'Greatly depressed',[167] like Borodin, he made a point of calling on Chiang and expressing the hope that this would not be the last time they met. Chiang still retained a soft spot for the veteran who had guided him through so many hard-fought campaigns. He said he hoped he and Blücher would have another chance to work together, and later recorded the meeting as being 'one of the most moving partings in my life'.[168]

With his KMT ties wholly ruptured Stalin now switched to the only option remaining – all-out support for the Chinese Communist Party. In late

July he decreed that 'the slogan of soviets is correct now',[169] and two months later he had the CCP formally withdrawn by the Comintern from the wreckage of the United Front. A young fellow Georgian, Besso Lominadze, was sent out to China in Borodin's place as the leading Comintern agent, and in the course of the autumn he and his colleagues presided over a series of armed insurrections attempted by the CCP against the Nationalists in the southern cities of Nanchang, Changsha and Canton. Each of these three insurrections ended ingloriously. In Nanchang, where on 1 August 20,000 CCP soldiers staged their rising at Blücher's suggestion, the Communists did briefly achieve a successful takeover. But Soviet funds weren't forthcoming, Soviet advisers were strictly forbidden to join in the battle, and the CCP force were in no position to build on their gains. Once again prompted by Blücher they headed south into Guangdong Province, where they were supposed to pick up a shipment of Soviet arms in the coastal district of Hailufeng. But the arms never turned up, and at the end of September the CCP soldiers suffered a crushing defeat at the hands of the Nationalists near the south-eastern city of Shantou. In the case of Changsha the Soviet commitment was more whole-hearted, or perhaps better organised. On 15 August the putative leaders of this 'Autumn Harvest' uprising were mustered by the local Soviet consul, Vladimir Kuchumov, who doubled as a Comintern agent, and bankrolled to the tune of 10,000 Chinese yuan. But the uprising launched on 9 September quickly proved a failure when neither the city's industrial workers nor the peasants in the surrounding farmlands showed any desire to come to the aid of the CCP troops. In Canton in December the Bolsheviks made their most substantial investment so far: 100,000 yuan were committed on this occasion, and the Soviet consulate was used as a command post and fountainhead of tactical advice for the Chinese rebels. On 11 December Canton awoke to a faithful re-enactment of the Petrograd Revolution of ten years before, with the proclamation of a 'Government of Workers', Soldiers' and Peasants' Deputies' and the slogan 'Bread for the workers! Land for the peasants!' (*sic*, 'bread', in a rice-growing region), while Soviet diplomats proudly drove to and fro in a sea of red flags. This insurrection, however, proved the most disastrous of all. A band of 3,000 Cantonese workers, randomly armed with whatever weapons they were able to find, were pitted against 45,000 regular troops of the local Nationalist commander, Zhang Fakui, thoroughly trained, as it happened, in past years by Blücher and his team at the Whampoa Military Academy. By 13 December it was all over. Almost 6,000 real or suspected CCP partisans were slaughtered by the vengeful Nationalists, including Borodin's former friend and interpreter, Zhang Tailei; and this time the blow also fell on the Russians themselves. Zhang Fakui's troops forced their way into the Soviet consulate, dragged out the vice-consul and four other members of the consular staff and lined them up on the pavement outside. Placards were hung on them bearing the legend, '*This person is a Russian Communist and anyone may do what he wants with him*.'[170] Passers-by accordingly spat on, beat and even knifed the Soviet captives, who were then hauled away to the nearest police station and shot. The local Comintern agent and a number of other survivors appeared, their faces black with gunpowder, in search of refuge at the gates of the western concessions where, no doubt in a reflex of racial solidarity, they were grudgingly taken in. All in all the adventures of autumn 1927 seemed to have achieved little more than to demonstrate that the new policy of confronting the Nationalists was no more productive than the original one of cosying up to them.

As the disasters unfolded the Soviet leader came under increasing attack from within his own Bolshevik camp. Leon Trotsky, who hadn't so far taken very much interest in Chinese affairs, now suddenly found China gave him a wonderful chance to lay into his rival. By March 1927 he was already denouncing the bankruptcy of Stalin's policies, calling for the CCP to pull out of the United Front with the Nationalists, where they enjoyed 'all the independence of Jonah inside the whale's belly',[171] and set up their own revolutionary councils instead. As the NRA entered Shanghai he observed that the Soviet Union was in the position of 'a hen who has hatched a duckling' and called for an emergency warning to be sent to the city's workers advising them that Chiang was a 'Chinese Bonaparte' who could turn his forces against them at any time.[172] After Chiang's coup of 12 April he mocked his rival's misplaced confidence in the Nationalist leader, noting that Stalin's speech likening the KMT leader to a squeezed-out lemon was never made public 'because a few days later the squeezed-out lemon seized power and the army',[173] and castigated 'those ill-fated revolutionaries who fear people's soviets but . . . have faith in the sacred ink-blots on the writing paper of the Nationalist Party'.[174] He went on to predict the suppression of the CCP by the KMT leftists, 'the Hankou Kerenskys and Tseretelis'.[175] In more general terms he assailed Stalin's constant attempts to manipulate events in China, declaring, '*The Chinese revolution cannot be stuffed into a bottle and sealed from above with a signet*.'[176] Even during the autumn, when Stalin's shift to supporting the CCP insurrections had largely stolen his clothes, he continued to ridicule witheringly his opponent's 'adventurist zigzags' and his creation of 'improvised' soviets.'[177]

Trotsky wasn't alone in his challenge. His supporters included Zinoviev, the first chairman of the Comintern, and Adolph Joffe, who had paved the way for the Soviet missionary drive in south China. They also included Karl Radek, the dishevelled but popular rector of Sun Yat-sen University, and the bulk of his faculty. And through Radek and his colleagues the Trotskyite influence rapidly spread into the Chinese student body. After Chiang's volte-face of 12 April a substantial minority of the students, conservatively estimated at around thirty or some 10 per cent of the total enrolment, came out firmly against Stalin and the United Front. Leading their ranks, spectacularly, was Chiang's own teenage son Chiang Ching-kuo, known by the Russian alias of Nikolai Yelizarov, who was described by his fellow students as 'the organiser of the Trotsky school.'[178] Publicly spurning his parent ('Revolution is the only thing I know, and I do not know you as my father any more'[179]), he is said to have busied himself with the production of posters and wall newspapers pushing the Trotskyite line. In mid-August the same path was taken by Feng Hongguo and Feng Funeng, son and daughter of the Christian General, who had likewise been deposited in Moscow for further studies. They rejected their father for his defection and his 'pretentious and pig-headed character' and aligned themselves with the Trotskyite faction.[180] The Trotskyite cause was also espoused by a significant number of the CCP youth. Young CCP intellectuals, as we have seen, had the currents of nationalism coursing through their veins every bit as strongly as their KMT counterparts; and to many of them the 'internationalism' and 'world revolution' promoted by Trotsky not surprisingly seemed to exhibit a stronger feeling for China than the 'socialism in one country' increasingly advocated by Stalin, which seemed to imply a narrow focus on Soviet interests alone. On 7 November the CCP students of Sun Yat-sen University took part in a grand parade in Red Square held to mark the tenth anniversary of the Bolshevik Revolution. As they approached Lenin's mausoleum a small band of them started shouting pro-Trotsky and anti-Stalin slogans. One young

Chinese woman was even rumoured to have unfurled a banner reading 'Long Live Trotsky!' in front of Stalin and his entire Politburo. The demonstration was rapidly stifled, but it must in the words of one student 'have seemed to Stalin as though someone had publicly spat in his face'.[181]

Most of the CCP leadership didn't support the Trotskyite theses, but they could scarcely ignore the huge losses their Party had suffered as it twisted and turned under Stalin's direction. At least 100,000 Party workers and activists are said to have been slaughtered in the great backlash of 1927, and one report by the CCP delegates to the Comintern claimed that 250,000 had fallen victim to the White Terror in April to June alone. Soviet influence was weakened, and indeed some authorities argue that the Chinese Communists never really recovered their faith in the Soviet Union. Already by the spring of 1927 there was clear incredulity: we are told that when the CCP Central Committee received Stalin's cable of 31 May urging them to launch an armed insurrection under the leadership of the Left KMT they 'didn't know whether to cry or to laugh'.[182] General Secretary Chen Duxiu commented that only lately the Comintern had been instructing them to help the Chinese middle classes, 'and now Stalin tells us to carry out an agrarian revolution in the next 24 hours'.[183] By July, when Lominadze arrived and began to blame *them* for the errors in policy, incredulity was shading into anger. One prominent leader, Zhang Guotao, described a talk with Lominadze as 'the worst conversation in my memory', and compared the young Georgian to a tsarist inspector-general haranguing the serfs.[184] And anger in turn was beginning to shade into insubordination. Flabbergasted when Moscow conveyed its withholding of funds and advisers just days before the planned launch of the Nanchang uprising, Zhou Enlai, who had been put in charge of the operation, agreed with his colleagues to go ahead with it whatever Stalin thought. Six weeks later, on 15 September, Mao Zedong, at the head of a small contingent in the Hunan countryside, judged that the advance on Changsha decreed by the local Comintern agent, Kuchumov, would be suicidal, and instead took his forces off to establish a defensible base in the mountains which straddled the border between Hunan and Jiangxi. Tall oaks from little acorns grow.

Over the decade that had elapsed since their October Revolution the Bolsheviks had endeavoured to present themselves to China as the representatives of a new and benevolent country – the Other Russia made flesh.

Some of the methods they used to endear themselves were familiar ones: money, arms, military training, even university places had all been bestowed by the tsarist regime on its Chinese clients at various points in the late nineteenth century. But there had also been something quite novel about their great secular mission with its borderless doctrines, its appeal to the grassroots, its commitment of talent and manpower and, yes, its real elements of dedication and humanistic zeal. That mission had now ended up in a bloody fiasco. The victorious Nationalist Party had been alienated, to all appearances for the foreseeable future, and indeed some authorities argue that the CCP never really recovered their faith in the Soviet Union. For all their exertions the Bolsheviks had never quite managed to allay the suspicion that the old tsarist ascendancy in China had simply been replaced by a Soviet one; that their Russia wasn't truly the Other Russia but the same old Russia under a different guise.

Judged from the point of view of their secondary, strategic objectives the Bolsheviks could be said to have done rather well. Using the old combination of diplomatic and military pressures they had restored Russia's position in the borderlands after the losses of the immediate post-revolutionary years – wholly in the case of Mongolia and substantially in the cases of northern Manchuria and Xinjiang. But they had dismally failed in their larger aim of uprooting the hostile foreign imperial powers from Chinese soil. Following the collapse of the Bolshevik mission Japan was left as strong as ever, both in southern Manchuria and along China's eastern seaboard. Under Nationalist pressure the British had felt obliged to disgorge their concession in Hankou and one or two of their other outlying strongholds. But the overall British position in southern China had not been substantially undermined, and as the backlash against Soviet meddling gained strength the decade had ended with Chiang Kai-shek seeking help from both Britain and the other western powers against what he saw as the graver Communist threat. Realpolitik had in other words proved quite effective for Soviet purposes; ideology had been the short road to ruin. There was a lesson to be drawn here, and the leadership in the Kremlin did not take long to assimilate it.

CHAPTER 5

STRATEGY IS KING

STALIN FIGHTS BACK (1927-31)

It can be argued that no foreigner ever made a more masterful impact upon Chinese history than Joseph Stalin. He never set foot in China, and some of the Chinese who met him found his knowledge of their country at best superficial. Yet from his rise to dominance in Moscow in 1922–4 the Soviet strongman exerted a decisive influence over Chinese affairs, shaping the outcome of a series of civil and external conflicts, coaxing or threatening some of the most prominent local leaders and tugging the country's political forces this way and that in pursuit of his crude but consistent goals. At first glance he would seem to have been wrenched off course, perhaps fatally, by the disasters of 1927. The collapse of his trademark project, the Nationalist-Communist United Front, the switch to exclusive support for the Chinese Communists and the slapdash calls for revolt so untypical of his usual wary proceedings all suggest a resounding defeat and a frantic underwater paddling to safeguard his domestic position. By 1927, however, his domestic authority was far too strong to be seriously challenged; and in spite of his apparent U-turn the evidence indicates that his underlying appraisal of China had not in fact changed. In July, as the last vestiges of the United Front fell apart in Wuhan, he wrote privately to his lieutenant, Vyacheslav Molotov, '*Our policy was and remains the sole correct policy*.'[1] It may even be that he adopted the course of armed uprising clamoured for by his adversaries in the cynical knowledge that it was certain to fail. The next four years would see him regaining his balance, recouping his losses and gradually reimposing the coolly pragmatic approach to Chinese affairs he would maintain for the rest of his decades in power.

He began by removing his Soviet opponents. Most of them had been marked for destruction for some time, but the China controversy helped to seal their fate. On 12 November 1927, less than a week after the Chinese student protest in Red Square, Leon Trotsky was expelled from the Bolshevik Party, and at the end of January 1928 he was put on a train to Alma Ata in Kazakhstan, the first step towards exile and a political afterlife as the execrated Lucifer of Soviet theology. Zinoviev was expelled from the Party along with his ally, and Adolph Joffe committed suicide in protest against Trotsky's expulsion, proclaiming to the last his internationalist credo, 'It is only when life is lived for humanity that it has any meaning.'[2]

Next came the turn of the Chinese student agitators. Behind the Trotskyite Radek Stalin had judiciously stationed, as deputy rector of Sun Yat-sen University, an ambitious young loyalist who went by the name of Pavel Mif – meaning 'Myth', though his presence was far from mythical to the students who crossed him. Already by the summer of 1927 Mif had been substituted for Radek as rector, and following the November disruption in Red Square Stalin gave him orders to root out the Trotskyites from the Sunovka student body. Mif accordingly issued directions to a nucleus of students who had taken the Stalinist line, and during the winter of 1927–8 these staged a mini-purge, beating up Trotskyites in the dormitories and helping to carry out 100 to 200 arrests. Over the next two years Mif and the GPU heavies continued to crack down periodically on further outbursts of Trotskyite discontent. In November 1928 a team organised by a supervisory committee of the Bolshevik Party were sent to the campus to look into the reported formation of a pro-Trotsky underground movement, and one year later, at the same time as the first major Stalinist political trials, a 'battery of iron-faced inquisitors' marched in to interrogate some eighty to ninety Chinese students who appeared still to cling to the Trotskyite heresy.[3] The methods used in these years were still relatively gentle. Incessant questioning was the favoured procedure, and physical violence doesn't seem to have been used on the students even in the dreaded confines of the Lubyanka Prison. But the crackdowns claimed one early suicide, and several dozens of young Chinese Trotskyites found themselves packed off to work in a factory or dispatched for hard labour in the Siberian camps or the gold mines of the Altai mountains.

The CCP leaders made excellent scapegoats for everything that had gone wrong in China under Stalin's supervision. Their General Secretary, the unfortunate Professor Chen Duxiu, who had opposed the merger with the Nationalists from the very beginning, was now found guilty of 'Right opportunism' for persisting obediently in precisely that course. In August 1927 he was sacked by Lominadze, and 'all the hounds of the Comintern were let loose upon him.'[4] Qu Qiubai, the young Russian-speaking translator and journalist, was installed in his place, only to take the rap for 'Left opportunism' following the failed insurrections of the autumn. For a number of months the knives were out for Mao Zedong also. Kuchumov, the Soviet consul and Comintern agent in Changsha, denounced him for 'exceptionally shameful behaviour and cowardice',[5] and efforts were made to track him down and transport him to Moscow to be put on trial for his 'military opportunism' and his stubborn disobedience of Comintern orders.[6] But Mao, in the depths of the Jinggang mountains, was beyond Moscow's reach.

In the meantime Stalin busied himself with the much needed polishing of his own revolutionary image. In June 1928 the Soviet government hosted a Sixth Congress of the Chinese Communist Party. For security reasons it was impossible to hold a conference of this now proscribed body on Chinese soil, and instead CCP delegates were smuggled across the Manchurian frontier along a kind of underground railroad of tunnels and safe houses before being forwarded, still in the utmost secrecy, to Moscow aboard the Trans-Siberian train. The congress was held in the comfortable seclusion of the Silver Villa, a large country mansion from tsarist times near Zvenigorod to the west of the capital. As in the past the proceedings took place under direct Comintern supervision. Stalin's ally Bukharin, now head of the Comintern, presided over the sessions, and although he seemed rather grotesquely concerned to blend in with the Chekhovian backdrop (he appeared on occasion in shooting clothes, with a hunting rifle and a falcon on his wrist), he worked hard to restore Stalin's grip on the demoralised Chinese Party, expounding the Soviet leader's line in a nine-hour speech. Virtually all the documents that emerged from the congress were drafted or overseen by Soviet officials. Stalin personally hand-picked a new CCP leadership to replace the discredited Chen and Qu, focusing in particular on a fiery young industrial agitator called Li Lisan. The Soviet chief reminded Li encouragingly, '*Even receding tides make waves*.'[7]

At a more junior level Stalin sought to mould a hard core of Chinese student devotees through the agency of his indefatigable acolyte, Pavel Mif. These thirty-odd students, who had made their mark during the anti-Trotskyite cleansing of 1927–8, were known variously as 'Mif's Fledglings' and 'Stalin's China Section'.[8] Typically they had a strong command of the Russian language plus a voluble grasp of Marxist dialectics. One particular favourite of Mif's was a certain Wang Ming, a short, tubby young man with 'the face of a streetwise urchin'. He acted as Mif's interpreter, and was said to be the one Chinese with whom Stalin conversed directly in Russian. Other prominent Fledglings included Luo Fu, the 'temperate, literary Bolshevik' who had translated Tolstoy and Turgenev,[9] and Qin Bangxian, alias Bo Gu, a domineering young zealot with wild hair, large glasses, a nervous laugh and a quavering voice who smoked a pipe in imitation of his Soviet idol. Together these cerebral youths would be ready, when the time came, to move into leadership posts and obey Stalin's orders to the letter.

Already in February 1928 Stalin had laid down that in spite of recent setbacks the policy of armed insurrection should be maintained, and this decision was duly endorsed by the CCP at their congress in the Silver Villa. The Moscow Politburo determined that up to 200 CCP members should be enrolled in Soviet military schools, in particular those specialising in aviation, artillery and engineering, and fifty of the delegates to the Sixth Congress were given a summer course in the use of arms, sabotage and street fighting techniques. Five thousand Mexican dollars a month were assigned for the military training of those CCP forces still in the field in such remote areas as Hainan Island and the Hailufeng district of Guangdong Province; and some thought was even given to strengthening Mao. As the months passed the survival of Mao's little band had begun to earn him a grudging respect from the Kremlin. By November 1928 he was bracketed with the hard-bitten soldier Zhu De as the joint leader of a 'Zhu-Mao Red Army', and by January 1929 General Janis Berzins, the Latvian head of the Soviet Army's military intelligence bureau, was conferring with the ever more influential Mif as to ways in which 'Zhu-Mao' could be given practical help. Finally Zhou Enlai, who had won kudos for his administrative skills, was entrusted with the task of stiffening the Party internally through the creation, with Soviet guidance, of a Public Security Bureau on the model of the GPU.

But . . . '*Our policy was and remains the sole correct policy.*' Amazingly, in the midst of these radical gestures, the Soviet boss persevered with his quest to maintain a working relationship with the Chinese Nationalists. Right through the autumn of 1927 he continued to hope for the 'formation of a truly revolutionary KMT government'.[10] Possible candidates for the leadership of such a government were the ever sympathetic Mme Sun Yat-sen and Eugene Chen, who had parted company with their Wuhan colleagues and taken ship from Shanghai to Vladivostok. Installed in a special train they were conveyed in triumph through Siberia, crowds cheering and bands playing at every station, and on their arrival in Moscow were promptly invited to take a well deserved holiday in the Caucasus. In early November, apparently with a view to cementing a new United Front, Stalin summoned to the Kremlin another Left KMT refugee, Deng Yanda, and proposed that Deng should become the new General Secretary of the Chinese Communist Party. When Deng protested that he wasn't even a Communist Stalin replied calmly, '*That can be arranged.*'[11]

More remarkable still was Stalin's persisting endeavour to keep a line open to Chiang Kai-shek. Ever since his suppression of the CCP in Shanghai in April 1927 Chiang had continued to manifest a detestation of 'Red imperialism'.[12] The new Nationalist government had declared their intention of severing diplomatic relations with the Soviet Union, and by December Chiang had closed down all the Soviet consulates in the area under his control. The KMT's Central Committee denounced Sun Yat-sen University for betraying Sun's principles and forbade their young people to study there any more. But Stalin seemed unfazed by this show of hostility. In a speech to the Sunovka students delivered on 13 May – one month *after* the slaughter in Shanghai – he went on putting the case for Chiang, arguing that the Nationalist supremo was 'warring, whether well or badly, against the enslavement of China' and was thus 'helping to weaken' the foreign imperial powers.[13] He for his part made no move to break diplomatic relations. He left open the Soviet embassy in Peking and the Soviet consulates in the northern Chinese provinces that hadn't yet fallen into KMT hands, and continued in the following months to reiterate the need for close Soviet ties with the Nationalist Party. Seemingly with the idea of bridging the gulf that had opened, he even suggested that Eugene Chen should go back to China and work at Chiang's side. In the meantime his hatchet man Mif took no step to maltreat the KMT students abandoning Sun Yat-sen University, concentrating his rage on the odious faction of Chinese Trotskyites; and even here Mif showed leniency in one striking case. Chiang Kai-shek's son, Chiang Ching-kuo, as we have seen, had spurned both his father and Stalin, emerging instead as a leading light in the pro-Trotsky movement. But the younger Chiang wasn't beaten or thrown into prison or packed off for hard labour in a Siberian camp. In 1928, after recanting his Trotskyite views, he was simply transferred to pursue advanced studies at the NG Tolmachev Military-Political Academy in Leningrad. At least one of his former classmates deduced that Ching-kuo was being held in reserve as a pawn to be played in some future deal with his father.

One year later the anti-Soviet frenzy of the Nationalist Party broke out yet again in a more acute form. Ever since the Bolsheviks had been granted joint management of the Chinese Eastern Railway under the treaties signed with the warlord regimes in 1924 their presence on the CER had been a continual source of Chinese vexation. Chinese constituted only 25 per cent of the railway employees and held fewer than a third of the administrative posts. The CER 'railway zone' helped the Russians preserve their old sphere of economic influence in northern Manchuria, while at the same time enabling them to pursue their new Soviet goals – serving them, in Bukharin's words, as 'our revolutionary forefinger pointing into China'.[14] For as long as Manchuria had remained a separate fiefdom in the grip of the Old Marshal, Zhang Zuolin, friction had been local. But in June 1928 the Old Marshal had been blown up, probably, though not certainly, by his former Japanese patrons; and his son and successor, Zhang Xueliang, inevitably called the Young Marshal, decided that his safest course was to nail his colours to the Nationalist mast. By the end of the year he was working closely with the KMT government on an all-out campaign to recover the railway. In early January 1929, as a first step, his troops took control of the telephone exchange that the CER management had installed in Harbin. On 25 May they broke into the Soviet consulate, arresting the consul-general and about thirty-five of the consular staff. On 10 July they took over the CER telegraph system and disbanded the Trade Bureau for the Far East, the Naphtha Syndicate, the Textile Syndicate and a number of other Soviet commercial concerns. And on 11 July they seized the entire railway, expelling some sixty senior Soviet officials and detaining 200 more. All of these measures were taken with the knowledge and approval of Chiang Kai-shek. On 10 July Chiang threw his full weight behind the Young Marshal, declaring, 'We should use force to take over the Chinese Eastern Railway and prevent sovietisation. Even if it means breaking relations with the Soviet Union we should not hesitate. If war breaks out between China and the Soviet Union the Central Government can send 100,000 men and raise several million yuan for military expenses.'[15] By this point the Young Marshal had deployed on the Soviet-Manchurian border some 60,000 troops including detachments of White Russians eager as ever to carry on waging their own civil war. At a meeting in Shanghai chaired by their leader, General F.L. Glebov, the local White Russian community resolved to ask General Khorvat, the former CER manager who now served as the titular head of the whole Far Eastern emigration, to convey their assurance of loyalty to the Nanking regime. From mid-July on White Guard units were vigorously engaging in cross-border raids.

This seizure of the CER was a provocation which Stalin could scarcely be expected to overlook. On 6 August a Special Far Eastern Army was formed at Khabarovsk under the command of none other than General Blücher, the revered 'General Galin' of the old Canton days, who was judged with good reason to know the arms, tactics and strategy of the Nationalist military like the back of his hand. On 7 September Soviet aircraft bombed the border town of Suifenhe, and by November Russia and China were at war in Manchuria, in what proved to be in many ways a re-enactment of their conflict in 1900. With a force that now totalled 300,000 Chinese troops and 70,000 White Guards Zhang Xueliang had his adversaries outnumbered by three to one; but the Soviet Army had the technological edge, rapidly overwhelming the Young Marshal's host with their artillery and aircraft and the strange and terrifying spectacle of thirty-four tanks. Blücher and his staff 'watched the Chinese soldiers lean about halfway out of their trenches when they caught sight of the tanks. We thought they were about to flee in panic, but their amazement was so great that not only their will but even their fear seemed to be paralysed.'[16] By 27 November two Manchurian towns near the border, Manzhouli and Hailar, were in Soviet hands and the brief war was effectively over. Nearly 20,000 of the Young Marshal's troops had been killed or wounded or captured. The episode had conclusively shown, in case anyone doubted, that Russian military superiority over China was as great as it had been in late tsarist times.

Yet the most striking feature of this Soviet riposte in Manchuria wasn't the victory but the consistent restraint. As the Nationalist challenge built up during the first few months of 1929 the Kremlin confined itself to a series of protests, requesting a conference to discuss the CER question, the release of detained Soviet citizens and an end to the harassments and the White border raids. It was only on 17 July, after Zhang Xueliang's campaign reached its climax, that Stalin at long last broke off diplomatic relations with the Nationalist government in Nanking. Even when the Special Far Eastern Army attacked in the autumn the blow was confined to a short, sharp shock in a strictly limited area. Blücher instructed his men to show leniency to the captured Chinese rank and file, and while there were field atrocities these appear to have been largely aimed at the Whites. No territory was detached from China by the victors, with the exception of Heixiazi (Black Bear), known to the Russians as Bolshoi Ussuriisky, a large island facing Khabarovsk at the confluence of the Amur and Ussuri rivers. Soviet stipulations embodied in the Khabarovsk peace protocol that was signed by the Young Marshal's emissary on 22 December simply echoed the earlier protests. The status quo at the start of the year was to be reinstated. Soviet citizens were to be freed, Soviet offices reopened, the White Guards disarmed and the Soviet Union restored to its original function as joint operator of the CER. Seldom if ever can war have been more of a continuation of diplomacy by other means.

This restraint, and the general kid-glove treatment of Chiang and his party, are best understood in the context of Stalin's strategic priorities. With the removal of Trotsky and the other fallen angels of the Bolshevik pantheon strategy had finally won out over evangelism; 'socialism in one country' over the international Marxist crusade. Stalin's concern was more clearly than ever with the threat to his eastern flank posed by the other great powers, and above all by Japan. Back in 1925, as we saw, he had warned the Politburo not to allow the National Revolutionary Army to advance into northern China for fear of provoking a Japanese intervention; and as the clash in Manchuria loomed four years later the same apprehension was at the front of his mind. The Kremlin took care to secure Japanese acquiescence before Blücher's troops marched across the Manchurian frontier, and indeed guaranteed to Japan that those troops would advance no further than Manzhouli and Hailar. It has even been conjectured that the whole show of force was intended as much for Japanese as for Chinese consumption. Given his fear of Japan Stalin needed China as an ally, not an enemy, and it is possible he was already eyeing the Nationalist government for precisely that role. In December 1929, as the fighting tailed off in Manchuria, a document purporting to be the memorandum of a former Japanese premier, Baron Tanaka Giichi, was published in Chinese in Nanking. The 'Tanaka Memorandum' set out a plan for the Japanese conquest of the Asian mainland, with an initial assault on Manchuria and Mongolia to be followed by an advance in Siberia up to or beyond Lake Baikal and a simultaneous invasion of China proper. The authenticity of this document has been widely discounted (though its contents accord well enough with the ideas we found circulating among the Japanese military at the time of the Russian Civil War), and some Russian scholars argue it may well have been a forgery concocted by the Soviet intelligence services. In this case the idea was presumably to frighten the Nationalist government into joining forces with Russia against the common threat. Stalin, like God, was on the side of the big battalions. If the Japanese did attack he would need a Chinese ally sufficiently strong to put up some effective resistance. And at this time the Nationalists were the only Chinese force with the remotest potential to play such a role.

As for the CCP, Stalin remained as convinced as ever that China was nowhere near ready for a socialist revolution. The chief task of the Chinese Communists now was to help to ensure the security of the 'one country' where socialism was to be built. '*An internationalist*', Stalin asserted in 1927, '*is one who unreservedly, without wavering, without conditions, is ready to defend the USSR*.'[17] When the conflict with the Young Marshal broke out two years later CCP leaders were enjoined 'to mobilise the whole Party and people to be ready to defend the Soviet Union with arms'.[18] Theirs was certainly not to reason why.

All of this was a difficult proposition for the CCP to swallow. On the face of it they had been asked to support a foreign country in shedding the blood of their fellow Chinese to restore that same foreign country's economic position on Chinese soil. The revamped Party leadership went ahead as requested with pro-Soviet demonstrations and strikes in Shanghai and the other big cities, but murmurs were heard. The deposed leader Chen Duxiu warned that this support for the Soviet Union 'only makes people assume that we dance to the tune of roubles',[19] and in August 1929 he published a letter announcing his conversion to the Trotskyite cause. Chen's breakaway largely fizzled out. By November he had been predictably cast out of the Party, and the Trotskyite flame which had blazed for a while among the Chinese students in Moscow doesn't seem to have caught on in China itself. The Trotskyite movement in China was split into four tiny factions, and even after Chen managed to merge these his new party's membership still only reached the grand total of 483.

Much worse was however to follow from Stalin's point of view. In the summer of 1930 he was confronted by a brazen challenge from his own hand-picked CCP leader, Li Lisan. This audacious young man was preparing to mount in the cities of Changsha and Nanchang a new uprising against the Nationalists which he expected to prove the climactic Chinese upheaval. To complement his efforts he called for direct intervention on the part of the Soviet Union. General Blücher should take command of a 'Southern Expedition' that would advance into China by way of Outer Mongolia and Manchuria to capture Peking. China, he explained, had replaced the Soviet Union as the centre of world revolution, and it was there that the 'volcano' was bound to erupt.[20] Back last November, he pointed out, the CCP had obediently supported the Soviet Union in its border war with the Young Marshal, and it was time for the Russians to return the favour. For good measure he noted that Outer Mongolia should become part of the Communist China of the future.

The Kremlin could scarcely believe its collective ears. In the first place the march on Peking of a Soviet army would have the certain effect of provoking a Soviet–Japanese war – the very scenario Stalin was most concerned to avoid. It was even suggested that Li might be trying deliberately to drag the Soviet Union into just such a showdown. Secondly Li's demand constituted a rejection of the basic tenet of Soviet primacy in the revolutionary movement, a claim to equality, a flagrant swipe at the doctrine of 'socialism in one country'. And finally Li had brought up once again the old chauvinist grievance about Soviet domination of Outer Mongolia. A whisper ran around the Comintern, '*Li Lisan has gone mad!*'[21] Mif confided to Stalin that Li was a temperamental 'semi-Trotskyite' who 'lacked flexibility'.[22] 'Bring him to Moscow, then,' Stalin grinned. 'We'll teach him to be flexible.'[23] In October, soon after the miserable collapse of his urban risings,

Li was duly summoned to the Soviet capital, and the following month he was hauled before the Comintern to account for his follies. He was lucky to be labelled as nothing worse than a *semi*-Trotskyite, and to be sentenced to nothing more than a course of political re-education.

This still wasn't the end of the story. The entire Chinese Communist leadership had shown signs of revolt. Even Zhou Enlai, who had been considered a safe pair of hands and had been granted the honour of delivering a special address to the Soviet Party's Fifteenth Congress in March 1930, had presumed to attempt a defence of Li and had had to be called back to Moscow for a reprimand. Stalin was now determined to crush the CCP's insubordination once and for all. During the second half of 1930 he sent Mif in person to China along with his whole brood of 'Fledglings' – the '28 Bolsheviks', as they were now called, or sometimes the '28½', to include one activist who was even younger than his classmates. In January 1931, at a CCP plenum held in Shanghai, Mif himself took the chair (something not even Borodin had ventured to do in his years as Special Adviser) and imposed, 'on his own authority',[24] the leadership of the twenty-eight Moscow trainees. Wang Ming was originally made the General Secretary, but by the summer he had decamped to the safer environment of the Soviet capital, where he gave speeches to factory hands and awaited the moment when he would return to China in triumph as Lenin had returned to Petrograd in April 1917. His position was subsequently assumed by Bo Gu at the venerable age of twenty-four. A rump of around twenty of the old CCP leaders resisted Mif's boardroom takeover, but were soon after arrested at their hotel by the KMT police and executed the following month. It has been strongly suggested that the police were tipped off by the 28 Bolsheviks.

FORTIFYING THE BORDERS (1931–7)

In September 1931, on the pretext of a 'Chinese' bombing which their own colonels had staged on a railway track on the edge of Mukden, the Imperial Japanese Army fanned out through Manchuria. In February 1932 they entered Harbin, and at the beginning of March they proclaimed the establishment of a puppet state, Manchukuo, under the nominal rule of the former Qing emperor, Puyi. It was the end of the tenuous grip which the Nationalist government had maintained through the Young Marshal on the Chinese north-east. It was also the end of nearly four decades of Russian dominance in the northern part of that region. For another three years Soviet staff continued to operate the Chinese Eastern Railway, but their work was a target for constant raids, bombings and sabotage incited by the Japanese, and it soon became clear that the CER was more trouble than it was worth. In March 1935, following talks in Tokyo, the Soviet leadership sold off the railway to Manchukuo (and thus to Japan) for 140 million Japanese yen or just one-eighth of the original cost of construction. Soviet railwaymen were quickly replaced by Japanese ones, and between May and August a final contingent of 25,000 Soviet personnel and dependants were packed on to trains in Harbin and sent home.

Japan's actions were all too consistent with the projects mulled over by the Imperial Army's staff officers during the years of the Allied intervention in Russia and spelt out, spuriously or otherwise, in the 'Tanaka Memorandum' of 1929. 'Glaring', to use a Chinese simile, 'like a tiger eyeing its prey', the ever more powerful Japanese military were clearly bent on the colonisation of Manchuria, with its rich farmlands, its oil, coal, bauxite and iron ore and its already substantial industrial base. But the Japanese were also moving to put into practice their long-cherished scheme of driving a territorial wedge between China and the Soviet Union to insulate China from the contagion of Bolshevism. One of the first steps taken by the Imperial Army following their assault on Manchuria in 1931 was to seal off the Soviet frontier, and large bodies of troops and consignments of heavy weapons were rapidly moved to the frontier zone. In February 1933 the head of the Japanese delegation to the League of Nations warned of the need to forestall a 'fateful alliance' between the Soviet Union and a future Communist China, and three years later a secret plan was said to have been found in north China for the creation of a Japanese-controlled buffer zone stretching all the way from Manchuria to Central Asia 'to prevent China and Russia from coming into contact with each other'.[25]

Japanese ambitions extended still further to the possibility of an all-out attack on the Soviet state. For the moment Japan's 'Guandong Army' in Manchuria were content to encourage the local White Russians in their continuing harassment of their Bolshevik foes. Many of the raids launched at Japanese prompting on the CER were conducted by White bands, and White intelligence agents controlled by a Colonel Dulepov slipped across into Soviet territory from the border town of Manzhouli. Down in Mukden the long-time Japanese protégé Ataman Semyonov was supplied with a bodyguard and maintained in style in a villa costing 90,000 Japanese yen, where he drew up plans for the creation of a 'second Manchukuo' in Transbaikalia and the Maritime Province. But it was clear all this might be the prelude to something much larger. The Japanese war minister General Araki Sadao, a leading anti-Soviet hawk, assured Konstantin Rodzaevsky, a more recent protégé who had founded a Russian Fascist Party, that 'Japan will save the Russian people'.[26] In 1933 Araki declared, '*If the Soviet Union does not cease to annoy us, I shall have to purge Siberia as one clears a room of flies*.'[27]

And in that same year, 1933, Adolf Hitler had come to power in Germany ready to implement, as soon as he had the armed forces to do so, his dream of an eastward expansion set out in *Mein Kampf*. Drawn together by their hatred of Bolshevism, Nazi Germany and Japan set the seal on their partnership through the Anti-Comintern Pact of 25 November 1936. For perhaps the first time Russia faced a real possibility of its nightmare scenario – a simultaneous onslaught by mortal enemies in both east and west. The result was that Stalin's preoccupation with strategy now became not merely the uppermost but virtually the sole thought in his dealings with China, the one constant factor which eclipsed every other concern. From 1934 he was getting a regular update on the Japanese threat from both the Red Army's intelligence branch and the Foreign Department of the OGPU security service, and by November 1936 *Pravda* was able to summarise, 'Comrade Stalin does not take his eyes off the Far East.'[28]

As before Stalin's instinct was to do whatever it took to head off a collision. In December 1931, three months after the Imperial Army's grab for Manchuria, the Soviet Foreign Ministry tried to interest the Tokyo government in a treaty of mutual non-aggression. One year later the Soviet military disarmed and interned upwards of 4,000 Chinese officers and men who had fled from Manchuria into the Russian Far East after a gallant but hopeless resistance campaign. In April 1933 Stalin turned down a request to receive the Young Marshal who, dislodged from his former Manchurian base by the Japanese forces, had been optimistic enough to suppose that his recent Soviet adversaries would be in a hurry to help him get back there again. And in March 1935 the sale of the CER to Manchukuo was intended at least in part to eliminate a potential source of friction with the conquering Japanese. In the meantime, however, a massive new effort was put into shoring up

Russia's eastern defences. Within days of the Japanese move on Manchuria General Blücher had called a halt to the demobilisation of the Special Far Eastern Army, and after the imperial forces entered Harbin in February 1932 reserve officers under thirty were called up for emergency service with the OGPU border troops in the Far East. Over the following years the Trans-Siberian Railway was double-tracked, and permanent fortifications began to be built the whole length of the Soviet–Chinese frontier. The Chinese resistance groups who had fled from Manchuria might not have been given active support, but nor were they extradited; and in due course they were amalgamated into Soviet Red Army units. Not content with fortifying their own borders, the Soviet leadership also took steps to strengthen their grip on the Chinese borderlands. Northern Manchuria was a lost cause, but there was still scope for bolstering both Xinjiang and Mongolia against the encroachment of the Japanese.

By the late 1920s, thanks to their ties with the cautious but amenable governor, Yang Zengxin, the Soviet government had slowly begun to rebuild the late tsarist economic position in Xinjiang. Progress was threatened momentarily in July 1928, when Governor Yang was mown down by a hail of bullets at a banquet in the provincial capital, Urumqi (the Soviet consul-general and his wife took refuge in a lavatory); but under the rule of Yang's successor Jin Shuren, economic relations not only continued but positively romped ahead. Xinjiang's transport links with Russia, always more developed than with China proper, were strengthened still further in 1930 with the completion by Soviet engineers of the Turkestan–Siberia Railway, parallel to the frontier and in places less than 200 miles away; and good roads were constructed at points along the 'Turk–Sib' line to the province's north-western 'Three Districts' of Yili, Tacheng and Ashan. 82.5 per cent of the province's trade was by now with the Soviet Union, dwarfing its trade with the rest of China, and an alluring market was open for Soviet manufactures such as metalware, cotton goods, cigarettes and matches in exchange for locally cultivated raw cotton, livestock and hides. In October 1931 Governor Jin formalised this new intimacy through the conclusion of a Temporary Trade Agreement that permitted Soviet representatives to do business in the Three Districts, Urumqi and the southern city of Kashgar, lowered duties on Soviet goods and provided for Soviet management of the province's wireless and telegraphic facilities.

Unfortunately Governor Jin was a figure of much lesser calibre than his murdered predecessor, and the policies he pursued of high taxes, confiscation of property, travel restrictions and general intolerance soon alienated the Muslim groups who made up the majority of Xinjiang's population. In 1930 a rising broke out among the Turkic Uighur citizens of the eastern town of Hami. Crushed for the moment by government forces, the rebels appealed for help to their Chinese Moslem co-religionists in the neighbouring province of Gansu. These Chinese Muslims responded by intervening in strength under the leadership of a dashing, twenty-year-old cavalry commander named Ma Zhongying, popularly known as Big Horse, who declared his intention of splitting Xinjiang off from China and turning it into an independent Muslim state; and by the beginning of 1933 Big Horse and his troops were within striking distance of Urumqi. The following autumn a separate Eastern Turkestan Republic was proclaimed in the south of the province by the Uighurs who lived in Kashgar and the other oasis towns on the edge of the Taklamakan desert. The prospects for continued Chinese rule in the province looked grim.

Soviet spymasters searched far and wide for the international operator behind these upheavals. There were still lingering suspicions of British designs. Rumour had it that Lawrence of Arabia, no less, was at work among the Chinese Muslims, and Sabit Mullah, emir of the oasis town of Khotan, was believed to be in contact with British India. But the more plausible bogey was Japan. Big Horse was reported to have Japanese on his staff, one of whom, a political agent named Onishi Tadashi, had been at his side ever since 1930. And Japanese weapons were said to have been shipped inland to Big Horse's followers through the port of Tianjin. Far more was at stake here for Moscow than the loss of a promising market. If the Japanese got control of Xinjiang they would be able to threaten the Soviet Central Asian republics, and would also be well placed to detach a large portion of Western Siberia. Japanese bombers would even be brought within range of the Baku oilfields on the Caspian Sea. Soviet action was urgently called for to preserve the authority of the Chinese provincial government and to make Xinjiang safe.

To begin with the Soviet countermove was made indirectly, through proxies. By 1932–3 the Red Army had redeployed some 10,000 to 15,000 of the Chinese resistance troops who had fled from Manchuria, shifting them the whole length of the Sino-Soviet border and reintroducing them to

China by way of Xinjiang. Fervently anti-Japanese, calling themselves the Manchurian Army of Salvation, these troops were placed under the leadership of a young officer named Sheng Shicai, who had arrived in the province in 1930 and risen to the eminence of chief of staff of the General Office of Xinjiang's Frontier Army. The second Soviet proxy force in Xinjiang was perhaps more surprising. Ever since their bedraggled retreat across the border in 1920 the defeated White Russians had made a home in the province; but by 1930 these Whites were no longer as white as all that. Surrounded by unfriendly Muslims, the Whites of Xinjiang, unlike their counterparts in Manchuria, had apparently made up their minds that blood was thicker than water. By the late 1920s they had already begun to share some intelligence with the Soviets, and by the time the insurgencies started three crack regiments of White troops were serving the Soviet purpose of propping up Governor Jin. They put down the initial uprising in Hami in 1930, and in February 1933 trapped and shattered a besieging Chinese Muslim force in a defile outside Urumqi. Incensed by Jin's miserliness and ingratitude, they proceeded to overthrow him in a coup two months later, but promptly replaced him with the chief of the Moscow-sponsored Manchurians, Sheng Shicai – the 'White' Russians, in the words of a passing British journalist, 'had more than earned their inverted commas'.[29] In August 1933 the new Governor Sheng marched forth at the head of a composite army of Whites and Manchurians to the east of the province, where he scored an initial success against Big Horse but was then badly mauled. By the end of the year Urumqi was again under siege, and Sheng was appealing to Moscow for rescue.

Faced with this crisis, Stalin and his entourage concluded that there was nothing for it but to step in themselves. In early January 1934 two brigades of 'Altai Volunteers', in reality troops of the OGPU, swept across the border to Urumqi and took the Chinese Muslim besiegers in the rear. Big Horse and his followers were no match for a Soviet expedition deploying artillery, armoured cars and according to one source light tanks; and his much vaunted cavalry were put to flight in short order by the attack of three Soviet planes which caused their mounts to stampede. Big Horse fled to the southern oases, where he managed to dislodge the rival Eastern Turkestan Republic before being finally routed by Sheng and his Soviet Army at Kashgar in early July.

It was another classic illustration of the Russian propensity for teaming up with the Chinese authorities in Central Asia against the rebellious local inhabitants. But we should notice a curious epilogue. On 7 July Big Horse was quietly allowed to retreat from the province, with an escort of Soviet diplomats, to the safety of Soviet Turkestan. From there he was transferred to Moscow, where he is said to have been put through a military training course and awarded the rank and uniform of a Soviet cavalry officer. Sheng demanded his extradition, but the demand was refused. Stalin didn't want to foreclose the possibility of future ties with the province's Muslim majority; and he liked to keep all the available pawns on the board.

In the meantime Moscow busied itself with the task of cementing the existing Chinese regime. In a cable sent at the end of July to the Soviet consul-general in Urumqi, Georgi Apresov, Stalin directed that 'so long as Sheng continues to fight the Japanese and the other foreign intelligence agents of Ma Zhongying's sort he can count on Soviet help';[30] and this help was now made available in a whole range of political, economic and military forms. A Public Safety Bureau was set up to serve Sheng as a secret police force, and a military academy and an aviation school were organised in Urumqi to train his troops. Under a secret agreement concluded in May 1935 the Soviet Union undertook to accord him a loan of 5 million gold roubles, and to supply him with arms and munitions in case of need. And in 1936 a Soviet Frontier Affairs Bureau was established in the province, in reality a military intelligence organ manned by seven officers of the Soviet General Staff.

All of this was still not quite enough to put paid to the Japanese menace. From his eyrie in Kabul the Japanese ambassador to Afghanistan, Kitada Matsumoto, kept in touch with the province's anti-Sheng elements. In June 1935 the emir of Khotan, Sabit Mullah, approached him with a request for Japanese arms and money to be used in the establishment of a second Eastern Turkestan Republic. Kitada forwarded the request to Tokyo with his own suggestion for a Japanese 'spiritual advance' into Xinjiang and a motor road to be pushed down there all the way from Manchukuo.[31] By 1936 the southern half of the province was once more ablaze, with uprisings led by a couple of Chinese Muslims, Ma Shaowu and Ma Hushan, the latter a brother-in-law of Big Horse. Whether these uprisings had direct help from Japan is unclear; but the Russians were taking no chances. In the course of 1936–7 upwards of

5,000 Soviet Red Army troops intervened in the province on four separate occasions, once again fearsomely mechanised with their combination of planes, tanks, artillery and armoured cars, and further reinforced by a body of stalwart 'White' Russians whom Sheng had sent to fight in the southern oases alongside the Reds. By the middle of 1937 the last embers of Islamic resistance to Sheng's rule in the province had been stamped out.

Sheng had however to pay a high price for his rescue. In accepting Soviet protection he had also submitted himself to a spectacular level of Soviet control. From the mid-1930s the Kremlin imposed on this vast if remote Chinese province the same micromanagement it had exercised over the Nationalist and Chinese Communist parties a decade before. The governor was obliged to consult with Consul-General Apresov on all political issues and appointments of personnel. Three hundred Soviet advisers were assigned to the various branches of the Xinjiang administration, and some of these advisers helped Sheng to draw up a 'Three Point Policy' – one point of which was support for the Soviet Union. On 7 November 1934, in a message sent to celebrate the seventeenth anniversary of the Bolshevik Revolution, Apresov reported happily to Stalin, 'Since we established relations [with Sheng] there has been no piece of advice or proposal from us that he would not have accepted.'[32]

An equally rigid grip was imposed in the economic sphere. A commission headed by Stalin's brother-in-law, Alexander Svanidze, was sent to Urumqi to help Sheng with the preparation of a Three-Year Plan. A team of geologists was dispatched to conduct a survey of the province's natural resources, in accordance with Stalin's drive to secure reserves of key minerals that could power his breakneck drive to industrialise the Soviet homeland and strengthen it for the eventual showdown with Japan and its other foreign foes. In his anniversary message of November 1934 Apresov positively drooled over the 'inexhaustible, fabled wealth' of Xinjiang, whose coal and oil could meet the needs of the Turk–Sib Railway, of the Soviet Central Asian republics and Western Siberia;[33] and the following spring the geologists duly came up with a map indicating the presence of vast amounts of coal, oil, manganese, copper, lead, tin and tungsten, particularly in the accessible Three Districts of the north-west. Under the secret agreement of May 1935 the Russians committed themselves to providing Xinjiang with help in the development of mining, animal husbandry, agriculture and other activities: the quid pro quo was a Soviet lien on the exploitation of oil and non-ferrous metals.

Soviet dominance even extended to culture. Russian was adopted as one of the province's official languages, and large numbers of Russian schools were set up teaching from Russian textbooks. The Arabic script used till then to transcribe the Turkic languages of the Uighurs, Kazakhs and other Muslim groups was replaced by Cyrillic. And a Sino-Soviet Cultural Association was opened in Urumqi to circulate Soviet periodicals, leaflets and books. Soviet soft power was rounded off with the provision of medical workers and hospital supplies.

By the mid-1930s, then, Soviet strategists had succeeded in thwarting Tokyo's ambition of turning Xinjiang into the western extremity of a Japanese-dominated buffer zone. They had done so quite simply by turning it into a buffer zone of their own. Soviet overlordship of the region had advanced way beyond the commercial supremacy of late tsarist times and was now all-encompassing. The question still facing the Russians was whether this state of affairs might in time prove too irksome for even their own chosen client. In his briefing to Stalin of November 1934 Consul-General Apresov cautioned that Sheng Shicai was 'not stupid' but 'a sophisticated and cunning man who has a good idea of the current circumstances'.[34] He was, moreover, possessed of a 'deeply restless and highly suspicious nature towards everyone and everything'.[35]

In Outer Mongolia the Soviet Union had of course been entrenched from as far back as 1921. Nominally still a province of China, this vast expanse had been moulded into a 'Mongolian People's Republic' (MPR), and Stalin himself is said to have referred to it as 'his puppet state'.[36] But the Soviet position there was by no means rock-solid. In March 1933, intent on their object of driving a territorial wedge between Russia and China, the Imperial Japanese Army advanced from Manchukuo into the Chinese-held Inner Mongolian provinces of Chahar and Jehol. By 1935 they had turned the MPR's flank and were poised in case of war to strike north across the Outer Mongolian deserts and grasslands with a view to cutting the Trans-Siberian Railway. In July of that year, at a meeting held with MPR representatives in the Manchurian border town of Manzhouli, Japanese spokesmen stepped up the pressure, demanding the right to station 'military observers' in Outer Mongolia and to set up a military telegraph there. This forward thrust was accompanied by a political game plan. The Japanese conquerors had found themselves widely welcomed in Inner Mongolia, where they were regarded as liberators from Chinese rule, and they had made every use of their popularity. They had cultivated the local leaders, in particular a Prince Demchugdongrub, whom they proposed to elevate in due course to the throne of a Greater Mongolia. And if the Inner Mongolians could be won over, why not the Outer ones too? Colonel Itagaki Seishiro, one of the trio of Japanese officers who had staged the 'Chinese' bombing in Mukden that had set Japan on the path to expansion, observed to his country's ambassador in Nanking, 'If Outer Mongolia unites with Japan's Manchukuo, it will be possible to eliminate the Soviet influence in the Far East without any fighting.'[37]

And indeed in the MPR there was a real risk that the local populace might seek to follow their Inner Mongolian cousins and throw in their lot with Japan. Disaffection was voiced at the highest level by the 'puppet' prime minister, a hard-drinking, pugnacious figure with the wonderfully Tolkienian moniker of Genden the Lame of Arvaheer. Genden was outspokenly bitter at Soviet domination, complaining of the way that his country was 'following the letter stamped with the signature of Stalin' and expressing his appetite for 'a duel with that Georgian with the knife-tipped nose.'[38] He was firmly opposed to the stationing of Soviet troops in the MPR, believed that Manchukuo envoys should be permitted to operate in the capital, Ulan Bator, and in general seems to have hoped to expand his country's freedom of movement by steering a middle course between the Russians and Japanese. Matters came to a head at the end of 1935, when Genden paid a visit to Moscow in the hope of extracting some (strictly civilian) Soviet aid. In the course of an alcohol-fuelled reception at the MPR embassy the obstreperous premier is said to have gone so far as to hint at the option of an Outer Mongolian alliance with Japan. Stalin sneered, 'Genden, you want to be king of Mongolia, don't you?', to which Genden retorted, 'You, bloody Georgian, have become a virtual Russian Tsar!'[39] According to some witnesses he then leant forward and *broke Stalin's pipe*. Genden's military commander, Demid, is said to have broadly shared the prime minister's attitudes, though he was willing to accept Red Army help in the form of training, equipment and technology. In the public at large unrest seethed among the 100,000-strong lama priesthood, who were repelled by Soviet atheism and drawn to Japan by the bonds of the Buddhist religion.

In Mongolia as on the other tense frontiers Stalin's aim was if possible to keep the peace. In July 1935, more in sorrow than in anger, the Soviet ambassador in Tokyo approached the Japanese Foreign Ministry about the Imperial Army's advance to the neighbourhood of the MPR, explaining candidly that his country had always been concerned for the territorial integrity of Outer Mongolia *for the purpose of defending its own borders*. It was a fairly obvious invitation to Japan to agree to the same kind of cold-blooded division of spheres of influence that had been achieved in the region between Japan and tsarist Russia in the years before the First World War. In the meantime a whole battery of defensive precautions was rolled into place. In November 1934 a loose understanding was reached between the Kremlin and the MPR government on cooperation in the event of a war, and the following January the existing Soviet garrison in Outer Mongolia was augmented by the arrival of 2,000 Red Army troops, ten artillery pieces and 300 armoured cars. On 1 March 1936 Stalin told an American journalist that if Japan invaded the territory, 'we shall have to help the MPR as we helped it in 1921',[40] and on 12 March a Soviet-MPR Mutual Defence Pact was concluded providing for mutual help in the event of an attack on either by any third party. The last link in the chain of physical and diplomatic defences on Russia's eastern frontiers had been hammered in. Measures were also taken to quell the threat posed by real or imagined Japanese sympathisers in the MPR. In 1932, and again in 1934, a combined expedition of Soviet army, air force and OGPU troops crossed the MPR border to suppress a developing lama revolt. The Kremlin blamed the disorders on Japanese agitation, and the rebel lamas are said to have been treated with relative leniency. In early 1936, back at home after his slanging match with the Soviet leader, Genden the Lame was, unsurprisingly, dismissed from all his official posts. He was sent to Moscow, and from there transferred to the Black Sea resort of Foros for a 'long holiday'.[41] His lieutenant Demid carried on for a time at the head of the MPR military, but was soon overshadowed by the new minister of internal affairs, Marshal Horoloogiin Choibalsan, whom the Russians had identified as a truly dependable 'Mongolian Stalin'.

ALL AGAINST JAPAN? (1931-7)

The more Japan gnawed its way into China, the more convinced it seems Stalin became of the need to mend fences with Chiang Kai-shek. Straight after the

Japanese colonels exploded their bomb in Mukden in September 1931 Lev Karakhan, once again number two in the Soviet Foreign Ministry, proposed to Mo Dehui, a Nationalist then serving as president of the Chinese Eastern Railway, that events now demanded the prompt restoration of Sino-Soviet diplomatic ties. In June 1932 a first round of talks was held behind the scenes of the International Disarmament Conference in Geneva, and on 12 December the two governments exchanged notes providing for a formal resumption of relations. In 1933 a Soviet embassy was opened in the new Nationalist capital. The Russians had actually stolen a march on their great power rivals: one British journalist noted that the Soviet Union was the only country at this stage to have moved the official seat of its representation from Peking to Nanking.

During the first few years the rapprochement progressed at a somewhat glacial pace. Stalin wasn't prepared to let Nationalist 'face' take priority over the vital task of defending the borderlands. In Xinjiang both the Temporary Trade Agreement of 1931 and the big loan agreement signed with Governor Sheng four years later, milestones in the creeping Soviet takeover of the Chinese north-west, were secret deals concluded behind the backs of the KMT central government. News of the former treaty was only conveyed to the Nanking authorities a year afterwards, and the text of the latter one never seems to have reached them at all. The Soviet–MPR Mutual Defence Pact of March 1936 was similarly concluded without any attempt to inform Chiang Kai-shek and his ministers, in spite of the fact that Outer Mongolia was still in theory a Chinese possession. Even more striking, perhaps, was the blithe Soviet disregard of Chinese government interests in Manchuria after the Japanese conquest. Not only did the Russians embark on the sale of the CER to Manchukuo without first obtaining Nanking's authorisation, they took the opportunity presented by China's loss of the territory to reinforce their own claim to the still disputed Manchurian border. In 1933, for example, the Moscow Politburo affirmed their position that control of the desolate islets in the Amur and Ussuri rivers should be based on the Tsarist-Qing treaties of Aigun and Peking, with the border to run along the Chinese riverbanks; and Soviet troops are said to have taken control of some 600 out of 700 islets which the Chinese had regarded as belonging to them.[42] This move was in part undertaken to check any further northward expansion on the part of the Japanese Army – but it also gave the Soviet Union a possessor's advantage in the event of any future Chinese demands.

All the same, we should note what the Russians did not do. They didn't annex Xinjiang, in spite of having established near-total control there. In August 1933 a Politburo directive ruled it inexpedient, at least for the moment, to back the local secessionists: rather the focus should be on maintaining the province's autonomy and improving the quality of the Chinese administration. The following month Consul-General Apresov gave a welcoming party in Urumqi for the Nationalist foreign minister, Dr Luo Wen'gan, who had arrived in the province on a tour of inspection. In July 1934 Stalin recoiled at a suggestion of the obsequious Governor Sheng that Communism should swiftly be implemented in Xinjiang and the province turned into a base for overthrowing the Nationalist government. Voicing his backing for Xinjiang's 'integrity' the Soviet leader wrote to Apresov, 'We consider your telegram on Sheng's Red views and conversation about the possibility of sovietising Xinjiang to be *alarming*!'[43] Nor did the Russians take any action to formalise their existing domination of Outer Mongolia. They contented themselves with explaining their pact with the MPR to the Nationalists as a matter of simple if not altogether flattering logic:

> The Soviet Union wishes to give Outer Mongolia military help to resist Japan, and this in no way conflicts with China's interests. Moreover Chinese forces are not in reality able to protect Outer Mongolia, while Japanese aggression against Outer Mongolia has already been manifested.[44]

Marked care meanwhile went on being shown in the Soviet handling of Chiang Kai-shek's missing son, Chiang Ching-kuo, who had by this time completed his course of study at the Tolmachev Military-Political Academy. Hostage though he was in effect, the younger Chiang wasn't molested, but was instead put through a series of work placements designed seemingly to turn him into the very model of a modern Marxist-Leninist. After a stint at the Dynamo Electrical Factory in Moscow he had been moved in May 1931 to a nearby village to serve as the chairman of the local collective farm and simultaneously 'to be used as part of the leadership at the level of the Regional Party Committee'.[45] In 1933 he was sent to the east for a spell in an Altai gold mine, but by the end of the year had been installed at Sverdlovsk in the Urals as head of the mechanical section of the Ural Factory of Heavy Machine Building, otherwise known as Uralmash or 'the Factory of

Factories'. A few months after that, in 1934, he was appointed deputy editor of the factory newspaper and began to give lectures to the workforce on international affairs. Even allowing for the hardships of the shop floor and the mineshaft, it is difficult to believe that his lot was an especially arduous one. He is known to have made Russian friends, one of whom recalled in an interview decades later, 'A smile never left his face. It always seemed that he was trying to open up to you completely. We never saw him unhappy.'[46] He enjoyed picnics and parties, sang Russian songs and performed a Georgian dance with a knife in his teeth. In March 1935 he was able to marry one of the factory hands, a shy, pretty blonde Byelorussian lathe operator named Faina Vakhreva.

With the political pathways still clogged an attempt was also made to achieve a rapport with the Nationalists in the realm of culture. In February–March 1935 a number of films emanating from Nationalist China were shown at the International Film Festival in Moscow, two of them starring the celebrated actress of the period Butterfly Woo (Hu Die). A professor of Oriental languages was brought in specially to unravel the plots for the Soviet audience. Miss Woo herself turned up in Moscow too late for the festival, but was nonetheless treated to a hearty welcome. This episode was immediately followed by the arrival of the great Chinese opera star Mei Lanfang, who came to Moscow at the invitation of the Soviet Association for Foreign Culture. In the course of his visit this second celebrity met both Meyerhold and Stanislavsky, the veteran theatre directors from pre-revolutionary days, and was introduced to Maxim Gorky and his fellow novelist, Alexei Tolstoy. The playwright Sergei Tretyakov declared that 'Dr Mei Lanfang's performances have burst out before our eyes like the multi-coloured fireworks the Chinese let off at their New Year.'[47]

Parallel with these overtures the Kremlin kept up its doctrinally indicated support for the underground Chinese Communist Party. Throughout the early 1930s Chiang Kai-shek and his generals launched wave after wave of 'extermination campaigns' against the rural bases the CCP had contrived to establish in outlying parts of Jiangxi and other southern provinces. The strategy needed to thwart these campaigns was worked out in the Soviet Union by a specially constituted Military Advisory Group, while the GRU, Stalin's military intelligence outfit, deployed no fewer than 100 agents in China to infiltrate Nationalist government offices and provide timely information to the beleaguered CCP. Thanks to these efforts the Chinese Red Army commanded by Mao Zedong were enabled to trap 9,000 troops of Chiang's first campaign in an ambush in December 1930,[48] and a second offensive the following April was foiled with the help of Soviet-trained radio technicians, who used a high-powered two-way radio obtained in Hong Kong to intercept the Nationalist communications. In the summer of 1932, when Chiang turned his attention to two of the smaller Red bases to the north of the Yangtze, Moscow supervised the resistance, directing the various CCP bands to join forces and relieve the pressure on these redoubts. A 'critical role' is said to have been played during these operations by Soviet arms and medicines, and by the continued flow of money that made its way from the Comintern to the CCP headquarters in Shanghai. Hundreds of thousands or even millions of roubles and dollars are said to have been channelled to Shanghai over the years, and though the flow seems to have slackened somewhat after 1931, in 1934 the CCP were still getting a subsidy worth the equivalent of 7,418 gold dollars per month.[49]

Soviet advisers also played a significant role in the bases themselves. In November 1931, when the principal base at Ruijin in Jiangxi was organised into a first Chinese Soviet Republic, Comintern envoys helped draft a political structure for the new rebel state. They also endorsed Mao's appointment as chairman of the new state's Central Executive Committee. Over the following years Mao persistently came under fire from Bo Gu, Luo Fu and the other young Stalinist whippersnappers whom Mif had installed in the Party leadership in Shanghai. In October 1933 Bo Gu and his colleagues secured Mao's removal from his military command on grounds of insubordination, and there was even talk of expelling him from the Party; and in January 1934 Mao was actually replaced by Luo Fu as premier (head of the Council of People's Commissars) of the Soviet Republic. But the Comintern intervened to demand that Mao should be kept in play. He was insubordinate, yes, but he was also a winner, and as such was too useful to drop altogether. In the Soviet press Mao was cited as one of the 'well-known heroes' of the Chinese Revolution, along with his military partner Zhu De, and Gao Gang who directed the northernmost 'Soviet area' in Shaanxi Province.[50]

By the spring of 1934 it was clear that in spite of all Soviet succour the wave-like assaults of the Nationalists were gradually wearing the CCP down.

The Red areas had now been ringed by barbed wire and blockhouses, and even the principal base in Jiangxi faced the prospect of being cut off and destroyed. In response to this crisis the Comintern resurrected a 'North-western Theory' that had originally been put forward by Borodin during the disasters of 1927. The idea was that the CCP should withdraw en masse from south China and re-establish themselves somewhere close to the north-western border where they would have ready access to Soviet shelter and arms. The Soviet counsellors consequently advised the CCP Central Committee to turn their minds to preparing the grand evacuation from Jiangxi that would become known to history as the Long March. During the summer a firm instruction was sent to the CCP to 'pull out and seek safety somewhere – as far away as Outer Mongolia, if necessary'.[51] By the time the Long March finally got under way in October Moscow is said to have contributed funds for the venture amounting to several million Mexican silver dollars. On 15 August 1935, as the Long Marchers struggled across the grasslands of western Sichuan, Stalin repeated the message that they should advance to the north and north-west – 'and you should not oppose drawing closer to the Soviet Union'.[52]

All this aid however presupposed that the CCP would stick closely to Soviet guidelines. In September 1933 the tight control that had been imposed on the Party by Mif three years earlier was reinforced by the arrival of a new Comintern aide in the shape of an officer of German origin called Otto Braun. (German aides were widely deployed by the Comintern in China at this period, in part seemingly to offset the powerful German advisers on Chiang Kai-shek's staff.) Braun had no knowledge of China and spoke no Chinese, but by April 1934 he had effectively taken over as the supreme commander of the Chinese Red Army. A classic Prussian martinet, he 'pounded his fists on the table' and told his Chinese clients that they 'knew nothing of military matters',[53] calling for a conventional stress on pitched battles in preference to the mobile warfare favoured by Mao. He considered Mao to have an inadequate understanding of Marxism and considered him 'too Chinese',[54] reserving his admiration for the doctrinaire – and Russian-speaking – Bo Gu, who 'permitted himself to be guided in military decisions by my suggestions'.[55]

This in turn meant that when CCP goals clashed with Stalin's strategic objectives, Stalin's strategic objectives would have to come first. Such a rule was already apparent in 1933, when the Kremlin refused to help CCP partisans to resist the Japanese in the Chahar Province of Inner Mongolia for fear of provoking a Japanese lunge at the MPR. By 1935 Stalin's quest for détente with the Nationalists had begun similarly to trump the CCP's focus on waging their own revolutionary war. In July–August that year the Comintern's Seventh Congress in Moscow proclaimed the new policy of an International United Front against Fascism, or in other words against the dreaded tandem of Germany and Japan. On 1 August the obedient Wang Ming, who now served as the chief Chinese delegate to the Comintern, was led on to the rostrum to endorse this new policy, identifying the CCP's central task as the military defence of the USSR.[56] The Party slogan was changed overnight with a truly Orwellian briskness from 'Oppose Chiang and Resist the Japanese' to 'Unite with Chiang and Resist the Japanese'.[57] This message was repeated incessantly over the following year. The CCP were to come together with the rest of China including Chiang's Nationalists in a second United Front to 'pin down' the Japanese and prevent their attacking the Soviet motherland.

Then, at the end of 1936, Stalin's priorities were driven home in the starkest possible way. Since the previous year, Zhang Xueliang, the Young Marshal dislodged from Manchuria, and his troops had been stationed by Chiang Kai-shek at Xi'an in the north-western province of Shaanxi to take on the CCP forces who had emerged in Shaanxi at the end of their epic Long March. But the Young Marshal and his men were disgruntled with Chiang's obsession with fighting the Communists and his seeming lack of interest in waging the war with Japan that might enable them to retake their home region. When Chiang arrived in Xi'an in December the Young Marshal decided to settle the issue by force. In the small hours of 12 December he had Chiang arrested at his hillside villa and held prisoner in an attempt to get him to change course. In their fastness of Baoan the Chinese Communist leaders, who had been in secret contact with the Young Marshal for months past, were cock-a-hoop. 'Laughing like mad' at the fall of his arch-enemy,[58] Mao proposed that a cable be sent to Zhang Xueliang requesting that Chiang should be handed over to the CCP, for a trial by a 'people's court' that would inevitably have resulted in his execution. When the news got to Moscow the following day the initial reaction was equally joyous. Even Wang Ming thought Chiang should be 'finished off',[59] and the general rapture was shared by no less a personage than Georgi Dimitrov, the Bulgarian General

Secretary of the Comintern. Stalin however had other ideas. In a furious midnight telephone call to Dimitrov he lashed out at the nearest CCP scapegoat: 'Who is this Wang Ming of yours? A provocateur? I hear that he wanted to send a telegram to have Chiang Kai-shek killed.'[60] In Stalin's judgement Chiang was the only figure capable of leading a united Chinese resistance to Japan. If anything happened to Chiang the Chinese body politic would split down the middle and any hope of a United Front would be gone. Worse still, the surviving Nationalist chiefs might ally with Japan and Germany in the ominous Anti-Comintern Pact that had been forged between those two powers less than three weeks before. On 16 December, at Stalin's prompting, a stern cable was sent by the Comintern to Baoan directing the CCP to secure Chiang's release and to work towards a peaceful resolution of the 'Xi'an Incident'. The cable was said to have reached Baoan in a garbled form, and had to be reissued on 20 December; but by 17 December Zhou Enlai was already in Xi'an to negotiate with the Young Marshal, and by 19 December the CCP Politburo had finally dropped their proposal that Chiang should be handed over to 'the people' for trial. Not to put too fine a point on it, the Soviet despot had saved Chiang Kai-shek's skin.

Throughout these years the response of the Chinese Nationalist government to Moscow's overtures had been one of mistrust. In 1932 the talks which began in Geneva on the resumption of diplomatic ties were held up for some months as the Nationalists tried to insist that the two sides conclude a non-aggression pact first – a commitment they hoped would restrain further Soviet help to the CCP. And after official relations were finally resumed that December the Nationalists went on doing their ineffectual best to block the Kremlin's strategic manoeuvres in their frontier zones. In 1933–4, for example, in the struggle for control of Xinjiang, the Nanking authorities gave covert backing to the Japanese protégé, Big Horse, against the Soviet-aided Governor Sheng Shicai; and in March 1935 they complained vociferously at the Soviet sale of the Chinese Eastern Railway to Manchukuo. The KMT were a broad church, and some of their leadership did indeed call for closer ties with Moscow. Prominent among these was Dr Sun Fo, the son of the Party's founder, Dr Sun Yat-sen. But such voices were generally drowned in the anti-Soviet chorus. Chiang Kai-shek himself was apt to allude in his diaries to 'our Russian enemy'. Every inch the traditional Chinese father, he was anguished by the absence in the Soviet Union of his own son

Ching-kuo, and appalled at the prospect of being left heirless if Ching-kuo were to be done away with by his Soviet hosts. He went so far as to put out a number of feelers to Stalin in the hope of securing Ching-kuo's release. But he was adamant that he would strike no political deals to attain that objective: 'I would rather have no offspring than sacrifice our nation's interests.'[61]

In spite of this deep-seated suspicion the Nationalists couldn't entirely ignore the strategic realities. With the Imperial Japanese Army pushing their way ever further across the Chinese provinces to the north of the Great Wall, with China in Winston Churchill's words being 'eaten up by Japan like an artichoke, leaf by leaf', some form of cooperation with the Soviets inescapably began to make sense. From the autumn of 1934 Chiang overcame his misgivings sufficiently to explore the possibility of a military agreement with the Soviet Union and the delivery of Soviet arms. He also tried several times to win Stalin's permission for his old mentor, General Blücher, to come back to China and work with him once more. By the last months of 1935 the Soviet embassy in Nanking were reporting that even the Right KMT had exhibited an unprecedented interest in dealing with them. Chen Lifu, one of Chiang's close confidants and a pillar of the Nationalist right, sat down quietly with the ambassador, Dmitri Bogomolov, and his military attaché with a view to concluding a secret alliance against Japan. This rapprochement was however blighted the following March after Stalin outraged KMT sensitivities by forging his Defence Pact with Outer Mongolia behind China's back. On 13 December 1936, when Chiang was held captive in Xi'an, the Nationalist acting premier, H.H. Kung (Gong Xiangxi) in the course of a talk with the Soviet chargé d'affaires in Nanking played on Stalin's worst fears by suggesting that if his master were killed the remaining KMT leaders might indeed join up with Japan in an anti-Soviet league. Looking back decades later, Chiang judged that from 1933 to 1937 Nanking's relations with Moscow had made 'no progress whatsoever'.[62]

In the spring of 1937 Stalin played what he possibly viewed as his trump card in winning Chiang over. On 3 March a decision was made by the Moscow Politburo to restore Ching-kuo, seemingly without preconditions, to his father's side. Recalled from the Urals to Moscow, the younger Chiang was received personally by both Stalin and Dimitrov of the Comintern and informed of his imminent departure for home. The idea, Dimitrov recorded in his diary, was that once in Nanking Ching-kuo would be able to influence his father to get a move on and team up with the Chinese Communists in the all-important anti-Japanese Front. Ironically, there is some question as to whether Ching-kuo really wanted to return to his native land. In November 1936 he had applied for membership of the Soviet Communist Party, turning down a suggestion that he should join the Chinese one, on the apparent assumption that he would be staying in Russia for good. He is said to have felt a genuine admiration for certain aspects of Soviet life – the equality, the absence of material greed, the mobilisation of the young. Finally he was still attached, on a personal level, to his Russian lifestyle and in particular to his Russian friends in Sverdlovsk, to whom he bid a cheerful farewell before boarding the Moscow train. ('In the cold winter air, they all had a tea party on the platform and danced the foxtrot.'[63]) Worked on however by both Stalin and the Comintern chief with a mixture of threats and blandishments, the young man had little choice but to fall into line and get on board a second train – to the Far East. From Vladivostok in April he cabled a pledge to the Comintern that 'he would strictly follow Party discipline',[64] and some days later he arrived in Nanking with his Russian wife Faina and a two-year-old rather oddly named Alan. To begin with it looked as though Stalin's gambit might turn out a total fiasco. Chiang Kai-shek declined to receive the prodigal son on the grounds that his Chinese was rusty and that he had failed in the basic Confucian obligation of filial piety, and is said to have stormed when Faina merely bowed to his mother instead of kneeling as Chinese tradition prescribed. Before long the younger Chiang and his spouse did win a degree of acceptance. The shy Russian daughter-in-law managed to turn herself into the very model of a demure Oriental wife. Ching-kuo for his part was given an initial appointment as district commissioner for the prefecture of Ganzhou in the southern province of Jiangxi, where he was reportedly moved by the desperate poverty of the local inhabitants to bring in a variety of social reforms. Over time he began to make himself heard as a dovish, Russia-friendly voice in the KMT's counsels and an unrivalled expert on Soviet affairs. But his return home still wasn't enough to outweigh the ingrained anti-Soviet instincts of his father and the Nationalist majority. In the summer of 1937 there was still no sign of a formal alliance between the KMT and the Chinese Communist Party; and though Chiang Kai-shek did embark on a further round of negotiations with Zhou Enlai as the CCP spokesman, this move had nothing to do with Ching-kuo and everything to do with the need to withstand the mounting Japanese threat to the old northern capital, Peking.

We may notice in passing that the KMT's deep suspicion of Soviet Russia also made itself felt in the cultural sphere. During the early 1930s bans were imposed on the publication of Soviet literature, and indeed on the works of some pre-revolutionary authors who had been blessed by the Kremlin, ranging from Chekhov to Maxim Gorky and the Symbolist poet and novelist Fyodor Sologub. Approval was largely reserved for certain White émigré authors who had by this time been rejected in Russia itself. In 1933, for instance, a play entitled *Neighbourly Love* by the late tsarist Silver Age writer Leonid Andreev, written after Andreev's 1917 departure for Finland, was performed in the northern province of Hebei under the auspices of the KMT government, and in 1936 an adaptation of the same play was published by the National School of Drama in Nanking. One critic in the KMT media praised Andreev's work for opening the eyes of the world to 'the terror and darkness of the revolutionary era in Russia'.[65] By the mid-1930s, however, parallel with their slow stirring of interest in Soviet military aid, the authorities seem to have judged it expedient to make some response to the cultural feelers from Moscow. In October 1935, just as Chen Lifu was sitting down to his first round of talks with Ambassador Bogomolov, a Sino-Soviet Cultural Association was formed in Nanking under the chairmanship of Dr Sun Fo. The association operated quite openly in KMT-held parts of China, and its members are said to have busied themselves with translations of Soviet artistic and 'socio-political' works. In February 1936 they hosted an exhibition of Soviet graphic art in Shanghai. For much of this period, though, leading writers and scholars of Nationalist China found it prudent to steer clear of Soviet culture. Their stance, as Lu Xun sardonically put it, was 'like that of a delicate young lady to tar – she not only disdains to soil her hands with it but even wrinkles her nose some distance away'.[66]

The Chinese Communists were by this time marinated in every aspect of Soviet political life. At a superficial level visitors to the Chinese Soviet Republic at Ruijin could register a Muscovite influence virtually every which way they looked. The very Chinese word for soviet, *suweiai*, was a direct transcription from the Russian, and the new state at Ruijin was formally established on 7 November 1931, the anniversary of the Bolshevik

Revolution. By 1934 the Ruijin government were issuing banknotes bearing the head of Lenin and coins embossed with the hammer and sickle. Small children were attending Lenin Primary Schools. A Gorky School was founded to train some sixty theatrical troupes for propaganda purposes, and a stage built in Soviet style took pride of place in the town's old clan temple; while many of the CCP's songs were set to Russian music. All of these trends were lovingly fostered by the 28 Bolsheviks group who came down from Shanghai to Ruijin to direct operations. Bo Gu, for example, ensured that traditional Chinese forms of address were replaced by plain 'comrade', and his very language reflected his Soviet frame of reference. In January 1934, when his colleague Luo Fu was installed in Mao Zedong's place as premier of the Ruijin government, he is said to have chortled in an allusion to the figurehead Soviet president, 'Old Mao is going to become a Kalinin now. Ha, ha!'[67] More substantially, the constitution of the Ruijin republic was modelled on the Soviet constitution of 1918. Government departments were organised with ponderous Soviet names such as the People's Commissariat for Internal Affairs, and the Peasants' Committees set up in the villages are said to have followed the precedent of the Soviet Poor Peasants' Corps. Creeping into CCP practice at this time was the Soviet technique of self-criticism (*samokritika*), promoted by Stalin since 1929 as a way to enforce Party discipline. Some scholars have also detected here the impact of Chinese tradition, from the Confucian stress on education to the Qing penal code; but it certainly was *samokritika* in a pretty pure form that was inflicted in Moscow on Li Lisan and the other CCP deviants who were being taught to mend their ways. Another Soviet custom which passed into CCP usage was the adoption by senior leaders of the orphaned children of revolutionary heroes who had lost their lives in the struggle for power. Stalin and his minister of defence, Kliment Voroshilov, had both set an example of this in the 1920s, and Zhou Enlai for one followed suit with his adoption of Li Peng, a future prime minister, and the future actress Song Weishi.

All the same there continued to be stirrings of independence – stirrings that were associated to a great extent with the maverick figure of Mao. Already by 1929 Mao's interests were starting to show signs of taking a slightly unorthodox turn: we catch a glimpse of him seated in a villa in an outlying hamlet in Fujian Province reading English (not Russian) out loud in his heavy Hunan accent. Looking back on the time he spent at Ruijin in the early

1930s, he recalled being subjected to 'pitiless attacks' by the likes of Bo Gu, Luo Fu and the military adviser Otto Braun. He was shunted into the Party's administrative offices where, in the words of one scholar, he 'drank his fill of Russian ink';[68] and it has been suggested by one later intimate that he may have conceived at this period the beginnings of a deep aversion to Stalin. However that may be, it certainly seems that the Stalinist zealots weren't able to prevent him from starting to slip the leash in theoretical terms. Already in these years he is said to have started to visualise the poor peasantry as the 'main force' in the coming Chinese Revolution, in opposition to the conventional Stalinist view that the urban working class were the 'main force' and that the peasantry, however massive, were merely auxiliaries. Mao apart, some of the most loyal devotees of the Kremlin had their restive moments. Even Bo Gu is said at one point in early 1934 to have exploded with anger at having Braun's military dogmas thrust down his throat.

The fact was that the Russians were trying to tighten their grip on the CCP at a time when their contacts with the Chinese movement were growing progressively weaker. The first blow to these contacts came as early as June 1931, with the arrest by the British Special Branch in Shanghai of a supposedly Belgian couple named Noulens who turned out in reality to be two leading Comintern operatives, Yakov Rudnik and Tatiana Moiseenko. Following this breakthrough the Shanghai Municipal Police and the gendarmes of the French Concession were able to roll up the Comintern's principal Far Eastern network, cutting off in the process a major channel for Soviet subsidies to the CCP. Three years later, in June 1934, the Nationalists managed to capture the Shanghai radio station which served as the vital link between Moscow and Ruijin. Chiang Kai-shek's men surreptitiously ran the radio station themselves for the next four months, closing it down in October just as the desperate CCP were about to abandon their Chinese Soviet Republic for the unknown hazards of the Long March. Soviet agents in Vladivostok told their bosses disconsolately, 'All radio contacts cut off. Last reports catastrophic, series of multiple betrayals.'[69] The result was that for nearly two years Soviet interaction with the main body of the Chinese Communists was effectively nil. The direction from Moscow which had been maintained, however erratically, since the 1920s was no longer possible. Stalin went to the trouble of sending Li Lisan down by train to broadcast to his comrades from a secret GRU military base near the border between

Kazakhstan and Xinjiang, but the attempt to communicate with the Long Marchers through the base's powerful radio transmitter proved unsuccessful. It wasn't until July 1936 that radio contact with Moscow was re-established by CCP technicians at their first post-Long March headquarters of Baoan in Shaanxi. And by this time the Chinese Party had started to go their own way.

The key transition took place in the midst of the Long March, at a Politburo meeting convened in the town of Zunyi in the south-western province of Guizhou in January 1935. In the course of this meeting Mao took the offensive. Bo Gu, the stripling imposed by Moscow as head of the Party, was charged with 'all mortal sins', and Braun the Comintern agent 'turned white' as Mao lashed out at him for his insistence on positional warfare and his monopolisation of military command.[70] Following this assault Mao was raised to the post of chairman of the Party's Military Affairs Committee. Nominally still subordinate to Luo Fu, who had replaced Bo Gu in the Party leadership, as well as to Bo Gu and the official military chief, Zhou Enlai, he was now, in reality, the supreme Party boss; and Chen Yun, one of his main supporters, was sent off to Moscow in the absence of radio contact to make his ascendancy clear to the Soviet government. In the meantime Mao started to stake out an independent position for the Party for the first time since Li Lisan's wild démarche in the summer of 1930. In July 1936 at Baoan he granted a series of interviews to a left-wing American journalist, Edgar Snow, in what would be the first of many attempts to reach out to the West. In his talks with Snow he played down any dealings the Party might have with the Soviet Union, declaring, 'We are certainly not fighting for an emancipated China in order to turn the country over to Moscow.'[71] Like Li Lisan he proclaimed that the Communist revolution in China was the 'key factor' in the world revolution as a whole, implying that the Soviet Union should be helping China and not the other way round.[72] And like Li, but more subtly, he voiced China's claim to Outer Mongolia, predicting that when the revolution in China was victorious 'the Outer Mongolian republic would undoubtedly become part of the Chinese federation of their own free will'.[73]

After the slaughter of 1927 and the years of repression that had followed, Mao and his Party had no inclination to enter a second United Front with the Nationalists in the interests of Stalin's strategic designs. In the absence of radio contact word of the new Comintern policy only reached them four months after its proclamation, through a solitary courier who arrived in Baoan in November 1935. The Party leaders mulled over the Comintern's message for several days, but in the end were unable to swallow the new formula of 'Unite with Chiang and Resist the Japanese', preferring to stick to the two-pronged 'Resist the Japanese and Oppose Chiang'.[74] When radio contact with Moscow was finally restored in the summer of 1936 Mao promptly cabled the Comintern seeking their endorsement for a breakaway state he proposed to set up in the north-western provinces and requesting in addition supplies of Soviet planes, heavy artillery, shells, infantry weapons, anti-aircraft guns and pontoons, and a financial transfusion of 2–3 million Mexican dollars. Such a breakaway state might indeed help to slow down the Japanese conquest; but by definition it would also be an entity opposed to the KMT central government, and any weapons that reached it might equally well be turned on Nanking. Moscow's response was predictably to crack the whip. On receipt of Mao's cable the Comintern chairman Dimitrov convened a session of his secretariat complete with Wang Ming and the other CCP delegates, and instructions were drafted for the Party leaders in Baoan demanding a change of course. On 15 August Stalin issued through Dimitrov an order to the Chinese Communists to stop treating Chiang as the enemy. 'Everything must be subordinated to the anti-Japanese cause.'[75]

Right through these same summer months secret talks, as we noticed, had been taking place between the CCP and the Young Marshal whose forces confronted them in Shaanxi Province – talks that bore fruit in December with the Young Marshal's kidnapping of Chiang Kai-shek in Xi'an. Mao had instigated these overtures behind Stalin's back, fully aware that the Soviet chief was against such an action and in defiance of his more conventional colleagues who felt that Moscow should at least be consulted. And when the Comintern cable restraining him from securing Chiang's trial and execution arrived in Baoan on 16 December his reaction was violent. We are told that he 'flew into a rage', that he 'swore and stamped his feet'.[76] Noting that Japan and the Soviet Union had each begun to argue that the 'Xi'an Incident' had been contrived by the other, he permitted himself possibly his first direct criticism of Soviet attitudes: 'Both sides are distorting the essence of the matter.'[77] According to one source this first cable from the Comintern wasn't in fact garbled, as reported elsewhere: Mao simply claimed that it was with the object of playing for time, and only gave way when the Comintern repeated their orders on 20 December. Summarising the Incident he declared, through gritted teeth doubtless, that 'the instructions of the Comintern more or less coincided with our views'.[78] Many other top CCP figures, both in Baoan and in Moscow, appear to have shared Mao's dismay at Stalin's last-minute rescue of Chiang Kai-shek. Even the hitherto faithful Stalinist Luo Fu is said to have commented, 'This is entirely in the interests of the Comintern and the Soviet Union.'[79]

And even after Stalin's clampdown the CCP still continued to kick up the traces. On 6 January 1937, with Chiang now free and back in Nanking and agreement reached in principle on the formation of a Second United Front, we still find Mao and Luo Fu dispatching a cable to Zhou Enlai and Bo Gu in Xi'an on the need 'to prepare boldly for war' with the Nationalist regime.[80] On 15 January, as the leaders decamped from Baoan to a more permanent base in the city of Yan'an, the Comintern sent a message complaining that the Chinese Party 'still hadn't shaken off their mistaken policy',[81] and on 19 January Stalin gathered his closest lieutenants for a meeting at which they agreed that the CCP's 'main task' at present was to achieve 'an effective end' to the Chinese Civil War.[82]

A similar kind of trajectory, from warm embrace of the Soviet model to mounting restiveness, can be traced in this period in the radical part of the Chinese literary world. During the late 1920s the first works of Soviet as distinct from pre-revolutionary Russian literature were beginning to percolate into the KMT-controlled cities, where they were read and translated in spite of the government's efforts to ban them – the Nationalist grip was autocratic rather than totalitarian. Lu Xun produced a Chinese version of Alexander Fadeev's *The Rout*, a novel recounting the lives of young Red guerrillas in Siberia during the Russian Civil War, and over the next few years translations followed of such revolutionary epics as Alexander Serafimov's *Iron Flood* and Mikhail Sholokhov's *Virgin Soil Upturned*. Interest in the old Russian classics declined, while translations of the Silver Age writers, condemned by the Kremlin as 'romantic' and 'individualistic', almost disappeared. A young Manchurian author, Xiao Jun, was inspired by Fadeev to write *Village in August*, a novel depicting the anti-Japanese struggle in his native region, incidentally finding a moment to praise Marx and Lenin as 'lovable because they are truly poets';[83] and a school of would-be Chinese poets aspired to write verse in the 'drumbeat style' of Vladimir Mayakovsky.[84] In March 1930 a League of Left-Wing Writers was founded in Shanghai by Lu Xun and others at the prompting of the CCP to bring together the various literary groups of the time to embark on the study of Soviet writing and Soviet literary theory. Admiration was also expressed for the Soviet visual arts. In February 1936 Lu Xun praised the Soviet woodcuts on show in Shanghai in language reminiscent of the famous eulogy given by Pericles of his native Athens, as 'truthful without pedantry, beautiful without effeminacy, joyful without wantonness, forceful without coarseness'.[85]

All of this time, however, a shadow of regimentation was creeping up. In a talk delivered in Moscow in October 1932 Stalin proclaimed the doctrine of Socialist Realism as the standard for all future revolutionary art, and the following year a CCP official named Zhou Yang was assigned to implant this new doctrine among the members of the Left-Wing Writers' League. By the mid-1930s, clear signs of discomfort with Stalin's cultural straitjacket were beginning to show, with dissent hinted at by none other than the celebrated Lu Xun. Pessimistic by instinct, the great satirist seems to have been unable to reconcile himself to the compulsory rosiness of Socialist Realism. He voiced regret at the withering of so much Russian literature after 1917 and the eclipse of his heroes Andreev and Artsybashev. He was deeply unmoved by the new proletarian literary style, suggesting that the Soviet idea of a perfect poem was

> Oh, steam whistle!
> Oh, Lenin![86]

Increasingly stifled by the atmosphere of the League of Left-Wing Writers he had helped to set up, he was oppressed above all by the looming presence of Zhou Yang: 'I always feel that I am bound in an iron chain while a foreman is whipping me on the back.'[87] Much admired by Russian critics, he declined repeated invitations to visit the Soviet Union. During his final years he reverted to his original work of translating the great Russian classics of the nineteenth century, focusing in particular on the stories of Gogol and Chekhov; and he was still busy on a translation of Gogol's *Dead Souls* when tuberculosis claimed him in October 1936. Qu Qiubai, the former CCP leader who had begun his career as a journalist and translator, seems in the same way to have turned back to the old Russian literature as 'the one field in which I always felt at home'.[88] Arrested in early 1935 by Nationalist soldiers on his way to Shanghai, he composed a long testament behind bars before being marched out to face a firing squad the following June. In the last paragraph he put forward a list of six books he considered 'worth reading':[89] three of these six books were Russian, and two of them, Turgenev's *Rudin* and Tolstoy's *Anna Karenina*, were products of the nineteenth century. (The third, *The Life of Klim Samgin*, was a novel by Maxim Gorky begun in the mid-1920s but dealing with pre-revolutionary rather than Soviet times.) Outside the purview of the league the liberal novelist Lao She struck a more acid tone with a fantasy which reads like a sketch for Orwell's *Animal Farm* – a tale called *Cat Country* in which the Chinese of the future are depicted as a feline colony living on Mars under the guidance of an ideology known as *Everybodyshareskyism*.

RESCUE AND REPRESSION (1937–41)

In July 1937 the Japanese Army seized on a clash which had taken place with Chinese troops on the Marco Polo Bridge to the west of Peking as a pretext for launching an all-out invasion of China proper. General Blücher, still serving as Soviet commander-in-chief in the Far East, proclaimed that in view of this open aggression the Soviet Union would be obliged to give China aid, and within a few weeks the roadblocks that had held up Russian military partnership with the Chinese Nationalists had been swept away. On 21 August the Soviet government signed with Chiang Kai-shek's diplomats the non-aggression pact that Nanking had so long hankered after, committing themselves at the same time to furnish Chiang's forces with both weapons and technical aid; and on 18 November Stalin confirmed in a talk with General Yang Ze, head of a KMT military mission to Moscow, 'We shall spare neither money nor arms to help you . . . All that we can do we will.'[90] The Soviet chief was as good as his word. During the four years from 1937 to 1941 the Soviet Union moved back from the wings to the centre of the Chinese stage, bolstering China's resistance to Japan with an aid package that dwarfed every previous military commitment Russia, either tsarist or Bolshevik, had made to the country. Contributions included between US $300 million and $450 million in war credits, plus weaponry in the form of some 1,000 aircraft, 1,000 artillery pieces, 1,000 machine guns, 50,000 rifles,

2,000 motor vehicles and eighty-six T-82 tanks. Upwards of 1,500 Soviet experts were sent to resume the work they had been obliged to suspend ten years earlier of modernising the Nationalist forces. They were headed by General A.I. Cherepanov, who had served in the 1920s as Blücher's deputy in Canton and who now came back to China to occupy Blücher's old post of chief military adviser to Chiang himself, and Lieutenant-General Vasily Chuikov, a rising star in the Soviet General Staff, who had travelled widely in China and picked up quite fluent Chinese before seeing service during the Manchurian war of 1929, and who took over from Cherepanov as chief military adviser in the autumn of 1940. Instructors from Russia gave lessons to over 100,000 Chinese officers and men, either directly or through the Nationalist military schools, in the techniques of handling modern Soviet weapons, while engineers supervised the construction of air bases and motor roads. Most important perhaps was the role played by some 2,000 Soviet pilots who effectively shouldered the task of defending Chinese air space at a time when no competent Nationalist air force existed. They strafed Japanese naval vessels and transports on the Yangtze, bombed Japanese airfields as far away as Taiwan and were said to have shot down a total of 986 Japanese planes. Many paid with their lives. Out of one group of sixty pilots who carried out bombing assignments between May and October 1938 only sixteen returned to their Russian homes.

And all this at a time when Shanghai, Nanking, Wuhan were falling successively to the Japanese legions, and when no significant help was forthcoming for China from any other outside power. The United States and Britain were both pursuing a studied neutrality, the United States largely concerned to maintain its lucrative Japanese trade and Britain anxious at all costs to steer clear of war in the Far East at a time it already faced the double menace of Hitler and Mussolini in Europe. Whatever Stalin's motives, it can be fairly conjectured that without Russian help and the boost to morale it engendered Chiang's regime would most probably have sued for peace with Japan, and that Chinese resistance might not have outlasted the first two years of the war.

But of course Stalin did have his motives. The Soviet foreign minister, Maxim Litvinov, hinted as much at the start of the conflict in a talk with the French vice-premier, Léon Blum. The Kremlin, he remarked, was delighted by the Japanese attack upon China and 'hoped that the war would continue for as long as possible'.[91] Stalin himself explained to Chuikov in a briefing he gave the general before his departure for China that even if Chiang Kai-shek couldn't drive back the Japanese he could 'tie them up for a long time', and that only in this way could Russia be freed from the nightmare scenario of a simultaneous Japanese–German attack.[92] Stalin, in other words, was proposing to fight Japan – to the last Chinese. Nationalist China had become a central part of his grand defence strategy, and the Nationalists had to be buttressed by every possible means even if this meant shedding the finer points of Bolshevik principle.

The CCP were now put well and truly on the back burner. By virtue of the new non-aggression pact the Soviet Union was constrained from augmenting the power of the Chinese Communists at the expense of Chiang's government, and in any case Stalin considered the CCP in Yan'an with their mere tens of thousands of troops and their backward equipment too feeble an outfit to spearhead a serious war of resistance against Japan. Under an agreement concluded with Moscow on 14 September 1937 the Nationalist government were required to pass on a fifth to a quarter of the Soviet weaponry they received to the CCP forces; but in practice there is little sign that any significant Soviet arms made their way through to Yan'an at all. Accounts speak of an early delivery of anti-aircraft guns, of a subsequent 120 machine guns and six anti-tank guns. Intermittent dollops of Soviet funds are reported, a donation of $500,000 authorised by Stalin at the start of the war, $300,000 supplied to Yan'an in July 1938 and a further $300,000 committed in February 1940; but even the total of $3.85 million which the CCP are said to have been granted between 1937 and 1941 compares rather pallidly with the $300 million to $450 million which the KMT were allotted in war credits.[93] Other Soviet deliveries to the CCP seem to have consisted of sundries – copies of *Pravda*, speeches and writings of Lenin and Stalin, a batch of printing machines to help circulate propaganda and 'three to five planeloads of blankets and medicine'.[94]

The Chinese Communists weren't altogether forgotten. The old evangelical mission of the 1920s still exerted a pull on the Soviet Russians (even some of Stalin's diplomats are said to have been shaken by the fulsome praise which their media now lavished on the former arch-villain, Chiang Kai-shek), and Chuikov was at pains to point out in his memoirs, 'We had treaty obligations to Chiang's government, but our *spiritual sympathies* lay with the CCP.'[95] Behind the lines, in the Soviet Union, various forms of back-up were deployed in these years to compensate the Chinese Party for the lack of any significant help in the field. Party leaders were frequently admitted to Russia for medical care. In 1939–40, for instance, Zhou Enlai came to Moscow for treatment after a riding injury sustained in Yan'an, while Lin Biao, a gifted but mentally unstable commander of the Chinese Red Army, was treated in Moscow and Kislovodsk for a series of ailments including headaches, vomiting, heart palpitations, insomnia and 'nervous disorders'. Neglected children of CCP leaders were given a home and an education at the No. 1 International Children's Home which had been set up by the Comintern at Ivanovo, 200 miles to the north-east of Moscow, in 1931. Among the more celebrated of the young Chinese taken in at Ivanovo were Mao Zedong's sons, Mao Anying and Mao Anqing, who had been found living rough on the streets of Shanghai in the spring of 1936. The two boys had been shipped around the world via Hong Kong and France to the Soviet Union with the knowledge and involvement of Stalin himself, and were known at Ivanovo by the affectionate Russian diminutives of Seryozha (Sergei) and Kolya (Nikolai). Also welcomed at Ivanovo was Liu Yunbin, the fourteen-year-old son of the early Party recruit Liu Shaoqi, who was sent to the school by his father in 1939, became known as Klim (Kliment) and developed a passion for Pushkin. The general handling by the Ivanovo staff of these uprooted children seems to have been kindly. We are told they remembered the children's birthdays, and marked their holidays by giving them little packets of fruit or sweets. In April 1940 'Seryozha' Mao wrote an article describing facilities worthy of a top English public school, complete with a library, a games room, a painting studio, a theatre, a football pitch, basketball, volleyball, tennis and 'special exercise' courts, a kitchen garden and a river where the children could swim, row and fish. 'Every day we have three meals and a snack. Every Saturday and Sunday we are shown at least one film.'[96] All of this thoughtfulness had of course its pragmatic side too. The medical visits by CCP leaders gave Stalin and his entourage a chance to build up their knowledge of the Chinese Party and to foster their ties with individual rising stars. And the rescued children could be used by Stalin as diplomatic pawns in the same way he had already used Chiang Ching-kuo. It is curious to reflect that for a few weeks in early 1937 the Soviet boss had his paws simultaneously on the offspring of both Chiang and Mao.

For all its displays of solicitude the message from the Kremlin to its CCP protégés was loud and clear. The CCP must team up with their Nationalist rivals. On 22 September 1937, after prodding by Stalin, the Second United Front was at last proclaimed. On 11 November Stalin summoned Wang Ming to remind him, 'The main thing now is the war against Japan',[97] and two weeks later he sent Wang off in a special plane to Yan'an to convey this injunction to the Chinese Politburo. Arriving, in the words of one colleague, 'like an Imperial envoy from Moscow, bearing high the Emperor's double-edged sword',[98] Wang proceeded to urge on his Party a policy of 'Fight Japan First' which entailed, among other concessions, a complete merger of the CCP armies with those of the KMT. Back in Moscow, on 18 November, Stalin made a somewhat startling promise to General Yang Ze, the head of the Nationalist military delegation: 'Don't the Communists prevent you from opposing Japan? Doesn't the [Communist] Eighth [Route] Army prevent you? *If there are disputes with the Eighth [Route] Army we shall help you.*'[99] Over the following years, as the tensions between the two partners in the Chinese alliance erupted periodically in open warfare, the Kremlin made a genuine effort to hold the balance between them. At the end of 1939, for instance, Moscow briefly suspended its aid to the KMT government after Nationalist forces launched a thrust into Mao's 'liberated areas'. Most of the heavier pressure, however, was reserved for the weaker CCP side. In November 1940 Stalin sent a message directing Mao: 'It is essential you do not initiate any military action [i.e. against the Nationalists]',[100] and at around the same time he observed in his briefing to Chuikov that nationalistic tendencies, with a small 'n', were quite strong in the CCP and that their feelings of 'international solidarity' were 'inadequately developed'.[101] Matters came to a head in January 1941 when the Nationalists attacked and wiped out a contingent of 7,000 troops of the Communist New Fourth Army who had been stranded in an exposed position to the south of the Yangtze in the central province of Anhui. When Zhou Enlai, who was at the time serving as senior CCP representative in the wartime Nationalist capital of Chungking, approached the Soviet ambassador Alexander Panyushkin on Mao's behalf for permission to retaliate the reaction was icy. Panyushkin even suggested that Mao had deliberately set up the debacle in Anhui in the hope that this would persuade Stalin to give him a free hand against Chiang's regime. He refused to believe Zhou's assertion that the KMT were intent on annihilating their Chinese Communist rivals. And he urged Zhou, '*Whatever happens you must maintain your alliance*.'[102] Two weeks later, in early February, Dimitrov the Comintern chief repeated this order with a hint of menace. 'We consider', he telegraphed Mao, 'that a rift [between you and the KMT] is in no way inevitable. Please clearly appraise the situation, *reexamine your current standpoint* and inform us of your views and proposals.'[103]

The same single-minded attention to thwarting the Japanese was apparent in the Kremlin's handling of its quasi-protectorate of Xinjiang. From the start of the Japanese onslaught on China in 1937 the Russians made use of their grip on the province to give every possible help to the KMT government's war of resistance. The huge volume of Soviet military aid that came through to the Nationalists was channelled along the old Silk Road as far as Lanzhou in Gansu, on a 1,700-mile highway especially built to facilitate the transit of hundreds of lorries and some 2,000 camels. This desert lifeline became more important than ever in the summer of 1940, when the beleaguered British gave way to pressure from Japan and closed the Burma Road which had previously brought the Nationalists a trickle of weapons from Western suppliers. In August 1939 Moscow reached an agreement with General Yang Ze for the construction in Xinjiang of Soviet military installations specifically intended to support the Nationalist war effort. A school for the training of Nationalist airmen was opened in the town of Yining, and a plant for the manufacture of fighter aircraft was built near Urumqi. Officially described as an agricultural machinery works and referred to by the innocent name of Factory No. 600, this aircraft plant was strongly fortified and protected by a special detachment of twenty tanks and 1,500 troops. In a meeting with Dr Sun Fo, who arrived in Moscow in March 1939 on a visit designed to extract still more Soviet assistance, Stalin observed that all Soviet activity in Xinjiang was 'indirectly helping the Nationalist government'.[104]

All of this didn't mean that the Soviet Union was intending to hand Xinjiang over to Chiang Kai-shek. In January 1938, at Governor Sheng Shicai's invitation, the Soviet 'Red Eighth Regiment', dressed in Chinese uniforms and accompanied by an air force squadron, was deployed as a semi-permanent garrison in Hami, at the province's eastern gateway. Dominating the Silk Road, this unit could serve as a barrier to any Japanese thrust towards Central Asia – and to any attempt by the Nationalists to develop their influence in the province at Sheng's expense. Nor for that matter were the Russians in any hurry to turn Xinjiang over to the Chinese Communist Party. In 1938 a contingent of CCP activists including Mao Zemin, Mao Zedong's younger brother, were sent to Urumqi to advise Sheng on various day-to-day issues like fiscal reform. But when Sheng, at the urging of these Chinese Communists, applied to Stalin for permission to enrol in the CCP, Stalin after some reflection turned down the proposal, suggesting that he take out membership of the *Soviet* Party instead. The truth was that Xinjiang was by now altogether too valuable to be entrusted to any non-Soviet hands. By the late 1930s successive teams of geologists had uncovered a wide range of strategic minerals which would be vital to Russia's economy in the event of the dreaded major war. By 1939 Soviet engineers had begun to exploit a substantial oilfield which had been found near the north-western town of Shihezi and which they expected to yield 50,000 tons of crude a year. In the north-west too they had started to extract tungsten, a metal of crucial importance in the manufacture of bullets, shells and missiles. And on 26 November 1940 Soviet emissaries signed with Sheng a culminating Tin Mines Agreement, which conferred on their country for fifty years the exclusive right to prospect and exploit the province's deposits of tin and other ancillary metals, with only 5 per cent of the output reverting to the province itself. Other provisions entitled the Soviet Union to set up and maintain power stations, telephone lines and communications facilities; to build railways and highways; to install offices, hospitals, schools and accommodation for Soviet personnel and their families and barracks for Soviet troops. The agreement in other words for all practical purposes handed Xinjiang to the Russians on a plate. To avoid hesitation on Sheng's part his Soviet interlocutor urged him in a curt, clipped discourse, 'We hope you will make a wise and cautious decision on a question which affects not only the future of Xinjiang *but also of yourself*.'[105]

Stalin can scarcely be faulted for doing whatever it logically took to maintain his country's security. During these same years, however, logic was giving way to paranoia as the Soviet tsar began to detect Japanese agents around every corner (or Trotskyites, which came to much the same thing). As the Great Purge engulfed Russia virtually every prominent diplomat or army officer who had been active in Chinese affairs since the Bolshevik Revolution fell under suspicion. One early victim was Dmitri Bogomolov,

1. Painting by a Chinese artist of an early Russian encampment in eastern Siberia. Dated to some time between 1689 and 1722, the work may in fact depict the Manchu siege of the Cossack fort of Albazin in 1685. Note the apparent arrival of Qing naval forces in the bottom right-hand corner.

2. Ivan Vlasov, the governor of Nerchinsk, gave staunch support to the Cossack attempt to hold on to Albazin, and even encouraged the Cossacks to expand their activities along the Amur.

3. Arguably one of the two or three ablest rulers of all time, the Kangxi emperor (1661–1722) masterminded the Qing siege of Albazin through a combination of skilful logistical and intelligence work, then went on to display a striking magnanimity to the defeated and starving Russians.

4. Imagined view of the 'Muscovite caravan' of Isbrandt Ides setting out from Peking in February 1694 and passing through the Great Wall on the long road home. Details of the caravan had apparently reached the novelist Daniel Defoe through the English translation of Isbrandt's diary and were woven by him into *The Farther Adventures of Robinson Crusoe* (1719).

5. From the late 1720s private Russian trade with China was conducted in the remote border settlement of Kyakhta. The 'Sandy Venice' developed into a place of great wealth and a centre where Russian and Chinese merchants mixed amicably together. This prosperous merchant was painted in 1851 in the adjoining Chinese settlement of Maimaicheng ('Trade Town') by the Swedish artist Carl Petter Mazer.

6. 'Tea on the Road to Kyakhta'. By the late eighteenth century tea had become a major Chinese export to Russia. After China was prised open by the great powers in 1860 Russian merchants were able to take control of all the stages of tea production, shipping processed tea from their factories in Hankou down the Yangtze, up the coast to Tianjin and from Tianjin overland to the border.

7. In 1897–8 the tsarist government abandoned their long-standing posture of solicitude towards China and joined the other great powers in an all-out grab for Qing territory. Here Tsar Nicholas II is shown seated among his British, German, French and Japanese rivals ready to carve himself a slice of the Chinese pie, while a distraught China looks on in the background.

8. In the summer of 1900, when the Qing court threw their weight behind the anti-foreign Boxer insurrection, tsarist troops overran the whole of Manchuria. The contest was an unequal one.

9. Emboldened by their successes, some of the tsarist commanders believed they could hold Manchuria indefinitely, and turn it into a 'Yellow Russia' in the teeth of British and US disapproval. They were especially scornful of puny little Japan …

10. … until the Japanese shattered their fleet at Port Arthur in February 1904. Further Japanese victories followed both on land and at sea. Here is the tsarist army in February 1905, in full retreat after the fall of Mukden.

11. The Bolshevik seizure of power in 1917 propelled into China a huge wave of upper- and middle-class émigrés: 25,000 of these White Russians took refuge in Shanghai alone. Many sank into beggary or prostitution, but others made their contribution to the city's cultural life. These dancing girls were recruited for Nikolai Sokolsky's local Ballets Russes.

12. The Russian Orthodox Church gave up their belated attempt to win Chinese converts, and focused instead on meeting the spiritual and material needs of the White refugees. Built in the French concession in Shanghai in 1931, the Cathedral of the Holy Mother of God is pictured here in a photograph from the late 1940s.

13. In the meantime the Bolsheviks were engaged in their own form of evangelism. Here Mikhail Borodin, Stalin's Special Adviser to the Chinese Nationalist Party, harangues a crowd in Wuhan in March 1927. Borodin knew no Chinese and instead delivered his gospel in English, with a Midwestern accent picked up in Chicago.

14. Borodin in repose. On his left is his much-loved interpreter, the young Chinese Communist Zhang Tailei, and on Zhang's left is Wang Jingwei, then leader of the Nationalist left. By the middle of 1927 Wang Jingwei had turned on his Communist allies, and in December Zhang Tailei was killed by the Nationalists during the suppression of the Canton Commune.

15. Many of the young Chinese who studied or worked in the Soviet Union during the 1920s and 1930s found romance as well as revolution. One of these was Chiang Kai-shek's son Chiang Ching-kuo, who married a pretty Byelorussian lathe operator named Faina Vakhreva. Here are Ching-kuo and his family at some unspecified date following their departure for China in 1937.

16. Thus far and no farther. In the late 1930s the Soviet Union and the Chinese Nationalists shared a common objective of halting Japan's expansion on the Asian mainland. In August–September 1939 the Soviet Army fought the Japanese to a standstill in the momentous battle of Khalkhin Gol on the edge of Mongolia, diverting Japan's energies towards South-East Asia and the Pacific.

17. Young Chinese Communists photographed in a workshop in Yan'an. Note the portraits of Stalin and, more surprisingly, Roosevelt. Mao Zedong and his followers were always careful to keep a line open to the United States and the West.

18. 14 August 1945. Chinese Nationalist negotiators sign the new Sino-Soviet Treaty while Stalin and Molotov look on. The Nationalist team were deeply unhappy with a document which provided for the independence of Outer Mongolia and restored Russian rights in Manchuria to the level of 1904, and their expressions are unsurprisingly sombre.

19. On 22 August 1945 Soviet forces entered the old tsarist naval base of Port Arthur, completing their occupation of Manchuria. Their advent was initially welcomed by local citizens happy with the eviction of their former Japanese masters …

20. … but this goodwill dissipated as the Soviet Army embarked on the systematic removal of all the industrial plant and equipment which the Japanese had installed in the region. Stalin and his commanders regarded this Japanese machinery as legitimate war booty, but both the Chinese Nationalists and Communists perceived its removal as theft.

21. Mao Zedong, the new ruler of China, seated at Stalin's right hand in the Bolshoi Theatre, Moscow, for the celebration of the Soviet leader's seventieth birthday, 21 December 1949. Mao was in a deep sulk, which neither Stalin nor Rakosi, the Hungarian Party boss on Mao's right, were able to penetrate.

22. After Stalin's death in 1953 the new Sino-Soviet alliance grew warmer as Soviet scientists and engineers poured into China to implement the 'biggest technology transfer in history'. The Soviet experts were genuinely revered by the thousands of Chinese they trained.

23. International Women's Day, 1954. Chinese women embraced Russian fashions and learnt from the Soviet efforts at gender equality. But the conviction expressed in this poster that 'Our Friendship is Unbreakable' proved sadly misplaced.

24. In October 1959 years of mounting tension between the Soviet and Chinese leaderships reached a climax at an acrimonious summit in Peking. 'I have an accusation for you,' Mao informed Nikita Khrushchev, '– that you are guilty of *Right Opportunism*.'

25. Within only four months of Khrushchev's withdrawal of scientists and technicians from China in July–August 1960, Soviet and Chinese leaders were striving to limit the damage. At a conference of eighty-one Communist parties in Moscow, Khrushchev has his arms around the chief Chinese delegates, Liu Shaoqi and Deng Xiaoping. Liu (on Khrushchev's right) worked quietly for a reconciliation, but Deng maintained the abrasive posture still favoured by Mao.

26. In January 1967 a group of Chinese provocatively recite Mao's *Quotations* at the Lenin Mausoleum in Moscow's Red Square. One source calls them 'students', but to judge from their ages they are more likely diplomats from one of China's European embassies recalled to Peking to take part in the Cultural Revolution.

27. 'Shame on the Chinese Sectarians!' A Soviet counter-demonstration in February 1967. The quarrel was couched in the language of Marxist-Leninist dogma, but the underlying tussle was one between nationalisms.

28. A 1969 rally of Chinese workers at the Baotou Iron and Steel Company in Inner Mongolia. Banners and placards denounce the 'New Tsars', the 'Soviet Revisionists' and the 'Soviet Social Imperialists'. One small contingent holds placards proclaiming the traditional condemnation of the United States, but the US has clearly been reassigned the less odious status of Enemy Number Two.

29. 'All Reactionaries are Paper Tigers!' During the frightening clashes on the disputed island of Damansky/Zhenbao in the River Ussuri in March 1969, Chinese troops hold up captured Soviet helmets on the points of their bayonets. Ironically they are all wearing Russian-style hats.

30. February 1979. Moscow rejoices as its Vietnamese ally gives the invading People's Liberation Army a bloody nose. But Soviet backing for Vietnam was restricted to threats and a few token military movements, and by April the Chinese were floating the possibility of a fresh set of Sino-Soviet talks.

31. Mikhail and Raisa Gorbachev befriend Deng Xiaoping, 16 May 1989. The great Sino-Soviet rapprochement didn't altogether live up to expectations. Deng privately considered Gorbachev an idiot, and Gorbachev confessed himself 'fed up with listening to this old man's sermons'.

32. Presidents Boris Yeltsin and Jiang Zemin. The two countries got on so much better without a shared ideology …

33. November 1992. The Sino-Russian border is now a visa-free zone as Chinese traders scramble to do business in the Russian Far East. Cut off from their traditional sources of supply in an anarchic European Russia, local Russian citizens are even willing to offer these Chinese their jewellery and other valuables in exchange for desperately needed clothing and food.

34. Bludgeoned by Western sanctions in 2014 following his annexation of Crimea, Vladimir Putin 'pivoted' eastwards, concluding a $400 billion deal to supply China with Russian natural gas for the next thirty years. This hoarding celebrates Gazprom's Power of Siberia pipeline, with a dotted line marking the route of the pipeline 'to China'.

35. Ever since the late nineteenth century Russia has acted as armourer to successive Chinese regimes. Here People's Liberation Army soldiers try out Russian guns during the first Sino-Russian joint military exercises in August 2005. The old dependence, however, may be ending, as the Chinese increasingly produce their own military hardware and Russia looks to China as a potential supplier of high-tech missiles and drones.

36. Gazing across the Amur from the run-down city of Blagoveshchensk, local Russians are apt to be mortified by the gleaming modernity of Chinese Heihe. Here they are confronted by a grand commercial centre with the Chinese name Yuandong (Far East) transcribed in Cyrillic letters.

37. Putin, Xi Jinping and the younger generation. Here the two leaders address Chinese and Russian children in Moscow Zoo. Will the children grow up favouring Sino-Russian autocracy or Western liberalism?

38. Demonstrators in Berlin in March 2022 condemn Putin's invasion of Ukraine. Many Western observers are looking for ways of loosening the close geopolitical embrace between China and Russia, or at least of persuading one partner to exert a restraining influence on the other.

the first Soviet ambassador to the Nationalist government, who was called home from Nanking to be executed in late 1937. In December Lev Karakhan, author of the famous Declaration, was shot in Moscow's Lubyanka Prison after refusing to confess at a show trial to crimes he hadn't committed. In November 1938 Chiang Kai-shek renewed his appeal for his old mentor Blücher to be sent back to China to serve at his side: the response was evasive, for the somewhat cogent reason that Blücher had been arrested, tortured and shot the previous August for a supposed love affair with a Japanese woman spy. Lominadze the Comintern agent committed suicide. Following an 'extravagant confession' Karl Radek, the former rector of Sun Yat-sen University, died in prison, possibly as the result of a brawl. Even Mif, Radek's successor, the Stalinist acolyte who had fostered the rise of the CCP's 28 Bolsheviks, was swept to his death in the terror.

The Great Purge soon encompassed the Chinese as well. Once again attention focused on the ready-made targets of the CCP expatriates on Soviet soil. One leading instrument in this process was the sinister Kang Sheng, a gaunt, bespectacled Party zealot who had made his way from Shanghai to Moscow in 1933. Over the years he had hobnobbed with officers of the NKVD (the new name for the OGPU), and had been trained in police work and intelligence by none other than Nikolai Yezhov, the NKVD chief known as Stalin's 'poison dwarf'. By the time the purge started in 1937 Kang was in a position to give the NKVD a long list of Chinese suspects; and the treatment accorded to them was appreciably harsher than that meted out to the turbulent Chinese students of ten years before. On 23 February 1938 Li Lisan was arrested in the Hotel Lux on suspicion of being a Trotskyite and a Japanese agent, and was incarcerated successively in the Lubyanka, Lefortovo and Butyrki prisons. Browbeaten and tortured, he preserved his sanity through reading Tolstoy and Dostoevsky in his cells 'by the anaemic glow of the only light bulb'.[106] A friend of Li's named Zhang Bao was picked up three days later and dispatched for an eighteen-year stint at a camp in the Arctic. 'It was hard, very hard,' he recalled. "They beat you . . ."'.[107] 'Nights of terror' were reported in the dormitories of the Ivanovo Children's School as police arrived to remove the offspring of the latest purge victims.[108] In the course of 1938 Stalin is said to have contemplated an eventual show trial of major CCP figures ranging from Zhou Enlai and Liu Shaoqi to Luo Fu, the former stalwart of the 28 Bolsheviks; but in the end he apparently dropped the idea.

Did the finger of Stalin's suspicion even point to Mao? We are told that as early as December 1936, following Mao's unwelcome attempt to have Chiang Kai-shek liquidated, an NKVD dossier was opened on the CCP leader as a likely Trotskyite and a Japanese mole. In the briefing he gave to Wang Ming in November 1937 on the eve of the latter's departure for China Stalin instructed this emissary that he should 'take measures' to eradicate Trotskyism in the conduct of the CCP, that the Trotskyites were to be 'hunted down, shot and destroyed'.[109] Kang Sheng, the secret policeman, was ominously assigned to accompany Wang on his flight to Yan'an. Some authorities argue that Stalin didn't intend Wang to take the place of the success story Mao, pointing out that the Comintern ordered Wang to be 'modest', and reminded him, 'The leader of the CCP is Mao Zedong and not you.'[110] Others however maintain that the replacement of Mao was precisely Stalin's intention, or at any rate that he supposed the mantle of leadership would descend upon Wang as soon as he arrived at the CCP's base. In April 1938, at all events, a disgraced Comintern intelligence chief, Osip Pyatnitsky, denounced Mao in the course of his 'confession' as a member of a 'Bukharin group' who had spied for Japan; and the NKVD dossier on Mao condemned him as being 'the leader of Trotskyism in the innermost depths of the CCP'.[111]

From Russia the Great Purge spread east and south into the Soviet-dominated Chinese borderlands. The 1937 Muslim rising against Sheng Shicai in Xinjiang was interpreted as a Trotskyite scheme backed by Germany and Japan with a view to creating a launch pad for an attack upon Soviet Central Asia, and Soviet officials were sent to Urumqi to help Sheng conduct the show trials of the 'Trotskyite-Fascist conspirators'. By 1938 the Xinjiang purge had claimed a mass of local victims estimated at anything from 200 to 100,000 or more. A further wave of repression followed two years later. In the meantime Stalin took a hand in expunging the last traces of political dissidence in the MPR. In the summer of 1937 Genden the Lame of Arvaheer was arrested at his enforced holiday home on the Black Sea coast. He 'confessed' to being a Japanese spy and a counter-revolutionary, and was brought back to Moscow for execution. In late August Genden's former ally, Demid, was found dead of food poisoning at the Taiga railway station in Siberia. Protesting a little excessively, the Soviet autopsy stated that he had been suffering from 'latent syphilis, chronic malaria, arteriosclerosis and a congenital drop-shaped heart'.[112] The way was now clear for Stalin's protégé,

Choibalsan, who promptly succeeded Demid as the MPR's commander-in-chief. On 3 September Choibalsan issued an order denouncing the influence of 'Japanese counter-spies', and one week later, under active Soviet guidance, the Outer Mongolian version of the Great Purge began. Suspect political leaders were made to sit on hot ovens or chairs spiked with nails to extract their 'confessions' before being sent up for trial. Particular energy went into smashing the lama Buddhist clergy, and in 1937–8 a total of 16,631 lamas are said to have been 'persecuted, mostly shot'.[113]

In the Soviet Far East the Great Purge assumed a more crudely demographic form. In the mid-1920s there had still been around 65,000 to 70,000 Chinese living in the region, traders and labourers left over from the migrations of late tsarist times. These numbers fell sharply after 1929, when the abandonment of the liberal New Economic Policy closed down most of the avenues for private business; but in the mid-1930s the local Chinese population still stood at just under 25,000. And to Stalin, who didn't always draw a fine distinction between different Oriental peoples, all of these Chinese residents were potential Japanese spies. At the end of 1937, consequently, the 'poison dwarf' Yezhov commanded the launching of a 'Chinese operation'.[114] Over the following months a total of 19,000 Chinese were rounded up in Vladivostok and other Far Eastern cities, many of them simply picked off the streets and hauled into lorries without so much as a request for their papers. They were then loaded straight on to westward-bound trains. Those who could prove they had Soviet citizenship were dumped at Alma Ata in Kazakhstan, while those without either Soviet or Chinese documents were deposited on the far side of the Central Asian border in Xinjiang. Any remnants were apt to be sent to the camps. In November 1938 a group of 270 Chinese from Manchuria who had been in the habit of crossing the border each summer to cultivate vegetable plots on the Soviet side were arrested as illegal immigrants and sentenced to eight years in a camp in Siberia. Their task was to shift virgin timber through the snows of the taiga to the nearest road. No one proved able to endure the burden of shouldering these immense logs for more than one week. By February 1939 269 of them were dead and 'the only survivor was one fellow in the kitchen'.[115] By the early 1940s Stalin had achieved his objective, and there were for all practical purposes no Chinese left in the Soviet Far East.

These fearsome cleansings ironically came close to provoking the very Armageddon that Stalin feared. In the late 1930s, emboldened by the swathes which the Great Purge had cut through the Soviet military from Blücher downwards, the Imperial Japanese Army began to probe Russia's eastern defences. The first challenge came in the summer of 1938, when Japanese forces attacked a small Soviet outpost on a disputed hilltop called Zhanggufeng, on the eastern edge of Manchukuo adjacent to the Soviet Maritime Province. The Russians were pushed off the hilltop; but the Japanese came up against unexpectedly stiff opposition and had to content themselves with what they called '40 per cent of a victory' for the loss of some 3,000 men. The following year the Imperial Army embarked on a larger offensive, directed this time at Siberia's underbelly, the Soviet fiefdom of the MPR. On 11 May 1939 a force of 11,000 Japanese soldiers advanced from the west of Manchukuo into Outer Mongolia as far as the banks of the River Khalkha (Khalkhin Gol), a desolate area filled with deep ravines, sand dunes and vicious mosquitoes. Confronted with this emergency the Kremlin ordered General Georgi Zhukov, a promising young commander who had been lucky enough to escape the Great Purge, to go east to Mongolia and bolster the existing Soviet garrison there. Over the following weeks Zhukov put together a powerful strike force including some 500 aircraft and 500 tanks. Broadcasting radio messages in easily breakable codes, he succeeded in giving the Japanese the impression that he was doing nothing more than maintain his position. On 20 August he launched a massive three-pronged assault across the River Khalkha, combining tanks, artillery, aircraft and men in an integrated thrust for the first time in modern warfare and encircling the Japanese in what Soviet experts later hailed as the most accomplished manoeuvre of its kind since Hannibal beat the Romans at Cannae. Mauled by the loss of 18,000 men the Imperial Army were forced to retreat, and on 16 September they accepted a ceasefire. One official in Tokyo remarked that the experience had been like 'putting Japan's hand in a charcoal brazier'.[116] It is still too little appreciated how at the exact time the Second World War was beginning in Europe one of the decisive battles of that war was drawing to its close at the far end of Asia. As a result of the battle of Khalkhin Gol (or Nomonhan, as it is sometimes called after a nearby village) the Imperial Army proponents of a 'Go North' attack on Siberia lost crucial ground to the elements in both the army and navy who favoured a 'Go South' advance into South-East Asia and the Pacific. If the battle had gone the other way it seems more than likely that the Japanese would indeed have invaded the Soviet Union in conjunction with Germany in the summer of 1941. It is hard to imagine under those circumstances how the Soviet Union could possibly have survived. Japan would not have 'gone South' and would not consequently have raided Pearl Harbor to safeguard its southern movement from the American fleet; in which case it has to be questionable whether the United States would have entered the war at all. For all the horrors of Stalin's rule, both Russia and much of the rest of the world have reason to be grateful to those tank formations of Zhukov's that turned the tide in the wastelands of eastern Mongolia.

Still, Stalin could not have foreseen this desirable outcome. On 23 August 1939 he concluded his sensational pact with Nazi Germany – among other reasons to head off the risk of a German attack while the fighting still raged along the River Khalkha, and to discourage any designs that Japan might still have on Siberia after the fighting came to an end. Soviet leaders remained deeply fearful as Japan pressed ahead with a (now perhaps largely defensive) build-up on their Far Eastern border, expanding its force in Manchukuo in the course of 1940 from nine to twelve divisions with a total strength of 350,000 men. In September that year Stalin authorised the opening of secret talks with the Japanese government, and on 13 April 1941, in a second diplomatic sensation, he presided over the signing of a Soviet-Japanese neutrality pact. As part of this deal the Soviet Union officially recognised the existence of Manchukuo, the first outside power to do so, in exchange for Japanese recognition of the MPR – once more blithely ignoring the views of the Chinese Nationalist government, which claimed sovereignty over both territories. After the signing Stalin paid Matsuoka Yosuke, the visiting Japanese foreign minister, the unique compliment of seeing him off at the Moscow railway station. 'Stalin and I', recalled Matsuoka's Soviet counterpart Vyacheslav Molotov, 'made Matsuoka drink a lot, and we almost carried him on to the train.'[117] The soul of amiability, Stalin assured the Japanese minister: 'We're Asiatics too, and we've got to stick together!'

The reaction of China to the Soviet rescue operation was less than ideal from the Kremlin's point of view. In the face of Japan's all-out onslaught in July 1937 there can be little doubt that the KMT government were eager, even desperate, for Soviet aid. Chiang Kai-shek said, 'No country in the world can help China apart from the USSR.'[118] On 23 July his finance minister, H.H. Kung, called on Ivan Maisky, the Soviet ambassador in

London, and 'with sharp gestures and rough manners' pressed for Russian help, emphasising 'rather clumsily' that the imminent seizure of Peking by the Japanese would be merely a prelude to an attack on the Soviet Union.[119] Once aid was forthcoming the Nationalist leaders were warm in their professions of gratitude. After the Soviet bombing raid on the Taiwan airfield in February 1938 Song Meiling (Mme Chiang Kai-shek), now effectively head of the Nationalist air force, praised the Russians for coming to China's rescue 'not in word but in deed'.[120] Chiang informed General Cherepanov that since the arrival of Soviet advisers his soldiers had 'begun to fight better',[121] and in June 1939 he wrote to thank the Soviet minister of defence, Marshal Voroshilov, for 'providing China with the material and moral aid which gives her the possibility of carrying on her long war of liberation'.[122] In a telegram sent two years later he told Stalin simply that 'Soviet help had been truly immense'.[123]

Under the surface, however, the mood of the KMT remained unmistakably 'once bitten, twice shy'. Some of the private musings in Chiang Kai-shek's diaries echo almost word for word the reflections on the tsarist empire jotted down by the Xianfeng emperor eighty years before. On 1 August 1937 he wrote, 'The diplomacy of Russia is one of unrivalled craftiness', speculating that the proposed Sino-Soviet non-aggression pact might be nothing more than a pretext for Moscow concluding a similar treaty with Japan.[124] On 30 August, after the pact had been finalised, he went on sighing, 'The Russians are crafty and the Dwarves [i.e. Japanese] are violent, and our China is caught in the middle.'[125] And on 1 January 1938 he summed up that the threat from the Dwarves was 'urgent but easy to guard against', while the Russian peril was 'hidden and unfathomable'.[126] Given this background it isn't surprising to find that the new corps of Soviet advisers never got to play the controlling role their predecessors had done in the 1920s campaigns. Soviet memoirs record that Cherepanov 'recommended' guerrilla-type tactics of 'fighting from ambush' and 'submitted a proposal' for a grand offensive in the Yangtze valley; that Chuikov urged on Chiang 'a wide range of corrective measures' designed to improve the coordination between the Nationalist army groups and the amount of artillery allotted to them.[127] But it isn't clear to what extent these suggestions were actually heeded, and the achievements explicitly chalked up to these two Soviet counsellors often seem rather minor – the opening of a centralised air weather service, or the dismissal of an obstructive Nationalist air force chief. At a more junior level care was taken to ensure that no Soviet instructors were attached to military schools where Chiang was retraining his officers, or given access to individual army units. When setbacks occurred, on the other hand, the Russians were often the first to be blamed. After the fall of Wuhan and Canton to the Japanese in October 1938 Cherepanov's team found that the Chinese with whom they dealt regularly, such as their interpreters, were sullen and withdrawn. 'Their eyes were bleak, their movements sluggish and they spoke through their teeth.'[128] By the turn of 1939–40 the latent reservations of the KMT leaders were clearly showing through. Chiang and his entourage were well aware by this time, if they hadn't been earlier, of Stalin's underlying strategic goal. The minister of foreign trade observed tartly to Chuikov, 'What you want is to defeat Japan by using the Chinese.'[129]

But the Nationalists too had their strategy. If Stalin's object was to fight Japan to the last Chinese, they were equally keen to fight to the last Russian. They aimed to draw Russia into outright war with Japan. On his visit to Moscow in November 1937 the KMT emissary General Yang Ze declared that China didn't want to involve the Soviet Union *immediately*, but expected that it would in due course step in 'to secure peace in the East'.[130] At the end of the year, after Nanking fell to the Imperial Army, Chiang Kai-shek ratcheted up the pressure, informing a Soviet plenipotentiary, 'The situation is such that if the Soviet Union does not come openly to China's aid with armed force the defeat of China is inevitable.'[131] Sun Fo made his journey to Moscow in March 1938 'to elucidate the possibility of closer Soviet-Chinese cooperation',[132] and in 1940–1 Mme Chiang reminded Chuikov frequently that 'the greatest support the Soviet Union could render China would be to declare war on Japan'.[133] This was of course the precise opposite of what Stalin intended. The Soviet autocrat made it clear that his country would stay on the sidelines as long as China seemed able to hold off the enemy, and pointed out to Chiang cunningly that if the Russians came in it would look as though they were preparing to Communise China, 'and that would do China no good'.[134] Far from drawing in Russia Chiang and his government were obliged to look on as their Soviet patrons moved steadily further away from a clash with Japan. Already disturbed by the Nazi–Soviet treaty, portent in his view of an upturn in ties between Moscow and Tokyo, Chiang was appalled by the Soviet–Japanese neutrality pact, which with its recognition by both sides of the MPR and Manchukuo smacked all too strongly of the secret deals tsarist Russia had signed with Japan for dismembering China during the years between 1907 and 1916. 'This is another example', he wrote in his diary, 'of the old Russian trick of harming others to benefit oneself . . . Although the Russian-Dwarf treaty can't obviously in practice do the least harm to our War of Resistance it is upsetting to a degree.'[135] In a talk with the Soviet ambassador, Alexander Panyushkin, he observed that the Chinese public and army were 'staggered' and had taken the news 'very keenly and painfully'.[136]

The CCP didn't even have the consolation of Soviet practical aid. Mao is said to have grumbled repeatedly, 'If so much can be given to Chiang Kai-shek, why can't we get a small share?';[137] and as the volumes of Lenin and Stalin arrived in Yan'an instead of armaments Soviet policy began to be labelled sarcastically, 'Weapons to the bourgeoisie, books to the proletariat.'[138] The potential for friction was made more acute by the fact that Mao, like Chiang, was pursuing a strategy clean contrary to the one Moscow wished. His plan was to keep well clear of any major engagements with the Japanese Army, and instead to husband his strength for the showdown with Chiang and the KMT which was bound to take place once the war with Japan had been brought to an end. He was thus dead against the instruction proclaimed by the newly arrived Wang Ming that the CCP should merge their armed forces with those of the Nationalists. By the spring of 1939 he was pushing explicitly for the Party to widen its territory and retaliate against any KMT incursions ('If others offend me I must offend them back'[139]). And by January 1941, after the KMT's massacre of the New Fourth Army in southern Anhui and the ferocious Soviet pressure to turn the other cheek, he is said to have moved finally into out-and-out deviation from the Moscow line. Using the somewhat apposite CCP slang for the Soviet Union he confessed frankly, 'The problem is that the policies of *The Distance* are at variance with our ideas.'[140] Once again the corollary was a tentative casting around for Western sympathy. In an interview granted in March 1938 to a left-wing British writer, Violet Cressy-Marcks, Mao explained that while the CCP was modelled on Marxist-Leninist principles it was 'quite separate from Russia'.[141] Zhou Enlai told Jack Chen, whose father Eugene had formerly served as the Left KMT foreign minister, that the Party needed him in Yan'an as the son of a seasoned Chinese revolutionary 'who, while allying with the Soviet Union, never neglected to reach out to the West'.[142]

And the bulk of the Party supported Mao's views. According to one Chinese source the secret police chief Kang Sheng, who arrived in Yan'an with Wang Ming in November 1937 to discharge Stalin's orders, took in at a glance where the real power lay in the CCP from the phalanx of leaders arranged around Mao in the welcoming group at the airfield. By the following spring he was courting Mao's favour. Wang Ming tried to establish a rival Party headquarters in the temporary Nationalist capital of Wuhan with a view to promoting active CCP participation in the United Front, and for a few months he managed to keep up a significant challenge to Mao in the Politburo. Mao however was able to call on the services of Ren Bishi, an Eeyore-like figure who was forever complaining about his illnesses but was unswerving in his devotion to the Party chief. In March 1938 Ren arrived with a delegation in Moscow, where he pleaded Mao's loyalty to the United Front and persuaded the Comintern to reiterate their backing for him. By October 1938 Wang was neutralised and undertaking 'to encircle Mao as the stars encircle the moon'.[143]

To all appearances the only figure who was wholly content with developments was Xinjiang's governor, Sheng Shicai. Possibly sharing some of the paranoid traits of his Soviet patron, Sheng implemented Stalin's Great Purge in his province with every sign of relish, even seizing the opportunity to label as Trotskyites certain Soviet officials who had in some way displeased him such as Georgi Apresov, the consul-general who had reported so shrewdly on his character, and Yekulov, a prosecutor who had been sent out to help him conduct the show trials. Both of these men were called back to Moscow to face the inquisitors. Over the next few years Sheng remained as obsequious as ever. In August 1938 he accepted Stalin's proposal that he take out membership of the Soviet Communist Party, and was duly presented with membership card number 1859118. In March 1939 he was observed by Sun Fo, then in Urumqi, to be making incessant visits to the Soviet consulate for consultations. And in January 1941 he went so far as to advocate the effective absorption of his province into the USSR as the 'Soviet Republic of Xinjiang'. At this final measure, however, Stalin demurred in the same way as his tsarist predecessors in the late nineteenth century. Well aware of the certain response of Chiang's government to such an act, he preferred the realities of economic, political and military domination in north-west China to the provocative trappings.

WHEN THE CAT'S AWAY . . . (1941–3)

Suspicious of everyone and everything except, so it seemed, the reliability of his agreement with Nazi Germany, Stalin was famously blind to the threat of a Nazi invasion right under his nose. Warnings poured in, from Winston Churchill and his foreign secretary, Anthony Eden, from the American under-secretary of state, Sumner Welles, from Richard Sorge, the Soviet master spy at the German embassy in Tokyo. And, yes, even from the Chinese. During the spring word was passed to Chungking by the Nationalist government's military attaché in Berlin that a German attack on the Soviet Union would take place in June, or July at the latest, and this information was conveyed to General Chuikov by the head of the KMT Central Executive Committee's International Relations Bureau. Then in mid-June the attaché submitted a more specific prediction, forecasting a German attack to begin on the night of 21–2 June. This alert was picked up by General Yu Baozheng, a top military adviser to Chiang Kai-shek who also happened to be a CCP mole. Yu apparently passed the intelligence on to Zhou Enlai, who on 18 June in turn forwarded it to Mao in Yan'an; and Mao directed that the message should be delivered to Nikolai Roshchin, the Soviet military attaché in Chungking, for communicating to Stalin. All of this Stalin dismissed as 'Oriental nonsense'.[144] Less than four days later, however, in the early hours of 22 June, Hitler's Wehrmacht did indeed attack Soviet territory with a force of 3,550 tanks, 2,770 aircraft and 3 million men in the most gigantic invasion in human history. Over the following months they raced eastwards, engulfing the Baltic states, Byelorussia and large tracts of the Ukraine and cutting Leningrad off from the rest of the country. In December they were held outside Moscow, thanks mainly to the outstanding military abilities of Georgi Zhukov, the victor of Khalkhin Gol; but in the summer of 1942 they resumed their offensive and pushed across southern Russia as far as the Volga and the Caucasus. Soviet Russia looked doomed. And just as had happened in the previous spell of Russian collapse, in 1917–20, the various political forces in China tried in their different ways to exploit the calamity and rid themselves of the Kremlin's embrace.

First to bolt was none other than Governor Sheng. Within a few weeks of the launching of Hitler's Operation Barbarossa the faithful Soviet client appears to have judged that German victory was certain, that Soviet power in Central Asia was bound to collapse and that he, consequently, was in an exposed position and had better do something about it. By the last months of 1941 he was starting to signal a change of course by obstructing the supply of local materials and provisions to the Soviet aircraft assembly plant near Urumqi. Early in 1942 he informed Moscow that he had found the Russian advisers in Xinjiang to be untrustworthy and could no longer cooperate with them, and in May he wrote to Stalin blaming the disorders which had broken out in the province on Soviet diplomats and technicians. At the beginning of July Stalin sent his vice-commissar for foreign affairs, Vladimir Dekanozov, on a special trip to Urumqi in a belated attempt to get Sheng back on the straight and narrow. Sheng told the stupefied commissar that he was renouncing his belief in Marxism, which he had found 'cruel and callous', and had decided instead to study the Three People's Principles of Sun Yat-sen.[145] And in October he called for the withdrawal of all Soviet military and technical personnel from Xinjiang in the space of three months. The way was thus prepared for a scurry back into the arms of the Nationalist Party. Four days after his spectacular slap in the face to Dekanozov Sheng wrote a letter to Chiang Kai-shek in which he referred to himself as Chiang's 'younger brother' and declared that he had been 'thoroughly awakened'.[146] He denounced Russian great power behaviour as reflected in the Nazi-Soviet treaty and the Soviet-Japanese neutrality pact, and disclosed the contents of the Tin Mines Agreement imposed on Xinjiang by the Soviet government, which he compared to the infamous Twenty-one Demands forced in 1915 by Japan on the infant Chinese Republic. As a token of good faith he launched a new purge of his very own against Mao Zemin and the other CCP activists whom the Russians had let into Xinjiang to work at his side. Already in the second half of 1941 the younger Mao and his comrades had been removed from all their official posts. In April 1942 they were flung into prison, where they are said to have been tortured with red-hot needles, and in February 1943 they were put to death.

'Just as I expected!' was Chiang Kai-shek's comment in his diary on learning the news of the German invasion of Russia.[147] For the first few days of the onslaught the KMT government issued appropriate statements of solidarity with their Soviet backers, even going so far as to break diplomatic relations with Germany and its Italian ally. But in the autumn of 1941 as the Wehrmacht pressed eastwards a change of attitude started to make itself felt. Anti-Soviet KMT officials were said to be privately 'taking delight' in the

Red Army's setbacks.[148] Soviet diplomats in Chungking were received with 'a show of contempt', while Soviet military instructors found that their working conditions suddenly became much less comfortable.[149] Most disturbing of all was the sharp decline in the Nationalist government's willingness to cooperate over economic affairs. Talks on a trade protocol for 1941–2 proved 'very difficult', as the Chinese side defaulted on their contracts, raised the prices of their goods and withheld from the Russians supplies of critical war materials such as tungsten, tin and antimony. Ordered by his superiors to drag his feet, slammed by his Soviet counterpart for his evasions, one KMT trade official behaved 'like a guilty child'.[150] And in the midst of all this the KMT still kept up their quiet drumbeat of pressure for the Russians to enter the war with Japan. In mid-October, as Stalin teetered on the verge of abandoning Moscow, Foreign Minister Guo Taiqi told Ambassador Panyushkin that he was not proposing to *rush* the Soviet Union into war with the Japanese, but . . . Chungking's growing indifference to its Soviet partner grew still more obvious after 8 December, when the Japanese southward lunge into South-East Asia and the Pacific brought the Western powers into battle with Tokyo instead. The way was suddenly open for Chiang's regime to obtain military training and weapons from more congenial sources, and in particular from the United States. The Russians were now of increasingly little value to Chungking unless they agreed to comply with Nationalist wishes by opening a (suicidal) second front in the East. The new pattern of Nationalist interest was soon revealed at a banquet held at the officers' club of the KMT military academy. Flags of all the Allied nations were proudly hung from the ceiling – except that of Russia. Chuikov, who was still functioning as Chiang's chief military adviser, complained to the Nationalist minister of war and commander-in-chief, He Yingqin. Minister He gave the order for a Soviet flag to be found, but none was available. Diplomatic convention left the strongly anti-Soviet He no choice but to have all the other flags taken down: Chuikov thought it was 'like forcing a dog to eat mustard'.[151] Mme Chiang remarked dismissively to her husband's American political counsellor, 'Of course our Soviet advisers are no good, because now that the Soviets are being attacked by the Germans they need every competent officer they've got. So anybody we've got must be third or fourth rate.'[152] Events would in fact show that Chuikov at least was rather considerably better than 'third or fourth rate'. In early 1942 however he indicated to Moscow that he and his colleagues were no longer able to play a leading role in China, and in February he was recalled to the motherland. His place as chief military adviser to Chiang was taken by the US general Joseph Stilwell.

The retreat of the Soviet Red Army before Hitler's Wehrmacht, followed six months later by the collapse of the Western powers in South-East Asia before the assault of Japan, had fostered in the KMT a new pride in their own long resistance and a new confidence in asserting their rights. By the end of 1941, as word got through of the growing rift between Sheng Shicai and the Russians, it was dawning on Chiang and his government that a golden opportunity had presented itself to recover Xinjiang. In March 1942 a KMT general named Zhu Shaoliang made a trip from Lanzhou to Urumqi, where he suggested that Sheng should return to his Nationalist allegiance, and in May he came back, this time in the company of the Nationalist minister of economics. The KMT were now ready to take formal steps. On 9 June Chiang received Ambassador Panyushkin to instruct him that from now on the Soviet authorities should address themselves to Chungking rather than to Urumqi on Xinjiang-related affairs, and in July he told Panyushkin further that he was sending General Zhu to the province to establish control over Sheng. A government military committee sat down to draft a Proposal for Resuming Sovereignty over Xinjiang. At the end of August, in response to the *mea culpa* which Sheng had addressed to his 'elder brother' in Chungking the previous month, Chiang and his wife headed out to the north-west in person to finalise the transfer of power. Chiang himself waited at Jiayuguan, at the western end of the Great Wall, while Mme Chiang went ahead to Urumqi, where she presented Sheng with a letter of absolution and discussed with him ways to stamp out the CCP in the province and to get the Soviet forces withdrawn. In January 1943 a Nationalist Party headquarters was installed in Urumqi, and on 9 February, dissatisfied with the pace of the Soviet evacuation, Chiang ordered Sheng to request the Russians to get a move on. Tensions for a while 'approached gunpoint',[153] but by October the forces of the Chungking central government had taken full charge. The Soviet 'Red Eighth Regiment' at Hami had been pulled back to their home turf, Soviet offices in Xinjiang had been closed, trade between Xinjiang and Russia had been prohibited and Soviet influence in the province had to all appearances been snuffed out. So far as Chiang was concerned the recapture of this immense territory was 'the greatest success since the establishment of the National Government';[154] and his irredentist ambitions did not stop there. Already in late 1941 his regime had adopted the 'clear-cut position' that Manchuria must be handed over to China in its entirety at the end of the war.[155] At the end of 1942 Panyushkin reported to Moscow on a rising Nationalist demand for territorial expansion at the expense of the Soviet Union, notably in those regions that had at one time or another 'acknowledged Chinese sovereignty'[156] – a concept which included not merely Outer Mongolia but large tracts of Transbaikalia and the Soviet Far East. From the Russian perspective it must have seemed a poor return for four years of tremendous if scarcely disinterested military aid.

The unkindest cut of all, however, was dealt by the CCP. The German assault had inevitably reawakened the Soviet terror of a simultaneous thrust by Japan in the East, and within days urgent messages were being sent to the Chinese Party enjoining them to use their troops in north China to keep the Japanese busy. On 7 July 1941 the Comintern chairman Dimitrov sent a cable to Yan'an announcing the imminent transfer of US $1 million to the CCP's coffers, and two days later the Comintern instructed the Chinese Communists to prepare 'concrete steps'.[157] In early October, with still no sign of movement from Yan'an, Dimitrov sent a more peremptory message demanding to know what the CCP were going to do; and at the end of the year and again in July 1942 when the Wehrmacht reached Stalingrad Stalin himself cabled Mao begging him to send his forces into action against Japan. But Mao never lifted a finger. He is said to have been deeply sceptical that the Soviet Union would prevail over Hitler, and seems indeed to have followed the Soviet reverses with some glee ('See what Stalin's babbling has led him to!'[158]). In any case he was still not disposed to abandon his basic strategy of sitting tight and husbanding his resources for the final showdown with the KMT. In a reply sent for Zhou Enlai in Chungking to pass on to Chuikov he lamented that the Chinese Red Army were in a daily worsening state owing to their shortage of weapons and war materiel, that their rifle bullets were 'like gold dust', that their military technology was altogether too primitive compared with Japan's – we may detect here a swipe at the minimal quantities of arms and money that Yan'an had been receiving from Moscow in recent years. The most they could offer was a little support in the fields of sabotage and intelligence.[159] To add insult to injury the CCP leader advised that the Soviet Union should resort to what to Russian ears sounded like sheer defeatism, giving up the three strongholds of Leningrad, Moscow and Stalingrad to withdraw to the Urals, from where they might launch guerrilla operations in true Maoist style. The Soviet chiefs were flabbergasted. Here they were in the darkest moment of Russian history, the very existence of their country at stake, denied vital succour by a movement which they themselves had created and had moulded and sustained for the past twenty years. One Russian observer expostulated of the Chinese Party, 'They are alive because the Soviet Union is alive!'[160]

Mao's reluctance to bolster the Soviet war effort wasn't initially shared by his senior colleagues. Liu Shaoqi, a rising leader deployed at that time in south China, wrote to him urging an offensive against the Imperial Army; Zhu De, his guerrilla associate from the late 1920s, thought Moscow should at least be assured of the Eighth Route Army's intervention if a Soviet–Japanese war were to start. More predictably, Moscow's perennial champion Wang Ming flared back into life. According to Wang's account Mao called on him personally on 4 October 1941 to discuss a response to the latest stern message from Dimitrov. Wang pressed for urgent steps to comply with the Comintern's wishes. Mao disagreed, but gave no reason. Wang suggested that Mao's line effectively meant working with Japan against the Soviet Union. Mao lost his temper and pounded the table. Over the next few days a number of other Politburo members were summoned to join in the argument, and Wang claims that these leaders all backed his position against a horrified Mao. However that may be, it seems clear that Mao's isolationist policy won through in the end. More than that, Mao decided to use the opportunity presented by Stalin's preoccupation with the German war and his own seclusion in the mountains of northern Shaanxi to cleanse the Party of Soviet influence once and for all.

Much of what followed has come down to us through the diaries of a certain Pyotr Vladimirov, who arrived in Yan'an with two Soviet colleagues in mid-May 1942. A fluent Chinese speaker, acquainted with some of the CCP leaders, Vladimirov had officially been assigned to Yan'an as a war correspondent for the TASS news agency. Unofficially he was to gather intelligence and report to Stalin on the goings-on at the CCP base. His diaries were finally published in Moscow a generation later, and while some retrospective Soviet editing is apparent the consensus now seems to be that they give a substantially accurate portrait of life in Yan'an as Mao plunged his Party into the throes of a Rectification Campaign.

The Rectification was launched to promote 'the creative Sinicisation of Marxism'.[161] Mao's own Thought was held up as the CCP's guiding ideology, and Mao himself was raised to the unprecedented eminence of Party Chairman. One account even claims he was openly styled 'the Chinese Lenin'.[162] As the native content of the Chinese Revolution was glorified, it followed that the Soviet contribution was sharply downplayed. According to Vladimirov Mao even went so far as to comment on Stalin in July 1942, 'He doesn't know and cannot know China, yet he pokes his nose into all matters. All of his so-called theories on our revolution are the blabberings of a fool.'[163] In May 1943 Mao's lunge for autonomy was further strengthened when as a gesture to the Western Allies the Soviet Union announced the dissolution of its evangelical organ, the Communist International. The Chinese Party were now rid of the incubus that had controlled their activities ever since their founding congress in 1921. Mao convened a memorial meeting at which he declared that the Comintern had existed for far too long and had failed to understand the CCP's conditions and needs.

This assertion of nativism was accompanied by a swingeing attack on the whole former CCP leadership. All of the Party chiefs who had studied in the Soviet Union, who had taken their cue from the Comintern, who had criticised Mao or stood in his way, all the likes of Wang Ming, Bo Gu, Luo Fu and the rest of the 28 Bolsheviks were now brought to book. They were stigmatised variously as the 'Moscow Group', the 'Muscovites', the 'dogmatists' and the 'Russian deviationist clique'. Mao lambasted their posture with typical earthiness: 'If Stalin chooses to fart you are prepared to sniff and admire it.'[164] Chastisement of a more drastic kind was applied by Kang Sheng. The secret policeman had now manoeuvred himself all the way to Mao's right hand, where as Vladimirov put it he had 'succeeded in divining the true aspirations of Mao Zedong, and had become his shadow, his will, his desire'.[165] Vladimirov called him the Fall Minister, dredging up from the old Chinese annals a term for 'a minister who sows death among his people'.[166] Certainly Kang deployed against his 'Muscovite' victims all the techniques of denunciation, torture and fabricated confession he had picked up in his own Moscow years from Yezhov and the NKVD. It is even possible that his activities extended to a systematic attempt on Wang Ming's life.

Shortly after his confrontation with Mao in October 1941 Wang is said to have fallen ill with a combination of ailments including a loss of blood from the stomach, a weak heart and dizziness. He was removed to Yan'an Central Hospital, where he spent most of the next two years being slowly poisoned on Kang Sheng's instructions with (according to different versions) either mercury or rotten calomel lotion. This story must be treated with caution: much of it derives from Wang's own testimony, and it begs the question of why such a competent operator as Kang should have failed to liquidate his victim over the course of a whole two years, even granted that the appearance of a natural death was considered desirable. By November 1942 however it was clear that the Rectification was taking a violent turn, and by July 1943 Vladimirov was commenting that the atmosphere in Yan'an was one of 'fear, fear and again fear'.[167]

The anti-'Muscovite' frenzy inevitably had repercussions for the handful of Soviet technicians and journalists attached to Mao's base. Already in the early autumn of 1941, as the Wehrmacht advanced towards Moscow, the attitude of the CCP leaders to the Russians among them was described as unfriendly, and by the end of November it was downright hostile. On their arrival in May 1942 Vladimirov and his group were assigned to the direct supervision of Kang, who repeatedly fascinated and sickened the Soviet diarist with his aura of chilling hypocrisy. At their first meeting the Fall Minister 'embraced and kissed me while others were looking on. I could not say I was delighted – Kang Sheng's kiss is a kiss of Judas . . . With a frozen smile he hissed into my ear, "*We are great brothers*"'.[168] 'Kang Sheng always smiles. It seems as if the smile has been glued to his thin, bilious face.'[169] 'As a rule he greets me with smiles, saying he has no secrets from the Soviet people. After that he flies into a rage . . .'.[170] Vladimirov's group were habitually denied access to the rest of the Chinese Party leadership, and unsurprisingly weren't invited to hear the speeches the leaders made as the Rectification began to unfold. They weren't even allowed to attend the plays, musicals and literary evenings that were organised periodically in the Yan'an cave houses, and were trailed everywhere by the Fall Minister's agents. Kang's staff seem to have made little effort to be welcoming or even polite: during one meal his secretary embarked on a discourse about the antiquity of Chinese civilisation compared with that of the Europeans which left a Soviet radio operator 'flushed with anger',[171] and Vladimirov described a cook who had been attached to the Russians' quarters as 'sloppy and dirty'.[172] In November 1942, as the Rectification intensified, Vladimirov noted despondently that even ordinary people 'refuse to look at us and start back as if we were contagious'.[173] On just one occasion in these years did Mao deign to offer a simple meal of rice, tea and *khanja* spirit to this TASS correspondent he regarded, with justification, as 'Moscow's Eye'. He held forth at some length on his favourite mealtime topic of how revolutionaries prefer spicy food. 'I'm sure Alexander the Great adored red pepper. As for Stalin, he surely eats red pepper too.'[174] But a question relating to the possibility of a Japanese attack on the Soviet Union rubbed him up the wrong way.

There were a few shafts of light in the gloom. From time to time Vladimirov was able to identify, in addition to the vilified 'Muscovites', certain CCP bigwigs who still seemed to harbour some trace of goodwill towards Russia. Liu Shaoqi, he recorded, was one of the chief managers of the Rectification along with the Fall Minister. Even he had however shown some discontent with the methods adopted by Kang Sheng, and had confided to Vladimirov that he considered the criticism of Wang Ming and his colleagues to be a mistake. Gao Gang, the former head of the northernmost Chinese soviet, was similarly 'a pleasant exception among those close to Kang Sheng. He is friendly and sincere with us. Holds himself independently.'[175] The old soldier Zhu De had initially given his active support to the 'Moscow Group'. As late as 1943, when the Rectification was well advanced, he still 'bore himself as a man who has his own values', and was 'always even, calm and friendly'.[176]

There was also an irony perhaps not immediately obvious to either the Chinese or Russian inhabitants of Yan'an. The fact was that the CCP were by this time so steeped in Soviet theory and practice that this very bid to establish their own independent identity could only be made in a Soviet idiom. Stalin's personality cult, for instance, had been dimmed in Yan'an only to be replaced by a similar cult of the Chinese Chairman, in which Mao was hailed as China's *Lenin* and the old Stalinist dogmatism was challenged by the new dogmas of Mao Zedong Thought. Suspect Party members were hounded for treason and espionage in a campaign clearly modelled on Stalin's Great Purge of the late 1930s, and the calumnies heaped on them were quite often identical to those aimed at their Soviet counterparts. One of the earliest victims of the Rectification, a translator of the Marxist classics, was accused by Mao of being a Trotskyite; and Wang Ming and Bo Gu and their faction were collectively branded as 'Mensheviks'. In May 1942 Mao delivered a celebrated set of 'Talks at the Yan'an Forum on Literature and Art'. These talks imposed much the same kind of restraints on artistic activity as Stalin had done ten years earlier in his speech advocating Socialist Realism. In the second half of 1943 the CCP extolled the virtues of a model worker they explicitly likened to the champion miner immortalised by the Soviet media eight years before:. 'The Soviet Union has a Stakhanov, we have a Zhao Zhankui.'[177] The organisational fetters proved easier to loosen than the conceptual ones.

RUSSIA RESURGENT (1943–5)

Against all apparent Chinese expectations the tide of war turned. In January 1943 the German Sixth Army were surrounded and captured at Stalingrad by the Soviet Red Army under the leadership of, among others, Zhukov and Chuikov. In July, in the greatest tank battle in history, Zhukov broke the back of the Wehrmacht at Kursk. In 1944 the Red Army fought their way back to the pre-war Soviet border and onwards into Central Europe; and in May 1945 Chuikov received the surrender of the remnant Nazi force in Berlin. Horribly bloodied but stronger than ever, the Soviet Union had emerged from the cataclysm and was once again turning its thoughts to the East.

The old dread of a Japanese stab in the back had at long last abated. On 10 October 1943 Vladimirov observed in his diary, 'Although the [Japanese] Guandong Army is deployed near our frontiers, the war threat for the Soviet Union in the Far East has disappeared.'[178] But Stalin's strategic attention was not letting up. His eye had been caught by a potential new menace in the form of his nominal ally, the United States, which was for the first time establishing a major military presence in China with the full support of its KMT protégés. How long was it likely to be before US forces were stationed in the Chinese borderlands? In September 1944 Stalin ordered his General Staff to start planning the concentration and supply of their troops in the eastern part of the country, and at the end of the year Vladimirov recorded, 'The time is now near when the Soviet Union can take measures to protect its frontiers in the Far East.'[179] The victorious Russians were also in desperate need of the mineral and industrial resources with which to rebuild their shattered economy. The Chinese borderlands, as they well knew, contained both; but their grip on those borderlands had been largely broken by the geopolitical upheavals of recent years.

Xinjiang was a case in point. Soviet troops and advisers had scarcely been expelled from the province before the American bogey was rearing its head. By April 1943 the Nationalist government were urging their US friends to set up a consulate in Urumqi 'to watch out for the Soviet Union',[180] and an American consulate (along with a British one) was duly established there. By spring 1943 too the Americans with Chungking's blessing were pressing the Kremlin to let them transport war supplies for the Chinese along the land route which ran from Iran through Soviet Central Asia and into Xinjiang, to make up for the Japanese occupation of the Burma Road. The Kremlin demurred on logistical grounds; but the Americans continued to press. In late 1944 they were seeking permission for a convoy of 500 trucks carrying arms plus 1,000 US military personnel to cross the Soviet Central Asian republics to the Xinjiang border town of Yining. Such an itinerary would bring a US presence into the heart of Xinjiang's north-western Three Districts, that mineral treasure-house which the Russians had till very recently been exploiting for tin and tungsten, and above all for oil.

As the war turned in their favour, accordingly, Stalin and his aides set to work to bring Xinjiang back into the Soviet orbit. On 4 May 1943 a Politburo meeting concluded, '*We must take steps to ensure that Sheng Shicai loses power in Xinjiang*.'[181] Betrayed by a Chinese general with the connivance of the Chinese central government, they calmly switched their support to the province's Turkic groups. The groundwork for this switch had been laid for a number of years. Ever since the 1930s young Uighurs and Kazakhs from the province had been invited to study in Tashkent and other cities of Soviet Turkestan, where they acquired fluent Russian along with a generous dosage of Marxism-Leninism. To cement their allegiance still further many of them were granted Soviet citizenship on the grounds that they had Russian or Soviet forebears or had been born or brought up on Soviet soil. With discontent against Chinese rule seething in much of the province, opportunities for a Soviet comeback didn't take long to present themselves. As early as June 1943, just weeks after the Politburo meeting, a rebellion led by a Kazakh leader named Osman Batur which had broken out in the Ashan district got Soviet backing, and in March 1944 Soviet aircraft and ground troops from the MPR helped Osman to inflict a severe defeat on Sheng's troops. By this point preparations for a major Soviet-sponsored insurgency in the province were well under way. A Xinjiang Turkish People's National Liberation Committee had been founded in Alma Ata, in Soviet Kazakhstan, and was supplying arms and ammunition to the Three Districts as well as a number of anti-Chinese periodicals which had been published in the Turkic languages by Soviet organs with titles such as *Home of the Kazakhs* and *Oriental Truth*. In the Three Districts themselves a whole network of liberation movements were founded by Soviet-trained Turkic radicals, of whom the most prominent was a young man named Ahmet Jan Kasim. The uprising was timed, significantly, for 7 November, the anniversary of the Bolshevik Revolution. That evening the Soviet consulate-general in Urumqi held an anniversary party to which they invited General Zhu Shaoliang, who had by now replaced Sheng as the Chinese military chief in Xinjiang. They plied the general with vodka so lavishly that he failed to take in the contents of an urgent telegram which had been sent to him from Yining. It was only the following morning he learnt that 500 Russians had led a rebellion there with machine guns and hand grenades, and that machine gunners inside the Soviet consulate had opened fire on a Nationalist reconnaissance plane. What followed was nothing less than a short but intense Sino-Soviet border war. On 16 November two 'White' Russian officers named Alexandrov and Polinov led a cavalry battalion from Soviet territory in an attack on the KMT positions in Yining. Under their direction in the course of the following days a steady pummelling was kept up at the Chinese defences. One eyewitness reported that every day at twilight long columns of trucks, flashing lights, rushed in from the west to the neighbourhood of the Air Force Academy, and kept up a barrage of artillery and machine gun fire the whole night before withdrawing at dawn.

On 12 November, while the fighting still raged, a new Eastern Turkestan Republic (ETR) was proclaimed in the Three Districts. Not content to be merely the midwives to this new Turkic government, the Russians proceeded to micromanage it even more thoroughly than they had the Chinese regime of Sheng Shicai. On 27 November they installed two advisory groups in Yining which became known as the Number One House and Number Two House. Based in the Soviet consulate, the Number Two House soon turned out to be the nerve centre of the ETR. Ahmet Jan Kasim acted as secretary, but appears to have taken his orders from a Lieutenant-General Vladimir

Kozlov, 'an old man with a bare head and a big moustache' who had arrived from Kazakhstan.[182] Under Kozlov's supervision the Number Two House drew up a Nine Point Declaration to serve as the political programme for the new regime: notable points included friendship with the Soviet Union and the extirpation of 'Chinese misrule'.[183] Soviet officials controlled the ETR's Economy Committee and made up a large part of the staff of a new Development Company, supplying the bulk of the company's chief accountants and heads of department. The Soviet system of business accounting was introduced, and the Russians operated their own state Gosbank. On 5 January 1945 a Yili National Army (YNA) was formed, to be built up in due course to a strength of some 45,000 men. The first commander of the YNA was a Soviet Kirghiz, and the Soviet military furnished the army with planes and artillery and trained around 450 local officers in the course of five months. When the Nationalist government sent in substantial reinforcements in the second half of January Soviet troops were promptly dispatched to the ETR's aid. A force of 3,000 Soviet Kazakhs and Kirghiz blocked the strategic passes leading to Yining, and on 21 January General Kozlov at the head of two Soviet regiments routed the fresh Chinese units and started to push them back east.

By this stage the Xinjiang operation had largely achieved Moscow's most pressing goals. US infiltration had for the moment been checked: Stalin had the satisfaction of turning down the proposed transit of US trucks and troops through Central Asia to Yining on the grounds of 'local unrest'.[184] And Soviet engineers had resumed (possibly without even formally consulting the ETR leaders) the extraction of oil and other minerals from the Three Districts on a far larger scale than before.

Having recovered a critical slice of Xinjiang by force of arms, Stalin now seized the chance to secure Russia's grip on the rest of the borderlands through skilful diplomacy. Both the United States and Britain were anxious that the Soviet Union should tear up its neutrality pact with Japan and take part in the war in the East as soon as the struggle with Hitler was over. At the Allied summit in Tehran in November 1943 Stalin had already consented to do this in principle. At Yalta in February 1945 he confirmed he would enter the war with Japan three months after the Germans surrendered, but this time submitted a hefty bill for his services. In the first place he wanted a guarantee that the status quo in Outer Mongolia, where the Soviet Union exerted control over a nominally Chinese territory, would continue to be upheld. Secondly, with regard to Manchuria, he demanded with a singular lack of Marxist justification that '*the former rights of Russia violated by the treacherous attack of Japan in 1904 shall be restored*'.[185] Yes, Stalin was calling explicitly for nothing less than the maximum position enjoyed in Manchuria by the tsarist empire at the turn of the century. Russia should once again be accorded a leasehold on the whole southern part of the Liaodong peninsula, including the naval base of Port Arthur; Dalian, China's largest commercial port apart from Shanghai; and the Chinese Eastern and South Manchurian railways, which could be jointly owned and managed with the Nationalist regime. In defence of these claims Stalin argued that the Soviet Union needed to reinforce its strategic position against the still unbeaten Japanese. He also pointed out (and we may perhaps sense a ring of truth here) that after four years of devastating war against Germany his people would need some incentive for being plunged into a second major conflict in the space of three months. Roosevelt and Churchill effectively raised no objection, stipulating only that Russia should seek the endorsement of Chiang Kai-shek's government. Stalin agreed, while insisting that Chungking should be kept in the dark for the moment about the whole deal. It was only in June, following an exploratory visit to Moscow by Harry Hopkins, the special envoy of Roosevelt's successor, Harry Truman, that Chiang and his colleagues were finally issued with a formal notification of the Yalta accords.

On 30 June Stalin welcomed to Moscow a KMT government team who had been duly sent to negotiate an appropriate treaty. The KMT had fielded as their chief negotiator T.V. Soong, Chiang's brother-in-law who was currently serving as his foreign minister, and the team also included Chiang Ching-kuo, the Nationalist leader's Russian-speaking son, who had been assigned to conduct unofficial discussions about the more sensitive issues. Talks ran on for the next seven weeks, punctuated by an interlude when Stalin went off to attend the third and last Allied summit at Potsdam. Taking personal charge of the negotiations, the Soviet boss pressed home his demands once again in a spirit of undisguised Realpolitik. From the outset he underlined that the question of Soviet control over Outer Mongolia was non-negotiable, and in a private discussion with Chiang Ching-kuo he explained clearly why. The exchange went as follows:

STALIN: To tell the truth, from a strategic point of view, if a certain military power attacks the Soviet Union from Outer Mongolia and cuts the Trans-Siberian Railway, the Soviet Union will be finished.
CHING-KUO: Not Japan or China, surely?
STALIN: Another third power.
CHING-KUO: The United States?
STALIN: Of course.[186]

Stalin even edged beyond his position at Yalta, suggesting that the Outer Mongolian 'status quo' he had talked of in February might be understood as implying Chinese recognition of the MPR as an independent state. With regard to Manchuria he stated, 'The new agreement will have to be an improved repetition of that contained in the Convention of 1898.'[187] The Soviet Union would need to have possession of both Port Arthur and Dalian 'so long as the Soviet ports in the north are underequipped', and to provide a solid platform for a Soviet military presence in the region. And again he edged forward beyond the proposed Yalta terms. Asked who he expected to own the restored Chinese Eastern Railway he replied tersely, 'The party that built it';[188] and he made it clear that he also envisaged the Soviet Union enjoying sole ownership of the South Manchurian Railway and all the coal mines and other enterprises that tsarist Russia had acquired in the region from the tottering Qing.

Stalin had a certain amount of leverage at his disposal that he didn't hesitate to use. At the start of the talks he warned darkly that if the Nationalist government didn't agree to grant independence to Outer Mongolia the MPR might begin to pursue independence for the whole Mongolian nation and 'the border between Inner Mongolia and Outer Mongolia would disappear.'[189] Added to that were the murky but threatening events in Xinjiang. In late June, a short time before T.V. Soong's delegation reached Moscow, the Soviet Politburo had passed a resolution to strengthen the ETR rebel force in that turbulent province through the dispatch of 500 Red Army officers and 2,000 troops. 'How seems to be the situation in Xinjiang?', Stalin asked Soong innocently. 'Do the rebels want to separate from China?'[190] To Soong's grim reply that the rebels were armed with weapons not available in China the Soviet leader gave the airy rejoinder, 'You can get weapons anywhere these days.'[191] By the late summer of 1945 the Yili National Army of the ETR were well on their way to Urumqi.

But the stick was accompanied by a full measure of carrot. At one point in the talks the Soviet chief did Chiang a small favour by casually shopping Sun Fo, the Left KMT leader of Russophile tendencies, who he disclosed had passed on surreptitiously to the CCP the contents of the Yalta decisions. When Soong complained of the Soviet revival of the colonial-sounding term 'lease' as applied to Manchuria Stalin promised to 'look for another formula';[192] and over Manchuria, though not Mongolia, the Soviet side eventually pulled back from their post-Yalta gambits, abandoning their bid for exclusive possession of Port Arthur, Dalian and the two railway lines. More important than any of this was an undertaking to recognise Chiang's regime as the sole legitimate government of China, and to refrain from giving help to any opposition group. Stalin guaranteed to prevent any further supply of Soviet arms to the ETR, by whatever mysterious means they might have got there. As regards the CCP he affirmed, '*We will not support them and we will not help them*';[193] and he even went so far as to ask if the Nationalists would like him to help in disarming Mao's troops. If Nationalist China formed an alliance with Moscow, he assured Soong that 'nobody would overthrow the government'.[194] As a final point he reminded the KMT envoys of the basic service that the Soviet Union would be doing them by evicting the Japanese from Manchuria on their behalf. 'As for the sovereignty of China [i.e. over Manchuria],' he remarked sardonically on 7 August, 'we are going to fight and shed blood for it, which you never did.'[195]

By early August the pace of events had increased exponentially. On 6 and 9 August the United States dropped its atomic bombs on Hiroshima and Nagasaki, and on 9 August, three months to the day after Germany's capitulation, the Soviet Army began its march into Manchuria as provided for in the Yalta accords. Japan's surrender was imminent, and the Soviet government faced a real danger that the Japanese war might be over before the basis of their participation had been signed and sealed. On 10 August Stalin observed pointedly to the KMT diplomats, 'It's time now to sign the agreement',[196] and on 14 August the signatures were affixed to a thirty-year Sino-Soviet Treaty of Friendship and Alliance. Subject to a plebiscite whose result no one doubted, the MPR was to be granted complete independence, detaching from China conclusively the central panel of the great border triptych. Russia had secured once again, for another three decades, all the rights it had lost in Manchuria since the start of the century, obtaining a strategic position to balance that of the United States in the central and southern Chinese provinces, plus unfettered access to the region's agricultural and industrial wealth. One eyewitness has left us a glimpse of the Soviet ruler's quiet satisfaction on being shown an updated map of East Asia. '"What have we here? . . . Port Arthur is ours, and Dalny is ours", Stalin waved his pipe over China, "and the Chinese Eastern Railway is ours. China, Mongolia – everything is in order".'[197]

We can see by this time unmistakably that from Stalin's perspective the Nationalist government were the only political grouping in China that really counted. So far as the CCP were concerned his main preoccupation was to bring them to heel. In late December 1943, some time after the Soviet Union had begun to recover its strength in the war against Germany, he made a first effort to stamp on the insubordinate tendencies that had sprung up in Yan'an. As the vehicle for his attack he employed a cable from Dimitrov, the Bulgarian former head of the Comintern, in spite of the fact that the Comintern with its hectoring manner had been dissolved over six months before. 'I think', the Bulgarian wrote to Mao, 'that the [CCP's] course of curtailing the struggle against the foreign occupier is politically wrong, and the current action to depart from the national United Front is also wrong.'[198] He deplored the activities of Kang Sheng, whom he regarded as 'helping the enemy', and the 'unhealthy' attitude taken towards the Soviet Union by Mao's acolytes during the Rectification Campaign. And he voiced alarm at the treatment of the CCP's 'Moscow Group', and Wang Ming in particular.[199] The Soviet leaders had fully believed Wang's claim to be getting systematically poisoned, and had twice sent a plane to collect him for treatment in Moscow, apparently in the hope of arranging a swap with Mao's elder son, 'Seryozha', who was still in residence there as half guest, half hostage, pursuing a course of military science at Moscow State University. But Mao had refused to play ball, probably out of fear that if Wang got to Moscow he would report all too eloquently on the goings-on in Yan'an.

By the final year of the war Stalin was making no secret of his profound lack of interest in the Chinese Communist Party. In August 1944, for example, his foreign minister Molotov told the US ambassador to Chungking, General Patrick Hurley, that 'the so-called Chinese Communists' were 'not in fact Communists at all'.[200] Stalin himself informed Roosevelt at Yalta that he judged the CCP to be 'radishes' (Red outside but White within),[201] and expressed in a talk with Truman's emissary, Harry Hopkins, his opinion that Chiang was the only figure capable of leading a post-war China. It has often been surmised that these statements were merely a ploy designed to hoodwink the Americans and prevent them from awakening to the true strength and intentions of the CCP, and the sheer insistence with which the Soviet leader disparaged the Chinese Party might indeed be thought to support such a view. But Stalin belittled the CCP in almost identical terms in private conversations with members of his own inner circle. To Beria, to Khrushchev he described Mao as being a 'radish', a 'caveman', a 'margarine Marxist'.[202] Insofar as ideology entered into Stalin's calculations at all in relation to China, he really does seem to have thought of the CCP as a bunch of amateurs grubbing about in a non-proletarian fashion in the north Chinese countryside. But above all they got in the way of his strategy.

Up to the point when the Nationalists signed the new treaty on 14 August 1945 the Soviet chief still had some use for the CCP as a lever, exploiting the Communist bogey to speed up Chungking's acquiescence in much the same way as he had exploited the Turkic advance in Xinjiang and the threat of a rising in Inner Mongolia. If T.V. Soong and his team didn't hurry and sign, he suggested, the Chinese Communists might seize the chance to move some of their troops from Yan'an to Manchuria before Chiang's armies could get there. But the moment the treaty was signed, the moment Stalin had pocketed his gains in the borderlands, the continuing CCP quest to dislodge Chiang became nothing more than a nuisance. Between 14 and 20 August Stalin sent Mao no fewer than three cables directing him not to oppose the KMT leader for fear of provoking a civil war which would ruin China and might even pit the Soviet Union against the United States in a Third World War. Rather Mao should accept an invitation which Chiang had issued to him personally to go down to Chungking and hold talks with a view to resolving the differences between the two parties. Stalin's attitude towards the further pursuit of a revolution in China was now said to be 'passive' and 'negative'.[203] On 26 August Vladimirov noted in his diary, 'The Soviet government's decision *not* to interfere in the internal affairs of China has been brought to the attention of the CCP leadership'.[204] Stalin, he observed, had refused to back Mao's 'adventurist' policies or to be drawn into war for the sake of Yan'an.[205]

As the Red Army began unexpectedly to prevail over Hitler from 1943 onwards the various Chinese political actors almost fell over in their haste to atone for their early misreading of Soviet prospects. One egregious example was that of Sheng Shicai. In August 1944, finding his control of Xinjiang getting steadily undercut by his new overlords in the Nationalist government, Sheng sent his chief of staff to the Soviet consulate-general in Urumqi with a message that all was forgiven. He asked the Russians to send their troops back to Xinjiang to take on the Nationalists, in return for which service he could offer them the Altai gold mines, some oilfields and 450,000 sheep. Stalin didn't even bother to reply, and the following month Sheng was called to Chungking and consigned to a post in the Ministry of Agriculture and Forestry. The two big Chinese parties followed a similar if rather subtler course. From late 1943, we are told, Nationalist diplomats in Moscow ended every conversation by voicing their hope that the friendship between the Soviet Union and China would soon be restored. Chiang Ching-kuo, 'always amiable', did his best to befriend the Soviet embassy staff in Chungking in the company of his Russian wife, Faina, and by the autumn of 1944 Foreign Minister Soong was preparing to travel to Moscow at the head of an ice-breaking mission. When the Turkic rising broke out in Xinjiang that November the local KMT authorities went to some lengths to pin the blame on Alexandrov, Polinov and other 'White' Russian officers to avert a new freeze in the attempted thaw with the Kremlin. In February 1943, after the little Soviet group in Yan'an gave a party to celebrate the triumph at Stalingrad, Kang Sheng reciprocated with a banquet of seventy dishes prepared by a senior chef who had worked for the last Qing emperor, Puyi. In July, as the Soviet forces won the clinching battle at Kursk, Vladimirov and his colleagues found themselves after months of exclusion invited to sit in on a meeting of CCP activists. Mao was badly shaken at the end of the year by the accusatory telegram he received from Dimitrov. Having fired off an instant rebuttal assailing Wang Ming and defending Kang Sheng he regretted his rashness, and on 7 January 1944 sent a second telegram assuring the Bulgarian, 'All your thoughts, all your feelings are close to my heart.'[206] Tense and exhausted, he even turned up at Vladimirov's lodgings, where he spoke of Wang Ming in an 'entirely different, almost friendly tone'.[207] And in February–March 1945, as the Soviet armies advanced on Berlin, he carried the goodwill so far as to ask Vladimirov, 'Haven't you liked a single pretty woman here? Don't be shy . . .', and to recommend that his colleague Dr Andrei Orlov should 'look around' for one of the many attractive and 'extremely healthy' girls. 'Really,'

Vladimirov recorded, 'I had never thought Mao Zedong would be a pimp!'[208] Two months later the Soviet journalist-cum-intelligence agent summed up Mao's change of posture in a savage quote from Lu Xun: 'In a dark corner he prepared a different face and a different banner so as to come upon the stage set for the new situation. You think that this is the gate of a temple, but instead you see the maw of a monkey.'[209]

And indeed the forced smiles of the two Chinese parties hid depths of dismay. Even as his officials affected to ignore the huge Soviet role in the Yili rebellion, Chiang Kai-shek fumed privately, 'If the Russian policy of aggression over the Xinjiang question cannot be abandoned, I shall have to achieve a comprehensive solution to it once the war with the Dwarves is over.'[210] Over the following months news of the Yalta agreements and the demands made by Stalin relating to Outer Mongolia and Manchuria hit the Nationalists like a blinding shock. At a time when the Western powers had shown their respect for their Chinese ally by giving up all their former concessions and extra-territorial rights, when even the Japanese in the regions they occupied had gone through the motions of following suit, here were the Soviet Russians, of all people, claiming the full reinstatement of the imperial presence that had been enjoyed in north China by their tsarist predecessors. At his first round of discussions in Moscow, on 2 July 1945, T.V. Soong tried to impress on Stalin the humiliation which the loss of Outer Mongolia in particular would mean for Chiang and his government. In a word it would look as though China had *lost the war*. Chiang was realist enough to accept that he had no alternative where Outer Mongolia was concerned. No support was in prospect from the United States. The Russians were hell-bent on detaching the MPR, and if he held out on this issue he would lose all hope of securing a tolerable settlement in the rest of the borderlands. Just one week into the talks, accordingly, on 7 July, he signalled his readiness to make 'the greatest sacrifice';[211] but elaborate measures now had to be negotiated to save his face. The detachment of Outer Mongolia was to be prettified by conducting a plebiscite (not that anyone had any doubt how the Mongols would vote), and the whole Mongolian deal was in the meantime to be kept under wraps. Like the Russians the Nationalists pressed to have the treaty signed quickly, on the grounds that the new concessions would be 'easier to explain' to the Chinese public while the war with Japan was still under way.[212] Even so Chiang was left feeling 'extremely sad and humiliated',[213] and his negotiators in Moscow made little effort to hide their distress. Soong had actually resigned his post as foreign minister during the interval created by Stalin's absence at Potsdam, in the apparent hope of sharing the odium for the treaty with his successor, Dr Wang Shijie. He took part in the signing ceremony, but comported himself in a 'strictly official' manner, 'as if he had fulfilled someone's orders but didn't agree with them'.[214] The Nationalist ambassador to Moscow, Fu Bingchang, 'couldn't even outwardly conceal his hostility'.[215]

Mao continued for some time to radiate goodwill for the Russians while quietly pursuing his own independent course. In July 1944 he at last gave practical expression to his long hinted desire for an outlet to the West by receiving an exploratory group of US diplomats – the so-called Dixie Mission. Over the following year the expatriate population of Yan'an numbered up to thirty-two Americans as opposed to precisely three Russians. Mao explained to Vladimirov that America's stance was of 'tremendous importance' to the CCP's future, and that he had even been thinking of changing the name of his Party to make it sound more attractive to American ears.[216] Vladimirov for his part had no doubt that Mao was offering himself as a partner to the Americans with a view to preventing the Soviet Union from 'participating in the solution of Far Eastern problems'.[217] In the spring of 1945 Mao presided over the CCP's Seventh Congress in a triumphant summation of his nativist Rectification Campaign. As Chairman of the Central Committee, the Politburo and the Party Secretariat he had now been exalted to a pre-eminence greater than even Stalin enjoyed; and his Thought was now formally enshrined in the Party's constitution. In late June, however, the CCP were brought up short in their turn by the staggering news that their Soviet patrons were about to sit down and negotiate a treaty with their arch-enemies in the KMT. One of the CCP team in Chungking, Wang Ruofei, went so far as to voice flat-out opposition, informing the Soviet chargé d'affaires that 'without special reservations and conditions . . . the CCP cannot approve the policy of the USSR regarding this question'.[218] The Party's fury was heightened still further when it emerged in mid-August that instead of encouraging them to sally forth from Yan'an and roll up the Nationalist armies, the Kremlin was directing them to knuckle under and make their peace with Chiang Kai-shek. Told by Stalin to proceed to Chungking for talks with the Nationalist Generalissimo,

Mao is said to have been 'so angry he didn't go out for two days'.[219] To add insult to injury the Soviet leaders were sucking their teeth over a CCP request that Mao should be put up at their Chungking embassy. There were real fears for his physical safety in the KMT capital. But the Kremlin was non-committal and so, consequently, was its new ambassador, Apollon Petrov. When Mao finally set off by plane for Chungking on 28 August he looked, observed Vladimirov, 'as if he was going to his Calvary'.[220] As a result of what they saw as treachery the CCP's relations with their Soviet mentors are said to have plunged to an all-time low, and it is perhaps no coincidence that Vladimirov detected in Mao at this juncture '*an organic dislike of the Soviet Union*'.[221]

A CHOOSING OF PARTNERS (1945–9)

The Soviet troops who set out to evict Japan from Manchuria crossed the border in overwhelming strength. 300,000 in all, they amounted to three times the size of the tsarist invasion army of 1900. They even included 'Stalin's Special Unit', an infantry force of Chinese who had been raised and trained within Soviet territory. Japanese resistance wasn't negligible even now, and the Soviet Army recorded a total loss of 8,200 men. But by 24 August, after only a fortnight, the fighting was over, and Manchuria lay once again at the feet of the Russians and their commander, Marshal Rodion Malinovsky. Most of the region was to be occupied on a temporary basis, with a deadline for departure fixed at three months. But the Russians marched proudly and proprietorially into their old possessions now once again leased to them in the southern half of the Liaodong peninsula. 'We of the older generation', said Stalin, 'have been waiting for this for the past forty years.'[222] At Port Arthur they knelt before the war memorial which had been raised there in honour of the tsarist defenders of 1904–5. The name of the central plaza in Dalian was changed to Stalin Square, and the gauge of the newly amalgamated Chinese Changchun Railway was widened to make it interface with the Soviet lines. The Russians were nonetheless conscious that their dominance of the region had definite limits. Their control didn't reach far beyond the main cities and the principal lines of communication. Even in Dalian and Port Arthur they were held back by the language barrier and their lack of local knowledge and forced (like the British arriving back in Hong Kong in these very same weeks) to rely on the help of the Chinese big businessmen who had kept the government ticking over while working in cahoots with the Japanese. In any case there were doctrinal constraints on how far they could push. Molotov, Stalin's right-hand man, recalled in an interview many years later, 'We couldn't take Manchuria. It was impossible. It contradicted our policy. We took a lot. But that's another matter.'[223]

The prime task of the occupation force was to keep the Americans out. The last thing Stalin wanted to see was a string of US bases rising up on his vulnerable Far Eastern frontier. At a Soviet Army Day reception in Changchun, the old Manchukuo capital, on 23 February 1946 the priority was spelt out with disarming frankness by Commander-in-chief Malinovsky. Described by the Chinese he dealt with as 'rugged, burly and outspoken', but at the same time 'agreeable' and even 'friendly',[224] the marshal declared in a slightly tipsy oration, 'Right now there is stretched between China and the Soviet Union the hand of a third party who wears suede gloves and has gold dollars in his pocket. Indeed we must get rid of him by chopping off his hand.'[225] But the Russians were also concerned at all costs to avoid a head-on confrontation with the United States which would plunge them into another cataclysmic war.

A second, related aim of the occupation was to lay Russian hands on the wealth of the region, which had been turned by the Japanese in the years of their rule into easily the most industrialised part of China. This state-organised plunder was seen as essential both for the rebuilding of the ravaged Soviet homeland and as a way of preventing US business from getting a finger in the Manchurian pie. Stalin and his assistants defended their grab for industrial wealth with the utmost candour as a collection of 'war booty' and as justified compensation for the thousands of lives they had lost in delivering Manchuria from the grip of Japan. And as Molotov put it, they 'took a lot'. In the course of their stay in Manchuria the Soviet Army are said to have helped themselves to just under US $900 million worth of industrial plant and equipment. Power generators, furnaces, motor vehicles, broadcasting apparatus, all were shipped home in Soviet vessels by the Russians who once again managed the port of Dalian. The city of Jilin lost its Japanese-built cement plant (Stalin explained it was being kept safe in the Soviet Union so the Americans couldn't take it), while in Mukden 'factories lay like raddled skeletons, picked clean of their machinery'.[226] In addition around

$3 million worth of gold was removed from the Japanese banks of the former Manchukuo, together with other precious metals, cash and negotiable securities. And the Soviet forces bought up vast amounts of supplies with the help of their own unbacked military scrip.

During the early days of the takeover, too, individual soldiers were given free rein to rampage on their own behalf. Brutalised by four years of unspeakable war with the Nazi invaders, the victorious Red Army men behaved very much as they had in their recent progress through Germany, looting, raping and killing, and often showing themselves unable or unwilling to distinguish between Japanese and Chinese. One report from Manchuria speaks of a Soviet trooper who after raping a woman 'tied her legs to a horse and dragged her until she died'.[227] During the three-day sack of Mukden Chinese women are said to have cut their hair short and dressed up in men's clothing to avoid being raped. By the end of August, however, the worst of the excesses seem to have been curbed. In the newly leased Soviet city of Dalian order was restored with particular briskness by the same moustachioed General Kozlov whom we last met directing the operations of the Number Two House in Yining. The focus there now switched to ensuring stability and production, and over the following year the leased zone of Dalian and Port Arthur turned into a haven of relative calm as the rest of Manchuria became engulfed in the final round of the long-drawn-out struggle between the Nationalists and the CCP.

Throughout the early months of renewed civil war Stalin brooded over the battlefield, like Zeus on Mount Olympus holding the fortunes of the warring Greeks and Trojans in the scales of Fate. As summer turned into autumn he took the first steps towards handing over the region to the Nationalist government on the basis laid down in the August Treaty of Friendship. By mid-October 1945 Malinovsky and his staff were embarking on talks in Changchun with a Nationalist Commission for the Recovery of Manchuria – a top-level team composed of Xiong Shihui, a senior general; Chiang Ching-kuo in his role as the KMT's Russia Hand; and a seasoned economist named Zhang Jia'ao. But this didn't preclude the extension of a helpful measure of support to the CCP too. In the confused early days of their advance through Manchuria Soviet officers found themselves unexpectedly faced with small groups of CCP guerrillas, part of a total force of 60,000-odd fighters whom Mao had dispatched, in defiance of Stalin's injunctions, to race the Nationalists for control of the Chinese north-east. Detailed policy guidelines seem not to have been laid down at this stage, and the response of the officers varied from unit to unit. Some of them hailed the CCP soldiers as ideological kindred spirits, and may even have been advised by the local Manchurian elders that the CCP, not the KMT, were the people to back; while others looked askance at the ragtag appearance of these partisans, and found it hard to believe they were really the troops of Mao's and Zhu De's fabled Eighth Route Army. Within a few days, however, we start to find indications that a boost to the Chinese Communists had been authorised from on high. On 29 August Soviet and CCP troops together took over the key town of Shanhaiguan, where the Great Wall meets the sea. The CCP men were warmly received by the Russian commander, who gave them permission to set up an administration and police force in the town; and a CCP cable from Shanhaiguan crowed, using the Chinese slang term for the Soviet Army, '*Brother Chen* has given us a big welcoming banquet, and is allowing part [of our forces] to enter the North-East.'[228] As the weeks passed the CCP were permitted to implant themselves in many rural areas where the Russians were unable to exert effective control.

Remember, Stalin liked to keep all his pawns on the board. Some future use may even have been envisaged for Puyi, the last Qing emperor and puppet sovereign of Japanese Manchukuo, whom the Russians had caught trying to make his getaway from the Changchun airfield. The ex-emperor was installed with all courtesy at a health resort in Khabarovsk, where he was addressed as 'Your Excellency' and ushered on to the verandah for afternoon tea. Stalin seems to have thought that Puyi might one day have a role again as a figurehead, either of an independent Manchuria or conceivably even of China as a whole. In the same way the CCP might be used as a check on the Nationalists if the latter continued to work, despite Soviet warnings, hand in glove with the dreaded United States. At the beginning of October, after the US had landed Marines at the northern Chinese ports of Tianjin and Qingdao, and a squadron of US naval transports had (unsuccessfully) sought the consent of the Soviet authorities to disembark KMT troops at Dalian, Stalin decided to transfer to the CCP in Manchuria part of the huge mass of weaponry the defeated Japanese Army had left behind. To avoid violating the terms of the new Sino-Soviet Treaty through giving aid to the KMT's enemies these arms weren't to be handed directly to Chinese

Communist units, but were instead to be collected and deposited in places where the CCP contingents could pick them up. On 25 October a representative of the Soviet Army is said to have instructed the CCP's newly established North-Eastern Bureau, 'We're giving you a free hand', and to have guaranteed that his army would help the Chinese Communists to fend off any KMT onslaught that might be attempted before they pulled back into Soviet territory at the end of the stipulated three months.[229]

Stalin's hopes were however still visibly pinned for all practical purposes on the Nationalist regime in Chungking. In mid-November, when Chiang Kai-shek, angered by Soviet obstruction in Dalian and elsewhere and covert support for the CCP enemy, threatened to pull his negotiators out of the Changchun talks, the Soviet side scrambled frantically to make good the damage. On 15 November the Soviet government reaffirmed that the Nationalist recovery of Manchuria would take place on the basis of the Sino-Soviet Treaty, and on 27 November they signed a specific agreement providing for the return of the region to KMT rule. At the Nationalist government's own request they twice agreed to extend the original deadline for the withdrawal to Russia of Malinovsky's legions, first till the end of the end of the year and then for another four weeks up till 1 February. This in effect gave the KMT time to rush more armies up to Manchuria and enhance their ability to handle any local resistance the CCP put up. And underscoring the value the Kremlin attached to the KMT partnership the Soviet economic negotiator, Mikhail Sladkovsky, unveiled during the second half of November a massive scheme for the joint operation by the Soviet Union and Nationalist China of 154 Manchurian industrial and mining enterprises, representing no less than 80 per cent of the region's heavy industry. Such a partnership would undoubtedly hold immense promise for the revival and modernisation of China's economy. At the same time it would have the beauty, in Moscow's eyes, of legitimising the Soviet Army's appropriation of the Manchurian factories, and still better would make it effectively impossible for American business to get a foot in the door. On 1 February 1946 Malinovsky acknowledged with his habitual bluntness the strategic calculation behind the scheme: 'Soviet Russia is not willing to see Manchuria used once again as an anti-Soviet base. This plan of economic cooperation is merely a precautionary measure for our own security.'[230]

Given these Russian priorities the CCP were inevitably relegated as usual to second place. Even in October the Soviet backing for their activities had been hedged about with restrictions. Stalin wasn't prepared to release to the Chinese Communists more than part of the Japanese arsenal. In particular he wasn't willing to let them have access to large amounts of heavy weaponry, as opposed to rifles and machine guns. Malinovsky in Changchun warned some local CCP activists that it was 'not permissible' to oppose the Nationalist government or to stick up anti-Nationalist posters,[231] and Soviet soldiers disarmed one of the CCP's rural guerrilla bands. And from mid-November, when Chiang Kai-shek looked like scuppering the entire Changchun process, the CCP found themselves getting stamped on hard. On 17 November the Soviet Army directed them to clear right out of the Manchurian cities and to dismantle their rural regimes. The Soviet commandant of Mukden, General I.A. Kovtun-Stankevich, told Peng Zhen, chairman of the North-Eastern Bureau, that the CCP had just one week to get out of his area, and '*If you do not leave we will use tanks to drive you out*.'[232] In the Soviet-leased southern Liaodong peninsula curbs on the Party's activities were introduced systematically. In Dalian General Kozlov cut the CCP down to size from the start, pointing out to the local Party chief a pair of government buildings and stating firmly, 'That's where I've put the Nationalists . . . That's where *you* will set up office.'[233] To avoid violating the terms of the treaty the CCP were forbidden to operate openly in either Dalian or Port Arthur; and in accordance with the Soviet stress on social stability they were discouraged both from agitating against the local fat cats who had worked with the Japanese but had been left in positions of influence and from trying to break the grip of landlords in the countryside. In the meantime the message for Mao and his Politburo was essentially what it had been for the whole of the last ten years, namely the necessity of working with Chiang Kai-shek. On 17 January 1946 Zhou Enlai sent a telegram from Chungking to Yan'an:

> The Soviet friends have requested us to inform them of the CCP Central Committee's position. Without a sufficient knowledge of the situation [they] cannot advance any specific point of view, but [they] believe that the CCP should not think of sovietisation but should rather with all resoluteness concentrate on prevention of the civil war and seek Chiang Kai-shek's agreement for the realisation of democracy.[234]

The same Russian willingness to favour Chiang's regime at the expense of its rivals was visible in the other chief area of sustained Soviet–Nationalist friction. In late August 1945 in Xinjiang the Moslem insurgents of the Eastern Turkestan Republic were still pressing eastwards with Soviet aid. One thousand five hundred Soviet troops were fighting a KMT garrison at Puli; Soviet-furnished ETR aircraft were bombing the Chinese-held town of Jinghe. Just two weeks later, however, the Kremlin was moving to bring its activities into line with the new Sino-Soviet Treaty. On 15 September Ambassador Petrov submitted a note to the Chungking authorities in which he declared that the ETR sought only autonomy, not independence, and were indeed seeking Soviet mediation with that end in view. The Yili National Army were ordered to halt at the River Manas, and Soviet officers called in the weapons for which the rebels had already paid them in gold and livestock and wool. By 10 October Soviet-sponsored peace talks were under way in Urumqi, and by 20 October one of the Soviet generals with the YNA was reporting to Molotov and Beria 'the implementation of your instructions to cease operations on the part of the insurgents'.[235] On 2 January 1946 the Urumqi talks reached a successful end with the signing of an eleven-point settlement. A Xinjiang Provincial Coalition Government was established under the chairmanship of the local KMT commander, General Zhang Zhizhong. The Three Districts remained an autonomous, Soviet-influenced territory, but the name Eastern Turkestan Republic was officially dropped at Stalin's insistence, and Xinjiang was formally recognised by the Soviet Union as an integral part of China. Once again the broad interests of China and Russia had trumped the aspirations of the scattered peoples between them, and the Soviet turnabout wasn't welcomed in the Turkic lands. ETR representatives, we are told, were 'surprised and disappointed' by Petrov's démarche,[236] and the Yili National Army fighters at the River Manas were said to have had 'murderous looks on their faces'.[237]

In the last days of 1945 the ubiquitous Ching-kuo was welcomed in Moscow as his father's personal envoy for one-on-one talks with the Soviet ruler himself. At a first meeting on 30 December Stalin spelt out for the younger Chiang's benefit the Soviet Union's bottom line. The Kremlin, he indicated, was willing to have close ties with the Nationalist government and to help in developing Manchuria and Xinjiang on one condition, namely that Chiang Kai-shek should pursue an 'independent' policy in the incipient

Cold War and *not allow a single US soldier to stay in China*.[238] Following the demise of the KMT–CCP peace talks, which had broken up inconclusively in early October, Stalin hastened to reassure his guest that the Kremlin was not contemplating any resumption of help to the KMT's foes: 'The Soviet Union is not giving advice to the Chinese Communists. We are dissatisfied with their behaviour.'[239] In any case the CCP were unlikely to turn to Moscow for advice any more: 'They know we don't agree with them.'[240] In the interests of stability, though, he proposed that Mao's party should be included in a coalition government (Stalin was all for coalitions at this time), launching in the course of a second discussion on 3 January 1946 into a positively angelic seminar on democratic procedures:

> You must introduce electoral principles in China . . . as in France, Poland, Yugoslavia, Britain and America. The parliament must be elected, and the government must be appointed by the parliament and confirmed by the president . . . In America and Britain governments are formed from the members of the party which constitutes the majority.[241]

Yes, a risk did exist that elections might let the opposition into power. During the Potsdam conference, he acknowledged, 'I myself thought that the Conservatives would win a majority in the [British] election, but Labour won.'[242] But he didn't anticipate any such outcome in China: 'The KMT is naturally a broader and more influential party than the CCP.'[243] Stalin rounded off his remarks with an invitation to Chiang *père* to meet him for a summit either in Moscow or at some point on the Sino-Soviet border – this second option a major concession on the part of the Soviet despot, who was accustomed to have foreign dignitaries travel all the way to Moscow to call on him. In May 1946 Stalin reissued the same invitation through the good offices of both Ching-kuo and Nikolai Roshchin, the Soviet ambassador to the restored Nationalist capital of Nanking.

But in spite of these Soviet efforts the Nationalists ultimately refused to play ball. As so often, the KMT spoke with many conflicting voices, and there were certainly some in their ranks who were prepared to give Moscow the benefit of the doubt. Chiang Ching-kuo, ever dovish, advised his father on 29 October 1945 that he thought the Russians would help the KMT armies to get back Manchuria, and on 12 November, as the Changchun talks teetered on the verge of breakdown, he continued to recommend patience with them. In Moscow at the turn of the year he went so far as to tell Stalin that he believed the Soviet Union to be the only outside power that genuinely wished to see China reborn. Zhang Jia'ao, the KMT's economist in Changchun, several times expressed admiration for the 'far-sightedness' of his opposite number, Sladkovsky, and the rest of the Soviet team. He agreed with Malinovsky that the Nationalists should aim at a 'spiritual understanding' with their Russian neighbours.[244] Over in Xinjiang the head of the new governing coalition, General Zhang Zhizhong, pursued what he himself called a 'pro-Soviet policy'.[245] He had every intention of maintaining Chinese sovereignty over the turbulent province, but felt it was only by working with the Soviet personnel there that any stability could be achieved. These friendly voices, however, were drowned in a chorus of scepticism. General Xiong, the military man at the head of the KMT team in Changchun, believed that the future was 'full of nettles',[246] and his forebodings were widely shared back at base in Chungking. T.V. Soong, who had played the leading role in the Moscow talks in the summer, displayed 'great indifference' to the Changchun process, and Wang Shijie, his successor as foreign minister, urged 'extreme discretion'.[247] Both men had come under heavy attack for their role in concluding the shameful Treaty of Friendship, and had no wish to be criticised once again. They insisted that the government must first recover Manchuria before any economic deal could be signed with the Russians – land first, partnership second. And on the right of the KMT was the whole Western-influenced phalanx of Party barons, represented most notably by Chen Lifu and his brother Chen Guofu – the 'CC Clique'. These rightists were quick to exploit the rising outrage of educated Chinese at the Soviet Army's misconduct in 'liberated' Manchuria. When news finally broke in addition on 11 February 1946 of the Yalta agreement a year before which had paved the way for the Chinese surrender of Outer Mongolia, Chen Lifu orchestrated a series of mass anti-Soviet protests staged by students in most of the principal cities. In one Manchurian rally students even held up a caricature of Stalin being stabbed with a knife. Local KMT activists often launched campaigns of their own without waiting for central direction, and in Manchuria some of them crossed the line into sabotage and terror. In Mukden, for instance, two attempts were made on the life of Commandant Kovtun-Stankevich, and when Soviet forces finally pulled out of the city on 9–12 March vicious reprisals were taken against a number of Russians who remained. The head of a Soviet trade mission, a certain M.A. Ivkin, was dragged out of his house and subjected to a mock execution. Around sixty Soviet citizens were tortured and executed in earnest, and some 200 families had their homes pillaged, as if in revenge for the Soviet Army's previous orgy of looting.

Somewhere in the midst of these cross-currents floated Chiang Kai-shek himself. To begin with Chiang seems to have felt some interest in exploring the scope for a modus vivendi with Russia (Ching-kuo's flying visit to Moscow at the turn of 1945–6 had been his idea), and certainly Stalin appealed to his vanity. On 15 January 1946 he observed in his diary, 'Stalin said to Ching-kuo that he has made a more thorough study of me personally than of any other leader and formed a closer knowledge of my character than that of anyone else. This shows how much attention he pays to me.'[248] On 28 February he is reported at Ching-kuo's request to have severely reprimanded Chen Lifu for organising the mass anti-Soviet rallies. But in the long run he couldn't resist the pressure of the Right KMT and more especially of his US backers. On 7 February the US secretary of state, James Byrnes, declared publicly to both the Soviet and Chinese Nationalist governments that his country wasn't prepared to accept their exclusive control of Manchurian industry. And Chiang couldn't afford to alienate the US. In the last resort it came down to a choice between the generous military and economic aid that was already in full flow from Washington and the vague promises emanating from the Kremlin; and a bird in the hand was worth any number in the bush. The Soviet Army postponed their withdrawal from Manchuria for four further weeks, from 1 February to 1 March, seemingly in the hope of imposing their formula, partnership first, land second – but by 1 March it was clear Chiang had put his foot down. The talks in Changchun had collapsed irretrievably, as the Nationalists showed themselves willing to cooperate only on a limited range of Manchurian industrial projects and insisted on having a 51 per cent share in the capital as against the Soviet demand for fifty-fifty joint ventures. As for Stalin's invitations to meet him in person, Chiang spurned both of them. On 11 May he recorded in his diary, '*Stalin is used to playing tricks with others, but I will not be his dupe*.'[249]

The Russians were in no better odour with the Chinese Communist side. Anger went on being voiced by the CCP leadership at Moscow's dalliance with the Nationalist regime. In the autumn of 1945 one Party organ, the *New Masses* (*Xin Dazhong*) publicly condemned the Soviet Union for its neglect of the CCP, while a regional military chief, Nie Rongzhen, told a meeting of Party officials in the Inner Mongolian town of Kalgan, 'Our Party will not be bound by the diplomatic relations between the Soviet Union and [Nationalist] China.'[250] One can imagine Zhou Enlai's lip curling as he penned his message to Yan'an containing the Soviet Party Central Committee's admission of being 'without a sufficient knowledge' of Chinese affairs. Yet again we find the top CCP leaders assuming a come-hither posture towards the West. At the end of 1945 Mao expressed his welcome to the US mission under General George C. Marshall which had arrived in Chungking to promote a reconciliation between the two Chinese sides, and Zhou pointed out to the American mediators, 'It has been rumoured recently that Chairman Mao is going to pay a visit to Moscow. On learning this Chairman Mao laughed and remarked half-jokingly that if ever he took a furlough abroad he would rather go to the United States.'[251] Soviet officers are said to have asked their CCP counterparts plaintively, '*Why is your Central Committee so polite to the US?*'[252] In Manchuria in late September the North-Eastern Bureau head Peng Zhen was complaining to the Mukden commandant Kovtun-Stankevich of the 'cold and detached' attitude of the Soviet Army headquarters to him and his colleagues, and in November he protested bitterly at the commandant's threat to use tanks to expel the army of another Communist Party. The Soviet Army's looting had caused as much rancour in CCP circles as it had among the KMT and the students: at least a million factory hands are said to have been left jobless after their plants were dismantled and carried off into Russia. In the leased south of the Liaodong peninsula CCP activists were incensed by the steps of the Soviet administration to curb their aggressive endeavours at land reform. When Russian soldiers broke up a rally staged in the countryside near Port Arthur in February–March 1946 to stir up the peasants against a local landowner the CCP Party secretary exploded at the presiding Soviet officer, 'Chiang Kai-shek doesn't grant the common people freedom to assemble, and you won't allow them to hold meetings either!'[253] The views of the CCP rank and file are more obscure, but old stereotypes would appear to have been dying hard. As the Soviet Army began to pull out of the region that spring and the CCP bands fled north before the advancing Nationalist forces, some disgruntled guerrillas are said to have pointed towards their commander, Lin Biao, yelling, 'Ask that chief, are we retreating to the land of the Old Hairy Ones?'[254]

Nonetheless Stalin had to accept the strategic realities. By the spring of 1946 his long-cherished Nationalist option was dead. Chiang Kai-shek wasn't going to seek the withdrawal of US troops from his territory or acquiesce in the plan for a Soviet–KMT economic partnership to keep US business interests out of Manchuria. US-backed Nationalist forces were moving into the south of the region and might soon be installed on the Soviet Union's Far Eastern frontier. There was just one way forward. From the spring of 1946 Stalin's scales at long last began to tilt bit by bit in the CCP's favour. In April Malinovsky's departing commissars were instructed to cooperate with Lin Biao and his officers, allowing them to take over as much as they could of the northern Manchurian countryside and to deploy their troops on the outskirts of Harbin and the other main northern cities. By the end of the year the entire border zone had been turned with Soviet help into a secure base where the battered CCP forces could recover their strength, flanked on west, north and east by friendly territories in the form of the MPR, the Soviet Far East and the Soviet-occupied northern half of Korea. Stalin's restrictions on arms supplies were lifted, and over the next three years the CCP's newly styled People's Liberation Army (PLA) were equipped with a panoply of heavy weaponry unsurpassed in the long history of Russian arming of China and totalling an eventual 900 captured Japanese aircraft, 700 tanks and 3,700 artillery pieces on top of the staple military fare of 740,000 rifles and 18,000 machine guns. Reinforcements were also supplied in the shape of some 200,000 Chinese POWs from the defeated army of Manchukuo and 180,000 troops from the future North Korea. Between June and October 1946 the Soviet Army opened at Dalian, Port Arthur and other centres upwards of sixteen substantial air force, artillery and engineering schools for the training of PLA officers, and Soviet military, intelligence and communications advisers were all laid on. This huge intervention, and above all the infusion of heavy weapons, played a vital role in enabling the CCP to survive the great Nationalist offensive of 1946–7. The new wave of Soviet experts also made a real effort to treat the Chinese Communists well and to make up for the misdemeanours of Malinovsky's occupation force. When Manchuria was engulfed by an epidemic of plague (the Black Death, no less) in the winter of 1947 a team of doctors were sent in and are said to have saved tens of thousands of Chinese lives. In the summer of 1948 Stalin made another critical move, dispatching as his special envoy to the CCP in Manchuria Ivan Kovalev, a former minister of communications who had directed the Soviet railway system during the Second World War. Backed by a team of fifty engineers, fifty-two railwaymen and 200 'skilled workers', Kovalev set about reconstructing the whole transport infrastructure of the region which had been ravaged during the past years of war. By December he had overseen the restoration of some 15,000 kilometres of railway track, 120 bridges and 885 locomotives, all of which were put to immediate use in the autumn offensive through which Lin Biao and his fellow generals smashed their way across southern Manchuria before pushing on to subdue the entire country north of the Yangtze. Just as a Soviet intervention, whatever its motives, had saved the Nationalist government from utter defeat by the Japanese Army in 1937–8, so now, whatever its motives, this second great Soviet thrust handed victory to the CCP over the Nationalists in the final round of the Chinese Civil War. Mao himself spoke appreciatively of the 'comfortable armchair' where his troops had been able to shelter with Russian assistance in northern Manchuria, with the Soviet Far East providing the backrest and the MPR and North Korea the two solid arms.[255] On 8 January 1949 he sent a cable to Stalin declaring, 'With the help of Comrade Kovalev and other Soviet comrades most of the railway network in Manchuria has been repaired',[256] and on 4 February he acknowledged, '*If there had not been any help from the Soviet Union we would hardly have been able to gain today's victories*.'[257]

Yet still Stalin nurtured his doubts. Taking the CCP 'half seriously, half sceptically',[258] he still didn't really believe they could take over China. When the Nationalists captured the CCP sanctum of Yan'an in March 1947 he offered to send a special plane to evacuate Mao and the rest of the leadership to Soviet territory, and he is said to have advocated a new round of peace talks between the Communists and the KMT regime. In September Nikolai Roshchin, the Soviet ambassador to Nanking, got back in touch with the top KMT policymakers, averring that his government could induce the CCP to accept a negotiated end to the war. Some shift of outlook was indicated in February 1948, when Stalin remarked to a delegation of visiting Yugoslavs that the Chinese Party had been right in pursuing their struggle with Chiang. But one year later, in January 1949, the grand strategist in the

Kremlin was still playing the mediation game, passing on to the CCP a last-ditch call for peace talks from the crumbling Nationalist government and suggesting a positive response. Did Stalin still not believe, at this late stage, that the CCP would be capable of crossing the Yangtze and overrunning the rest of the country? Or was he pushing for a settlement precisely because he *did* believe it and feared the emergence of a united and powerful eastern neighbour that might one day pose a threat to both Russia and Russia's control of the new Marxist empire carved out by the Soviet Army in Eastern Europe in the aftermath of the Second World War? Did he, like the old tsarist foreign minister Sazonov, hope to see 'a happy and a contented and a prosperous China – but not a *strong* China'.?

The chessboard was now rearranged, with the CCP as the main piece and the Nationalists relegated to a secondary role. But still Stalin liked to hang on to his pawns. In January 1949 Moscow ordered Ambassador Roshchin, alone of the foreign diplomatic corps, to accompany the retreating Nationalist leadership from Nanking to Canton; and it was only in May, after the PLA marched into the old Nationalist capital, that Roshchin was finally called back home. In distant Xinjiang contacts were maintained almost to the last moment with the friendly KMT authorities as the Russians sought to preserve their traditional influence in the province and access to its enormous mineral wealth. In January 1949 talks opened with General Zhang Zhizhong on a range of commercial and economic issues, and in May the existing airline agreement between the Soviet Union and the provincial government was renewed for five years. The Soviet consul-general in Urumqi is even said at one point to have buttonholed a second KMT commander, General Tao Zhiyue, and proposed that he should declare Xinjiang independent on the lines of the MPR: '*If you will do this we will order the CCP not to continue their advance into Xinjiang*.'[259]

And still Stalin mistrusted Mao. 'What kind of man is this Mao Zedong?', he is said to have grumbled to his cronies. 'I don't know anything about him. *He's never been to the Soviet Union*.'[260] Mao, as we saw, unlike virtually all of his senior colleagues had never jumped through the hoops of Soviet training at Sun Yat-sen University or the Communist University of the Toilers of the East; and he had these pretensions to being an independent source of Marxist-Leninist wisdom. As early as 1947 Stalin banned the circulation on Soviet territory of an adulatory life of the CCP Chairman that had been written by a left-wing American journalist named Anna Louise Strong. In the following year, 1948, the Soviet boss received from the western fringe of his new Marxist empire an unpleasant reminder of the threat that might be posed to his authority by local non-conformists when Marshal Tito's government in Yugoslavia refused to accept Moscow's dictates and had to be cast into the outer darkness as a regime of *kulaks* (rich peasants). It didn't take much of a leap of the imagination to size Mao up as a possible second Tito. At the end of June the Kremlin abruptly turned down a request for a CCP delegation to travel via Moscow to Warsaw for a meeting of the Communist-sponsored World Federation of Democratic Youth. Stalin is said to have feared that 'just one sneeze from a Chinese would infect the Soviet Union with the germs of the *kulak* line'.[261] In January 1949, for the first time in the CCP's thirty-year history, a senior Kremlin leader was sent to China in the form of the Politburo member Anastas Mikoyan, who as an Armenian was seemingly felt to be more attuned than his colleagues to the workings of the Oriental mind. Travelling under the name of Andreev to the CCP's new headquarters in the mountain village of Xibaipo, Mikoyan came in part to discuss the programme of a future Chinese Communist government; but he was also plainly intended to pass back to Stalin a close-up appraisal of the Chinese Party's long-standing chief. Unimpressed by Mao's efforts to present himself as Stalin's faithful disciple, the Armenian drily reported, '*This does not correspond to what Mao Zedong is in reality, nor to what he thinks about himself*'.[262] During February, as Mikoyan thrashed out policy details with the CCP inner circle, a further hammer blow was directed at the attempt to boost Mao in the eyes of the Soviet public. The main victim was none other than Mikhail Borodin, who on returning home after the catastrophe of 1927 had found a niche as editor of an English-language daily, the *Moscow News*, and had somehow emerged unscathed from the Great Purge of the late 1930s. Borodin had been trying to help Anna Louise Strong in her continuing drive to get her Mao biography published in Moscow. He was now at last hauled in and tortured in the Lubyanka as the NKVD tried to extract a confession that during his glory days in south China he had recruited Mao for US intelligence. Strong for her part was detained and deported. Dr Orlov, who had served in Yan'an, was likewise arrested and savagely tortured for his supposed links with Mao, 'that American and Japanese spy'.[263]

If Stalin was in the end converted to unambiguous backing for the victory of the Chinese Communist Party, his conversion must be assigned to the astonishingly late date of June 1949. At the end of that month the Kremlin received a top-level CCP delegation headed not by Mao but by Mao's number two, Liu Shaoqi. It seems clear that for Stalin Liu unlike his master ticked all the right boxes. He hadn't merely spent time in Soviet Russia but had been one of the first batch of Chinese students sent there for instruction in the spring of 1921. He had voiced no heretical notions about the role of the peasantry, but was best known for a series of lectures he had delivered at Yan'an under the title *How to Be a Good Communist*, which had focused largely on the uncontroversial topics of self-cultivation and discipline. And he managed unlike Mao to give a convincing impression of the humble, respectful Confucian pupil. At any rate he and his entourage were treated like winners. Arriving in Moscow on 28 June, they had scarcely got to their hotel from the airport before being whisked off to the countryside for a feast given by the assembled members of Stalin's Politburo. Over the next few weeks Stalin personally received Liu no fewer than six times; he is said to have studied with keen attention a report Liu had drawn up for him on the tentative domestic and foreign policies of the future People's China, and to have made fifty-three underlinings and notes. Liu and his team were also introduced to a series of ministers and factory managers who might be able to provide the new China with economic aid. And on 27 July the team were accorded the ultimate honour of a banquet at Stalin's country dacha of Kuntsevo. In excellent humour, the Soviet boss did something he had seldom if ever done previously in the whole of his tortuous career – he *apologised*. '*We feel*', he declared, '*that perhaps we hampered you in the past. We did not know a lot about you and for this I am very regretful*.'[264] And he offered a toast to a future in which the Chinese Party would *emulate their Soviet elder brother*.[265]

This show of benevolence was followed up with a gift of a more solid kind. By the time Liu came to Moscow the Kremlin had plainly dropped any lingering thoughts of hiving Xinjiang off from China proper. The advance of the People's Liberation Army into the east of the province was now imminent and unstoppable, and in the meantime Stalin had been having second thoughts about his sponsorship of the autonomous Three Districts of the far north-west. Ever since 1946 various Turkic leaders in the Districts, including one or two who had previously received Moscow's blessing, had staged anti-Soviet risings with the encouragement of US officials; and Stalin's emissaries considered the apparent growth of American influence 'a knife thrust into the back of the Soviets in Central Asia'.[266] His advice to Liu was accordingly that the CCP should go ahead and absorb the whole region with all convenient speed. On 14 August Liu's political secretary, Deng Liqun, was sent straight from Moscow to Yining to impose Chinese Communist leadership on the erstwhile Eastern Turkestan Republic. Deng handed Ahmet Jan Kasim and the other top ETR leaders a letter from Mao inviting them to a Political Consultative Conference in newly 'liberated' Peking, and Stalin directed them to cooperate with the CCP Chairman. On 27 August Ahmet Jan and three of his associates took off for the conference from Alma Ata in Kazakhstan in a Soviet aircraft – only to be killed shortly afterwards when their plane came down in the neighbourhood of Lake Baikal. Deng was informed a week later of the accident by the Soviet consulate-general in Urumqi, who reported additionally that the Xinjiang situation was 'already under proper control'.[267] Whether or not Ahmet Jan and his colleagues were deliberately liquidated on Stalin's orders, the effect was to decapitate the region's Turkic leadership and to frustrate yet again local cravings for an independent, Islamic Xinjiang. Once more Russia and China had closed ranks at the expense of the people in the middle. In his talks with Liu Stalin recommended the use in Xinjiang of a method which has sometimes been referred to as 'ethnic cement'. Pointing out that the current Chinese population of Xinjiang was no more than 5 per cent of the total, he suggested that this figure should be brought up to 30 per cent through a systematic process of resettlement. In fact, he pursued, not just Xinjiang but all of the border regions – Tibet, for example – should be settled by Chinese migrants 'in the interests of strengthening China's frontiers'.[268]

As Stalin gradually threw his weight behind the cause of the Chinese Communists, so the CCP came round, step by step, to the notion of a renewed partnership with their former Soviet guides. At the forefront of this trend were the leaders of the North-Eastern Bureau which the Party had set up in Manchuria. Cut off from the rest of the CCP forces in China proper, the Bureau were largely dependent on the military and economic support which officials in the nearby Soviet-controlled zones channelled through to their northern Manchurian 'armchair'. By late 1946 they were seeking Soviet help for a wide range of purposes, from arms deliveries to the circulation of currency to the export of Manchurian soyabeans and the supply from Vladivostok of grain, vegetable oil, sugar and other Soviet produce; and the teamwork that resulted gave rise in its turn on the Chinese side to a distinct reawakening of interest and goodwill. One leading figure to show an appreciative face to the Soviet Union was Lin Biao, the gifted, neurotic commander of the People's Liberation Army. Early in January 1947 the Soviet trade official Mikhail Sladkovsky was presented to Lin at one of a series of dance evenings the Bureau had arranged in Harbin to enable their personnel to get to know the new influx of Russian assistants. Lin wasn't an entirely easy person to talk to (Sladkovsky remarked on his sickly, feminine appearance, his strained expression and soft, breathless speech); but he spoke 'rapturously' of his time in the Soviet Union and the military training he had received there during the first few months of the German invasion.[269] In the course of 1947 he busied himself making ready his great Manchurian offensive on the basis of the various Soviet battle plans he had studied in Moscow and of the Soviet Army's campaigns in Eastern Europe in the final stages of the Second World War; and in 1948, we are told, he was 'regularly' turning to the Soviet authorities with questions on different aspects of military aid.[270] Even more warmly disposed, it appeared, was the tall and bespectacled Gao Gang, who had risen in June 1946 to the post of Deputy Secretary of the North-Eastern Bureau and Deputy Political Commissar of the North-Eastern People's Army. At the dance evening in January 1947 he struck Sladkovsky as being the life and soul of the festivity, laughing, joking and coming over after each dance to greet the Russian guests and talk 'sincerely' to them. He proudly drew attention to his seventeen-year-old son, who had just returned from years of study in Soviet schools during which he had wholly forgotten the Chinese language, clapping the boy on the shoulder and urging him, 'Learn from the Soviets! Learn from them!'[271] On another occasion he casually described to Sladkovsky how he had been tortured with red-hot irons during Mao's anti-'Muscovite' Rectification Campaign. Over the following years Gao developed close ties with large numbers of Soviet officials and military men, while his star went on rising spectacularly. By 1949 he had been appointed First Secretary of the North-Eastern Bureau and was informally known as the 'King of Manchuria'. In June that year he travelled to Moscow at the head of a separate Manchurian contingent of Liu Shaoqi's delegation, and proceeded to sign the first major economic agreement between a CCP organ and the USSR, for the exchange of Manchurian soyabeans for Soviet military equipment and materials.

In the central Politburo too, many CCP leaders were keen to see a shift back to an intimate Russian alliance. One leading proponent of this view was certainly Liu Shaoqi, who is said to have concluded quite swiftly that the United States couldn't be weaned off its attachment to Chiang Kai-shek. Renewed partnership with the Soviet Union was consequently the only course that made sense, and if that meant assuming an air of submission so be it. At the Kuntsevo banquet on 27 July 1949 Liu played to perfection the role of the modest disciple, refusing dramatically to accept Stalin's toast to 'the younger brother emulating the elder'. 'The elder brother', he proclaimed, 'will always be the elder brother and the younger brother will always be the younger. We shall always learn from our elder brother.'[272] Stalin seemed mildly surprised by this Confucian sentiment, but agreed he had only meant that the younger brother should endeavour to overtake his sibling. One week later Liu assured Stalin, 'I am ready to carry out any task you wish to set me.'[273]

Underlying these protestations was a jockeying for Soviet favour in the topmost ranks of the CCP. Gao and Liu were both angling for Stalin's approval of the opposing economic programmes they had in mind for the new People's China, Gao's based on the drastic Stalinist collectivisation of agriculture in the late 1920s, Liu's on the more moderate Soviet New Economic Policy of the years before that. And Gao was apparently bidding for still higher stakes. By this date he was routinely passing confidential information to Stalin about the inner ructions in the Chinese Politburo, and specifically about rivals like Liu. He was certainly seeking a Soviet helping hand up the CCP ladder, and may even have hoped to emerge with a fief of his own. At the Kuntsevo banquet, if an account left by Kovalev is to be believed, he arose from his seat to put forward the staggering proposition that Manchuria should be declared the seventeenth socialist republic of the USSR. Some of the Soviet Politburo members applauded, but the canny Stalin didn't jump at the offer, any more than he had at the offer of Xinjiang briefly dangled before him by Sheng Shicai in January 1941. Fixing his eyes upon Gao he got up, and after an 'awkward pause' addressed the daring CCP man sardonically as the reincarnation of the Old Marshal of 1920s Manchuria – '*Comrade Zhang Zuolin*'.[274] In the meantime Liu sat in his chair 'black as night'.[275] As soon as the banquet was over he rushed to the telephone to alert his colleagues in the Chinese Politburo and demand that Gao should at once be recalled to the motherland for an 'act of treason'.[276] Stalin did his best to act as mediator, holding a drinks reception to bring the two rivals together and prodding them, in an atmosphere of utter frostiness, to drink each other's health. Three days later, however, Gao set off for home on his own. Liu himself incidentally may not have been quite such a pillar of virtue as he wished to appear. According to some sources he too was passing confidential information to Stalin, and may have been doing so ever since the 1930s.[277]

The hold-out against all this was, predictably, Mao. In June 1946 the Chairman was still urging Lin Biao not to rely on Soviet military aid but instead to be 'entirely self-reliant'.[278] By the autumn he had accepted the need for such aid, but insisted that it should be paid for with 1 million tons of food from the CCP-controlled areas. He was not going to be beholden to the Soviet Union. Unlike Gao Gang he didn't rejoice when his two sons, 'Seryozha' and 'Kolya', returned home in 1945 and 1947 respectively from their years of study at Ivanovo and other Soviet centres largely ignorant of Chinese life, and in 'Kolya''s case able to speak only Russian. 'In the Soviet Union', he admonished 'Seryozha', 'you slept in a bed, but from now on it'll be a mat on a *kang*';[279] and he asked 'Seryozha' to translate a letter he had written to his younger son into 'the foreign language'.[280] The 'rectification' of pro-Soviet elements in the CCP hadn't yet run its course, and in June 1948 the hapless Wang Ming once again complained that his doctors were trying to poison him through the administration of doses of lysol. And as the civil war entered its final convulsions Mao reacted with fury to any sign of reserve or double-dealing on the Soviet part. Stung by Stalin's apparent attempt in January 1949 to promote the KMT government's offer of peace talks, suspecting that the Soviet aim was to replicate the arrangement of the Northern and Southern Dynasties (AD 420–589) when China had been divided between regimes to the north and south of the Yangtze, he cabled tartly back that the 'KMT peace swindle' should be 'flatly rejected', and even went so far as to instruct the Soviet autocrat, '*We think you should give the following answer*' to the KMT.[281] When Mikoyan arrived at Xibaipo three weeks later Mao declined to receive him for two days as a gesture of pique at the Kremlin's having directed Ambassador Roshchin to take part in the Nationalist government's exodus from Nanking to Canton – Mikoyan and later Stalin were forced to explain themselves, arguing that they had merely been following standard diplomatic practice while taking the opportunity to extract useful intelligence from senior Nationalist and US personnel. In his exchanges with Mikoyan Mao brought up among other topics the vexed territorial question of the MPR, asking innocently whether after the CCP victory Outer and Inner Mongolia might not be merged into a single autonomous region of the new Chinese People's Republic. And one evening in February he caught the seasoned Armenian off guard with a bitter and cryptic tirade:

> Friends are divided into true and false ones . . . False friends are friendly on the surface. They tell you one thing but do another and even devise some evil designs. They fool the people and afterwards take joy in the people's disaster.[282]

But Mao didn't yet have complete control of Party foreign policy. Nor could he ignore the fact that despite all his feelers the US government remained implacably hostile to the CCP, and that consequently the Soviet Union was the only place he could look for the arms and technology he needed to defend and develop the new Chinese state. In addition, as the Party's ties with the Soviet Union tightened, he seems to have felt a degree of anxiety about his own standing. In November 1947 he suddenly brought up with Stalin for the first time the suggestion that he should visit Moscow in person to learn from the Soviet 'experience of nation-building' – a request he repeated twice in the course of the next eighteen months. He had apparently started to fear that his lack of personal knowledge of the Socialist Motherland might place him at a disadvantage, complaining to Kovalev that the other CCP leaders had all spent time in the Soviet Union while he had been nowhere. By the end of 1948 he was also afraid of being lumped by Stalin with the apostate Tito, wondering possibly whether the Soviet chief still remembered his refusal to help Russia out at the time of the Nazi invasion and his purge of the Chinese 'Muscovites' in Yan'an. From 1947, at any rate, he began to display a new deference in the bulk of his dealings with Stalin, hailing him as the 'Supreme Master' and diligently pruning the Chinese Party's documents of their previous references to 'Mao Zedong Thought'. Possibly to put Mao in his place Stalin fended off his repeated requests for a visit, with excuses ranging from the plausible (that Mao ought to stay at his post at this crucial stage of the civil war) to the ridiculous (that the members of the Soviet Politburo were all busy overseeing the grain harvest). But Mao took it all lying down, reiterating to Mikoyan in February 1949 that the new People's China would be built on the basis of Soviet experience and Stalinist teachings. Like Stalin he finally crossed the Rubicon of rapprochement that summer, dispatching the mission led by Liu Shaoqi with a hefty list of military, economic and financial requests. And on 30 June, as Liu and his team settled into their talks in the Kremlin, he published a celebrated article proclaiming that the new China would 'lean to one side' in its diplomatic affairs, towards the Soviet Union and away from the Western world. In a sense it seems extraordinary that there could have been any question about it. The Chinese Communist Party was a Soviet creation moulded in the Soviet image – where else was it to lean? Yet Mao's formula even now looked ambiguous. The Chairman had only promised to tack for a time in a certain direction; and if he could tack in one direction he could just as easily tack in another.

Still, for the moment at least there was no doubt that the CCP had crept back under Soviet patronage. And as always that patronage came at a price. As the old ties were reforged the anti-Soviet grumbles which had issued from the Party in recent years were comprehensively stifled. In May 1947, for instance, the Manchurian novelist Xiao Jun, the same who had once extolled the poetic essence of Marx and Lenin, had published an article in a new Party journal, the *Cultural Gazette*, in which he condemned Malinovsky's troops for their uncouth behaviour in his home region and for shipping home industrial raw materials which were vitally needed in China itself. By the end of 1948 Xiao had been accused of equating the comradely operations of the Soviet Army with the predatory conduct of the tsars and had been packed off to work in the Fushun coal mines; and the *Cultural Gazette* had been closed. In Soviet-governed Dalian two of the Party's activists had brought up a whole litany of complaints ranging from the higher wages paid to workers in Soviet-run enterprises as compared with Chinese ones to the oppressive presence of Soviet liaison officials at Party meetings and the administration's insistence that all their employees including Chinese ones should turn up to work in Western suits, ties and leather shoes. (How times had changed since the Qing had imposed Chinese dress on the Russian Orthodox Mission!) In October 1947 these two malcontents were shunted out of the Soviet leased zone to postings elsewhere, and a new slogan was adopted by the CCP in Dalian and Port Arthur – '*Put the Soviets First!*'[283]

In addition the CCP once again took their seats at the feet of their Soviet teachers. From 1947 the watchword was once again 'Learn from the Soviet Union'. Once again Party cadres were sent off to Moscow in sizeable numbers to be trained. Once again Stalin began to dispense advice to his Chinese disciples reflecting his perception of China's backwardness on the long road to Communism and his overriding concern to maintain strategic security in Russia's backyard. In November 1947, in terms not dissimilar to those he had used to Chiang Ching-kuo less than two years earlier, he counselled Mao that on coming to power he would have to make room for rival parties in a coalition government. The future China would necessarily be a 'New Democracy' rather than a Communist state, and would remain so for many years to come. In a series of other suggestions put forward in 1948–9 he directed Mao variously *not* to do away with private property, *not* to expropriate Western-owned enterprises, to win the support of the local middle classes and to make good use of the Western-trained experts left over from the old regime. And in April 1949 he urged the Chairman on no account to break off diplomatic relations with the United States and other Western powers for fear of provoking an American landing in northern China. Mao was by no means happy with these counsels of moderation. His idea was to skip 'New Democracy' and instead to eliminate all his potential opponents as part of the 'final victory' of the Chinese Revolution. But whatever his private gripes, Mao himself found it only appropriate to give his Soviet sponsor a voice in determining both the starting date and the seat of the new People's Government. In August 1949 Stalin recommended that the CCP should bring forward the date planned for the inauguration of their regime from New Year's Day to 1 October. Otherwise, he observed, the delay might give rise to a political vacuum which could be exploited by 'hostile foreign powers'.[284] This proposal was duly adopted, and 1 October became the birthday and eventual National Day of the new Chinese state. On another occasion Mao asked whether Stalin agreed that the capital of the future China should be moved back from Nanking to Peking. This would, as he noted explicitly, bring it closer to Russia and thus within easier reach of Soviet influence. And the Supreme Master did not say no.

CHAPTER 6

REBELLION

A COLD BETROTHAL (1949–53)

It was, officially, the best of times. On 21 December 1949, in Moscow at long last after years of requests and postponements, the leader of the newly proclaimed People's Republic of China (PRC) sat at Stalin's right hand in the former tsar's box in the Bolshoi Theatre, at a gala performance to celebrate the seventieth birthday of the all-powerful Soviet chief. The audience rose three times from their seats and cheered, 'Glory to Stalin! Glory to Mao!'. Early in 1950 a hymn entitled 'Moscow-Peking' received its first airing in the Hall of Columns of the Kremlin building which housed the Soviet Union's parliament, the Supreme Soviet. The singer exulted,

> A Russian and a Chinese are brothers forever;
> The unity of peoples and races is strengthening;
> Stalin and Mao are listening to us![1]

The Russians had now, it seemed, finally won the role of benign overlords they had sought in China since the mid-nineteenth century, first as avuncular conquerors and later, since 1917, as apostles of revolutionary change. In the 1920s they had micromanaged the rise of China's first political parties. In the 1930s and 1940s they had exerted control, at different times and with differing degrees of authority, over the three great border regions of Xinjiang, Outer Mongolia and Manchuria. Now, as they moved in to answer the

Chinese Communist Party's appeal for support in constructing the new People's Government, they were getting their hands on the levers that activated the country as a whole.

They began by attending to the new regime's needs for defence and security. During the first few months of its existence the infant PRC remained vulnerable to the still smouldering challenge of the beaten Chinese Nationalists. By the end of 1949 878 Soviet air force specialists had arrived in China to train local pilots and to strengthen the air defences of the big eastern cities of Shanghai, Nanking and Xuzhou as well as the south-eastern province of Fujian which lay opposite the Nationalists' last refuge of Taiwan. During the spring of 1950 these Soviet airmen shot down five KMT aircraft over Shanghai. A second group of ninety experts were sent in to help the new government with the creation of a modern navy. In the restored northern capital Soviet security men set about ensuring the physical safety of Mao and the rest of the CCP leaders in Zhongnanhai, the compound they had occupied next to the old Forbidden City – what some of the Russians called 'the Kremlin of Peking'.[2] Soviet mine detectors were used to sweep the ground everywhere Mao and his colleagues might tread, and a pair of Russian toxicologists who had been attached to the new regime's Central Bureau of Guards organised a food-tasting procedure complete with two special laboratories to check for poison all the dishes served to the leadership. Assurances were incidentally given to the CCP that the skills of the Soviet security organs would no longer be used for intelligence-gathering within China.

These protective steps cleared the way for a huge intervention on the civilian side. In mid-August 1949 Liu Shaoqi had arrived back from his month-long sojourn in Moscow with a trainload of 250 Soviet political advisers and technicians: a further 650 had joined this group by the end of the year. Hand-picked by Stalin himself, the advisers helped their Chinese colleagues to formulate the basic structures of the new administration, to determine the functions of the newly founded departments and to work out a system of state planning. Within a few months they were present in all the new central ministries and all the provincial and regional governments, offering guidance in areas ranging from financial and economic policy to law, policing, transport, education and cultural affairs. One of only two of the new regime's organs which did not have its quota of senior Soviet consultants was the Foreign Ministry; but even here it seems Russians were active at a humbler level, showing the rustic guerrillas turned diplomats how to put on a Western suit and tie and how to dance. Schooling received the most striking attention. One hundred and twenty-seven advisers (the largest of any of these consultancy teams) were installed in the Ministry of Higher Education, where they helped to push through a complete over-hauling of the country's university system. During the winter of 1949–50 Soviet experts drew up the blueprint for a new People's University based on the traditional Russian model of chairs, faculties and hard if rather narrow specialisation; and Soviet instructors went on to train future Chinese officials at both the People's University and the CCP's Central Party School.

The technicians meanwhile got to work assessing the new regime's needs for economic aid and directing the operation of some of the larger factories. Much of their effort went into Manchuria, now officially known as the North-East, where Soviet engineers had already been building on the existing Japanese industrial base and where they could best apply their traditional strength in the heavy industrial sectors of coal and electric power generation, chemical engineering and the production of iron and steel. Thirty out of forty-two projects completed with Soviet help in the following three years were located in the Chinese North-East. Overall charge of assistance to China was placed in the hands of the Soviet State Planning Commission, and in 1950 a metallurgical expert named Ivan Arkhipov, also hand-picked by Stalin, was sent out to serve as chief economic adviser to the Chinese government. The Planning Commission were leery about extending their remit into the vast arena of Chinese agriculture, on the grounds that their specialists were unfamiliar with the local crops and the natural environment; by 1950 nonetheless Russian consultants had taken the lead in a meeting about the establishment of Soviet-style state farms and had arranged the supply of some tractors, and by 1951 some Russian agronomists had appeared on the scene. Medical care was also made part of the programme, a natural follow-up to the decades of treatment already accorded to CCP leaders, and in June 1952 a Soviet Red Cross Hospital with sixty doctors and nurses was established in Peking.

And the CCP showed every sign of receiving this bounty with open arms. On 31 October 1949 their newly appointed ambassador to Moscow, Wang Jiaxiang, an erudite former member of the Moscow-trained 28 Bolsheviks, told the Soviet deputy foreign minister Andrei Gromyko quite simply, 'The

Soviet Union is China's teacher, and the Chinese people should become pupils of the Soviet People.'[3] To facilitate this apprenticeship a new Russian Language Institute was founded in Peking, and a second one was set up in Shanghai in February 1950. Before long Russian was being taught at a total of fifty-nine schools in the capital, and had been made a compulsory subject at secondary level throughout the North-East. This linguistic campaign was accompanied by the translation of thousands of books, as the CCP sought to implant the model presented by Soviet society in Stalin's last years – a model known variously to historians as Late, or High, or Bureaucratic Stalinism, with its massive administration, its tight central control of economic planning, its stress on heavy industry and defence, its preference for autarky and limited foreign trade and its insistence on the absolute supremacy of the Communist Party over the government. On the political side Stalin's *Short Course*, a history of the Bolshevik Party, became holy writ for large numbers of the new regime's administrative trainees, while Soviet economic ideas were absorbed through the translated texts of such titles as *Party Control in the Factory* and *The Origins of Industrial Management in the USSR*. (The Russians supplied some more general fare in the form of biographies of Lenin and Stalin and an introduction to the Soviet Union quaintly entitled *What the Scottish Miners Saw*.) The next step was to recreate Soviet institutions. Moscow's Seven Principles of Industrial Management were adapted in China into an Industrial Management Mechanism, with ten principles instead of seven. State companies for the direction of internal and foreign trade were organised on the Soviet pattern, and in November 1952 the CCP formed their own State Planning Commission, tasked with preparing their first Five Year Plan. In September 1951 the regime greatly strengthened their grip on the urban population by introducing the *hukou*, once described to me by a Chinese friend as 'the most important thing in China' – the household registration card which governed access to food, goods and jobs and is said to have been inspired in part by the *propiska* or internal passport imposed in Russia under Stalin in 1932. As early as October 1949 the CCP's Central Military Commission decided to streamline the organisation of their field armies, substituting the Soviet hierarchy of ranks and salaries for the haphazardly egalitarian structure of the PLA, and in 1950 the Commission chose to adopt the Soviet code of military regulations until such time as they could thrash out a code of their own. The legal system was largely transplanted from Soviet jurisprudence, though some help had to be invoked from the legal advisers from the former KMT government in wedding Soviet practice to the existing Chinese judicial base. In the realm of education a literacy campaign was explicitly modelled on the post-revolutionary Soviet one, while a First National Higher Education Conference was held in June 1950 to promote the complete revamping of Chinese universities on Soviet lines. A clone of the Soviet Academy of Sciences was brought into being, with a similar method for the election of scholars; and research was concentrated, Soviet-style, in the Academy and the various industrial research centres connected with it, with the universities mostly restricted to teaching. In Shanghai in September 1951 work started on the Caogang New Village, a settlement modelled on Soviet workers' compounds with its own schools, kindergartens, shops, banks and cinemas. A journal, *Women of New China*, was launched to inform Chinese women of the emancipated lives of their Russian sisters, with particular reference to Soviet methods of family planning and the Soviet effort at gender equality represented by job opportunities and equal pay. 1n 1951–2 a congress of 'youth cadres' was convened in Shanghai to study the experience of the Soviet Young Pioneers. Chinese authors, like Soviet ones, were corralled into a Writers' Union.

All this against a background roar of pro-Russian enthusiasm. Just four days after the proclamation of the PRC a new Sino-Soviet Friendship Association was formed that went on to claim an eventual 120,000 branches. One early Chinese report publicised the rejoicing of a bank manager in Tianjin who was said to have gushed, 'We don't wish to regard the USSR and China as two states.'[4] 'The Soviet Union's Today', ran the ubiquitous slogan, 'is China's Tomorrow!'

Not surprisingly, in the context of the deepening Cold War the overwhelming new Soviet presence in China stirred panic in Western and above all in American circles – panic not unlike that which had been generated among British observers by the tsarist advance into Qing territory in the late 1890s. On 12 January 1950, in a speech to the National Press Club in Washington, the US secretary of state, Dean Acheson, accused the Russians of 'detaching the northern provinces of China' and 'attaching them to the Soviet Union'.[5] This process, he declared, was 'complete' in Outer Mongolia, was 'almost complete' in Manchuria and was 'under way' in Inner Mongolia and Xinjiang.[6] One year later, in May 1951, Acheson's subordinate, Dean Rusk, the under-secretary of state for Far Eastern affairs, chimed in with a still more alarming claim. The regime in Peking, he argued, was '*a Russian colonial government* – a Slavic Manchukuo on a larger scale. It is not the government of China. It does not pass the first test. *It is not Chinese*.'[7]

Despite and because of this surging US hostility the Soviet Union and the new PRC marched forward in lockstep. On 14 February 1950, after three weeks of talks, Mao and his Moscow hosts formalised their ties in a new, thirty-year Treaty of Friendship, Alliance and Mutual Assistance that inevitably became known to some Western commentators as the Valentine's Day Treaty. Nominally directed at the beaten Japanese enemy, with which both countries were still technically at war, but in reality aimed at the United States ('any other state which may collaborate with Japan in acts of aggression'), the treaty committed both signatories to render each other military aid 'with all the means at their disposal' if either of them should come under attack.[8] China. it seemed, had been taken snugly under the Soviet wing.

But it was still the same old Stalin.

Oddities had begun to present themselves from the very start of the new Chinese order. On the historic date of 1 October 1949 when the new People's Government was proclaimed in Peking no Soviet leaders or even officials were in attendance to celebrate the birth of their ideological offspring. The only notable Russians on hand were two writers, Alexander Fadeev and Konstantin Simonov, plus Galina Ulyanova of the Bolshoi Ballet and her accompanying troupe. On 2 October a cable of congratulations was dispatched from the Kremlin – but only at the relatively modest level of Deputy Foreign Minister Gromyko. And when a first Soviet ambassador to the PRC was appointed it turned out to be not a weighty new figure but a retread from the pre-revolutionary period, Nikolai Roshchin, the former Soviet envoy to Chiang Kai-shek. It is surmised by an ex-Soviet diplomat that the ever cautious Stalin, fearful of a violent reaction from the United States if his country were seen to be too conspicuously at the CCP's side, had preferred to create an impression of 'business as usual'. One might perhaps also speculate that to the ageing and cynical despot who had witnessed the passing of so many transient Chinese regimes it may have seemed far from certain that Mao's administration would represent any sharp break from those of its predecessors.

Certainly Stalin's suspicion of Mao was as acrid as ever. After a first interview at the Kremlin on the evening of his arrival, 16 December 1949, the

Chinese Chairman was swept away to a dacha in the countryside and there left to cool his heels for four and a half days, probably to remind him of his subordinate status while the Soviet boss tried to form an opinion of 'what sort of fellow Mao was'.[9] During those days three of Stalin's lieutenants, Molotov, Mikoyan and Nikolai Bulganin, turned up intermittently to question him, sitting stiffly 'on the edge of their chairs',[10] only to come back to their master with much the same conclusion they had all reached already during the Second World War. Mao, according to Molotov, was a clever man, a peasant leader not unlike the eighteenth-century Cossack rebel Yemelyan Pugachev – but not a Marxist. By his own admission he had never read a line of *Das Kapital*. For an insight into Mao's true feelings the NKVD had a bug installed in his room. His quarters were further equipped with a special lavatory, which had secret boxes attached to it: his stools were routinely whisked away for analysis, with a lack of potassium judged to betoken a nervous and volatile disposition.[11] Small wonder the British press started to speculate that the CCP leader had been placed under house arrest. At a subsequent meeting, when access to Stalin had once again been granted, the Soviet chief's paranoia was on full display. As the Kremlin's Chinese-speaking interpreter, a young Sinologist named Nikolai Fedorenko, struggled to make sense of Mao's Hunan accent, complicated still further by a sprinkling of classical Chinese expressions, Stalin cut in, '*Is this conspiracy going to go on much longer?*'.[12] It was only when Stalin had been soothed by the explanation that the subject under discussion was nothing more sinister than a story about the Song dynasty general Yue Fei that the hapless interpreter had 'an almost physical sense of the guillotine moving away'.[13] Incensed by Dean Acheson's allegation of 12 January 1950 that the USSR was in the process of swallowing up northern China, the Soviet ruler demanded that Mao should arrange for a formal rebuttal to be issued through the Chinese Foreign Ministry, and was further enraged to discover a few days later that the promised statement had been issued not through the Foreign Ministry but at the less weighty level of the director of the New China News Agency: this was clearly regarded as signalling a tacit Chinese agreement with the American charge. On 21 January Mao was hauled to the Kremlin for a savage tongue-lashing jointly administered by Stalin, Molotov and the NKVD chief, Lavrenty Beria. 'Keeping promises', Molotov told him, 'is an important part of our cooperation.'[14] The suggestion was made to Mao's face that he was a 'national

Communist' and a 'semi-Tito'.[15] On the evening that followed the signing of the Valentine's Day Treaty Stalin accepted the invitation of Mao and his colleagues to a celebratory banquet which the Chinese had organised at the Metropole Hotel. The acceptance was startling, as the autocrat never usually emerged for festivities outside the Kremlin walls. But he brought his own bottle (no doubt from a terror of poisoning); and he pointedly used the occasion for a further attack upon Tito, condemning the Yugoslav Party for their abandonment of the socialist camp. Their road, he observed, was a dead end, and the renegades would only return to the fold *under a different leader*. The company listened 'with bated breath'.[16]

The same old Stalin was visible in both the talks that took place with the Chairman and the new treaty that resulted from them. Stalin didn't initially want a new treaty at all. Focused as always on Russia's strategic advantage, he had no wish to replace the existing Treaty of Friendship he had signed with the KMT government in August 1945, which had left the Soviet Union in such an eminently comfortable position in Manchuria and the rest of the borderlands. 'We with our inner circle', he informed Mao at their first meeting on 16 December 1949, 'have decided not to modify any of the points of [the existing] treaty for now.'[17] While acknowledging that the 1945 treaty had 'unequal' features he explained that to alter it would mean violating the terms of the Yalta accords with the wartime Allies, and would give the United States and Britain a pretext for tampering with the terms of the other Yalta provisions. Two weeks later, after a New Year's Eve visit from his 'inner circle' in the persons of Molotov and Mikoyan, the Soviet boss unexpectedly shifted his ground. He had apparently been persuaded that it would be less dangerous to conclude a new treaty with the CCP than to let Mao return home unhappy. Mao was accordingly given the green light to summon from Peking the indispensable Zhou Enlai, now become premier and foreign minister, to work out the details of a new document, and on 22 January 1950, the day after Zhou's arrival in Moscow, Stalin airily brushed aside his own previous qualms about Yalta and negotiations began. Yet the changes eventually conceded by the Soviet Union in the Valentine's Day accord were remarkably slight. The Russians agreed to hand over the Chinese Changchun Railway to the PRC government by the end of 1952, and to withdraw from the Port Arthur naval base by the end of 1952 or following the conclusion of a peace treaty with Japan, if that happened sooner. But that still left the prospect of a quasi-colonial body of Soviet troops and railwaymen in Manchuria for another three years. And in the meantime the treaty provided for certain new institutions designed to buttress, not weaken, the Soviet presence in the border territories. Sino-Soviet joint stock companies modelled on the enterprises set up by the Soviet Union in Sheng Shicai's days were to be founded in Xinjiang to exploit the vast region's resources of petroleum and rare and non-ferrous metals. (Similar joint enterprises in civil aviation and shipbuilding were later established in the Manchurian port of Dalian.) In all of these ventures the Soviet side would contribute 50 per cent of the capital and be rewarded with 50 per cent of the profits, and in all of them Stalin insisted on parity of management, which in practice meant virtually exclusive Soviet control. In stipulations recalling the tsarist-Qing secret treaty of 1896 no citizens of any country but Russia and China were to be allowed into either Xinjiang or Manchuria, and the Soviet Red Army were to be permitted to use the Chinese Changchun Railway as a short cut for transporting their troops from Siberia to the Maritime Province in time of war. All of this smacked of a designation of Soviet spheres of influence little short of the wholesale Russian ingestion of northern China that Acheson had depicted in his speech of foreboding on 12 January. Other clauses providing for Soviet economic aid to the new Chinese government had a whiff of the tight-fistedness with which Stalin had meted out his supplies to the CCP forces in wartime Yan'an. Funds allotted to enable the PRC leadership to pay for their purchase of Soviet equipment and technology came to the scarcely munificent total of US $300 million. This money came, furthermore, as a loan, not a grant, to be repaid over five years in Chinese agricultural and mineral produce, and it even carried an interest rate of 1 per cent: Stalin compared this to the 2 per cent interest rate carried by Soviet loans to the satellite countries of Eastern Europe, adding sardonically, 'We can raise the interest for you as well, if you like.'[18] Finally Stalin demanded that China should pay handsome compensation for the services of his aid personnel, to a total of 2,000 to 4,000 roubles per month per technician, representing four to six times the monthly income of the most senior CCP leaders. Compensation was also to be paid to those Soviet enterprises that were making technicians available for Chinese use, along with stipends for the upkeep of the wives and children whom they were leaving at home. In fairness we should bear in mind that the Soviet Union was still severely cash-strapped as it strove to repair the immense devastation of the Second World War; but the overall package was still a long way from enough to propel a country as massive as China on the road to its first Five Year Plan. Still apparently with one foot in the past, Stalin further insisted that any of his experts who committed a misdemeanour in China should be subject to Soviet rather than Chinese jurisdiction. In so doing he was upholding the old colonial principle of extra-territoriality which the Western powers had relinquished in 1943.

And it was still the same old Mao. Right at the start the Chairman was upset by the failure of Stalin to send him a personal message of congratulations on the birth of the new Chinese state. He was further angered by the reappointment of Roshchin as Soviet ambassador to China – that same Roshchin who had tagged along with the Nationalist government in their last-ditch retreat from Nanking to Canton. When Roshchin threw his first dinner for the CCP Politburo Mao is said to have sat in silence throughout the whole meal, displaying a 'mocking-indifferent' attitude.[19] Once again a close study of the Chairman's visit to Russia from December 1949 to February 1950 yields a different picture from the ecstatic official reports. Mao was venturing outside his comfort zone in more ways than one. He was travelling abroad for the first time in his life. He was making an honorific call on a foreign potentate, paying tribute as it were, when all Chinese tradition demanded that the victorious founder of a new regime should have foreign potentates calling on him. And to win the support he required, military, political and economic, he was likely to have to make some concessions which would be regarded as deeply humiliating by a considerable number of his new subjects. Even before he set out he was showing clear signs of anxiety. In apparent concern for his personal safety he insisted on making the journey by train rather than by air – was he recalling the fate of the Xinjiang Muslim leaders whose plane had crashed on Stalin's territory just four months before? He took with him a minimal entourage so that any deal he struck might be concluded effectively without Chinese witnesses. By the time his train got to Sverdlovsk in the Urals his anxiety was beginning to take a psychosomatic form. Taking a stroll down the platform he was observed to be 'white-faced' and pouring with sweat in the freezing December air.[20] And on arrival in Moscow he was bristling with the consciousness of real and imagined slights. At the Yaroslavl Station he found no Stalin to greet him, and was aggrieved by the coolness of Molotov and Bulganin, who appeared on their master's behalf but were dry and official and turned down an invitation from the Chinese delegation to share their lunch. When the two titans finally approached one another in the Kremlin that evening Stalin greeted his guest affably, praising him as 'a fine son of the Chinese people'.[21] Mao's response was a querulous raking up of old resentments: 'I have been beaten and pushed around for a long time and had nobody to complain to.'[22] There then followed four and a half days of crushing indignity as the Chairman was left in the countryside to await Stalin's pleasure. In the space of less than three months he had gone from receiving the adulation of the Chinese masses at Tiananmen to sitting in a Russian dacha looking out at a wintry garden and waiting for the phone to ring. To those Russians he did get to see, notably Kovalev the adviser and Fedorenko the interpreter, he complained with his typical earthiness that he had come to Moscow to work but had 'nothing to do except eat, shit and sleep';[23] and he declined with contempt an invitation to go sightseeing. Correctly assuming that his quarters were bugged he took the opportunity to give Stalin a piece of his mind, telling the bug pointedly that he was prepared to do business with Britain, Japan and the United States. Finally he exploded to Kovalev that he 'simply couldn't stand it any more', and for all the world like a teenager 'locked himself in the bedroom and let no one in'.[24] Even the honours that were belatedly paid him at Stalin's birthday gala on 21 December failed to dispel a protracted case of the sulks. Both Stalin on his left and Mátyás Rákosi, the Hungarian Communist chief, on his other side, did their best to engage him in conversation; but no matter how hard they tried they 'couldn't get the least smile out of him'.[25] The Chairman's mood lightened somewhat in the New Year, when Stalin at last agreed to negotiate a new treaty and Zhou Enlai was sent for to sort out the details (though Mao insisted that Zhou too should travel by train, not by air). Mao was even persuaded to spend a few days sightseeing in Leningrad. But the sulks returned in a big way on 21 January, when Stalin, Molotov and Beria took it in terms to lambast the Chairman, in the presence of the newly arrived Zhou, for China's low-key response to the Acheson speech. 'I laughed at them in my nose', Mao recalled, 'but did not say a word.'[26] Following this confrontation the Soviet boss spirited Mao and Zhou off for a prearranged dinner at his dacha in Kuntsevo; but a deathly silence persisted throughout the thirty-minute drive. Seeking to lower the tension the Chairman's interpreter, Shi Zhe, reminded Stalin of a promise he had made to call on the Chinese delegation, only to have Mao break in, 'What are you talking to him about? Don't invite him to visit us!'[27] The same 'cold and dreary' atmosphere prevailed through the dinner.[28] At one point Stalin turned on the gramophone to generate a festive mood. Zhou and Shi Zhe allowed themselves to be hauled to the dance floor by Stalin's courtiers (all men), but in spite of a number of efforts to rally him Mao refused to budge, and 'the whole thing ended in bad odour'.[29] Even at the supposedly celebratory dinner the Chinese gave Stalin on the evening of Valentine's Day the Chairman barely exchanged a word with his VIP guest.

The substantive discussions got off, in Mao's eyes, to an equally unpromising start. The Chairman began the first exchange of views on 16 December with the bizarre declaration, '*From this trip we hope to bring about something that not only looks nice but also tastes delicious*.'[30] The Kremlin leaders looked nonplussed as visions of noodles danced in their heads, and Beria actually laughed out loud. Mao unlike Stalin urgently needed a new treaty of alliance which would secure Soviet military (including nuclear) protection for his regime. But his hopes were apparently dashed at the outset by Stalin's refusal to alter the terms of the Soviet-Nationalist treaty of 1945, to which he replied, one suspects with some sullenness, 'It is already becoming clear that the treaty should not be modified at the present time.'[31] He went on to propose various 'tasty' projects, all of which promptly ran up against Stalin's habitual strategic caution. For example he tried to secure the dispatch of Soviet 'volunteer' pilots plus a secret Soviet military detachment to speed up the capture of Nationalist-held Taiwan, and to win Stalin's backing for a lunge by the PLA into Vietnam to support the uprising of the local Communists against their French colonial masters. Stalin however demurred in both cases: 'What is most important here is not to give the Americans a pretext to intervene.'[32] Even after Stalin's change of heart over the treaty question, when formal talks on a new treaty got under way on 22 January 1950, extracting concessions from the Soviet despot was like drawing blood from a stone. Mao still cherished hopes of recovering Outer Mongolia, even in spite of his past disavowals to Mikoyan and others, even in spite of the fact that his government under Soviet pressure had already established diplomatic relations with the MPR. But when Zhou Enlai unexpectedly resurrected this ultra-sensitive issue the Soviet leaders at once tensed up. Molotov accused the CCP of infringing the 1945 Sino-Soviet deal on Mongolian independence, and Stalin asked virtuously, 'What right have we to decide other people's destiny?'[33] Mao is said to have been enraged by this negative outcome. On his way back to China in February he got off his train several times to visit the Siberian towns, but conspicuously turned down an invitation to tour Ulan Ude, the local capital of the Buryat Mongols, to which he was probably laying a symbolic claim. No greater progress was made in the talks on the other two borderlands. In an effort to keep China's end up Mao and Zhou held out for a controlling stake of 51 per cent in both the Xinjiang joint stock companies and the Chinese Changchun Railway, but without success. Again in the interests of equality they sought the right for their troops to be ferried all the way from Xinjiang to Manchuria on the Trans-Siberian Railway in case of war, as a quid pro quo for Soviet use of the CCR; but this idea was rejected amid 'heated argument'.[34] Mao referred privately to both Xinjiang and Manchuria as 'Soviet colonies', and 'unpleasant feelings' are said to have been exhibited in the course of the discussion on these points by the Chinese team.[35]

There were a few silver linings. Mao did, after all, come out with the military alliance he needed to protect his regime against the American threat. Soviet weapons were there for the asking: in the course of his visit the Chairman was able to order a hefty consignment of 586 military aircraft, and two days before his departure from Moscow he was emboldened to write to Stalin for a further 628, the costs in both cases to be covered by the Kremlin's loan of $300 million. After Acheson's speech of 12 January, which failed to include Taiwan in the US defence perimeter the secretary of state had decreed in the western Pacific, Stalin began to encourage Mao to launch an attack on the renegade province, though he didn't pledge either naval or air support for such a campaign; and he endorsed plans that the Chairman was drawing up to take over Tibet, well away from the centres of geopolitical tension ('The Tibetans need to be subdued'[36]). When the Soviet leader, still probing the borderlands, asked whether Moscow would in future be signing separate trade agreements with Xinjiang and Manchuria or whether all trade should from now on be conducted through the Chinese central government, the CCP chiefs were able to take a firm line. Mao declared that Xinjiang could conclude separate deals with the Soviet Union for the moment, but that these must be signed in the name of the Peking government, while Zhou stated flatly, 'A separate agreement with Manchuria can be ruled out.'[37] Mao was strangely unruffled by the modest $300 million dollop of Soviet funds. Preferring, as he had consistently done since the mid-1940s, to minimise his indebtedness to the Soviet Union, he argued that any more generous loan would enable the Russians to extend their influence even further (if that were possible) over China's domestic affairs. Over the question of the salaries for the Soviet experts Zhou managed to get their remuneration brought down from the hair-raising level of 2,000–4,000 roubles per month to a slightly more palatable 1,000–1,500.

Nonetheless this was Mao's Brest-Litovsk. Just as Lenin and Trotsky in 1918 had found it necessary to sign a humiliating peace treaty with imperial Germany, giving up huge expanses of the defunct tsarist empire to ensure the survival of their frail revolutionary regime, so Mao swallowed an almost equally demeaning agreement with his Soviet patrons to lock in Russian military protection against the United States. Such huge concessions as the barring of all foreigners other than Russians from Xinjiang and Manchuria and the right to extra-territorial jurisdiction for Soviet experts were tucked away in a series of secret protocols, and Mao even cabled Liu Shaoqi, who was minding the shop in Peking, to delete any reference to these terms from the CCP's press and publicity: '*This is extremely important, extremely important!*'[38] From an outsider's perspective Harrison Salisbury, the pioneering correspondent of the *New York Times*, who was in Moscow during these months, detected a number of 'curious and inexplicable signs' as the Chairman lingered on in Moscow for week after week, disappearing altogether for part of that time, and as the talks resulted in a treaty eerily similar to the ones with the Qing and the KMT which had gone before it;[39] while Stalin is said to have remarked to his intimates, 'Comrades, the battle of China isn't over yet. *It's only just beginning.*'[40]

And so for the next three years it went on, surface unanimity masking a persistent underlying friction. The Korean War was a case in point. At the end of March 1950, less than two months after the Stalin–Mao encounter, Kim Il-sung, Stalin's satrap in North Korea, arrived in Moscow to seek his master's blessing for an invasion of the American-sponsored South. The grand strategist in the Kremlin was amenable to this idea, which at best might eliminate the United States presence on his eastern flank and at least might distract the Americans from Europe and bog them down in a prolonged Asian war. But there was no way he was risking a superpower collision. 'If you get kicked in the teeth', he told Kim, 'I shall not lift a finger. You have to ask Mao for all the help.'[41] After Kim launched his invasion on 25 June, and the Americans girded themselves for a counter-attack under the banner of the United Nations, Stalin actively encouraged the CCP to move in on behalf of the North, guaranteeing a large arms supply and promising in particular the dispatch of a division of 122 jet fighters to provide air cover for the advancing PLA troops. At the end of September, after the Americans and their allies had landed at Inchon and sent Kim Il-sung's forces reeling back into their own territory, the Soviet leader stepped up the pressure on China, urging Mao to send in at least five or six divisions under the anodyne label of 'volunteers', to advance on the 38th Parallel separating North and South and repeating the critical promise of air cover. Back at his old technique of the 1930s and 1940s, Stalin was once again getting ready to fight a geopolitical foe to his east . . . to the last Chinese.

The CCP had little appetite for such an adventure. After decades of fighting the Nationalists and the Japanese the majority of them craved a breathing-space, free of major conflict, in which to lay the foundations of their new society. On 2 October Mao cabled to Stalin, 'Many comrades in the CCP Central Committee judge that it is necessary to show caution here.'[42] Under strong Kremlin pressure the Chairman took steps to beat down the resistance of his Politburo colleagues, and sent off a two-man delegation in the form of his premier, Zhou Enlai, and Lin Biao, his top military commander, to call on Stalin at his holiday villa at Sochi on the Black Sea coast and discuss the practicalities of a Chinese intervention. Both Zhou and Lin, however, were personally opposed to the project, and Zhou opened the talks on the night of 10 October by repeating that in the light of their own strategic vulnerability the Chinese government thought it best not to send troops to save North Korea. If, as seems likely, Zhou's opening statement was a gambit meant to elicit still greater Soviet armed support for a Chinese campaign, the premier was in for an unpleasant surprise. Stalin reaffirmed that the Soviet Union was willing to supply the Chinese 'volunteers' with planes, artillery, tanks and other equipment; but the vital air cover over Korea would after all not be available for another two and a half months. Zhou is said to have 'gasped'.[43] Apart from anything else this was a clear violation of the pledge made under the Valentine's Day Treaty that the two signatories would come to each other's aid in case of war 'with all the means at their disposal'.[44] As Zhou and Lin dug in their heels the Kremlin supremo is said to have given way to exasperation, shouting at his guests, 'In that case, if you've decided you don't want to send troops, socialism in Korea will collapse in no time',[45] and commenting sullenly to his entourage, 'Well, what of it? We didn't send our troops to Korea, and so now the Americans will be our neighbours on our Far Eastern border, that's all.'[46] Molotov was even instructed to cancel the newly agreed programme for the delivery of Soviet arms. At this juncture, however, Mao quite unexpectedly chose to play ball. On 13 October he sent a cable to Zhou, now in Moscow, declaring that with or without air cover the PLA should go in: '*We believe that we should enter the war and that we must enter the war*.'[47] The long-suffering Zhou is said to have 'buried his head in his hands'.[48] But Mao had apparently concluded he had little choice. Showing a cable from Stalin he told the Politburo, '*The Old Man considers that we have to act*.'[49] Playing ball seemed the only way to sustain Stalin's trust in the CCP, such as it was, and more concretely to preserve Chinese access to the vital Soviet arsenal. On 19 October PLA 'volunteers' in Manchuria crossed the River Yalu into Korea, and by early December they had driven the US-UN forces from the North Korean capital of Pyongyang.

Up to a point it paid off. Stalin is said to have received the news of the Chinese intervention 'close to tears', and with a mawkish sentimentality quite out of character to have murmured, 'The Chinese comrades are so good . . .'[50] (Well, he had got what he wanted.) For the first time he seems to have been satisfied that the CCP weren't dancing to the American tune, and his help for the Chinese war effort was correspondingly brisk. The Russians continued to steer well clear of any overt role in the fighting on the Korean peninsula, but were active participants behind the scenes. While air cover for the 'volunteers' was denied for the whole first twelve weeks of the war, Soviet fighters and bombers did at least patrol China's north-eastern borders and shielded Shanghai. Most important, from Mao's angle, the Soviet Union sent enough tanks, artillery and MiG fighter planes to equip sixty-four infantry and twenty-two air divisions, incidentally endowing the PLA with the backbone of a modern military force.[51] The Chinese in return showed themselves to be compliant allies. Peng Dehuai, an experienced general whom the CCP had appointed commander-in-chief of their Korean operation, was surrounded by Soviet advisers, and while disagreements were frequent he is said in the main to have deferred to their views. Mao's own elder son, the Soviet-educated 'Seryozha', served for a short time as Peng's Russian language translator at meetings with these counsellors before being killed in a US bombing raid on 25 November. Peng sent battle reports to Mao, who passed them up the line to Stalin, and in June 1951 Mao wrote to Stalin expressing the need for still more Soviet advisers on tactics and strategy to be sent to Peng's side. To help conceal their nationality two Soviet airmen named Vanyushkin and Sinitsyn were decorated for their services under the Chinese aliases of Wang Yujin and Xin Yiqin, and Zhou Enlai and his diplomats maintained to the world that the Soviet troops spotted by some American POWs were in fact merely members of the old ethnic Russian community in Xinjiang. In September 1952, with no end to the war yet in sight, the CCP proved sufficiently conscious of the value of Russian protection to seek a three-year extension of the Soviet presence at the Port Arthur naval base. In agreement broadly on the need to keep the Korean War simmering and Western forces pinned down there, Stalin and Mao linked arms for a few final years in a rough sort of harmony as Russia and China combined their resources in this first ever joint expedition outside the borders of both.

But Stalin's military aid had a sting in its tail. Mao and Zhou were incensed to discover that their regime would be called on to *pay* for its Soviet weapons – the money to be drawn to begin with from the $300 million credit the Kremlin had allotted to China in economic support. China, after all, was bearing the overwhelming brunt of the Korean adventure, with a commitment of 3 million troops of whom at least 400,000 would be killed, and sustaining heavy economic damage and loss of property; and it seemed only fair that its Soviet arms should come free. This grievance rankled more deeply as the war dragged on and China's military indebtedness rose to $650 million, while Soviet exports to China climbed happily from $338 million to $554 million. There were grumbles, too, about the quality of some of the Soviet weapons supplied. One Chinese officer in Shenyang (the former Mukden) was heard to complain, 'The Russians have dumped a lot of old, beat-up tanks on us!'[52] The Soviet military were said to be fobbing the PLA off with obsolescent MiG-9 fighters which were no match for advanced American aircraft, while turning out for their own use a new line of more sophisticated MiG-15 planes. Soviet officials for their part complained of a Chinese tendency to disparage the arms they were sending, but Stalin eventually judged it expedient to furnish the PLA with a mollifying batch of 372 MiG-15s.

In the borderlands a quiet tussle ensued as the Russians strove to maintain their existing influence and the Chinese sought to erode it. This tug-of-war was especially noticeable in Xinjiang. In 1949–50, in keeping with Stalin's policy shift of the previous summer, Soviet ground and air forces were deployed to help the CCP enter into their Central Asian inheritance. But this help only underlined the huge Soviet presence that had built up in Xinjiang over the years. In Urumqi, the capital, 'convoys of lorries with Soviet troops in full winter clothing rumbled through the streets at night', while Soviet traders and engineers were active in every part of the province. Ninety per cent of the province's exports of wool and other animal produce were sent to the Soviet Union, and 80 per cent of its imports of capital goods were brought in from there. Above all in the Three Districts of the north-west, site of the former Soviet-backed Eastern Turkestan Republic, Moscow's imprint was deep. Soviet-trained officials, many of them indeed holding Soviet citizenship, dominated the senior ranks of the local government. The local Turkic Muslim culture had acquired a Russian overlay, particularly in the towns: Russian loan words had crept into the Kazakh, Uighur and other Turkic languages, and the Cyrillic alphabet was used to transcribe them in print. The Kremlin did what they could to perpetuate this happy state of affairs. As leaders to replace the former ruling group who had been killed in the 1949 air crash they put forward another two of their own long-term protégés, Burhan Shahidi, who held a Soviet passport, and Saifudin Azizi, who had been a member of the Soviet Communist Party. And they recommended transferring the province's capital from Urumqi to the principal Three Districts town of Yining.

To begin with the CCP showed every sign of accepting the status quo. They recognised the existing government of the Three Districts, and retained around 17,000 former employees of the ETR. They even allowed the Kazakhs, Uighurs and other Turkic peoples to carry on using the Cyrillic script. Their objective was nonetheless to eradicate Soviet influence, and within a few months they were already taking some steps to that end. By the second half of 1950 they had reorganised the Three Districts government and placed it firmly under Urumqi's control. In 1951 key officials in the area were liquidated as part of a major purge of 'counter-revolutionaries'. 'Many problems' were discovered in the management of the Three Districts Development Company:[53] Soviet employees of the company began leaving for home, and in 1952 the Soviet system of business accounting which had been used to run it was dropped. By the following year a Xinjiang People's Democratic Protection League which had functioned as an engine for Soviet-sponsored separatism had been transformed into a body for advocating provincial unity under the leadership of the CCP.

The picture in Manchuria is less clear, but there too we find hints of bad blood. While the Soviet government honoured their pledge in the Valentine's Day Treaty to relinquish their stake in the Chinese Changchun Railway by the end of 1952, some of their staff on the railway appear to have made the surrender with a distinct lack of grace. On 30 August that year the Chinese vice-minister of foreign affairs, Wu Xiuquan, complained to the Soviet chargé d'affaires in Peking that the Russian officials on the CCR were refusing to give their Chinese counterparts any help in drawing up plans for the railway's operations in 1953.

With regard to the borders themselves Stalin and his subordinates moved hard and fast to prevent any bid by the new Chinese government to dredge up old disputes. In January 1951 they extracted an agreement from the leadership in Peking obliging them to accept Soviet military control over all disputed zones in Xinjiang and the North-East. In Xinjiang herdsmen living on the Chinese side of the border were required to get special Soviet authorisation to move their livestock into traditional grazing lands which the Russians considered to lie within Soviet Kazakhstan, and in Manchuria similarly Chinese river fisherfolk needed permission to ply their trade in supposedly Soviet waters. The Russians remained in control of over 600 of the 700-odd islets in the Amur and Ussuri, and insisted on their view that the border ran along the Chinese side of the two riverbanks rather than along the main navigation channels of the rivers. The CCP leaders accepted this document, but declined to concede that it spelt out the genuine borderlines.

In the meantime the new economic relations between the two countries bred gripes of their own. Stalin's Chinese aid programme was implemented at a distinctly slow pace. By early 1953 the Kremlin had given its final approval to only fifty out of 147 proposed industrial projects and seemed in no hurry to launch even these. This sluggishness contrasted with Stalin's transparent impatience to lay his hands on the natural resources of his Asian ally. We are told that on one occasion he asked his Politburo where China's gold and diamond mines could be found. Ever keen to please, Beria advised him that the PRC contained immense mineral wealth which Mao was hiding from his Soviet patrons. Certainly the dictator is known to have pressed for the extraction of tungsten and molybdenum by the Non-Ferrous Metals joint stock company in Xinjiang as soon as might be. Above all he sought rubber, a substance with many military uses whose production was unfortunately concentrated in Western-ruled territories such as Ceylon and Malaya and subject to the Cold War embargo on the supply of strategic goods to the Soviet camp. At his very first meeting with Mao in December 1949 he had asked, 'Can rubber-bearing trees be grown in southern China?',[54] and on 31 March 1952 his Council of Ministers ordered the Soviet embassy in Peking to reach an agreement with the Chinese government on the production of this 'liquid gold'. The idea was to win Mao's consent for a Soviet team to set up a rubber plantation in a suitably tropical part of southern China such as the Leizhou peninsula of Guangdong Province or the adjacent island of Hainan. More surprisingly, Stalin also sought Mao's permission to set up a cannery in China to turn out tinned pineapple. The old tyrant is said to have developed a personal taste for this foodstuff: possibly he had also spotted an easy way to compensate the Soviet consumer for the eternal shortages of fresh fruit. At any rate he instructed his deputy, Georgi Malenkov, to inform the Chinese of his wishes; and the topic of tinned pineapple was included in the agenda for a forthcoming negotiation with Zhou Enlai.

Much of this sat uneasily with the CCP leadership. The new Chinese rulers could hardly fail to appreciate the contribution made by the early Soviet aid teams: between 1949 and 1952, to take just one example, Soviet engineers in Manchuria are said to have increased China's total coal production by 60 per cent. But they were keenly aware that the overall aid that reached them was less than they had been led to expect. There were complaints at the large-scale shipments of food to the Soviet Union that were found essential to pay for the aid projects: Zhou is said to have remarked to his intimates that Chinese trade with Russia 'boils down to our selling agricultural products to buy machines'.[55] Some resentment was also expressed that China should be obliged to pay anything whatever for the rebuilding of Manchurian industry, given the quantity of machines and equipment the Soviet Red Army had removed from the region in 1945–6. As for Stalin's requests for a rubber plantation and pineapple cannery, these were seen as frankly colonial projects. The CCP wanted foreign trade but not foreign investment, least of all at a time when they were moving gradually to close down the huge number of Western-owned factories on their soil. Mao and Zhou counter-proposed an arrangement that would leave control of the projects in Chinese hands. The Soviet Union would provide China with the appropriate start-up loans: the Chinese would set up the projects themselves and would pay back the loans out of the finished produce. Stalin is said to have 'cursed and fumed'.[56]

Other stresses emerged at the grass-roots level. Soviet experts arriving in China in the early 1950s are said often to have been irked by the secretiveness of their Chinese hosts. They complained that they found themselves barred from solid or creative work in the departments to which they had been seconded, and were instead allotted routine tasks. Some of these Russians appear in addition to have had the same trouble adapting to their new environment as their forbears in the Orthodox Mission of the early eighteenth century. They were reported to have got drunk, to have failed to show up for work and even to have attracted the attention of the Chinese police. In January 1951 the Soviet authorities themselves carried out an investigation of 466 specialists who had been deployed in China by their air force. Eighty-two of these men were sent home for drunkenness and 'immoral behaviour'. The Soviet chief investigator, a Colonel Rogov, observed that 'sending workers abroad without their families creates an inclination towards moral decay'.[57] The Chinese for their part praised their Soviet helpers for their experience and their advanced technology, and for generating a whole new atmosphere. But they too had complaints about secretiveness. In the joint stock companies of Xinjiang and Manchuria, for example, the Russians were said to be keeping the technologies they were applying out of reach of the attendant Chinese technicians. At the People's University set up to train the New China's officials trainees reported that some of their Soviet instructors had 'very strong personalities', 'insisted on their own opinions' and were 'hard to reason with'.[58] Sometimes Russian experts appear to have given offence while acting with the best of intentions. In 1951 in the course of a tour of the new PRC the Soviet journalist and novelist Ilya Ehrenburg called in at a factory where machine tools were being installed. It turned out these machine tools had been designed for Russian operators, who were on the whole somewhat taller than their Chinese counterparts, and the Soviet engineers duly busied themselves putting platforms up for the Chinese to stand on. The Chinese started laughing and said they would install the machine tools themselves, which they accomplished without difficulty by digging the machinery into the ground. But the laughter may have indicated embarrassment rather than mirth. Ehrenburg was convinced 'there was something about the platforms they found insulting'.[59]

In spite of these ructions Mao and his followers were obliged to accept the basic reality of Kremlin control. The New China had taken its place side by side with the Eastern European members of the Soviet ideological camp. These members were knit together by the Marxist-Leninist doctrine its leaders all shared; but the Soviet Union interpreted the doctrine, through its high priest Stalin; and the head and the hoof of the Law, and the haunch and the hump was – Obey! During his visit to Moscow in 1949–50 Mao found it judicious to ask Stalin for the help of a Soviet expert on Marxist theory in editing his *Selected Works*. Stalin's choice fell on Pavel Yudin, a 'famous Soviet philosopher' who had made his name by prevailing in an obscure doctrinal squabble with a rival school called the Deborinists whom he had damned as a 'Menshevising ideological deviation'. Yudin was duly installed in a house in Peking, where the Chairman is said to have paid him frequent visits for hours of affable Marxist discussion. The same meekness was still on display in the summer of 1952, when Zhou Enlai came to Moscow at the head of a large Party and government delegation for talks on a wide range of military, political and economic matters. Among other points Stalin made clear that he didn't approve of the CCP's draft of a first Five Year Plan. He declared that the annual growth rate of 20 per cent envisaged by the Chinese leaders was altogether excessive: the Soviet Union at the same stage had contented itself with a growth rate of 18.5 per cent, and a rate between 13 per cent and 15 per cent should be sufficient for China. Towards the end of these conversations an exchange took place:

ZHOU: We would like to receive instructions concerning all these issues.
STALIN: Instructions or suggestions?
ZHOU: From Comrade Stalin's perspective this would be advice, but from our perspective these would be instructions.
STALIN: [modestly]: We know China too little, and that is why we are cautious in giving instructions.[60]

The Kremlin for its part went to some trouble to police the New China's acceptance of Soviet leadership. During the early days of the new dispensation the Soviet programme was greeted with stubborn hostility by what the CCP called 'the survivors from the old society' – the Western-trained, city-dwelling professionals, merchants and academics whose urban habitats had been the last to fall under the sway of Mao's peasant armies. Moscow's representatives sought to keep track of such people. In December 1950, at the end of a trip round the country, Mao's ideological counsellor Pavel Yudin reported the views of 'non-Marxist intellectuals' in the Christian missionary-run universities of Hangzhou and Canton who openly expressed their conviction that 'United States culture is the highest level of culture';[61] while Ambassador Roshchin was briefed about the pro-Western bias that prevailed among artistic, scientific and educational personnel, especially those who had studied in Britain and the United States. During a tour of Soviet factories and collective farms made by a Chinese government delegation in April 1950 a deputy head of the new Department of Industry, a certain Lü Dong, was observed by accompanying Russian security staff to have shown himself 'unfriendly' to the USSR. He had manifested less interest in Soviet machines and machine tools than in the occasional 'old foreign ones' which he had tried to point out to his colleagues. Told that the workers on a collective farm had earned a total of 20,000 to 25,000 roubles in 1949 he had snorted, 'These earnings are extremely small and insignificant.'[62] Why, grumblers wanted to know, did the medicines on sale at the new Soviet Red Cross Hospital in Peking cost more than their US equivalents? Increasing the country's coal production by 60 per cent was all very well, but if Western technology had been applied might not the results have been even better? News of the four joint stock companies in Xinjiang and Manchuria was said to have caused 'tremendous concern' among Peking students alarmed for China's sovereignty,[63] while a sampling of young workers in privately owned shops and factories whose views were canvassed by officials in Shanghai lamented, 'The Soviet Union wants to turn Port Arthur into another Hong Kong!'[64] Stalin inevitably discerned in these anti-Soviet outbursts the hand of his Western geopolitical foes. In September 1952 he warned Zhou Enlai that agents of the United States and Britain would seek to infiltrate the Chinese government apparatus, and in November a draft directive drawn up by the Kremlin for the benefit of the newly appointed ambassador,

Alexander Panyushkin, laid down that while sticking to the promise made by the Soviet Union not to gather intelligence inside the New China the ambassador should nonetheless keep a close eye on the doings of American and British envoys and spies.

Still more demanding of vigilance were the views of the CCP themselves. In an interview with Ambassador Roshchin in October 1951 Mao stated bluntly that 'not everyone in the country, *in fact not all the members of the Party*, agree with our policy of friendship with the Soviet Union.'[65] Activists taking part in a series of CCP-sponsored seminars had raked up a whole series of anti-Russian grievances, from the early Bolshevik takeover of Outer Mongolia to the entrenchment of Soviet influence in the North-East, from the 'unequal treaty' of 1945 to the murky annexes that were smuggled into the new agreement on Valentine's Day. Gripes of this kind reinforced the belief of the Soviet leadership that while they themselves were committed to the goals of the worldwide Communist movement the Chinese Party were suffused with the virus of nationalism. Certainly there was reason to think that perhaps the CCP saw Communism less as an end in itself than a means to the still more exalted goal of a Chinese resurgence. On 18 August 1952, in a talk with Andrei Vyshinsky, Stalin's fearsome public prosecutor now serving a stint as the minister of foreign affairs, Zhou Enlai noted that in their thirty-year struggle for *national liberation* Marxism-Leninism and the 'scientific' prescriptions of Stalin had been the Chinese people's most powerful *tool*.[66] There were also certain indications even at this early date that Moscow's new Chinese pupils might not be submissive for long. At the Central Party School some trainees impishly asked their Soviet instructors why so little mention was made in Stalin's historical *Short Course* of the great leader's rivals, Trotsky and Bukharin. (The response was a harsh put-down: 'There is no need to know about those men.'[67]) The young workers surveyed in Shanghai made it clear that they didn't subscribe to the concept of the Soviet Union as the PRC's 'Elder Brother', and in 1951 one young man in Peking informed Ilya Ehrenburg, 'Soon we will outstrip Elder Brother in the building of Communist society.'[68] In the light of these tendencies the Soviet leaders directed their incoming envoy Panyushkin to monitor, in addition to the intrigues of the West, the Chinese Party's fulfilment of the political obligations they had incurred under the Valentine's Day Treaty and the economic obligations they had assumed in connection with the joint stock companies. In January 1953 Mao discovered that Stalin had bugged not merely the dacha where he had stayed outside Moscow but even his bedroom and other apartments in the Chinese leadership compound, the Zhongnanhai. Soviet technicians working for the KGB had installed the devices at the end of 1950 in a clear violation of the promise the Kremlin had made to desist from espionage within the new Chinese state.

This is not to say Stalin had no Chinese friends. Mao's deputy, Vice-chairman Liu Shaoqi, continued to show unbridled enthusiasm for the Soviet political and economic construct. Swiftly appointed chairman of the new Sino-Soviet Friendship Association, he had proclaimed in an opening address to that body on 5 October 1949, 'The path already traversed by the Soviet people is exactly the path we should take.'[69] Unlike Mao he was friendly towards Ambassador Roshchin, holding many talks with him and even confiding to him on one occasion in 1950 that Mao's Rectification Campaign in Yan'an had been a 'perversion which cost a great number of victims'.[70] Still displaying the knowledge of the Russian language which he had acquired as a student in the early 1920s, he referred in a speech at the opening of the People's University to the presence in its prospectus of 'some Russian nouns which in my opinion have not been translated correctly',[71] and was a frequent visitor to the Soviet Union where he talked at great length while repeatedly puffing on Russian cigarettes. As the years passed he was foremost in pressing for an increase in the number of Soviet specialists sent to China: in September 1952 he told the Russian chargé d'affaires in Peking that the CCP were placing immense hopes on Soviet aid, and in February 1953 he urged on the newly arrived Ambassador Panyushkin the need for the Kremlin leaders to speed up their study of China's request for help with its first Five Year Plan. More flamboyant in his parade of allegiance to Moscow was Gao Gang, the North-Eastern Party boss who had earned the sobriquet of 'King of Manchuria'. When Mao and his suite passed through Gao's domains on their train trip to Moscow in December 1949 they found the towns plastered with portraits of Stalin – and none of the Chairman himself. As the head of one of the six Regional Bureaux into which the New China had been divided, Gao continued to foster his own direct contacts with Russian officials in Manchuria, Korea and the Soviet Far East. His objective was not, seemingly, to intrigue against Mao, but to win the support of the Russians for an eventual bid to replace his hated rival,

Liu, as Mao's heir apparent. In May 1951 he told Andrei Ledovsky, the Soviet consul-general in Shenyang, that he had to be careful in his dealings with Russian representatives as he 'wasn't encouraged to mix with them',[72] and in May 1952 he complained to Ledovsky that Liu and other opponents were seeking to evict him from his Manchurian power base. Ledovsky and his colleagues thought highly of Gao as a pro-Russian personage, and the young diplomat Mikhail Kapitsa perceived him as being 'genuinely loyal to the Soviet Union'.[73]

There seems little doubt Stalin was sifting through his Chinese sympathisers for a leader who might be pushed forward as an alternative to the refractory Mao. In September 1952, still apparently mindful of the deferential terms Liu had used during his visit to Moscow three summers before, he approved a request the vice-chairman had made to be allowed to meet the heads of other Asian Communist Parties during the forthcoming Nineteenth Congress of the Communist Party of the Soviet Union (CPSU): '*Older brothers cannot refuse their younger brother in such a matter*'.[74] And at the congress itself he accorded Liu a series of favours which astounded Liu's retinue and contrasted sharply with his cavalier treatment of Mao in 1949–50. On 9 October *Pravda* published a speech Liu had made at the congress, labelling him in large type as the 'General Secretary' of the CCP, a position the Russians well knew the CCP didn't have but which strongly implied that Liu rather than Mao was his Party's paramount leader: Liu had to issue a hasty disclaimer to the effect that he wasn't a 'General Secretary' and that the Chinese Party were united behind their Chairman. After the congress was over Stalin even rang Liu for a personal chat during which he disclosed how exhausted he felt; and he kept the vice-chairman in the Soviet Union for a further two months, sending him to the Black Sea for a holiday and convening him and his aides to receive some advice about China's economic reforms. Gao Gang was by contrast judged to be expendable, and indeed the Soviet leader discarded him right at the start. In late January 1950, at one of the talks which were held during Mao's stay in Moscow, he shopped Gao to the Chairman in exactly the way he had shopped Sun Fo to Chiang Kai-shek in the summer of 1945 – as a gesture designed to elicit a few extra scraps of goodwill from a difficult opposite number. He supplied Mao with a secret report put together by Kovalev of the intelligence Gao had fed to his Soviet contacts regarding the anti-Soviet, pro-American and Trotskyite tendencies at the top of the CCP. The difference was that Liu, as the second in command of the Central People's Government, was a distinctly more valuable piece on the chessboard than Gao the regional boss. He was also amenable to Stalin's views on the need for the CCP to move forward gradually, to be slow and discreet in dismantling the power of the urban middle class and the wealthier peasants and not to go racing ahead to collectivise agriculture. 'Your ideas are correct', Stalin told him.[75] Gao on the other hand had aligned himself with Mao's more radical leanings, and had even advocated the eviction to the countryside of the entire population of Shanghai – a policy of de-gutting the cities that was horrifically implemented twenty years later by the Khmer Rouge in Cambodia. Following Stalin's tip-off Gao was in due course prised out of his Manchurian fiefdom. In November 1952 he was recalled to Peking to head the CCP's new State Planning Commission: a promotion in name, as he ruefully commented, a demotion in fact. But Mao didn't dare strike at this one-time Soviet protégé while Stalin still lived.

One other senior figure of apparent interest to Stalin was Peng Dehuai, the commander-in-chief of the PRC's 'volunteers' in Korea who travelled to Moscow as part of the big Chinese delegation in the late summer of 1952. At one point during this visit the Soviet leader drew Peng aside for a tête-à-tête out of earshot of Zhou Enlai and the rest of the delegation. Peng subsequently explained that the talk had dwelt on the innocuous topic of Western prisoners of war; but the Chairman in Peking is said to have been incandescent.

PRESSING THE RESET BUTTON (1953–6)

On 5 March 1953 the Soviet personage who had loomed over China for a whole generation was carried off by a stroke. Stalin's death was followed by a three-way succession struggle among his intimates, Beria, Malenkov and Nikita Khrushchev. Whichever of these men won out would in all probability have made changes in Stalin's approach towards China, just as all three of them showed signs of changing the dead boss's policies in other areas: at all events, it was Khrushchev who won and Khrushchev who emerged as the agent of change. Impulsive where Stalin was wary, open-handed where Stalin was stingy, the new Soviet leader seems genuinely to have wished to return to the first, fine, careless rapture of the Soviet mission to China in the 1920s, before the relationship became overwhelmed by his predecessor's relentless pursuit of strategic gain. 'We will be like brothers with the Chinese', he declared. 'If it comes to that, we will divide in half our last piece of bread.'[76] Already in 1953 as a gesture to Mao he appointed the Chairman's ideological crony Pavel Yudin ambassador to Peking in place of Panyushkin, like Roshchin a diplomatic retread from Nationalist times. And in the autumn of 1954, his position now strengthened following the arrest and execution of Beria and the sidelining of Malenkov, he arrived in Peking at the head of a top-level delegation to celebrate the fifth anniversary of the PRC and to promote 'the establishment of closer and more trusting relations'.[77] At a series of meetings in early October he cancelled the secret annexe to the Valentine's Day Treaty that had enshrined Soviet spheres of influence in Xinjiang and the North-East by barring the entry of all other foreigners to these borderland regions. Deploring the fact that 'for centuries the French, English and Americans had been exploiting China, and now the Soviet Union was moving in',[78] he arranged for the liquidation as from 1 January 1955 of the Sino-Soviet joint stock companies in Xinjiang and Dalian, with all the Soviet Union's shares in these enterprises to be transferred to the Chinese government. 'Fully agreeing' that Port Arthur was Chinese territory,[79] he arranged for the naval base to be handed over to China by the end of May, and for the facilities Russia had built there to be given up simultaneously without any claim for compensation. As a confidence-building step he provided a list of all the KGB's secret agents in China, who were rapidly and predictably removed from the scene.

Above all Khrushchev shovelled in aid. This wasn't an easy about-turn to sell to his colleagues. Most of the Moscow Politburo were opposed to large hand-outs: Marshal Voroshilov, the minister of defence, complained not unreasonably, 'After the terrible anti-Fascist war, when the shell holes are still all around us, our people are not equal to this kind of major undertaking in China.'[80] Nonetheless the new boss got his way. As early as May 1953 the post-Stalin leadership signed an agreement with a PRC economic team for the construction of ninety-one new projects on top of the fifty which had already received the Kremlin's approval. During his stay in Peking in the autumn of 1954 Khrushchev added another fifteen projects, making a total of 156, and underpinned the whole programme with a new long-term credit of US$130 million plus US$100 million to finance the delivery of extra construction equipment. Thousands more Soviet technicians were sent out to China to help implement the country's 1953–7 First Five Year Plan, and the total number of secondments would climb to 10,000 by the last years of the decade. Still focused on the heavy industrial sector, Soviet-aided projects now stretched well beyond Manchuria to cover the entire northern half of the PRC. One list compiled by a Soviet source for the years of the Plan records twenty-six metal processing factories, twenty-five hydroelectric and other electrical power installations and seventeen ferrous and non-ferrous metallurgical works along with twelve coal and seven chemical plants and a single petroleum venture. Among the most celebrated Soviet achievements were the Anshan Iron and Steel Company, whose key components became operational in December 1953; the Wuhan Iron and Steel Company, brainchild of the Leningrad Design Institute, which went into production in 1956; the Changchun No. 1 Automobile Factory, also 1956, modelled on the Stalin Automobile Factory in Moscow; and the 1,670-metre, double-decker Great Yangtze Bridge at Wuhan, the creation of a Soviet engineer named Konstantin Silin. (Times had certainly changed since the seventeenth-century Tsar Alexei had petitioned the Qing court to supply him with Chinese bridge builders.) Russian, PRC and Western sources agree that the Soviet Union supplied in these years nothing less than the backbone of modern Chinese industry. Much of the Soviet help came in manufacturing areas quite new to China, from aircraft and lorries to mining equipment, radios, aluminium and synthetic rubber; and the Russians no longer seemed chary of sharing their knowledge. In December 1954 Khrushchev decided to furnish the Chinese at no cost with an eventual total of 1,400 technical blueprints for major industrial enterprises and 24,000 sets of scientific and technical documents. It was, quite simply, in the words of one Western authority, 'the biggest technology transfer in history'.[81]

In the framework of this revived aid programme military equipment was dispensed to the Chinese as never before. Khrushchev recalled in later years that 'virtually our entire defence industry had been at their disposal'.[82] Forty-four of the 156 projects earmarked for completion under the First Five Year Plan were defence-related. In August 1955 the Soviet government notified their Chinese counterparts of their readiness to help build fifteen new defence enterprises, and in 1955–6 the PLA was progressively modernised through the provision of up-to-date Soviet weapons including MiG-17, MiG-19 and MiG-21 fighter aircraft, Mil Mi-4 helicopters and a whole assortment of air-to-air, air-to-ground, ground-to-ground and ship-to-ground missiles. Light as well as heavy industry received a modicum of attention with the completion of a textile mill, a paper mill and a couple of food-processing plants. Even agriculture got a look-in. In 1954 a Sino-Soviet Friendship Farm was set up in Heilongjiang Province on the Manchurian border with the help of Russian soil experts, and the Russians provided blueprints for the establishment of future Chinese state farms. Finally Soviet architects addressed themselves to the reconstruction of Chinese cities. In the spring of 1953 the CCP published under Soviet guidance the first draft of a General Plan for Peking. The initial idea was to take Stalin's 1935 Great Plan for Moscow and superimpose it comprehensively on the old Ming city grid. In the event this didn't happen; but the old city walls were torn down and replaced by a succession of monumental structures in the classic Stalinist style, some of which are still visible in the Beijing of today. They included the Exhibition Hall of 1954, the Youyi (Friendship) and Minzu (Nationalities) hotels, and a little later the Great Hall of the People, created to host state occasions on the western flank of Tiananmen Square. Shanghai meantime received a Sino-Soviet Friendship Building, which was subsequently transformed into an Industrial Exhibition Centre.

From 1954 too the Soviet Union opened its arms even wider to Chinese trainees. In the mid-1950s, according to one recent study, some 40,000 students were accepted there annually for a higher education, with 2,000 going to Moscow and the remaining 2,000 allotted to other major cities such as Leningrad, Kiev, Odessa and Sverdlovsk.[83] For the first time ordinary Chinese workers were brought in as well to get technical training in the country's larger industrial plants. Over the whole 1950s at least 38,000 Chinese 'technicians and workers' are said to have benefited from this Soviet apprenticeship.

At a more rarefied level the new Kremlin bosses also did their bit to accelerate cultural exchange. Soviet publishing houses poured out translations of Chinese literature, from classical prose and poetry to the recent fiction of twentieth-century authors such as Lu Xun, Mao Dun and Lao She. By the end of the decade this output would reach a total of 976 translated works. Successive delegations of Soviet writers and artists were sent eastwards, like Ilya Ehrenburg in 1951, to make contact with their Chinese counterparts and to celebrate the glories of the PRC's Revolution. A Professor Konstantin Maximov of the Surikov Fine Arts Academy in Moscow who had been attached as consultant to the Peking Central Fine Arts Academy helped to introduce oil painting to China, and Soviet artistes trained the first Chinese ballet troupes.

As a result of these different exertions we begin finally, in the mid-1950s, to find signs of a genuine mutual warmth. In the upper echelons Ivan Arkhipov, who continued to serve as the chief economic adviser to the Chinese government, felt that he and Chen Yun, the principal economic brain in the CCP leadership, 'understood each other and had a common language'.[84] But the most striking indications came from the grass roots. Interviews conducted decades later with former Soviet experts suggest that many of them, like the young Bolshevik missionaries of the 1920s, set out with a real sense of adventure, a fervour to travel and pass on their knowledge to the people of this needy Oriental land. On their arrival in China they were pleasantly surprised by some aspects of their living and working environment. 'The people are poorer than those in Moscow, but the shop windows richer' was one reaction to Wangfujing, the main shopping street in the Chinese capital.[85] A former military aircraft engineer deployed in Shenyang reminisced glowingly about the local government Friendship Store where you could use special coupons to buy consumer goods unavailable in the Soviet Union. Scattered around the vast country, the experts were able to work on their projects free from the minute supervision of their Soviet chiefs: Konstantin Silin, for instance, the builder of the Great Yangtze Bridge at Wuhan, tried out techniques that he hadn't been allowed to attempt back at home. And they took pride in their contributions. Silin's tomb in a Moscow cemetery was adorned on his death, whether on his own instruction or that of his family, with a picture of the Yangtze Bridge; and a Soviet academic in Harbin recalled an upsurge of respect and a sense that he was doing a valuable job. This feeling was accompanied by a widespread esteem for the Chinese tutees. A professor of geography, Alexei Stozhenko, wrote in 1956 of the talent and discipline of his students, of their honesty and politeness not only to their Russian teachers but even to each other, '*The most valuable thing in China is the Chinese themselves*.'[86] One teacher in Moscow was so impressed by the overall grades of his students that he chivvied a slacker who had failed to complete his homework, '*Did you come from China or not?*'[87] One official Soviet report noted how much closer the aid workers were to the ordinary Chinese than the staff of the embassy and other representative bodies who had a tendency to behave in an arrogant manner. There were expressions of general sympathy. Stozhenko castigated his fellow Russians for their 'voracious eating, sleeping in luxury [hotel rooms] and travelling in the international [railway] cars' at the expense of the Chinese state.[88] And there were personal friendships, formed both at the workplace and some way outside it. Already by early 1953 Soviet experts were being allowed to bring their families to China with them, which must have reduced the early incidence of 'moral decay'; but there were still some young Russians who sought out the company of Chinese of the opposite sex. Decorous evening dances were laid on from time to time at the International Club in Peking. Oleg Glazilin, who came to China in 1956 as interpreter for a team of geologists in search of uranium, recalled being 'friendly with this young girl, such a nice girl, and I . . . didn't do anything, didn't even embrace her, we just flirted a little . . .'.[89]

Equal appreciation was voiced by Chinese on the receiving end of the aid programme. In July 1955 Li Fuchun, who had headed the Chinese team at the signing of the big agreement for new projects two summers before, was quoted as saying, 'The main achievement of our economic reconstruction cannot be separated from the assistance of Soviet experts.'[90] Once again, however, it seems to have been at the grass roots that the real warmth was felt. Chinese trainees looked up with classic Confucian deference to their Soviet teachers, whom they perceived as erudite, dedicated and efficient. On the Yangtze Bridge project engineer Silin was remembered as having 'taken part in every aspect of the work, adopted a very pleasant working style and worked very closely with the Chinese comrades' who 'learnt a great deal from him.'[91] Many years later, when the relations between the two governments were in deepest freeze, personnel from the Wuhan Iron and Steel Company were unable to hold back a measure of praise for their former Soviet mentors. There had been, they recounted to an American journalist, only the most trivial friction between them and the Russians, and the relationship had by and large been perfectly good. They had accepted 93 per cent (*sic*) of the Soviet proposals, and the Russians had amicably given way when they vetoed a scheme to turn their main canteen into a bakery, on the grounds that they were eaters of rice, not bread. They had 'grown fond of the Russian experts, and the feeling was reciprocated'.[92] Most of the Chinese students who went to the Soviet Union during these years seem to have had a happy experience.

Sustained by Kremlin stipends, they enjoyed a standard of living superior to both their Soviet classmates and their Chinese contemporaries back at home. One student who arrived in Moscow in August 1954 with a twenty-strong group to attend the school of the Central Communist Youth League thought the staff there 'warm-hearted'. Finding that her charges were partial to peanuts, the Russian-language teacher appeared with a whole consignment one day, 'face wreathed in smiles', and the class interpreter, Valya, 'did what she could to help them with their problems'.[93] They had adequate time for leisure pursuits ranging from roller skating to nature-sketching to opera and music, and (the student noted gleefully) their PE course would include skiing in winter. They also had adequate time for romance.[94]

On the cultural side the successive groups of Soviet writers and artists were enthralled by what they saw, though not perhaps in the way their CCP hosts would most have appreciated. Sent to acclaim the triumphs of the new PRC, they fell head over heels in love with traditional China. In the autumn of 1954, for example, Valentin Ovechkin, a playwright, novelist and leading personality of Khrushchev's cultural 'thaw', found himself 'caressed' by the beauties of old Chinese architecture.[95] In October 1956 Boris Galin, a member of a journalists' group, looked on with fascination as a pair of Chinese lovers exchanged sweet nothings along the Echo Wall of the Temple of Heaven in Peking, murmuring as he moved off, 'Farewell, you old, kind, wonderful Wall!';[96] while his colleague Sergei Zalygin, a hydraulic engineer by training, was 'plunged into a sacred trance' by the jointed ceramic pipes built into the Ming dynasty Drum Tower in Xi'an, and could be torn away from them only with the greatest difficulty.[97] A deputation of painters and sculptors who arrived two months later were entranced by the old quarters of Chinese cities, and sought out as subjects for their work such emblems of continued backwardness as rickshaws and peasants carrying water. This predilection for old things naturally affected the visitors' responses to Chinese art. Already in 1951 Ilya Ehrenburg is said to have 'rediscovered' the great traditional painter Qi Baishi, rescuing him in his eighties from the oblivion in which he had languished since the CCP takeover two years before. The artists who arrived in December 1956 were delighted to encounter old-style Chinese compositions, with mountains, birds and trees being painted 'exactly the same as in classical works',[98] while Galin, Zalygin and their group were charmed by the 'traditional, strictly classical' style of a

Chinese opera they saw performed in Shaanxi Province.[99] Conspicuously lacking from the response of these visitors are celebrations of factory smokestacks or praise for such early manifestations of Chinese cultural radicalism as the 1953–4 campaign to disparage the great eighteenth-century novel *Dream of the Red Chamber*. Like the aid workers these transient intellectuals undoubtedly struck up a rapport with many of their Chinese counterparts. On his departure from China in November 1954 Ovechkin recorded how he and his fellow delegates had made a number of Chinese friends with whom it had now become difficult to part. These friends included certain figures who probably also would not have enjoyed the wholehearted approval of the CCP leadership. Ovechkin singled out for special mention a young Chinese critic and editor, Liu Binyan, already known for his outspokenness, who would emerge decades later as a leading dissident and a thorn in the side of the CCP regime. The Soviet writer concluded that his thoughts and dreams were the same as Liu's, that Liu didn't just 'translate someone else's words' but spoke 'from himself, from his heart, from his convictions'.[100]

The Chinese printing presses were even livelier than the Soviet ones. By December 1956 a total of 2,746 volumes of Russian and Soviet literature are said to have been published in the PRC. To begin with these included a strong pre-1917 component, with some fifty of Tolstoy's works brought out in new translations along with a wide range of novels, stories and poetry by other tsarist-period giants such as Pushkin, Gogol, Turgenev, Nekrasov and Saltykov-Shchedrin. This choice clearly reflected the taste of Chinese intellectuals from the 1920s and 1930s who had so far weathered the change of regime. In 1951 the renowned woman novelist Ding Ling had written,

> Russian literature is probably our favourite. In it we regularly make discoveries about our problems, our fate and our people. We love those Cossacks, Byelorussians, Ukrainians and Tatars; we love those guerrilla fighters with bushy beards; those freckled youths and girls with plaited hair; those old men, cobblers and coach drivers. We have feelings about those little huts in the village, the birch woods, the blizzards and the fine sunny days. We can feel, too, the emotions that are hidden inside the woods, by the fireside or the samovar, or covered with a shawl . . .[101]

As the years passed the forces of political dogmatism were gathering strength, and the great nineteenth-century classics began to lose ground to the products of Socialist Realism. Ostrovsky's Bolshevik novel *How the Steel Was Forged* was held up in the PRC as a 'textbook for life', and in November 1954 Mikhail Sholokhov's *Virgin Soil Upturned* was described as a 'standard text' for Chinese engaged in agrarian reform.[102] In 1955 the novelist and translator Zhou Libo produced *The Molten Iron Rushes Out*, a work written in imitation of a Soviet novel entitled *Cement*, and later that year the journal *China Youth* serialised Galina Nikolaeva's *The Newcomer: The Manager of a Machine Tractor Station and the Chief Agronomist*. Still, tsarist-era or Soviet, there seems no doubt that Russian writing did make a significant impact on the public of the new Chinese state. One small indication of this was the vogue during these years for Chinese boys to be given the name Haiyan, meaning 'petrel' – a tribute to Maxim Gorky, who was celebrated in his homeland as the 'stormy petrel' of the approaching Russian Revolution. Classical Russian culture was also imported in a number of other forms. Sun Weishi, the adopted daughter of Zhou Enlai who had studied drama in Moscow, took part in translating *The Directing Lessons of K.S. Stanislavsky*, and in November 1956 the former Shanghai Conservatory, which White Russian exiles had helped to found in the 1920s, built on that old link by hiring a small team of Soviet conductors and sought permission to employ the wife of one of them, Nina Nikolaeva, as academic director of the opera faculty.

Various other exchanges took place of a more banal kind. Soviet experts in China developed a faith in Chinese medicine, from Tiger Balm ointment for treating headaches and rheumatism to an assortment of herbal remedies supposed to lower the blood pressure, relieve constipation and restore the sexual powers. Their wives made extensive use of acupuncture and took frequent Chinese 'cures', mostly, in the sardonic view of a male compatriot, for imaginary ailments. Chinese women embraced the fashions of their Russian sisters that were publicised in the journal *Women of New China*, cutting their hair short like the girls trained in Moscow in the 1920s, and sporting Lenin-style jackets and one-piece Soviet dresses. Out on the frontier, on Bolshoi Ussuriisky, aka Heixiazi or Black Bear, the large island at the confluence of the Amur and Ussuri rivers which the Soviet Special Far Eastern Army had detached from China in 1929, Russians and Chinese rubbed shoulders in a bazaar which was opened on weekends and holidays. Once again, as in the nineteenth and early twentieth centuries, use was made of a Russian-Chinese pidgin. The Chinese word for 'to eat' (*chifan*) was adapted into both a Russian verb (*chifanit'*) and a Russian noun (*chifan*, meaning 'Chinese restaurant'). And once again there were cases of intermarriage.

These growing signs of a grass-roots convergence were unhappily offset by new strains at the top. With Stalin's passing in 1953 Mao had lost his residual awe of the Kremlin. Khrushchev and his rivals appeared to the Chairman mere juniors, pen-pushers: how could they be compared with him, Mao, leader of a great revolution which had propelled almost a quarter of humanity into the Marxist-Leninist camp? And why anyway should the Soviet Union carry on automatically at the head of that camp? Some of the CCP leaders are said to have stated explicitly to a Soviet interpreter, 'Now that Stalin is dead the leader of the international revolutionary movement is Mao Zedong';[103] and posters appeared in Peking showing the apostolic succession of Marx, Engels, Lenin, Stalin – and Mao. At a banquet thrown for him by the Kremlin leadership at Spiridonovka House in Moscow in July 1954 Mao's right-hand man, Zhou Enlai, behaved in a manner strikingly different from the deference with which he had asked for Stalin's 'instructions' less than two years before. The journalist Harrison Salisbury, who attended the banquet as part of the press corps, remembered,

> When I came upon Zhou he was circling the table of his Russian hosts – Malenkov, Molotov, Bulganin, Khrushchev, Mikoyan, Kaganovich and the others – offering toasts to each. But he was speaking in *English* – a language none of them understood. I thought it strange, and apparently the Russians did too, for when Zhou approached Anastas Mikoyan and offered a toast in English Mikoyan said through an interpreter, 'Why don't you speak in Russian, Zhou? – you know our language perfectly well.' Zhou rejoined saucily, 'Look here, Mikoyan, it's time you learnt to speak Chinese. After all, I have learnt to speak Russian.' Zhou's remarks had to be interpreted for Mikoyan, who sullenly grumbled, 'Chinese is a difficult language to learn.' 'Not harder than Russian', Zhou snapped back. 'Come down to our embassy in the morning. We'll be glad to teach you Chinese.' Kaganovich then intervened with a rude remark in Russian, but Zhou, continuing to speak English, said, '*There's no excuse for you people*.'[104]

From the CCP's angle the Soviet rivals were much of a muchness. Mao had no obvious preference among them, and indeed told his interpreter, Shi Zhe,

'We will support whoever comes out on top.'[105] The salient feature was that they were *weak*. And because they were weak they were suppliants. Jostling for power, they sought the lustre of association with Mao and the endorsement of his massive Party. On 9 March 1953 Malenkov is said to have made an early bid for supremacy by arranging for *Pravda* to carry a photograph of himself with Stalin and Mao at the signing of the Valentine's Day Treaty, carefully cropped to omit all the other Soviet chiefs; and on 3 June 1954, apparently at Malenkov's prompting, the CPSU Central Committee sent a message to Peking asking to consult their Chinese counterparts about 'an important question.'[106] Then in September along came Khrushchev, victorious in the tussle for power but not irreversibly so, prepared to be generous but also keen to secure Chinese backing, descending on Peking like Father Christmas with a sackful of economic and political gifts. Despite Khrushchev's lavish concessions the trip in itself was a fatal mistake, and one Stalin surely would never have made. By coming to Peking instead of waiting for the Chairman to pay him a visit in Moscow the new Soviet boss had cast himself in the role of a tribute bearer arriving to pay homage at the foot of the Dragon Throne, and had thus reinforced Mao's already marked tendency to look down on him. Once in Peking he compounded his error, showering the Chairman with hugs and kisses that seemed shocking to the not very tactile Chinese and struck Mao as a further indication of weakness. Mao emerged with the feeling that Khrushchev was 'a big fool.'[107]

Sensing this new Soviet weakness, the CCP leaders went on to exploit it for all they were worth. During the talks that took place in October 1954 they pushed for still further concessions on top of those Khrushchev had already made. Yet again they brought up the vexed question of the MPR. Zhou Enlai asked brightly, 'What would you think if Mongolia became part of the Chinese state?',[108] while Mao drew attention to the region's long history as an integral part of the Qing domains. Taking his leave of Khrushchev, he is said to have held up a finger of one hand signifying Mongolia Irredenta. In addition the CCP duo sought to expand Moscow's arms package through the inclusion of nothing less than the Bomb. Already following his sojourn in Moscow in 1949–50 Mao had commented to a bodyguard, 'The United States has it, the Soviet Union has it and we can make one too,'[109] and in early 1953 Zhou had tried to arrange for a team of Chinese nuclear scientists to be admitted to Russian research institutes. Now, invited by Khrushchev to say what help China would like besides economic, Mao answered, 'We're interested in atomic energy and nuclear weapons . . . If you aren't willing to share these kinds of weapons with us it will be enough if you provide us with the technology to make an atomic bomb.'[110]

In the meantime the Chairman began in one way and another to edge China quietly out from the Soviet shadow. Stalin's body was barely cold before he was once again moving to crush the principal Russophiles at the top of his Party. During the first few days after the death of the old dictator in March 1953 he took a series of steps seemingly designed to ensure that his deputy, Liu Shaoqi, couldn't make the transition from Stalin's favourite Chinese leader to the favourite Chinese leader of Stalin's heirs. Liu as it happened was currently in hospital having his appendix removed, and Mao took advantage of this coincidence to keep him immobilised and prevent him from getting news of the Master's decease. When Liu finally emerged from confinement the Chairman is said to have denied him permission to call on the Soviet embassy, to have excluded him from the memorial gathering at Tiananmen and to have kept his name off the list of condolences from the CCP leadership that was published in the Party organ, the *People's Daily*. Over the following months he continued to go after Liu, making preparations for a closed-door Party conference on financial and economic policy that would 'unmask' the vice-chairman and his 'rightist' allies. Though the issues to be discussed at this forum were strictly domestic there was nonetheless an anti-Soviet subtext in that Mao still hankered after a rapid plunge into socialism whereas Liu and his allies continued to follow the slow and steady approach prescribed by the Kremlin. To chair the conference Mao chose none other than Liu's deadly enemy Gao Gang, the chairman of the new State Planning Commission, whose own enthusiasm for Moscow was offset by his ardent support for Mao's radical economic ideas. During the sessions, which started in mid-June, Gao lashed out viciously at the assembled 'rightists'. Much of his venom was directed at Bo Yibo, the minister of finance, who had introduced a new tax held to be excessively favourable to the private sector; but the ultimate target was Liu and his alleged desire to perpetuate the pre-socialist order. The sword of Damocles hung over Liu's head.

At this point, however, the unexpected occurred. In July, in response to an anxious letter from Zhou Enlai, himself currently getting tarred with the same 'rightist' brush, the Chairman expressed his rejection of 'innuendo' and 'covert hints'.[111] On 12 August he brought the conference to an end, proclaiming it a success and commending Liu and his backers for having 'acknowledged some mistakes'.[112] The anti-Liu drive was over. What precisely had happened remains unclear. Perhaps Mao felt he had made his point and sufficiently cowed the Soviet-leaning 'rightists'. Perhaps Liu was too senior and well respected for Mao to feel able to purge him – for the moment, at least. And perhaps too Mao was following Stalin's classic playbook of the 1920s and 1930s, setting one group of victims on another before swivelling round to destroy them as well. For at this point he turned his attention to Gao. Already on 9 August, at a meeting of the Politburo, he is said to have criticised Gao explicitly for his zeal in the anti-'rightist' campaign. Gao seems to have had for some weeks an uneasy sense that 'the clouds were gathering around him';[113] but he disregarded Mao's strictures and instead doubled down on his radical stance. Right through the autumn he kept up his feud with the 'rightists', claiming the encouragement of both Mao and the Kremlin, canvassing the support of other Party leaders (who passed the word to the Chairman) and divvying up with a confederate the senior posts he expected to fall to them once Liu and his allies had been removed. In December Mao finally pounced. At a Politburo meeting he noted that there were now two separate headquarters in Peking. The first was his own. The second, operating clandestinely, had '*stirred up a sinister wind and lit a sinister fire*'.[114] And he accused Gao of 'splittist activity' as his former acolyte sat 'red as a lobster' before him.[115] On 5 February 1954, at another closed-door Party gathering, it was Gao's turn to face the judges and Liu's turn to prosecute. The vice-chairman castigated his enemy in true Stalinist style, likening him to historical villains such as Trotsky and Bukharin; but the full-blooded indictment followed two weeks later in the report of a Special Commission headed by Zhou. No attempt was now made to disguise the fact that the principal crime being tried was collusion with the USSR. Gao was condemned as a 'traitor to the motherland'.[116] The indictment harked back to the 'independent kingdom' he had carved out in Manchuria; to the way he had curried favour with the 'Elder Brothers' at the expense of China's national interests; to the portraits of Stalin he had displayed in Manchurian cities where Mao's should have hung; to the outrageous proposal he was said to have made in Moscow for the transfer of Manchuria to the Soviet Union as the newest SSR; to the secret briefings he had given to Stalin's envoy Kovalev slandering Liu and Zhou and assailing the Chairman himself for his 'anti-Soviet' and 'right Trotskyite' tendencies. Even Gao's private life was found to have had a Russian dimension. The Chairman described him as a 'sordid individual', whose sexual escapades had involved 'enemy elements' in the form of a bevy of White Russian women. The former 'King of Manchuria' quickly broke down in the face of this barrage. On 17 February, while Zhou's commission were still gathering evidence against him, he tried to shoot himself only to be prevented by one of his bodyguards. Six months later he finished himself off successfully by taking an overdose. Looking back on the episode in March 1955 Mao reflected, 'What predominant bright side is there in Gao Gang's case? There is darkness through and through, a mass of murkiness which neither moonlight nor sunlight can penetrate.'[117]

Some explanation had naturally to be given to the Elder Brothers for this first disgrace of a CCP leader since the New China was formed. In January 1954 Ambassador Yudin called on Mao at his holiday retreat in Hangzhou to apprise him of the execution in Moscow of Lavrenty Beria. Mao deftly seized the chance to account for Gao's purge as a 'similar problem' which had arisen in the upper ranks of the CCP. Even so there was no escaping the central message of Gao's fall: the Chairman would no longer tolerate any Soviet meddling in the Chinese Party's internal affairs. Following Gao's disgrace orders were issued that any information passed recently by anyone to a Soviet official should be reported and that all further dealings with the Soviet Union should be channelled through the CCP's Central Committee. The six Regional Bureaux into which the PRC had been divided for political and military purposes five years before were abolished and replaced by a tight, highly centralised administrative structure. There would be no more 'Kings of Manchuria'.

The CCP meanwhile took advantage of Soviet weakness to further China's numerous borderland claims. In 1954 a *Short History of Modern China* that appeared in the name of a certain Liu Peihua carried maps showing as Chinese territory the maximum extent of the old Qing empire, including Outer Mongolia, the Amur-Ussuri region and the Soviet Maritime Province, the North Pacific island of Sakhalin and the Soviet Republic of Kazakhstan. During the following year, even as Mao held up a finger to Khrushchev to register his continuing claim to the MPR, Peking sought to win the goodwill of the MPR public through a plan to build a mausoleum for Genghis Khan on the frontier between Inner and Outer Mongolia. In 1955 this gambit was followed up by the PRC's first venture as a foreign aid donor: 10,000 Chinese labourers were to be sent to the MPR to help in construction projects and factories. Over in Xinjiang fresh efforts were made to cement that recalcitrant province to the Chinese heartland and to erase the last traces of the Soviet presence there. In 1954 Mao arranged the formation and dispatch to the province of a Xinjiang Production and Construction Corps. Made up of demobilised Chinese soldiers, this body was intended partly to engage in farming and make the desert bloom, and indeed received a good deal of instruction and material help from the Russians for that very purpose. Another part of its duty, however, was to 'defend the borders of the motherland', and the soldiers were ordered to keep their guns to fend off potential incursions which logically could only come from the Soviet-ruled territories next door. The Corps was also required to 'envelop' the border towns where Soviet influence had been at its strongest. In November 1954 a 'Yili Kazakh Autonomous Prefecture' was created in the old Three Districts as a sign of the final establishment of Chinese authority over that Russified area. As the Prefecture's title suggests an attempt was made to present the substitution of Chinese for Soviet control as a form of emancipation for the local Turkic majority, and in October 1955 the province as a whole was renamed the Xinjiang Uighur Autonomous Region.

Other moves were designed to shape a new, independent diplomacy for the PRC on the broader world stage. As the Kremlin's self-confidence faltered Mao and his colleagues began once again to eye up their long-time alternative option – the West. In April 1953, just one month after Stalin's death, the CCP's Central Committee observed, 'Learning from the advanced science and technology of the Soviet Union does not exclude the possibility of absorbing certain things from the technology of the capitalist countries that are good and useful to us';[118] and by 1954 the Chinese were putting out recognisable feelers. Early that year Foreign Ministry officials accepted to widespread surprise an invitation from the British chargé d'affaires to watch a film of the recent coronation of Queen Elizabeth II. In the spring, at the conference held in Geneva to settle a number of issues arising from the Korean War and the Vietnamese insurrection against the French, Zhou

Enlai offered both to return the remaining US prisoners captured in Korea and to sort out various other obstacles to détente with America, only to have his way blocked by the implacable hostility of John Foster Dulles, the US secretary of state. Zhou's bizarre goading of his Soviet hosts at Spiridonovka House in July begins to make sense if we bear in mind that while the Kremlin leaders didn't understand English there were others present who did – members of the foreign press corps and an assortment of diplomats from the United Kingdom, Sweden and elsewhere. Zhou's show of disrespect was quite clearly put on for the benefit of the Western powers. Any interest in a breakthrough with the United States then apparently vanished with the orchestration that autumn of the 'First Taiwan Straits Crisis', when Mao, possibly without warning his Soviet mentors, courted Washington's fury by launching a months-long bombardment of Quemoy and Matsu, two Nationalist-held islands off the coast of Fujian Province. Some scholars have seen the 'crisis' as a ploy on the Chairman's part to step up the pressure on Khrushchev to supply the PRC with atomic weapons, on the grounds that this would be more palatable to the Russians than getting dragged into a head-to-head confrontation with the United States. By April 1955, however, Mao again seemed to show signs of hankering after his Western alternative. In a chat with his newly appointed physician, the United States-educated Dr Li Zhisui, he remarked,

> I like having American- or British-trained people working for me. I am interested in foreign languages. Some people think that I should learn Russian but I don't want to. I'd rather learn English. You can teach me.[119]

The following August brought with it the start of discussions on matters of mutual concern which were held in Warsaw between 'ambassadors' of China and the United States. The talks achieved little but carried on in a desultory way right up to 1970. In the meantime the PRC started exploring a wholly new role, as a leader of what would soon be known as the Third World. In June 1954, on his way back from Geneva, the ubiquitous Zhou went to India, where he proclaimed with Prime Minister Nehru 'Five Principles of Peaceful Coexistence' based on the sturdily nationalistic concepts of equality between countries and non-interference in each other's internal affairs; and in April 1955 he dazzled the first conference of 'non-aligned' Asian and African states in Bandung, Indonesia – a conference to which the Soviet Union had not been invited on the grounds that it was a European power. In counterpoint to these manoeuvres the Chinese declined certain efforts by Khrushchev to integrate them more into the Soviet camp. In October 1954 Mao turned down a proposal that the PRC should join the Soviet-East European economic community, and in May 1955 he resisted a push to enlist China in the newly organised Warsaw Pact.

Finally the Chairman ventured into a first open break with the Kremlin's doctrinal prescriptions. Early in 1955 he embarked on a rapid and forcible collectivisation of Chinese agriculture. This campaign flew in the face of the constant reminders from Soviet sources that China should proceed gradually and avoid reproducing their own past mistakes. 'So what?' Mao told Dr Li in his usual scatological manner: 'When I say "Learn from the Soviet Union" we don't have to learn to piss and shit from the Soviet Union too, do we?'[120] In July he acknowledged the 'impetuosity and rashness' of Stalin's collectivisation, which had led to the hideous Ukrainian famine. But that didn't mean China should move 'at a snail's pace': rather, 'our cooperatives must be better than those of the Soviets'.[121] In a talk on 21 December he enlarged on this suggestion that the Chinese might actually outperform their Soviet tutors, inquiring, 'What is the most suitable figure for the total number of cooperatives in the countryside – 300,000, 400,000 or 500,000? The figure is over 100,000 in the Soviet Union: would over 300,000 or 400,000 be more suitable for us?'[122]

Over the first year or two Stalin's heirs showed themselves surprisingly willing to accommodate the new Chinese pretensions. In March 1953 Zhou Enlai was accorded the honour of being the sole foreign pall-bearer at the Supreme Master's funeral, escorting the cortège side by side with Beria and Malenkov. Mao's wife Jiang Qing, who happened to be in Moscow for medical treatment, was admitted to the Hall of Columns in the Kremlin and allowed to stand guard by the bier. In 1955 even Stalin's rhinoceros-like former foreign minister Molotov is said to have referred to China as the 'co-leader' of the socialist camp.[123] During the Peking negotiations that autumn the Soviet team proved to be uncoordinated and at times even malleable in their reaction to Chinese demands. At the PRC's National Day celebration on 1 October Khrushchev's bearded sidekick Bulganin is said to have muttered to the Chinese interpreter Shi Zhe that so far as he had been able to see from the air Outer Mongolia was a barren wasteland and it would be better for the

Russians to let China have it back. Mao triumphantly seized on this comment, and it was left to Khrushchev to restate the old Soviet line that the status of the MPR was non-negotiable and to snap at Bulganin, 'All because you chatter too much!'[124] Khrushchev's initial reaction to Mao's request for atomic bombs was one of bewilderment. 'What do you want with such weapons?', he asked. 'So long as we have them we can use them to protect China at any time.'[125] A nuclear weapons programme would consume huge amounts of both money and electricity, and the PRC should instead focus on economic construction. By the end of the talks, however, he had given ground so far as to promise to help China set up a small-scale nuclear reactor for research into the peaceful use of atomic energy: in April 1955 the appropriate protocol was concluded, and in March 1956 the Soviet Union and China unveiled a Joint Institute for Nuclear Research in the small town of Dubna near Moscow. Khrushchev even made a show of knowing the CCP's necessities before they asked them. To relieve unemployment in the PRC he proposed to import a large number of Chinese seasonal labourers to fell timber in Siberia and the Soviet Far East. Mao was initially leery, remembering the demeaning coolie traffic of colonial times, but subsequently came round; and in 1955 Mikoyan went to Peking to finalise an agreement for a first batch of 200,000 woodcutters, with a total of 3 million expected to follow over the next several years.

As the months passed though, and Soviet leaders began to perceive the immensity of Mao's ambitions, a deepening apprehension began to set in. Possibly the first shock was the CCP's purge of Gao Gang in February 1954. Gao's close friend, the diplomat Andrei Ledovsky, recalled being 'filled with dismay and anger' at this development.[126] Doubtless thinking of Gao, Khrushchev noted how Mao 'treated the people around him like pieces of furniture, useful for the time being but expendable',[127] and the Kremlin bosses in general are said to have viewed Gao's removal as an act of vindictiveness directed at them. The account in Khrushchev's memoirs of the October talks in Peking seethes with mistrust. Written years later in the light of huge political changes, these memoirs must of course be treated with caution; but it does look as though Khrushchev felt at least a kind of peasant discomfort with the ultra-civilised ways of the East:

> Everyone was unbelievably courteous and ingratiating, but I saw through their hypocrisy. It was all too sickeningly sweet. The atmosphere was

> nauseating . . . I remember, for instance, that the Chinese served tea every time we turned round – tea, tea, tea![128]

Under the impact of Mao's requests for Mongolia and nuclear weapons, he warned his colleagues in Moscow, '*Conflict with China is inevitable*.'[129] The CCP's tentative steps towards an independent foreign policy caused unease in the Kremlin whatever form they took. In the winter of 1954–5, for example, the Soviet leaders were unsettled by Mao's first military adventure in the Taiwan Straits, describing the Chinese as 'too trigger-happy' and comparing their regime to 'an intractable wild horse'.[130] Khrushchev is said to have gone so far as to hint that the nuclear umbrella he had offered to hold over China would not extend to the Taiwan area in the event of a Sino-American clash. Almost as worrying were the sporadic Chinese flirtations with the West, and especially the opening of 'ambassadorial' talks with the United States in Warsaw: the Russians are said at one point to have prodded their Polish vassals to bug the negotiating venue order to find out what was going on. The Kremlin leaders looked on with dismay as their influence carried on being squeezed from Xinjiang, and as Mao jumped the Marxist-Leninist gun by creating his rural cooperatives against their persistent advice. Still more drastic concerns were expressed by the Soviet China Hands whose ears were closest to the ground. Some of these Sinologists sought to draw their leaders' attention to the 'cartographical aggression' in Liu Peihua's history book, only to be told reprovingly that no territorial question existed between the two Communist powers. 'The higher the positions they occupied', the Sinologists grumbled, 'the more deeply they buried their heads in the sand.'[131] Foreign Ministry staff were appalled by Khrushchev's project to import Chinese labour, which reawakened all the Yellow Peril anxieties of late tsarist times. The proposed 3 million lumberjacks, they maintained, would inevitably settle in Soviet territory and intermarry with Soviet women; and in twenty years the Soviet Union would find its population augmented by 20 million Chinese or half-Chinese. Hag-ridden by this combination of strategic, demographic and ideological terrors, Khrushchev was by 1955 reaching out for the sympathy of his supposed adversaries in the West. Harold Macmillan, then British foreign secretary, recalled how at a conference of the former wartime Allies which took place in Geneva in June of that year 'the Russian leaders had not disguised from us in their private talks the drain on their resources which the Chinese connection involved and their concern about the future.'[132] In September, when the West German chancellor Dr Konrad Adenauer paid a visit to Moscow, Khrushchev asked him repeatedly 'to help us deal with the New China'. 'You imagine', he urged, 'China now has a population of some 600 million. Every year it will increase by a further 12 million. These people will all have to live off a handful of rice.' He told Adenauer that the Soviet Union faced two enemies, the United States and China; but the greater of these was China.[133]

These growing tensions between the elites had a chilling effect on the grass roots as well. Despite the mingling reported in the frontier market on Bolshoi Ussuriisky/Heixiazi Island the Soviet–Chinese border remained fundamentally closed. Every time, we are told, that a resident of the Soviet Far East wanted to visit China the trip had to be registered and coordinated through Moscow. Travelling to Eastern Siberia on a journalistic assignment in 1954 Harrison Salisbury had the impression of a garrison state, with military concentrations in Chita, Khabarovsk and all the other cities along the route. The number of troops was enormous, and the border with China appeared to be guarded 'as vigilantly as the demarcation line in Berlin'.[134] Russian aid workers in China soon found that the scope for fraternisation had definite limits. Oleg Glazilin, interpreter for the geologists' mission, recalled,

> We were all the same, well, they were Communists and we were Communists, for God's sake. But we were also conscious of some sort of estrangement, as if some kind of wall stood between us, transparent, invisible, but some kind of wall.[135]

So far as the CCP were concerned the name of the game was to minimise informal contact between the Russian experts and the local people they came to serve. In May 1954 the State Council issued a decree forbidding all Chinese other than the 'foreign affairs departments' of official bodies to meet Soviet experts except on business. Soviet specialists were confined to their hotels and hotel restaurants; their smallest activities were monitored, their suitcases searched. 'The Chinese', Glazilin reported, 'treated us honestly, but among the regular people there were always Party leaders, who smiled on the outside but with eyes that were cold.'[136] Officials of both countries did everything in their power to discourage romance. The Chinese girl with whom Glazilin had enjoyed a mild flirtation was 'worked over' by her superiors 'until she cried'.[137] At one of the dances in the International Club a newly arrived Russian chemistry teacher fell head over heels in love with his Chinese partner. He sent his beloved a series of 'agitated declarations', which the girl passed on to her bosses and the bosses in turn passed on to the Cultural Group of the Soviet embassy. The Cultural Group had the teacher in for a 'fatherly talk', which however failed to 'extinguish the flames of passion'; and the unfortunate teacher was packed off home.[138] On another occasion Chinese martinets passed on gossip to a Soviet embassy counsellor, who proceeded to grill some interpreters for 'improper behaviour' with Chinese girls.[139] Unmarried experts were solemnly warned by the staff at the embassy of the 'dangerously artful' Chinese women.[140] The CCP were equally bent on stopping the students they sent to the Soviet Union from sowing wild oats in the way their precursors had done in the 1920s. Students were told by their minders, 'It's best not to fall in love and get married while studying',[141] and thousands of young Chinese men are said to have had to return to the motherland leaving their Russian girlfriends behind. The Moscow authorities seem to have been rather more easy-going, and now and again couples slipped through the net. One professor from Peking University succeeded both in marrying a Soviet woman and bringing her back to China; and a student of mechanical engineering who had fallen for the daughter of a high-ranking Soviet intelligence officer was allowed to remain at her side – on condition that he undertook to do his bit for the KGB. But the course of true love very rarely ran smooth.

A TURN OF THE TIDE (1956–60)

On 24 February 1956, in a secret speech at the Twentieth Congress of the Communist Party of the Soviet Union, Khrushchev rounded on Stalin, excoriating the dead dictator for his crimes and his gross 'personality cult'. The CCP delegation to the congress, like the other delegations of foreign Communist Parties, had not been forewarned, and indeed their chief delegate, the aged Marshal Zhu De, had innocently sung Stalin's praises to the assembled company a few days before. Official word of Khrushchev's stunning move only reached them a full three days later, when a copy of the speech was brought along by a Kremlin messenger, and partly translated, partly summarised before being whisked away again. A full text of the speech only got to Peking in mid-March, in the form of an English-language translation which had been published by the *New York Times*. Faced with these indignities Mao however appears to have been surprisingly calm. 'I read Khrushchev's report from head to tail', he remarked to his aides, 'without losing my appetite.'[142] The point was Khrushchev's speech had shown that the Kremlin was no longer a monolith. Its teachings could no longer be considered infallible. Mao could now enjoy the luxury of sitting in judgement on the Soviet leaders as they had once sat in judgement on him, of acting as arbiter between the new orthodoxy and the old. Over the following weeks he proceeded to do just that, in a series of talks with Ambassador Yudin and other Soviet emissaries, in discussions with his colleagues and in a speech he delivered on 25 April on 'The Ten Major Relationships'.

Certainly Khrushchev in Mao's view had 'taken the lid off'.[143] The Chairman jumped at the chance to vent all the pent-up grievances he had nursed against Stalin for the past thirty years, charging him with all manner of 'serious mistakes' in his handling of the Chinese Revolution, from the fully arguable (Stalin's repeated attempts to prod the CCP into coming to terms with the Nationalist government) to the preposterous (Stalin's supposed failure to supply arms to the PLA in the late 1940s, 'not even a fart'[144]). To this catalogue Mao added all the slights he had had to endure at Stalin's hands since the PRC's founding, the 'ugly atmosphere' and pressures he had experienced in Moscow during the winter of 1949–50, the insistence that he had presided over nothing more than 'a victory of the Tito type', the 'two bitter pills' he had been made to swallow of continuing Soviet spheres of influence in Xinjiang and Manchuria.[145] But Khrushchev had also 'made a mess'.[146] Mao couldn't help underlining the irony: 'In the Soviet Union those who extolled Stalin to the skies have now in one swoop consigned him to Purgatory.'[147] And he added significantly, '*Here in China too some people are following their example*.'[148] For here was the rub. In the Chinese context Mao *was* Stalin. He too was all-powerful: he too was the object of a luxuriant personality cult. And if Khrushchev and his allies could turn on Stalin with impunity, what might not Mao's successors do to *him*? It followed that the Chairman couldn't come out in wholehearted support of Khrushchev's hatchet job. 'Out of Stalin's ten fingers', he concluded that spring, 'only three were rotten.'[149] His mistakes were of a 'partial' and 'temporary' nature, and 'could be set right'.[150] At the Labour Day celebration which was held in Tiananmen on 1 May a huge portrait of Stalin was still being carried.

Mao was now striking out for complete independence. In a comment made to Yugoslav visitors that September he gave a glimpse of the Oedipal struggle going on in his brain:

> Is the [Sino-Soviet] relationship a father and son relationship or one between brothers? It was between father and son in the past: now it more or less resembles a brotherly relationship, but the shadow of the father and son relationship is still not completely removed.[151]

By late autumn he was shifting from Olympian judgement to naked partisanship. The 'sword of Stalin', he observed in a talk to the CCP Central Committee on 15 November, had now been discarded by the Soviet leadership. So, possibly, had the 'sword of Lenin' as well.[152] Some of the other new themes which Khrushchev had unveiled at the Twentieth Congress, such as the concepts of a peaceful transition to socialism by parliamentary means and of peaceful coexistence with the Western powers, had a distinctly un-Leninist feel. '*Is the October Revolution still valid?*'[153] Mao was beginning to carve out a niche for the CCP as the champions of the old, hardline Communist orthodoxy. 'The Soviet Union', he remarked to his doctor, 'may attack Stalin, but we will not. Not only that, we will continue to support him.'[154]

From this point we begin to detect a change in the whole dynamics of Russian–Chinese interaction. Ever since the 1850s, under both tsarist and Soviet regimes, it had been the Russians who took the initiative, pushed the limits, set the agenda, with the Chinese largely confined to reacting in either a positive or a negative way. From now on we find more and more that it is the Chinese who are making the running, with the Russians increasingly passive and on the defensive.

This change became visible for the first time as the CCP unexpectedly took a hand in the politics of Eastern Europe. It is possible Mao had identified at quite an early stage the scope he might have for enlarging China's freedom of movement by manoeuvring among the other Soviet vassal states. Already in 1947–8 he had hoped to include a tour of the new Eastern European People's Republics as a supplement to his proposed trip to Moscow. The idea came to nothing, but eight years later a more promising opportunity for Chinese intervention arose. In October 1956 Khrushchev's liberal course heralded by the secret speech began to rebound on him with a vengeance, as two of the seven Eastern European vassals were emboldened to start asserting themselves. A new Polish Communist leader, Władysław Gomułka, touched off the unrest by demanding the withdrawal of Soviet officers from Poland's armed forces. Khrushchev's instinct was to stamp on the trouble, and on 19 October he directed the Soviet troops in the country to march upon Warsaw. Gomułka and his team sent a message to the Chinese comrades appealing for help, and the plight of the Polish nationalists struck an immediate chord with the Chairman. On the night of 20 October he summoned the Soviet ambassador, Yudin, receiving him, not altogether respectfully, in his bedroom in a dressing-gown, and gave the perspiring envoy a piece of his mind. 'We resolutely condemn what you are doing: I request that you immediately telephone Khrushchev and inform him of our views. *If the Soviet Union moves its troops, we will support Poland*.'[155] This support was presumably meant to be political rather than military; but it was enough to panic Khrushchev, who had already been hesitant over whether or not to advance. On 21 October, after hearing from Yudin, he decided to drop the idea of a military solution. For good measure he also decided to consult with a number of other Communist Parties, 'and first and foremost with the CCP'.[156] On 23 October a deputation of Chinese leaders headed by Liu Shaoqi flew into Moscow, where they were greeted in person by an agitated Khrushchev, so anxious to secure Peking's backing that he rushed them straight from their guest house to a conference chamber without leaving them so much as a few minutes for a rest, a wash or a cup of tea. A bloody crackdown in Poland had effectively been forestalled by Mao's veto.

But while Poland simmered down, Hungary was boiling over. That same day, 23 October, a backlash that had toppled the country's Stalinist leadership expanded into an all-out revolt against Communist rule. Over the following week Khrushchev and his Praesidium huddled with their CCP guests in a series of emergency meetings, with Mao steering the course of the on-the-spot Chinese advisers from the end of a telephone line. Mao initially rooted for the insurgent Hungarians, as he had for the Poles, recommending that the Soviet leaders resist their instinct to step in; and once again the Russians complied with his counsel and pulled back their troops. On 30 October, however, the Chairman experienced a change of heart, as news came through from Budapest of the lynching of state security officers and the increasingly obvious aim of the rebel Hungarian chief, Imre Nagy, to take his country right out of the Communist sphere. The Polish upheaval, Mao seems to have judged, was acceptable insofar as it was anti-*Soviet*; the Hungarian rising was anti-*Communist*, and that was a different matter altogether. Put another way, we may guess that a change of tack seemed important at this stage if the CCP were to assume the posture Mao intended for them as the champions of the old, hardline Stalinist cause. At any rate the Chinese delegates in Moscow switched abruptly that day to insisting that the Soviet leaders should keep their forces in Hungary and suppress the rebellion there if they were not to go down as 'historical criminals'.[157] Liu Shaoqi tried, perhaps rather sheepishly, to make a joke out of it: 'Well, yesterday we advised you to withdraw your troops from Hungary, and you were against it, and now we advise you not to . . .'.[158] Khrushchev, amazingly, veered around yet again in response to this latest guidance, and the following evening he informed Liu and the other Chinese delegates on their way to the airport that the Praesidium had decided to 'restore order' in Hungary. This time Mao had helped to precipitate a bloodbath. On 4 November Soviet tanks entered Budapest.

Buoyed up by their new, seemingly indispensable role as chief counsellors the CCP leaders began to assert themselves as never before. While the crisis was still unfolding they urged Khrushchev and his entourage to accept as the basis for dealings between states the Five Principles which Zhou Enlai had agreed on with Nehru, with their stress on equality and non-interference in one another's affairs; and on 30 October they extracted from Khrushchev's Praesidium a pious statement along these lines on future relations 'between the Soviet Union and other socialist countries'.[159] At the beginning of 1957 Khrushchev, still anxious for Chinese cooperation, asked for Zhou to make a tour of the Kremlin's two turbulent vassals to clear up the mess from the previous year. It was 'easier for the Chinese than the Russians to talk to the Poles', and there were hopes the emollient Zhou might help build support for the new Soviet-instituted Hungarian leadership. The Chinese premier duly carried out this assignment. Back in Moscow, however, and egged on by Mao to administer 'a good round of stinking curses',[160] he took his Soviet hosts well and truly to task, blaming the whole convulsion in Eastern Europe on traditional Russian great power behaviour. At a banquet in the Chinese embassy on 17 January he brought up the vexed subject of Stalin, twitting the tyrant's denouncers with their own Stalinist past in the same tetchy style he had used two years previously at Spiridonovka House:

> You people worked with Stalin for twenty years. Can you really bear no responsibility for encouraging Stalin's tendency to make his own decisions, his rigid thinking, his arrogance, conceit and other mistakes? . . . *Why don't you do a bit of self-criticism?*[161]

China, in Zhou's view, 'was now in a position to discuss any problems with the Kremlin on an equal basis'.[162] Mao agreed with his lieutenant: 'As much as they intend to influence us we want to influence them too.'[163]

Mao now conceived the idea of arranging a grand international conference of Communist Parties to restore solidarity after the recent disorders. His original thought was that the CCP should co-sponsor the event with the equally independent-minded Yugoslav Party, leaving the Soviet Union out of the loop. On 18 January, the day after Zhou Enlai's dressing-down of the Soviet bosses, the Chinese premier duly approached the Yugoslav ambassador to Moscow at a diplomatic function to put Mao's suggestion across. In early February it emerged that the Russians had somehow got wind of the project, and Mao hastily reassured them that the CPSU should of course be the sponsors and organisers; but when the conference finally met in November it became evident that the Chairman intended to be the dominant force. Arriving in Moscow at the head of a huge delegation he rapidly asserted himself, declining to provide his Soviet hosts with the advance text of his speeches as per the usual procedure on the grounds that he 'wanted to be able to speak freely'.[164] When he did come to speak his remarks took the form not of speeches but impromptu monologues, and unlike everyone else he delivered them sitting down, as it were *ex cathedra*, pleading a history of anaemia of the brain. The thrust of his comments reads like one sustained provocation, with Khrushchev as its target. He took the opportunity to wash a whole bundle of the Kremlin's dirty linen in public, referring openly to the fresh power struggle which had convulsed it in June when Khrushchev had survived an attempt to overthrow him by Molotov and other members of an 'Anti-Party Group'. Assuming his judgemental mantle he noted that the now disgraced Molotov had been 'an old comrade with a long history of struggle'. Yes, Molotov had been mistaken this time; but Khrushchev's line had been only 'relatively correct'.[165] The Chairman proceeded to urge on Khrushchev the importance of turning to other people for help and advice. 'You have a quick temper', he pointed out, 'which tends to make enemies . . . Let people voice their different views and talk to them patiently.'[166] Even the best leader had to have back-up, he pursued, quoting a Chinese proverb which said that with all its beauty the lotus still needed the green of its leaves to set it off. 'You, Comrade Khrushchev, even though you are a beautiful lotus, you too need the leaves to set you off.' (Khrushchev didn't entirely resemble a beautiful lotus.[167]) These barbs were accompanied by Mao's cryptic boast that 'the East Wind was prevailing over the West Wind'. This pronouncement was widely interpreted in the obvious sense of implying the ascendancy of the Communist over the capitalist camp, as displayed in the recent launch by the Soviet Union of the world's first artificial satellite, Sputnik, and its development of intercontinental ballistic missiles. But it was also open to another possible interpretation: what if the East Wind meant China and the West Wind included the Soviet Union? Wearing his Stalinist hat Mao took aim at Khrushchev's policy of détente with the West through a series of chillingly casual prognoses about nuclear war. 'Taking an extreme case', he opined, 'if half the world's population died there would still be the other half left. Imperialism would be smashed and the whole world would become socialist.' China itself might lose 300 million people, but 'the years will pass, and we'll get to work producing more babies than ever before'.[168] When the Italian Party leader Palmiro Togliatti interrupted to ask how many Italians Mao expected to survive a nuclear conflict, the Chairman replied briskly, 'None at all. But why do you think that *Italians* are so important to humanity?'[169] In spite of these startling utterances the conference closed with a bland communiqué in which the participants, to use a favourite Chinese phrase, 'sought common ground while reserving their differences'. The Soviet Union was still agreed to be the head of the Communist fellowship, with China aspiring to nothing more than the role of a guide based on its more recent experience of revolution. The Soviet Union set its sights on overtaking the United States in the production of steel within fifteen years, while China with its relatively backward economy contented itself with the more modest goal of overtaking Britain. But there was no doubt in Mao's mind that when China's economy took off the leadership of the world Communist movement would be bound to change. And just how long did that need to take?

In January 1958 the Chinese media suddenly launched a campaign to promote 'self-reliance'. In place of the constant injunctions to 'learn from the Soviet Union' the CCP started preaching the danger of blind faith in foreign ideas. At a gathering of Party workers that took place in March in the south-western city of Chengdu Mao deplored in particular the psychological effects of long-term reliance on the Soviet model: the Chinese people, he complained, 'had got so used to being slaves that they seemed to want to go on'.[170] From May to July, at a conference of the Military Affairs Commission, he berated his top brass for their dependence on Soviet weapons and Soviet military doctrine, exhorting them rather to put their trust in China's inexhaustible manpower and its mastery of revolutionary war. And in the meantime he was busy preparing spectacular changes in both the economic and social domains. Already in March he was sketching the outlines of the drive that became known as the Great Leap Forward – the fantastic attempt to industrialise the country overnight by setting the whole rural population to work smelting steel and prospecting for iron ore. Under way by the summer, the Great Leap was followed by the creation of People's Communes. All the old private plots and cooperatives in the countryside were swept up into huge new collectives of 10,000 households or more which took charge of all agricultural, commercial, social and even family life with the single-minded aim of increasing production. Even in his experiments Mao showed the imprint of Soviet thought. Lenin had tinkered with setting up communes in 1919, at the height of the Russian Civil War, and both Lenin and Stalin had used the term 'leap forward' in connection with the policy shifts of the 1920s. The Great Leap still enshrined the Stalinist quest for advanced heavy industry. Nonetheless the break made with contemporary Soviet practice was sharp. Out of the door went the Second Five Year Plan which the CCP had pursued under Soviet guidance since 1956, and with it the whole plodding stage-by-stage approach into which the Kremlin had been steering Mao's fledgling regime. As his experiments hurtled forward the Chairman even dared to imagine that the new self-reliant China might end up by outstripping its Soviet patron. By June he had so far diverged from the modest economic target he had set in Moscow as to suggest that the PRC could draw close to Soviet steel production within five years. In October he claimed to have identified in the Great Leap a short cut to socialism, and in December, at a banquet held to celebrate the success of the mighty endeavour, he crowed, 'For decades the Soviets have tried to develop an advanced form of socialism, but always they have failed. We have succeeded in less than a decade!'[171] The formation of the People's Communes encouraged a still wilder hope. That same autumn Mao ventured to speculate that the PRC might be able to skip the transitional socialist stage altogether and vault straight into full-blown Communism – ahead of the Soviet Union. The Russians had bragged of their progress, but nothing more: '*One hears footsteps without seeing anyone coming down the stairs*.'[172] The Chairman even felt able to speak of his Soviet tutors with a certain contemptuous magnanimity. Perhaps, he mused, China should actually let the Soviet Union make the transition to Communism first. 'No matter how fast we're going we must still leave the Russians a bit of face.'[173] In the heady climate of the period any Soviet triumph became a goal to be aimed at. 'Whatever happens', Mao told his associates in May 1958, '*we* must have Sputniks. Not the one or two kilogram kind . . . They will have to be several thousands of kilograms.'[174] Contemplating the grandeur of Red Square during his visit to Moscow in November 1957, the Chairman is said to have decided that Tiananmen Square in Peking would have to outdo it, and in 1959, in the run-up to the PRC's tenth anniversary, a million Chinese workers were employed in enlarging Tiananmen into the biggest square on Earth. 'Anything you can do I can do better,' Mao seemed to be singing in the words of the musical; 'I can do anything better than you.'

Given this outlook it was hardly likely that Mao would appreciate any new Soviet effort to confine him to a subordinate role. On 18 April 1958 Marshal Malinovsky, newly raised to the post of defence minister, wrote to his Chinese counterpart Peng Dehuai proposing the construction on PRC soil of a long-wave radio station which would enable the Kremlin to keep track of its far-flung naval squadrons in the Pacific and Indian oceans. The Soviet government would contribute 70 million roubles out of the 110 million overall cost of the scheme. Mao promptly raised the same kind of objection he had put up six years earlier to Stalin's plans for a rubber plantation and a pineapple cannery in Guangdong Province. Foreign trade, yes; foreign investment, no. The Russians could provide the technology and equipment, but the Chinese side would have to bear the whole cost of the project and retain complete ownership. Subject to these stipulations the Chairman would probably have acquiesced in the scheme; but on the evening of 21 July Ambassador Yudin appeared in the Zhongnanhai leadership compound with a second proposal, this time from Khrushchev himself, advocating the creation of a Joint Fleet, commanded by Russians and manned by Chinese, which would operate out of China's warm-water ports as part of an integrated East Asian defence system designed to resist the American threat. Coming on top of the radio project, this new scheme collided spectacularly with the CCP's aspirations to self-reliance. Once again Russian troops would be stationed in China, just three years after the last of the Soviet garrison had been withdrawn from Port Arthur. Once again China would be obliged to accept a joint venture with the Soviet Union, just three years after the liquidation of the hated joint stock companies in Xinjiang and Dalian. The Chairman erupted. On the following day, 22 July, he summoned Yudin back to his quarters and told him, 'You made me so angry that I didn't sleep all night and I have been unable to eat.'[175] He went on to subject the wretched ambassador to a sustained rant of five and a half hours in which all the pent-up Chinese rage of the last century seemed to come boiling out. '*You don't trust the Chinese; you only trust the Russians! . . . You want us to subject our 10,000-kilometre coastline to your protection and leave us only capable of fighting guerrilla war! . . . What you want is joint ownership, you'll want joint ownership of everything, the army, the navy, the air force, industry, agriculture, culture, education, all of it, right?*'[176] In response to the Soviet charge that the CCP were irredeemable jingoes by contrast with the selfless internationalists in the Kremlin he added, '*My counter-argument is that you have extended* Russian *nationalism to China's coast.*'[177] Refusing to have any further dealings with Yudin, he brusquely insisted that Khrushchev should come in person to China instead. And when Khrushchev did indeed turn up in Peking on a damage limitation trip nine days later Mao accorded him a reception from which the last shreds of respect had been peeled away. The General Secretary of the Soviet Communist Party was installed in an outlying villa in the Fragrant Hills with no air conditioning at the height of the Peking summer, obliging him to drag his bed on to the terrace where he immediately got bitten by swarms of mosquitoes. Next day, 1 August, the Chairman greeted his guest in Zhongnanhai clad in his bathing trunks by the side of a swimming pool. Well aware that Khrushchev was no swimmer, he invited the Soviet leader to borrow a pair of trunks and take to the water with him – swimming up and down effortlessly while Khrushchev floundered after him in a doggy-paddle, a knotted handkerchief tied around his bald pate and a rubber ring round his middle, and interpreters scurried along the pool's edge. (Mao subsequently described this as 'sticking a needle up Khrushchev's arse'.[178]) Similar treatment persisted when the two leaders finally sat down for talks. Aware that Khrushchev loathed tobacco, the Chairman took the opportunity of blowing smoke in his face. When Khrushchev expressed hope that a Joint Fleet might yet be organised Mao, we are told, 'banged his large hands against the sofa and stood up angrily. His face turned red and his breath turned heavy.'[179] Pointing a finger at Khrushchev's nose he yelled, 'I asked you what a joint fleet is and you still haven't answered me!'[180] In his final response to the Soviet overtures he put the whole issue in a broad historical context as he understood it:

> The answer is no, and I don't want to hear anything more about it. We don't want you here. The British, the Japanese and the other foreigners who stayed here for a long time have already been driven away by us. I'll repeat it again: we will never again allow anyone to use our land for their own purposes.[181]

Talking afterwards to his doctor he summarised; 'Their real object is to control us. They're trying to tie our hands and feet. But they're full of wishful thinking, like idiots talking about their dreams.'[182]

Side by side with this ever more brazen defiance of Moscow's authority Mao and his colleagues began to unpick the key links in the chain that bound them to the Kremlin. From late 1956 onwards, apparently at China's request, the Russians gradually withdrew the political advisers who had been attached to the PRC ministries ever since 1949, and in late 1958 the post of Soviet adviser was formally abolished. From the second half of 1957 Chinese officials abandoned the custom of supplying the Soviet embassy with confidential written briefings on the PRC's internal affairs, and by 1959 Soviet diplomats were complaining that they no longer had the opportunity for meetings with Mao or Zhou or the other top leaders.

Indirect methods were found to deflate the Soviet Union's image in the eyes of the Chinese public. One early set of pinpricks was applied under cover of the 'Hundred Flowers' campaign, first proclaimed by the Chairman in May 1956 but not activated until February of the following year. Ostensibly meant to encourage the Chinese population to ventilate their pent-up grievances in the spirit of Khrushchev's secret speech, the campaign proved to be a device for flushing out those pro-Western elements who had still not succumbed to the charms of CCP rule. But there was yet another dimension. Among the complaints which were voiced in wall posters and meetings convened in response to Mao's call were a number specifically aimed at the Russians, at the Kremlin's continuing failure to compensate China for the industrial loot the Red Army had carried away from Manchuria during the occupation of 1945–6, at Moscow's expectation that China should bear the full cost of the weapons supplied to it during the war in Korea. The CCP media censured such views as 'absurd', but by reporting them in the first place were of course drawing screaming attention to them. One Peking University student demanded the right for the country's young people to read Byron rather than second-rate Soviet authors. The Chairman's cultural watchdogs were certainly not about to indulge China's youth with a mass perusal of *Don Juan*; but they didn't mind airing the thought that there might be something less than seductive about certain Soviet works.

Mao went on finding ways to exploit the continued in-fighting among Stalin's successors. In June 1957, following Khrushchev's purge of the Anti-Party Group of Molotov, Malenkov and Kaganovich, the Chairman deliberately took his time extending congratulations to the emergent supremo. Worried by the idea that the Chairman might make common cause with his enemies, Khrushchev sent his ally, Anastas Mikoyan, to Mao's retreat in Hangzhou to extract an endorsement from him. Mao seized the chance to renew the request he had made three years earlier for Soviet help in equipping the PRC with nuclear arms. Mikoyan duly came up with a verbal offer, and the end of it was that he got what he came for: the Chairman turned, somewhat 'languidly', to Wang Jiaxiang, his former ambassador to Moscow, and asked for the CCP's cable of support for Khrushchev.[183] By the autumn, however, no solid Soviet nuclear commitment had yet been forthcoming, while Khrushchev still needed all the backing the Chairman could give him at the forthcoming Moscow conference of the Communist world. The Soviet boss also wanted to move against Marshal Zhukov, his minister of defence, who had stood by him in the June crisis but whom he had come to fear as a potential 'Bonaparte'; and he needed China's blessing for that as well. Mao accordingly ratcheted up the pressure another notch by conveying that

China would only take part in the conference if the Soviet Union first gave a firm guarantee to supply 'the materials and the models for the production of an atomic weapon and the means to deliver it'.[184] On 15 October Khrushchev's representatives signed an Agreement on New Defence Technologies under which the Russians would provide China with a sample A-bomb and the technical data required for a bomb's manufacture along with the technologies needed to make guided missiles and advanced fighter planes. The Chinese more or less kept their side of the bargain. By 27 October Khrushchev felt free to sack Zhukov, and at the conference in November Mao uttered, as we have seen, a not very ringing acknowledgement of Khrushchev's leadership of the CPSU. At the end of the year the Chinese leader was rewarded with the first tangible results of his long quest for advanced weaponry. On 20 December a Soviet train containing two P2 ground-to-ground missiles together with forty-five items of vital technical equipment and 102 officers and men crept into the border station of Manzhouli. Nuclear arms were specifically excluded from the self-reliance doctrine imposed on the Military Affairs Commission the following summer, and in June 1958 Zhou Enlai wrote to ask Khrushchev to furnish additionally submarines capable of delivering nuclear weapons, aircraft carriers and large, fast-moving vessels that could carry rockets.

Further unobtrusive advances were made in the borderlands. The CCP persevered with their effort to coax the MPR back into Peking's orbit by economic means. In 1956 a second large contingent of Chinese labourers was dispatched to the country, and Chinese trade with the MPR increased to the point where the PRC looked like replacing the Soviet Union as Outer Mongolia's chief trading partner. Chinese settlers were in the meantime encouraged to move into Inner Mongolia as a way to ensure that at any rate the southern part of the great grassland territory would remain in the PRC's grasp. The last traces of Soviet influence were conclusively expunged from Xinjiang. In 1957 the Chinese government ordered that the Latin rather than the Cyrillic alphabet should from now on be used to transcribe the languages of the Kazakh and Uighur communities, with a view to hampering future contact between disaffected Kazakhs and Uighurs and their cousins in Soviet Kazakhstan. Most of the Soviet citizens who had held posts in the defunct Eastern Turkestan Republic had returned home by this time, and in 1958 a further purge was conducted of those Moscow-friendly officials who had worked under them. In Moscow in 1957 Zhou Enlai unexpectedly brought up the issue of border disputes which had been suppressed six years earlier by the agreement providing for Soviet military control of disputed zones, and for the rest of the decade the PRC called repeatedly for the correction of 'unequal' border arrangements in such areas as the Manchurian rivers.

Finally the Chairman pressed ahead still further with his drive to construct an independent diplomacy. Any return to the brief overture he had tried with the United States in the middle of the decade was ruled out by both US hostility and the hardline stance he himself had adopted in reaction to Khrushchev's secret speech; though in a talk delivered in January 1957 he dismissed the Americans in a curiously wistful tone, saying, 'I still think it preferable to put off the establishment of diplomatic relations for some years . . . One day the United States will have to establish diplomatic relations with us.'[185] On 23 August 1958, this time unquestionably without notifying his Soviet allies, he launched a second round of bombardments of the Nationalist-held offshore islands of Quemoy and Matsu, thereby provoking a huge concentration of US air and naval power off the coast of Fujian Province as the Eisenhower administration hurried to safeguard these outlying possessions of their exiled protégé, Chiang Kai-shek. For a few weeks a massive collision seemed imminent. Mao's objective, however, was not a showdown with America but the discomfiture of the Soviet Union and above all the sabotage of the Kremlin's attempt at superpower détente. 'Khrushchev wants to improve relations with the US?', he asked his doctor rhetorically. 'Good, we'll congratulate him with our guns.'[186] Quemoy and Matsu, he went on, were 'two batons that keep Khrushchev and Eisenhower scurrying this way and that. Don't you see how wonderful they are?'[187] When Andrei Gromyko, just starting his immensely long tenure as Soviet foreign minister, arrived in Peking on 7 September for urgent consultations about this Second Taiwan Straits Crisis, the Chairman treated him to another blood-curdling discourse about the insignificance of nuclear war. 'You [and the United States]', he observed, 'may well be wiped out. China too will suffer, but will still have 400 million people left over.' Those 400 million Chinese survivors, furthermore, 'would be able to extend the influence of Communism throughout Asia and Africa.'[188] Mao's bravado was also intended as part of the Chinese effort to build up a constituency in the developing countries, at Russia's expense. As early as 1956, at the time of the Suez crisis, the Chairman urged the Egyptian ambassador to Peking to 'study the experience of China'.[189] China as well as the Soviet Union, he declared, would like to help Egypt, and Chinese aid (i.e. unlike Soviet) came free and gratis and with no strings attached. In 1959 the ninety-first birthday of the black American intellectual Dr W.E.B. DuBois was celebrated in China as a public holiday. DuBois was widely revered among African nationalists, in West Africa especially, and this accolade was one sign among many that the new Chinese evangelism had crossed the Sahara. The Chinese had begun the decade with the slogan 'The Soviet Union's Today is China's Tomorrow!'; they ended it proclaiming, 'China's Today is Africa's Tomorrow!'. In August that year Mao summed up the great shift in initiative which had taken place from Russians to Chinese, commenting to Wang Jiaxiang, '*I think they* are *in a passive position, whereas we are in an extremely active position*.'[190]

The Soviet leaders were undoubtedly caught off guard by this blistering challenge. Goaded by Zhou Enlai in January 1957 for their failure to stand up to Stalin during his lifetime Khrushchev and Bulganin could only plead, 'If we had tried to arrest Stalin at a secret meeting it wouldn't have been Stalin who would have been arrested, it would have been us!'[191] At the Moscow conference of Communist Parties the following November the Soviet hosts repeatedly quivered under the impact of Mao's provocations. The Chairman's public analysis of the CPSU's inner ructions, his respectful allusion to the disgraced Molotov and the faint praise with which he damned the victorious Khrushchev were greeted with a 'deathly silence' in the conference hall, and Mikoyan rose from his seat and regarded Mao with a 'distinctly unfriendly expression'.[192] Hearing himself compared to a beautiful lotus Khrushchev, we are told, 'hung his head and went very red'.[193] Whatever outside observers may have made of Mao's reference to the East Wind prevailing over the West Wind, many Soviet pundits detected a hint of the future ascendancy of China over themselves. At the most basic level the East Wind had unpleasant connotations for Russians: it brought dry air and threatened the harvest while the West Wind brought fertilising rain. And the East conjured up visions of Genghis Khan and the Mongolian hordes. With the benefit of hindsight it seems fairly obvious that Mao's airy dismissals of the consequences of nuclear war were not meant to be taken at face value – that he was playing a game of chicken designed to show up the Soviet bosses as cowards by contrast with the fearless revolutionaries in Peking. But for the

Russians, who had lost 20 million dead barely ten years before in the most terrible war in history, Mao's blithe assumption of nuclear wipeout sounded all too serious. 'Paper tiger?', demanded Khrushchev. 'Mikoyan, did you hear that? He says nuclear weapons are a paper tiger!'[194] Once again Mikoyan rose from his seat, staring 'angrily' at the Chairman; and once again a 'deathly silence' prevailed in the hall.[195] As the CCP's self-reliance drive got under way in the early months of 1958 Soviet diplomats slowly began to appreciate that the Chinese were no longer interested in their economic model and that instead 'stones were flying into our kitchen garden'.[196] Khrushchev was predictably 'jolted' by the wild Chinese claims that accompanied the promotion of the Great Leap Forward and the People's Communes, and the implication that China was surging ahead of the Soviet Union on the road to the Communist paradise.[197] In spite of these shocks he still seems to have thought that the Joint Fleet proposal he submitted to the PRC that July would be warmly received as an answer to the request Zhou Enlai had just made for advanced military technology. After all, the Joint Fleet would consist in large measure of nuclear submarines. He and his colleagues were totally unprepared for the xenophobic diatribe with which Mao lashed back. Ideological crony no longer, poor Ambassador Yudin is said to have had 'a great fright': a few days after Mao's tirade he took to his bed with an aneurysm and a partial paralysis of his left side.[198] Khrushchev came back from his dash to Peking spluttering to his comrades, 'Just where do you think Mao Zedong received me? In a swimming pool! He received me in a swimming pool!'[199] Three weeks later he was incensed by Mao's failure to give him notice of the second shelling of Quemoy and Matsu, detecting in the Chairman's secrecy an attempt to twist his arm into providing diplomatic and military support. And even the ice-cool Gromyko is said to have been flabbergasted by Mao's continuing levity on the brink of the nuclear abyss.

Yet in spite of widespread dismay the most striking feature of these episodes is the patience, even the indulgence with which the Kremlin responded to Mao's new pugnacity. For a short time at the turn of 1956–7 there are signs of a slowdown in Soviet economic aid. Possibly as a riposte to the Chinese request for the withdrawal of Soviet political advisers from the ministries, the Russians are said to have sought the return of their technical experts as well, to reduce the strain on their domestic economy; and the number of experts is said to have been reduced by a third to a total of 947.

This trend had however been halted by the summer of 1957, when Khrushchev once more found himself in need of Peking's political backing, and for the best part of two years the Soviet chief showed himself as concerned to keep the Chinese in the fold as Mao and his followers were to break out of it. Anxious clearly to make up for the indignities the Chairman had suffered at Stalin's hands during his first trip to Moscow in 1949–50, Khrushchev received him there in November 1957 with every sign of respect. He escorted Mao personally to the former Kremlin residence of Catherine the Great, where the Chairman was installed in the empress's bedroom. (Mao's aside to his doctor: 'Look how differently they're receiving us now . . . What snobs!'[200]) Taunted by Mao for his short fuse, he sat uncomplainingly through the conference sessions while the Chairman subjected him to slight after slight. During the following spring he expressed some initial support for Mao's Great Leap Forward and the economic take-off it seemed to presage. From May onwards reports pouring in from the Soviet experts in China indicated that the Great Leap was in fact a catastrophe in the making, that the steel being turned out by the backyard furnaces was good for nothing and the diversion of peasants from agriculture threatened a hideous toll in human lives. But he forbore to exploit this intelligence, and maintained a discreet public silence as the Leap was supplemented by the still more provocative People's Communes. In late July, rushing off to Peking in response to Mao's rage at his Joint Fleet proposal, he again cast himself in the demeaning role of a vassal prostrating himself before the Dragon Emperor. Whatever his inner fury he followed Mao into the swimming pool, consoling himself with a notional victory when he finally clambered out and could look down on Mao from above. At the beginning of the substantive exchanges he pleaded defensively, 'There was no thought of a Joint Fleet',[201] seeking to blame the whole hullabaloo on a garbled transmission on the part of Ambassador Yudin. Later he tried to turn Mao's wrath aside with the offer of various sweeteners, from help with the construction of a large factory to produce nuclear submarines to the use of the Soviet Arctic port of Murmansk as a submarine base. He did make one visible gesture of displeasure at his treatment by cutting his visit short and returning to Moscow after three days instead of one week as originally planned. But even after that the concessions continued. On 8 August an agreement was signed between Soviet and Chinese representatives for the design and installation in China of forty-seven new industrial plants in the sectors of metallurgy, chemicals, coal-mining and machine-building: a similar deal, this time for seventy-eight projects, was concluded by Khrushchev with Zhou Enlai on 7 February of the following year. Angered though the Kremlin leaders were by Mao's unheralded pounding of the Nationalist-held offshore islands, they did slowly rally to China's side against the US threat in keeping with the terms of the Valentine's Day alliance. A vague warning to Washington carried in *Pravda* on 5 September was followed two days later by a personal letter from Khrushchev to Eisenhower warning that any attack upon China would be treated as an attack on the Soviet Union too.

If Khrushchev's retrospective account is to be believed the turning-point finally came in the next few months in the form of a tussle over the spoils of war. On 24 September 1958, in the course of the Taiwan Straits conflict, CCP and Nationalist aircraft engaged in a dogfight over the east Chinese country-side not far from the coastal city of Wenzhou. The KMT squadron were equipped with five of the latest American Sidewinder air-to-air missiles, one of which was brought down but failed to go off. The CCP authorities put the wreckage on show in Peking, to the keen interest of Soviet military experts who were having trouble developing their own air-to-air missile technology and who asked the Chinese to deliver the wreckage to them to take home for research. The CCP dragged their feet, claiming that they could not for the moment lay their hands on the missile while (the Russians imagined) sequestering it for their own private study. In February 1959, the month in which Khrushchev concluded the second new aid deal, they at long last came up with the missile – but with the critical guidance system removed. For Khrushchev this was the last straw, the ultimate, unforgivable display of mistrust. By the summer he had begun to take significant action to rein China in. On 20 June the Kremlin formally cancelled the 1957 agreement on nuclear cooperation. No sample atom bomb would now be supplied to Peking, and in August a total of 233 Soviet scientists who had been sent to implement the agreement were pulled out of China along with their data and blueprints. Gloves off in earnest, Khrushchev now permitted himself a public swipe at the Chairman's economic and social experiments. On 18 July, in a speech in the Polish city of Poznań, he declared that the losses from Mao's Great Leap Forward exceeded the gains, that the advocates of the People's Communes had 'a poor understanding of what Communism is and how it is to be built'.[202]

Far from exercising forbearance Khrushchev and his colleagues were now visibly courting Chinese displeasure. In late August 1959 clashes broke out between Chinese and Indian troops in a disputed region of the Himalayas. Marxist-Leninist principle as well as the Valentine's Day Treaty dictated that the Russians should stand four-square behind their Chinese comrades in opposition to the 'bourgeois' Indian government of Jawaharlal Nehru. Instead the Kremlin adopted a posture of steadfast neutrality between their Chinese 'brothers' and their Indian 'friends'. In addition a note sent by the Central Committee of the CPSU to their CCP counterparts strongly hinted that the Chinese had been deliberately muddying the international waters on the eve of a forthcoming visit by Khrushchev to Washington for a summit meeting with President Eisenhower. Intended by Khrushchev to serve as a breakthrough in his quest for superpower détente so disliked by the Chairman, this visit, which went ahead in the second half of September, amounted to another slap in Mao's face. Less conspicuous but perhaps more intriguing were signs of a new Soviet ambivalence over the hypersensitive question of Nationalist-held Taiwan. Ever since his withdrawal to Taiwan in 1949 Chiang Kai-shek had been consistently demonised in the Soviet media in an apparent attempt to make amends to the Chinese Communists for Stalin's long years of support for the KMT. At Chiang's right hand, nonetheless, was his son Ching-kuo, with his Soviet education, his Russian wife and his track record of goodwill towards Moscow. In the early 1950s Ching-kuo had introduced on Taiwan a mixed economy seemingly modelled on the Soviet New Economic Policy of the 1920s, and on a more sinister note had created for security purposes what US intelligence agents deplored as a 'highly objectionable system of Political Commissars'.[203] In 1953 the State Department and Pentagon had combined to invite him to Washington with the aim of expanding his 'intellectual horizons on which Soviet Russia looms so large',[204] and two years later the US secretary of state, John Foster Dulles, was still reported to view him as the 'possible leader of an anti-American defection'.[205] By the end of the decade, as Soviet ties with Peking became ever more strained, it would seem that the Kremlin had started to see possibilities in a Taiwan connection. At the most senior level the Kremlin chiefs remained firmly supportive of the PRC's claim to be the one and only China, and they protested along with their ally at the admission of Nationalist delegates to a series of international bodies, including the Red Cross, the Red

Crescent, the Worldwide Hydrometeorological Commission and most contentiously the International Olympic Committee. They did not, however, follow Peking in walking out of these offending organisations. And nor do they seem to have exerted themselves to make sure that the Taiwan issue was fully explained further down in the Soviet hierarchy, where a junior functionary assigned to play host to a visiting PRC deputation might not necessarily grasp what the 'One China' neuralgia was all about. In the summer of 1958 a Nationalist party actually showed up in Moscow for a UN-sponsored International Geology Conference, where the leading Soviet delegate, a geologist named Dr Dmitri Pushkov, cheerfully urged the PRC representatives to join up with the Nationalists in a unified team. The outraged PRC group boycotted the meeting, and Pushkov was obliged to issue a personal apology confessing that he 'had failed to appreciate his actions' broader implications'.[206] Over the following year Khrushchev mulled over the idea of Soviet recognition of the Taiwan regime. Two Germanies, two Koreas, two Vietnams . . . so why not two Chinas? In any case he made clear to the Peking authorities that the Soviet Pacific Fleet wouldn't help them to take Taiwan over by force.

By the last years of the decade relations between the two powers were plunging into a spiral of fear and hostility. On 11 July 1959 Harrison Salisbury of the *New York Times* attended a reception at Ulan Bator in the MPR held to celebrate the country's Naadam Festival. He recalled:

> As I entered the ballroom I saw a strange spectacle. On one side of the room stood the Russian guests, on the other the Chinese. Between the two groups, rushing back and forth with determined hospitality, were the Mongol hosts, doing their best to make it appear that the party was gay and joyous. But alas, the evidence was inescapable. One half of the party was not speaking to the other half. The Russians and the Chinese were drawn up in aloof ranks of icy hostility.[207]

In the absence of diplomatic ties between his country and the PRC, Salisbury realised there was no point in his even trying to socialise with the Chinese contingent:

> I quickly strode to the Russian side, where the Soviet diplomats and military men greeted me with great joviality. Before the evening was

> over I found myself confronting a massive Soviet officer who insisted on my drinking to Soviet–American friendship. Then, putting one great paw around my shoulder, he leaned over confidentially and said, 'Now, honestly, don't you feel more at home on *our* side? We must stand together against *them*.' And lest there be any mistake, he waved grandly toward the Chinese standing politely silent on the other side of the room.[208]

It would be wrong to imagine that the CCP establishment were unanimously in favour of Mao's anti-Soviet revolt. One renowned champion of Kremlin policy, Wang Ming, had indeed disappeared from the scene. In and out of hospital again from the early 1950s, still complaining of suspicious ailments from hepatitis to inflammation of the gall bladder, still under fire for his 'slavish' adherence to 'foreign dogma',[209] Wang had withdrawn to Moscow in 1956 at the start of a lasting political exile. But there were other and weightier figures in the CCP leadership who still held the Soviet Union in high regard. Prominent among them, as always, was Mao's deputy, Liu Shaoqi, elevated at this time from vice-chairman of the government to first vice-chairman of the CCP. Taking his cue from Khrushchev's secret speech, Liu spoke out with enthusiasm in support of collective Party leadership and against Stalin-type personality cults at the CCP's Eighth Congress in September 1956 – a gathering which went so far as to delete all references to Mao Zedong Thought from the Party's constitution. Too much shouldn't be read into this: Mao himself may have thought it judicious to excise allusions to his Thought, as he had done before in the late 1940s. But Khrushchev certainly felt that Liu 'seemed to agree with the point of view held by the leaders of our own Party';[210] and Mao subsequently had caustic remarks for those colleagues who had bowed to Soviet pressure and wished to learn how to overthrow the personality cult. A Soviet specialist who arrived in Peking in early 1958 recorded that Liu was thought to be the leading light in a pro-Russian group. Orthodox Leninist that he was, Liu is said to have hoped to keep China within the mainstream Communist movement in the interests of Party-building and economic advance. At a time when Mao preached self-reliance he is known to have admired the calibre of the scientists and engineers, managers and economists that the Soviet system produced. He even had family ties with Russia. His son Liu Yunbin (Klim), whom we last met at the International Children's Home in Ivanovo, had stayed on in the Soviet

Union after completing his schooling to pursue research in nuclear physics. Yunbin had found romance there, as his father before him is said to have done: he had fallen in love with a girl named Mara from the chemical faculty of Moscow State University, and had married and had two children by her. For good measure Liu's second son Yunruo had also studied in the Soviet Union and had also fallen in love with a Russian girl. Back in China he sought his father's agreement to let him rejoin his Muscovite sweetheart with a view to matrimony. But Liu Senior had very definite limits. He had come so near damnation in 1953. As relations with Russia grew steadily worse his position was vulnerable, and he had to protect it. At the end of 1957 he found it expedient to recall Yunbin from Moscow to carry on his research work at home – not, however, permitting the young man to bring with him his Russian wife and his half-Russian children. And Yunruo's request for permission to be reunited in Moscow with his Soviet girlfriend was turned down flat.[211] Such gestures as Liu felt able to make towards Soviet contacts were typically small and discreet. In September 1959, for instance, he agreed to receive the Soviet chargé d'affaires in Peking, who wished to pass on an Indian government statement on the Himalayan conflict and had repeatedly failed to get access to Mao. But that was as far as he went.

Stiffer resistance entirely came from the minister of defence, Marshal Peng Dehuai, the former commander-in-chief of the PRC's troops in Korea, who had attracted Stalin's interest briefly during his visit to Moscow in the summer of 1952. Peng represented a generation of top-ranking officers who had judged that if China were to be able to stand up to a Western attack it must have a modern conventional army equipped with the best Soviet weapons plus a fully integrated alliance with the Soviet Union as its nuclear protector. 'If war breaks out', Peng asserted in 1956, 'we will send troops and the Soviet Union will provide the atomic bomb.'[212] This outlook was diametrically opposed to Mao's concept of an independent Chinese nuclear deterrent coupled with continued reliance on rural guerrilla techniques, and the watershed meeting of the Military Affairs Commission convened by the Chairman from May to July 1958 was correspondingly 'stormy'.[213] Undeterred, Peng pressed Mao in October to place a new order for 130,000 field guns and 40,000 shells with the Soviet Union; but the Chairman advised Zhou Enlai 'not to hurry' with the required correspondence.[214] In the meantime Peng had begun to form his own private assessment of Mao's Great Leap Forward, as reports started to seep in of the mass production of useless metal and of the hideous famine which would in due course claim a total, according to some authorities, of up to 45 million lives. By the first months of 1959 the marshal appears to have reached the conclusion that Mao must be stopped, and that Soviet help might be needed to stop him. With this aim in mind he accepted an outstanding invitation to visit the Soviet Union and Eastern Europe. At a farewell reception given in his honour on 20 April by the embassies of the prospective host countries he took Ambassador Yudin aside and 'cautiously' embarked on a conversation about the Great Leap; Yudin recalled 'the Marshal's mournful eyes expressing a gamut of feelings'.[215] In the course of his tour Peng made contact with Khrushchev on at least two occasions, in Albania in late May and again in Moscow in early June. What transpired is unclear, but it seems very possible he sought the Kremlin's support for a move against Mao. On 14 July, at an enlarged session of the CCP Politburo held in the mountain resort of Lushan in Jiangxi Province, he set the ball rolling with a carefully penned memorandum to the Chairman in which he deplored the wild claims of industrial output being made for the Leap and the 'rather large losses' that had resulted from 'the nation-wide smelting of steel'.[216] But Peng's broadside was fatally unsupported. After some hesitation Luo Fu, the former member of the 28 Bolsheviks who was currently serving as deputy foreign minister, came out on his side, and so did the PLA's chief of staff, Huang Kecheng, and one or two other officials of medium rank. But no support was forthcoming from Liu Shaoqi, who whether from conviction or out of a simple instinct for survival was backing the Leap and who even reversed his own stance at the time of the Eighth Congress three years earlier by upholding the Chairman's personality cult. By 23 July Mao and his loyalists were lashing back, with particular focus on Peng's rather obvious Soviet ties. Much was made of the closeness in timing between Peng's Eastern European tour and his démarche at Lushan; between his démarche at Lushan and Khrushchev's public disparagement of the Great Leap and the People's Communes in his Poznań speech a mere four days later. Peng was denounced as a 'Soviet agent', whose object had been to depose the Chairman and place China under the direct control of the Soviet military. In September the marshal was fired from his post as defence minister, and he and his handful of adherents were cast into the outer darkness as (Mao still a prisoner of Soviet jargon) . . . an Anti-Party Group.

Nor were all Russians by any means in accord with Khrushchev's retribution. The hardline Stalinists Khrushchev had dislodged, for example, continued to look upon Peking as a natural ally. The disgraced Molotov, whom the Soviet boss had dispatched (rather mercifully) to Outer Mongolia to serve as ambassador there, soon established a cosy rapport with his Chinese counterpart, and recalled later on that he had been both physically and conceptually 'too close to Mao Zedong for Khrushchev's comfort'.[217] Some middle-ranking officials considered Khrushchev's counter-moves to be reckless, deploring in particular his abrupt scrapping of the 1957 nuclear agreement as a damaging violation of the principle of international law that pacts must be honoured. And to begin with at least Mao's ploys had a distinct fascination for Soviet liberals. Many of them initially saw the Hundred Flowers campaign as a genuine 'call for pluralism, freedom of expression and opinion in ideology, science and culture'.[218] The Great Leap at its outset was viewed as a creative and democratic phenomenon in contrast with the stagnant conservatism of Soviet development plans. In the frontier regions of the Soviet Far East a number of regional committees were said to have taken up Chinese slogans, and Chinese propaganda about the Leap began creeping into the local press. For the first time since the eighteenth century Russians were starting, however misguidedly, to look towards China as a model of governance, and Khrushchev didn't like it. In January 1959, at the Twenty-first Congress of the CPSU, he inveighed against 'the temptation to imitate Chinese economic measures blindly'.[219] 'The slogans of the Chinese reforms', he told his colleagues, 'are very alluring. You're mistaken if you don't think the seeds of these ideas will find fertile soil in our country.'[220] 'To be honest,' he confessed in his memoirs, 'I'd have to say we were frightened by the Chinese attempts to get us to adopt their slogans and their policies.'[221]

By this time, however, the two powers were on a collision course that no scattered dissent could reverse. On 30 September 1959, flushed with success from his American tour and his summit with President Eisenhower, Khrushchev arrived in Peking to attend the festivities marking the tenth anniversary of the PRC. His reception was chilly. There was no welcoming crowd at the airport, no rapturous choir singing 'Moscow-Peking'. At a state banquet that evening the Soviet leader delivered a forty-minute address extolling 'the spirit of Camp David'. The Chinese responded with two days of brickbats. At a series of meetings held in the newly completed Great Hall of the People, amid the new and provocative grandeur of Tiananmen Square, they laid into Khrushchev over a series of major issues, from the United States and détente to the Kremlin's studied neutrality during the Sino-Indian border clash. 'I have an accusation for you,' Mao declared to his Soviet guest, '– that you are guilty of *Right Opportunism*.'[222] It was exactly the label that the Kremlin had bestowed thirty years earlier on the CCP's founder, Chen Duxiu; only this time the Chinese were doing the labelling. Marshal Chen Yi, who had replaced Zhou Enlai as foreign minister, called Khrushchev a 'time-server' and 'kept repeating over and over again, as though he had been wound up like a machine, "Nehru! Nehru! Nehru!" '.[223] Even the normally urbane Zhou dismissed a remark made by Khrushchev as 'totally irrelevant'.[224] On the defensive again, Khrushchev complained rather pathetically that he and his retinue were outnumbered: 'This negotiation is unfair and *unequal* [*sic*].'[225] 'Why can you criticise us', he protested, 'but the Elder Brother can't criticise you?'[226] Nonetheless he got in a few jabs of his own. When Mao, castigating détente, urged him to provoke a war with America, offering to send 100, 200 or even 1,000 divisions to his aid, he informed the Chairman that under modern conditions 'two missiles would suffice to transform those divisions of his into radioactive offal'.[227] He asked his hosts to consider the possibility of accepting an independent Taiwan, provoking Chen Yi to ask if he was trying to speak for the KMT. He appealed for the reinstatement of the disgraced Peng Dehuai, whom the Russians had taken to calling 'the Marshal of Truth' and 'the voice of one crying in the wilderness'.[228] And he slapped down the Chinese foreign minister: 'In military matters I listen to you because you are a marshal. Now, within the Party, I am a First Secretary and you are only a Politburo member. You should listen to me.'[229] This whole protracted slanging match took place behind closed doors, out of sight of the celebrating public. But we do have a close-up observation by Sidney Rittenberg, one of a handful of Western radicals who had made their home in Peking. In an interval between two sessions the leaders emerged, and Rittenberg was on hand to report the after-effects of this culminating explosion:

> Khrushchev's [face] was twisted into something between a scowl and a sneer, and he flashed a look at the people milling about as if his anger took in every citizen in China. As for Mao, I had never seen him so

> angry. Usually his anger was controlled, sarcastic, biting, needling. But at that moment his fury was unchecked. His face was black and tense and the atmosphere around him snapped and crackled with the force of his emotion.[230]

The talks are said to have broken up amid 'complete disorder'.[231] Khrushchev set off for home three days early, just as he had the year before, and the send-off at the airport was even icier than the welcome had been. On 6 October, from the safe distance of Vladivostok, the Soviet leader charged Mao with behaving 'like a fighting cock' in his clamour for war.[232] Looking back on the visit his colleague Mikhail Suslov deduced more reflectively that Chinese heads had been turned by the fact that China was 'back on its feet' and was 'visibly stronger'.[233]

From this point it was downhill all the way. The Chinese were now busy preparing an all-out assault in the ideological sphere. The Sino-Soviet conflict, we should bear in mind, was never primarily about ideology. It was about dominance; it was about independence; it was about the raw issues of political, economic and military strength. But given the quasi-religious context in which these regimes operated, the teachings of Marx and Lenin provided a natural weapon with which to maul one's opponents and undermine their support. On 22 April 1960, on what would have been Lenin's ninetieth birthday, the CCP published an article entitled 'Long Live Leninism!' in their theoretical journal *Red Flag*, claiming Lenin's mantle for themselves, damning Khrushchev and his team for the deadly sin of 'revisionism' and for the first time exposing the bitter dispute to the outside world. At the same time they started to take up the ideological cudgels at each successive international forum of Communist groups. Mao himself preferred to keep a dignified distance from this verbal brawling, leaving the diatribes to his subordinates, the 'new gladiators' as the Russians called them, and in particular to Kang Sheng, the former NKVD trainee turned Maoist police chief, and Deng Xiaoping, the Party's diminutive but feisty secretary-general. In February Kang led the charge at a meeting of the Political Consultative Committee of the Warsaw Pact. In early June Deng delivered a hundred-minute harangue on 'revisionism' at a gathering of the World Federation of Trade Unions (WFTU) in Peking, and the CCP began for the first time to disseminate leaflets and canvass support among the international guests. Later the same month they kept up the challenge at a congress of the Romanian Party in Bucharest, with a statement publicly berating Khrushchev for his 'patriarchal, arbitrary and despotic attitude'.[234] And back in China they launched an attempt to win over the Soviet aid workers and turn them against their own government. The Soviet leadership responded in kind. Unlike Mao Khrushchev happily placed himself at the front of the action. Already by late October he had started, like Stalin before him, to equate Mao with Trotsky, pointing out that the Chairman's calls for 'continuing revolution' in the context of the Great Leap sounded very much like the 'permanent revolution' espoused by the Soviet outcast. At the Warsaw Pact meeting in February 1960 he likened Kang Sheng to Malyuta Skuratov, the hatchet man of Tsar Ivan the Terrible; and he showed himself every bit as capable of earthy speech as the Chairman, whom he referred to as 'a used condom'.[235] During the spring, in a gesture surely meant for effect rather than out of real expectation, he invited Mao to pay a 'friendly visit' to the Soviet Union. But Mao 'expressed no desire personally to acquaint himself with the life of our country',[236] and before long it was hammer and tongs again. At the Bucharest congress Khrushchev denounced Mao personally as an 'ultra-leftist' and accused the CCP of 'spitting in our face'.[237] Once again he took up the cause of a purged Chinese leader, condemning the CCP for their treatment of Gao Gang, whose 'only crime' had been to oppose the Party's anti-Soviet course.[238] And he and his colleagues jeered harshly at the Chinese delegates for their bizarre choice of hero which had marked the start of the open rift: '*Since you love Stalin so much why don't you take his corpse to Peking?*'[239]

With his curious penchant for biblical imagery Khrushchev emphasised in his memoirs, 'We took great care never to offend China until the Chinese actually started to crucify us.' But when they did start to hammer the nails in, he pursued, 'well, I'm no Jesus Christ, and I didn't have to turn the other cheek'.[240] On 16 July he struck back dramatically. In a note to the Peking authorities the Kremlin announced that the whole current batch of 1,390 scientific and technical experts would be withdrawn from China with their families in the space of a month. There would be no replacements; 343 major contracts and 257 technical projects would be scrapped with immediate effect, and the supply of important equipment and materials was to be discontinued. By 24 August the whole body of civilian experts had left, stripping their offices, shredding their documents and carrying off their blueprints; by 31 August the remaining military advisers had followed suit. Out of 336 big industrial enterprises which had been earmarked for construction over the past six years only 154 had yet been completed. The great Soviet effort to modernise China had been stopped halfway through.

At one level the move could be seen as an understandable payback for the incessant goading that Khrushchev and his allies had endured at Mao's hands. The thankless child had indeed proved sharper than a serpent's tooth. But it was also a savage blow, whose worst repercussions were liable to be felt not by Mao but by an already starving Chinese population. Once again many Russians looked on with dismay. Stepan Chervonenko, who had succeeded Yudin as ambassador to Peking, was 'amazed' and expressed the private opinion that Khrushchev had thrown away what little influence he still had in China. In a telegram sent to Moscow he protested against this further violation of the principle that international treaties are to be honoured. If Soviet aid to the Chinese really had to cease, he entreated, at least let the current contingents stay on till their contracts expired.[241] More intense opposition was voiced by Mikhail Klochko, a research scientist of Ukrainian origin who had been seconded to China by the Moscow Institute of Chemistry. Earlier in the year, as the official relationship nosedived, he had made up his mind to ignore his instructions to observe full professional secrecy 'and to do whatever I considered most useful for Chinese science'.[242] Assigned to an institute in the south-western city of Kunming, he had deliberately given four lectures on the metallurgy of precious metals instead of the prescribed one. Now, ordered home, he complained bitterly to the Soviet embassy that he and his colleagues had been working with 'real, live people'; that they had been doing their best to make themselves useful to China and did not appreciate being shunted around 'like a bundle of firewood on a train'.[243] He fought tooth and nail to delay his departure, only finally boarding a train to Moscow on 13 August, and returned home convinced that he should 'devote the years left to him to the service of Chinese science'.[244] Klochko had undoubtedly, in the parlance of the British Foreign Office, 'gone native' in a big way. Other accounts do, however, suggest that he was not a mere outlier, that his reaction was shared by other Soviet personnel to a greater or lesser degree. Russian technicians still working at the Wuhan Iron and Steel Company announced their departure glumly to their Chinese hosts: 'We don't know why. Orders are orders.'[245] Some of them, we are told, even wept. Klochko maintained in a memoir that he had 'never heard a single Soviet adviser in China speak approvingly of the brutal Soviet note or of our sudden recall home'.[246] Inside the Soviet Union ordinary Russians were proud of their country's epic assistance to the PRC and by no means delighted to see it curtailed. Back at his Moscow institute, Klochko found that his colleagues were astonished at his reappearance. None of them voiced approval of Khrushchev's act, and some were even bold enough to express mild criticism.

Under far tighter control than the scattered Soviet aid workers, the staff of the Chinese host bodies were in no position to carp openly at the CCP's Russophobe line. But if the account left by Klochko is anything to go by one or two of them did show their feelings either through a sudden outburst or (more usually) through a quiet display of goodwill. In April 1960 Klochko found himself assigned a replacement interpreter who treated him brusquely and asked him aggressive questions about his comings and goings. Reproached by the scientist for this behaviour, the young man cried, 'Do you think I act that way because I like it? I'm just carrying out orders . . .'. Klochko noted, 'There were tears in the poor fellow's eyes.'[247] On 16 July Professor Tan, the director of Klochko's host institute in Kunming, reported the Kremlin's démarche to him with the words, 'I have sad news for you and sad news for us.'[248] On 27 July the professor and his staff gave a farewell party for their departing adviser in a friendly atmosphere 'not imposed by political decree but based on warm, human solidarity'.[249] At the top of the Chinese pyramid, however, one figure remained unmoved by the implications of the fearsome rift he had done so much to provoke. Mao Zedong had now finally achieved his objective of driving the last dominant foreign presence from Chinese soil. So far as he was concerned this was China's second Liberation, whatever the collateral damage to the country's science, industry and foreign trade.[250] 'This will force us to be self-reliant', he commented. 'It's a blessing in disguise, no?'[251] As if validating Mao's opinion Chinese boffins were busily piecing together a number of blueprints left shredded by the departing Soviet nuclear scientists and embarking on their own independent research programme which they mockingly called Project 596 after the year and month when the Kremlin had broken off its assistance to them. In October 1964 their efforts were crowned by the detonation of an atomic bomb.

CHAPTER 7

CONFRONTATION

LAST APPROACHES (1960–6)

During the first two years of the 1960s one of the loudest noises to be heard from the Sino-Soviet arena was the screeching of brakes. Faced with the shattering outcome of the Great Leap Forward, the huge damage inflicted on both agriculture and industry, the unspeakable famine, Mao Zedong, as the principal author of the catastrophe, found it judicious to retreat for the moment to the 'second line' of the CCP leadership and devote himself to theoretical work. In his relative absence the task of repairing the devastation devolved on his more pragmatic associates – Liu Shaoqi, his proclaimed heir apparent and since 1959 the PRC's ceremonial head of state; Deng Xiaoping, the Party's secretary-general; and the premier and factotum, Zhou Enlai. It was evident to these men, and to many besides them, that to climb out of the wreckage China had to receive economic aid and particularly food aid from outside, and that in view of the country's isolation from the non-Communist world the only plausible source of such aid was the Soviet Union. By as early as November 1960 Chinese officials were pleading with the Soviet authorities to send their advisers back.

But if Soviet aid was to be regained the gaping cracks which had opened in the former partnership had to be papered over at the very least. In the autumn of 1960 yet another Marxist-Leninist synod was held in Moscow, attended by eighty-one of the world's Communist Parties. At the head of the Chinese delegation was Liu Shaoqi. Always well disposed to the Soviet

Union, Liu is said to have been deeply troubled by the drastic worsening of inter-Party ties, and on a personal level by the possible implications for his half-Russian grandchildren who continued to live in the Soviet capital. He was seen pacing gloomily, chain-smoking, up and down in the woods that surrounded the dacha where the CCP team were housed. On 6 November, shortly before the conference opened, he paid a call on Khrushchev in the Kremlin in which he expressed his intention of taking a back seat in the coming debates and agreed that if the meeting ended successfully he would carry out a tour of the Soviet Union in his capacity as head of state. Over the following weeks he remained largely silent, and the few interventions he did make appeared to point strongly to his wish for a settlement. On one occasion he echoed Khrushchev's own thesis, anathema to the Chairman, that war between the Communist and capitalist worlds was unthinkable; on another he spoke of Mao's provocative People's Communes as being no more than a 'temporary expedient'.[1] It fell to his deputy, Deng Xiaoping, to maintain China's doctrinal challenge, which Deng did with some brio, condemning Khrushchev's 'mistaken methods' and at one point even engaging in a 'violent personal quarrel' with the Soviet chief.[2] Back in Peking Mao sent a message urging his delegates to 'fight to the death and not fear a breakdown';[3] but he seems somehow to have been circumvented. On 25 November the CCP Politburo 'unanimously' resolved that their team at the conference should make some concessions on doctrine with the object of averting a split, and on 30 November Liu paid a further call on Khrushchev to seal the deal. The CCP team agreed that the conference Declaration should enshrine once again the contents of Khrushchev's transformational Twentieth Congress with its vision of a peaceful worldwide transition to socialism by the parliamentary road. And Liu duly made his state visit. Over nine days in December he travelled amicably to Leningrad, Minsk and Irkutsk on the shores of Lake Baikal, in the company of a certain Leonid Brezhnev who was currently serving as ceremonial head of state on the Soviet side. In one speech at this period he proclaimed, 'Solidarity – that is the source of our strength.'[4] In another he prophesied that 'just as people have never seen the sun rise in the west', so the world would never witness a Sino-Soviet rupture.[5]

Right through the following year and well into 1962 the CCP pragmatists kept up their emollient line. As the ravages of the Great Leap became more and more evident fingers pointed increasingly at the policies which had brought them about. In January–February 1962, at a gathering of officials from all over China that became known as the Conference of the Seven Thousand, Mao came probably closer to being denounced by his colleagues than at any other point in his reign. Liu Shaoqi, who had been shaken to the core the previous April by a glimpse of the mass starvation in his (and Mao's) native province of Hunan, abandoned his usual discretion to confront the Chairman directly with the shortages of food and clothing, the slump in agricultural output and the general Great Lurch Backward, and was followed by scores of participants who condemned the Great Leap policies and insisted that they must be scrapped. And if Mao's domestic programme had been found wanting, what did that say for his management of foreign affairs? In March 1961 Vice-premier Li Fuchun, one of the leaders most closely associated with the Sino-Soviet economic partnership, went so far as to apologise to a group of Soviet visitors for the part China had played in the 'complications' of the previous year, and a Work Bulletin of the People's Liberation Army which fell into Western hands in April stressed the need to maintain good relations with Moscow, pointing out that the CCP couldn't expect to agree with the Russians on everything. In February 1962, in the aftermath of the Conference of the Seven Thousand, Wang Jiaxiang, the professorial figure who had served as the PRC's first ambassador to Moscow and was now heading the CCP Central Committee's International Liaison Department, submitted a plan for the Party to follow a new and more moderate foreign policy course. His idea was to bring about 'Three Reconciliations and One Reduction' – reconciliations with the Soviet Union, the United States and India and a reduction in Chinese military and economic commitments to the developing world. This project received the approval of Liu and the rest of the pragmatists. Even Zhou Enlai, so often the Chairman's alter ego, was reported to have declared to the National People's Congress, the PRC's parliament, that China would necessarily develop cooperation and friendship with the Soviet Union and its Eastern European sister states. By the end of 1961 moves were afoot in high Party circles to secure the return to favour of Khrushchev's supposed confederate, Marshal Peng Dehuai, and the following summer the marshal himself lodged a formal appeal for rehabilitation. In July 1962 Mao Dun, the eminent novelist of the 1930s, led a Chinese delegation to a World Disarmament Conference in Moscow, where the group unexpectedly took an approach so positive that the sponsoring World Peace Council even proposed giving them a gold medal.

The Kremlin bosses too showed a distinct inclination to bury the hatchet. It was one thing to chastise the CCP for their insubordination; quite another to have them drop right out of the Soviet orbit. On 7 November 1960, at the parade in Red Square which took place just before the opening of the Communist synod to mark the anniversary of the Bolshevik Revolution, the Russians gave conspicuous proof of their regard for Liu Shaoqi by allowing him to mount the Lenin Mausoleum ahead of everyone else and placing him in the central spot on the Mausoleum reviewing stand between Khrushchev and Brezhnev. The Declaration which issued from the synod bore the imprint of Chinese as well as Soviet views. The Yugoslav Party, habitually used by Chinese propagandists as a rhetorical punchbag in place of their real target, the CPSU, were slated for their 'revisionism', the predatory nature of the Western powers was agreed to be immutable and stress was placed on the 'free and sovereign peoples' who made up the socialist commonwealth.[6] In the course of the talks Mikoyan indicated that the Soviet Union was willing to discuss sending food and reassigning specialists to the stricken PRC; and within weeks some steps were already being taken in that direction. In early February 1961 Ivan Arkhipov, the former economic adviser to the Chinese government who had since been appointed vice-chairman of the State Committee for Foreign Economic Relations, was dispatched to Peking at the head of a mission to talk about economic and trade ties, and on 27 February Khrushchev himself wrote to Mao observing that the Chinese famine reminded him of the dreadful starvation and cannibalism in post-war Ukraine and promising a massive shipment to China of 500,000 tons of Cuban sugar and a million tons of grain – this at a time when the Soviet Union was itself undergoing severe food shortages. Following the arrival of a Chinese delegation in Moscow in April a deal was struck that provided not only for food but also for the postponement for four years of the repayment of China's outstanding debt to the Soviet Union, which now stood at $288 million. Fresh help was forthcoming to satisfy a continued Chinese demand for Soviet military hardware. In 1961–2 the Kremlin provided the PRC with a total of up to twenty-six of their new MiG-21 fighter aircraft, licensing their production in China with the assistance of Soviet experts and continuing to deliver the appropriate spare parts and special materials. Technical documents were also supplied to enable the Chinese to start the production of Ilyushin Il-14 passenger planes. Even the KGB showed a trace of benevolence. In August 1961 the authorities were confronted with a pair of star-crossed lovers. Romeo was a Russian student at Leningrad University, Juliet a visiting Chinese student attached to the same institution. When Juliet was obliged to go home at the end of her course Romeo followed her all the way to the Manchurian border. Juliet sent word of her determination to cross back illegally into Soviet territory, but the ensuing scheme was discovered and the pair threatened suicide unless they were permitted to reunite. The Soviet security chiefs advised the CPSU Central Committee that if the Chinese were willing to admit Romeo they had no objection to letting him go.

But Mao was having none of all this. Even at his lowest ebb he remained the ultimate authority over Chinese affairs and not least over Chinese dealings with Moscow. And he hadn't the slightest desire for the two great Communist powers to kiss and make up. The economic agreement arrived at in April 1961 was hedged in on all sides by Mao's stubborn determination to minimise his dependence on Soviet help. The document took the form of a trade protocol rather than a simple dollop of aid. The Chinese side accepted Khrushchev's offer of Cuban sugar, to be paid for through an interest-free loan, but declined the accompanying handout of a million tons of grain, despite China's desperate need and in recognition, as Zhou Enlai put it gracefully, of the Soviet Union's own economic hardships. During the following year the PRC was obliged after all to accept a transfusion of 360,000 tons of grain from the Russians – on the understanding, however, that this would be paid for with 150,000 tons of Chinese rice. The debt moratorium provided for in the agreement was in fact a good deal shorter than the Russians had envisaged: the original idea had been that the repayments should be staggered over sixteen years, but Mao was insistent on clearing the debt in just four – a result he had indeed accomplished by 1965. And in the very days the agreement was being finalised the Chairman's associates continued to subject the Kremlin to some vicious rhetorical jabs. Yuri Gagarin's pioneering space flight on 12 April was announced to the Chinese public by Foreign Minister Chen Yi in the following terms:

> Today two events have taken place. The first, *the principal one*, is the victory of the PRC in the world ping-pong championships. The second is the new scientific and technical achievement of the Soviet Union.[7]

In the early autumn of 1961 Khrushchev and his colleagues were busy preparing for the Twenty-second Congress of the CPSU, a meeting designed to confirm yet again the denunciation of Stalin and to proclaim once more the feasibility of a peaceful worldwide transition to socialism. This whole project was anathema to the Chairman, who pronounced the draft programme of the congress to be 'like the foot-binding bandages of Wang's wife, not only long but also stinking',[8] and sent Zhou Enlai off with a delegation to Moscow to uphold the hard Maoist line. The congress was accordingly subjected to a harsh Chinese onslaught, with Zhou interjecting provocative questions 'like a needle in wool' and lambasting his hosts for their condemnation of the Albanian Party (a punchbag used by the Russians for the CCP[9]). It is probably to this event that we should assign the (maybe apocryphal) story of Zhou's riposte to Khrushchev. On one occasion, when Khrushchev compared Zhou's mandarin antecedents unfavourably with his own peasant origins, the Chinese premier is said to have rejoined acidly, 'Well, at least you and I have one thing in common – *we've both betrayed our class*.'[10] One step Zhou certainly did take, on 21 October, was to lay a wreath inscribed 'To the Great Marxist-Leninist, J.V. Stalin' at the Red Square Mausoleum where the mummified remains of both Lenin and Stalin still lay side by side. It was a further slap in the face for the Soviet leaders, who were on the point of transferring Stalin's corpse from the Mausoleum to the relative obscurity of the Kremlin wall.

By this time Mao was ready to take some initial steps to deter his domestic Soviet lobby. Early in 1962 he unleashed his bloodhound, Kang Sheng, to sniff out any persons in the CCP who had shown signs of an unhealthy intimacy with the Russians. Li Lisan, Mao's precursor in the Party leadership, came under pressure to divorce Lisa Kishkina, the Soviet wife he had married in the 1930s, who had now fallen under suspicion of espionage. A compromise was eventually reached under which Lisa would be left unmolested on condition that she agreed to renounce her Soviet citizenship. But a warning shot had been fired, and Kang aimed an additional threat at Li's half-Russian daughters, whom he accused of being un-Chinese, wearing 'short skirts, much shorter even than in Moscow',[11] and 'always hanging out with their revisionist pals'.[12] Kang moved on to investigate several hundreds of thousands of Chinese citizens who were held to have fraternised with the departed Soviet experts. In the late summer, during the Party leadership's annual retreat at the seaside resort of Beidaihe, the Chairman decisively re-emerged from the 'second line' and resumed active power. For the first time he explicitly linked the 'revisionism' of the Kremlin with the doctrinal backsliding of his own Party colleagues. Liu Shaoqi was berated for having started along the 'revisionist' road. Wang Jiaxiang's 'Three Reconciliations and One Reduction' were castigated as having 'continued to draw close to Khrushchev's ideas',[13] and the sometime 'Red Professor' was dropped from his post in the Party's International Liaison Department and disappeared altogether from public life. Mao Dun and his team at the World Disarmament Conference in Moscow were directed to make an about-turn to a belligerent posture; a switch they performed so effectively that the Chairman felt able to praise them, '*Wrong in July, corrected in August*.'[14] At a Party plenum held in September Marshal Peng Dehuai's application for a return to favour was 'forcefully' rejected, while Xi Zhongxun, father of the future Chinese president Xi Jinping, was 'savagely' criticised by Kang Sheng for having pressed for the posthumous rehabilitation of that disgraced friend of Russia, Gao Gang.[15] Looking back in the following year on the various efforts made by the CCP pragmatists to mend fences with Moscow, Mao could only conclude that a minority of his comrades had gone rather mad.

Having muzzled his own Moscow-leaners the Chairman went on to proclaim a full-scale doctrinal offensive against the backsliders in Moscow itself. A perfect starting point was provided that autumn of 1962 by the Cuban Missile Crisis. Holding back for a few days in response to an offer from Khrushchev of support for the PRC's simultaneous war with India in exchange for Chinese support over Cuba, the Chinese went for the jugular after the Soviet leader agreed to withdraw his rockets from the island on 28 October. The Kremlin leadership were accused of 'adventurism' for having got into the crisis and 'capitulationism' for having got out of it. On the following New Year's Day the *People's Daily* in Peking carried for the first time a public denunciation of Khrushchev by name, and for the first time it bracketed US 'imperialism' and Soviet 'revisionism' as a pair of twin evils. On 24 June 1963 the CCP issued an Open Letter to the Soviet Party, with twenty-five theses aimed at both Soviet foreign and domestic policy and an explicit condemnation of the sacred Twentieth Congress. Early in July a CCP delegation arrived in Moscow with the ostensible purpose of ironing out their differences with the CPSU, but showed no sign whatever of giving ground. Once again Deng

Xiaoping led the charge. 'Look', he admonished Khrushchev, 'at the chaos into which you have plunged the beautiful socialist camp!'[16] He derided the Kremlin's pretensions to 'internationalism' and described his own strictures as 'a bitter but necessary medicine'.[17] Then from early September right through to early July 1964 the CCP's theoretical journal, *Red Flag*, published a series of 'Nine Criticisms' designed to expose the whole record of Soviet perfidy. 'Not all the water in the Volga', the *Peking Review* told Khrushchev, 'can wash away the great shame you have brought upon the CPSU and upon the Soviet Union.'[18] These Great Polemics, as the Chinese called them, were accompanied by a couple of striking new features. In the first place the conflict had gone global. By merely posing their doctrinal challenge the CCP had made an assertion of independence from their Soviet overlords for all the world to see; by letting fly with their arguments they undermined, in the eyes of the world, the rival Party's legitimacy and its international standing. Their bid for the sympathy of the Eastern European satellite states, already apparent in the late 1950s, was now unmistakable, with Mao contending in February 1964 that the Soviet 'revisionist' line was 'rebuffed in Romania and not listened to in Poland'.[19] In the new radical forums of the non-aligned world they pressed ahead with their drive to have the Soviet Union excluded as a *European* power: in January 1963 the chief Chinese delegate at a meeting of the Afro-Asian People's Solidarity Organisation icily told his Soviet opposite number, 'We regret that you came here at all, and to think that you were needed here is an insult to the solidarity movement of the Afro-Asian countries.'[20] And in both these arenas they busied themselves with the attempted formation of anti-Soviet splinter groups. The Polemics were also underpinned by behaviour of a spectacularly provocative kind. In Moscow Chinese diplomats and visiting Chinese citizens handed out copies of the CCP's Open Letter of June 1963 to any passing Russians who would take them, and members of a Chinese group attending a World Women's Congress disrupted the proceedings so effectively that the congress had to be adjourned. Incensed by the confiscation of their polemical pamphlets, some Chinese students crossing into the Soviet Union from Mongolia at the border station of Naushki were reported by Soviet sources to have pulled down their trousers and systematically fouled the station platform.[21]

Nor was Mao's offensive restricted to doctrine. In the course of the early 1960s the Sino-Soviet quarrel began to expand from Party versus Party to the larger dimension of State versus State. Already in June 1960 one of the old territorial issues referred to by Zhou Enlai during his visit to Moscow three years earlier had been deliberately fanned into life. On the orders of their local People's Commune a band of some hundreds of shepherds who lived near the Buz-Aygur Pass in Xinjiang drove their combined flock of 15,000 sheep across the frontier with the Kirghiz SSR to a depth of three or four kilometres and resisted for some weeks every effort by the Soviet border guards to make them budge. Officials at the Foreign Ministry in Peking told a protesting Soviet diplomat, '*You* think this is Soviet territory but *we* think it belongs to the People's Republic of China.'[22] Over the next few years squabbles of this kind began to take place repeatedly on the Xinjiang and Manchurian borders, with the Soviet side reporting a total of 5,000 Chinese border violations in 1962 alone. On 8 March 1963 an editorial in the *People's Daily* made the first public CCP allusion to the 'unequal' nature of the nineteenth-century treaties between tsarist Russia and the Qing, and on 27 September the Foreign Ministry formally brought up the 'unequal treaties' as a subject that had to be addressed.

In every sphere of activity Mao seemed intent on expunging the last traces of Russia from Chinese soil. Trade declined steadily by a factor of 18 per cent in 1962, 20 per cent in 1963 and 25 per cent in 1964 as the Chairman sought to detach the Chinese economy from its Soviet moorings and form new business partnerships with Western Europe and Japan. Early in 1964 he compared Soviet exports unfavourably with those of France. 'We can do a little business', he remarked, '[with the Soviet Union], but we can't do much, for Soviet products are heavy and crude, highly priced, and they always keep something back.'[23] Cultural ties were likewise in free fall. By November 1960 even Tolstoy, beloved by generations of Chinese readers, was under attack from the CCP radicals as a 'landowner' and a 'defender of the status of the nobility'.[24] Modern Soviet authors such as Sholokhov, Simonov and Ehrenburg were equally judged to be 'bad' and 'subversive'. By 1962 Russian literature of all kinds had effectively been banned in China, and the only works still imported for local consumption were children's stories. In 1964–5 Soviet contributions to the performing arts were damned in their turn, as the opera *Eugene Onegin* and the ballets *Swan Lake* and *Giselle* were discovered to 'stupefy and corrupt the workers'.[25]

Raked by these broadsides the Russians assumed their now characteristic reactive stance. In the words of one Soviet diplomat in Peking they 'frequently acted on the principle of a fire brigade', waiting for challenges to arise and then taking what steps seemed appropriate in each situation.[26] In some cases they gave as good as they got. At the CPSU's Twenty-second Congress in October 1961 Khrushchev told Zhou Enlai bluntly that while the voice of the CCP had once carried weight in international Communist circles, 'things were different now'.[27] He mocked Mao's apparent egalitarian ideal of a populace 'squatting in rags round a communal tin bowl drinking watered soup', and contrasted with this his own vision of an affluent collectivised society providing 'a plate of goulash for everyone'.[28] (Mao mocked back by vocalising the word 'goulash' as *gou lashi* – the Chinese for 'dog shit'.) The July 1963 parley in Moscow turned out to be, as Deng Xiaoping put it, a 'dialogue of the deaf',[29] as the Soviet team headed by the Kremlin's ideological pontiff, Mikhail Suslov, rebuffed the Chinese diatribes by simply reading out their own long prepared statements, and the parley broke up after two weeks without any agreement being reached. In the meantime the CPSU had replied to the CCP's Open Letter, denouncing the Chinese Party for their 'erroneous and fatal' belligerence and firmly rejecting their call for another world war;[30] and the Chinese diplomats and other citizens who had distributed copies of the Open Letter were promptly expelled. Over the following year Suslov led the Soviet counter-attack against the Chinese Nine Criticisms, flaying the CCP for their nationalism and for 'adopting the methods and line of the Trotskyites' through their attempts to foster anti-Soviet splinter groups in Parties and radical movements around the world.[31] In this context Khrushchev and his colleagues defended themselves stubbornly against the Chinese charge of betraying the anti-colonial struggle. Khrushchev insisted in biblical mode, 'You can see we are true Christians, so to speak, who obey Christ's commandments.'[32]

The Soviet bosses also stood their ground in the borderlands. In April–May 1962 a host of some 62,000 Kazakhs and members of other minority groups poured over the Xinjiang border from the Yili district into Soviet Kazakhstan – not this time on the orders of their local commune but in full flight from the great famine and the suffocation of the commune system under which 'life [was] measured by the ringing of a gong' while the least show of political disaffection would see them consigned to 'reeducation' camps.[33] The Kremlin's response in this case was to shift to its old default posture of backing the Turkic minorities against their Chinese overlords.

Propaganda broadcasts were made to entice the fugitives across the border by reminding them of the Soviet Union's 'traditional' friendship and its support for the 'Eastern Turkestan Republic' of 1944–9. The Soviet consulates in Yining and Urumqi began once again to hand passports out to all comers, and Soviet agents facilitated the exodus by opening gaps in the wire entanglements laid along the border and guiding the fugitives to them with the help of searchlights, signal flares and vehicle headlamps. Soviet border guards seem to have kept their end up in the periodic scrimmages that took place along both the Xinjiang and Manchurian frontiers: Chinese officials claimed that 1,674 incidents that took place on the frontiers between 1960 and 1964 were provoked by the Soviet side. And the Russians also took vigorous action to strengthen their dominant position in Outer Mongolia. In the late summer of 1960 the Kremlin bestowed on the MPR an aid package that easily trumped the economic support with which Peking had attempted to win back the region's allegiance, and the political dividends soon became clear. In an interview with Zhou Enlai in December 1962 the MPR leader, Yumjaagiin Tsedenbal, bluntly declared his country's neutrality in the conflict between China and India. Unprepared seemingly for this show of defiance from a territory that had formed part of the Chinese empire for generations, the premier lost his habitual cool, and the two men are said to have virtually descended to fisticuffs as Tsedenbal pleaded with his host to 'calm down, calm down'.[34] One year later, in December 1963, the MPR government formally complained of the pressure they had been put under to accept Chinese influence, and in June 1964 they requested the recall of the 20,000-odd labourers whom the PRC had planted in their midst. Outer Mongolia's status as a Soviet protectorate had by now been confirmed beyond any further doubt.

Yet in spite of these pushbacks the Kremlin was still, unlike Mao, seeking pathways to reconciliation. On 21 February 1963, six months into the Chairman's doctrinal offensive, the CPSU Central Committee sent an 'even-tempered' letter to their CCP counterparts calling for an end to polemics and talks on the whole range of troubled bilateral issues.[35] This démarche led eventually to the two-week parley in July. In the course of the general stonewalling Suslov gave an account of the scope for possible Sino-Soviet cooperation in the spheres of trade, science and technology and currency policy – a recital described as 'boring' by one of his own Russian colleagues and of no interest whatever to the pugnacious Chinese,[36] but which none less suggests some desire to accentuate the positive. The July parley coincided with a more productive discussion that was taking place, also in Moscow, between representatives of the Soviet Union, Britain and the United States on the conclusion of a Nuclear Test Ban Treaty. In the course of these talks President Kennedy's special envoy, Averell Harriman, showed Khrushchev US intelligence data on Mao's nuclear programme and quietly put the case for a joint US–Soviet operation to bomb China's nuclear facilities before it was too late. Khrushchev however declined to be drawn into such an adventure, telling Harriman firmly that the Chinese nuclear programme posed no threat. Even now, in the thick of the ideological quarrel, there were still upwards of 1,000 Chinese students and technical trainees in the Soviet Union, including, amazingly, a contingent at the Dubna Nuclear Research Institute.

The Kremlin was even prepared to give ground on the territorial question. In May 1963, two months after the *People's Daily* had first raised the subject of the nineteenth-century treaties, the Soviet leaders declared themselves willing to enter into talks on the disputed sections of the Sino-Soviet border, and in February 1964 a delegation assigned to that purpose arrived in Peking. Over the next five months, against all expectation, the delegates managed to reach agreement with their Chinese counterparts on almost the entire eastern section of the border, 4,200 out of a total 4,280 kilometres, with differences only remaining about one or two places such as Bolshoi Ussuriisky/Heixiazi, the large island opposite Khabarovsk. The Soviet team went so far as to concede for the first time that the border should run along the main navigation channel of the border rivers, the *thalweg*, to give it its technical German name, in accordance with international law, rather than along the Chinese riverbanks as the Russians had been insisting from tsarist times onwards: this would have the effect of transferring around 400 of a total of 700 islets in the Amur and Ussuri to Chinese control. By early July an agreement appeared to be in the bag, and the Soviet negotiators were encouraged to relax at Beidaihe in the pleasant expectation of a signing.

But at this point Mao struck once again. On 10 July he declared to a visiting delegation of the Japanese Socialist Party that the Russians had occupied 'too many places' in Europe and Asia since the Second World War. They had imposed their rule upon Outer Mongolia. 'Some' of them had suggested that Xinjiang should be absorbed into the Soviet Union. Looking deeper into the past, the Chairman continued that China had not yet 'presented the bill' for Vladivostok, Khabarovsk, Kamchatka and other towns and regions east of Lake Baikal which had become Russian territory 'about a hundred years ago'.[37] The point was that the talks in Peking had concentrated exclusively on the PRC claims to disputed tracts of the border itself, amounting to a relatively modest 35,000 square kilometres, whereas Mao was apparently moving the goalposts by bringing up for discussion the whole vast Manchurian hinterland taken from the Qing dynasty by tsarist Russia under the 'unequal treaties', totalling a fantastic 1.5 million square kilometres, and throwing in for good measure the Kamchatka peninsula in the far northern Pacific to which China hadn't the ghost of a claim. Mao subsequently explained to an Albanian minister that he had 'merely been firing a blank' with the object of keeping the Russians in a state of tension: Khrushchev was 'the kind of person who doesn't feel good if you don't fire a few blank shots at him'.[38] But the fact was that the Chairman had deliberately sabotaged a process which looked like delivering a major improvement in Sino-Soviet ties. The Soviet team left for home in high dudgeon on 28 August, and Khrushchev threw away a Chinese supporting map 'in disgust'.[39] He pointed out that the Qing rulers of China had proved every bit as predatory as their tsarist opposite numbers, and had indeed been responsible for the Chinese annexation of Mongolia, Tibet and Xinjiang. In any event he found little merit in the standpoint of those who persisted in citing 'the frontiers of the Old Testament'.[40]

In the midst of this stalemate, however, another way forward seemed suddenly to be presenting itself. For some time now the ground in the Kremlin had been slipping from under the feet of the ageing Khrushchev. His associates had been displeased by his handling of many issues, from the Cuban Missile Crisis to the failed Virgin Lands agricultural scheme for developing Kazakhstan, and not least by his management of the quarrel with China. Suslov the high priest argued that while Khrushchev couldn't be blamed for the downturn in the Party-to-Party relationship, he had worsened the feud by allowing it to sink to the level of personal vituperation between himself and Mao. In recent years he had even surpassed the Chairman's capacity for gutter language: Western journalists in Moscow believed that his description of Mao as 'a man with a worm writhing and wriggling in his arsehole' had caused almost as much offence in the Soviet Union as in China itself.[41] And by attracting Mao's diatribes he had simply succeeded in bringing humiliation on himself and the country as a whole. A joke circulated:

> Q: Who discovered the Earth was round?
> A: Our beloved leader, Nikita Sergeevich Khrushchev. He pissed on the West and it came back from the East.[42]

Any residual Soviet sympathy for the Chinese had been largely extinguished by the extreme behaviour they had exhibited during the quarrel, but there was a sense that on one or two issues they had perhaps got it right. Alexander Shelepin, a former KGB chief, condemned Khrushchev's 'adventurism' and 'capitulationism' over Cuba in virtually the identical terms used by Mao's propaganda machine. On 15 October 1964 the old man was quietly deposed in a boardroom coup engineered by Suslov and the KGB top brass, and replaced by a leadership tandem of Leonid Brezhnev and Alexei Kosygin.

This switch of leaders at once aroused worldwide expectation of a fresh Soviet effort to end the feud. In spite of the nine days he spent showing Liu Shaoqi around Soviet cities in December 1960, Brezhnev seems at this stage to have shown little interest either in China or in foreign policy in general. Instead the banner of conciliation was raised by his colleague Kosygin, the lugubrious-looking economic planner, so self-effacing he managed to serve as the Soviet premier for the next sixteen years without earning more than an entry or two in the index of the average Western history book. Kosygin however appears to have been, not unlike Liu in China, a staunch mainstream Communist, convinced that any differences which might arise between Parties must and easily could be overcome. He is said to have been filled with 'a sense of euphoria' (if it's possible to imagine a euphoric Kosygin) at the news that Zhou Enlai would be coming to Moscow to attend the festivities marking the forty-seventh anniversary of the Bolshevik Revolution.[43] For all Zhou's occasional sallies at their expense the Soviet leadership had maintained a continuing faith in the Chinese prime minister as 'a bright, flexible and up-to-date man with whom we could talk sensibly'.[44] Here surely at last was the chance for a breakthrough. But once again it ended in tears.

Mao and his entourage seem to have given the news of Khrushchev's deposition a tepid reception at best. Briefed by Ambassador Chervonenko on the night of 15 October, the Chairman is said to have commented, 'Nice move you have made, but this is not enough . . . There are still a few things that need fixing.'[45] The CCP leaders clearly thought the events in the Kremlin worth monitoring, and Zhou is said to have solicited an invitation to the Moscow festivities with that aim in view. But the presence in his assigned escort of Mao's hatchet man, Kang Sheng, didn't give cause for optimism; and Soviet diplomats noted in Zhou's demeanour in the run-up to his visit a strange haughtiness that likewise didn't bode well. Trouble erupted on virtually the first possible occasion, at the grand anniversary reception held at the Kremlin on the evening of 7 November. In the course of a conversation with Zhou and his entourage Marshal Malinovsky, the Soviet minister of defence, toasted the Chinese guests with the jovial suggestion, '*Now that we've kicked out our Nikita why don't you do the same to your Mao Zedong? Then we'll get along just fine!*'[46] What did Malinovsky think he was doing? Most accounts of the episode (including most Russian accounts) are agreed that the marshal was just plain drunk, and we recall from his time as commander-in-chief of the Soviet occupation force in Manchuria in 1945–6 that he was capable of being both boozy and garrulous. Other scholars however have seen a deliberate if very crude attempt to test the political waters. They find it unthinkable that a top-ranking military man, at an ultra-sensitive period, could have blurted out an idea so provocative out of sheer inadvertence, and point out that the marshal never got demoted or even censured as a result of his conduct that night. Perhaps there is room for a middle interpretation – that the marshal was under orders to make an overture while acting drunk. If his Chinese listeners showed any sign of receptiveness, well and good; if not his outburst could simply be dismissed as the alcohol talking. Zhou must of course have been terrified. One moment's hesitation in rejecting the gambit might easily spell ruin for him if Kang Sheng passed the word back to Mao. But it also seems clear that he jumped at this first chance to shatter the tentative atmosphere of goodwill. Snapping 'I don't understand what you're talking about', he stalked out of the banqueting hall at the head of his delegation, stopping on the way to vent his fury on the new Soviet head of state, Mikoyan.[47] He spent the night putting together an explanatory cable to the Chairman, and the following morning submitted a formal protest at the outrage to Brezhnev and other members of the new Moscow leadership who had called on him to pay their respects The Russians predictably dissociated themselves from Malinovsky's proposal and laid the blame on the vodka: Zhou lashed back with the Chinese equivalent of '*in vino veritas*'. Scheduled discussions went on for a few days, but were doomed from the outset, and Zhou's attitude made it apparent that nothing short of a complete doctrinal surrender on the part of the CPSU would be acceptable to the Chinese side. Back in Peking Mao was plainly delighted by the collapse of another rapprochement he had never wanted to see. 'Right,' he told the Standing Committee of the CCP Politburo on 8 November, 'we've got their pigtail in our hands and we can use this affair to take the offensive';[48] and he dismissed the new Soviet policy with a scathing new label – '*Khrushchevism without Khrushchev*'. After three days of talks an exhausted Mikoyan even acknowledged, 'On the question of relations with the CCP we and Khrushchev fully agree: one might even say we do not have any shades of opinion';[49] to which Zhou retorted, 'Since there is no difference between you what is there for us to talk about?'[50] It was left to Kosygin to try to persuade his Chinese guest on the way to the airport that he and his colleagues must have some differences with Khrushchev – or why else would they have sacked him? On 14 November the premier arrived back in Peking to a hero's welcome. Looking back decades later a Russian intelligence expert summed up the message of the episode: '*We learnt that we could not divide Zhou and Mao*.'[51]

But the Soviet China lobby had not yet been silenced. In January 1965 at a meeting of the new Moscow Politburo, Kosygin pressed earnestly for a fresh overture to be made to Peking. Specifically he urged that Brezhnev should pay a visit to China in his capacity as the new General Secretary of the CPSU. The premier's views were received with some enthusiasm by Shelepin, the KGB man, with scepticism by almost everyone else. 'If you think it's that important,' grumped Brezhnev, 'why don't you go yourself?'[52] The upshot was an agreement that Kosygin would make a stopover in the Chinese capital in the first half of February, on his way back from a visit to North Vietnam. The war in Vietnam was intensifying, with the United States weighing in heavily in support of the South, and the Kremlin's ruling duo had made up their minds to give major backing to the Communist war effort. The Chinese were already involved, and Kosygin thought that the

Soviet Union and China would naturally be brought together by a joint commitment of military aid to Hanoi. As for the doctrinal squabbles, he believed he could sort them out and restore the old friendship in a couple of hours. He was quickly disabused of both notions. Arrived in Peking, he was kept waiting for almost an hour on the threshold of Mao's Zhongnanhai residence before the Chairman would deign to receive him. Mao's greeting was perfunctory, and the conversation that followed was 'pointed and rather unpleasant'.[53] So far as the Chairman was concerned Vietnam fell within the PRC's sphere of influence, and he had no desire for the Russians to muscle on to the scene. A proposal mooted by Kosygin for the establishment of a Soviet air base at Kunming, within easy reach of the North Vietnamese border, looked all too much to Mao like a rerun of Khrushchev's Joint Fleet suggestion in 1958 – an attempt to bring China under Soviet military control. To Kosygin's appeal for an end to the public polemics he replied that he was quite prepared to continue them for another 10,000 years, but would reduce this to 9,000 in acknowledgement of the Soviet premier's visit. (One is reminded of King Harold Godwinson at the Battle of Stamford Bridge offering the king of Norway, Harald Hardrada, 'six feet of English earth for a grave, or as much more as he may be taller than other men'.) Kosygin left in frustration, with a reproachful stare at the attendant Soviet diplomats, whom he appears to have blamed for his lack of progress.

The Chinese Soviet lobby too still showed signs of life even after the crackdown Mao had inflicted on them in the summer of 1962. The chief Chinese negotiator at the so nearly successful 1964 border talks, Zeng Yongquan, was a known ally of Liu Shaoqi. Working behind the scenes, Liu is thought to have coaxed the Russians towards the major concessions they made over the eastern border; and the draft document which emerged from the talks is even referred to by one Russian historian as the 'Khrushchev–Liu Shaoqi Agreement'. Liu is actually said to have been on the point of signing the document in his capacity as head of state of the PRC – when Mao moved the goalposts. Over the following year Liu continued to make a display of goodwill towards Moscow's representatives. In April 1965 he received the departing Soviet ambassador, Chervonenko, for a friendly farewell interview, avoiding all polemics and instead reminiscing wistfully about his stay in Soviet Russia in the early 1920s and his experience of seeing Lenin and hearing him speak. In May he had an equally affable talk with Chervonenko's successor, Sergei Lapin, who conveyed the hopes of his Kremlin masters for more contact with the CCP leadership. Liu replied, 'This is good. In the future we can and will meet.'[54] The veteran guerrilla leader, Zhu De, also met Lapin at his own request, and expressed the view that hostility to the Soviet Union was 'unacceptable'.[55] But behind all these promising signs there still lurked the grim stumbling-block of the Chairman. Liu's farewell to Chervonenko was attended by the ubiquitous Kang Sheng, 'His Majesty's Eye', as one Soviet diplomat called him,[56] who said nothing but quietly sat puffing one cigarette after another. Aides of Zhu De tried to block any eavesdropping on the Lapin meeting by Kang or his agents by rapping repeatedly with a metal object on a nearby radiator.

During the first months of 1966 the Kremlin made a final, despairing effort to bring the relationship back to something like normality. On 24 February Ambassador Lapin approached Liu Shaoqi on the tarmac at Peking Airport, where the PRC leaders had mustered to see off the visiting President Nkrumah of Ghana, with the news that he had 'something important' to hand over – an invitation to the CCP to take part in the CPSU's imminent Twenty-third Congress. Liu said 'Give me the letter.'[57] The invitation was back at the Soviet embassy: whether and how Lapin got it to Liu is unclear, but the Chairman later recalled that Liu had proposed the dispatch of a CCP delegation to the Moscow congress and he had said no. A parallel overture was attempted by the former KGB boss, Alexander Shelepin, who like Kosygin a year before stopped off in Peking on his way back from a trip to North Vietnam. Shelepin had tried unsuccessfully for a meeting with the Chinese Party's top leadership, whom he hoped to persuade of the Kremlin's desire to bridge the ideological gulf. On arrival he was indeed greeted by a vice-premier, Li Xiannian; but Li wasn't prepared to discuss anything of substance and instead . . . took him to the circus. On 23 March the CCP brusquely rejected the Soviet invitation to the Twenty-third Congress. This snub marked the final severance of ties between the two Parties. From now on any dealings between the Soviet Union and the PRC were conducted by government officials, and low-level officials at that. The last vestiges of economic teamwork were discontinued, and economic relations were reduced to the bare exchange of goods. Mao repeated once more his refusal to depend on the Russians: 'Our banners must be fresh, they must not be soiled in mud.'[58] And Foreign Minister Chen Yi supplied a practical justification: 'The Soviet Union is one of those dangerous friends without whom China feels more secure.'[59]

AT DAGGERS DRAWN (1966–9)

On 16 May 1966 Mao Zedong used a meeting of the CCP Politburo to launch his people into the ten-year frenzy known as the Great Proletarian Cultural Revolution. The Cultural Revolution had many targets. At the most literal level it was aimed at traditional culture, both Chinese and foreign, and at the 'bourgeois' educators through whom such culture was diffused. Beyond that it was aimed at the technocratic reformers, Liu Shaoqi and Deng Xiaoping in particular, who had tried to reverse Mao's rural collectivisation and were held by the Chairman to have steered the country back on to the 'capitalist road'. It was aimed at the Party bureaucracy. And yes, it was also aimed at the Soviet Union, both in an indirect sense and head-on. Mao intended to settle scores once and for all with the CCP moderates who had sought so persistently to frustrate his endeavours to tear China out of the Soviet orbit. Even after the severance of ties with the Soviet Party the danger remained that 'people like Khrushchev' who were 'still nestling beside us' might transmit the virus of Soviet 'revisionist' thinking to the CCP itself.[60] Even sooner than that they might work in cahoots with their Soviet patrons to pose a political and military challenge to Mao's rule. It was a question of treason. The West Wind, Mao claimed (now unmistakably meaning the Kremlin) was blowing 'fallen leaves' into the Chinese capital: 'if we don't sweep them up the dust will not disappear by itself'.[61] By the spring of 1966 the brooms were already at work.

First of the dead leaves to be cleared was Peng Zhen, the mayor of Peking. Already in trouble for having approved the performance of a new play which was seen as a veiled attack on the Chairman, Peng was now bombarded with fresh accusations of a Soviet-related kind. He was said to have urged the dispatch of a CCP delegation to the Soviet Party Congress – itself a display of what Mao regarded as 'treacherous behaviour'.[62] On a visit to Sichuan Province in February he was reported to have held a 'secret' meeting with his namesake, the disgraced Marshal Peng Dehuai, who was currently rusticated there. The PLA chief Marshal He Long was also in Sichuan at this juncture, and Peng Zhen was suspected of having conspired with both the two marshals in a 'military plot' which entailed making contact with a 'foreign embassy' and overthrowing the Chairman in a coup d'état.[63] The familiar damning phrases began to roll out. By March the mayor was under fire for running an 'independent kingdom', and on 16 May, when the Chairman proclaimed the Cultural Revolution, he was labelled an 'out-and-out revisionist' and stigmatised as a member of an 'Anti-Party Group'.[64] A worse fate awaited the marshals. Peng Dehuai was brought back from Sichuan to Peking, where he is said to have been interrogated some 260 times about his nefarious dealings with Khrushchev and beaten till his ribs were broken. He Long had never lived down the unfortunate report that he had been the first Chinese delegate at the Moscow reception in 1964 to be addressed by Malinovsky with his boozy invitation to overthrow Mao. He too was arrested and interrogated, and died in prison in 1969 in 'appalling circumstances'.[65] In the meantime Mao's attention had focused on Ulanhu, an ethnic minority satrap who had been left in charge for the past seventeen years in the sprawling border region of Inner Mongolia. In June 1966 the 'Mongolian Khan' was summoned to Peking to be 'struggled against' for having allegedly connived with the Kremlin to detach his region from China and merge it with Outer Mongolia in an expanded version of the MPR. Ulanhu didn't lack support locally, and by the spring of 1967 a near civil war was reported in Inner Mongolia as some 16,000 of his partisans battled with PLA units that had been sent from Peking to quell the unrest.

The arch-villain, however, was of course Liu Shaoqi. Stripped of his post as the PRC's head of state in August 1966, the 'Number One Capitalist Roader' had by October acquired the additional label of 'China's Khrushchev' – an epithet which identified him in particular as the hidden betrayer 'nestling' in the leadership while associating him subliminally with the Soviet Union and all that it stood for. In March 1968 he was denounced by Kang Sheng as a traitor, and in October that year he was formally expelled from the Party as a 'renegade, traitor and scab' and a 'running dog of revisionism'.[66] In the meantime he was subjected to the whole gamut of Cultural Revolution torments, beaten up and jeered at by Red Guards in the Zhongnanhai complex before being committed to solitary confinement under the supervision of gaolers who were under explicit instructions to treat him harshly and doctors who went through the motions of treating him for pneumonia and diabetes, cursing him as they did so. Haggard and dishevelled, he was moved in October 1969 to the north-central province of

Henan, where he was housed in conditions of bitter cold and denied both X-rays and hospital treatment. Covered in bed sores, his leg muscles atrophied, he was unable by this time to get out of bed or to change his clothes, and no one dared help him. He died the following month in 'squalid misery'.[67]

By the summer of 1967 the brooms had swept wider, and any trace of involvement with anything Soviet was apt to be pounced on as treasonable. On 18 June fate finally caught up with Li Lisan and his Russian wife Lisa, who were hauled before rallies of Mao's screaming acolytes, the Red Guards, for denunciation as 'Soviet revisionist spies'. Tortured and humiliated, Li was reported to have put an end to himself four days later with an overdose of sleeping pills. Lisa was packed off to serve eight years of solitary confinement in the Qincheng Prison, a top-security complex on the edge of the capital which had been built, ironically enough, with Soviet help in the late 1950s. Similar treatment was meted out to Shi Zhe, a fluent Russian speaker with a Soviet wife and children who had served as the leading interpreter for Mao and his colleagues in their dealings with Moscow in the early years of the PRC. Now suspected of having been privy to secret exchanges between Stalin and Peng Dehuai, he too was immured in the Qincheng Prison and kept busy composing several hundred copies of his alleged crimes. Yet another victim was Sun Weishi, the adopted daughter of Zhou Enlai, who had served as a top-flight Russian language interpreter before launching into a career as a theatrical producer who brought the works of Gogol and Chekhov to the Chinese stage. Arrested as a 'Soviet spy', tortured and according to some accounts repeatedly raped, she died behind bars. Zhou is said to have registered no emotion at her downfall, any more than Molotov had done when his wife Polina was consigned to the Gulag in Stalin's last years. Doubly tainted by both his parentage and his Soviet education was Liu Shaoqi's son Liu Yunbin, the young nuclear scientist who had once been known to the Russians as 'Klim'. Branded a 'Soviet spy', spat on and beaten at his place of work, he came home to his family one evening in November 1967, filthy but forcing a smile, and quoted a couplet from his beloved Pushkin:

> If life deceives you, don't be sad, don't be gloomy;
> Believe, and the days of brightness will come.

A week or two later he headed off into the night, laid himself on a railway track and was killed by an oncoming train that smashed half of his head in. His death was described by the press as a 'guilty suicide'.[68] His brother Yunruo, who had begged to rejoin his Russian girlfriend in Moscow, was likewise persecuted to death for pursuing 'illicit relations with a foreign country'.[69]

Not all the top leaders experienced the extremes of the purge. Not Zhu De, for example. Despite his frequent professions of warmth towards the Soviet Union Mao's one-time guerrilla confederate was still probably too revered to subject to the most vicious humiliations. The worst that befell him was a four-year suspension from the Standing Committee of the Politburo. And not Deng Xiaoping. The 'Number Two Capitalist Roader' was saved from Number One's fate by his anti-Soviet track record. Already in June 1968 Mao remarked about Deng, 'Some say that he colluded with the [Soviet] enemy, but I don't set much store by this',[70] and in April 1969 he insisted that a distinction must be drawn between Deng and Liu Shaoqi.[71] In later years he elaborated that Deng had been an anti-Soviet hero who had led the CCP delegation to Moscow in 1963 to do battle with revisionism, and had held his own under Soviet pressure.[72] Rusticated to work in a tractor repair station in Jiangxi Province, the little pragmatist lived on to fight another day.

The wrath of the Cultural Revolution was also directed at what little still remained of the Soviet presence in China. On 20 August 1966, three weeks after the Chairman gave his teenage fanatics licence to rebel, the first Red Guard demonstrations took place in front of the Soviet embassy in Peking. The thoroughfare outside the embassy was renamed Anti-Revisionism Street, and a wall poster promised the inmates, '*When the time comes we will skin you, we will strip out your veins, we will burn your corpses and scatter the ashes to the winds*.'[73] In late January 1967 several thousands of Red Guards embarked on a two-week siege of the embassy. Imitation gibbets and coffins were fixed to the embassy gates, together with effigies of the Soviet leaders and posters exhorting, '*Hang Brezhnev!*', '*Boiling oil for Kosygin!*'.[74] The demonstrators subjected the Soviet diplomats to a fiendishly relentless programme of torture by noise, using loudspeakers to blare slogans into the embassy right through the day. Around midnight the noise stopped – only to resume fifteen minutes later when the exhausted diplomats were just dropping off to sleep, and so on at fifteen-minute intervals for the rest of the night. The beleaguered staff could no longer eat out, as the walls of the hotel restaurants (the only ones open to them) were smothered in hostile graffiti and the waiters refused to take their orders. In early February they managed to drive their women and children through the surrounding mob to the airport to fly them out; but the Red Guards were waiting there too. Around 200 protesters marched up and down the departure zone bawling anti-Soviet invective; and the women and children were made to crawl beneath huge portraits of Lenin, Stalin and Mao and to run a gauntlet of youths who spat and shook their fists at them and pulled their hair. The following August the embassy siege resumed with still greater intensity. A band of Red Guards drove around the perimeter of the embassy compound in a lorry filled with cobblestones and smashed 200 of the embassy window panes. On 17 August 100 or so of the most aggressive protesters broke every conceivable bounds. Bursting into the compound they set fire to a sentry box and a number of cars, stormed the consular section and burnt some documents, a radio receiver and a quantity of furniture. The diplomats were threatened with violence, and at least one was severely beaten up. It was the 1900 siege of the foreign legations all over again. As in 1900 it engendered a brief solidarity among the diplomatic corps. On the following day Donald Hopson, the British chargé d'affaires, called on a Soviet diplomat to express his sympathy over the mayhem. 'Well, this'll never happen to us,' he observed.[75] (Two days later it did.) And again, as in 1900, the Chinese authorities let it all happen. The Foreign Ministry sighed that they couldn't guarantee the Soviet diplomats' safety, and the police and the military sat on their hands.

Russophobe outbursts weren't confined to the capital. In August 1966 a Soviet merchantman, the *Zagorsk*, was detained by the local authorities in Dalian, the Manchurian port where the Russians had been periodically dominant in both tsarist and Soviet times. The vessel was said to have violated the rules of the port, and its captain to have 'behaved provocatively'. One year later, again in Dalian, a second vessel, the *Svirsk*, was detained, the crew browbeaten and the captain imprisoned. It turned out that the ship's second officer had refused to put on a Mao badge.

Nor were Russophobe outbursts exclusively aimed at the Soviets. In Xinjiang and Manchuria the fast-shrinking White Russian communities found themselves classified as 'politically unreliable elements' and 'Soviet revisionist spies'.[76] One night in August 1966 the much loved Russian Orthodox church of St Nicholas in Harbin, the 'Chocolate Church' of generations of emigrants, was 'mercilessly battered into firewood' while the church bells were jangled for hours by triumphant Red Guards.[77] The Albazintsy, descendants of those Cossack prisoners who had been settled in Peking by the Kangxi emperor, came under suspicion along with everyone else. Their homes were ransacked, and they were forced out of the north-eastern quarter of the old city where their people had lived ever since Kangxi's time and dispersed in a haphazard fashion around the other parts of town.

Last, the Red Guards trampled joyously on what little they could still find of the old Russian culture. By the end of 1966 a mob had demolished the Pushkin memorial which had been put up thirty years earlier by White Russian emigrants in Shanghai. Copies of Tolstoy's great novels, *War and Peace*, *Anna Karenina* and *Resurrection* were consigned to bonfires along with the works of Lermontov and Turgenev and other 'poisonous weeds'. Modern Soviet works fared no better. The stirring Second World War poems of Konstantin Simonov were compared by one literary journal to 'the braying of a donkey'.[78] Only *How the Steel Was Forged*, the impeccably Socialist Realist novel by Nikolai Ostrovsky, escaped execration.

Yet in casting out all things Russian the Chairman was as much as ever in thrall to his Soviet heritage. The very idea of a 'cultural revolution' had been developed before his time by both Lenin and Stalin, the latter of whom had envisaged it as a backdrop to his first Five Year Plan. Heroes extolled by the CCP media during this period such as Chen Yonggui, the model peasant leader and 'Iron Man' Wang Jinxi, the model oil driller, were merely the most recent incarnations of Stakhanov, the Soviet demigod of the late 1930s; and Mao's own grotesque personality cult, the worship of hysterical millions in Tiananmen Square, the veneration throughout the country of mangoes presented to the Chairman by the government of Pakistan, can be seen as competing with the adulation of Stalin's seventieth birthday, the dictator looming up in the night sky above Moscow as searchlights picked out his features in a giant portrait suspended by balloons. Even the villains, the 'Soviet spies' hunted down by Kang Sheng and the Red Guards, were in a sense nothing more than an updated version of the supposed German and Japanese agents who fell victim to Stalin's Great Purge. In this context the

CCP under Mao were reliving the adolescence of their now matured Soviet 'elder brother', and their rage at the CPSU can be put down to a certain extent to a generation gap.

As the Cultural Revolution approached and boiled over so the friction on the borders increased. The Russians maintained that the Chinese had violated their frontier over 2,000 times in 1967, more than twice the total for the previous year; the Chinese alleged that the Russians had committed no fewer than 4,189 violations between 1964 and 1969. Most of the time the two border guard forces observed certain tacit restraints. Confrontation was limited to oral protests, to pushing and shoving and tearing off one another's buttons. Sometimes, we are told, Chinese border guards on the Amur and Ussuri would pull down their trousers and 'moon' their Soviet counterparts on the opposite riverbank; the local Soviet officers countered by supplying their men with large photographs of Mao which they brandished, thus putting the Chinese in the appalling position of 'mooning' the Chairman.[79] But the clashes were getting uglier. On 5 January 1968 blood was shed for the first time when a Soviet force drove armoured vehicles into a Chinese crowd on the islet of Qilishan in the frozen Amur, killing four Chinese in the process. Over the following year tensions started to mount on another small island, this time in the Ussuri, known to the Russians as Damansky and to the Chinese as Treasure Island – Zhenbao. Damansky/Zhenbao had in fact been awarded to China under the abortive border agreement of 1964, and perhaps for this reason the Chinese seem to have been especially adamant that they were entitled to occupy it. In the last days of 1968 border guards from both sides fought a skirmish on the island with sticks and clubs. Mao apparently made up his mind that this was a suitable place for subjecting the Soviets to an armed onslaught, and on 15 February 1969 a plan for an ambush was approved by Premier Zhou Enlai, the Foreign Ministry and the PLA General Staff. During the night of 1–2 March a specially trained and equipped elite unit of some 300 PLA troops was smuggled on to Damansky/Zhenbao. The following morning a party of Soviet patrols arrived on the island for a tour of inspection and were met, according to a now familiar pattern, by a squad of their Chinese opposite numbers. The stand-off developed routinely – until the Chinese squad drew aside to reveal the 300-strong PLA company who were lurking behind them and who now opened fire on the Russians at point-blank range. In the ensuing melee the Soviet commander, a Senior

Lieutenant Ivan Strelnikov and upwards of thirty of his men were killed for a total of fifty to 100 on the PRC side. Soviet sources complained that the rampaging Chinese had shot wounded Russians close-up, or had stabbed them with knives or bayonets; that the faces of some of the victims were 'distorted beyond recognition'.[80] Liquor bottles found scattered around the island suggested that the attackers had purposefully fuelled themselves for the carnage. Sino-Russian relations had come full circle and were back in the seventeenth century, with far-flung garrisons scrapping over the Manchurian waterways.

The consensus view seems to be that Mao's motives for the onslaught were chiefly domestic. Ever since 1967 the Chairman had been taking steps to rein in the Red Guards, whose excesses had been making China ungovernable, and to restore order with the help of the PLA. A short, successful attack on a bewildered Soviet border force would busy giddy minds with foreign quarrels, boost the army's prestige and enable him to bring the Cultural Revolution to a triumphant close at the CCP's forthcoming Ninth Congress. But the fact remains that he had sanctioned a deliberate strike against a neighbouring foreign power. The Chairman hadn't bargained for the scale of the Russian reprisal. On 15 March several thousand Soviet troops took part in a retaliatory action on Damansky/Zhenbao. Local Soviet forces deployed many dozens of tanks and armoured vehicles, aircraft, artillery and Grad missiles capable of hitting targets some twenty kilometres inside Chinese territory. By the time they had finished their ambush 800 Chinese had been killed, while Soviet losses were recorded as no more than sixty. The Chinese had still not been wholly dislodged from Damansky/Zhenbao, but the island had been reduced to a 'moonscape of craters' and 'virtually erased from the map'.[81] Forty years since the last substantial clash between the two powers in Manchuria the Chinese had been dealt another reminder of the overwhelming superiority of Soviet arms.

Mao was sufficiently shaken by the outcome to issue an immediate order: 'We should stop here. Do not fight any more!'[82] Within a few weeks, however, he had apparently recovered his nerve. Beginning in April a further round of clashes broke out along the western part of the border, where Xinjiang adjoined Soviet Kazakhstan, and once again the general picture seems to have been one of Chinese provocation followed by heavy Soviet counter-strike. On 2 May the Chinese reprised their gambit of 1960, prodding local

Kazakh shepherds to drive their flocks across the existing border under cover of PLA troops with machine guns as a way of asserting Peking's territorial claims. The Russians responded in early June with a large armoured thrust into Xinjiang's Yumin county. In August Mao is said to have authorised an attack to be made in the neighbourhood of the Soviet border settlement of Zhalanaskol. A hundred PLA troops crossed the frontier under cover of darkness with intelligence-gathering equipment including a video camera and occupied the surrounding hills. The next day, 13 August, a local Soviet force of 300 men complete with armoured personnel carriers and a couple of helicopters cleared out the intruders, assailed the PRC border posts and advanced two miles into a portion of Yumin county which they effectively annexed. One Soviet official declared the idea was to show the Chinese that they couldn't expect to get away with these border pinpricks. Casualty figures for the Xinjiang border fighting are strangely modest. One Chinese report refers merely to an unfortunate shepherdess who was killed in the course of a shooting incident on 19 June, and Chinese figures for the battle at Zhalanaskol record an exiguous total of twenty-eight Chinese and two Soviet dead. Other sources suggest that the Zhalanaskol collision was far more serious, with heavy losses on both sides, a Chinese battalion wiped out and a general sense that the momentum was building inexorably towards an all-out war. On 28 August, two weeks after the fighting at Zhalanaskol, the CCP issued orders to the Chinese public to prepare for hostilities. Citizens were instructed to 'dig tunnels deep' and to 'store grain everywhere'. In late September Mao is even said to have authorised the testing of a couple of hydrogen bombs in Xinjiang. Though Chinese nuclear testing was nothing new such an exercise carried out at a time of acute tension could have been suicidally dangerous, and the Chairman apparently had to be prevailed upon to rescind his directive.[83]

Yet there was method in Mao's madness. To understand what, we must pause for a moment to trace the development of the Chairman's strategic thought. Ever since 1964 he had been taking steps to prepare China for a hypothetical foreign invasion. Whole industries were transplanted from the border regions and coastline to the interior, out of reach of enemy troops. The Chairman's sights weren't yet focused on one particular adversary: instead he talked in terms of a simultaneous onslaught by the Russians in the northern provinces and the Americans in the south. But then came

August 1968 and the Soviet crackdown in Czechoslovakia, followed three months later by the issuing of the 'Brezhnev Doctrine', with its ominous affirmation of Moscow's right to intervene in any Communist country where the Party had diverged from the straight and narrow. Chinese sources agree that from this point on the Soviet Union was indisputably Enemy Number One in Mao's eyes. The old slur of 'revisionist' cast at the Soviets for their perceived abandonment of Marxist-Leninist thinking was now supplemented by two further insults reflecting the Chairman's new focus on the Soviet military threat: the Russians were castigated as 'social imperialists', and Brezhnev and Kosygin were proclaimed 'the new tsars'.

In the light of this new thinking the Chairman now started to execute a strategic shift which one suspects he had meditated for a good many years. In March 1969, as the fighting flared up on Damansky/Zhenbao, Mao summoned a quartet of senior military men and instructed them to 'research the international situation'.[84] Over the following months these four 'old marshals' conferred with the Chairman no fewer than twenty-three times, and on 11 July they came up with an initial report. Highly timorous (how they must all have feared advocating a heresy!), they clung to the established line that the United States and the Soviet Union were equally pernicious, while concluding that the likelihood of an attack on China either by the two together or by one of them separately was not very great. In September, however, after Soviet forces drove back the PLA raiding band near Zhalanaskol, the 'old marshals' reported again. This time they spoke up a little more boldly, venturing the opinion that the United States 'would not wish to see a Soviet victory over China'.[85] They discerned a strategic benefit for the PRC in 'making use of the tension between the United States and the Soviet Union to strengthen our position', and observed that the Soviets would never dare fight a war on two fronts.[86] Finally one of the four, the former foreign minister Chen Yi, drew a deep breath and mooted the 'wild idea' that China might pursue a diplomatic breakthrough with the United States.[87] This was of course what Mao wanted to hear. At around the same time he informally canvassed the view of his physician, Dr Li Zhisui. Dr Li was even more chary about committing himself than the marshals; but the Chairman came clean. '*Think again . . . Didn't our ancestors recommend negotiating with faraway countries while fighting with those that are near?*'[88] The US and the Soviet Union, he continued, were different cases. 'The

United States never occupied Chinese territory . . . While Britain, Japan and Russia had imperialistic designs and became deeply involved in China's internal affairs, the United States remained aloof.'[89] Here, surely, was a force that could be relied on to offset the danger from the 'Polar Bear in the North'. Seen from this angle Mao's brinkmanship in 1969 starts to make sense as a way of signalling to the Americans that the PRC was available as a staunch reinforcement in their anti-Soviet struggle.

For some time now the Russians had been preparing a long-term military response to the Chinese rage. One early step was to plug the gap in their Chinese border defences represented by the MPR. In January 1966 Brezhnev travelled to Ulan Bator with his minister of defence and signed with the Outer Mongolian leadership a twenty-year Treaty of Friendship, Cooperation and Mutual Assistance remarkably similar to the defence pact concluded by Stalin with the MPR thirty years previously, when the perceived threat had come not from China but from Japan. The effect of this treaty was to lodge a Soviet army of 100,000 to 200,000 troops on the MPR–PRC border, just 560 kilometres to the north of Peking. Between 1966 and 1969 the Soviet military presence along the northern fringes of China expanded dramatically from seventeen to twenty-seven divisions, making an estimated total of 800,000 men, and new command posts were established at Alma Ata (facing Xinjiang) and Khabarovsk (facing Manchuria). The stage was set for a titanic collision.

Confronted with Peking's sudden military challenge in 1969 the Kremlin reacted in three different ways. Just as the Kennedy White House had come under pressure during the Cuban Missile Crisis from a small but vocal military clique represented by air force General Curtis LeMay, who urged an immediate invasion of the Soviet island protectorate even if this would provoke the Third World War, so now in Moscow a hawkish minority headed by the defence minister, Marshal Andrei Grechko, clamoured for drastic steps – for a 'surgical strike' against Chinese nuclear installations or a 'nuclear blockbuster' targeting Chinese industrial centres that would put paid to the China threat 'once and for all'.[90] On 15 March 1969, the day of the Soviet counter-attack on Damansky/Zhenbao, Moscow Radio noted, 'The Soviet Union's weapons are powerful and will perhaps inflict tens of millions of casualties'; and by mid-August, soon after the fighting at Zhalanaskol, the hawks were apparently gaining the upper hand as the Kremlin began clearing the path to apocalypse. On 18 August a second secretary at the Soviet embassy in Washington named Boris Davydov gave lunch to William L. Stearman, a middle-ranking Soviet expert in the State Department, and asked how he thought the United States would respond if Soviet forces took out the Chinese nuclear facilities at Lop Nor in Xinjiang. '*Yes, this is a real question, I am not making a joke.*'[91] Over the following weeks the approach was taken up at a higher level by the Soviet ambassador, Anatoly Dobrynin, who repeatedly tried to extract from Dr Henry Kissinger, national security adviser in the new Nixon administration, a US commitment to remain neutral in the event of a Soviet attack on the PRC. The US reaction was sternly negative, and on 15 October Kissinger finally declared to Dobrynin that not only would the United States not remain neutral, it would launch a missile attack on 130 Soviet cities the moment the first Soviet rocket was fired at China.[92] Serious or not, the Kissinger warning had the desired effect. Dobrynin warned the Politburo in Moscow of the American attitude, and restraint won the day. But a question remains in the air. Back in 1963, we recall, the United States had sought Soviet acquiescence in a strike against China's nuclear facilities, but the Russians had demurred. Now, in 1969, the Soviet Union had sought US acquiescence in a similar action, but the Americans had demurred. What might the outcome have been if one side or the other had proposed the idea at some point in between these two dates – say in 1967, when the Red Guards were running amok and besieging the Soviet and British embassies in Peking?

At the opposite end of the Soviet spectrum was the indefatigable dove, Alexei Kosygin. On 21 March 1969, in a bid to head off further conflict on Damansky/Zhenbao, the Soviet premier put through a call on a long disused hotline between Moscow and Peking and asked to speak to Chairman Mao. The operator retorted, 'You are a revisionist and therefore I will not connect you.' Kosygin tried again meekly, 'Well then, will you connect me to Premier Zhou?' The operator called him a revisionist again and hung up.[93] At the end of the summer, with full-scale war apparently imminent, Kosygin once more roused himself for a last-ditch attempt to resolve matters peacefully. An opportunity was provided by the death on 2 September of Ho Chi Minh, the revered leader of North Vietnam who had trodden a delicate line between the Soviet and Chinese camps. Arriving in Hanoi for the funeral on 6 September, the Soviet premier sent a message to Zhou Enlai through his

North Vietnamese hosts indicating that he was willing to stop in Peking for discussions on his way back home. Zhou had already paid his respects to the late Uncle Ho in advance of the funeral ceremony precisely so as to avoid running into Soviet mourners, and now he kept Kosygin waiting for days on end for a response to his message. Finally giving up hope, Kosygin set off back to Moscow on 10 September, stopping to refuel first at Calcutta and then at Dushanbe in Soviet Tajikistan – where at last he received the desired invitation to Peking. His initial reception was bleak enough. Talks were held in the departure lounge at Peking Airport, since it was not considered appropriate to let the revisionist boss enter town. (One of his retinue even found significance in the fact that the visitors were installed in the neighbourhood of the lavatory.) The talks were said to have opened in a 'very tense' atmosphere, and the usually courteous Zhou even failed to call his guest 'Comrade', addressing him as plain 'Kosygin'.[94] The Soviet premier nonetheless made a spirited appeal for common sense, declaring that while he had no objection to polemical discussion as such, exchanges of insults could only lead to estrangement and bitterness, and urging that progress would be easier 'if we tie all the past into a bundle and throw this bundle out'.[95] He denied that the Soviet Union had any intention of attacking China, and may even have given a verbal promise that China would not be subjected to a nuclear strike. In the course of a parley of three to four hours he reached agreement with Zhou for a ceasefire on the borders and the withdrawal by both sides of troops from the 'disputed areas'. Talks on the border dispute were to be resumed at vice-ministerial level, with an opening round to be held in Peking on 20 October. The Soviet ambassador to Peking and the Chinese ambassador to Moscow were to return to the posts from which they had been recalled at the start of the Cultural Revolution, and as a further step back to normality Kosygin proposed a renewal of discussions on trade and economic affairs. It seems likely that this meeting really did help to pull the two countries back from the terrifying brink. Certainly the parley seems to have ended more amicably than it had begun: we find references to a 'calm' and 'constructive' atmosphere, and Zhou is said to have summarised, 'Although you came by a roundabout route your journey will not have been in vain . . . A good start has been made.'[96] The proceedings concluded with a hearty meal of Peking duck and *maotai* spirit, accompanied by 'pleasant toasts' and 'cheerful conversation'.[97] On the flight home Kosygin was once again in an untypically celebratory mood, even proposing to an accompanying China Hand, Mikhail Kapitsa of the Foreign Ministry, that they crack open a bottle of whisky which had been taken on board in Calcutta. Back in Moscow, however, the long-suffering premier found no senior colleagues on hand at the airport to greet and congratulate him. For Brezhnev had by this time long since eclipsed his partner in the ruling duumvirate. And Brezhnev and his allies were inclined to suspect that Kosygin had been taken for a ride.

Brezhnev and the Politburo mainstream stood for a middle course, halfway between devastating reprisals and placid pow-wows, that can best be described as a policy of overwhelming defence. Following the March clashes at Damansky/Zhenbao Brezhnev is said to have decided on a somewhat more vigorous expansion of Russia's already enormous conventional forces in the Far East combined with a deployment of battlefield nuclear weapons: six divisions equipped with such weapons were installed on the borders, two of them being assigned to the MPR sector. The idea was however not to attack but rather to intimidate, and in the meantime Brezhnev had other options in mind. In an address delivered to an international conference of Communist Parties on 8 June 1969 the Soviet leader proposed the establishment of 'a system of collective security in Asia'.[98] What he envisaged was a grand strategic encirclement of the PRC, a policy of containment remarkably similar to the one the United States and its allies had adopted against the Soviet Union in the early years of the Cold War. True, there were as yet very few potential partners for such an encirclement; but India at least seemed a promising candidate, and the Soviet chiefs lost no time in dispatching an exploratory mission to New Delhi.

These defensive steps didn't preclude an attempt to exploit any cracks that the Kremlin could find in the Chinese political monolith. As relations with Peking got worse Brezhnev and his team pressed ahead with the courtship of the PRC's ethnic minorities. In a Uighur-language broadcast directed at Xinjiang in 1967 a Soviet propagandist pointed out to his listeners that their struggle for independence from China had never been more effective than it was when it had Moscow's backing in the years 1944–9; and in 1969 further broadcasts encouraged the indigenous peoples of Xinjiang, Inner Mongolia and Tibet to rise up against Mao's 'inhuman chauvinism'.[99] In China proper, however, the Chairman's purge of 'traitors' in the course of the Cultural Revolution had silenced the last Soviet-friendly voices at the top of the CCP. There remained, to be sure, Wang Ming, in exile in Moscow since the mid-1950s and keen as ever to supplant his old rival. In January 1967 Wang offered to assemble a force of Central Asians and Mongols to cross the Xinjiang border, make contact with local minority leaders and set up a base with a view to staging a coup against Mao. The Kremlin wasn't impressed. During the spring and summer of 1969 Wang was used to make broadcasts into China and to turn out material detrimental to Mao for the benefit of other broadcasters; but that was as far as his usefulness was perceived to extend.

Greater promise was apparently glimpsed in Moscow's old alternative – the Chinese Nationalist Party. In October 1968 Victor Louis, an urbane KGB operative who doubled as a stringer for the London *Evening News*, paid a call in his journalistic capacity on the information office of the Chinese Nationalist embassy in Tokyo and requested a visa to visit Taiwan. His appearance soon afterwards on the Nationalist-ruled island was witnessed by local people with some incredulity. As he wrote down his Moscow address in the Taipei hotel register most of the hotel staff assumed that he must be an American having a joke. Unfazed by the sensation, he sought and on 29 October was granted the first of three interviews with Stalin's former interlocutor, Chiang Ching-kuo, the son of the Generalissimo who by this time was serving as the Nationalist minister of defence. In a show of goodwill and no doubt to establish his own bona fides he handed over a package of letters from relatives for Ching-kuo's Russian wife, Faina, before steering the conversation to weightier topics. He is said to have brought up with Ching-kuo the idea of a Nationalist assault on the Chinese mainland, promising in that event Soviet neutrality and even limited cooperation. As a first step towards re-establishing diplomatic relations he also proposed that the Soviet and Nationalist governments should set up trade offices respectively in Taipei and Moscow. Ching-kuo for his part is said to have greeted this shadowy visitor with some affability, reminiscing in still serviceable Russian about his 1930s stint in Moscow's Dynamo factory and bombarding Louis with questions about present-day life in the Soviet capital. In response to Louis's concrete ideas he suggested that the Soviet Union should abrogate the Valentine's Day Treaty and should create some disturbances on the Xinjiang and Manchurian frontiers to coincide with the mooted Nationalist descent on the PRC coast. In the spring of 1969 a former

Nationalist vice-minister of education became the first non-Communist Chinese dignitary to visit Moscow in twenty years, and agreement was reached on developing an exchange of information between Soviet and Nationalist agencies on military and intelligence matters. Louis meanwhile received an invitation from Ching-kuo to return to Taiwan. This second visit was planned for September, but was postponed at the last moment at the request of Kosygin, who was afraid that word of the Kremlin's subterranean dealings with the Nationalists might leak out and damage the prospects for the renewed border talks he had agreed to organise during his parley at Peking Airport with Zhou Enlai.[100]

THE DEAD OF NIGHT (1969–76)

In the last months of 1969 the CCP leaders were suddenly gripped by a state of collective panic. Part of the reason would seem to have been the opaqueness of Soviet intentions. The CCP had observed with unease the lack of a welcome accorded to Kosygin by his colleagues on his return from his airport discussion with Zhou. They were still more unsettled by the Kremlin's failure to confirm the understandings arrived at by Kosygin with Zhou in the course of their talks, and in particular the oral promise Kosygin is said to have made that the Soviet Union wouldn't drop nuclear weapons on China. On 18 September Zhou sent a follow-up letter to his Soviet counterpart, but all he received in return was an enumeration of the various steps that the Kremlin had taken to ease tensions on the border. On 30 September Lin Biao, Mao's defence minister, put the PLA on alert against a possible Soviet blitz on 1 October, the PRC's National Day; and as the time approached for Soviet negotiators to arrive in Peking for the new border talks the awful notion occurred to the Chinese authorities that the Soviet plane might be carrying not negotiators but nuclear bombs. On 17 October, three days before the expected descent of the Russians, Defence Minister Lin issued an 'Order No. 1' for the evacuation of the entire Party leadership from the capital. Mao was to withdraw to Wuhan on the Yangtze, and Lin himself was to go to Suzhou. Only Zhou Enlai was to be left to mind the shop in Peking, and a large gap in his desk diary indicates that he too abandoned his Zhongnanhai office on 20 October and didn't return until February of the following year. Lin also removed from their bases and dispersed round the country a total of 940,000 troops, 4,000 planes and 600 naval vessels.

In the event the CCP's fears proved groundless. A Soviet aircraft duly delivered negotiators, not nukes, to Peking, and on 11 November the talks opened on an almost jocular note, as the chief Soviet spokesman, Vice-minister V.V. Kuznetsov, asked his Chinese counterpart, Vice-minister Qiao Guanhua, 'You won't mind if I hang my revisionist coat next to yours?'[101] (Qiao is said to have responded with his 'loud, liquid, characteristic laugh.'[102]) By February 1970 the CCP's scattered leaders were back at their desks, and on 1 May Mao himself in the course of a seven-minute conversation in Tiananmen Square pronounced an apparent blessing on the deputy head of the Soviet team, '*Just carry on with the negotiations, then all will be well.*'[103] Such incidents as took place between the two powers over the next half-decade were of a relatively trivial kind. At the end of 1972 further clashes were reported on the border between Xinjiang and Soviet Kazakhstan. In March 1974 a Soviet helicopter, purportedly on a medical mission, came down in bad weather on the Xinjiang side; the crew were imprisoned for espionage, but were unexpectedly released at the end of the following year. But there was no real improvement. The hair-trigger tension that had prevailed for the greater part of 1969 had been replaced merely by a deathly rigidity on the part of both antagonists. Armageddon had been avoided, but relations had chilled to the lowest possible temperature short of war.

War or no war, there was ample cause for the CCP leaders to feel apprehensive. They had, to be sure, their new atomic weapons, supplemented in June 1967 by their first detonation of a hydrogen bomb. But to deliver these weapons they were dependent on an arsenal of thirty to forty intermediate-range ballistic missiles (IRBMs) with a modest range of 1,500 miles and a similar number of medium-range ballistic missiles (MRBMs), both types of rockets agreed by NATO specialists to be 'highly inaccurate',[104] plus a force of eighty elderly TU-16 bombers supplied by the Russians in earlier years. In theory they could destroy several Soviet cities within easy reach of their borders such as Vladivostok and Novosibirsk. But they couldn't hope to deter a Soviet 'first strike'; and if the Russians struck first with all the power and accuracy of their enormous missile forces there would likely be very little of the Chinese arsenal left to hit back. The CCP duly continued to pin their hopes on their manpower, the one domain in which they enjoyed an undoubted advantage over the other side. With a total of seventy-five divisions containing 1.5 million men under arms they dinned into their populace, as one British diplomat put it, the superiority of Chinese soldiers armed with Mao Zedong Thought over 'Soviet troops equipped with a clutter of modern weapons, which in their poor Thoughtless hands is no better than a heap of scrap iron'.[105] An equal flimsiness was apparent in the exhortation to 'dig tunnels deep'. Cities buzzed with activity as the people dug air raid shelters, but the earliest ones were primitive in the extreme, not even enough, in the judgement of Western observers, to withstand a hit or near-miss from a conventional bomb, let alone one of Grechko's 'nuclear blockbusters'. Even after the techniques and materials had grown more sophisticated and 'underground cities' had begun to appear (an idea which may have been inspired, incidentally, by the network of shelters built up around the Moscow Metro on Stalin's orders in the late 1940s), their effectiveness in withstanding a nuclear strike remained open to question. A booklet distributed in Shanghai instructed the public pathetically how to shoot with rifles at incoming aircraft and how to 'take shelter from a nuclear attack'. Another British diplomat reckoned that the Chairman's object in all this was not so much to protect the citizenry as to generate 'a controlled atmosphere of crisis' which would help put an end to the continuing internal strife.[106]

To make up for these weaknesses Mao now began to develop his opening to the United States. It wasn't entirely plain sailing at this early stage. Even now, with the obvious Russophiles in the CCP crushed beneath the wheels of the Cultural Revolution, there were still certain leaders who found themselves unable to stomach the colossal U-turn entailed in Mao's shift to the West. One such is said to have been Chen Boda, the Chairman's long-time secretary, who occupied the fifth place in the Party hierarchy. A second, more spectacular hold-out was Defence Minister Lin Biao. Appointed in 1959 to succeed Khrushchev's supposed accomplice Peng Dehuai, Lin had spent much of the following years presiding over the extirpation of Soviet influence from the PLA, and by the mid-1960s he had emerged as the most vocally anti-Soviet of all the CCP chieftains. Hailed as Mao's 'closest comrade-in-arms', at the Ninth Party Congress of April 1969 he was formally anointed as the Chairman's heir apparent. By the start of the new decade he is said nonetheless to have argued that the United States should continue to be Enemy Number One and that the dispute with the Soviets should be regarded as nothing more than a 'family quarrel'.[107] There were other factors involved. Chen and Lin were both locked in a feud with Mao's wife Jiang Qing and her coterie of doctrinal extremists, and Mao's relations with Lin were beginning to show the strains that are apt to develop between an autocrat and his designated successor. But whatever precisely the balance of grievances, it seems clear from the vitriol later hurled at both of these men that their stance on the Soviet question wasn't considered the least of their crimes. In October 1970 Chen Boda was disgraced and arrested, and a campaign was launched to denounce him for 'treason and espionage'.[108] By August 1971 the knives were out for Lin too, as Mao toured the provinces in his special train canvassing official and military support for a purge. Lin's son Lin Liguo, a well-connected young air force officer who headed a secret anti-Mao faction known as the Joint Fleet, discussed with his fellows the possibility of staging a military coup in which Mao would be liquidated, either by bombing his train or by dousing him with germ weaponry or poison gas. But it was all hopelessly unrealistic, and by the following month Lin Senior was a desperate man. On the night of 12–13 September he and his wife and son commandeered an aircraft at Shanhaiguan, where the Great Wall meets the sea, and made a dash to the north with the apparent intention of reaching Irkutsk; but their plane ran out of fuel and crashed in the grasslands of Outer Mongolia. Five days later an internal CCP document reviled Lin for 'capitulating to the enemy' and 'betraying our country'.[109]

In spite of these stirrings of protest the opening to the West was unstoppable. In 1970 came the establishment of diplomatic relations with a number of secondary Western countries (notably Canada and Italy), followed in April 1971 by the dramatic invitation to a team of American ping-pong players to visit Peking and in July by the secret mission of Dr Henry Kissinger. In February 1972, in the culminating breakthrough, US President Richard Nixon was received with honour in the Chinese capital, and at their meeting on 21 February Mao had the satisfaction of confiding to his visitor, 'In our country there was a reactionary group who were opposed to our contact with you. The result was that they got on an aeroplane and fled abroad.'[110]

Mao wasn't proposing to highlight the weakness of China's strategic position through a crude immediate appeal for US support. At his meeting with Nixon on 21 February he insisted on limiting the talks to a discussion of 'philosophical questions'; and he is said to have deflected no fewer than three attempts by Nixon and Kissinger to bring up the subject of the Soviet Union. Instead he and Zhou Enlai opted for the subtler approach of a charm offensive – for prettifying their own image and that of the PRC in the eyes of their guests, and for doing so in such a way as to make the Soviet Union look dowdy and brutish. The results were immediate. Already in July 1971 Kissinger had come back in rapture from his preparatory meetings with Zhou, describing the Chinese premier as 'an intellectual equal' and 'an extraordinary and subtle negotiator',[111] and telling the president what a pleasant change he had found his discussions with Zhou from the habitual 'pettiness, bullying and bluster' of the Soviet leaders.[112] After their summit the following February both the president and his national security adviser spoke in glowing terms of the Chairman himself: Nixon lauded Mao's 'remarkable sense of humour' and 'mind that moved like lightning',[113] while Kissinger was fascinated by his 'Socratic' style of conversation and his 'raw, concentrated willpower'.[114] Lower-ranking Americans who followed in Nixon's and Kissinger's footsteps were embraced with a hospitality that took their breath away. In May 1972 Harrison Salisbury, the veteran Moscow correspondent of the *New York Times*, penned his first impressions of arriving in the PRC from Hong Kong, contrasting the 'shy grin' and 'tired smile' of the PLA border guards and the politeness of the 'gentle little Chinese Customs lady' with the 'sullen Russian frontier' and its 'eternal suspicions'.[115] In the dining room at Shenzhen (then a small border village) he observed,

> The waitresses were clean, neat, friendly. They did not seem to think that it was an indignity that I had interrupted their leisure by sitting down at a table – as Russian waitresses usually seemed to do. They brought the food with a smile. And it was good food. Hot. Chinese. Clean. Eggdrop soup, chicken with green peppers, breaded oysters, pungent pork meatballs and orange pop. The tablecloth was clean. The chopsticks clean. I felt myself relaxing. Why, I suddenly thought, it's pleasant to be in this country![116]

Skilful compliments were lavished on visiting dignitaries from the United States and other Western powers. In a nod to his alma mater, the British foreign secretary, Sir Alec Douglas-Home, was serenaded at a banquet by a PLA band with a spirited rendition of the 'Eton Boating Song'. Parties of Westerners ranging from hard-bitten businesspeople to questing academics and Maoist groupies were wowed with earnest teach-ins and choruses of schoolchildren chanting '*Huanying, huanying, relie huanying!*' ('Welcome, welcome, warmly welcome!'). Few of these Western visitors were apparently conscious that only half a dozen years had passed since the murderous peak of the Cultural Revolution, or indeed that the Cultural Revolution in a more subdued form was still going on.

The dividends for Peking were tremendous. In a dozen ways Mao's initiative had brought China out of its long isolation. The new diplomatic architecture being fashioned for the United States by Nixon and Kissinger envisaged a simultaneous advance in relations with both the two Communist rivals, but with a distinct tilt in favour of the newly lovable PRC. In December 1971 Kissinger confided to a senior Chinese diplomat, '*We tell you about our conversations with the Soviets; we do not tell the Soviets about our conversations with you*.'[117] China had been received into a 'quasi-alliance' with the US – not a formal defence pact, but a solidarity strong enough to give pause for thought to any hawks in the Kremlin who might still be contemplating a 'surgical strike' against Chinese bases. In the course of Nixon's visit Kissinger treated top-ranking Chinese officials to a detailed briefing consisting of reams of classified US intelligence material on the current Soviet arsenal, from bombers to missiles, complete with satellite images of the Soviet dispositions along the PRC's borders – a briefing he supplemented over the next two years. Thanks to these new ties the CCP were even able to work out the rudiments of an answer to Brezhnev's containment strategy. In February 1973 Mao suggested to Kissinger the idea of creating a 'horizontal line' linking the US and China by way of Western Europe, Turkey, Iran, Pakistan and Japan, through which they could 'work together to deal with the bastards';[118] and incessant efforts were made by Peking to draw attention to the Soviet threat facing *Western Europe*, with a view to galvanising NATO and thereby if possible inducing the Russians to shift at least some of their pressure from their eastern to their western flank. Admitted at last to the United Nations in 1971, the PRC was able to pursue its doctrinal vendetta against the Russians in front of the entire world community: in October 1974 Deng Xiaoping, now released from his rustication and back as vice-premier, had the pleasure of informing the United Nations General Assembly that there had been three great revolutions in world history – the American, the French . . . and the Chinese. The Sino-Soviet feud had by now become globalised in strategic as well as ideological terms, as the CCP worked in tandem with the US to provide arms and money to forces competing with Soviet clients for power in far-flung corners of the Third World. In Angola, for instance, in 1975 the Chinese helped the CIA to make contact with the UNITA faction of Jonas Savimbi, which was locked in struggle with the Soviet-backed MPLA movement in the country's post-colonial civil war. At a meeting in December that year with President Nixon's successor, Gerald Ford, the Chairman personally affirmed with regard to Angola that he was 'in favour of driving the Soviet Union out'.[119]

One result was that the CCP grew markedly less afraid of the Soviet Union as time went on. After the spasm of fright in the final months of 1969 a note of increasing confidence began to be sounded. Already in early 1970, as his lieutenants returned from their provincial hideouts to their offices in Peking, the Chairman began to express his conviction that no foreign country, including the Soviet Union, would really dare to invade China; and the ensuing rapprochement with the United States can only have strengthened him in that view. In February 1973 he scoffed to Henry Kissinger of the likelihood of a Soviet onslaught, 'How could that happen? How could that be? Do you think they would feel good if they were bogged down in China?';[120] and the following July David Bruce, head of the new United States Liaison Office in Peking, observed in his diary that the Chinese 'no longer believed a Soviet attack to be at all likely, or at least imminent'.[121] This confidence was reflected in a distinctly feisty attitude towards the PRC's new American partners. Discontented with Kissinger's efforts to improve relations with the Soviet Union as well as with China, Mao and Zhou both accused him of trying to climb to the Kremlin on China's shoulders; and the unexpected release in December 1975 of the captured Soviet helicopter crew has been interpreted as a quiet way of reminding the Americans that China did still have other options besides themselves.

Ordinary Chinese may not have been altogether so sanguine about the danger of war. One future diplomat, Fu Ying, who grew up near the Manchurian border, recalled her fear as a teenager that fighting might break out at any time between the hundreds of thousands of Chinese and Soviet troops who glowered at each other in her vicinity; and many other Chinese citizens must surely have shared her apprehension. Yet there are also hints in this darkest of times of a certain insouciance. British embassy staff in Peking at the turn of 1969–70 recorded their impression that some of the Chinese public who had been called upon to 'dig tunnels deep' didn't take the war scare very seriously.[122] In around 1973 a young diplomat, Qian Qichen, who was serving in the PRC's Moscow embassy, had the opportunity to visit a Soviet provincial town. Walking one day around the streets with a group of his colleagues, he decided to have a little gentle fun at the expense of the KGB operative who was dogging their steps. 'It must be hard for you', he declared, 'to trudge around behind us, and it happens that we don't know the way. Please come in front and lead the way for us.'[123] A British visitor to China in 1975 met a swineherd on a commune who called his pig Brezhnev.

Throughout this time the Moscow leaders pressed on with their grim defence build-up. Between 1969 and 1971 the number of Soviet divisions on the Chinese frontier increased still further, from twenty-seven to forty-four, a figure reckoned to correspond to about a quarter of total Soviet military strength. A million Soviet troops were said to be on the alert 'in deep concrete ravelins along the Amur and the Ussuri, in mobile missile bases south of the Gobi [desert] in Mongolia, at strategic air stations east of Baikal, in armoured concentrations near Khalkhin Gol, in rocket silos positioned in the mountains of Mongolia, in hardened installations in eastern Kazakhstan'.[124] The Soviet high command had at their disposal the most powerful mechanised army China had ever faced. With 100 submarines and sixty major warships in their Pacific ports they possessed the ability to sweep the seas clear of all Chinese naval and merchant shipping. They had at least 500 military aircraft and perhaps as many as 1,400 deployed in the East. And above all they enjoyed an overwhelming superiority over their Chinese opponents in guided nuclear missiles. In 1974 Brezhnev ordered the construction of the Baikal-Amur Magistral' (BAM), a new long-distance railway line to be laid to the north of the existing Trans-Siberian. First proposed in the early years of the century by the tsarist general Anton Denikin, the BAM was conceived of as offering a second line of defence against Chinese invasion: the Trans-Siberian was too close to the border and too vulnerable to guerrilla attack. A new railway would also enhance the ability of the Soviet General Staff to send reinforcements to the Far Eastern front. Brezhnev meantime continued to press ahead with his plan for uniting the rest of the East in a grand containment of China. In 1970 he floated the idea of an 'Asian defence pact'.[125] One Chinese wag is said to have commented that it looked as though the ghost of John Foster Dulles had taken up residence in the Kremlin.[126]

Brezhnev and his colleagues undoubtedly did crave a thaw in relations with China if this could be achieved at no cost to themselves. 'Seeking hope in the dead of night', as one diplomat put it,[127] they came up with repeated proposals for new departures – for a treaty on the non-use of force (July 1970 and January 1971), for a mutual non-aggression pact (June 1973 and February 1975). Progress was however blocked steadily by a body of hardline pundits who had been assembled in 1966 to advise the Moscow Politburo on Chinese affairs. Head of this group was a certain Oleg Rakhmanin, a protégé of Mikhail Suslov, the Soviet Party's high priest, who held the position of deputy head of the CPSU Central Committee's Department for Liaison with Socialist Countries. Another prominent figure was Mikhail Kapitsa, the head of the Foreign Ministry's First Far Eastern Department, who had accompanied Kosygin on his Peking parley without sharing the Premier's rosy view of the outcome. These hardliners saw their main task as pursuing with all due pugnacity the doctrinal quarrel with 'Maoism'. Any new talks with Peking, they insisted, must begin with a discussion of 'questions of principle' at which the Chinese could recant their heretical line. Close to the Soviet military-industrial complex, they stood four-square behind the great build-up of troops and arms on the PRC border (Rakhmanin is said to have been one of its earliest advocates) as well as the Brezhnev containment drive. There were a few dissentient voices. Lev Delyusin, a maverick scholar at the Institute of Oriental Studies, argued that the doctrinal quarrel wasn't really central to Sino-Soviet relations and condemned the great military build-up as 'an unparalleled squandering' of resources.[128] But it was Rakhmanin's way or the highway.

The flirtation with Taiwan continued. In November 1971, December 1974 and June 1975 Victor Louis was able to pay three more visits to the Nationalist island. On 12 May 1973 a squadron of 'three to five' Soviet warships including a destroyer and a submarine was reported to have passed through the Taiwan Straits for the first time since 1949 with the permission of the Nationalist authorities before completing a circumnavigation of the island; and the Russians even asked (unsuccessfully) if they could use the Pescadore Island group, also Nationalist-held, as a naval refuelling base. While Moscow was steadfast enough in its diplomatic allegiance to support the 1971 resolution that propelled the PRC into the United Nations at Taiwan's expense, it appears the 'two Chinas' scenario still hadn't lost its attraction in Soviet eyes. In November 1975 the Foreign Ministry China

Hand, Kapitsa, was overheard by the Canadian ambassador telling his US colleague at a Kremlin reception that the US should urge Taiwan to declare independence from China and should recognise it as an independent state. The Soviet Union would then follow suit and he, Kapitsa, would be happy to go to Taiwan as Moscow's first ambassador there.[129] But these remarks were seen, no doubt correctly, as having been first and foremost intended to sabotage the developing intimacy between Washington and Peking.[130]

Moscow's problem by this stage was that it no longer had any clear notion of what was going on in the PRC. When a Soviet ambassador returned to Peking in 1970 in the person of Vasily Tolstikov the Foreign Ministry cabled him a reminder 'to exert every effort to gather intelligence'.[131] Tolstikov confessed that he had practically no access to reliable information in the Chinese capital, and that such information as reached him came largely from other members of the diplomatic corps. In May 1971 a second secretary at the Soviet embassy in London called on the editor of the *China Quarterly* in search of any materials he might have about China, observing that nothing substantial came out of Peking. While the CCP leaders were spoon-fed precious data on Soviet military deployments by Dr Kissinger in person the Russians had to grub around for intelligence using the somewhat primitive methods of traditional espionage. In August 1972 British Special Branch in Hong Kong caught a couple of KGB agents in the act of conferring with the manager of an import-export business named He Hong'en. It turned out that the KGB had been penetrating the colony in the guise of crew members of visiting Soviet merchant vessels; one of the two men arrested on this occasion, the 'stoker', was in reality a lecturer at a top Soviet university, while his contact man, He Hong'en, a stateless Chinese, had been recruited in 1969 and implanted in Hong Kong to gather whatever intelligence might be forthcoming about local conditions and Sino-British relations as well as about the PRC and Taiwan. Anxious at all costs to avoid disturbing the PRC government, the British marched the two infiltrators back to the docks in short order and lodged a formal protest with the ship's home base in Vladivostok. On the night of 15 January 1974 two Soviet diplomats drove out from their Peking embassy to a gloomy rendezvous under a bridge some three miles from the centre of town. Disguised in local 'Mao suits' they were shortly accosted by a pair of Chinese, one of whom identified himself by calling out 'I'm Unicorn!'. The senior Soviet diplomat responded, 'I'm Silver Birch!'. 'Unicorn' was in fact Li Hongshu, a Soviet-born Chinese who had been trained in 1970 at a military intelligence branch of the Ministry of Defence in Moscow before being smuggled into China by way of Xinjiang. He handed the two Russians a package of materials he had obtained on subjects ranging from the general (the inner workings of the CCP) to the rather minute (the activities of the PLA in the Mudanjiang region of Heilongjiang Province). In return he was given a large suitcase containing a letter with further instructions, 5,000 yuan for expenses and spare parts for assembling a short-wave radio to enable him to keep in touch. This operation, however, like the Hong Kong one, came to grief: the police swooped, and the upshot was that no fewer than five Soviet diplomats were expelled from the country. Moscow's reliance for these missions on deracinated Chinese illustrates incidentally how hard the Kremlin now found it to train a cohort of home-grown Russian Mandarin speakers. In 1973–4 a contingent of young Russians could be found taking a Mandarin language course at Nanyang University in Singapore. The PRC was out of the question now for Soviet students; Taiwan was impossible in the absence of diplomatic relations; Hong Kong was barred to Soviet personnel. Singapore was the only Chinese-speaking territory prepared to accommodate them.[132]

While the Chinese, in other words, were emerging from isolation the Russians were rapidly sinking down into it. News of the Kissinger trip to Peking in July 1971 is said to have generated in the Kremlin a state of 'confusion and indeed, almost hysteria'.[133] Amid the cascade of Western diplomatic recognitions of the PRC government the Soviet Union was now beginning to look like the global pariah: in the spring of 1972 Kosygin is said to have inquired plaintively of a Danish visitor, '*Is everyone ganging up on us?*'[134] In May 1973, as Kissinger sought to exploit the US's new China option to extract some concessions from the Soviet Union on the road to détente, Brezhnev urged on the American master diplomat his impression of Chinese squalor and barbarism. He seems to have been genuinely incredulous that the US might be willing to sacrifice all the benefits of improved ties with Moscow for an intimacy with these 'cannibals' in the East. A more imaginative Soviet team might have tried to increase their appeal, as the Chinese were doing, to both Western policymakers and the Western public at large. But under the deeply uncharismatic leadership of Brezhnev and Kosygin the Russians either couldn't or wouldn't compete in the prettiness stakes.

And while Chinese apprehension of Russia seemed to lessen as time went on, the Soviet leadership's sense of a Chinese threat was profound and unchanging. Brezhnev for one had no doubt that Mao was a maniac; and he and his Politburo colleagues are said to have been 'driven almost frantic' by the vision of millions of Chinese invaders pouring over their Far Eastern border at this maniac's command.[135] If any difference in outlook can be distinguished among them it was between those officials who were seeking to fashion a more or less rational defensive strategy and those who were roused by their sense of the Chinese danger to sheer pugnacity. In July 1972 Foreign Minister Gromyko was busy trying to craft a resolution to be pushed through the United Nations General Assembly which would have the effect of permitting the Soviet Union to use nuclear weapons in the event of a Chinese attack. With this object in view he warned his ambassador to the UN, Yakov Malik, to restrain his seething hatred of China: 'We don't want to bark like mad dogs at every word they say.' Malik, we are told, 'looked as if he had swallowed a lemon'. After a further stiff reminder from the foreign minister 'not to exacerbate polemical exchanges with the Chinese' he fumed to his staff that Gromyko was a 'marshmallow': 'You have to be tough with those yellow bastards.'[136]

True to their long tradition of *sotto voce* irreverence the Soviet public poked fun at the Chinese obsession of their leaders. Various jokes went the rounds:

Q: Why are there mice in the Kremlin?
A: Because there are no cats.
Q: Why are there no cats in the Kremlin?
A: Because they say *mao* . . .[137]

AIDE TO BREZHNEV: Comrade General Secretary, I have good news and bad news. Which would you like first?
BREZHNEV: I'll have the bad news first.
AIDE: The bad news is that the Chinese have gone to the Moon.
BREZHNEV: And the good news?
AIDE: The good news is that *all* the Chinese have gone to the Moon.[138]

But the fact was that the same visceral dread of a Chinese invasion pervaded the whole society, rulers and ruled. The intelligentsia, whose ranks included both outspoken critics and outright opponents of the Soviet regime, sounded the same notes of warning as the CPSU. In 'On the Red Snow of the Ussuri', lines inspired by the fighting at Damansky/Zhenbao, the charismatic poet Yevgeny Yevtushenko elided Chinese and Mongols in the same way as Vladimir Soloviev had done at the turn of the century in his poem 'Pan-Mongolism', calling his readers to arms with a defiant reminder of the 1380 victory of the Muscovites over the Golden Horde:

> You can see in the smoky twilight
> The new Mongol warriors with bombs in their quivers;
> But if they attack the alarm bells will ring,
> And there will be more than enough fighters
> For a new Battle of Kulikovo.[139]

On a more sombre note Alexander Solzhenitsyn, shortly to be deported to America as an insufferable thorn in the Kremlin's side, used his *Letter to the Soviet Leaders* of 5 September 1973 to warn of the human implications of such a conflict:

> War with China is bound to cost us 60 million people at the very least – all our finest and purest people are bound to perish . . . You will have against you a country of almost 1,000 million people, the like of which has never yet gone to war in the history of the world.[140]

Ordinary folk in small towns all over Siberia were said to believe that war with China was inevitable. After the fighting at Zhalanaskol 'people went about with ashen faces, and the women already felt themselves to be widows'.[141] Asked in August 1971 what he thought should be done about China a local journalist in Khabarovsk answered with spirit, but not altogether constructively, 'I have my sword.'[142] Nor was the foreboding confined to the east of the Urals. One piece of black humour predicted, 'Twenty-first century radio bulletin: "All Quiet on the Sino-Finnish Border".'[143]

Halfway through the new decade Sino-Soviet relations were barely a step further forward than they had been at the start. At the top level all of the Soviet proposals for talks on a mutual non-aggression pact or a treaty on the non-use of force were brusquely rebuffed. The CCP were prepared to discuss matters of substance but not to be browbeaten over 'questions of principle' by the likes of Rakhmanin. As for the border talks, they meandered on hopelessly for year after year. Vice-minister Qiao Guanhua threw a major obstacle in at the outset by demanding Soviet recognition of the 'disputed areas' as Chinese and the disengagement in those areas of Soviet from Chinese troops. For the Russians 'disputed areas' referred merely to those spots on the border where physical clashes had been taking place, but for the Chinese the expression meant the entire 35,000 square kilometres of land which they claimed had been filched from them under the 'unequal treaties'; so that Qiao was effectively asking the Russians to give up those territories as a precondition for any further talks. The Russians for their part retreated from the big concession they had made in the 1964 negotiations when they agreed to accept the *thalweg* of the rivers Amur and Ussuri as the eastern border between the two states. It is possible that the talks may have served as a mechanism for settling various minor problems and incidents that arose in these years; but substantial progress there was none, and the claim made by one senior Soviet negotiator at a farewell banquet in his honour that his team's efforts had not been in vain was greeted with roars of laughter. Trade crawled up from a negligible 41 million roubles in 1970 to a still minuscule 314 million in 1976, and the Kremlin turned down an appeal from the Khabarovsk branch of the CPSU to be allowed to reopen their border trade with the Chinese, suspended since the start of the Cultural Revolution, to enable them to dispose of a quantity of surplus or unsaleable goods. A 'thin flow' of scientific and technical publications is said to have continued between certain universities and research institutes;[144] it's surprising to find even that. On the cultural side Mergen Mongush, a boy growing up in Siberia, struggled to lay his hands on any reading material translated from the Chinese. In the end he succeeded in tracking down precisely one book – a translation of *Strange Tales from Liaozhai*, a Qing dynasty work first published in 1740. In China the authorities still denied access, except in the most exceptional cases, to any Russian or indeed any foreign publications whatsoever. This bleak picture shows up in a rather different light the apparently benign advice dispensed by Mao to the deputy chief of the Soviet border talks team in May 1970, '*Just carry on with the negotiations, then all will be well.*'[145] What the Chairman actually seems to have meant, in this last conversation he ever had with a Soviet official, was that failing a total surrender by Moscow the talks could go on forever so far as he was concerned. There would be no reconciliation so long as Mao lived.

THE LONG ROAD BACK (1976–89)

Nor was there any immediate sign of improvement when the Chairman was finally gathered to his ancestors on 9 September 1976. The new CCP leader, the ineffectual Hua Guofeng, proclaimed his simple creed of the Two Whatevers, '*Whatever* Chairman Mao said we will say and *whatever* Chairman Mao did we will do', and that applied to dealings with the Soviet Union as much as to everything else. In May 1977 the CCP brought out amid fanfare the fifth volume of Mao's *Selected Works*, including conspicuously the speech of 25 April 1956 on the Ten Major Relationships in which the Chairman had issued his first public challenge to Soviet overlordship with simultaneous swipes at Stalin and Khrushchev. Hua expressed his opinion that the Soviet Union had 'not shown one iota of good faith about improving state relations';[146] and at banquet after banquet in the Great Hall of the People the Chinese host launched a ritual diatribe against the Kremlin, on hearing which any Soviet diplomats present were obliged to get up and walk out. On 11 June 1978, we are told, Soviet representatives had to exit from a banquet for the second time in four days. (One wonders idly what it was like to be a Soviet diplomat going to a banquet in the full knowledge that you would have to walk out of it. Were sandwiches laid on at the embassy?)

Between 1977 and 1980 Hua was progressively elbowed aside by a far more formidable figure. Back on to centre stage came Deng Xiaoping, twice purged, twice rehabilitated, powerful now beyond any possible challenge. This wasn't, however, necessarily a step forward where relations with the USSR were concerned. Ever since 1960, as we have seen, the diminutive leader had been at the forefront of Chinese doctrinal polemics with Moscow, and it had been his consistent display of anti-Soviet fervour that had won him the Chairman's protection during the witch-hunt of the Cultural Revolution years. Now his own man, Deng pursued Mao's vendetta with Moscow while shifting his emphasis on the issues at stake. Ideological quarrels, he explained to Pierre Trudeau, the prime minister of Canada, were not at the root of the Sino-Soviet hostility; rather the cause lay in 'Russian chauvinism, which is worse now than the chauvinism of Tsarist times'.[147] Deng's focus was above all on countering the Soviet strategic challenge. Calling publicly for a 'world united front' against Moscow, he entered with vigour into the global duel of containment and counter-containment.[148] In August

1978 he secured the dazzling coup of a Treaty of Peace and Friendship with Japan, even persuading the Japanese to include in this document an 'anti-hegemony clause' – Chinaspeak for a statement of veiled opposition to the Soviet Union. The Soviet leaders were faced with the appalling combination of Chinese arms with Japanese wealth and technology. In early November they answered Deng's move by concluding a Treaty of Friendship and Cooperation with the now unified and increasingly Sinophobe Vietnam, which was duly emboldened the following month to invade Cambodia and topple the Chinese-backed Khmer Rouge regime. This time it was the Chinese not the Russians who faced the nightmare scenario of a war on two fronts, with the Soviets to their north and the battle-hardened and expansionist Vietnamese on their southern border; and on 17 February 1979 Deng hit back hard by dispatching a force of 85,000 PLA troops across that southern border to 'teach the Vietnamese a lesson'. At the end of the year the Soviet invasion of Afghanistan added a further link in the far south-west to the Kremlin's developing encirclement of the PRC. Within weeks, in January 1980, Deng received in Peking Harold Brown, secretary for defense in the US administration of Jimmy Carter. The PRC now accepted the installation, first suggested by Kissinger in 1975, of a US electronic intelligence base at Aksu in Xinjiang to monitor Soviet missile tests, and agreement was reached on expanding the supply to Peking of American military technology, including advanced surveillance equipment and vehicles. For a time it looked very much as though the US–China 'quasi-alliance' had mutated into the real thing.

But Deng had other and deeper priorities. Unlike Mao he was intent above all on the modernisation of China, a goal set forth clearly at the watershed conference of the CCP's Central Committee in November–December 1978, in the course of which he proclaimed a shift in the Party's focus from politics to economics. But to achieve this he needed a '*peaceful international environment*'.[149] His attack on the Soviet Union's Vietnamese ally in February 1979 might seem at first glance an appallingly dangerous provocation to Moscow, but it was in fact carried out with great caution. He made no attempt to detach any Vietnamese territory, and set a deadline of one month for the entire operation, even starting to pull his troops back across the southern Chinese border after less than three weeks. As well as squaring the United States, with which the PRC had just established full diplomatic relations, he made a tour to rally support among other South-East Asian countries that shared his fear of Vietnamese expansion. And he even made an appreciable effort to reassure the Kremlin itself. The British ambassador to Peking reported to the Foreign Office that on 'social occasions' Chinese officials had gone to some lengths to explain to their Soviet opposite numbers that the PRC had no wish to go to war with Russia.[150]

All the same an attack on Vietnam might still seem like an odd way to set about building a 'peaceful international environment'. It wasn't even successful, in strictly military terms: the PLA emerged with a bloody nose after losing a total of 20,000 men. This may not however have mattered unduly from Deng's point of view. It seems possible that, like Anwar el-Sadat of Egypt in the Middle East five years before, he was deliberately making war in order to be able to make peace; that by taking on the Vietnamese in the first place he was signalling that the PRC would not tolerate a Soviet strategic encirclement, and that having established that point he was ready to take the first opportunity that presented itself for a diplomatic advance. Whatever the truth the Chinese now proceeded to set a new diplomatic ball rolling with remarkable speed. The question had to be settled of whether the Valentine's Day Treaty of 1950, which was due to expire in a year's time, should be scrapped or renewed for another three decades. On 3 April 1979 the PRC Foreign Ministry made it predictably clear that they had no intention of renewing that suffocating agreement which had been a dead letter for years. They would, however, be open to holding a fresh set of talks '*with the object of resolving the unsettled problems between our two countries and improving our state-to-state relations*'.[151] The Russians were clearly perplexed by this unexpected coda to the Chinese announcement, but they accepted the gambit, and on 27 September a first round of the new talks took place in Moscow at vice-ministerial level. Overseeing the talks, Deng took what looked curiously like a leaf out of the playbook of his Qing dynasty predecessor three centuries earlier. Back in 1676, we recall, the Kangxi emperor had set out three preconditions for allowing Russian merchants to trade with the Chinese empire, namely (i) the return of the fugitive Evenki prince, Gantimur, (ii) the dispatch of a 'reasonable' man to replace the pig-headed Milescu as the Muscovite envoy to Peking and (iii) an end to the Cossack marauding in the Amur basin. Deng now in his turn highlighted 'Three Great Obstacles' that had to be cleared away if Soviet relations with China were to be normalised. These were (i) Soviet support for the Vietnamese expansion into Cambodia, (ii) the Soviet military presence in Outer Mongolia and (iii) the Soviet military build-up along the Chinese frontier. The way ahead to a settlement had at last been sketched out. To encourage the Russians to start on the clearance of obstacles the ideological feud was effectively abandoned that autumn as the CCP media ceased to besmirch the Soviet Party with the slur of 'revisionism'.

In January 1980 the new talks were suspended indefinitely in response to the Soviet march into Afghanistan. But the hiatus that followed proved to be surprisingly short. By the summer of 1982 CCP analysts had begun to suspect that the Soviet Union had shot its bolt. Bogged down in Afghanistan, drained by their economic commitments to Eastern Europe, the Russians were overstretched to the point where they no longer looked like a serious threat. In the meantime Chinese amity with the United States had cooled suddenly with the advent in Washington of the Reagan administration, bent seemingly on revitalising the old US ties with Taiwan, which had been downgraded when President Carter extended diplomatic recognition to the PRC. At the CCP's Twelfth Congress in September proposals were made for a posture of 'equidistance' between the two superpowers. In October the new Sino-Soviet talks resumed in Peking, with Deng putting forward for Soviet attention a revised set of Obstacles, viz. (i) Soviet support for the Vietnamese occupation of Cambodia, (ii) the Soviet military presence in Afghanistan and (iii) the Soviet military build-up along both the Soviet-Chinese and the MPR–Chinese frontiers. By the mid-1980s a drive for retrenchment in the People's Liberation Army was well under way. Deng abandoned his call for a worldwide anti-Soviet front, and in 1985 he declared himself ready to travel to Moscow (or anywhere else) to spur the process of 'normalisation', if only the Russians would take steps to rein in Vietnamese expansion – in Deng's mind apparently the major Obstacle with its implicit threat of a war on two fronts.

Various background signs also pointed to a fresh Chinese perception of the Polar Bear. At the transformative CCP conference of November–December 1978 Chen Yun, the Party's economic brain who had worked closely with Soviet advisers in the 1950s, re-emerged in the top leadership after years in retreat, summing up the emerging assessment of recent decades in a neat little mantra:

Mao Zedong was a man, not a god.
Kang Sheng was a devil, not a man.
Liu Shaoqi was a man, not a devil.[152]

Posthumous absolution began to be granted to a number of now-deceased Party leaders who had suffered for their Soviet ties. In August 1979 Zhang Wentian (Luo Fu), the PRC's former ambassador to Moscow who had supported Peng Dehuai's supposedly Soviet-instigated challenge to the Chairman, was rehabilitated after two decades of disgrace in what Soviet diplomats interpreted as a gesture of goodwill. In March 1980 Li Lisan (he with the Soviet wife) had his record swept clean at a special memorial meeting, and in August none other than Liu Shaoqi, demonised for so long, was restored to his place as one of the Party's immortals. Some of the Party theorists even began once again to consider the case for adopting a Soviet model. A switch to a market economy was not yet thinkable, but some way had to be found of freeing the country from the dead weight of collectivisation which Mao had imposed following the example of Stalin. Hope was glimpsed in a different Soviet approach – in the New Economic Policy (NEP) of a state-directed mixed economy with scope for private peasant production which had been introduced by Lenin as a temporary expedient in 1921 and thereafter maintained right up until Stalin embarked on his ruthless campaign to collectivise agriculture in 1928–9. Champion of the NEP throughout this period had been the amiable 'darling of the Party', as Lenin had called him, Stalin's ally and subsequent victim, Nikolai Bukharin; and it was Bukharin who was now held up as the sage who would light the way to the PRC's future. By July 1979 members of the Chinese Academy of Social Sciences had embarked on the study of Bukharin's works, and in September 1980 a national Bukharin symposium held in Peking led to the creation of an All-China Scholarly Council to pursue this research. Volumes of foreign essays about the great man were published in Chinese translation, and lectures on Bukharin were given all over the country in 'jam-packed halls' where some of the attendees even sat on the windowsills.[153] By 1981 Chinese scholars had started to produce their own articles on the NEP, and some of them went so far as to spot an equivalence between Bukharin and Liu Shaoqi. In countenancing this movement Deng Xiaoping is said to have been prompted by memories of his time in Moscow at the height of the NEP in 1926, and it has even been suggested that the economic reforms he launched in the Chinese countryside in the early 1980s owed something to Bukharin's ideas. Certainly he acknowledged, in a remark made in public in 1985, that the NEP was 'perhaps' the most correct model of socialism.[154]

On a more down-to-earth level officials in the north-eastern provinces of Heilongjiang and Jilin were pressing for a resumption of border trade with the Soviet Far East, which would enable them to invigorate their stagnant economies and perhaps even let them compete one day with the Special Economic Zone which had been launched in the south of the country, on the banks of the Shenzhen River across from Hong Kong. By October 1982 they were sitting down to discuss this idea with their Soviet counterparts in Khabarovsk. Cultural links were also being reforged. In 1979 the veteran novelist Ba Jin published a first volume of his translation of *My Past and Thoughts*, the memoir by the nineteenth-century writer, thinker and anti-tsarist campaigner Alexander Herzen; and in the course of the 1980s he went on to reintroduce the Chinese public to the classics of Russian fiction. Tolstoy and Turgenev, he recalled, had been 'the first to teach me how to be a good, upright person, to face life honestly and tell the truth to readers'.[155] In the most trivial contexts it seemed as though memories of the old 1950s intimacy were forcing their way to the surface. In the summer of 1979 an elderly Chinese chef, clearly Soviet-trained and still active at a reopened Russian restaurant opposite the Peking Zoo, beamingly recommended his version of Chicken Pozharsky. A member of a Chinese technical study group on a visit to the United Kingdom, offered a paper cup of Maxpax coffee on the platform at Paddington Station, solemnly read out the brand name in the Cyrillic alphabet – '*Makhrakh*'.

The Russians had moved in eagerly to seize the first opportunity for a thaw that appeared to present itself as soon as Mao died. They at once indicated their readiness to advise on the embalming of the Chairman's remains. After all, they had done it for Lenin, and more recently for Ho Chi Minh. All hostile references to the PRC were dropped for the moment from the Soviet media. On 27 October 1976 Brezhnev sent a letter congratulating Hua Guofeng on his rise to the Chairmanship, and in December a special emissary arrived in Peking with proposals, some of them old, some novel, for easing the tension in the border areas. The response was stony. Li Zhisui, Mao's former doctor, who had been put in charge of the embalming arrangements, recalled that while the CCP undoubtedly wished to preserve Mao's body, to send a research team to Moscow for guidance on the technicalities was out of the question. The congratulations addressed to Hua were rejected, and the proposals conveyed by the emissary were likened to 'poisoned arrows disguised as an olive branch'.[156]

There followed a time of mixed signals. The Russians were deeply hostile to Deng Xiaoping, 'that yellow dwarf' as some of them distastefully called him,[157] who was trying to forge a worldwide coalition against their country. When Deng sent his troops into Vietnam in February 1979 they responded with menace. Foreign Minister Gromyko declared that the Chinese should 'stop their aggression against Vietnam before it is too late – *I repeat, before it is too late*'.[158] An airlift of Soviet weapons was organised for the Vietnamese army, and a Soviet naval task force was dispatched to the South China Sea. Military exercises were held along the whole length of the Soviet–Chinese and MPR–Chinese borders, and the Xinjiang authorities even judged it advisable to evacuate several tens of thousands of local residents from the Soviet border zone. But it was all so much bluster. The Soviet leaders were no more inclined for a head-on collision with China than they had been ten years previously: Deng's calculation that he could get away with a punitive raid on Vietnam of limited scope and duration was proved correct. By September, in keeping with the principle that they were always ready to accommodate 'rational' PRC wishes, a Soviet team of negotiators were settling down for the start of the new talks proposed by Peking; and the team leader, Leonid Ilyichev, offered the poignant reflection that he and his colleagues were 'not so old as to forget and not so young as not to remember' the halcyon days of Sino-Soviet concord.[159] When it came to the core issues, though, the Soviet side were as wooden as ever. They wouldn't discuss Deng's Three Great Obstacles, and in particular wouldn't touch on any matters affecting the interests of third countries such as the MPR and Vietnam. And the dead hand of the Rakhmanin group continued to block any progress on 'questions of principle'. The New China News Agency reported sadly from Moscow, 'It seems the Soviet Union still regards itself as the instructor of the Chinese people, with the right to teach them how to think, live and what way to choose.'[160]

The first unequivocal sign of a shift in the Kremlin's approach came in a speech delivered by Brezhnev on 23 March 1982, in the course of a ceremonial trip to Tashkent, the capital of Soviet Uzbekistan – within earshot, as it were, of the PRC. In a series of comments addressed to the CCP leaders the veteran Soviet boss affirmed China's right to describe itself as a socialist country, in effect dropping the Kremlin's long-standing insistence on thrashing out 'questions of principle' before any progress could be made on substantive disputes. He denied that the Brezhnev Doctrine had been meant as a threat to use force against China, and indeed that the Soviet Union had ever intended to threaten China or meddle in Chinese affairs, and spoke of his wish for the re-establishment of normal relations between the two powers. Credit for this initiative should probably not be ascribed to Brezhnev, who was by now moribund, but to his more vigorous colleague Yuri Andropov, who had largely taken over the direction of Soviet policy. After Brezhnev died in November and Andropov replaced him as the CPSU General Secretary further movement came fast. In remarks made less than two weeks after the old leader's passing Andropov spoke of the need to 'overcome the inertia of prejudice'.[161] Open-minded figures such as the maverick scholar Lev Delyusin and Georgi Arbatov, director of the Institute for USA and Canada Studies, were brought in to help redesign China policy, and Foreign Ministry officials are said to have chided one stick-in-the-mud at the Soviet embassy in Peking, 'Nobody in Moscow thinks any more in this stupid way about China!'[162] A plan was developed for sending Ivan Arkhipov, the chief economic adviser to the Chinese government in the 1950s who had now risen to the post of vice-premier, on a goodwill mission to the PRC, where he might among other things hope to renew contact with his old friend, Chen Yun.

But the Rakhmanin group weren't yet finished. In the first place, as allies of the Soviet military-industrial complex, they wanted to stoke the Kremlin's fear of China in order to keep up the country's enormous defence spending; and secondly they were concerned for their own careers, which had been built up over years on the basis of Sinophobia. According to another story from this period the Foreign Ministry diehard Mikhail Kapitsa hissed at a diplomat from the Soviet embassy who had talked of a possible rapprochement, 'Are you crazy? Our two countries are geopolitical enemies and this factor will never go away.'[163] Further hardline resistance was voiced by the military. At a Politburo meeting in May 1983 Andropov spoke in favour of economic cooperation with China, and even Gromyko saw the need for a measure of diplomatic advance; but all positive steps were halted by the implacable opposition of the defence minister, Marshal Dmitri Ustinov, who refused to contemplate any reduction whatever in the forty-five divisions deployed on the Chinese frontier. Over the following months Andropov became moribund, like Brezhnev before him. In February 1984 he too died and was succeeded by Brezhnev's former counsellor Konstantin Chernenko, under whose feeble leadership the diehards once more had the wind in their sails. In May the ice-breaking Arkhipov trip was abruptly put off. The Chinese foreign minister, Wu Xueqian, reported bleakly to his colleagues that the resumed talks were stagnant because the Soviet negotiators were still unprepared to discuss the Three Obstacles.

This time, however, the hold-up was brief. Chernenko was moribund too, and by the end of 1984 the diehards seem to have lost their ability to act as a drag on events. In late December Arkhipov at last got to make his goodwill visit to the PRC. The one-time economic adviser was received with great warmth. One senior Chinese diplomat recalled in a memoir that Arkhipov had 'never said an unpleasant word about China, not even in the most difficult period of bilateral relations'.[164] When Arkhipov was brought face to face with Chen Yun for the first time in twenty years the two old friends embraced tearfully in front of the television cameras, and Chen marked the occasion by inscribing a couplet of the Song dynasty poet Lu You (1125–1210):

> The hills and streams have no end, and there seems to be no road beyond,
> But veiled by willows, bright with flowers, another village appears.[165]

By way of a peace offering Arkhipov signed with his CCP hosts an economic agreement providing for help with the renovation of seventeen industrial plants built by the Soviet Union in the 1950s, and he also extended a loan of $82 million for the completion of the Xinjiang part of the Alma Ata–Urumqi railway which had been left significantly unfinished in 1960 at the time of the rift. A longer-term agreement was signed for the setting up of a Committee for Cooperation in Economics, Trade and Science and Technology. After Chernenko's demise in March 1985 leadership in the Kremlin finally passed to a younger and healthier statesman in the shape of Mikhail Sergeevich Gorbachev: it was in large part to meet Gorbachev that

Deng Xiaoping declared himself willing to travel to Moscow or any other Soviet rendezvous. During his first year in office the new Soviet leader was in fact more intent on cultivating Indian than Chinese friendship, and his relative inattention gave Rakhmanin the chance for one last attempt at sabotage. Still in control of the Soviet media's coverage of Chinese affairs, he went behind Gorbachev's back in July 1985 with an article in *Pravda* assailing the reformer Georgi Arbatov for a recent visit he had made to the PRC, during which he was said to have praised the 'capitalist tendencies' he observed there. Gorbachev was incensed but took no immediate action. By 1986, though, the new leader and his new foreign minister, Eduard Shevardnadze, were ready to make a clean sweep of the Sinophobe old guard. Rakhmanin was sacked outright. Under fire for a combination of conservatism and bingeing, Mikhail Kapitsa was shunted out of the Foreign Ministry to the innocuous post of director of the Institute of Oriental Studies. Arbatov, Delyusin and the other progressive advisers had the field to themselves. On 28 July Gorbachev delivered a major speech in Vladivostok, once again as it were within earshot of Peking, in which he at last began to make the concessions the CCP had waited to hear. He reasserted the generous line the Soviet spokesmen had taken during the border negotiations in 1964, publicly accepting the *thalweg* as the international boundary on the Amur and Ussuri rivers. And most important, he promised some initial steps to remove the Three Obstacles. Six regiments were to be withdrawn from Afghanistan, and a 'significant number' of troops would be pulled out of both Outer Mongolia and the Soviet Far East. The clouds of decades were dispersing.

On the Soviet as on the Chinese side diplomatic progress was reflected in some striking new trends. Officials in the Soviet Far East were keen once again to resume border trade with the provinces of north-eastern China, which would enable them to take advantage of the rapid surge in production of Chinese consumer goods, greatly craved by a population whose government had consistently given priority to heavy industry and armaments over satisfying consumer needs. Following the talks held in Khabarovsk with representatives of Heilongjiang and Jilin provinces border trade duly reopened in 1983, and between 1983 and 1988 the value of this trade increased by 4,000 per cent to a dizzying level of $1.8 billion. Related to this was the growth for the first time of a really serious Soviet interest in the

Chinese economic model. In December 1984 Ivan Arkhipov was taken to visit the Special Economic Zone which the CCP leaders had set up in Shenzhen to boost exports and attract foreign investment. The veteran Soviet adviser was awed by the speed of development in an area which had been just a muddy village a few years before. 'He could not', his hosts noted, 'help marvelling at what the Chinese had accomplished, and often revealed his disappointment and dissatisfaction with the current situation in the Soviet Union.'[166] Within a couple of years Arkhipov's perception had become common ground at the highest levels of the Soviet leadership. In 1986 Foreign Minister Shevardnadze directed the newly appointed ambassador to Peking, Oleg Troyanovsky, to follow China's reforms with attention and in particular those aspects which might be of interest to the USSR. On arriving at his post Troyanovsky observed that the Chinese had made a full-blooded start on reforms while the Russians were only tinkering: 'One might say I was converted to a new faith.'[167] Fast-forward another two years and the Soviet leaders were actively setting off in the PRC's footsteps. Plans were drawn up by 1988 for a 'Soviet Shenzhen' to be founded in the Far Eastern provinces, and the port of Nakhodka was designated a free economic zone.

With tourist visits and student and artistic exchanges all stirring back into life, the PRC by the late 1980s was also beginning to make a fresh cultural impact on Soviet minds. Young Russians were rediscovering China just as young Americans and other Westerners did following the Nixon-Kissinger breakthrough of fifteen years before. But whereas the attention of Westerners at that time had been fixed very largely on Maoism this new generation of Russian Sinophiles were drawn, like their predecessors in the late tsarist period, to the more esoteric features of traditional China – to martial arts and *qigong* breathing exercises, to fortune-telling from the *Book of Changes*, to Daoist and Buddhist mysticism. They dreamt of making the pilgrimage to the Shaolin Monastery, to searching for Shangri-la in the wilds of Tibet. When they got sick they treated themselves with Chinese or Tibetan herbal medicine, which had even received the official imprimatur of the Soviet government.

Between 1986 and 1988 Gorbachev and his team got to work systematically removing Deng's Obstacles. By the end of 1988 Soviet troops were withdrawing on schedule from Afghanistan, and a partial withdrawal had also been completed from Outer Mongolia. Deng's priority, that the Kremlin secure a Vietnamese pull-out from Cambodia, was more of a headache. The Soviets had enjoyed major strategic benefits from their close alliance with Vietnam which they were reluctant to jeopardise, and in any case Vietnam wasn't a malleable client like the Afghan and MPR regimes. Shevardnadze observed wryly to his Chinese interlocutors, 'Our ability to influence Vietnam has limits. We can't even influence the Estonians!'[168] In June 1988 nonetheless Gorbachev indicated his willingness to halt the supply of Soviet military aid to Hanoi and in general use his best efforts to get the Vietnamese out of Cambodia. By December Deng judged that enough 'visible progress' had been made on removing the Obstacles to justify moving ahead to a summit of 'normalisation' between the two leaders, and in the course of the winter the groundwork was laid through an exchange between Shevardnadze and his counterpart Qian Qichen, whom we last met in the 1970s gently teasing his KGB tail in a Soviet street. Here one small adjustment had to be made. Back in 1985 Deng had offered to travel to Moscow to make the acquaintance of Gorbachev and assess the prospects for improving relations with this new, youthful Soviet chief. In the intervening years, however, he had watched as the liberalised Soviet Union started coming apart at the seams, with ethnic minorities fighting each other or clamouring for independence and the newly decentralised economy tanking amid widespread shortages and production bottlenecks. Under these circumstances there seemed no reason why he should demean himself by making the traditional pilgrimage to Moscow as the source of all Marxist-Leninist wisdom. Instead Gorbachev could come to Canossa.

Which the Soviet chief duly did, stepping into Peking on 14 May 1989 in the first formal visit by a top Kremlin leader since Khrushchev's last rancorous appearance thirty years before. Gorbachev now intended to put an end to the great feud with China, an initial step in a broader design of engaging the Soviet Union with the rising economies of the East. Taken on the inevitable excursion to the Great Wall he offered a comment rather markedly different to those of the average visitor: '*It's a very beautiful work, but there are already too many walls between peoples*.'[169] With regard to the scheduled meeting with Deng he proposed to respect Asian concepts of seniority and approach his eighty-four-year-old Chinese host 'as a younger person would consult an elder'.[170] Deng's own approach was less delicate. He instructed that there should be none of the comradely hugging traditional between Party leaders – a handshake would do. And when the meeting took place on 16 May he delivered a forthright analysis of Soviet shortcomings over the past few decades. He conceded that the doctrinal polemics in which he had played such a prominent part had been largely hot air, and the Chinese themselves didn't now believe that their positions had always been the right ones. The main fault of the Soviets had lain not in that, but in their *failure to treat the Chinese as equals*, subjecting them to humiliating coercion and pressure. The two powers, Deng proposed, should now 'close the past and open the future';[171] but it was clear he himself wasn't altogether ready to let the past go. During a talk in February with the visiting US president, George Bush the Elder, he had brought up the still festering grievance of Outer Mongolia, recalling the old days when the map of China had looked like a maple leaf, with Xinjiang, Mongolia and Manchuria its three protruding segments; only now the central segment of Outer Mongolia had been torn away. In the same spirit he treated his Soviet guest to a ninety-minute harangue on the history of foreign predation in China. Japan, he observed, had inflicted the greatest damage, but the power that had benefited the most had been Russia in both its tsarist and Soviet incarnations, from the 1.5 million square kilometres of land grabbed under the 'unequal treaties' to the Soviet seizure of Black Bear Island in 1929 and the Manchurian concessions secured by Stalin at Yalta and thrust down the throats of the Nationalist regime. It isn't entirely surprising to learn that Gorbachev ended up grumbling to his aides he was 'fed up with this old man's sermons'.[172] By the time Gorbachev left Deng's presence his basic objective had been secured. The great quarrel was over, and normal relations had been restored. But these relations, between the Soviet and Chinese governments, between the CPSU and the CCP, had been restored on a basis of strict equality. The Russians had been compelled to shed the assumption, implicit and explicit, of superiority they had made ever since the 1850s, whether casting themselves as China's well-meaning imperial uncle or its revolutionary elder brother. For the earnest Soviet reformer, normalising relations with the PRC was a genuine triumph; but it was a triumph that came at a price.

NEW WINE, OLD BOTTLES (1989–91)

The first two years after Gorbachev's visit presented the same appearance of outward harmony as the 1950s had done. At Deng's side there had risen up a new generation of CCP leaders who had received a professional training in the Soviet Union during that period, who had acquired and retained a fluent command of the Russian language and who looked back on their Soviet experiences with genuine warmth. They included Jiang Zemin, the Party's General Secretary from 1989, who had trained in Moscow at the Stalin Automobile Works, and Li Peng, the prime minister since 1987, an alumnus of the Moscow Power Engineering Institute. Both of these men now paid visits to Moscow, Li in April 1990 and Jiang in May 1991; and Jiang, a bubbly extrovert, took the opportunity of a gala reception at the Chinese embassy to burst into his own rendition of the old anthem, 'Moscow-Peking'. Certain of the old patterns were re-emerging. Back came teams of Soviet technicians all set to upgrade the outdated equipment in factories their predecessors had installed in the PRC some forty years earlier. Back came the old Chinese appetite for Soviet weapons. During his visit to Moscow in April 1990 Li Peng expressed interest in cooperating with the Soviet Union in aircraft manufacture, and the following year an agreement was reached for the Chinese government to buy a squadron of twenty-four Sukhoi Su-27 fighter jets. All of a sudden old barriers were falling away. As trade along the borders continued to surge the Soviet leadership for the first time threw open the closed frontier areas: visas were no longer required for business trips, and Chinese traders fanned out into the Soviet hinterland from dozens of newly opened entry points, including forty in the Maritime Province alone. Vexatious issues were suddenly turning out to be soluble. On 16 May 1991, during Jiang's Moscow visit, an agreement was signed settling the territorial squabbles along virtually the entire eastern section of the Sino-Soviet border. The deal largely followed the lines of the 'Khrushchev–Liu Shaoqi' settlement torpedoed by Mao in 1964. The island of Damansky/Zhenbao, scene of so much bloodshed, was transferred to China without further difficulty, along with the other islets on the Chinese side of the *thalweg* in the Amur and Ussuri rivers, and only one or two places like the large Black Bear Island remained in dispute. What had all the fuss been about? One veteran Chinese official remarked to Ambassador Troyanovsky, '*When you read the messages our countries exchanged not so long ago you don't know whether to laugh or cry*.'[173] As a number of new Russian restaurants began to sprout in Peking groups of ageing Chinese citizens who had studied in the 1950s in Soviet institutions or received instruction locally from Soviet experts began to turn up to sample Russian cuisine once again and to hear Russian singers belt out the old nostalgic favourites, 'Kalinka', 'Katyusha', 'Moscow Nights' . . .

Under the surface, however, the whole balance of the relationship had changed. Just how much so was illustrated in the aftermath of Gorbachev's 1989 Peking visit when the Soviet leadership asked their CCP counterparts for *economic aid*. The collapse of the Soviet economy had by this time resulted in a chronic shortage of consumer goods, in the Far East in particular. The authorities needed to bring in such goods in large quantities, but lacked the hard currency with which to buy them. Gorbachev and his colleagues proposed a barter arrangement under which a large volume of Chinese consumer necessities would be paid for with Soviet raw materials. The proposal was rich in irony. Back in the 1950s Sino-Soviet trade had consisted essentially of the exchange of Chinese foodstuffs and other raw materials for Soviet manufactured goods. Now it was the other way round. The Chinese were breaking into the Soviet market not merely with foodstuffs but also with a wide range of light industrial products, from textiles and footwear to medical equipment and consumer electronics, while the Russians were obliged to supply raw materials such as timber and fertiliser in the face of a general Chinese lack of interest in Soviet manufactures (with the exception of armaments). The Soviet leadership also asked for some *loans*. The CCP chiefs were 'quite taken aback', in the words of Foreign Minister Qian, by the dramatic reversal of roles this implied, but 'agreed to extend some money to them',[174] and commodity credits to the value of 500 million and 1 billion Swiss francs respectively were dispensed to the Russians in early 1990 and March 1991, enabling Soviet storekeepers to restock their shelves with vital staples such as grain, meat and tea. In the Soviet borderlands meanwhile the irruption of Chinese was making an impact with more than just goods. Between 1989 and 1991 over 30,000 Chinese labourers found jobs helping out on farms and in factories in the Soviet Far East. There were also some entrepreneurs. In 1989 a property developer named He Weinan crossed the Amur to the Soviet border city of Blagoveshchensk. Finding the local construction business to be in the doldrums, he first set about revitalising a stalled hospital project and then went on to put up apartment and office blocks and shopping centres the length and breadth of the town. Other magnates from the Chinese North-East introduced their

Soviet clients to the technology of food processing, and by the middle of 1991 around thirty Sino-Soviet joint ventures had taken shape in the region. In 1990 a report in the *New York Times* judged the economic output of China and the Soviet Union to be approximately equal, and it is possible we can identify in this short period the watershed moment at which the Chinese *caught up* and the Russians were forced to accept economic as well as political equality with their eastern neighbour.

New political strains were meanwhile creeping in. From 1986 Gorbachev and his team of reformers were promoting their signature concept of *glasnost* (transparency in government), pointing the way towards freedom of speech and a pluralistic democracy. This struck an immediate chord in the PRC, where young people were growing increasingly restive at the downside of Deng's economic reforms, the corruption, the social inequality, the lack of status and opportunity for students in particular by comparison with the business elite, while radical intellectuals were calling for a political as well as an economic transformation. All of a sudden the Soviet Union was beginning to look like the cradle of liberty. The dissident Chinese astrophysicist Fang Lizhi, an outspoken advocate of Western-style democracy, hailed the dissident Soviet nuclear physicist Andrei Sakharov, whom Gorbachev was at this time recalling to Moscow after six years in internal exile, and was himself lauded as 'the Chinese Sakharov'. But it was Gorbachev who became the icon of this last great craze for things Russian to sweep China during the twentieth century. As fate would have it the simmering discontent of young people and liberals with the CCP regime finally boiled over in May 1989, at precisely the time Gorbachev set out for Peking on his mission of reconciliation. The Soviet leader arrived, to the acute embarrassment of his CCP hosts, in a city paralysed by the tens of thousands of student protesters who had occupied Tiananmen Square. His official welcoming ceremony had to be staged at the airport rather than downtown, out of reach of the demonstrators; he had to be smuggled into the Great Hall of the People through a rear entrance, as the ceremonial entrance opened on to the Square; the Great Hall had to be protected during the state banquet given in his honour by three concentric rings of armed guards. And outside on the Square the protesters awaited their idol. On 13 May, the day before his arrival, a deputation of student leaders handed to the Soviet embassy a petition with 60,000 signatures requesting a meeting with him, and plans were discussed for organising a march in his honour. Slogans held up on the Square included 'Swap Deng for Gorbachev!' and 'Hurrah for Gorbachev!'.[175] (One is irresistibly reminded of the schoolboys acclaiming the saintly Alyosha 'Hurrah for Karamazov!' at the end of Dostoevsky's great novel.) Gorbachev was unwilling to jeopardise the gains of his visit by addressing the students, as a few of his more enthusiastic aides would have liked him to do. But he did at one point climb out of his car and plunge into the welcoming throng of protesters; and there was little doubt where his sympathies lay. His rather less than congenial meeting with Deng on 16 May was followed that evening by a very different session with Zhao Ziyang, General Secretary of the Party since 1987. Zhao had already signalled his endorsement of Gorbachev's policies by raising the call for 'transparency'. Closet social democrat warmed to closet social democrat, and 'by the end of the evening it was as if they had known one another for years'.[176] Zhao even confided to Gorbachev his doubts about the merits of one-party rule. With regard to the protests, he told the Soviet leader that the Chinese intelligentsia had been following his political reforms 'with the great interest and attention' and had 'demanded that China learn from you and emulate your experience'.[177] But it would all end in tears. Zhao was a lonely figure, his visible feeling for the students outweighed by the stony hostility of Deng, Li Peng and the rest of the Politburo. On the very next day, 17 May, while the Soviet delegation were still in the capital, he was obliged to relinquish his post as the CCP's General Secretary, to be replaced in due course by Jiang Zemin; and he quickly vanished from prominence to spend the rest of his life under house arrest. Two weeks after the Russians departed, on the night of 3–4 June, the dreams of the student protesters and their liberal backers were crushed beneath the bloodied treads of the PLA tanks.

Deng Xiaoping and Li Peng were no keener than Gorbachev to put at risk the newly proclaimed Sino-Soviet concord. Western disgust at the slaughter on Tiananmen Square had left China politically isolated and subject to sanctions on the supply of advanced technology and above all of weapons, and the Soviet Union was the only power available to fill the gaps: hence in part Li Peng's visit to Moscow in April 1990 and the renewed Chinese quest for Soviet military aircraft. But Deng and Li couldn't ignore the fact that the tumult in their capital had been inspired to a significant degree by Gorbachev's *glasnost*, which they hated and feared as a threat to the CCP's rule. And dismissive as Deng might have been about the inanity of the former doctrinal polemics, they and their colleagues remained Marxist-Leninists, looking out at the world through a Marxist-Leninist prism. In the autumn of 1989 the chickens of *glasnost* came home to roost as country after country in Eastern Europe broke out of the socialist straitjacket without Gorbachev lifting a finger to stop them. In an interview granted to a West German magazine that November Li Peng declared ominously, and in direct contradiction of several assurances given by Deng six months earlier about the resumption of Party ties, that with regard to the Soviet Union 'only the relations between *states* have been normalised'.[178] In March 1990 a document circulating within the CCP maintained that the Gorbachev line amounted to 'a betrayal of the fundamental principles of Marxism',[179] and in November another Party homily that made its way to Hong Kong labelled Gorbachev 'a traitor to the socialist cause'.[180] Deng even appears at one point to have reverted to his strategic preoccupations of the late 1970s, saying 'What we have to worry about is the North. The danger from the North is very great.'[181]

By this time of course the social chaos within the Soviet Union was provoking intense opposition to Gorbachev from diehards in the Kremlin itself. There is a certain amount of evidence for contact between the malcontents in the Kremlin and the CCP leadership in Peking. In early May 1991 Dmitri Yazov, the Soviet minister of defence, made a trip to the Chinese capital during which he assured his hosts that the Soviet armed forces would 'defend the gains of socialism';[182] and in August, when members of an 'Emergency Committee' including Yazov tried to grab power from the Soviet leader in a coup d'état, the Chinese ambassador in Moscow was instructed to call on the chairman of the 'Committee', Vice-president Gennady Yanaev, to convey the Chinese Party's approval of their act. Following the collapse of the coup two days later the CCP retreated to a position of 'cool observation';[183] but Deng fumed privately at the 'stupidity', the 'idiocy' of Gorbachev in embarking on a programme of economic reform without taking care to maintain his Party's political grip.[184] Some might argue that the CCP's approach to reform was proved right by events, that it was a case, in the immortal formulation of *1066 and All That*, of Gorbachev, 'Wrong but Wromantic' versus Deng Xiaoping, 'Right but Repulsive'. But Gorbachev always claimed that in Soviet circumstances economic reform could never have been attempted while leaving the political lid on. Whatever the truth it seems probable that the CCP would sooner or later have issued a public anathema against Gorbachev as they had against Khrushchev before him. But the anathema never came, for suddenly at the end of December Gorbachev resigned his office as president and the Soviet Union ceased to exist.

CHAPTER 8

EQUILIBRIUM RESTORED?

A NEW CONVERGENCE (1991–2001)

In the opening months of 1992 the new Russian government led by President Boris Yeltsin proclaimed their wholehearted allegiance to the West. The new, post-Soviet Russia aspired to take its place alongside the United States, Europe and the rest of the 'civilised world', and even hoped for admission to NATO. At a session of the United Nations Security Council on 31 January Yeltsin personally declared Russia's guiding principles to be from now on 'democracy, human rights and freedoms and legal and moral standards'.[1] There was little place for the People's Republic of China in this scheme of things. Yegor Gaidar, the economic whizz-kid who administered Russia's new free market 'shock therapy', dismissed China as a 'dangerous and useless neighbour'.[2] Visiting Beijing in March Russia's new foreign minister, Andrei Kozyrev, added his voice to the familiar Western critique of the PRC's failings, bringing up both the human rights issue and the ever-sensitive question of Taiwan. Where Taiwan was concerned a significant step was now taken to forge a permanent Russian link-up with the rebel island. In April Oleg Lobov, a former deputy premier and vigorous lobbyist with personal ties to the president, met a Taiwanese envoy in the shape of Deputy Foreign Minister Chang Hsiao-yen, an illegitimate son of the Soviet Union's long-time Nationalist interlocutor, Chiang Ching-kuo. Together the two men signed a protocol for establishing a couple of 'unofficial' Economic and Cultural Coordination Commissions, one to operate in Moscow and the other in Taipei. Some months later, in early September, Lobov persuaded the president to sign an authoritative document to the same purpose, thereby subscribing apparently to the 'two Chinas' policy vehemently denounced in Beijing; and the victorious lobbyist was said to have secured a Taiwanese loan, ostensibly to be put towards the establishment of Russia's future Taipei Commission. With a haphazardness characteristic of this zany period neither Yeltsin nor Lobov had bothered to consult on this step with the rest of the Russian government, let alone with the PRC embassy. Two days later the Chinese ambassador called on Foreign Minister Kozyrev to demand if these new commissions could really be considered 'unofficial', while representatives of both the Foreign and Defence Ministries, of the Foreign Intelligence Service and the fledgling state parliament, the Duma, all piled into the president's office to express their alarm. On 15 September Yeltsin was obliged to issue a presidential decree emphasising the Kremlin's commitment to the 'one China' orthodoxy and affirming that the two commissions to be housed in Moscow and Taipei would be strictly non-governmental.[3]

Yeltsin wasn't in fact indifferent to the future of Russian relations with the PRC. To him can apparently be ascribed the credit of realising that the two countries would get on much better *without* a shared ideology. On 31 January 1992, on the fringe of the same UN gathering at which he spelt out the new Russia's principles, he explained to the Chinese premier, Li Peng, that while the world views of Russia and China were now very different, 'we are neighbours and can and must cooperate'.[4] By the summer he was beginning to pull his ministers back from their extreme pro-Western attitudes, and on 7 June *Time* magazine was already voicing its anxiety that 'Russia could go the Asiatic way'.[5] In December he made a trip to Beijing, where he signed a Joint Declaration with the PRC's head of state, Yang Shangkun. The Declaration took as its premise that China and Russia were '*friendly countries*', and Yeltsin observed at a press conference that 'the ideological barrier' (*sic*) had been removed.[6] The Declaration was reinforced by the signing of some twenty-five documents looking forward to future joint technological projects, up to and including the exploration of space.

Over the next few years Yeltsin and his team spoke increasingly of a 'balanced' foreign policy. Russia in their view should look West and East simultaneously, facing both ways like the double-headed eagle on the old tsarist coat of arms. Different interest groups naturally pulled in one direction or the other, and the great nineteenth-century contest between Westernisers and Slavophiles seemed to have taken on a new shape, with the Westernisers replaced by a new breed of liberal-minded 'Atlanticists' such as Gaidar and Kozyrev and the Slavophiles by an assortment of China-friendly 'Eurasianists'. Allied to the Atlanticists were some strategic thinkers who still nursed the deep Soviet-era suspicion of Chinese intentions: in a speech of December 1996, for example, the current defence minister, Igor Rodionov, without having consulted either the president or the Foreign Ministry (more haphazardness!) listed China among the 'potential threats' to his country.[7] The Eurasianists constituted a mixture of advocates of the Deng-era Chinese economic reforms and the ideological old guard from Soviet days. Prominent in the latter category were Oleg Rakhmanin, former scourge of the Maoists, for whom even a flawed and heretical socialist China was better than a Russia with no socialism at all, and the leader of what remained of the Communist Party, Gennady Zyuganov, who argued that 'to a great extent Russia belongs to the East'.[8] For a time the 'balance' was upheld, and the new China lobby remained a minority in the Yeltsin administration. But the Eurasianist concept was gaining ground.

For a start China was propping up the economy. Following the collapse of the Soviet Union Gaidar and his colleagues embarked on a policy of drastic retrenchment. The arms sector was a particular target. The military budget was slashed, and the decision was taken that any recently signed government contracts for supplying weapons should not be fulfilled. For an economy as heavily militarised as that of the former USSR the impact was devastating. A number of basic industries were in peril; hundreds of thousands of workers were laid off; and arms producers were desperate 'to sell virtually anything to anybody'.[9] Into this chaos stepped the Chinese, still debarred from acquiring Western arms by the sanctions imposed in the aftermath of the Tiananmen massacre, their appetite for Russian arms whetted by the deals they had managed to strike during the final two years of Soviet rule. Between 1992 and 1994 they bought 97 per cent of their military imports from Russian suppliers, and between 1993 and 1997 they spent at least $5 billion on Russian weaponry, making the PRC overwhelmingly the biggest customer for Russian arms. One Russian scholar has stressed that this Chinese business was 'crucial for Russia's short-term survival as an industrial power'.[10] Another credits the PRC with nothing less than the rescue of Russia's entire military-industrial complex.[11]

The post-Soviet devastation was felt with particular keenness in the Russian Far East. Gaidar and his associates put a stop to the huge subsidies with which the Soviet leadership had sustained their Far Eastern possessions. Internal transport began to break down, which triggered an unaffordable rise in freight charges, which in turn cut the region off from its traditional sources of consumer goods in European Russia. Grossly neglected by Moscow, the region felt 'orphaned',[12] and a widespread demoralisation set in; one symptom of this was the reappearance, for the first time since the 1920s and 1930s, of Russian prostitutes in the hotels and nightclubs of East Asian cities. Relief once again came from the Chinese, this time in the form of the cross-border traders who had for years been stepping up their activities to the north of the River Amur. Through the grim early post-Soviet years of 1992–4 these traders filled the empty shelves in the shops from Irkutsk to Vladivostok supplying desperately needed food and clothes at affordable prices. It has been conjectured that if it hadn't been for Chinese 'shuttle traders' peddling their wares across the Manchurian frontier large numbers of Russians would not have survived the onset of Moscow's 'shock therapy'. Other Chinese took jobs, like their forebears in the same region a century earlier, in local factories and on local farms, where they planted watermelons and vegetables and were said to have taught their Russian employers how to 'coax crops out of poor soil using the traditional Chinese style of back-breaking labour'.[13]

The principal force edging Yeltsin's government in a 'Eurasian' direction was not however Chinese help so much as the attitude of the West. In spite of much talk of a second Marshall Plan, large-scale Western aid for the new Russia never really materialised. Between 1993 and 1999, for example, the total aid forthcoming from a booming United States is said to have been equivalent to just 1 per cent of the US defence budget for the single year 1996;[14] while at the same time the Russians were being expected to keep taking the West's economic medicine by cutting spending and raising more taxes. Far from admitting Russia to NATO, the Western powers were by 1996 to the anger and alarm of the Kremlin planning vigorously to expand the alliance into the former Soviet sphere of control in Eastern Europe – this in spite of an informal but definite pledge given to Mikhail Gorbachev in 1990 that the alliance would not expand east.[15] By 1997 NATO had incorporated the former Warsaw Pact member states of Poland, Hungary and the Czech

Republic; by 2004 it would have taken in the former Soviet-ruled Baltic nations of Estonia, Latvia and Lithuania and crept up to the borders of Russia itself. Conceived with the no doubt benevolent aim of providing security for Moscow's former vassals, this gambit was bound to lead sooner or later, as anyone with the least knowledge of Russian history and psychology could have predicted, to a return of the Cold War. Probably this was clear enough to the Western officials and analysts who pushed for NATO's expansion. But one suspects that their mindset was similar to that of the Soviet diehards who refused in the early 1980s to accept the reality of a changed PRC. They had built their careers on the Cold War. They didn't want it to end.

Be that as it may, as the 1990s advanced Yeltsin's tilt towards China became increasingly marked. In 1994 he persuaded the PRC leaders to upgrade the status of Sino-Russian relations from the 'friendly countries' formula of two years before to a '*constructive partnership*'.[16] In 1996 he upped the ante still further, winning China's consent to the proclamation of a new and grandiloquent '*strategic partnership of equality and mutual trust for the twenty-first century*'.[17] From this point on he began to exchange visits annually with his Chinese counterpart, President Jiang Zemin, and to do his utmost to cultivate ties of personal warmth with the PRC chief. On arrival in Beijing in November 1997 he was photographed clasping Jiang in a bear hug. 'We are united', he declared, 'by our love for our grandsons . . . we do not have to spend time testing each other. We trust each other.'[18] In Moscow in 1998 he proposed an informal dress code for his meeting with Jiang, 'without ties',[19] and on his last trip to Beijing, in December 1999, he described having woken up in his hotel room unsure where he was, and then remembered that he was in China – 'among friends'.[20]

The Chinese had meanwhile been moving towards the same destination, by a rather different trajectory.

For true believing Marxists in the CCP the events that unfolded in Moscow in the last months of 1991 had come as a hideous shock. The collapse of the Party of Lenin! In the country of Lenin! A pro-Western government in the Kremlin! Post-mortems debating the fall of the CPSU and its lessons for the Chinese Party began at once, and in the form of conferences and treatises continued for years. Russia was now identified as a negative example, with blame focused largely on Gorbachev and his folly of launching into economic reform while neglecting to keep the political lid on. As for Yeltsin, he was dismissed as an anti-Communist and a traitor. Deng Xiaoping, now approaching his nineties but still China's paramount leader, declined to receive Yeltsin during his ice-breaking Beijing trip in December 1992 and is said to have been unwilling to refer to Yeltsin's country by its new names of Russia and the Russian Federation 'even through gritted teeth'.[21]

Even so there were practicalities that couldn't wait. On 27 December 1991, with the ink barely dry on Gorbachev's resignation, a team of Chinese Foreign Ministry officials arrived in Moscow to firm up diplomatic relations with the new post-Soviet government, while Foreign Minister Qian Qichen cabled recognition of the five former Soviet Central Asian republics of Kazakhstan, Kyrgyzstan, Tajikistan, Turkmenistan and Uzbekistan which had just emerged blinking into the daylight of independence. Speed was essential to prevent Taiwan from getting in first, as the Lobov episode clearly demonstrated a few months later. On 15 January 1992 a Politburo meeting leaked to the Hong Kong media took a line in essence very similar to that conveyed by the Russian president to Li Peng in New York at the end of the month: '*Even if Yeltsin is very reactionary we can internally curse him and pray for his downfall, but we shall still have to maintain normal state relations with him*'.[22] One result was the issuing as early as March of an invitation to Yeltsin to visit Beijing, though the project was nearly torpedoed by the Lobov affair and the president didn't arrive in the Chinese capital until December.

In the first place there was unfinished business to settle. In particular the Chinese were keen to lock in the agreement concluded with the former Soviet Union in May 1991 which had handed them back such a generous helping of territory on the eastern part of the Sino-Soviet border along the Amur. In February 1992, well before their misgivings about Yeltsin's government had dissipated, the Chinese National People's Congress ratified the agreement, with the new Russian Duma gratifyingly following suit. Over the following years, with continuing cooperation from Moscow, the Chinese pressed ahead with the demarcation of the eastern border, and by November 1997, when a further agreement was signed, the only areas still in dispute were Black Bear Island and Tarabarov, aka Yinlong Island, across from Khabarovsk, and Bolshoi Island in one of the Amur's tributaries, the River Argun. The western border presented a different problem. The Sino-Russian portion of that border was now minute, a fifty-five-kilometre sliver of land between Kazakhstan and Mongolia which was quickly sorted as one of the first fruits of the new 'constructive partnership' in September 1994. The rest of the western frontier was now shared by the PRC with three of the Soviet Union's Central Asian successor states – Kazakhstan, Kyrgyzstan and Tajikistan. And the Beijing authorities were fearful of the impact which the Islamic religion and the Turkic or Persian ethnicity of these new neighbours might have on the Uighurs, Kazakhs and other minority groups in their ever-troubled border region of Xinjiang. In the last days of 1991, Wang Zhen, a CCP elder and the general who had presided over the Party's conquest of Xinjiang in 1949–50, reappeared in the region and called on its people to build a 'steel wall' to 'safeguard the country's unification'.[23] At some point in the following year, though, the CCP seem to have grasped the superior wisdom of building bridges to the 'Stans' with the help of their one-time Russian overlords. In November 1992 a combined delegation of Russian, Kazakh, Kyrgyz and Tajik representatives were received in Beijing at the start of series of talks to determine the whole western borderline. These negotiations dragged on for some years, but the kinks in the western border had largely been ironed out by the turn of the century.

Another outstanding issue from the PRC point of view was that of 'military confidence-building'. Troop reduction and disarmament on the Sino-Soviet border had been one of the major conditions stipulated by Deng Xiaoping for the normalisation of relations with Moscow; but serious progress in that area had still not been made. In November 1992 the talks between China, Russia and the three Stans set off simultaneously on this separate track. In April 1996 at a meeting in Shanghai the participants signed a Five Country Agreement on the Building of Mutual Trust in the Border Regions. Under this pact each signatory was to inform the others of any troop movement or deployment of weaponry within 100 kilometres of their border with the PRC. No more than 40,000 troops could be used in military exercises on the eastern border (the agreement applied to the Manchurian frontier as well), and no more than 4,000 on the western one. Some Russians were apparently irked by the Chinese insistence on appointing military inspectors to supervise the fulfilment of these obligations – 'manipulating', as they saw it, the movement of Russian troops on Russian soil.[24] But the talks carried on, and in April 1997 a culminating agreement was signed in Moscow on the Reduction of Military Forces in the Border Regions, with a maximum of 130,400 Chinese troops and 130,400 Russian and Central Asian troops to be stationed within their frontier zones. In this area too, then, the PRC had largely achieved its objectives. And in the meantime the negotiating countries had quietly morphed into a bloc known from the site of the 1996 breakthrough as the Shanghai Five.

But the new Russia had more to offer than just the redress of past grievances. We have already touched on the voracious Chinese appetite for Russian arms. In 1992, once again overcoming their initial aversion to Yeltsin's rule, the PRC leaders contracted to purchase a total of seventy-two Sukhoi Su-27 advanced fighter jets, buying twenty-six on the spot and the remaining forty-six four years later. In that same year, 1996, the Chinese navy acquired two Sovremenny-class destroyers equipped with surface-to-air and ship-to-ship missiles, and placed an order for four Kilo-class diesel submarines. Other sophisticated hardware bought during these years included up to 100 S-300 ground-to-air missiles and rocket launchers thought capable of propelling cruise missiles. What the Chinese wanted even more than the hardware was the underlying technology which would save them the time needed to develop these arms by themselves, and here too the Russians seemed willing to oblige. In 1996, for example, they agreed to sell the PRC the knowhow required to produce its own Sukhoi Su-27 jet fighters at a factory in Shenyang. With a readiness that contrasted with Khrushchev's attempt to deny China the Bomb, they committed to helping the Chinese build two new nuclear plants and to supplying Beijing with the latest technology for enriching uranium.

And while all this was happening a whole new realm of commercial opportunity was opening up. In 1993 a swiftly industrialising China made the transition from being a net exporter to a net importer of oil. To ensure a continuing flow of the black gold the Chinese needed sources of supply more dependable than the volatile Middle East, and neighbouring Russia, with its enormous energy resources, was an obvious potential supplier. Already by 1994 the Chinese were starting to raise with the Kremlin the proposition that Russia might help meet the PRC's needs. In 1997 the China National Petroleum Corporation (CNPC) signed three contracts with the Russian oil firm Yukos under which Yukos agreed to sell 1.5 million tons of oil to China in 1999 along the existing railway routes, and discussions were launched about the possibility of building a pipeline from the Yukos oilfield near Tomsk in Siberia to the Chinese North-East. Similar projects began to be mooted for natural gas. In June 1997 CNPC reached an agreement with another Russian company, Sidanko, under which 3 to 3.5 billion cubic metres of natural gas would be exported annually from the Kovyktinskoe gas field near Irkutsk over the next thirty-six years, with an eventual 20 billion going to China and other Asian states once a proposed pipeline had been completed. Energy experts began to quip that Marx and Lenin had been replaced in the Sino-Russian relationship by the more compelling deities of Oil and Gas.

Russian science remained an attraction. Even the remote-sounding goal of joint space exploration began to take on substance within a few years. In 1992 the Chinese launched a manned space programme entitled Project 921. By the second half of the decade Russian experts were busy helping Beijing to train cosmonauts ('taikonauts' in Chinese parlance), to design spacesuits and to build the PRC's Shenzhou spacecraft and its accompanying booster rockets.

PRC strategists didn't relinquish their apprehensions of Russia overnight. As late as the summer of 1996 a Western academic reported discovering on Google Earth that Chinese missiles stationed in the north-western province of Qinghai continued to point in Russia's direction.[25] Sage advisers, however, were now counselling that the threat to the PRC came not from Russia, but from the United States. In March 1996 the US Seventh Fleet moved into the Taiwan Strait to deter a PRC missile campaign designed to intimidate the Taiwan authorities, thereby prompting the PLA's subsequent order for Russian destroyers and submarines. And in April the US and Japan issued a Joint Declaration on Security, clearly pointing to a future anti-China coalition – a development not much less alarming to the Beijing leadership than the expansion of NATO was to the Kremlin.

So the Chinese chiefs gradually responded to Yeltsin's embraces. Personal ties did in fact take a little time to adjust. President Jiang Zemin is known to have been perturbed, for example, by the Russian leader's notorious drinking habits. One Chinese diplomat has left an account of a banquet given by Jiang for his opposite number at the Great Hall of the People in Beijing in April 1996 to celebrate the creation of the new 'strategic partnership'. No spirits were set out on the banqueting table at the specific request of Yeltsin's doctors in Moscow. The ensuing scene went as follows:

YELTSIN [broad hint]: Do you remember the last time I came to China we drank a kind of spirit?
JIANG [reluctantly]: Do you want some?
YELTSIN: You bet!

[Waiters produce a bottle of twenty-year-old vintage *maotai*. YELTSIN 'excitedly' downs three glasses in succession.]

Mme YELTSINA [to JIANG]: Don't let him drink any more.
YELTSIN [rounding on wife]: Don't you meddle with me! Do it again and I won't bring you next time![26]

The extrovert in Jiang does seem nonetheless to have warmed to the extrovert in Yeltsin; more conspicuously after the death in February 1997 of Jiang's patron Deng Xiaoping, who had probably carried his suspicion of Russia to the grave.

By the late 1990s, then, the two powers had effected a full transition from mutual aversion to solidarity. In April 1997, at the summit marked by an agreement to cut down their troops on the old Sino-Soviet frontier, China and Russia issued for the first time a joint statement on foreign policy in the form of a *Declaration on the Trend to a Multi-polar World and the Establishment of a New International Order*.[27] Translated into plain language this proclaimed the two countries' shared opposition to US dominance of the post-Cold War world. Then in spring 1999 NATO launched its bombing campaign against the Serb rulers of the rump Yugoslavia to secure independence for the Albanian-majority province of Kosovo. NATO's assault enraged both the two partners – Russia because it saw itself as the natural protector of its Serb cousins in the same way it had done in 1914, and China because NATO planes had inadvertently dropped five bombs on the Chinese embassy in Belgrade, killing three Chinese journalists who had taken shelter there. Both the two countries abruptly severed what military links they still had with the West, and plunged into discussions on how to add muscle to their 'strategic partnership'; and Yeltsin reiterated in December on his final visit to Beijing, 'A multi-polar world – that's the basis of everything.'[28] In the following year, with Yeltsin retired and replaced by the reassuringly sober Vladimir Putin, the Chinese took the initiative as Jiang proposed to the new Russian leader the conclusion of a major treaty for the first time since the ill-fated Valentine's Day compact of fifty years before; and on 16 July 2001 the two men appended their signatures to a new *Treaty of Good Neighbourliness, Cooperation and Friendly Relations*.

A NEW PARTNERSHIP (2001–22)

The new agreement was cautiously phrased. 'Drawing on the lessons of history',[29] Jiang and his colleagues made clear that they weren't prepared to be locked into another formal alliance with Russia – a reluctance the Russians were happy to share. No target countries were specified, and no commitments were written into the document which either signatory might find irksome in future. Instead stress was placed on the *durability* of the new relationship, with the two countries pledging themselves to be 'always friends and never enemies', living and working together 'from generation to generation'.[30] This new era of amity was ushered in over the next ten years by the joint efforts of Putin and Hu Jintao, who succeeded Jiang Zemin as the CCP's General Secretary in November 2002. In the run-up to their first meeting in Beijing that December both men were eager to signal their predilection for the partner country. Putin expressed his hope of practising Chinese kung fu during his first visit to the PRC, disclosing for good measure that both his two daughters were martial arts enthusiasts and that one of them was taking a Chinese language course. Hu for his part revealed that one of his favourite books was *The Story of Zoya and Shura*, an epic account of the Soviet resistance to the Nazi invaders of Russia in the Second World War. If the rapport between the two leaders lacked the effusiveness of the Yeltsin–Jiang interaction it was enhanced by the similarity of their cool, reserved temperaments and the sheer frequency of the meetings between them as they conferred face to face five or six times a year. One Western journalist commented that the pair 'couldn't seem to stay out of each other's capitals',[31] and they earned themselves in some circles the collective label of 'Pu and Hu'.[32] Their prime ministers met with a similar regularity, with Hu's premier Wen Jiabao remarking in 2007 of a session with Putin's premier Dmitri Medvedev, 'We didn't even use prepared speeches.'[33]

Under these auspices a whole range of joint institutions sprang up, with the appearance successively during the first decade of the new century of a Sino-Russian Business Council, a Sino-Russian Research Centre, a Russo-Chinese Centre of Trade and Economic Cooperation and a Russian–Chinese Commission on Cooperation in Military Technology. Joint scientific projects unfolded in spheres ranging from biotechnology, high-energy physics and petrochemistry to microelectronics, new materials, laser technology and nanostructures. Following the successful flight of the first

(Russian-trained) Chinese taikonaut in October 2003 the two powers prepared the way for a hugely ambitious joint leap into space. The Russians had developed a spacecraft intended to land on Phobos, one of the two moons of Mars, and collect soil samples to bring back to Earth: the mission was accordingly named Phobos-Grunt, '*grunt*' being the Russian word for soil. Under an agreement concluded in 2007 the space vehicle would also carry China's first inter-planetary probe, Yinghuo-1, to be released from the main craft and sent into orbit around Mars itself to study the planet's external environment.

Swords went on getting beaten into ploughshares. In October 2004 during one of Putin's incessant trips to Beijing the Russian president signed a Supplementary Agreement on the Eastern Section of the Border. The western half of Black Bear Island was at last recognised as belonging to China (the Chinese graciously conceded the eastern half), along with Tarabarov Island, henceforth and forever to be known as Yinlong, and Bolshoi Island in the River Argun. Four years later, in 2008, the final handover took place. The PRC flag was hoisted on Black Bear Island, on 'the easternmost tip of China',[34] and glowing predictions were made about how the island might be transformed into an ecological resort like Hainan Island off the south coast, or alternatively into a big border city like Shenzhen. The handover was billed as the final settlement marking the end of four decades of Sino-Russian border disputes. Territorial clashes now gave way to an abundance of twinning arrangements linking Russia's Maritime Province with Jilin Province in Manchuria, the Irkutsk region with Liaoning Province, the Russian Altai mountain region with Xinjiang.

The stage was now set for the two powers to take up their role as Leaders of the Opposition in a world dominated by the United States.

Superficially reminiscent of the Sino-Soviet tandem of the 1950s, the new partnership differed from it in fundamental ways. It was not a revolutionary combination but a deeply traditional and conservative one. The two partners took their stand in effect on the principles of the 1648 Treaty of Westphalia, of unfettered national sovereignty and the right of national governments to do as they pleased in their own backyards without interference from outside, in defiance of the growing opinion in the United States and the West that governments were answerable to a global tribunal for the treatment of their populations. And this simple creed of Leave Us Alone bound them together with a more potent glue than Marxism-Leninism had ever been. It followed that each of them sprang to the other's defence against external brickbats. China supported the Russians over their wars in Chechnya and their hostility to the expansion of NATO, while the Russians voiced their understanding of China's position regarding Taiwan, Xinjiang and Tibet. And when popular uprisings broke out in other countries, from the 'colour revolutions' in Georgia in 2003–4 and in Ukraine in 2005 to the protests in Burma in 2007 and in Iran following the elections of 2009, the two partners repeatedly threw their weight behind the embattled regimes. As permanent members of the United Nations Security Council both of them wielded veto powers which they used to protect their favoured despotisms against outside pressure. In July 2009, for instance, they jointly vetoed a US resolution calling for economic sanctions to be imposed on Robert Mugabe's regime in Zimbabwe. By 2011 they were patently coordinating their UN votes in advance, first supporting the initial Security Council decision imposing sanctions against Qadhafi in Libya, then swivelling to abstain over the establishment of a no-fly zone in the country and authorisation of the ensuing NATO air strikes. Over Syria they vetoed a whole series of motions condemning the Assad regime for its violations of human rights and calling on member states to refrain from supplying it with money and arms. To draw another analogy with European history, it was a posture remarkably similar to that of the Holy Alliance of Russia, Prussia and Austria in the post-Waterloo years, Metternich's forces hurrying to shore up the beleaguered tyranny of the Bourbons in the Kingdom of the Two Sicilies. At the same time the partners touted their own model of state-guided capitalism coupled with stringent political control. It was a model the Chinese had made their own ever since Deng's time and which Russia also was beginning to tack towards under the new Putin government. It was a formula not unattractive to the developing world at a time of global financial crisis, when the Western free market model appeared to be coming apart at the seams.

On 15 June 2001, one month before the conclusion of the new Sino-Russian treaty, the Shanghai Five signed a document transforming themselves into a permanent Shanghai Cooperation Organisation (SCO). It was a first attempt by the partners to set up a political camp under their combined leadership. The camp now included not merely the three original Central Asian 'Stans' that shared borders with China, but also Uzbekistan, which had no Chinese border but was the most developed and populous of the Central Asian successor states. The SCO members pledged themselves to combat 'terrorism, separatism and religious extremism', or in other words any spread of Islamic fundamentalism in Central Asia which might infect the Chechens and Tatars in southern Russia or the Uighurs and Kazakhs in Xinjiang. By 2003 an elaborate institution had been created, including a Council of Heads of State, a Council of Heads of Government and a Council of Foreign Ministers, plus a permanent Secretariat based in Beijing. Various arrangements were made linking up the ministries of the member states responsible for foreign trade and economic relations, education and culture and so forth, but the stress remained firmly on security issues: the second permanent body created after the Secretariat was the Executive Committee of an entity known in English as the Regional Anti-Terrorist Structure, evocatively abbreviated to RATS. Taking shape here was a subtler variant of the old familiar pattern, China and Russia joining forces to keep control of the restless peoples between them. The SCO offered something to both the two partners. The Russians got a fresh lease of life for their long-standing military and cultural pre-eminence in the former Soviet Central Asia. The Chinese were free to develop an influence in the Stans which they hadn't enjoyed since the high tide of Qing conquest in the mid-eighteenth century, and were happy, it seemed, for this influence to be largely confined to the economic sphere. The Central Asians themselves were ambivalent. On the one hand they benefited from a flood of investment and the possibility of playing off their two patrons against each other. On the other hand they weren't entirely comfortable sandwiched between the two behemoths. Already in the 1990s a prime minister of Kazakhstan was lamenting that his country was 'bottled up in a semi-stable space between Russia and China',[35] and a furore arose among the Kyrgyz when the owner of a new Chinese restaurant in their capital, Bishkek, was found to have named his establishment 'Northern Province'. The name was hastily altered to 'Silvery Moon'.[36]

The two partners also began to construct a grander if looser network with a worldwide dimension. In June 2009 a first formal summit was held in the Russian city of Ekaterinburg of an emerging quartet of powers consisting of China, Russia, India and Brazil. During the following year the quartet was joined by South Africa, thereby acquiring the handy acronym of BRICS. The idea was to bring together a number of major developing nations that were dissatisfied with the Western dominance of global financial bodies. The BRICS members called for the creation of a new global reserve currency to compete with the US dollar, and by 2013 they had started to plan the establishment of a New Development Bank to rival the World Bank and the International Monetary Fund. The BRICS didn't constitute any kind of alliance, and indeed one of them, India, was periodically at daggers drawn with the PRC. But they were at least all content to subscribe to the Sino-Russian objective of a multi-polar world free of US hegemony, and the other members seem at times to have tilted towards the Sino-Russian position on more concrete issues: thus for example in March 2011 Brazil and South Africa joined the partners in withholding support for the United Nations imposition of a no-fly zone over Libya. The BRICS headquarters was housed in a tower block in Shanghai.

These strategic manoeuvres were felt to call for some judicious underpinning in the realm of defence. In August 2005 military cooperation between the partners took a dramatic new turn as 8,000 troops of the PLA's army, navy and air force teamed up with a 1,000-strong Russian naval contingent in a joint exercise. Following 'military and political consultations' at the headquarters of the Russian Pacific Fleet in Khabarovsk,[37] the participants headed southwards to the Shandong peninsula and the Yellow Sea. The exercise was billed as a Peace Mission tasked with 'restoring order' in an imaginary third country; to some Western observers it looked more like a dress rehearsal for an eventual invasion of Taiwan. Over the next few years similar exercises went on being staged to a biennial rhythm. In August 2007 1,600 PLA troops were dispatched by train to Chelyabinsk in the Urals, joining up with 2,090 Russian counterparts for the first Chinese military exercise on Russian soil, the operation concluding with a final round of drills on the PRC side of the border in Xinjiang. And in July 2009, after 'strategic' talks in Khabarovsk, the two powers contributed 1,300 troops each for joint 'counter-terrorism' practice in the Russian Far East and the Shenyang Military Region.

In other sectors progress was more sluggish. For all the mushrooming of commissions and councils, major economic transactions took a long time to materialise. Starting from the still-modest level of $10 billion in 2001, two-way trade had crept up to no more than $59.3 billion by the end of the decade. Emblematic of this slowness was the PRC's struggle to gain access to the Russian energy market. By December 2002 Chinese hopes were soaring for a deal between the CNPC and its Russian partner, Yukos, to build a 3,400-kilometre pipeline to carry Siberian oil to China's 'oil capital' at Daqing in Manchuria. Weeks later, however, in January 2003, a competitor appeared on the scene in the form of Japan, which was willing to finance a pipeline crossing the whole Russian Far East up to the Pacific port of Nakhodka. The Japanese proposal had the attraction of delivering Russian oil not just to Japan but to a range of Far Eastern and Pacific consumers, whereas China's pipeline would be destined for China alone; and the ensuing half-dozen years saw what the media labelled a 'Sino-Japanese scramble' for Russian crude. The Kremlin's attitude seemed to be, in the words of the opera, 'How happy could I be with either / Were t'other dear charmer away'. Putin expressed a personal preference for the Japanese scheme, and the Chinese plan took a further buffeting in October 2003, when the Russian president closed down Yukos and arrested its owner, the oligarch Mikhail Khodorkovsky. In any event the 'scramble' afforded Russia a delectable opportunity to play off the two would-be customers against one another. The Beijing authorities are said to have greeted the Japanese challenge with 'intense fury',[38] and their impatience grew steadily as the Kremlin continued to drag its feet between the two bids. In March 2006 a Chinese vice-minister summed up the impasse: 'Today is cloudy with a chance for sun, while tomorrow is sunny with a chance for clouds, just like a weather forecast.'[39] China's path to a contract for natural gas supplies proved equally thorny. By 2000 the original deal with the Sidanko company had already foundered, with Sidanko going bankrupt and the Kovyktinskoe gas field fenced off by the Duma as a 'strategic asset', out of bounds to foreign investors. In 2006 Putin promised to build two gas pipelines for China for a cost of $10 billion, but progress was hobbled by disputes over pricing, as Moscow wanted the Chinese to pay for their gas supplies at European prices, while the Chinese were only prepared to pay at developing country rates.

Not all of the joint scientific schemes bore the anticipated fruit. Phobos-Grunt was duly launched from the Baikonur cosmodrome in November 2011 – but came to an inglorious end when its booster rockets failed to propel it in the direction of Mars and instead left it stranded in low Earth orbit before plunging into the Pacific Ocean. This debacle seems not surprisingly to have cooled the ardour of the partners for extra-terrestrial ventures for several years.

There were times when the two partners even seemed to be pulling in opposite directions. In September 2001, just two months after the signing of the new Sino-Russian treaty, Putin abruptly wrenched his country back into alignment with the United States. In response to the 9/11 attacks on New York and Washington he gave his blessing to the deployment of US forces at the old Soviet air bases in Uzbekistan, Kyrgyzstan and Tajikistan as part of America's drive into Afghanistan against al-Qaeda and its Taliban hosts. The PRC didn't approve of this provocative US lunge into a Muslim country or of the Russian support for it, which flew in the face of the newly signed treaty with its implicitly anti-American commitment to building a 'multi-polar world'. In a veiled but unmistakable rebuke of the Kremlin the Chinese media noted that US forces had entered Afghanistan with the tacit consent of the Russians. In August 2008 Russia fought a short war with its southern neighbour, Georgia, partly with a view to detaching the disaffected regions of Abkhazia and South Ossetia from Georgian overlordship and securing their recognition as independent states. This too was unpalatable from the PRC's standpoint, since it meant condoning secession from an established nation, and secession was the last thing the PRC wished to encourage with the example of Taiwan before it and the seething unrest in Tibet and Xinjiang. In a more general sense it upended the Westphalian doctrine of the sanctity of borders which both China and Russia were pledged to uphold. When the Kremlin sought the blessing of China and the SCO for its Georgia policy the response was accordingly a flat no, and the Chinese Foreign Ministry confined itself to a vague and platitudinous statement appealing for dialogue. The same pattern repeated itself in 2014, amid the still larger diplomatic furore that broke out over Russia's annexation of Crimea. Once again for Westphalian reasons the Chinese couldn't bring themselves to endorse Russia's seizure of this territory from Ukraine, no matter how much it might have enjoyed the support of the local population; and they certainly didn't want to draw the attention of the public in Taiwan, Tibet or Xinjiang to Russia's use of a referendum in the annexed area as a device for legitimising a transfer of sovereignty. In the aftermath of the takeover the Russian foreign minister, Sergei Lavrov, held a meeting with his Chinese opposite number, Wang Yi, from which he emerged to state blandly that Beijing was in complete agreement with the Russian position: Wang Yi promptly placed a telephone call to the US secretary of state, John Kerry, to assure him that this was not the case.[40]

Most of these contretemps, however, turned out to have happy endings. As early as May 2003 a compromise was proposed over the vexed question of Russian oil supplies. The new pipeline would indeed be laid to the Pacific; but a spur would be added from a town called Skovorodino to carry oil to Daqing as originally planned. In August 2004 Putin's current prime minister, Mikhail Fradkov, acknowledged that Russia needed to honour its promise to provide China with oil, and in September 2005 Putin himself announced that the spur to Daqing would be laid before the main pipeline was extended to the Pacific coast. The Chinese cause may have benefited from the contrast between Beijing's show of readiness to close the books on the border issue and Japan's continued insistence on regaining the Kurile Islands which the Soviet Army had occupied in the final stages of the Second World War. In February 2009 the Chinese finally clinched their deal by signing a 'loans for oil' agreement under which the PRC would pay the Russian side $25 million for the construction of the pipeline in return for a Russian pledge to deliver 300 million tons of oil over the next twenty years. On 10 September 2010 the spur was completed, and on New Year's Day 2011 it began to pump crude. In the meantime the statistics were surging at last. In 2010 the PRC became for the first time Russia's largest trading partner, accounting for 10 per cent of the country's foreign trade, and in 2010–11 Sino-Russian bilateral trade made its first big jump, from $59.3 billion to $80 billion.

Ways were also found to avoid political discord. In the aftermath of 9/11 CCP foreign policy experts explained to their readers that it was in Beijing's interests to talk the Russians round; to persuade them patiently that the US was cosying up to them for tactical reasons and still largely viewed Moscow as a strategic opponent. During the next few years the partners were quietly drawn together again by a shared alarm at the spread of US influence in Central Asia, and by July 2005 they were calling through the SCO for America to withdraw from the region and encouraging the Uzbek government to evict their contingent of American troops. In spite of its refusal to take Russia's side over the Georgia conflict the PRC played down the whole issue and declined to join in the chorus of outrage from Western countries at Russia's show of force. In 2014 similarly the Chinese didn't endorse the Russian annexation of Crimea; but nor did they denounce it. Over the following month they quietly supplied the Russians with an electricity cable which could be run through to Crimea to undermine an attempt being made by Ukraine to mount an energy blockade of its lost territory. And as the Kremlin proceeded to back a secessionist bid to throw off Ukrainian rule in the Donbass they turned a blind eye, in exchange for the Russians turning a blind eye to Beijing's growing effort to enforce its claim to the whole of the South China Sea.

From the turn of the decade events combined to propel the two partners even closer together. In November 2012 Xi Jinping replaced Hu Jintao as General Secretary of the CCP, and in March 2013 he also succeeded Hu as China's president. During meetings the following winter, Xi and Putin exchanged the now ritual professions of warmth and affinity. Xi recalled his enjoyment of numerous Russian writers from Pushkin to Sholokhov,[41] while Putin recounted how during his birthday the previous October the two men had 'drunk a little vodka together: we even had sandwiches like university students'.[42] But Xi also reported feeling 'as though our personalities had a lot in common';[43] and certainly he and Putin seemed still better matched than the previous Sino-Russian pairings, with the shared taste for autocracy which would lead both to work towards the indefinite extension of their personal rule. By 2019 Xi was referring to Putin as 'my best friend and colleague'.[44] In the meantime the mounting hostility of the United States and its allies was driving Putin towards the classic Russian default option selected both by the tsarist regime after its defeat in the Crimean War and by the Bolsheviks after their failure to ignite revolution in Europe: *Blocked in the West, try the East*. Already in 2013 the Russian president had taken a leaf out of Barack Obama's playbook by announcing a 'pivot to the East',[45] and the following spring, hemmed in by the Western sanctions imposed on his government in reaction to the Crimean takeover, he sped to Beijing with the object of sealing the elusive contract for Russian deliveries of natural gas. The negotiations were plainly not easy. One Western commentator reported a 'nail-biting session of late-night brinkmanship',[46] and Putin was obliged to accept a steep discount in the prices to be charged; but he emerged from the talks nonetheless with an 'indescribable grin' on his face.[47] Even after granting the discount he had still sewn up a $400 billion deal, the largest in the history of the Russian gas industry, and had locked China into an economic embrace that was scheduled to last for the next thirty years. By September 2014 the engineers of the Russian gas giant, Gazprom, were already at work on the China-bound pipeline to be known as the Power of Siberia.

In May 2015 Xi and Putin signed a joint statement on the deepening of what was now labelled a '*comprehensive* strategic partnership'.[48] Agreements followed on the launching of thirty ambitious new projects, from the joint assembly of a long-range passenger aircraft to the construction with Chinese help of a high-speed railway line from Moscow to Kazan, to form part of an eventual high-speed line all the way to Beijing. In their relentless quest for energy the Chinese had started to focus on the region the English had once referred to as the 'North-east Frostie Seas' – the 24,000-kilometre Arctic coastline of Russia with its vast underlying deposits of oil and gas. In 2013 the PRC had succeeded in gaining observer status on the international Arctic Council on the grounds of its being a 'near-Arctic state' (one commentator remarked that this was rather like calling New York a 'near-Caribbean city'[49]), and in the following years it began to push for an Arctic shipping route which would give access to these deposits as they were opened up by global warming. In particular Beijing showed interest in the natural gas reserves underneath the Yamal peninsula, which juts out of northern Siberia into the Arctic Ocean by the mouth of the River Ob. And the Russians played ball. By 2014 the governor of the Yamal Nenets Autonomous District was already enthusing 'China tells us, Give us gas!'.[50] Russia's problem was that it couldn't afford the computer technology needed to exploit its own Arctic resources; and this was where the Chinese came in. By the end of 2019 the PRC had acquired a 30 per cent and a 20 per cent stake respectively in two liquefied natural gas projects being developed by Russia in the Yamal District for a total cost of $45 billion; 2019 also saw the launch of a Sino-Russian Arctic shipping company. In the meantime the joint space endeavour was stirring back into life after some years in the doldrums following the fiasco of Phobos-Grunt. In October 2017 a conference was held to examine a number of joint projects to be undertaken in the coming five years, and in March 2021 an agreement was signed between Roskosmos and the China National Space Administration to set up and operate a joint research station on the Moon. Reality seemed to be catching up with the fantasy penned back in 1838 by Prince Odoevsky in which Russia and China joined hands in the far-distant future to prevent the Earth colliding with Halley's Comet.

Above all the cooperation between the two militaries was visibly going from strength to strength. During Xi Jinping's first trip to Moscow in 2013 Putin encouraged his Chinese guest to visit the Operational Command

Headquarters of the Russian armed forces – the first time this sanctum had ever been thrown open to a foreign leader. After the 2014 nosedive in Russian–Western relations he also began to relax the restrictions on arms supplies to Beijing. For the first time the PRC was supplied by the Kremlin with some truly cutting-edge military hardware in the form of an S-400 missile defence system and a squadron of twenty-four Sukhoi Su-35 fighter jets – the latter reckoned by one Russian expert to be enough to tip the balance of air power in Beijing's favour in the Taiwan Straits. In a talk at the Valdai International Discussion Club in Moscow in October 2019 the Russian strongman went on to declare publicly the Kremlin's intention of providing the PRC with an early warning missile defence system. From 2012 on the former biennial military exercises were taking place at least once a year, and the locations were becoming increasingly startling. Sino-Russian naval manoeuvres were held in May 2015 in the Mediterranean, in July 2017 in the Baltic near the Russian exclave of Kaliningrad and in November 2019 off Cape Town in the company of the South African navy. In July 2019 a first Sino-Russian joint air patrol sallied forth into the Sea of Japan, to the indignation of both the Japanese and South Korean governments which complained the patrols had violated their air space. A similar exercise was conducted in December 2020. Seasoned observers were inclined to view these activities as a political warning ('Leave Us Alone') to the United States and its allies rather than a statement of intended aggression. Still, the show of force was dramatic enough. The partnership looked by now like a military alliance in all but name, and Putin himself spoke in terms of an 'allied relationship',[51] though the Chinese still seemed chary of making that final commitment.

All these advances took place against a steady drumbeat of celebration. As early as 2002 the Chinese prime minister at the time, Zhu Rongji, judged that Sino-Russian relations had entered 'their best period ever',[52] and in 2004 Putin agreed that ties between the two countries had soared to 'unparalleled heights'.[53] The following year Hu Jintao's premier, Wen Jiabao, reiterated that the relationship was passing through its 'best period in history',[54] and in 2010 Putin's stand-in as president, Dmitri Medvedev, opined that 'never before had relations between the two powers been characterised by such a high level of mutual trust'.[55] The superlatives only intensified after the Xi-Putin axis emerged. In late December 2020, in a telephone call to his 'best friend' in Moscow, Xi affirmed that the ties between China and Russia could not now be broken by any third party, and could weather all kinds of international turmoil;[56] and in January 2021 Foreign Minister Wang Yi declared, 'In developing Sino-Russian strategic cooperation we see no limits, no forbidden areas, no ceiling to how far the cooperation can go.'[57]

One year further on and the partnership was subjected to its stiffest test yet. In February 2022 Putin sent his armies into Ukraine in a bloody and anachronistic attempt to bolster his country's security and to restore its historical frontiers by force. It was the Russian leader's most flagrant breach to date of the Westphalian principle, a savage blow struck at the existence of an internationally recognised state, and one with which China enjoyed friendly commercial ties. It also potentially laid China open to economic disruption as the appalled West imposed hundreds of billions of dollars' worth of sanctions on both Russia and any outside power coming to Russia's support. This time the fissures in Chinese opinion were apparent for all to see. Critics on Chinese social media drew comparisons with Japan's seizure of Manchuria in 1931–2 and poured scorn on the way Russia had 'attacked another person's house and talked about a "peaceful settlement" '.[58] In March both the Bank of China and the Industrial and Commercial Bank of China restricted financing for the purchase of Russian commodities out of fear of Western reprisals, and in April for similar reasons the telecommunications giant Huawei suspended the operations of its Russian branch. Discontent with the Russian offensive was voiced at a very senior political level. The Chinese ambassador to the United Nations declared that 'The situation has evolved to a point which China does not wish to see',[59] and as Putin's troops flagged in their early attempt to take Kyiv the former Chinese ambassador to Ukraine predicted Russia's eventual defeat.[60] In early March a startling commentary was published by a distinguished scholar named Hu Wei, vice-chairman of the Public Policy Research Centre which formed part of the Counsellor's Office of the State Council under Prime Minister Li Keqiang. Hu declared bluntly that China should dump Putin in favour of a full-scale rapprochement with the Western world. Hu's broadside was carried on the Chinese internet for the whole of ten days. Some sources even speculated that the topmost Party leadership, the Standing Committee of the Politburo, was split down the middle.[61]

Yet in spite of all this the partnership held firm once again. In Beijing for the Winter Olympics on the eve of his onslaught Putin elicited from the CCP leadership a reaffirmation of the 'no limits' character of the Sino-Russian partnership. The PRC media obediently followed Moscow's designation of its Ukrainian campaign as a 'special operation' rather than an invasion, and expressed understanding for the very real Russian fear of NATO expansion to the East. At a conference of the BRICS grouping in June Xi Jinping lambasted the United States and the West for 'weaponising the global economy', 'expanding military alliances' and 'seeking security for oneself at the expense of the security of other countries'.[62] Critics such as Hu Wei were censored or obliged to register their dissent from the safe distance of Singapore. The PRC refused to condemn Putin's invasion at the United Nations, and instead called for peaceful dialogue – though apparently without departing from its solid backing for Russia so far as to offer itself as a neutral mediator. Once again as in 2014 the PRC held out an economic lifeline to its partner, through the import (at heavily discounted prices) of greatly expanded quantities of Russian oil, the purchase of nearly 8.42 million tons in May alone turning Russia immediately into the country's biggest oil supplier. Natural gas purchases rose similarly by 60 per cent on the previous year in the first few months of 2022.[63] The CCP leadership steadfastly rebuffed allegations that they were supplying Putin with arms; but they continued to advertise the deepening military teamwork between the two powers. In May 2022 Chinese and Russian strategic bombers conducted a fresh patrol over the Sea of Japan and the East China Sea, to the agitation of both the US and the Japanese governments. And in July PLA troops, tanks and armoured vehicles were spotted crossing the Russian border at Manzhouli on their way to take part in the latest round of war games to be held in the company of friendly states such as Iran and Venezuela, the latter of which was arranging for a part of the exercises to be staged in the Western hemisphere for the first time.

DESTINATION UNKNOWN (2022–)

Many Westerners seemed slow to grasp what was taking place under their noses. The unfolding from 2015 of the 'comprehensive strategic partnership' was seized on with excitement by Western journalists seemingly unaware that the partnership had been in the making for over twenty years (nearly thirty if one counts the ice-breaking phase under Yeltsin). Among those officials and pundits who did take a longer view the reaction looked a little like the response to news of a personal disaster. Initially there was denial. The present cosiness between the two powers, they maintained, couldn't possibly last: look at the Sino-Soviet 'honeymoon' of the 1950s and the decades of bitter hostility that replaced it. The current trumpeting of good relations could be disregarded as mere propaganda. And in any case China and Russia would always be closer to the United States, economically and culturally, than they would be to each other. Then, as the reality of the new alignment sank in, denial gave way to anger and alarm. China and Russia began to be bracketed, as the Soviet Union and China had been in the 1950s, as a twin-headed menace to the US and to democracy throughout the world. By 2014 rumour had it that the two partners were fostering the Shanghai Cooperation Organisation as a 'second Warsaw Pact'.[64] The Sino-Russian naval exercise in the Mediterranean was interpreted as the start of a seaborne challenge to the Western alliance, and the joint space programme was seen as portending a wartime attempt to disable American satellites. In 2018 the Trump administration identified the partnership publicly as Washington's 'strategic rivals', and NATO signalled its readiness to pay more attention to the proliferating Sino-Russian ties. In June 2021 a Pentagon report expressed the mounting dread by declaring that while UFOs were unlikely to be of extra-terrestrial origin they could well be 'technologies from other nations like China and Russia'.[65]

Some of the earlier Western assumptions about the relationship have indeed turned out wide of the mark. Economic exchanges haven't proved negligible: by 2018 two-way trade had climbed to a total of $100 billion. Nor has it proved a foregone conclusion that any rapprochement between the two powers is bound to break down in short order. It bears repeating that the current sunny period of official relations has already lasted more than twenty years – twice to three times as long as the doomed 1950s alliance. Looking back beyond the 1950s we remember, too, the largely tranquil period ushered in by the treaties of Nerchinsk and Kyakhta – all 170 years of it, from 1689 right up to the 1850s when Muraviev started dispatching his flotillas of colonists down the Amur. Even after that, when first the tsarist regime and later the Bolsheviks tried to impose their will on an enfeebled China, the new tensions were accompanied by remarkably little in the way of physical conflict. Several times in these years, during the Yili valley crisis of 1880, the clash over the Chinese Eastern Railway in 1929 and the 1969 border fighting in Manchuria and Xinjiang the two powers have peered over the brink, as it were, only to draw back as if daunted by the latent potential of the other side. One former Soviet China Hand has observed that during the entire four centuries of their interaction China and Russia have *never fought a major war*.[66] And the evidence strongly suggests that in laying the foundations of their twenty-first-century partnership the leaders on both sides have taken great pains to ensure that nothing like the breakdown of the mid-twentieth century will happen again. In this sense the relations between the two governments really do seem to be 'the best ever'. All the same the question is obvious and legitimate: *Will the partnership last?*

We may begin by peeling away routine sources of friction such as might arise between any two states. Obvious examples are the PRC's struggle to gain access to Russian oil supplies in the teeth of Japanese competition and the wrangling over gas prices in the years before agreement was reached on the Power of Siberia pipeline. In February 2009 a cargo ship registered in Sierra Leone but crewed by Chinese tried to bolt from the Russian Pacific port of Nakhodka following a dispute with the local customs authorities; Russian coastguards boarded the vessel and killed seven of the eight crew members. The outcome was sufficiently serious for the Chinese Foreign Ministry to request an emergency meeting with the Russian ambassador, but the ministry seem to have carried the matter no further than voicing discontent with the obdurate attitude of the Russian side. Three years later, in July 2012, the coastguards at Nakhodka boarded a PRC fishing vessel and detained seventeen Chinese sailors for fishing illegally; but no wider consequences were reported, and neither of these incidents had the potential to derail the partnership. The sheer length of the 2,700-mile Russian–Chinese border virtually guaranteed that occasional ructions would take place. In November 2005 an explosion devastated a PRC petrochemical plant, one of 100-odd Chinese factories that lined the River Songhua in the north-eastern border province of Heilongjiang. A hundred tons of benzene and other toxic chemicals spilt into the river, which swept them downstream towards its confluence with the Amur and the Russian cities on the Amur's northern bank. Angry Russian residents demonstrated outside the Chinese consulate in Khabarovsk, brandishing a poster that read '*U nas poryadok takoi: Nagadil, uberi za soboi!*' – a couplet which translates very simply, '*We* clean up after ourselves!'[67] But all was settled harmoniously. The Chinese foreign minister of the time, Li Zhaoxing, made a formal apology to Russia, the PRC government agreed to spend 10 billion renminbi on cleaning up the Songhua over the next few years, and in 2006 a new Sino-Russian sub-commission was set up for Cooperation in Environmental Protection.

More problematic were some of the longer-term trends. The Sino-Russian rapprochement was designed above all to restore the old equilibrium between the two powers. *Equality* was the basis of Deng Xiaoping's understanding with Gorbachev in the twilight years of the former Soviet Union, of the embryonic 'strategic partnership' agreed by Jiang Zemin and Yeltsin in 1996. No longer would Russia be allowed to lord it over its neighbour as it had done for decades under both the tsarist and Soviet regimes. But what if the pendulum swung too far in the other direction, if the PRC now attained a supremacy Russia found unable to stomach? By as early as 2000 China's GDP was reckoned by Western analysts to be four times that of the Russian Federation. By 2021 it was judged to be eight or even ten times as large, and Russia's GDP was said to have been outstripped by that of Guangdong Province alone. The trade figures reflected this contrast, with China now accounting for 15 per cent of Russia's foreign trade, Russia only 1 per cent of China's. For years China had shown a consistent lack of interest in Russian industrial products, to the chagrin of Russian officialdom; but it had at least kept up its traditional appetite, conspicuous as far back as the late nineteenth century, for Russian arms. Even that staple, however, showed signs of losing its attraction. China's arms purchases from its northern neighbour declined from $3.2 billion worth at the turn of the century to near zero by 2006 – a 'strategic pause', as one Russian commentator described it,[68] that lasted for the next several years. Essentially the Chinese no longer sought to buy complete Russian military equipment. More than ever they wanted the core technologies, not the individual pieces of hardware they could perfectly well make themselves, and were ready to seek those technologies by fair means or foul. By the second decade of the century they were exporting vital spare parts for advanced Russian weapons systems and were poised to export naval engines to Russian fleets. And with their forces bogged down before Kyiv in March 2022 Putin and his associates were reported by US intelligence to have covertly asked China for military hardware ranging from surface-to-air missiles to armoured and logistical vehicles and intelligence-related equipment. Particular Russian interest was said to have been aroused by the PRC's new Yiling II military reconnaissance drone, known for its gaunt and sprawling appearance as the Pterodactyl.[69] A similar shift in the balance was visible in other sectors as well. During one of Putin's incessant trips to Beijing the *People's Daily* newspaper crowed, 'China's past importation of technology from Russia has come to an end: now it is China's turn to help Russia build high-speed railways.'[70] Amid the glamour of the new Sino-Russian space partnership the PRC was quietly pursuing its own independent space ventures. In December 2020 a Chinese robot retrieved a soil sample from the lunar surface in the first such operation since the last US manned expedition nearly fifty years before, and in May 2021 the China National Space Administration landed their home-made Zhurong rover on the surface of Mars, in direct competition with the US and with Russia left nowhere.

And as the Chinese colossus moved forward, the partner was consistently nudged to one side. One case in point was Outer Mongolia, that long-standing arena for Sino-Russian rivalry which had spent seventy years in the Soviet grip. Even after the fall of the Soviet Union the Mongols were still said to prefer being dominated by the Russians, who would at worst throw their weight around, than by the Chinese, who threatened to obliterate them by sheer numbers. But the Chinese had set their sights on Mongolia's huge resources of coal and copper. By 2010 they had gained effective control of the country's coalmining industry, and by 2017 they were said to account for 65.8 per cent of its foreign trade. A still more dramatic picture unfolded in Central Asia. Driven by their quest for energy, the Chinese effectively redirected the flow from the Stans into Russia of Kazakh oil and Turkmen gas. In 2009 they completed with local partners the laying of a pipeline to carry oil from Kazakhstan eastwards into Xinjiang, and at the end of the same year they celebrated the completion of a pipeline for carrying gas in a great S-shaped trajectory from Turkmenistan through Uzbekistan and Kazakhstan into Xinjiang, to be extended in due course all the way to Shanghai. By 2013 the PRC was said to be the largest foreign investor in Uzbekistan and Tajikistan, and the largest trading partner of all the Stans but Uzbekistan, as total trade with the region, a mere $1.8 billion at the start of the century, surged to $50 billion a decade later. In 2013 Xi Jinping proclaimed on a visit to Kazakhstan his grandiose vision of a Belt and Road Initiative (BRI), spreading Chinese infrastructure and investment projects across Central

Asia and on into Europe. Kazakhstan was especially favoured, with fifty-five projects earmarked for development there, and the country proudly declared itself the 'buckle' on Xi's new Silk Road Economic Belt.[71] Up to this point the PRC had respected the tacit understanding that it should confine its activities in Central Asia to the economic sphere, but by the second decade of the century there began to be hints of a wider ambition. Marked attention started to be paid to Tajikistan, poorest of the five Stans and an outlier among them in the sense that its people's ethnic roots were Persian rather than Turkic. Chinese contractors built schools, roads and tunnels for the Tajiks as well as a parliament building, a government palace and a Palace of Officers in the capital, Dushanbe. By 2016 the PRC was also beginning to station upwards of 3,000 troops in the country. 'Dozens' of PLA personnel were engaged in training the Tajikistan National Army at camps in the Pamir mountains, and on the Tajik border with Afghanistan.[72] The apparent reason was straightforward enough. Afghanistan is connected with China by a narrow corridor of land known as the Wakhan Salient, and Beijing wished to monitor and eventually block the potentially dangerous flow of Islamic extremism down the corridor into Xinjiang. But the Chinese didn't consider it necessary to consult their Russian partners about the arrangement.

Every so often these signs of a Chinese ascendancy did cause grave disquiet in some Russian circles. Early in the post-Soviet rapprochement, in 1993, Viktor Ishaev, the governor of the Khabarovsk region, and Yevgeny Nazdratenko, the governor of the Maritime region, joined forces in an attempt to thwart the implementation of the new eastern border treaty with its heavy concessions to Beijing. Ishaev wrote a letter of protest to the prime minister in Moscow, and unilaterally imposed restrictions on Chinese ships sailing down his stretch of the Amur. His more flamboyant colleague mobilised local Cossacks to stand guard on the banks of the Ussuri, thereby performing their traditional role of defending the frontier; and in 1996 he made a public avowal that 'Yevgeny Nazdratenko, while there appears to be the smallest single chance, intends to fight against the transfer to a foreign jurisdiction of land that has been Russian since time immemorial.'[73] The eastern border agreement of 2004 was supposed to have 'finally settled' the old Sino-Russian territorial issue.[74] But, some Russians wondered, was it really a 'final settlement'? Teachers in China were still said to instruct their classes about the tsarist annexation of 1.5 million square kilometres of

'Outer Manchuria' for which Mao had threatened to 'present the bill'. The CCP had never officially relinquished Mao's larger claim; and a professor at the Shanghai branch of the Chinese Academy of Social Sciences warned Russian visitors that the PRC public still nursed hard feelings about that colonial land grab. In this context the 'strategic pause' in Chinese arms purchases started in 2006 seems to have been not unwelcome to certain Russian observers who doubted the wisdom of supplying Beijing with sophisticated military hardware which might one day be used against them.[75] By this time however a more pressing concern for most analysts was the prospect of Russia's being reduced to a mere 'resource appendage' of an industrialising PRC. During the first decade of the new century the sporadic transfer of technology to China which had taken place in the confused Yeltsin period seems to have given way to a tougher regime. In 2005 and 2007 two Russian scientists were convicted of selling satellite and other space-related knowhow to Chinese firms, and in 2008 a Chinese academic reported, not without sympathy,

> We want to buy better quality weapons, but they refused. If I were Russian I would do the same thing. We are a country that is very capable of using their technology to build our own version and competing with them.[76]

As the PRC knit together its vast worldwide economic and security networks the Kremlin took what looked like discreet countermeasures intended to dilute its partner's overwhelming hegemony. Unhappy with China's predominance in the Beijing-based SCO, the Russians are said to have blocked the creation of an SCO bank which would inevitably have fallen under Chinese control, and in 2017 they pressed successfully for the admission of two weighty observer states, India and Pakistan, as full members of the organisation. In January 2015 they set up their own separate Eurasian Economic Union (EAEU) composed of a bevy of former Soviet republics including Kazakhstan and Kyrgyzstan – partly, it was suggested, in order to protect their own market from the influx of Chinese goods expected to accompany Xi Jinping's Belt and Road Initiative. Broadly acceptant though they had been of China's economic supremacy in the new Central Asia, they continued to cherish Moscow's military dominance there. The arrival of PLA units in Tajikistan in 2016 was another matter altogether, and the Kremlin is said to have been 'rattled'.[77] In 2018 the Russian minister of defence, Sergei Shoigu, was dispatched to Dushanbe to inspect the 7,000-strong Russian garrison and conduct Russia's own military exercises with the Tajikistan National Army. It was Russia's oblique way of standing its ground.

Yet these traces of Russian unease didn't necessarily add up to much. The anti-China campaign spearheaded by governors Ishaev and Nazdratenko, for instance, was essentially a reflection of the near-anarchy that prevailed in Russia in the immediate post-Soviet years, when regional bosses strove to assert their authority in the face of a weak central government and struck jingoistic poses designed to bolster their own prestige. Insofar as a PRC military threat still played a role in its thinking the Kremlin could draw comfort from its massive continuing superiority in nuclear arms. Many Russians at different levels seem to have been surprisingly relaxed about their new status as junior members of the Sino-Russian partnership. In July 1995 Boris Yeltsin expressed himself happy to 'lean on China's shoulder' in his dealings with the West.[78] A professor of metallurgy who had served as an adviser in the PRC in the 1950s emerged from a return visit in 2006 with the affectionate verdict, 'Little Brother is all grown up',[79] while a Moscow journalist remarked drily, 'Everyone here sees China as the model because Russia is not the model.' One pundit in 2010 delivered the no-nonsense verdict that 'China has clearly overtaken Russia on all parameters.'[80] Russians weren't quite as stressed about keeping their high-tech secrets from China as might appear at first glance. The two scientists who were convicted of selling space-related technology to PRC companies were sentenced respectively to fourteen and eleven years behind bars, the former being released on parole after only six – rather lenient punishments, one might think, for conniving in acts of industrial espionage; and from 2014 onwards, as we saw, Putin was starting to give China access to advanced missile systems as the strategic partnership became more vital for him. Rather than merely sulking at their loss of potential contracts as the Chinese focus narrowed from equipment to technology, Russian arms dealers poured into China to sell what equipment they could while they still had the chance. One leading Russian scholar of the relationship, Professor Alexander Lukin, has described as a 'myth' the idea of a Sino-Russian struggle for influence in Central Asia. There was, he observes, little reason for the Kremlin to be aggrieved at Chinese domination of the SCO structures, seeing that China and Russia made equal contributions to the entity's budget and seeing that its most active branch, the RATS counter-terrorism unit, had its headquarters not in Beijing but in the Uzbek capital, Tashkent.[81] One might add that there was little sign of rancour arising from Beijing's siphoning off of the region's oil and gas reserves, unreasonable as this would have been in any case given Russia's own abundance of energy resources. The stationing of PLA troops in Tajikistan to guard against Islamic extremists couldn't easily be interpreted as an anti-Russian manoeuvre, and the small Chinese and Russian contingents there seemed to discharge their duties without visibly grating on each other. Far from resenting the advent of the Belt and Road Initiative, the Kremlin seemed eager to latch on to the opportunities it might provide for attracting badly needed Chinese investment. By May 2015 the newly created Eurasian Economic Union was already pursuing integration with the BRI's Silk Road Economic Belt (SREB), and putting forward proposals to it for forty infrastructure projects. Unfortunately for the Russians the main thrust of the SREB's infrastructural drive was directed towards Kazakhstan and the historical Silk Road rather than following the northern route through Siberia that the Kremlin had been hoping for; and the Chinese are said to have turned down every one of the forty proposals.[82] But Putin and his associates continued to work on bringing together the EAEU and the SREB in an overarching Greater Eurasia free-trade zone.

Another possible partnership-breaker could be demographic. In the summer of 1971, to inject a short personal note, I and two friends paid a visit to the Siberian city of Bratsk, site of the great hydroelectric power station on the River Angara. We were greeted on arrival by a large lady who marched up to us and delivered at point-blank range an aria entitled 'Here People Live!' ('*Zdyes' lyudi zhivut!*'). It was a point that would probably not have been made on the Chinese side of the border, where the presence of people was too obvious a fact to be worth alluding to. But Russians were, and are, keenly aware of their own small numbers in the great wilderness beyond the Urals, and of the contrast between those numbers and the Chinese multitudes to the south. In the Russian Far East in particular a modest Russian population of around 6 million faced some 110 million Chinese in the PRC's three Manchurian provinces: a population that threatened to dwindle still further as people deserted the derelict Far Eastern cities in search of a higher standard of living in European Russia. And a portion of the 110 million Chinese appeared to be seeping across the border in the shape of those enterprising traders and labourers who had moved in to meet the material needs of the Russian inhabitants. By as early as 1992–3 the initial Russian appreciation of these helping hands was beginning to give way to panic. Wild rumours began to be bandied about in the local press, allegations that up to 8.5 million Chinese had settled in Russia illegally. Some analysts were even said to have forecast that by 2050 the Chinese would constitute the second largest ethnic group in the country after the Russians themselves.[83] It was the old nightmare of demographic swamping which had been caused by the previous influx of Chinese from Manchuria in the late nineteenth and early twentieth centuries; with the obvious difference that at that time they were seen as competing for the riches of the new Russian frontier whereas now they were rather imagined as coming to scavenge among the ruins. Some commentators hypothesised that the CCP were pursuing a policy of 'quiet expansion', a deliberate 'Move to the North' which would enable them to occupy Russian territory without actually resorting to arms: one wit claimed that all the Chinese would need to do to achieve their objective would be to walk across the border and surrender.[84] The main cause of alarm in this case was however not geopolitical but bread-and-butter issues. People feared for their livelihoods. In February 2002 hundreds of women stallholders in the remote Kamchatka peninsula blocked the main highway in protest, demanding the expulsion of Chinese traders who they claimed were undercutting their businesses. Chinese goods were now excoriated as shoddy and worse as illegal, many of them apparently being brought in through the 'grey trade' under which the owners bribed Russian mafiosi or other shady middlemen who in turn bribed the customs to turn a blind eye. Again on the pattern of 100 years before, Chinese migrants were advancing beyond the Far East and showing up in the cities of European Russia. During the early 2000s 80,000 Chinese merchants made up the dominant presence in Moscow's Cherkizovsky Market ('Cherkizon' for short), the largest wholesale market in the country. A Shanghai consortium got to work directing the construction of a commercial and residential complex on the coast of the Gulf of Finland south-west of St Petersburg – an 'urban glamour zone' to be known as the Baltic Pearl. By 2005 public anger was mounting in these two cities as well. Muscovites complained variously about the poor-quality Chinese goods in Cherkizon and the unending din.

Citizens of St Petersburg feared that the Chinese at work on the Baltic Pearl would bring chains of compatriots in there to settle. Rumour had it that the complex was to be Sinified through the installation of a Buddhist temple and a Peking opera house.

Local demagogues were quick to jump on the bandwagon. In the Far East the duo of governors Ishaev and Nazdratenko supplemented their campaign against the new border treaty with claims that there were now more Chinese than Russians in parts of Khabarovsk, that the Chinese irruption into the Maritime Region included large numbers of 'criminals, sick people and drug addicts'.[85] In 1996 the mayor of Vladivostok, an ally of Nazdratenko's, wrote a 'very positive' review of a new publication bluntly entitled *The Yellow Peril*. Leading figures in Moscow were calmer, but even there Dmitri Rogozin, a nationalist politician and future head of the Russian space programme, used a radio broadcast to recycle a grim joke about 'Chinese crossing our state border in small groups of five million people'.[86] From time to time the authorities found it judicious to take concrete measures to stem the perceived Chinese tide. In January 1994 the visa-free regime which had been introduced in the last Soviet years on the Far Eastern frontier was scrapped, and in June 2009 the Moscow police were sent in to evacuate the Cherkizon Market with a view to protecting local Russian producers of consumer goods. Several hundred Chinese traders were detained and deported as illegal immigrants, and \$2 billion worth of goods, many of them smuggled in through the 'grey trade', were confiscated in what was described as the largest haul of contraband in Russian history. The Beijing authorities were incensed by counter-measures of this kind. In May 2004 they took advantage of their recent admission to the World Trade Organization to make their backing for Russia's admission conditional on its granting free entry to Chinese workers. In response to the Cherkizon crackdown they sent an angry delegation to Moscow, demanding compensation for those traders who had lost their jobs, the release of some 200 of them who were still in detention and the construction of a Chinatown on the site of the wrecked market stalls. If their demands went unheeded they threatened a 'complication' in the Sino-Russian partnership,[87] by which they meant among other things the suspension of the loans they had promised the Russian oil giant Rosneft as part of the 'loans for oil' agreement the previous February. One aggrieved PRC citizen foretold on a website that without its supply of good

Chinese clothing and footwear Russia would turn into a 'naked bear' when the first frosts set in.[88]

The main thrust of Kremlin policy, however, was to damp down the Yellow Peril scare. In December 1996 Yeltsin issued a formal warning to Governor Nazdratenko, who had continued his Sinophobic invective for some time after his colleague Ishaev had quietened down. The governor was told from now on to coordinate his remarks about international issues with the Foreign Ministry in Moscow. Nazdratenko duly back-pedalled, conceding sullenly that Russia and China were 'doomed to cooperate'.[89] In October 2002 Foreign Minister Igor Ivanov declared at a press conference that 'no Chinese expansion' was taking place,[90] and in December the Russian ambassador to Beijing maintained that there were more Russians going to China than the other way round.[91] In 2005 the governor of St Petersburg delivered a no-nonsense rebuttal to critics of the Baltic Pearl scheme, pointing out that the project was due to create 35,000 new Russian jobs: a local teacher concurred that the object was to develop the district, 'and it's not important if it's the Russians, the Chinese or aliens who do so'.[92] A greater impact was probably made by the release of some sober statistics. National censuses conducted in 2002 and 2010 yielded totals respectively of just 34,577 and 28,943 Chinese who reported themselves to be part of the permanent Russian population. Figures produced by the Federal Migration Service told a rather different story, recording the presence of 248,000 Chinese citizens in Russia in 2010 and 300,000 in 2015; but these included large numbers of people who merely happened to be in the country at those particular times – wheeler-dealers and merchants, seasonal farm workers and factory hands. Surveys made of these migrants suggested that the vast majority of them had no intention of staying in Russia long-term. Put off as they were by the climate, the bureaucracy, the corruption and the widespread unfriendliness of local people, their idea was simply to make their pile and then go home.[93]

By the second decade of the century these government reassurances seem to have had some appreciable impact. Nothing more was heard – publicly – of the wilder Yellow Peril assertions. But at least in the Russian Far East it seems clear that the old dread still lingered. Western travellers who visited the Amur border cities chatted with local Russians who claimed there were 8 million Chinese immigrants in their region *alone*, that 20 per cent of the land to the north of the Amur was rented or owned by Chinese.[94] Way back in 1988, in the late Soviet period, talks had started about the construction of a first road bridge across the Amur to link up the cities of Blagoveshchensk and Heihe; but the discussions dragged on with a slowness that betokened a dreadful reluctance on the Russian side, and agreement was only reached, after 'prolonged' negotiations, in 2015. Even then the bridge took four years to complete, with the Chinese pushing briskly ahead with their part of the project while the Russian side crawled. And the Russian, unlike the Chinese, frontier bristled with watchtowers and barbed wire. In the long run the risk of collision could clearly not be dismissed. The independent British scientist James Lovelock has speculated that by the middle of the century global warming might have turned much of north China into a desert, leaving the inhabitants little choice but to push their way northwards into Siberia – 'and how will the Russians feel about that?'.[95] As of 2022, though, demographics were not at the forefront of Sino-Russian concerns.

A third possible stumbling-block had to do with the human underpinnings of the partnership. Back in the 1950s, during the previous spell of official brotherhood, the relations between the two governments had been shot through from the start with suspicion and acrimony, while at the grass roots the dealings between the Soviet advisers and their Chinese pupils had taken place in an atmosphere of considerable warmth. The situation now was precisely the opposite. While the political leaders acclaimed the all-time high in their interactions the rapport between ordinary folk had dissolved. At the dawn of the new century people in Moscow and European Russia weren't necessarily ill-disposed to the great Eastern power; they simply didn't think much about China any more. Chinese studies were in decline. Media coverage of the PRC was slight by comparison with the attention devoted to the United States and the European Union. Films about China were few and far between. In an opinion poll conducted in 2000 52 per cent of respondents placed China top of a list of 'friendly countries' – but that only after the PRC had been pointed out to them as a possible option.[96] And in view of China's economic advance people were no longer inspired, as so many had been in the 1950s and earlier, by a generous impulse to come to the aid of a more backward neighbour. In the Russian Far East the picture was even more glum. Citizens were reported remarkably ignorant of their own country's history of encounters with China, including even a development as recent as the eastern border treaty of 1991. Aware of the PRC's presence, they looked on it resentfully from the perspective of poor relations, peering across the Amur at the blaze of modernity in the Chinese cities opposite where 'even the street sweepers had mobile phones'.[97] One young woman in Blagoveshchensk remarked sourly as she gazed at the gleaming high-rise buildings on the Heihe side, 'And we're the same dirty old village we've always been.'[98] Western press reports spoke of groups of forlorn Russian traders 'bickering over the price of fur coats and leather boots'. Truly the wheel appeared to have come full circle, right back to the early seventeenth century, Petlin and his small band of Muscovite emissaries gawping at the wealth and sophistication of the Ming domains.

Among ordinary Chinese the traditional Confucian respect of pupil for teacher no longer applied where Russia was concerned. The new attitude showed through very clearly in a survey conducted in 2002 among students at Beijing University. There were no Russian products to be seen, they noted, in PRC shops nowadays, and the old Lada and Volga cars had disappeared from the streets. In general Russia 'did not interest' many people.[99] Only a few Chinese now wanted to learn Russian or study in Russian universities: most preferred to head to the United States, Europe or Japan. Russia was now a country in decline, and ties with the West were vastly more important for China than the Sino-Russian partnership. Grass-roots Chinese indifference made itself felt even more strikingly in September 2004, when Chechen terrorists seized a school in Beslan in the Russian north Caucasus, and the ensuing shoot-out with Russian troops claimed the lives of some 300 hostages including 186 children. As the story unfolded one PRC television channel invited its viewers to take part in a mobile phone competition to guess the eventual number of victims. Russians who learnt of this game were aghast at the callousness.

Both the Chinese and Russian leaderships were keenly aware of this lack of rapport at the grass roots and what it might portend for the long-term future of their ties. Their pairing, they agreed, was '*warm on the outside but cold within*';[100] and they sought by all possible means to thaw out the frozen interior of this Baked Alaska of a relationship. On his visit to China in December 2002 Vladimir Putin extended a hand to the sceptical undergraduates of Beijing University, stating winningly, 'If I were allowed to choose a great culture worthy of the name my first choice would be Chinese culture.'[101] In the autumn of 2004 the CCP chiefs went into overdrive to repair the damage inflicted by the Beslan TV competition. Heads rolled at the offending television station; 10 million renminbi were committed to helping the victims of the Chechen atrocity; and Premier Wen Jiabao quoted the Russian equivalent of the saying, 'A trouble shared is a trouble halved.'[102] A whole year later, in November 2005, the PRC Health Ministry announced that they were sending doctors to Beslan to provide free medical treatment for any survivors who still needed it. In the meantime the two regimes were getting ready to launch on their subjects a campaign to rekindle interest and goodwill. 2006 was proclaimed the Year of Russia in China. A Russian National Exhibition was held in Beijing, and over 200 events were staged the length and breadth of the PRC, from a Sino-Russian youth forum to a display of Russian art treasures from the Tretyakov Gallery in Moscow and a glittering performance of ballet and folk dancing before an audience of 5,000 in the Great Hall of the People. 2007 was correspondingly the Year of China in Russia, once again featuring some 200 'activities' in what was reported to be the largest display of Chinese culture ever mounted abroad. Attractions included treasures from the Forbidden City in Beijing, Chinese ballet, acrobatic and martial arts troupes and a special Women's Cultural Week with concerts and discussions. And so it went on. 2009 was the Year of Russian Language in China, 2010 the Year of Chinese Language in Russia. 2012 was the Year of Russian Tourism in China, 2013 the Year of Chinese Tourism in Russia. 2016 was the Year of Russian Media in China, 2017 the Year of Chinese Media in Russia . . . a line stretching out seemingly to the crack of doom.

It is hard to gauge the impact of all these exertions based on a few random data. In both countries there have been indications that popular sympathy for the strategic partner has grown with the years. In 2021, for example, 74 per cent of respondents to another all-Russia survey expressed a positive view of the PRC and felt that the partnership strengthened Russia's place in the world. Against this must be set the continuing bitter chorus reported by Western visitors to the Amur border, Russian traders in Blagoveshchensk describing the Chinese they dealt with as ruthless, aggressive, dishonest and having 'closed hearts'.[103] One woman had a new take on the glittering modernity of Heihe, calling it a Potemkin village deliberately set up to make the Russians feel miserable.[104] On the Chinese side people were already said by 2006 to be looking on Russia with greater respect as the country began to recover its political and economic strength under Putin's leadership, and a survey conducted in 2014 found that 55 per cent of respondents now took a favourable view of their northern neighbour; this finding however was challenged by a report the same year of a *Financial Times* correspondent whose Chinese interlocutors 'remained unimpressed' at Russia's continuing 'failure to modernise'.[105] There is clearly no reason to take at face value opinion surveys conducted under the auspices of two increasingly autocratic regimes. Equally there is no reason to assume that the gripes of a remote Russian border community and the judgments passed by the business elites in Beijing and Shanghai necessarily reflect the feelings of the wider public in either country.

Nothing is eternal in human affairs. It is possible that the Sino-Russian partnership could be undone in the near future by a change of regime at one end or the other or even by a change of individual leaders. Perhaps Putin's military will inflict on Ukraine an atrocity so horrific that the Beijing leadership will feel compelled to abandon the Russian cause. Perhaps some unforeseeable conflict will arise over Central Asia or Mongolia, or some violent ethnic collision will take place in the Siberian taiga. It could also be that the partnership will be good for another generation. The two powers are now knit together by a thick web of agreements and institutions which would not be easy to unravel. In an article published in *Foreign Affairs* in December 2015 Mme Fu Ying, a former deputy foreign minister of the PRC and ambassador to the United Kingdom, insisted for the benefit of her Western readers that the Sino-Russian entente was 'by no means a marriage of convenience' but was '*complex, sturdy and deeply rooted*'.[106] On the Russian side Professor Lukin has observed in addition that the basis of the 'near-alliance' is now so strong that '*any differences can be effectively resolved through the existing mechanism of consultations*'.[107] An illustration of this appeared to present itself after the COVID-19 pandemic hit Moscow in February 2020. The PRC embassy lodged an indignant protest with the Moscow city government, complaining that Chinese citizens were being singled out for violating the quarantine rules and were being subjected to violence, abuse and deportation. Eighty Chinese were said to have been earmarked for deportation as opposed to just eight people from other countries; and the embassy didn't fail to remark on the contrast with the cordial top-level ties. Within days, however, the diplomats had executed a complete about-turn. A statement was issued declaring that the reports they had heard were untrue, and calling on Chinese citizens not to 'create, believe or spread rumours'.[108] Wherever the blame lay, a nascent quarrel had been deftly snuffed out.

Where then does this leave the West? Back in 2011 a professor at the National Defence University in Beijing warned bluntly, '*As long as American pressure remains the Sino-Russian partnership will endure*.'[109] Over the last dozen years his prediction has been amply borne out. The United States and its allies have slapped sanctions on Russia following the Crimea annexation and more and fiercer sanctions following the all-out attack on Ukraine, and have deployed warships and fighter planes to deter Chinese expansion in the western Pacific and the South China Sea. In response both the Russian and Chinese regimes have grown harsher, and the political, military and economic ties between them have become even closer than they already were. By 2021 pundits in Washington were concluding that it would be foolish to wait for the partnership to collapse of its own accord, and were instead looking for ways of *splitting* the partners, or more precisely of luring Russia, as the junior partner, from its growing dependence on its ever more formidable Chinese neighbour. One school of thought advocated a 'modest and incremental' approach designed to persuade Putin's entourage of the advantages of working with the United States and to proclaim the merits of democracy versus autocracy: this would however be punctuated by regular war games pitting the US and NATO against China and Russia.[110] A second proposal rejected any kind of doctrinal crusade as being likely to drive the two partners still closer, and instead favoured offering Moscow cooperation in certain concrete areas. Russia would be invited to commit itself to a diplomatic settlement of the conflict in eastern Ukraine and to desist from its mischief-making in cyberspace; in return the United States and its allies would look at reducing their sanctions and would in due course endeavour to help Russia combat climate change, to wean it off its dependence on exports of fossil fuels and to steer it in the direction of a knowledge economy.[111] Following the assault on Ukraine in 2022 Russia was restored to its usual position of Enemy Number One and the United States camp were now viewing the PRC, with its place at the heart of global trade, as the more obvious candidate for detachment. The US national security adviser, Jake Sullivan, exhorted Beijing to put pressure on Putin to halt the invasion, and the secretary of defense, Lloyd Austin, warned his Chinese opposite number that any material backing for Russia would be 'deeply destabilising'.[112]

Various US and European notables appealed to the Chinese authorities to use their influence with Putin's government to bring about a ceasefire.[113] All these various gambits, however, appeared to beg certain questions. Why, from the Kremlin's perspective, should Russia exchange the embrace of a country which has shown it a generally friendly face for the last thirty years for that of a power which has pushed NATO up to its western borders, constricted its economy and opposed it around the globe? Why should Russia cut loose from a partner that operates in a steady and largely predictable fashion in favour of one that is capable of changing its entire international outlook every eight years or even every four? Why, from the CCP's point of view, should they rush headlong into the arms of the West at a time when the US has subjected them to a grinding trade war it shows no sign of relaxing; when American power continues to impede their cherished objective of reabsorbing Taiwan; when NATO has announced its intention of adjusting its focus to take account of Chinese manoeuvres in the Indo-Pacific region; and when the chiefs of the FBI and MI5 have combined to denounce the 'immense threat' posed by China to their nations' security?[114] Why, finally, should either partner welcome designs which explicitly set out to 'check both countries' ambitions',[115] and which are grounded additionally in a (justified) repugnance at the policies of internal repression and external aggressiveness that both the two partner regimes have seen fit to pursue?

If neither of these powers can be detached as desired through these gambits the prospects for Western relations with a surviving Sino-Russian partnership look distinctly bleak. In a comparatively benign scenario confrontation will begin to give way to reasoned dialogue. Fears in both camps will subside, disarmament will resume, the partners will lighten up to a certain extent in the treatment of their dissidents and their ethnic minorities, and all will join forces in the critical battle against climate change. The Western attitude to the partners will be roughly that of the British from 1815 to around 1850 to the East European autocracies of Russia, Prussia and Austria – disapproving, perhaps, but non-confrontational. In a darker scenario, which unhappily seems to be that now unfolding before us, the arms race will accelerate, repression within the partner states will persist or grow worse, and the behaviour of both sides will be characterised by the incessant sabre-rattling, alliance-building and demonisation of the perceived enemy that in the pre-nuclear age was so often the precursor of war. What we are looking at here, in other words, is the approximate climate in Europe between 1890 and 1914. Under these circumstances some of the wisest advice may be that offered recently by Dr Henry Kissinger from the summit of his ninety-nine years: not to try to 'generate disagreements' between the two powers but instead to wait for history to 'provide an opportunity in which we can apply the differential approach'.[116] Pending this development an equally sensible guideline is that offered by Sir Stephen Lovegrove, the national security adviser to the United Kingdom, in a recent lecture in Washington: keep talking, above all keep talking to both China and Russia, at this very dangerous time when nuclear war has begun to look all too conceivable and when the mutual comprehension among the nuclear-armed adversaries appears to be less than it was at the height of the original Cold War.[117] Whether the West acts with wisdom or folly, one prediction at least can be made with some confidence. It seems clear that the dealings between China and Russia, twin Leaders of the Opposition, will remain for the rest of this century of decisive importance to the world as a whole.

NOTES

INTRODUCTION

1. See Odd Arne Westad, *Brothers in Arms: The Rise and Fall of the Sino-Soviet Alliance, 1949–1963*, Washington DC and Stanford, CA, 1998, Introduction, p. 2.

CHAPTER 1: WORLDS IN COLLISION

1. Chancellor was deputy chief of a squadron of three vessels under the command of Sir Hugh Willoughby. After passing the North Cape, however, the squadron was broken up by a storm; Willoughby, unlike Chancellor, failed to discover the entrance of the White Sea that led towards Muscovy and died, along with the crews of two of the vessels, in the wastes of the Kola Peninsula.
2. Some sources date the start of work on the map to as early as 1537. See N.F. Demidova and V.S. Myasnikov, *Pervye russkie diplomaty v Kitae*, Moscow, 1966, p. 13.
3. See Mark Mancall, *Russia and China: Their Diplomatic Relations to 1728*, Cambridge, MA, 1971, p. 41.
4. In 1557 Tsar Ivan the Terrible gave an English merchant adventurer named Anthony Jenkinson permission to travel through Russian territory to the Central Asian emirate of Bokhara, where Chinese goods were said to be available. By the time Jenkinson got there, however, Chinese goods were no longer reaching the Bokhara market. Mancall, *Russia and China*, p. 37.
5. Demidova and Myasnikov, *Pervye russkie diplomaty*, p. 19.
6. The year when Muscovy finally freed itself from Mongol domination. The first step in this direction had been taken in 1380, when the Muscovites under the Grand Prince Dmitri I defeated a portion of the Mongol Golden Horde at the Battle of Kulikovo.
7. Not, however, the district of Moscow known as Kitaigorod, which looks as though it ought to mean 'Chinatown' but in fact derives from *kita* ('wattle'), a reference to the wattle palisade with which the newly settled district was fenced off from the thirteenth century onwards. The Mongol term *Kitai* derives from the Khitan, a nomad people akin to the Mongols who controlled a large area of Manchuria and northern China in the tenth and eleventh centuries. It was transmitted by the Mongols in the thirteenth century into western European languages in the form *Cathay*.
8. Wang Shicai, 'Qianxi Zhongguo Dongbei yu Eluosi de wenhua jiaoliu', in Guan Guihai and Luan Jinghe (eds), *Zhong E guanxi lishi yu xianshi*, Beijing, 2009, p. 678.

9. References made in this tale to a 'Chinese tsar' suggest that it probably dates from no earlier than Ivan the Terrible's assumption of the title of tsar (Caesar) in 1547, while the vagueness with which China is depicted points to a date no later than the mid-seventeenth century. The attacks by Polkan perhaps indicate a memory of the Mongol conquests, traumatic for Russians and Chinese alike. Finally, it is tempting to guess at a Chinese origin for the three daughters' names, garbled perhaps by some Mongol intermediary. Laota in particular invites comparison with *Lao Da*, the Chinese term for the eldest in a succession of siblings; though in this case the storyteller will have muddled the daughters up, as Laota should be the eldest, not the youngest, of the three. And the name of the middle daughter, Spasa, which is given in other versions of the tale as Siaza and Skao, might possibly suggest a struggle to reproduce the Chinese *xiaode*, the 'younger'. But this is of course the merest speculation. See Robert Steele (ed.), 'Ivan, The Peasant Son', in *The Russian Garland of Fairy Tales*, New York, 1916, p. 44; Jack V. Haney with Sibelan Forrester (eds), *The Complete Folktales of A.N. Afanas'ev*, vol. 3, Jackson, MS, 2021, accessed via Project Muse and Google Books, p. 394. See also David Schimmelpenninck van der Oye, *Russian Orientalism: Asia in the Russian Mind from Peter the Great to the Emigration*, New Haven, CT, and London, 2010, p. 29.
10. Afanasy Nikitin, *Khozhdenie za tri morya Afanasiya Nikitina*, Moscow, 1958.
11. See John F. Baddeley, *Russia, Mongolia, China: Being Some Record of the Relations between them from the Beginning of the XVIIth Century to the Death of the Tsar Alexei Mikhailovich, 1602–1676*, vol. 2, London, 1919, p. 39.
12. O. Edmund Clubb, *China and Russia: The Great Game*, New York and London, 1971, p. 16; Morris Rossabi, *China and Inner Asia: From 1368 to the Present Day*, London, 1975, p. 116; M.I. Sladkovsky, *History of Economic Relations between Russia and China*, Jerusalem, 1966, p. 8.
13. Clubb, *China and Russia*, p. 17. This remark reads at first glance like an exhibition of comical ignorance on the part of the Russians, but should perhaps rather be seen as part of a calculated attempt to make China look as unattractive as possible to the English merchants.
14. For quotations given in this paragraph see Petlin, official report (*stateiny spisok*), reproduced in Baddeley, *Russia, Mongolia, China*, vol. 2, pp. 79–83. A *sazhen* was a Russian measure of length of 2.13 metres.
15. Ann Paludan, *Chronicle of the Chinese Emperors*, London, 2004, p. 182. In keeping with general practice I have referred to Chinese emperors by their reign titles, i.e. 'the Wanli emperor' rather than 'Emperor Wanli'.
16. Baddeley, *Russia, Mongolia, China*, vol. 2, p. 83; Sun Fang, Chen Jinpeng et al., *Eluosi de Zhongguo xingxiang*, Beijing, 2010, p. 6.
17. *Yuan shi* (History of the Yuan Dynasty), *juan* (vols) 34–6.
18. Mancall, *Russia and China*, p. 36. The map was discovered in the mid-nineteenth century by Archimandrite Palladius Kafarov, head of the Thirteenth and Fifteenth Russian Orthodox Missions in Peking.
19. Ibid.
20. Baddeley, *Russia, Mongolia, China*, vol. 2, p. 82.
21. Demidova and Myasnikov, *Pervye russkie diplomaty*, p. 25; Ye Baichuan, *Eguo lai Hua shituan yanjiu (1618–1807)*, Beijing, 2010, p. 20.
22. Baddeley, *Russia, Mongolia, China*, vol. 2, pp. 72, 82.
23. Mancall, *Russia and China*, p. 43; Rossabi, *China and Inner Asia*, p. 125; Demidova and Myasnikov, *Pervye russkie diplomaty*, p. 38.
24. The collection of *yasak* was a practice originally instituted by the Mongols.
25. Quoted in Peter C. Perdue, *China Marches West: The Qing Conquest of Central Eurasia*, Cambridge, MA, 2005, p. 87.
26. Igor Popov, *Rossiya i Kitai: 300 let na grani voiny*, Moscow, 2004, p. 46. Compare the tribulations of the Donner party in the Sierra Nevada, 1846–7.

27. Baddeley, *Russia, Mongolia, China*, vol. 1, p. 66; Mancall, *Russia and China*, p. 24. See also B.L. Putnam Weale, *Manchu and Muscovite, Being Letters from Manchuria Written during the Autumn of 1903*, London, 1904, pp. 19–22.
28. Mancall, *Russia and China*, pp. 20–1.
29. Quoted in V.V. Barthold, *La découverte de l'Asie: Histoire de l'Orientalisme en Europe et en Russie*, Paris, 1947, p. 218.
30. See John J. Stephan, *The Russian Far East: A History*, Stanford, CA, 1994, pp. 16–17. Stephan notes further (p. 14) that Chinese contacts with the Amur region are said to date from as far back as the Eastern Zhou and Han dynasties.
31. For the myth of Alexander's presence in the region see Barthold, *La découverte de l'Asie*, pp. 224–5. The late seventeenth-century map of Siberia composed by Semyon Remezov marks a point on the mouth of the Amur where Alexander of Macedon 'hid a rifle and left a bell'.
32. Quoted in Popov, *Rossiya i Kitai*, p. 62.
33. Weale, *Manchu and Muscovite*, pp. 26–7; Clubb, *China and Russia*, p. 23.
34. Weale, *Manchu and Muscovite*, p. 27.
35. Quoted in Fu Lo-shu, *A Documentary Chronicle of Sino-Western Relations*, Tucson, AZ, 1966, p. 25.
36. Ibid. The original Manchu report just says 'dogs' but the reference is to the sleds.
37. Suggestion made by Professor Jonathan Spence, *The Search for Modern China*, New York and London, 1990, p. 65.
38. See O.N. Vilkov, 'Kitaiskie tovary na tobolskom rynke', *Istoriya SSSR* 1, January–February 1958, p. 118.
39. Not to be confused with the celebrated city of gardens in Jiangsu Province.
40. John Webster, *The Duchess of Malfi*, Act II Scene 5.
41. Vilkov, 'Kitaiskie tovary', p. 119; Sun, Chen et al., *Eluosi de Zhongguo xingxiang*, pp. 29–30.
42. Demidova and Myasnikov, *Pervye russkie diplomaty*, pp. 87–8.
43. See V.N. Usov, *Sovietskaya razvedka v Kitae v 20e gody XX veka*, Moscow, 2011, p. 309.
44. I am indebted to Dr Philip Mansel for stressing this point.
45. Mancall, *Russia and China*, p. 47; Nigel Cameron, *Barbarians and Mandarins: Thirteen Centuries of Western Travellers in China*, Hong Kong, 1997, p. 226.
46. Baddeley, *Russia, Mongolia, China*, vol. 2, p. 134.
47. Quoted by Fr Joseph Sebes, SJ in *The Jesuits and the Sino-Russian Treaty of Nerchinsk (1689): The Diary of Tomas Pereira, SJ*, Rome, 1961, p. 207; V.S. Myasnikov, *The Ch'ing Empire and the Russian State in the Seventeenth Century*, Moscow, 1985, p. 115.
48. For the foregoing see Baddeley, *Russia, Mongolia, China*, vol. 2, pp. 144–52; Sebes, *The Jesuits*, pp. 60–1; Mancall, *Russia and China*, p. 50.
49. The Russians continued to use this term for the Qing emperor right up to the end of the dynasty in 1911.
50. Cameron, *Barbarians and Mandarins*, p. 226.
51. Mancall, *Russia and China*, p. 52.
52. Ibid.
53. Ibid., p. 51. The Soviet economic historian Mikhail Sladkovsky gives a far higher figure of 30,000 roubles for the value of these Chinese imports. One possible explanation of this huge discrepancy may be found in the work of the Chinese scholar Ye Baichuan, who repeats Sladkovsky's figure while describing the goods as gifts for the tsar and his family. A value of 30,000 roubles is certainly in line with the records of gifts brought back for the Russian imperial household in the following century, and it is perhaps only to be expected of an absolute monarchy that the lion's share of the luxuries brought back from afar by a trade mission should have gone to the monarch himself. See Sladkovsky, *Economic Relations*, p. 10; Ye Baichuan, 'Lun Eguo zaoqi dui Hua maoyi zhong tuixing de guanfang maoyi longduan zhengce', in Guan and Luan (eds), *Zhong E guanxi*, p. 142.

54. For the foregoing see Baikov official report in Baddeley, *Russia, Mongolia, China*, vol. 2, pp. 147–50.
55. He Qiutao, *Shuofang beicheng, juan* 37; Myasnikov, *The Ch'ing Empire and the Russian State*, p. 117.
56. Mancall, *Russia and China*, p. 30.
57. Baddeley, *Russia, Mongolia, China*, vol. 2, p. 153. See also Cameron, *Barbarians and Mandarins*, p. 232.
58. Baddeley, *Russia, Mongolia, China*, vol. 2, p. 202; Mancall, *Russia and China*, p. 63.
59. Mancall, *Russia and China*, pp. 55, 58; Ye, 'Lun Eguo zaoqi', in Guan and Luan (eds), *Zhong E guanxi*, p. 142; Perdue, *China Marches West*, p. 165.
60. A *pood* was a weight equivalent to 16.38 kg.
61. This envoy's name is often rendered as Spathar-Milescu. 'Spathar', however, was not a name but an old Byzantine title meaning 'sword-bearer'. I have consequently followed Mancall in calling the envoy plain Milescu.
62. See Pereira diary in Sebes, *The Jesuits*, p. 209.
63. For a detailed biographical sketch of Milescu see Mancall, *Russia and China*, pp. 70–4.
64. Baddeley, *Russia, Mongolia, China*, vol. 2, p. 304.
65. For the foregoing see Milescu original official report published as Milescu, *Sibir i Kitai*, Kishinev, 1960 pp. 307–8; Baddeley, *Russia, Mongolia, China*, vol. 2, p. 295; Mancall, *Russia and China*, pp. 85–6.
66. Milescu, *Sibir i Kitai*, pp. 309, 405; Baddeley, *Russia, Mongolia, China*, vol. 2, pp. 303, 332, 337, 347–9, 359–60; Mancall, *Russia and China*, pp. 86–7, 92, 94.
67. Milescu, *Sibir i Kitai*, pp. 478–9; Baddeley, *Russia, Mongolia, China*, vol. 2, pp. 397–401, 403–6, 410–13; Mancall, *Russia and China*, pp. 106–7.
68. Baddeley, *Russia, Mongolia, China*, vol. 2, pp. 344, 369; Mancall, *Russia and China*, pp. 91, 95–7.
69. Milescu, *Sibir i Kitai*, pp. 464, 485; Baddeley, *Russia, Mongolia, China*, vol. 2, pp. 340–1, 356, 409; Mancall, *Russia and China*, p. 108.
70. Mancall, *Russia and China*, p. 34.
71. Mala quoted in Milescu, *Sibir i Kitai*, p. 319; Baddeley, *Russia, Mongolia, China*, vol. 2, p. 301; Mancall, *Russia and China*, p. 89.
72. Manchu was written in a Mongolian-derived alphabetic script rather than in the complex Chinese ideograms.
73. Baddeley, *Russia, Mongolia, China*, vol. 2, p. 330; Mancall, *Russia and China*, p. 92.
74. Milescu, *Sibir i Kitai*, p. 479; Baddeley, *Russia, Mongolia, China*, vol. 2, p. 403; Mancall, *Russia and China*, p. 105.
75. Alexander Lukin, *The Bear Watches the Dragon: Russia's Perceptions of China and the Evolution of Russian-Chinese Relations Since the Eighteenth Century*, New York, 2003, p. 9.
76. For the foregoing quotations see Milescu, *Sibir i Kitai*, pp. 153, 155, 200–1, 205; Baddeley, *Russia, Mongolia, China*, vol. 2, pp. 326, 440; Mancall, *Russia and China*, pp. 77–8.
77. Mancall, *Russia and China*, pp. 117–19; Popov, *Rossiya i Kitai*, pp. 73–4.
78. See Fu, *A Documentary Chronicle*, p. 58. A *picul* was a Chinese measure of grain corresponding to 133⅓ lbs.
79. Ibid., p. 79.
80. Mancall, *Russia and China*, p. 119.
81. Ibid., p. 127; Popov, *Rossiya i Kitai*, p. 82.
82. Cossack deserters especially are said to have been disenchanted with their way of life on the Amur. See Weale, *Manchu and Muscovite*, p. 43.
83. Fu, *A Documentary Chronicle*, p. 62.
84. Details given in A.R. Colquhoun, *The 'Overland' to Peking*, London, 1900, p. 25; Myasnikov, *The Ch'ing Empire and the Russian State*, p. 201; Popov, *Rossiya i Kitai*, p. 83.
85. Mancall, *Russia and China*, p. 129.

86. Fu, *A Documentary Chronicle*, pp. 78, 79.
87. Mancall, *Russia and China*, p. 132. See also R.K.I. Quested, *Sino-Russian Relations: A Short History*, Sydney, 1984, p. 38; Popov, *Rossiya i Kitai*, p. 84.
88. Fu, *A Documentary Chronicle*, p. 80.
89. Ibid., p. 87.
90. Popov, *Rossiya i Kitai*, p. 99.
91. As Venyukov and Favorov would have remembered, a pair of gerfalcons had been presented to the emperor by Milescu in 1676. These two birds had failed to survive the heat of the Peking summer, but Kangxi had managed to obtain a replacement pair which he evidently wished to display.
92. Immanuel C.Y. Hsü, 'Russia's special position in China during the early Qing period', *Slavic Review* 23, (December 1964), pp. 688–700; Popov, *Rossiya i Kitai*, p. 121; diary of Fr Tomas Pereira, in Sebes, *The Jesuits*, pp. 179, 181.
93. Zhang Pengge, *Feng shi Eluosi xingcheng lu*, in He Qiutao, *Shuofang beicheng, juan* 42.
94. Fu, *A Documentary Chronicle*, p. 97.
95. Pereira diary, in Sebes, *The Jesuits*, p. 181.
96. Fu, *A Documentary Chronicle*, p. 102.
97. Myasnikov, *The Ch'ing Empire and the Russian State*, p. 272; Perdue, *China Marches West*, p. 169. Perdue gives Golodin's force as 1,500: I prefer Myasnikov's more angular figure of 1,450.
98. Description by Fr Jean-François Gerbillon, quoted in *The Chinese Repository*, Canton, vol. VIII, 1839–40, art. III.
99. Pereira diary in Sebes, *The Jesuits*, p. 237.
100. Myasnikov, *The Ch'ing Empire and the Russian State*, p. 274.
101. Ibid., pp. 275, 276.
102. Pereira diary in Sebes, *The Jesuits*, p. 301.
103. Ibid., pp. 225, 257.
104. Ibid., p. 247.
105. See N.V. Skritsky, *Pervy kavalier ordena svyatogo Andreya Admiral F.A. Golovin (1650–1706): biografichesky ocherk*, Moscow, 1995, p. 7. It isn't clear that Golovin was blamed by the Russian government, and his career doesn't seem to have suffered any long-term damage.
106. Gerbillon, quoted in *The Chinese Repository*, vol. VIII, 1839–40, art. III.
107. Pereira diary in Sebes, *The Jesuits*, p. 281.
108. In June 1690 a party of Manchu officers are said to have travelled right up to Yakutsk. The Russians were anxious to establish whether they meant to make war or merely to pacify the local taxpayers. Episode recorded in Ye, *Eguo lai Hua shituan*, p. 54.

CHAPTER 2: THE GREAT EQUILIBRIUM

1. Peter was nominally co-ruler with his feeble-minded half-brother Ivan V until the latter's death in 1696.
2. Adam Brand, *A Journal of the Embassy from Their Majesties John and Peter Alexeievits, Emperors of Muscovy &c., Over Land into China through Siberia, Dauria and the Great Tartary to Peking, the capital city of the Chinese Empire, by Everard Isbrand, their Ambassador in the years 1693, 1694 and 1695*, London 1698, p. 2.
3. *The Chinese Repository*, Canton, vol. VIII, no. X, article IV, 1840. See also Brand, *A Journal of the Embassy*, pp. 70–1.
4. Mancall, *Russia and China*, p. 194; Quested, *Sino-Russian Relations*, p. 45.
5. Immanuel C.Y. Hsü, 'Russia's special position in China during the Early Ch'ing Period', *Slavic Review*, vol. 23, no. 4, 1964, pp. 688–700; Ye, *Eguo lai Hua shituan*, p. 226.
6. Sladkovsky, *History of Economic Relations*, p. 33.
7. Ye, *Eguo lai Hua shituan*, p. 226.
8. The firms were those of O. Filatev and S. Luzin.

9. Fu, *A Documentary Chronicle*, p. 121.
10. With apologies to the late Mr John le Carré, 'Russia House' seems the most fitting translation of *Eluosi guan*.
11. Strictly speaking it was a yellow banner with a red border.
12. For the quotations in this paragraph see Tulisen, *Narrative of the Chinese Embassy to the Khan of the Tourgouth Tartars in the Years 1712, 13, 14 & 15*, London, 1821, pp. 44–5, 61, 62, 69–71, 77, 83, 133, 135–6, 138–9. Note that Tulisen wasn't the leader of the embassy, as is often assumed: that post was held by an obscure figure called Yuzhana.
13. Ibid., pp. 116, 122.
14. Ibid., pp. 95, 200–1.
15. See Milescu in Baddeley, *Russia, Mongolia, China*, vol. 2, p. 299; Lev Izmailov quoted in Eric Widmer, *The Russian Ecclesiastical Mission in Peking During the Eighteenth Century*, Cambridge, MA, 1976, p. 56.
16. Hieromonk Nikolai Adoratsky, 'Istoriya Rossiiskoi Dukhovnoi Missii v Kitae v pervy period yego deyatelnosti', in S.L Tikhvinsky et al. (eds), *Istoriya Rossiiskoi Dukhovnoi Missii v Kitae*, Moscow, 1999, pp. 56–7.
17. Ibid., p. 55. See also V.G. Datsyshen, *Istoriya Rossiiskoi Dukhovnoi Missii v Kitae*, Hong Kong, 2010, pp. 78–9; Zhang Xuefeng, 'Qingchao chuqi Zhong E jiaowang wenhua zhang'ai de kefu yu Eguo zongjiao chuandaotuan lai Hua', in Guan and Luan (eds), *Zhong E guanxi*, p. 134.
18. Adoratsky, 'Istoriya', in Tikhvinsky et al., *Istoriya*, p. 60; Barthold, *La découverte de l'Asie*, p. 226.
19. Adoratsky, 'Istoriya', in Tikhvinsky et al., *Istoriya*, pp. 65–7, 71; Datsyshen, *Istoriya*, pp. 83–4. Datsyshen records eight rather than seven language students. The latter were formally designated *tserkovniki*, or minor church officials.
20. Kangxi, 24 November 1693, quoted in He Qiutao, *Shuofang beisheng*, *juan* 1, pp. 612–13; Mancall, *Russia and China*, pp. 356–7 n.70.
21. John Bell of Antermony, *A Journey from St Petersburg to Pekin, 1719–22*, Edinburgh, 1965, p. 52. See also Morris Rossabi, *China and Inner Asia: From 1368 to the Present Day*, London, 1975, p. 134.
22. Peter C. Perdue, *China Marches West: The Qing Conquest of Central Eurasia*, Cambridge, MA, 2005, p. 212.
23. Adoratsky, 'Istoriya', in Tikhvinsky et al., *Istoriya*, p. 77 n.68.
24. Mancall, *Russia and China*, p. 218; Ye, *Eguo lai Hua shituan*, pp. 64–5.
25. Fr Matteo Ripa, SJ, quoted in Nigel Cameron, *Barbarians and Mandarins: Thirteen Centuries of Western Travellers in China*, Hong Kong, 1997, p. 278.
26. Hsü, 'Russia's special position'.
27. Adoratsky, 'Istoriya', in Tikhvinsky et al., *Istoriya*, p. 93. See also Widmer, *The Russian Ecclesiastical Mission*, pp. 64–5.
28. Laurence de Lange (Lorents Lange), *Journal of the Residence of Mr. de Lange, Agent of his Imperial Majesty of all the Russias, Peter the First, at the Court of Pekin, during the Years 1721 and 1722; Translated from the French*, in John Bell, *Travels from St. Petersburg in Russia, to Various Parts of Asia, in 1716, 1719, 1722, &c*, in John Pinkerton (ed.), *A General Collection of the Best and Most Interesting Voyages and Travels in all Parts of the World; many of which are now first translated into English; digested on a new plan*, London, 1811, vol. VII, p. 438; Barbara Widenor Maggs, *Russia and 'le rêve chinois': China in Eighteenth-century Russian Literature*, Oxford, 1984, p. 74.
29. Lange, *Journal of the Residence*, in Pinkerton, *A General Collection*, vol. 7, p. 449; Mancall, *Russia and China*, p. 226; Widmer, *The Russian Ecclesiastical Mission*, p. 58; Maggs, *Russia and 'le rêve chinois'*, p. 74.
30. Lange, *Journal of the Residence*, in Pinkerton, *A General Collection*, vol. 7, p. 477; Mancall, *Russia and China*, p. 232.
31. Mancall, *Russia and China*, p. 233.
32. Adoratsky, 'Istoriya', in Tikhvinsky et al., *Istoriya*, p. 93; Widmer, *The Russian Ecclesiastical Mission*, p. 65.

33. Clifford M. Foust, *Muscovite and Mandarin: Russia's Trade with China and Its Setting, 1727–1805*, Chapel Hill, NC, 1969, p. 38.
34. Ibid., p. 47.
35. Adoratsky, 'Istoriya', in Tikhvinsky et al., *Istoriya*, p. 101; Datsyshen, *Istoriya*, p. 86; Widmer, *The Russian Ecclesiastical Mission*, p. 73.
36. Mancall, *Russia and China*, pp. 245, 253–4; Foust, *Muscovite and Mandarin*, pp. 48–9.
37. Foust, *Muscovite and Mandarin*, p. 48.
38. Ibid., p. 56; Mancall, *Russia and China*, p. 257.
39. Ye, *Eguo lai Hua shituan*, p. 62.
40. Foust, *Muscovite and Mandarin*, p. 110.
41. Ye Baichuan, 'Lun Eguo dui Hua maoyi zhong tuixing de guanfang maoyi longduan zhengce', in Guan and Luan (eds), *Zhong E guanxi*, p. 153.
42. Foust, *Muscovite and Mandarin*, pp. 141–2.
43. Originally called Troitskaya, the fortress was renamed to include the first syllable of Sava's own moniker.
44. Foust, *Muscovite and Mandarin*, p. 134.
45. Already in the 1720s the Russian government had lifted the state monopolies on gold, silk, rhubarb and tobacco.
46. Foust, *Muscovite and Mandarin*, p. 229.
47. Ibid., p. 230.
48. Ibid., p. 245.
49. Adoratsky, 'Istoriya', in Tikhvinsky et al., *Istoriya*, p. 149; Datsyshen, *Istoriya*, p. 93.
50. Adoratsky, 'Istoriya', in Tikhvinsky et al., *Istoriya*, pp. 127–8. See also Foust, *Muscovite and Mandarin*, p. 130. According to Foust Father Antony claimed a slightly bolder total of twenty-five baptisms. For equally unimpressive results reported by Protestant missionaries in the nineteenth century see Donald Treadgold, *The West in Russia and China*, vol. 2, Boulder, CO, 1985.
51. Datsyshen, *Istoriya*, p. 93.
52. Adoratsky, 'Istoriya', in Tikhvinsky et al., *Istoriya*, pp. 47–8. See also Datsyshen, *Istoriya*, p. 80.
53. Widmer, *The Russian Ecclesiastical Mission*, p. 107.
54. Adoratsky, 'Istoriya', in Tikhvinsky et al., *Istoriya*, p. 92; Datsyshen, *Istoriya*, p. 90.
55. Widmer, *The Russian Ecclesiastical Mission*, pp. 117–18.
56. Archimandrite Antony report to College of Foreign Affairs, 25 July 1731, quoted in ibid., pp. 119–20.
57. Adoratsky, 'Istoriya', in Tikhvinsky et al., *Istoriya*, p. 137; Datsyshen, *Istoriya*, p. 90.
58. Adoratsky, 'Istoriya', in Tikhvinsky et al., *Istoriya*, p. 162; Schimmelpenninck van der Oye, *Russian Orientalism*, p. 142; Widmer, *The Russian Ecclesiastical Mission*, p. 133.
59. Foust, *Muscovite and Mandarin*, p. 51; Widmer, *The Russian Ecclesiastical Mission*, pp. 6–7.
60. Adoratsky, 'Istoriya', in Tikhvinsky et al., *Istoriya*, p. 125; Widmer, *The Russian Ecclesiastical Mission*, p. 117.
61. Adoratsky, 'Istoriya', in Tikhvinsky et al., *Istoriya*, p. 136.
62. Ibid., p. 162; Widmer, *The Russian Ecclesiastical Mission*, pp. 133, 140.
63. Adoratsky, 'Istoriya', in Tikhvinsky et al., *Istoriya*, pp. 136, 162; Widmer, *The Russian Ecclesiastical Mission*, pp. 119, 133–4; Foust, *Muscovite and Mandarin*, p. 149.
64. Rossabi, *China and Inner Asia*, p. 162. This *Eluosi xue* should not be confused with the *Eluosi wenguan* (Russian Language School) previously set up by the Qing to enable their own people to study Russian.
65. He Qiutao, *Shuofang beisheng*, *juan* 37. See also Widmer, *The Russian Ecclesiastical Mission*, pp. 101–2, 160; Fu, *A Documentary Chronicle*, pp. 169–70.
66. Widmer, *The Russian Ecclesiastical Mission*, p. 138.
67. Datsyshen, *Istoriya*, p. 102.
68. See Yanagisawa Akira, 'Some Remarks on the Addendum to the Treaty of Kyakhta in 1768', *Memoirs of the Toyo Bunko* 69, 2005, pp. 65–8.

69. Foust, *Muscovite and Mandarin*, p. 61.
70. See Widmer, *The Russian Ecclesiastical Mission*, p. 169 n.2. Daughter of Peter the Great, Elizabeth reigned as empress from 1741 to 1762. Note that from Peter's time on Russian monarchs used the title of emperor/empress as well as tsar/tsaritsa.
71. See Tulisen, *Narrative of the Chinese Embassy*, p. 185.
72. Bell, *A Journey from St Petersburg to Pekin*, p. 181. See also Maggs, *Russia and 'le rêve chinois'*, p. 72; Lukin, *The Bear Watches the Dragon*, p. 42.
73. 'Dzhog' was possibly a Russian attempt at 'Zhuge'. The double-barrelled surname Zhuge is evocative of Zhuge Liang, the wily Odysseus of Chinese legend. It would have been an appropriate name for a Chinese secret agent, and one wonders whether it may not have been adopted for that reason.
74. Observation of General Alexei Kuropatkin in *Russko-kitaisky vopros* (The Russo-Chinese Question), 1914, quoted in Lukin, *The Bear Watches the Dragon*, p. 60.
75. There remained the Great Horde, which was only subdued in 1844.
76. Odd Arne Westad, *Restless Empire: China and the World Since 1750*, London, 2012, p. 10. For references to a 'final solution' in this context see also Perdue, *China Marches West*, p. 285; James A. Millward, *Eurasian Crossroads: A History of Xinjiang*, London, 2007, p. 95.
77. The term Xinjiang is said to have been introduced in the late eighteenth century, but it is not clear at what precise date (if any) this occurred. See Millward, *Eurasian Crossroads*, pp. x, 97.
78. Qianlong, 8 November 1757, quoted in He Qiutao, *Shuofeng beisheng, juan 1*, p. 619.
79. Widmer, *The Russian Ecclesiastical Mission*, p. 174; see also Fu, *A Documentary Chronicle*, pp. 210–13.
80. Widmer, *The Russian Ecclesiastical Mission*, p. 174.
81. Quoted in Lukin, *The Bear Watches the Dragon*, p. 12.
82. Ibid., p. 11.
83. Quoted in Widmer, *The Russian Ecclesiastical Mission*, p. 173. See also Perdue, *China Marches West*, p. 288.
84. Quested, *Sino-Russian Relations*, p. 56.
85. Fu, *A Documentary Chronicle*, p. 238.
86. Ibid., p. 212.
87. Quoted in Liu Dexi, 'Shijiu shiji zhongye yiqian de Zhong E guanxi', in Guan and Luan (eds), *Zhong E guanxi*, p. 168.
88. Ibid.
89. Fu, *A Documentary Chronicle*, pp. 262–3.
90. Ibid., p. 264. In 1791 Qianlong remained scornful of rumours that the Russians were out to recapture the Torguts, declaring that Russia 'would never dare attack the [Chinese] border by force'. Ibid, p. 313.
91. Ibid, p. 274.
92. Ibid., p. 287.
93. Ibid, p. 322; Widmer, *The Russian Ecclesiastical Mission*, p. 178.
94. Schimmelpenninck van der Oye, *Russian Orientalism*, p. 39.
95. I am indebted for this point to Professor Alexander Woodside.
96. Phrase of Dr Loretta Kim.
97. Fu, *A Documentary Chronicle*, p. 302.
98. Ibid., p. 312; Widmer, *The Russian Ecclesiastical Mission*, p. 110.
99. Widmer, *The Russian Ecclesiastical Mission*, p. 165.
100. Ibid; Datsyshen, *Istoriya*, p. 111; Ye, *Eguo lai Hua shituan*, p. 322.
101. Maggs, *Russia and 'le rêve chinois'*, p. 20; Widmer, *The Russian Ecclesiastical Mission*, p. 144.
102. Quoted in Maggs, *Russia and 'le rêve chinois'*, pp. 108, 138; Schimmelpenninck van der Oye, *Russian Orientalism*, p. 52; Lukin, *The Bear Watches the Dragon*, p. 12.

103. Quoted in Maggs, *Russia and 'le rêve chinois'*, p. 108; Schimmelpenninck van der Oye, *Russian Orientalism*, p. 52; Lukin, *The Bear Watches the Dragon*, p. 12.
104. Quoted in Schimmelpenninck van der Oye, *Russian Orientalism*, p. 52, Maggs, *Russia and 'le rêve chinois'*, p. 108.
105. Quoted in Maggs, *Russia and 'le rêve chinois'*, p. 110; Lukin, *The Bear Watches the Dragon*, p. 11.
106. Maggs, *Russia and 'le rêve chinois'*, p. 107.
107. Isabel de Madariaga, *Catherine the Great: A Short History*, New Haven, CT, and London, 2002, p. 101; Maggs, *Russia and 'le rêve chinois'*, pp. 107–8.
108. See Leo Tolstoy, *War and Peace*, Book I, Chapter XXIV.
109. Widmer, *The Russian Ecclesiastical Mission*, pp. 178–9. Quoted in Maggs, *Russia and 'le rêve chinois'*, p. 108; Lukin, *The Bear Watches the Dragon*, p. 12.
110. Maggs, *Russia and 'le rêve chinois'*, pp. 87, 91, 126–7; de Madariaga, *Catherine the Great*, pp. 100, 110; Lukin, *The Bear Watches the Dragon*, p. 12.
111. Maggs, *Russia and 'le rêve chinois'*, pp. 24–6, 29.
112. He Qiutao, *Shuofang beisheng*, *juan* 37. See also A.L. Galperin, 'Russko-kitaiskaya torgovlya v XVIII – pervoi polovine XIX veka', in *Problemy Vostokovedeniya*, no. 5, 1955, p. 216
113. Quoted in Foust, *Muscovite and Mandarin*, p. 323.
114. Wu Yuxing, 'E chuan shou hang Guangzhou maoyi fengbo zai yanjiu', in Guan and Luan (eds), *Zhong E guanxi*, p. 174.
115. Ibid., p. 26; Foust, *Muscovite and Mandarin*, pp. 327–8.
116. Qianlong had already abdicated in 1796 so that the length of his reign should not exceed that of his revered grandfather Kangxi, but had continued to wield influence till his death three years later.
117. R.K.I. Quested, *The Expansion of Russia in East Asia, 1857–1860*, Kuala Lumpur and Singapore, 1968, p. 11.
118. Foust, *Muscovite and Mandarin*, pp. 327–8.
119. Ye, *Eguo lai Hua shituan*, p. 102.
120. Wu Yuxing, 'E chuan shou hang', in Guan and Luan (eds), *Zhong E guanxi*, p. 178.
121. I.e. the anti-Qing insurrections in central and southern China, and in particular the rebellion of the White Lotus sect.
122. Quoted in Wu Yuxing, 'E chuan shou hang', in Guan and Luan (eds), *Zhong E guanxi*, p. 177.
123. Maggs, *Russia and 'le rêve chinois'*, p. 51; Lukin, *The Bear Watches the Dragon*, pp. 43–4.
124. Quested, *The Expansion of Russia*, pp. 16, 21–2.
125. Georgi Timkovsky, ed. Julius von Klaproth, *Travels of the Russian Mission through Mongolia to China and Residence in Peking in the Years 1820–1821*, London, 1827, vol. 2, p. 329.
126. The vet warned that these 'traders' were really military men. See Peter Hopkirk, *The Great Game*, Oxford, 1990, pp. 90–1.
127. Quested, *The Expansion of Russia*, pp. 16–17.
128. Fu, *A Documentary Chronicle*, p. 340.
129. Quested, *The Expansion of Russia*, p. 16.
130. Chen Kaike, 'Eluosi guan yu Taiping Tianguo shiqi Sha E de dui Hua waijiao', in Guan and Luan (eds), *Zhong E guanxi*, p. 191.
131. Timkovsky, ed. Klaproth, *Travels*, vol. 2, p. 65.
132. M.P. Alexeev, '*Pushkin i Kitai*', in *A.S. Pushkin v Sibirii*, Moscow and Irkutsk, 1937, pp. 139–45.
133. Ibid.
134. Review of *Travels in Siberia: Including Excursions Northwards Down the Obi to the Polar Circle, and Southwards to the Chinese Frontier* by Dr. Adolph Erman in *The Chinese Repository*, Canton, vol. XX, no. I, art. II, 1851.
135. Ibid.

136. For the foregoing see Timkovsky, ed. Klaproth, *Travels*, vol. 1, p. 9, describing 30 August 1820; diary of Fr Hyacinth Bichurin, 11 August 1830.
137. Timkovsky, ed. Klaproth, *Travels*, 10 February 1821.
138. Diary of Fr Hyacinth Bichurin, 6 September 1830.
139. Ibid.
140. Yet another possibility could be that *pelmeni* and *jiaozi* have a common origin in the plain Mongolian meat dumplings known as *buuz*.
141. The Qing didn't think it appropriate that the Ninth Mission should arrive in Peking along with the embassy, and the mission were consequently obliged to wait in Irkutsk.
142. Inventor in 1812 of the first practical electromagnetic telegraph.
143. I.I. Panaev, quoted in V.S. Myasnikov, 'Izbranie otsa Iakinfa (Bichurina) v Akademiyu Nauk', in Tikhvinsky et al., *Istoriya*, p. 213.
144. For the foregoing quotations from Fr Hyacinth see S.F Tikhvinsky and G.N. Peskova, 'Vydayushchiisya russkii kitaeved o Iakinf (Bichurin)', in Tikhvinsky et al., *Istoriya*, pp. 173–4, 194; Schimmelpenninck van der Oye, *Russian Orientalism*, p. 148.
145. Alexeev, 'Pushkin i Kitai', in *A.S. Pushkin v Sibirii*, Irkutsk 1937.
146. S.F Tikhvinsky and G.N. Peskova, in Tikhvinsky et al., *Istoriya*, p. 175.
147. Alexeev, 'Pushkin i Kitai', in *A.S. Pushkin v Sibirii*.
148. Ibid.; Alexander Bezzubtsev-Kondakov and Ilya Drokanov, *Nado li Rossii boyatsya Kitaya?*, St Petersburg, 2011, p. 34.
149. See Lukin, *The Bear Watches the Dragon*, p. 15.
150. Ibid., p. 62.
151. Datsyshen, *Istoriya*, p. 153.
152. O.V. Shatalov, '*Arkhimandrit Pyotr (P.I. Kamensky) – nachalnik 10oi Russkoi Dukhovnoi Missii v Pekine*', *Pravoslavie na Dal'nem Vostoke*, vypusk 3, St Petersburg, 2000, pp. 85–98.
153. The Daoguang emperor had succeeded his father Jiaqing in 1820. Jiaqing shares with the fourth-century Roman emperor Carus the distinction of being one of the only two monarchs reported to have been killed by lightning.
154. P.E. Skachkov, 'Russkie vrachi pri Rossiiskoi Dukhovnoi Missii v Pekine', *Sovietskoe Kitaevedenie*, no. 4, 1958, pp. 136–48.
155. Ibid.
156. Quested, *The Expansion of Russia*, p. 27; Datsyshen, *Istoriya*, p. 174.
157. Quested, *The Expansion of Russia*, pp. 26–7.
158. Quoted in Schimmelpenninck van der Oye, *Russian Orientalism*, p. 149.
159. Shatalov, '*Arkhimandrit Pyotr*', in *Pravoslavie na Dal'nem Vostoke*, vypusk 3, pp. 85–98.
160. Mikhail Musin-Pushkin, quoted in Schimmelpenninck van der Oye, *Russian Orientalism*, p. 104.
161. See *The Chinese Repository*, Canton, vol. VIII, no. VIII, art. II, 1839.
162. Quoted in Iosif Antonovich Goshkevich, 'Hong Kong: From the notes of a Russian traveller', *Journal of the Hong Kong Branch of the Royal Asiatic Society*, vol. 38, 1998–9, pp. 230–6.

CHAPTER 3: THE TSARIST SUPREMACY

1. Letter of Archimandrite Polycarp, 26 July 1846, in A.S. Ipatova, 'Archimandrite Polycarp's Letters', *Far Eastern Affairs*, no. 3, 1991.
2. Letter of Archimandrite Polycarp, 15 September 1847, ibid.
3. Archimandrite Palladius to Muraviev, 1 June 1850, in V. Kryzhanovsky (ed.), Palladius-Muraviev correspondence, *Russki Arkhiv*, no. 8, Moscow, 1914, p. 493.
4. B.A. Romanov, *Russia in Manchuria (1892–1906)*, Ann Arbor, MI, 1952, p. 3.
5. Chen Kaike, 'Eluosi guan yu Taiping Tianguo', in Guan and Luan (eds), *Zhong E guanxi*, p. 192.
6. Quoted in Shatalov, 'Arkhimandrit Pyotr', in *Pravoslavie na Dal'nem Vostoke*, vypusk 3, p. 96.

7. Palladius report 2 March 1851, Kryzhanovsky (ed.), Palladius–Muraviev correspondence, *Russki Arkhiv*, no. 8, pp. 502–3.
8. Quoted in Ipatova, 'Archimandrite Polycarp's Letters', *Far Eastern Affairs*, no. 3, 1991.
9. S.L. Tikhvinsky and G.N. Peskova, 'Vydayushchiisya russky kitaeved', in Tikhvinsky et al. (eds), *Istoriya*, p. 194. See also Lukin, *The Bear Watches the Dragon*, pp. 17–18.
10. Osip Senkowski, extract from 'Kitai i Kitaitsy', in A.D. Romanenko (ed.), *Kitai u russkikh pisatelei*, Moscow, 2008, pp. 54–5.
11. Datsyshen, *Istoriya*, p. 174.
12. Contemporary description provided in Anna Kovalenko, 'Rol' kazachestva v ukreplenii granitsy Rossii s Mongoliei i Kitaem v XVIII-pervoi polovine XIX vv', in *Problemy Dal'nego Vostoka*, no. 3, 2009, pp. 110–18.
13. Quoted in Foust, *Muscovite and Mandarin*, p. 320 n.104.
14. Quested, *The Expansion of Russia*, pp. 31–2.
15. Sladkovsky, *History of Economic Relations*, p. 77; Popov, *Rossiya i Kitai*, p. 133.
16. Clubb, *China and Russia*, p. 80; Stephan, *The Russian Far East*, p. 45; Popov, *Rossiya i Kitai*, p. 133.
17. Palladius report 2 March 1851, Kryzhanovsky (ed.), Palladius–Muraviev correspondence, *Russki Arkhiv*, no. 8, p. 502.
18. For Goncharov remarks see Romanenko (ed.), *Kitai u russkikh pisatelei*, p. 100; V.S. Kuznetsov, 'Kitai glazami russkikh pisatelei, XIX – nachala XX veka', in *Problemy Dal'nego Vostoka*, no. 5, 2010, pp. 132–40.
19. Lifanyuan to Russian Senate, Xianfeng 3rd year, 6th month, 16th day, document 61, *Qingdai Zhong E guanxi dang'an shiliao xuanbian, di san bian*, vol. 1, Beijing, 1979.
20. Shengbao memorial, Xianfeng 1st year, 8th month, 25th day, document 11, ibid.
21. Ibid.
22. Cai Hongsheng, *Cai Hongsheng shixue wenbian*, Guangzhou, 2014, p. 145.
23. Quested, *The Expansion of Russia*, p. 46.
24. Letter to Tsar Nicholas I, May 1849, quoted in Victor Zatsepine, *Beyond the Amur: Frontier Encounters between China and Russia, 1850–1930*, Vancouver, 2017, p. 72; Popov, *Rossiya i Kitai*, pp. 131–2.
25. Lukin, *The Bear Watches the Dragon*, p. 45.
26. Stephan, *The Russian Far East*, p. 48.
27. Quested, *The Expansion of Russia*, p. 148.
28. Ibid.
29. Ibid., p. 114.
30. Ibid., p. 75.
31. Ibid., p. 117 n.1.
32. Clarendon to Russell, 23 September 1859, quoted in Quested, *The Expansion of Russia*, p. 232.
33. Ibid., p. 257.
34. Clarendon to Russell, 23 September 1859, quoted in ibid., p. 232.
35. Memorial from Tepuchin and others, Xianfeng 9th year, 6th month, 28th day, document 601, *Qingdai Zhong E guanxi dang'an*.
36. Chen Kaike, 'Eluosi yu Taiping Tianguo', in Guan and Luan (eds), *Zhong E guanxi*, p. 194.
37. Ibid., p. 203.
38. Ibid. See also Popov, *Rossiya i Kitai*, p. 153.
39. See account of draft treaty in Quested, *The Expansion of Russia*, p. 147.
40. See Kryzhanovsky (ed.), Palladius–Muraviev correspondence, *Russki Arkhiv*, no. 9, Moscow, 1914, p. 15.
41. Memorial from Yu Cheng and others on document received from Archimandrite Palladius, Xianfeng 7th year, 4th month, 3rd day, document 248 appendix, *Qingdai Zhong E guanxi dang'an*.
42. Quested, *The Expansion of Russia*, p. 112.

43. Memorial of Wulehonge and others, Xianfeng 7th year, 8th month, 2nd day, document 314, *Qingdai Zhong E guanxi dang'an.*
44. Palladius to Muraviev in Kryzhanovsky (ed.), Palladius–Muraviev correspondence, *Russki Arkhiv*, no. 9, p. 168.
45. Cai Hongsheng, *Cai Hongsheng shixue wenbian*, pp. 139–40, 141.
46. Quested, *The Expansion of Russia*, p. 110.
47. Dispatch to Russian minister from the Grand Council with attached Ignatiev letter to Grand Council, Xianfeng 10th year, 7th month, 26th day, document 760, *Qingdai Zhong E dang'an.*
48. Memorial of Prince Gong and others with attached letter from Archimandrite Gurii, Xianfeng 10th year, 8th month, 29th day, document 762, *Qingdai Zhong E guanxi dang'an.*
49. Quested, *The Expansion of Russia*, p. 67.
50. Memorial of Delekedorji and others, Xianfeng 7th year, 5th month, 26th day, document 258, *Qingdai Zhong E guanxi dang'an.*
51. Ibid.
52. Ibid.
53. Memorial of Prince Gong, 10th year, 10th month, 9th day, document 786, *Qingdai Zhong E guanxi dang'an.*
54. Palladius report from Peking, 22 April 1856, in Kryzhanovsky (ed.), Palladius–Muraviev correspondence, *Russki Arkhiv*, no. 9, p. 167.
55. For comments by Xianfeng, Delekedorji and other Qing functionaries see Quested, *The Expansion of Russia*, pp. 53, 70, 74, 170, 225; memorial of Tan Tingxiang et al. Xianfeng 8th year, 4th month, 6th day, document 403, *Qingdai Zhong E guanxi dang'an.*
56. Isidore Cyril Cannon, *Public Success, Private Sorrow: The Life and Times of Charles Henry Brewitt-Taylor (1857–1938)*, Hong Kong, 2009, p. 32.
57. Quested, *The Expansion of Russia*, p. 45.
58. Ibid.
59. Memorial of Tan Tingxiang and others, Xianfeng 8th year, 4th month, 6th day, document 403, *Qingdai Zhong E guanxi dang'an.*
60. Memorial of Prince Gong and others, Xianfeng 10th year, 8th month, 25th day, document 762, *Qingdai Zhong E guanxi dang'an.*
61. Quested, *The Expansion of Russia*, p. 267.
62. Xianfeng order to Delekedorji, Xianfeng 5th year, 2nd month, 26th day, document 353, *Qingdai Zhong E guanxi dang'an.*
63. Memorial of Prince Gong and others, Xianfeng 10th year, 10th month, 11th day, document 787, *Qingdai Zhong E guanxi dang'an.*
64. Memorial of Yuan Jiasan, Xianfeng 10th year, 12th month, 2nd day, document 815, *Qingdai Zhong E guanxi dang'an.*
65. Ibid.
66. Quested, *The Expansion of Russia*, p. 185 n.4.
67. Ibid., p. 206.
68. Xianfeng order to Tan Tingxiang and others, Xianfeng 8th year, 2nd month, 25th day, document 351, *Qingdai Zhong E guanxi dang'an*. See also Lukin, *The Bear Watches the Dragon*, p. 67.
69. Quested, *The Expansion of Russia*, p. 5.
70. Ibid., p. 182; Luan Jinghe, 'Jindai yilai Eluosi dui Hua zhengce shulun', in Guan and Luan (eds), *Zhong E guanxi*, p. 61.
71. Lifanyuan to Russian Senate, Xianfeng 9th year, 3rd month, 5th day, document 528, *Qingdai Zhong E guanxi dang'an.*
72. Quested, *The Expansion of Russia*, pp. 123–5; Chen Kaike, 'Eluosi guan yu Taiping Tianguo', in Guan and Luan (eds), *Zhong E guanxi*, p. 204.
73. Xianfeng Imperial Command to Prince Gong and others, Xianfeng 10th year, 9th month, 6th day, document 765, *Qingdai Zhong E guanxi dang'an*; Quested, *The Expansion of Russia*, p. 263.

74. Memorial of Zeng Guofan, Xianfeng 10th year, 11th month, 8th day, document 803, *Qingdai Zhong E guanxi dang'an*.
75. Datsyshen, *Istoriya*, pp. 190–1.
76. Ibid., p. 193.
77. Rosemary Quested, *The Russo-Chinese Bank*, Birmingham, 1977, p. 46.
78. Quoted in B.A. Romanov, *Russia in Manchuria*, p. 44.
79. Cai Hongsheng, *Cai Hongsheng shixue wenbian*, p. 245.
80. A similar ploy was adopted in 1898, when the Qing were induced to lease to Britain the stretch of Hong Kong's hinterland known to the British as the New Territories. The Qing insisted on retaining jurisdiction over one enclave in the form of the Walled City of Kowloon.
81. See Louis Livingston Seaman, *From Tokyo through Manchuria with the Japanese*, New York, 1904, p. 148. The term was however applied sometimes to a smaller number of Russian thugs. See Zatsepine, *Beyond the Amur*, p. 49.
82. Cai Hongsheng, *Cai Hongsheng shixue wenbian*, p. 238.
83. Ibid., p. 239; Nikolai Samoilov, 'Little Known Facts About Russian–Chinese Relations: Visit of the Mission of the Qing Empire to St Petersburg in 1870', *Far Eastern Affairs*, no. 1, 2009, pp. 98–104.
84. Wang Zhichun, *Wang Zhichun ji*, vol. 2, Hunan, 2010, p. 685.
85. Schimmelpenninck van der Oye, *Russian Orientalism*, p. 180.
86. Ibid., p. 181.
87. 'Tolstoi i Kitai', section 1 in A.I. Shifman, *Lev Tolstoi i Vostok*, Moscow, 1971.
88. Ibid.
89. Ibid., section 2.
90. Ibid.
91. Ibid.
92. Ibid., section 4.
93. Quoted in Schimmelpenninck van der Oye, *Russian Orientalism*, p. 212.
94. Chapter 13 of Przhevalsky, *From Kyakhta to the Headwaters of the Yellow River*, cited in Dmitri Kapustin, 'Hong Kong: The First Port of Chekhov's Foreign Journey', *Far Eastern Affairs*, no. 3, 2009, pp. 118–33. See also Sergey Radchenko, *Two Suns in the Heavens*, Washington DC and Stanford, CA, 2009, p. 118.
95. Lukin, *The Bear Watches the Dragon*, p. 49.
96. Ibid.
97. See Potanina in Romanenko (ed.), *Kitai u russkikh pisatelei*, pp. 156, 159–60.
98. Ibid., p. 165.
99. Zatsepine, *Beyond the Amur*, p. 42.
100. Natalia Novgorodskaya, 'A Chinese Envoy to Russia', *Far Eastern Affairs*, no. 5, 1991, pp. 148–57.
101. Ibid.
102. Ibid.
103. Wang Zhichun, *Wang Zhichun ji*, vol. 2, p. 689.
104. Ibid., p. 694.
105. Ibid., pp. 671, 677.
106. Memorial of Sekelong'e, Xianfeng 11th year, 7th month, 10th day, document 914, *Zhong E Guanxi Dang'an*.
107. Ibid.
108. E.M. Ivanova, quoted in V.S. Kuznetsov, 'Kitai glazami russkikh pisatelei', in *Problemy Dal'nego Vostoka*, no. 5, 2010, pp. 132–40.
109. Ibid.
110. Zatsepine, *Beyond the Amur*, p. 51.
111. Ibid.; Sören Urbansky, *Beyond the Steppe Frontier: A History of the Sino-Russian Border*, Princeton, NJ, 2020, pp. 57–8.
112. Urbansky, *Beyond the Steppe Frontier*, pp. 27, 31, 38.

113. Zatsepine, *Beyond the Amur*, p. 15.
114. For the foregoing see Mark Gamsa, 'California on the Amur: The Zheltuga Republic in Manchuria (1883–1886)', *The Slavonic and East European Review*, April 2003, pp. 236–66; Zatsepine, *Beyond the Amur*, pp. 64–5.
115. Quoted in Lukin, *The Bear Watches the Dragon*, p. 47.
116. Ibid., p. 49.
117. Immanuel C.Y. Hsü, *The Ili Crisis: A Study of Sino-Russian Diplomacy, 1871–1881*, Oxford, 1965, pp. 30–33.
118. Ibid., p. 52.
119. Ibid., p. 81. See also James A. Millward, *Eurasian Crossroads: A History of Xinjiang*, London, 2007, p. 134
120. Hsü, *The Ili Crisis*, p. 87.
121. Ibid., p. 131.
122. Fyodor Martens, quoted in Lukin, *The Bear Watches the Dragon*, p. 37.
123. Hsü, *The Ili Crisis*, p. 157.
124. Ibid.
125. Ibid., p. 159.
126. Ibid., p. 163.
127. Ibid., p. 176.
128. Ibid., p. 181.
129. Ibid., p. 188. See also Peter Hopkirk, *The Great Game: On Secret Service in High Asia*, Oxford, 2001, pp. 409–10.
130. Sladkovsky, *History of Economic Relations*, p. 89.
131. Miao Pusheng, Ma Pinyan and Li Sheng (eds), *Lishishang de Xinjiang*, Xinjiang, 2006, p. 285.
132. Ibid.
133. Quoted in C.P. Skrine and Pamela Nightingale, *Macartney at Kashgar: New Light on British, Chinese and Russian Activities in Sinkiang, 1890–1918*, Oxford, 1987, p. 90.
134. Count Sergei Witte, trans. and ed. Abraham Yarmolinsky, *The Memoirs of Count Witte*, Garden City, NY and Toronto, 1921, p. 83.
135. Wang Zhichun, *Wang Zhichun ji*, vol. 2, p. 674.
136. Quoted in Witte, *Memoirs*, p. 88.
137. Sladkovsky, *Study of the History of Economic Relations*, p. 89.
138. R.K.I. Quested, *'Matey' Imperialists?: The Tsarist Russians in Manchuria, 1895–1917*, Hong Kong, 1982, pp. 21, 25.
139. Weale, *Manchu and Muscovite*, p. 60.
140. Witte, *Memoirs*, p. 85.
141. Romanov, *Russia in Manchuria*, p. 101.
142. Popov, *Rossiya i Kitai*, p. 191.
143. G.E. Morrison to J.O.P. Bland, 26 March 26, 1897, in Lo Hui-min (ed.), *The Correspondence of G.E. Morrison, 1895–1912*, Cambridge, 1976, p. 52.
144. Romanov, *Russia in Manchuria*, p. 71.
145. Quested, *'Matey' Imperialists?*, p. 25.
146. Romanov, *Russia in Manchuria*, p. 125.
147. Ibid.
148. Quoted in Lukin, *The Bear Watches the Dragon*, p. 68.
149. Quoted in Don C. Price, *Russia and the Roots of the Chinese Revolution, 1896–1911*, Cambridge, MA, 1974, p. 67.
150. Ibid., p. 76.
151. Ibid., p. 75.
152. P.A. Badmaev, *Rossiya i Kitai: K voprosu o politiko-ekonomicheskom vliyanii*, Moscow, 2011; see also Hopkirk, *The Great Game*, p. 503; Baabar, *History of Mongolia*, Cambridge, 1999, p. 116; Lukin, *The Bear Watches the Dragon*, pp. 31–2.
153. Hopkirk, *The Great Game*, p. 503; Lukin, *The Bear Watches the Dragon*, p. 32.

154. Witte, *Memoirs*, p. 86.
155. Quoted in Clubb, *China and Russia*, p. 121. Comment not included in the most recent edition of Witte's *Memoirs*. Witte is also said to have referred to the tsar and his entourage as having the 'prehensile instincts' of an infant. See Romanov, *Russia in Manchuria*, p. 177.
156. Quoted in Skrine and Nightingale, *Macartney at Kashgar*, p. 92.
157. Datsyshen, *Istoriya*, p. 304.
158. Ibid., p. 212.
159. Witte, *Memoirs*, p. 100.
160. Ibid.
161. Skrine and Nightingale, *Macartney at Kashgar*, p. 94.
162. A.E. Hippisley to Morrison, 6 February 1898, in Lo Hui-min (ed.), *Correspondence of G.E. Morrison*, p. 67.
163. Quoted in Price, *Russia and the Roots*, p. 97.
164. Romanov, *Russia in Manchuria*, p. 168.
165. A.S. Ipatova,'Rossiiskaya Dukhovnaya Missiya b Kitae: vek dvadtsaty', in Tikhvinsky et al., *Istoriya*, p. 295.
166. Fr Dionisy Pozdnyaev, 'Skazanie o muchenikakh kitaiskoi pravoslavnoi tserkvi, postradavshikh v Pekine v 1900g.', *Kitaisky Blagovestnik*, 1, 2000, p. 6.
167. Ibid., p. 15.
168. Datsyshen, *Istoriya*, p. 253; Popov, *Rossiya i Kitai*, p. 259.
169. Peter Fleming, *The Siege at Peking*, London, 1959, p. 152.
170. Zhang Li, 'Eguo Weite yu Yihetuan yundong shiqi dui Hua zhengce', in Guan and Luan (eds), *Zhong E guanxi*, p. 242.
171. Weale, *Manchu and Muscovite*, p. 326.
172. Quested, *'Matey' Imperialists?*, p. 49; Zatsepine, *Beyond the Amur*, p. 122. See also Popov, '*Rossiya i Kitai*', p. 283.
173. Quoted in Seaman, *From Tokyo through Manchuria*, p. 170.
174. Quested, *'Matey' Imperialists?*, p. 204.
175. Clubb, *China and Russia*, p. 128.
176. Price, *Russia and the Roots*, p. 171.
177. Leo Tolstoy, draft *Address to the Chinese People*, in Romanenko (ed.), *Kitae u russkikh pisatelei*, p. 210.
178. Romanov, *Russia in Manchuria*, p. 217.
179. Quested, *'Matey' Imperialists?*, p. 100.
180. Weale, *Manchu and Muscovite*, p. 166.
181. Ibid.
182. Quested, *'Matey' Imperialists?*, p. 78.
183. L.S. Skidelsky was a Russian-Jewish merchant and Władyslaw Kowalski a Polish merchant.
184. Ibid., p. 134.
185. Ibid., p. 28.
186. Quoted in Zhang Chang and Liu Yue, 'International Concessions and the Modernisation of Tianjin', in Laura Victoir and Victor Zatsepine (eds), *Harbin to Hanoi: The Colonial Built Environment in Asia, 1840 to 1940*, Hong Kong, 2013, p. 98.
187. Quested, *'Matey' Imperialists?*, p. 126.
188. Weale, *Manchu and Muscovite*, p. 409.
189. Ibid., p. 408; see also Quested, *'Matey' Imperialists?*, p. 132.
190. Dugald Christie, *Thirty Years in Moukden 1883–1913*, London, 1914, p. 165.
191. Weale, *Manchu and Muscovite*, p. 514. See also Quested, *'Matey' Imperialists?*, p. 125.
192. Weale, *Manchu and Muscovite*, pp. 68–9. See also Quested, *'Matey' Imperialists?*, p. 125.
193. Quested, *'Matey' Imperialists?*, p. 126.
194. Ibid., p. 137.
195. Quested, *'Matey' Imperialists?*, p. 63.

196. Ibid.
197. Ibid., p. 72.
198. Weale, *Manchu and Muscovite*, pp. 527–8.
199. Ibid., p. 180.
200. Ibid., p. 384.
201. Weale, *Manchu and Muscovite*, p. 143.
202. Quoted in Bezzubtsev-Kondakov and Drokanov, *Nado li Rossii boyatsya Kitaya?*, p. 85.
203. Wang Shicai, 'Qianxi Zhongguo Dongbei yu Eluosi de wenhua jiaoliu', in Guan and Luan (eds), *Zhong E guanxi*, p. 681; Zatsepine, *Beyond the Amur*, pp. 89–90.
204. Quested, *'Matey' Imperialists?*, p. 101.
205. Stephan, *The Russian Far East*, p. 72.
206. Quoted in Bezzubtsev-Kondakov and Drokanov, *Nado li Rossii boyatsya Kitaya?*, p. 85.
207. Quoted in Lukin, *The Bear Watches the Dragon*, p. 21.
208. Quoted in Clubb, *China and Russia*, p. 125.
209. A.G. Larin, *Kitaitsy v Rossii*, Moscow, 2000, p. 27.
210. Clubb, *China and Russia*, p. 133.
211. Ibid., p. 139. See also Xu Wanmin, 'Gengzi Zhong E Dongbei zhi zhan fansilu', in Guan and Luan (eds), *Zhong E guanxi*, p. 256.
212. Morrison to L.G. Fraser, 22 May 1905, in Lo Hui-min (ed.) *Correspondence of G.E. Morrison*, vol. 1, p. 305.
213. Price, *Russia and the Roots*, p. 178.
214. Zeng Guangzhuan to Morrison, 5 June 1905, in Lo Hui-min (ed.), *Correspondence of G.E. Morrison*, vol. 1, p. 315.
215. Romanov, *Russia in Manchuria*, p. 391 n.25.
216. Morrison to V. Chirol, 5 May 1905, in Lo Hui-min (ed.), *Correspondence of G.E. Morrison*, vol. 1, p. 299.
217. Quested, *The Russo-Chinese Bank*, p. 59.
218. Quoted in Orlando Figes, *A People's Tragedy*, London, 1998, p. 168.
219. Quoted in Lukin, *The Bear Watches the Dragon*, p. 40. See also Bezzubtsev-Kondakov and Drokanov, *Nado li Rossii boyatsya Kitaya?*, p. 36.
220. For the foregoing see Sladkovsky, *History of Economic Relations*, pp. 119–20; Quested, *'Matey' Imperialists?*, p. 221.
221. Romanov, *Russia in Manchuria*, p. 380.
222. Yuan Jizhou, 'Lun Ri E si ci miyue yu Eguo de yuandong zhengce', in Luan Jinghe (ed.), *History and Reality of Sino-Russian Relations*, Henan, 1991, pp. 137–50.
223. Romanov, *Russia in Manchuria*, p. 386.
224. Ibid., p. 23.
225. Yuan Jizhou, 'Lun Ri E', in Luan Jinghe (ed.), *History and Reality*, pp. 137–50; Romanov, *Russia in Manchuria*, p. 386.
226. Romanov, *Russia in Manchuria*, p. 386.
227. Ibid., p. 420 n.35; Baabar, *History of Mongolia*, p. 116.
228. Baabar, *History of Mongolia*, p. 133.
229. Liu Cunkuang, quoted in Alexandra Sizova, 'Russkie konsulstva Mongolii v rossisko-kitaisko-mongolskom politicheskom vzaimodeistvii nachala XXv', *Problemy Dal'nego Vostoka*, no. 6, 2009, pp. 100–110. See also Spence, *The Search for Modern China*, p. 283.
230. P.M. Ivanov, 'Pravoslavnye missionerskie stany v Kitae v nachale XX veka', in Tikhvinsky et al. (eds), *Istoriya*, p. 271.
231. Datsyshen, *Istoriya*, p. 295.
232. See Ivanov, 'Pravoslavnye missionerskie stany', in Tikhvinsky et al. (eds), *Istoriya*, p. 280; see also A.S. Ipatova, 'Rossiiskaya Dukhovnaya Missiya', in Tikhvinsky et al. (eds), *Istoriya*, p. 300.
233. Skrine and Nightingale, *Macartney at Kashgar*, p. 223.
234. J.O.P. Bland to Morrison, 29 May 1907, in Lo Hui-min (ed.), *Correspondence of G.E. Morrison*, vol. 1, p. 415.

235. Quoted in Quested, *'Matey' Imperialists?*, p. 261.
236. Mark O'Neill, *From the Tsar's Railway to the Red Army: The Experience of Chinese Labourers in Russia during the First World War and Bolshevik Revolution*, Camberwell, Australia and Beijing, 2014, p. 11. See also Lukin, *The Bear Watches the Dragon*, p. 59.
237. O'Neill, *From the Tsar's Railway*, pp. 4, 24.
238. Ibid., p. 25.
239. Ibid., p. 30.
240. Morrison to D.D. Braham, 21 February 1911, in Lo Hui-min (ed.), *Correspondence of G.E. Morrison*, vol. 1, p. 580. See also Lukin, *The Bear Watches the Dragon*, p. 65.
241. Morrison to D.D. Braham, 30 May 1911, in Lo Hui-min (ed.), *Correspondence of G.E. Morrison*, vol. 1, p. 609.
242. Morrison to R. Wilton, August 23, 1911, ibid., p. 618.
243. Morrison to D.D. Braham, 21 February 1911, ibid., p. 582.
244. Ivanov, 'Pravoslavnye missionerskie stany', in Tikhvinsky et al. (eds), *Istoriya*, p. 265 n.27; Datsyshen, *Istoriya*, p. 281.
245. Quoted in Ivanov, 'Pravoslavnye missionerskie stany', in Tikhvinsky et al. (eds), *Istoriya*, p. 273.
246. Quoted in Stephan, *The Russian Far East*, p. 80.
247. Larin, *Kitaitsy v Rossii*, p. 20.
248. Lukin, *The Bear Watches the Dragon*, p. 58.
249. Ibid., p. 66.
250. Quoted in Stephan, *The Russian Far East*, p. 74.
251. O'Neill, *From the Tsar's Railway*, pp. 1, 29.
252. Yueh Sheng, *Sun Yat-sen University in Moscow and the Chinese Revolution: A Personal Account*, Lawrence, KS, 1971, p. 32; Zhang Guotao, *The Rise of the Chinese Communist Party*, vol. 1, 1921–7, Lawrence, KS, 1971, pp. 183–4.
253. Zhang Guotao, *The Rise of the Chinese Communist Party*, vol. 1, p. 121.
254. See Margaret MacMillan, *Seize the Hour: When Nixon Met Mao*, London, 2006, p. 125.

CHAPTER 4: LIGHTHOUSE OF THE MIND'S SEA

1. See 'Tolstoi i Kitai', section 7 in Shifman, *Lev Tolstoi i Vostok*.
2. Ibid., section 9.
3. Ibid., section 7.
4. Gu Hongming (Ku Hung-ming), *Papers from a Viceroy's Yamen*, Shanghai, 1901; Leo Tolstoy, 'Letter to a Chinese Gentleman', *The Saturday Review of Politics, Literature, Science and Art*, 1 December 1906, vol. 102, pp. 670–2; Derk Bodde, *Tolstoy and China*, Princeton, NJ, 2015, pp. 49–58. I am grateful to my son-in-law, Mr Pierce Lai, a descendant of Gu's, for drawing my attention to this exchange, which he discovered from a blog post: 'Tolstoy: Letter to a Chinese Gentleman (Ku Hung-ming)', *The Bamboo Sea*, 9 May 2014, https://thebamboosea.wordpress.com/2014/05/09/tolstoy-letter-to-a-chinese-gentleman/, accessed 29 August 2022. See also Shifman, 'Tolstoi i Kitai', section 8.
5. Price, *Russia and the Roots*, p. 134.
6. Clubb, *China and Russia*, pp. 141, 144.
7. Shifman, 'Tolstoi i Kitai', sections 7, 8.
8. Ibid.
9. Lukin, *The Bear Watches the Dragon*, p. 66.
10. Quoted in Yueh Sheng, *Sun Yat-sen University*, p. 7.
11. Quested, *'Matey' Imperialists?*, p. 178.
12. Ibid., p. 303.
13. Lukin, *The Bear Watches the Dragon*, p. 97; Larin, *Kitaitsy v Rossii*, p. 55; O'Neill, *From the Tsar's Railway*, pp. 51–2.
14. Circular letter from Moscow Central Orgburo of Chinese Communists, 6 May 1920, RGASPI 495-154-5, p. 1.

15. Figes, *A People's Tragedy*, p. 599.
16. Clubb, *China and Russia*, p. 173.
17. Circular letter from Moscow Central Orgburo of Chinese Communists, 2 July 1920, RGASPI 495-154-5, p. 2.
18. Larin, *Kitaitsy v Rossii*, p. 58.
19. Quested, *'Matey' Imperialists?*, p. 315.
20. Stephan, *The Russian Far East*, pp. 233–4.
21. Quoted in Michael Meyer, *In Manchuria*, New York and London, 2015, p. 123.
22. Harry A. Franck, *Wandering in Northern China*, New York and London, 1923, p. 164.
23. M.I. Sladkovsky, *Znakomstvo s Kitaem i Kitaitsami*, Moscow, 2006, p. 34.
24. James Palmer, *The Bloody White Baron*, London, 2008, pp. 91, 113.
25. Gennady Litvintsev of Voronezh, 'Manchzhurskaya Atlantida: Vospominanya russkogo repatrianta', in *Rossiiskaya Gazeta, Dal'ny Vostok*, no. 3537, 29 July 2004.
26. Oleg Lundstrom, oral reminiscences, 'Big Band from Harbin', in 'China', *Ekspert*, special issue 17 June 2000.
27. Wang Zhicheng, *Shanghai Eqiao shi*, Shanghai, 1993, p. 315.
28. Harriet Sergeant, *Shanghai*, London, 2002, p. 51.
29. Wang Zhicheng, *Shanghai Eqiao shi*, p. 334.
30. E.N. Rachinskaya, quoted in E. Oglechneva, 'Russky yazyk vostochnogo zarubezhya v pervoi polovine XX v.; k voprosu o svoeobrazii', *Problemy Dal'nego Vostoka*, no. 6, 2008, pp. 135–49.
31. Wang Zhicheng, *Shanghai Eqiao shi*, p. 315.
32. Ibid., pp. 314–15.
33. Lundstrom, oral reminiscences, 'Big Band from Harbin'. See also Meyer, *In Manchuria*, p. 123.
34. Missionaries Mildred Cable, Eva French and Francesca French, June 1927, quoted in *South China Morning Post* (*SCMP*), 12 June 2007. For a similar observation by an Italian diplomat see the novel by Daniele Varè, *The Maker of Heavenly Trousers*, London, 1943, p. 198.
35. Karakhan Declaration quoted in O.B. Borisov and B.T. Koloskov, *Soviet-Chinese Relations, 1945–1970*, Bloomington, Ind., 1975, p. 35. 'Borisov' was the pseudonym of Oleg Rakhmanin, the mouthpiece of Soviet orthodoxy during the Sino-Soviet ideological dispute.
36. Quoted in Chiang Kai-shek, *Soviet Russia in China: A Summing-Up at Seventy*, New York, 1957, p. 309; Conrad Brandt, *Stalin's Failure in China, 1924–1927*, Cambridge, MA, 1958, p. 175.
37. Quoted in Orlando Figes, *Natasha's Dance*, London, 2002, p. 418. See also Schimmelpenninck van der Oye, *Russian Orientalism*, p. 222; Rachel Polonsky, *Molotov's Magic Lantern*, London, 2010, p. 208.
38. Yuan-tsung Chen, *Return to the Middle Kingdom: One Family, Three Revolutionaries and the Birth of Modern China*, New York, 2008, p. 98. See also Jung Chang and Jon Halliday, *Mao: The Unknown Story*, London, 2005, p. 27; Alexander V. Pantsov with Steven I. Levine, *Mao: The Real Story*, New York, 2012, p. 105.
39. Jonathan Spence, *Mao*, London, 2000, p. 67.
40. A.I. Kartunova, 'K zavershenyu izdanii serii sbornikov dokumentov, "VKP (b) Komintern i Kitai", 1920-mai 1943 gg', *Problemy Dal'nego Vostoka*, no. 1, 2008, pp. 103–18; Lin Jun, 'Yue Fei yu Huangpu junxiao: Su E dui Zhongguo Guomindang zhengce neimu', in Guan and Luan (eds), *Zhong E guanxi*, p. 296.
41. A.I. Kartunova, review article, 'Politichesky obraz Sun Yat-sena v perepiske I.V. Stalina i G.V. Chicherina s L.M. Karakhanom (1923–1926 gg.)', *Problemy Dal'nego Vostoka*, no. 1, 2010, pp. 124–35.
42. Usov, *Sovietskaya razvedka*, p. 207.
43. Sergeant, *Shanghai*, p. 25.
44. Karakhan quoted in Kartunova, 'Politichesky obraz'.

45. Quoted in Peng Shu-tse, Introduction to Trotsky, *Leon Trotsky on China*, New York, 1976, p. 39.
46. Chang and Halliday, *Mao: The Unknown Story*, p. 32; Lin Jun, 'Yue Fei', in Guan and Luan (eds), *Zhong E guanxi*, p. 303.
47. Lin Jun, 'Yue Fei', in Guan and Luan (eds) *Zhong E guanxi*, p. 296.
48. Kartunova, 'Politichesky obraz'; Lin Jun, 'Yue Fei', in Guan and Luan (eds), *Zhong E guanxi*, p. 305.
49. Chicherin to Karakhan, 24 October 1923, in M.I. Titarenko (ed.-in-chief), *Perepiski I.V. Stalina i G.V. Chicherina s Polpredom SSSR v Kitae LM Karakhanom, Dokumenty avgust 1923–1926*, Moscow, 2008, p. 99.
50. Karakhan to Chicherin, 27 August 1923, in Titarenko (ed.), *Perepiski*, p. 67.
51. Vincent Sheean quoted by M.I. Kazanin in Y.V. Chudodeev (ed.), *Soviet Volunteers in China, 1925–1945*, Moscow, 1980, p. 180.
52. Chen, *Return to the Middle Kingdom*, p. 105.
53. Brandt, *Stalin's Failure in China*, p. 40. Compare Cicero's famous assessment of Octavian as 'a young man to be praised, promoted, and erased'.
54. Chen, *Return to the Middle Kingdom*, pp. 106–7.
55. Peng Shu-tse, Introduction to Trotsky, *Leon Trotsky on China*, p. 44.
56. Dan N. Jacobs, *Borodin: Stalin's Man in China*, Cambridge, MA, 1981, p. 132.
57. Karakhan to Stalin, 8 January 1924, in Titarenko (ed.), *Perepiski*, p. 157; Kartunova, 'Politichesky obraz'.
58. Stalin to Karakhan, 16 June 1924, in Titarenko (ed.). *Perepiski*, p. 237.
59. The US journalist Bill Prohme, quoted in Jacobs, *Borodin*, p. 261.
60. Politburo instructions for Borodin, 31 July 1923, quoted in Kartunova, 'Politichesky obraz'; Usov, *Sovietskaya razvedka*, p. 210. Usov gives the date as 2 August.
61. Zhang Guotao, *The Rise of the Chinese Communist Party*, vol. 1, p. 512; Patrick Lescot, *Before Mao: The Untold Story of Li Lisan and the Creation of Communist China*, New York, 2004, p. 71; Brandt, *Stalin's Failure in China*, p. 76.
62. Blücher report for the period December 1924 to July 1925, quoted in Usov, *Sovietskaya razvedka*, p. 226.
63. Blücher cable to Karakhan, 7 December 1924, quoted in ibid., p. 220.
64. A.I. Kartunova, 'Blücher in China', in Chudodeev (ed.), *Soviet Volunteers in China*, p. 54.
65. Karakhan, 1 March 1925, quoted by A.I. Cherepanov in ibid., p. 33.
66. Trotsky quoted in Yueh Sheng, *Sun Yat-sen University*, p. 32; Jay Taylor, *The Generalissimo's Son: Chiang Ching-kuo and the Revolutions in China and Taiwan*, Cambridge, MA, 2000, p. 30.
67. Stalin to Karakhan, 6 March 1925, in Titarenko (ed.), *Perepiski*, p. 474.
68. Karakhan to Chicherin, 1 February 1925, in ibid., p. 426; Kartunova, 'Politichesky obraz'.
69. Jacobs, *Borodin*, p. 170.
70. Ibid., p. 177.
71. Zhang Guotao, *The Rise of the Chinese Communist Party*, vol. 1, p. 204.
72. Quoted in Usov, *Sovietskaya razvedka*, p. 105.
73. Quoted in Chudodeev (ed.), *Soviet Volunteers in China*, p. 28; Jacobs, *Borodin*, p. 195.
74. Quoted in Usov, *Sovietskaya razvedka*, p. 40.
75. Yuan-tsung Chen, *Return to the Middle Kingdom*, New York, 2008, p. 236.
76. Laura Tyson Li, *Madame Chiang Kai-shek*, New York, 2006, p. 67.
77. Quoted by M.Y. Shass in Chudodeev (ed.), *Soviet Volunteers in China*, p. 137.
78. Alexei Ivanov (A. Ivin), extract from *Pis'ma iz Kitaya*, in Romanenko (ed.), *Kitai u russkikh pisatelei*, pp. 264–5.
79. Vera Vladimirovna Vishnyakova-Akimova, *Two Years in Revolutionary China, 1925–1927*, Cambridge, MA, 1971, p. 2.
80. Ibid., pp. 79, 181.
81. Ibid., p. 62.

82. Ibid., p. 226.
83. Quoted in Lukin, *The Bear Watches the Dragon*, p. 99.
84. See Yu. M. Galenovich, *Pyatdesyat let s Kitaem*, Moscow, 2011, p. 110.
85. Trotsky to Joffe, 1922, quoted in Lukin, *The Bear Watches the Dragon*, p. 85.
86. See Karakhan to Chicherin, 13 October 1923, in Titarenko (ed.), *Perepiski*, pp. 88–9; Usov, *Sovietskaya razvedka*, pp. 122–3.
87. Baabar, *History of Mongolia*, p. 221.
88. Karakhan to Chicherin, 3 November 1923, in Titarenko (ed.), *Perepiski*, p. 105.
89. Karakhan to Chicherin, 10 March 1924, in ibid., pp. 177–8.
90. Franck, *Wandering in Northern China*, p. 166.
91. Joffe, 27 September 1922, quoted in Lukin, *The Bear Watches the Dragon*, p. 85.
92. Usov, *Sovietskaya razvedka*, p. 124.
93. Chicherin to Karakhan, 16 March 1926, in Titarenko (ed.), *Perepiski*, p. 610; Lukin, *The Bear Watches the Dragon*, pp. 88–9; Baabar, *History of Mongolia*, p. 250.
94. Chicherin to Karakhan, 16 March 1926, in Titarenko (ed.), *Perepiski*, p. 610; Lukin, *The Bear Watches the Dragon*, p. 85.
95. Quoted in Baabar, *History of Mongolia*, p. 272.
96. C. Martin Wilbur and Julie Lien-ying How, *Documents on Communism, Nationalism and Soviet Advisers in China: Papers Seized in the 1927 Peking Raid*, New York, 1956, Document 1.
97. See A.V. Blagodatov, 'With the Chinese Revolution', in Chudodeev (ed.), *Soviet Volunteers in China*, p. 99.
98. Quoted by A.N. Kartunova in ibid., p. 57.
99. Song Qingling letters to Borodin, 23 October 1923 and 14 May 1924, in Konstantin Shevelev, 'The Unknown Letters of Song Qingling and Sun Yat-sen to Mikhail Borodin', *Far Eastern Affairs*, no. 2, 2003, pp. 121–6.
100. Quoted in Sladkovsky, *Znakomstvo*, p. 32.
101. See M.I. Kazanin in Chudodeev (ed.), *Soviet Volunteers in China*, p. 181; Spence, *The Search for Modern China*, p. 338; Tyson Li, *Madame Chiang Kai-shek*, p. 66.
102. Chiang Kai-shek, *Soviet Russia in China*, p. 18; Clubb, *China and Russia*, p. 230; Spence, *The Search for Modern China*, p. 335.
103. Chiang Kai-shek, Diaries, 4 November 1923.
104. Chiang Kai-shek, *Soviet Russia in China*, p. 21.
105. Ibid., p. 22.
106. Ibid., p. 51; Brandt, *Stalin's Failure in China*, p. 117.
107. A.V. Blagodatov in Chudodeev (ed.), *Soviet Volunteers in China*, p. 113.
108. Chiang Kai-shek, Diaries, 28 November 1923.
109. Chiang Kai-shek, *Soviet Russia in China*, pp. 23–4.
110. Ibid., p. 35.
111. Spence, *The Search for Modern China*, p. 308.
112. Jonathan D. Spence, *The Gate of Heavenly Peace: The Chinese and Their Revolution 1895–1980*, London, 1982, p. 75. A pun is intended here: the Chinese for 'hunger' (*e*) is a homonym of 'Russia' (*E*).
113. Spence, *The Search for Modern China*, p. 309.
114. Zhang Guotao, *The Rise of the Chinese Communist Party*, vol. 1, p. 208.
115. Du Weihua and Wang Yiqiu (eds), *Zai Sulian zhangda de hongse houdai*, Beijing, 1999, p. 97.
116. Pantsov with Levine, *Mao: The Real Story*, pp. 83–4; Chang and Halliday, *Mao: The Unknown Story*, p. 20.
117. Pantsov with Levine, *Mao: The Real Story*, p. 65.
118. Yueh Sheng, *Sun Yat-sen University*, pp. 63–4.
119. Ibid., pp. 64–5.
120. Ibid., pp. 68, 77–80.
121. Ibid., p. 35.

122. Ibid.; Taylor, *The Generalissimo's Son*, p. 31.
123. Yueh Sheng, *Sun Yat-sen University*, p. 35; Taylor, *The Generalissimo's Son*, p. 31.
124. Yueh Sheng, *Sun Yat-sen University*, p. 89; Elizabeth McGuire, 'Between Revolutions: Chinese Students in Soviet Institutes, 1948–1966', in Thomas P. Bernstein and Hua-yu Li (eds), *China Learns from the Soviet Union, 1949–Present*, Lanham, MD, 2010, accessed at ProQuest Ebook Central, pp. 367–8.
125. Chang and Halliday, *Mao: The Unknown Story*, p. 224.
126. Yueh Sheng, *Sun Yat-sen University*, pp. 166–7. For a more detailed account of the romantic entanglements of Chinese students in 1920s Moscow, see Elizabeth McGuire, *Red at Heart: How Chinese Communists Fell in Love with the Russian Revolution*, Oxford, 2020, pp. 131 and 135 and *passim*.
127. For an account of the transmission of Russian works into China, see Mark Gamsa, *The Chinese Translation of Russian Literature: Three Studies*, Leiden and Boston, MA, 2008.
128. See Douwe W. Fokkema, 'Lu Xun: The Impact of Russian Literature', and Leo Ou-fan Lee, 'Genesis of a Writer: Notes on Lu Xun's Educational Experience, 1891–1909', in Merle Goldman (ed.), *Modern Chinese Literature in the May Fourth Era*, Cambridge, MA, 1977, pp. 99, 184.
129. Lu Xun, 'Foreword to *The Harp*', 9 September 1932, in Lu Xun, *Selected Works*, vol. 3, Beijing, 1980, pp. 183–4.
130. Lu Xun, 'Literature and Sweat', 23 December 1927, in ibid., vol. 2, Beijing, 1980, p. 382.
131. Quoted in Mark Gamsa, *The Reading of Russian Literature in China: A Moral Example and a Manual of Practice*, New York, 2010, p. 31.
132. Pantsov with Levine, *Mao: The Real Story*, p. 89.
133. Ibid., p. 100; Zhang Guotao, *The Rise of the Chinese Communist Party*, vol. 2, p. 139.
134. Chang and Halliday, *Mao: The Unknown Story*, p. 26.
135. RGASPI 532-1-4, pp. 22, 26.
136. Chang and Halliday, *Mao: The Unknown Story*, p. 27.
137. Vishnyakova-Akimova, *Two Years*, p. 268.
138. Tyson Li, *Madame Chiang Kai-shek*, p. 72.
139. Chiang Kai-shek, *Soviet Russia in China*, p. 38; Usov, *Sovietskaya razvedka*, p. 262.
140. Lescot, *Before Mao*, p. 75.
141. Pavlov report, 9 August 1926, in Wilbur and How (eds), *Documents on Communism*, Document 43. The reporter added the qualification, 'He must be hypocritical about this since two fingers on his right hand are stained as dark as smoked sausages.'
142. Pantsov with Levine, *Mao: The Real Story*, p. 165.
143. Chen, *Return to the Middle Kingdom*, p. 204.
144. Borodin quoted by Blücher in A.V. Blagodatov, 'With the Chinese Revolution', in Chudodeev (ed.), *Soviet Volunteers in China*, p. 115.
145. M.I. Kazanin in ibid., p. 169.
146. Lescot, *Before Mao*, p. 76.
147. Brandt, *Stalin's Failure in China*, p. 76.
148. Jiang Yongjing (Chiang Yung-ching), *Baoluoding yu Wuhan zhengquan*, Taipei, 1963, pp. 116–17; Pantsov with Levine, *Mao: The Real Story*, p. 178.
149. Jiang Yongjing (Chiang Yung-ching), *Baoluoding yu Wuhan zhengquan*, p. 117. The activist in question was a certain Luo Yinong.
150. Quoted in A.M. Grigoriev, 'Joseph Stalin's Unpublished Speech on China', *Far Eastern Affairs*, no. 1, 2001, pp. 64–79.
151. Trotsky, *Leon Trotsky on China*, p. 225; Taylor, *The Generalissimo's Son*, p. 42; Tyson Li, *Madame Chiang Kai-shek*, p. 175.
152. Quoted in Lukin, *The Bear Watches the Dragon*, p. 84.
153. See M.Y. Shass in Chudodeev (ed.), *Soviet Volunteers in China*, pp. 141–2.
154. Ibid., p. 142.
155. Vishnyakova-Akimova, *Two Years*, p. 300; Usov, *Sovietskaya razvedka*, p. 278.
156. Kazanin in Chudodeev (ed.), *Soviet Volunteers in China*, p. 174.

157. Blagodatov in ibid., p. 123.
158. Ibid.
159. Ibid., p. 124
160. Yueh Sheng, *Sun Yat-sen University*, pp. 105, 161.
161. Brandt, *Stalin's Failure in China*, p. 137.
162. Jacobs, *Borodin*, p. 271.
163. Ibid.
164. Spence, *The Search for Modern China*, p. 358.
165. Brandt, *Stalin's Failure in China*, p. 153; Jacobs, *Borodin*, p. 295.
166. Blagodatov in Chudodeev (ed.), *Soviet Volunteers in China*, p. 129.
167. Usov, *Sovietskaya razvedka*, p. 293.
168. Ibid.; Chiang Kai-shek, *Soviet Russia in China*, p. 52.
169. Brandt, *Stalin's Failure in China*, p. 162.
170. Michael Share, *Where Empires Collided: Russian and Soviet Relations with Hong Kong, Taiwan and Macao*, Hong Kong, 2007, p. 76.
171. Trotsky, *Leon Trotsky on China*, p. 328.
172. Ibid., pp. 126, 134.
173. Trotsky, *Leon Trotsky on China*, pp. 225–6.
174. Ibid., p. 192.
175. Ibid., p. 247.
176. Ibid., pp. 214, 233; Spence, *The Search for Modern China*, p. 357.
177. Trotsky, *Leon Trotsky on China*, pp. 274, 321–2. Trotsky acidly compared the Canton Soviet to 'an ancient Chinese dragon simply drawn on paper'.
178. Taylor, *The Generalissimo's Son*, p. 36.
179. Ibid., p. 43; Tyson Li, *Madame Chiang Kai-shek*, p. 147.
180. Yueh Sheng, *Sun Yat-sen University*, pp. 141–2. Feng Funeng was the first wife of Chiang Ching-kuo.
181. Ibid., p. 207.
182. Zhang Guotao, *The Rise of the Chinese Communist Party*, vol. 1, p. 637. See also Jacobs, *Borodin*, p. 269.
183. Pantsov with Levine, *Mao: The Real Story*, p. 182.
184. Zhang Guotao, *The Rise of the Chinese Communist Party*, vol. 1, pp. 669–70.

CHAPTER 5: STRATEGY IS KING

1. Stalin to Molotov, 11 July 1927, quoted in Kartunova, 'K zaversheniyu izdanii serii sbornikov dokumentov', pp. 109–18.
2. Quoted by Lin Jun, 'Yue Fei', in Guan and Luan (eds), *Zhong E guanxi*, p. 309.
3. Yueh Sheng, *Sun Yat-sen University*, pp. 174–5.
4. Trotsky, *Leon Trotsky on China*, p. 451.
5. Pantsov with Levine, *Mao: The Real Story*, p. 205.
6. Ibid., pp. 205–6; Chen, *Return to the Middle Kingdom*, p. 282.
7. Lescot, *Before Mao*, p. 109.
8. Pantsov with Levine, *Mao: The Real Story*, p. 276; Richard Evans, *Deng Xiaoping and the Making of Modern China*, London, 1995, p. 30.
9. Yueh Sheng, *Sun Yat-sen University*, p. 261.
10. See Chen, *Return to the Middle Kingdom*, pp. 274–5, 277–8.
11. Ibid., p. 275.
12. As distinct from traditional 'gunboat imperialism' practised by 'friendly countries' such as Britain, the US and Japan. See Xue Xiantian, 'Nanjing zhengfu de "geming waijiao" yu Sulian dui Dongbei de "chengfa zhanzheng"', in Guan and Luan (eds), *Zhong E guanxi*, p. 258.
13. Yueh Sheng, *Sun Yat-sen University*, pp. 104–5.
14. Chang and Halliday, *Mao: The Unknown Story*, p. 74n.

15. Xue Xiantian, 'Nanjing zhengfu de "geming waijiao"', in Guan and Luan (eds), *Zhong E guanxi*, p. 260.
16. Vasilii I. Chuikov, *Mission to China: Memoirs of a Soviet Military Adviser to Chiang Kai-shek*, Norwalk, CT, 2004, p. 169.
17. Quoted in Austin Jersild, *The Sino-Soviet Alliance: An International History*, Chapel Hill, NC, 2014, p. 9.
18. Chang and Halliday, *Mao: The Unknown Story*, p. 75.
19. Ibid.
20. Lescot, *Before Mao*, p. 123.
21. Ibid., p. 126.
22. Ibid., pp. 126, 132.
23. Ibid., p. 133.
24. Pantsov with Levine, *Mao: The Real Story*, p. 235.
25. Clubb, *China and Russia*, p. 299.
26. Yuri Melnikov, 'Russian Fascists in Manchuria', *Far Eastern Affairs*, no. 4, 1991, pp. 178–209.
27. For Araki attitude see Sladkovsky, *Znakomstvo*, p. 199. For quotation see also Philip Snow, 'Nomonhan: The Unknown Victory', *History Today*, July 1990.
28. *Pravda*, 11 November 1936, quoted in Stephan, *The Russian Far East*, p. 200.
29. Peter Fleming, *News from Tartary*, London, 1936, repr. 1995, p. 250.
30. Stalin, Molotov and Voroshilov to Apresov, 27 May 1934, in R.A. Mirovitskaya and A.M. Ledovsky, 'The Soviet Union and the Chinese Province of Xinjiang in the mid-1930s', *Far Eastern Affairs*, no. 4, 2007, pp. 92–103.
31. Allen S. Whiting and Sheng Shih-ts'ai, *Sinkiang: Pawn or Pivot?*, East Lansing, MI, 1958, p. 37.
32. Apresov to Stalin, 7 November 1934, in Mirovitskaya and Ledovsky, 'The Soviet Union and the Chinese Province of Xinjiang in the mid-1930s'.
33. Ibid.
34. Ibid.
35. Ibid.
36. S.G. Luzyanin and R.A. Mirovitskaya, 'SSSR i Kitai (1931–1939)', in V.V. Naumkin (ed.), *SSSR i strany vostoka nakanune i v gody Vtoroi Mirovoi Voiny*, Moscow, 2010, pp. 125–64; Baabar, *History of Mongolia*, p. 318.
37. Baabar, *History of Mongolia*, p. 340.
38. Ibid., p. 344.
39. Ibid., p. 348.
40. Ibid., p. 342.
41. Ibid., p. 348.
42. See Elizabeth Wishnick, *Mending Fences: The Evolution of Moscow's China Policy from Brezhnev to Yeltsin*, Seattle, WA, paperback edn 2014, p. 26.
43. Quoted in Mirovitskaya and Ledovsky, 'The Soviet Union and the Chinese Province of Xinjiang in the mid-1930s'.
44. Quoted by Sun Caishun, 'Wai Menggu duli guocheng shuping', in Guan and Luan (eds), *Zhong E guanxi*, p. 350.
45. Taylor, *The Generalissimo's Son*, p. 62.
46. Ibid., pp. 62–3, 65–6.
47. Huang Dingtian in *Zhong E wenhua guanxi chugao (17 shiji–1937)*, Changchun, 2011.
48. Chang and Halliday, *Mao: The Unknown Story*, p. 102.
49. Ibid., p. 128n.
50. Yang Kuisong, *Mao Zedong yu Mosike de enen yuanyuan*, Nanchang, 1999, p. 16. For reported early Soviet praise of Gao Gang see Nikita Khrushchev, *Khrushchev Remembers: The Last Testament*, trans. and ed. Strobe Talbott, Boston, MA, 1974, p. 237.
51. Taylor, *The Generalissimo's Son*, p. 65.

52. Yang, *Mao Zedong yu Mosike*, pp. 197, 198. The instructions were delivered to Baoan the following November.
53. Dick Wilson, Introduction, in Otto Braun (Li De), *A Comintern Agent in China, 1932–1939*, London, 1982, p. x.
54. Ibid., pp. 55–6; Lescot, 'Before Mao', p. 173.
55. Braun, *A Comintern Agent in China*, p. 58.
56. Ibid., pp. 134–5; Quested, *Sino-Russian Relations*, p. 102; Evans, *Deng Xiaoping*, p. 47; Pantsov with Levine, *The Real Story*, p. 291.
57. Zhang Guotao, *The Rise of the Chinese Communist Party*, vol. 2, 1928–1938, Lawrence, KS, 1972, p. 446.
58. Chang and Halliday, *Mao: The Unknown Story*, p. 190.
59. Ibid., p. 192.
60. Pantsov with Levine, *Mao: The Real Story*, p. 300.
61. Taylor, *The Generalissimo's Son*, p. 74.
62. Chiang Kai-shek, *Soviet Russia in China*, p. 230.
63. Taylor, *The Generalissimo's Son*, p. 75.
64. Ibid., p. 77.
65. Yuan Jiahua, 1929, quoted in Gamsa, *The Chinese Translation of Russian Literature*.
66. Lu Xun, 'The Exhibition of Soviet Graphic Art', in Lu Xun, *Selected Works*, vol. 4, Beijing, 1980, p. 253.
67. Chang and Halliday, *Mao: The Unknown Story*, p. 124.
68. Yang, *Mao Zedong yu Mosike*, p. 18.
69. Lescot, *Before Mao*, p. 171.
70. Braun, *A Comintern Agent*, p. 103; Rana Mitter, *China's War with Japan 1933–1945*, London, 2014, p. 62.
71. Edgar Snow, *Red Star over China*, London, 1972, p. 504.
72. Ibid., p. 505; MacMillan, *Seize the Hour*, p. 69.
73. Snow, *Red Star over China*, p. 505.
74. Yang, *Mao Zedong yu Mosike*, p. 57.
75. Chang and Halliday, *Mao: The Unknown Story*, p. 185.
76. Ibid., p. 193; Pantsov with Levine, *Mao: The Real Story*, p. 301.
77. Pantsov with Levine, *Mao: The Real Story*, p. 302.
78. Yang, *Mao Zedong yu Mosike*, p. 60.
79. Zhang Guotao, *The Rise of the Chinese Communist Party*, vol. 2, p. 486.
80. Pantsov with Levine, *Mao: The Real Story*, p. 302.
81. Yang, *Mao Zedong yu Mosike*, p. 61.
82. Pantsov with Levine, *Mao: The Real Story*, pp. 302–3.
83. Spence, *The Gate of Heavenly Peace*, p. 328.
84. Ibid., p. 341.
85. Lu Xun, 'The Exhibition of Soviet Graphic Art', in Lu Xun, *Selected Works*, vol. 4, p. 255.
86. Quoted in Spence, *The Search for Modern China*, p. 412 and *The Gate of Heavenly Peace*, p. 253.
87. Spence, *The Search for Modern China*, p. 413 and *The Gate of Heavenly Peace*, p. 294.
88. Ellen M. Widmer, 'Qu Qiubai and Russian Literature', in Merle Goldman (ed.), *Modern Chinese Literature*, p. 123.
89. Spence, *The Gate of Heavenly Peace*, p. 293; Gamsa, *The Reading of Russian Literature in China*, p. 72.
90. Luzyanin and Mirovitskaya, 'SSSR i Kitai (1931–1939)', in Naumkin (ed.), *SSSR i strany vostoka*.
91. Quoted in Chang and Halliday, *Mao: The Unknown Story*, p. 210.
92. Chuikov, *Mission to China*, pp. 16–17.
93. For the foregoing figures see Yang in Shen Zhihua (ed.), *A Short History of Sino-Soviet Relations, 1917–1991*, Shanghai, 2018, p. 74; Mitter, *China's War with Japan*, p. 194; Kartunova, 'VKP (b) Komintern i Kitai 1920-mai 1943gg'; Share, *Where Empires Collided*, p. 177.

94. Odd Arne Westad, *Cold War and Revolution: Soviet-American Rivalry and the Origins of the Chinese Civil War, 1944–1946*, New York, 1993, p. 62.
95. Chuikov, *Mission to China*, p. 52.
96. For the foregoing see Du and Wang (eds), *Zai Sulian zhangda de*, pp. 63–81, 82–9, 109–31.
97. Yang, *Mao Zedong yu Mosike*, p. 70; Chang and Halliday, *Mao: The Unknown Story*, p. 213.
98. Zhang Guotao, *The Rise of the Chinese Communist Party*, vol. 2, p. 572.
99. Quoted in R.A. Mirovitskaya, *Kitaiskaya gosudarstvennost i Sovietskaya politika v Kitae, gody tikhookeanskoi voiny, 1941–1945*, Moscow, 1999, p. 46.
100. Chang and Halliday, *Mao: The Unknown Story*, p. 235.
101. Chuikov, *Mission to China*, p. 15.
102. Luzyanin and Mirovitskaya, 'SSSR i Kitai (1931–1939)', in Naumkin (ed.), *SSSR I strany vostoka*.
103. Yang, *Mao Zedong yu Mosike*, p. 111.
104. Whiting and Sheng, *Sinkiang: Pawn or Pivot?*, p. 63.
105. Ibid., p. 224.
106. Lescot, *Before Mao*, p. 224.
107. Ibid., p. 290.
108. Ibid., p. 273.
109. Pantsov and Levine, *Mao: The Real Story*, pp. 332–3.
110. Yang, *Mao Zedong yu Mosike*, p. 68.
111. Chang and Halliday, *Mao: The Unknown Story*, p. 216.
112. Baabar, *History of Mongolia*, p. 356.
113. Ibid., p. 363.
114. Elena Chernolutskaya, 'The Expulsion of Chinese Nationals from the Soviet Far East and their Deportation in 1938', *Far Eastern Affairs*, no. 3, 2008, pp. 109–22.
115. Pyotr Korovyakovsky, 'Chinese Victims of Stalinist Repression', *Far Eastern Affairs*, no. 3, 1991, pp. 170–5; L.E. Razgon, quoted by Zhang Zonghai, 'Miuzhong liuchuan de "huang huo" lun – Zhongguo ren zai Eluosi lizu de lishi genyuan', in Guan and Luan (eds), *Zhong E guanxi*, p. 112. Huge though it was this deportation was dwarfed in scale by the simultaneous eviction of Koreans, 173,000 of whom were transplanted from the Soviet Far East to Kazakhstan and other parts of Soviet Central Asia.
116. Quoted in Philip Snow, 'Nomonhan – The Unknown Victory', *History Today*, July 1990. For a detailed account of the battle of Khalkhin Gol/Nomonhan see Alvin D. Coox, *Nomonhan: Japan against Russia, 1939*, Stanford, CA, 1985.
117. See Vyacheslav Molotov, ed. Albert Resis, *Molotov Remembers: Inside Kremlin Politics, Conversations with Felix Chuev*, Chicago, 1993, p. 21.
118. Sladkovsky, *Znakomstvo*, p. 253.
119. Ivan Maisky, 1 August 1937, in *The Maisky Diaries*, New Haven, CT, and London, 2015, p. 85.
120. Quoted by S.V. Slyusarev, 'Protecting China's Airspace', in Chudodeev (ed.), *Soviet Volunteers in China*, p. 254.
121. A.Y. Kalyagin, 'Along Unfamiliar Roads', ibid., p. 210.
122. Quoted in Harrison E. Salisbury, *The Coming War between Russia and China*, New York, 1969, p. 78.
123. Luzyanin and Mirovitskaya, 'SSSR i Kitai (1931–1939)', in Naumkin (ed.), *SSSR i strany vostoka*.
124. Chiang Kai-shek, *Diaries*, vol. 2, 1 August 1937.
125. Ibid., 30 August 1937.
126. Ibid., 1 January 1938.
127. Kalyagin, 'Along Unfamiliar Roads', in Chudodeev (ed.), *Soviet Volunteers in China*, pp. 210–11, 215; Chuikov, *Mission to China*, p. 113.
128. Kalyagin, 'Along Unfamiliar Roads', in Chudodeev (ed.), *Soviet Volunteers in China*, p. 218.

129. Chuikov, *Mission to China*, p. 81.
130. Mirovitskaya, *Kitaiskaya gosudarstvennost*, p. 45.
131. Ibid., p. 47.
132. Ibid., p. 49.
133. Chuikov, *Mission to China*, p. 80.
134. Chiang Kai-shek, *Diaries*, vol. 2, 4 December 1937.
135. Ibid., 2 April 1941.
136. Mirovitskaya, *Kitaiskaya gosudarstvennost*, p. 69.
137. Zhang Guotao, *The Rise of the Chinese Communist Party*, vol. 2, p. 566.
138. Braun, *A Comintern Agent*, p. 209.
139. Yang, *Mao Zedong yu Mosike*, p. 89.
140. Ibid., p. 108.
141. Pantsov with Levine, *Mao: The Real Story*, p. 320.
142. Chen, *Return to the Middle Kingdom*, p. 324.
143. Yang, *Mao Zedong yu Mosike*, p. 79.
144. Mitter, *China's War with Japan*, p. 286.
145. Whiting and Sheng, *Sinkiang: Pawn or Pivot?*, p. 246; Clubb, *China and Russia*, p. 325; Mirovitskaya, *Kitaiskaya gosudarstvennost*, p. 90.
146. Whiting and Sheng, *Sinkiang: Pawn or Pivot?*, p. 79; Yang, in Shen Zhihua (ed.), *Zhong Su guanxi*, Beijing, 2011, p. 71.
147. Chiang Kai-shek, *Diaries*, vol. 2, 22 June 1941.
148. Chuikov, *Mission to China*, p. 145.
149. Sladkovsky, *Znakomstvo*, p. 268; Chuikov, *Mission to China*, p. 145.
150. Sladkovsky, *Znakomstvo*, p. 268.
151. Chuikov, *Mission to China*, pp. 153–4.
152. Ibid., David P. Barrett Introduction, p. xxix.
153. Whiting and Sheng, *Sinkiang: Pawn or Pivot?*, p. 91.
154. Chiang Kai-shek, *Diaries*, vol. 2, 21 July 1942.
155. Chiang Kai-shek political adviser Owen Lattimore, quoted in Mirovitskaya, *Kitaiskaya gosudarstvennost*, p. 80.
156. Ibid., p. 149.
157. Chang and Halliday, *Mao: The Unknown Story*, p. 245; see also Borisov and Koloskov, *Soviet–Chinese Relations*, p. 119.
158. Vladimirov, 29 July 1942, in Pyotr Vladimirov, *The Vladimirov Diaries, Yen'an, China, 1942–1945*, Moscow, 1974, English translation 1975.
159. Yang, *Mao Zedong yu Mosike*, p. 121 and 'Sino-Soviet Wartime Cooperation and Conflict', in Shen Zhihua (ed.), *A Short History of Sino-Soviet Relations, 1917–1991*, Singapore, 2016, p. 82.
160. Leonid Dolmatov, Soviet radio operator in Yan'an, quoted in *Vladimirov Diaries*, 18 July 1942.
161. Phrase used by Chiang Kai-shek, *Soviet Russia in China*, pp. 110, 367.
162. Borisov and Koloskov, *Soviet-Chinese Relations*, p. 117.
163. Vladimirov, *Diaries*, 29 July 1942.
164. Ibid., 26 October 1942.
165. Ibid., 16 June 1943.
166. Ibid., 4 February 1943.
167. Ibid., 29 July 1943.
168. Ibid., 11 May 1942.
169. Ibid., 12 May 1942.
170. Ibid., 30 May 1942.
171. Ibid., 18 June 1942.
172. Ibid., 12 May 1942.
173. Ibid., 11 November 1942.
174. Ibid., 30 August 1942.

175. Ibid., 13 December 1942.
176. Ibid., 19 December 1943.
177. Yu Miin-ling, '"Labour is Glorious": Model Labourers in the PRC', in Bernstein and Li (eds), *China Learns from the Soviet Union*, pp. 231–58.
178. Vladimirov, *Diaries*, 10 October 1943.
179. Ibid., 30 December 1944.
180. David D. Wang, *Under the Soviet Shadow: The Yining Incident*, Hong Kong, 1999, p. 67.
181. Quoted by Li Sheng, 'Sulian yu Xinjiang San Qu geming', in Guan and Luan (eds), *Zhong E guanxi*, p. 372.
182. Wang, *Under the Soviet Shadow*, p. 150.
183. Ibid., pp. 130, 150. The actual drafting of the Declaration has been ascribed to a Soviet consul named Borisov.
184. Ibid., p. 125.
185. Clubb, *China and Russia*, p. 337; Mirovitskaya, *Kitaiskaya gosudarstvennost*, p. 199.
186. Quoted in Wang, *Under the Soviet Shadow*, p. 93.
187. Mirovitskaya, *Kitaiskaya gosudarstvennost*, pp. 251–2.
188. Ibid., p. 254.
189. Sun Caishun, 'Wai Menggu duli guocheng shuping', in Guan and Luan (eds), *Zhong E guanxi*, p. 359; Yang, 'Sino-Soviet Wartime Cooperation and Conflict', in Shen Zhihua (ed.), *A Short History*, p. 87.
190. Mirovitskaya, *Kitaiskaya gosudarstvennost*, p. 269.
191. Ibid.
192. Ibid., p. 253.
193. Yang, 'Sino-Soviet Wartime Cooperation and Conflict', in Shen Zhihua (ed.), *A Short History*, p. 89.
194. Quoted in Westad, *Cold War and Revolution*, p. 41.
195. Ibid., p. 49.
196. Mirovitskaya, *Kitaiskaya gosudarstvennost*, p. 231.
197. Quoted in Molotov, ed. Resis, *Molotov Remembers*, p. 8.
198. Chang and Halliday, *Mao: The Unknown Story*, p. 268.
199. Yang, *Mao Zedong yu Mosike*, p. 160; Chang and Halliday, *Mao: The Unknown Story*, p. 268.
200. Clubb, *China and Russia*, pp. 334, 341.
201. Taylor, *The Generalissimo's Son*, p. 122.
202. Khrushchev, *Khrushchev Remembers*, p. 512; Pantsov with Levine, *Mao: The Real Story*, p. 343; Sergey Radchenko, *Two Suns*, p. 5. A 'radish' was someone who was Red on the outside but White within.
203. Zhang Shengfa, 'The Main Causes of the Return of the Changchun Railway to China and Its Impact on Sino-Soviet Relations', in Bernstein and Li (eds), *China Learns from the Soviet Union*, pp. 61–78.
204. Vladimirov, *Diaries*, 26 August 1945.
205. Ibid.
206. Chang and Halliday, *Mao: The Unknown Story*, p. 270.
207. Vladimirov, *Diaries*, 8 January 1944.
208. Ibid., 26 February 1945 and 5 March 1945; Chang and Halliday, *Mao: The Unknown Story*, p. 293.
209. Vladimirov, *Diaries*, 21 April 1945.
210. Chiang Kai-shek, *Diaries*, vol. 2, 29 January 1945.
211. Westad, *Cold War and Revolution*, p. 41.
212. T.V. Soong observation, 10 August 1945, Luzyanin and Mirovitskaya, 'SSSR i Kitai (1939–1945)', in Naumkin (ed.), *SSSR i strany vostoka*.
213. Sun Caishun, 'Wai Menggu duli guocheng shuping', in Guan and Luan (eds), *Zhong E guanxi*, p. 357.

214. Sladkovsky, *Znakomstvo*, pp. 285–6.
215. Ibid., p. 286.
216. Vladimirov, *Diaries*, 15 July 1944; Chang and Halliday, *Mao: The Unknown Story*, p. 304.
217. Vladimirov, *Diaries*, 21 April 1945.
218. Quoted by Luzyanin and Mirovitskaya, 'SSSR i Kitai (1939–1945)', in Naumkin (ed.), *SSSR i strany vostoka.*
219. Yang, 'China's Civil War', in Shen Zhihua (ed.), *A Short History*, p. 97, and Yang, *Mao Zedong yu Mosike*, p. 216.
220. Vladimirov, *Diaries*, 28 August 1945.
221. Ibid., 2 August 1945.
222. Christian A. Hess, 'From Colonial Jewel to Socialist Metropolis, Dalian, 1895–1955', dissertation, University of California, San Diego, 2006, p. 183.
223. Molotov, ed. Resis, *Molotov Remembers*, p. 71.
224. See for example Zhang Jia'ao (Chang Kia-ngau), ed. Donald G. Gillin and Ramon H. Myers, trans. Dolores Zen, *Last Chance in Manchuria: The Diary of Chang Kia-ngau*, Stanford, CA, 1989, diary entry 23 November 1945.
225. Ibid., diary entry 24 February 1946.
226. Frank Dikötter, *The Tragedy of Liberation: A History of the Chinese Revolution, 1945–57*, London, 2013, p. 15.
227. Meyer, *In Manchuria*, p. 159.
228. Yang, *Mao Zedong yu Mosike*, p. 220.
229. Ibid., p. 235.
230. Chiang Kai-shek, *Soviet Russia in China*, pp. 169–70.
231. Westad, *Cold War and Revolution*, p. 123.
232. Ibid., p. 125.
233. Hess, 'From Colonial Jewel to Socialist Metropolis, Dalian, 1895–1955', p. 191.
234. Mirovitskaya, *Kitaiskaya gosudarstvennost*, p. 241.
235. Valery Barmin, 'Xinjiang in the History of Soviet–Chinese relations from 1937 to 1945', *Far Eastern Affairs*, no. 1, 1 January 2000.
236. Wang, *Under the Soviet Shadow*, p. 170.
237. Ibid., p. 171.
238. Taylor, *The Generalissimo's Son*, p. 139; Sergei Goncharov, John W. Lewis and Xue Litai, *Uncertain Partners: Stalin, Mao and the Korean War*, Stanford, CA, 1993, p. 299 n.55.
239. Report of Stalin meeting with Chiang Ching-kuo meeting 30 December 1945, document appended to A.M. Ledovsky, 'Stalin i Chan Kaishi sekretnaya missiya syna Chan Kaishi v Moskvu, Dekabr dekabr 1945–Iyanvar ianvar 1946', *Novaya i Noveishaya Istoria*, no. 4, 1996, pp. 100–29.
240. Ibid.
241. Ibid.
242. Ibid.
243. Ibid.
244. Zhang Jia'ao, *Last Chance in Manchuria*, diary entries pp. 110 (11 November 1945), 149 (6 December 1945), 298–300 (27 March 1946).
245. Wang, *Under the Soviet Shadow*, p. 228.
246. Quoted in Zhang Jia'ao, *Last Chance in Manchuria*, diary entry p. 159 (8 December 1945).
247. Ibid., p. 208 (18 January 1946).
248. Chiang Kai-shek, *Diaries*, vol. 2, 15 January 1946.
249. Ibid., 11 May 1946.
250. Westad, *Cold War and Revolution*, p. 90.
251. Quoted in Chang and Halliday, *Mao: The Unknown Story*, p. 305.
252. Yang, *Mao Zedong yu Mosike*, p. 244.
253. Hess, 'From Colonial Jewel to Socialist Metropolis, Dalian, 1895–1955', p. 219.

254. Chang and Halliday, *Mao: The Unknown Story*, p. 303.
255. Ibid., p. 307.
256. Quoted in Andrei Ledovsky, 'Correspondence between Mao Zedong and Joseph Stalin', *Far Eastern Affairs*, no. 6, 2000, pp. 89–96.
257. Mao observation to Mikoyan, quoted by Sergei Goncharov, 'Sino-Soviet Military Cooperation', in Westad (ed.) *Brothers in Arms*, p. 144.
258. Mao Zedong, *Selected Works*, vol. V, Beijing, 1977, p. 304.
259. Whiting and Sheng, *Sinkiang: Pawn or Pivot?*, p. 117.
260. Khrushchev, *Khrushchev Remembers*, p. 239.
261. Yang, *Mao Zedong yu Mosike*, p. 257.
262. Quoted in Chang and Halliday, *Mao: The Unknown Story*, p. 356.
263. Ibid., p. 358.
264. Stalin remarks widely quoted, but with slight variations in the wording. See memoir of the Chinese interpreter, Shi Zhe, *Zai lishi juren shenbian*, Beijing, 1998, pp. 370–1; Steven M. Goldstein, 'Nationalism and Internationalism: Sino-Soviet Relations', in Robinson and Shambaugh (eds), *Chinese Foreign Policy: Theory and Practice*, Oxford, 1994, p. 233; Goncharov, Lewis and Xue, *Uncertain Partners*, p. 73; MacMillan, *Seize the Hour*, p. 127.
265. Shi Zhe, 'I Accompanied Chairman Mao', *Far Eastern Affairs*, no. 2, 1989, pp. 125–39. See also Goldstein, 'Nationalism and Internationalism', in Robinson and Shambaugh (eds), *Chinese Foreign Policy*, pp. 233–4.
266. Wang, *Under the Soviet Shadow*, p. 71.
267. Ibid., pp. 380–1. See also Lukin, *The Bear Watches the Dragon*, p. 120.
268. A.M. Ledovsky, 'The Moscow Visit of a Delegation of the CCP in June–August 1945', *Far Eastern Affairs*, no. 4, 1996, pp. 64–86.
269. Sladkovsky, *Znakomstvo*, p. 323.
270. Yang, *Mao Zedong yu Mosike*, p. 277.
271. Sladkovsky, *Znakomstvo*, pp. 327–8.
272. Shi Zhe, 'I Accompanied Chairman Mao', *Far Eastern Affairs*, no. 2, 1989.
273. Ibid.
274. Kovalev report, Goncharov, Lewis and Xue, *Uncertain Partners*, p. 68.
275. M.S. Kapitsa, *Na raznykh parallelyakh: zapiski diplomata*, Moscow, 1996, p. 45.
276. Ibid.; Paul Wingrove, 'Gao Gang and the Moscow Connection: Some Evidence from Russian Sources', *Journal of Communist Studies and Transition Politics*, vol. 16, no. 4, 2000, pp. 88–106; Goncharov, Lewis and Xue, *Uncertain Partners*, p. 68.
277. See Pantsov with Levine, *Mao: The Real Story*, p. 395.
278. Chen Hui, 'Ma xie er tiao chu shiqi Sulian dui Hua zhengce de yanbian', in Guan and Luan (eds), '*Zhong E guanxi*', p. 393.
279. Quoted in Du and Wang, *Zai Sulian zhangda de*, p. 74. A *kang* is a traditional heated brick platform used in north China for sleeping and general living purposes.
280. Ibid., p. 84.
281. Chang and Halliday, *Mao: The Unknown Story*, p. 354.
282. Shi Zhe, *Zai lishi juren shenbian*, pp. 343–4; Goncharov, Lewis and Xue, *Uncertain Partners*, p. 41; Jersild, *The Sino-Soviet Alliance*, p. 177.
283. Hess, 'From Colonial Jewel to Socialist Metropolis, Dalian, 1895–1955', pp. 230–4.
284. Goncharov, Lewis and Xue, *Uncertain Partners*, p. 74.

CHAPTER 6: REBELLION

1. Quoted in Lukin, *The Bear Watches the Dragon*, p. 118.
2. Chang and Halliday, *Mao: The Unknown Story*, p. 334; Galenovich, *Pyatdesyat let s Kitaem*, p. 169.
3. Jersild, *The Sino-Soviet Alliance*, p. 11.
4. AVPRF 100-43-305-721.

5. Chang and Halliday, *Mao: The Unknown Story*, p. 367.
6. Ibid.
7. Quoted in Harrison E. Salisbury, *To Peking – and Beyond: A Report on the New Asia*, New York, 1973, p. 8.
8. For full text of the treaty see Goncharov, Lewis and Xue, *Uncertain Partners*, document 45, pp. 260–1.
9. Chang and Halliday, *Mao: The Unknown Story*, p. 365; Vladislav Zubok, Commentary on Stalin–Mao meetings in 1949–50, *CWIHP Bulletin*, issues 6–7, winter 1995–6, pp. 24–7.
10. Kovalev quoted in Pantsov with Levine, *Mao: The Real Story*, p. 369.
11. BBC News report, 28 January 2016.
12. Nikolai Fedorenko, 'The Stalin–Mao summit in Moscow', *Far Eastern Affairs*, no. 2, 1989, pp. 134–48.
13. Ibid.
14. Shi Zhe, *Zai lishi juren shenbian*, p. 407.
15. Yang, *Mao Zedong yu Mosike*, p. 304.
16. Shi Zhe, *Zai lishi juren shenbian*, pp. 415–16; Chang and Halliday, *Mao: The Unknown Story*, p. 369.
17. See record of Stalin–Mao meeting, 16 December 1949, appended to Westad (ed.), *Brothers in Arms*, p. 315.
18. See record of Stalin–Mao meeting, 22 January 1950, ibid., p. 327.
19. Chang and Halliday, *Mao: The Unknown Story*, p. 355.
20. Shi Zhe, *Zai lishi juren shenbian*, p. 387.
21. Steven M. Goldstein, 'Nationalism and Internationalism', in Robinson and Shambaugh (eds), *Chinese Foreign Policy*, p. 234.
22. Ibid. See also Shi Zhe, *Zai lishi juren shenbian*, p. 388; Goncharov, Lewis and Xue, *Uncertain Partners*, p. 86.
23. Quoted in Shi Zhe, *Zai lishi juren shenbian*, p. 391.
24. Pantsov with Levine, *Mao: The Real Story*, p. 371.
25. Shi Zhe, *Zai lishi juren shenbian*, p. 394.
26. Yang, *Mao Zedong yu Mosike*, p. 304.
27. Shi Zhe, *Zai lishi juren shenbian*, p. 408. See also Yang, *Mao Zedong yu Mosike*, p. 305; Goncharov, Lewis and Xue, *Uncertain Partners*, p. 104; Chang and Halliday, *Mao: The Unknown Story*, p. 368.
28. Shi Zhe, *Zai lishi juren shenbian*, p. 408.
29. Ibid., pp. 408–9; see also Chang and Halliday, *Mao: The Unknown Story*, p. 368.
30. Quoted in Shi Zhe, *Zai lishi juren shenbian*, p. 389.
31. Record of Stalin–Mao meeting, 16 December 1949, appended to Westad (ed.), *Brothers in Arms*, p. 315.
32. Ibid., p. 316.
33. Shi Zhe, *Zai lishi juren shenbian*, pp. 401–2; Goncharov, Lewis and Xue, *Uncertain Partners*, p. 120.
34. Shi Zhe, *Zai lishi juren shenbian*, p. 398; Yang, *Mao Zedong yu Mosike*, pp. 309–10.
35. Chen Jian, 'Comparing Russian and Chinese Sources: A New Point of Departure for Cold War History' and Mark Kramer, 'The USSR Foreign Ministry's Appraisal of Sino-Soviet Relations on the Eve of the Split, September 1959', *CWIHP Bulletin*, issues 6–7, winter 1995–6, pp. 20, 172. See also Michael Yahuda, *China's Role in World Affairs*, London, 1978, p. 51.
36. Record of Stalin–Mao meeting, 22 January 1950, appended to Westad (ed.), *Brothers in Arms*, p. 328.
37. Ibid. See also Pantsov with Levine, *Mao: The Real Story*, p. 372.
38. Chang and Halliday, *Mao: The Unknown Story*, p. 369.
39. Salisbury, *To Peking – and Beyond*, pp. 6–7.
40. Quoted in Simon Sebag Montefiore, *Stalin: The Court of the Red Tsar*, London, 2004, p. 618.

41. Goncharov, Lewis and Xue, *Uncertain Partners*, p. 145; Chang and Halliday, *Mao: The Unknown Story*, p. 376.
42. Pantsov with Levine, *Mao: The Real Story*, p. 381.
43. Sebag-Montefiore, *Stalin*, p. 622. An alternative account has Zhou 'gasping' in response to a broader disquisition by Stalin on why the Soviet Union couldn't enter the war in Korea and China should. See Goncharov, Lewis and Xue, *Uncertain Partners*, pp. 188–9.
44. Ibid., p. 260.
45. Quoted in Yang, *Mao Zedong yu Mosike*, p. 337.
46. Pantsov with Levine, *Mao: The Real Story*, p. 384.
47. Shi Zhe, *Zai lishi juren shenbian*, p. 446.
48. Ibid. See also Chang and Halliday, *Mao: The Unknown Story*, p. 379.
49. Goncharov, Lewis and Xue, *Uncertain Partners*, p. 197.
50. Ibid., p. 195.
51. Chen Jian and Yang Kuisong, 'Chinese Politics and the Collapse of the Sino-Soviet Alliance', in Westad (ed.), *Brothers in Arms*, p. 284 n.58.
52. Quoted in Khrushchev, *Khrushchev Remembers: The Last Testament*, p. 243.
53. Wang, *Under the Soviet Shadow*, p. 331.
54. Record of Stalin–Mao meeting, 16 December 1949, appended to Westad (ed.), *Brothers in Arms*, p. 318.
55. Chang and Halliday, *Mao: The Unknown Story*, p. 398.
56. Khrushchev, *Khrushchev Remembers*, p. 464.
57. Quoted in Austin T. Jersild, 'Soviet Bloc Komandirovka and its Consequences in China, 1950–1960', paper delivered at University of Hong Kong conference February 2012, *Mao's China: Non-Communist Asia and the Global Setting, 1949–1976*. See also Jersild, *The Sino-Soviet Alliance*, pp. 44–5.
58. See Douglas Stiffler, '"Three Blows of the Shoulder Pole": Soviet Experts at Chinese People's University, 1950–1957', in Bernstein and Li (eds), *China Learns from the Soviet Union*, p. 311.
59. Ilya Ehrenburg in Romanenko (ed.), *Kitai u russkikh pisatelei*, pp. 378–9.
60. Report of Stalin–Zhou meeting, 19 September 1952, appended to Westad (ed.), *Brothers in Arms*, pp. 333–4; Chang and Halliday, *Mao: The Unknown Story*, p. 388.
61. Zhang Shengfa, 'The Main Causes for the Return of the Changchun Railway to China and its Impact on Sino-Soviet Relations', in Bernstein and Li (eds), *China Learns from the Soviet Union*, p. 74.
62. AVPRF 100-46-306-40.
63. Chang and Halliday, *Mao: The Unknown Story*, p. 369n.
64. SMA C 210-2-310-20.
65. Borisov and Koloskov, *Soviet-Chinese Relations*, p. 124.
66. AVPRF 100-46-342-9.
67. Li Hua-yu, 'Instilling Stalinism in Chinese Party Members: Absorbing Stalin's *Short Course* in the 1950s', in Bernstein and Li (eds), *China Learns from the Soviet Union*, p. 122.
68. Ehrenburg in Romanenko (ed.), p. 382.
69. Quoted in Cheng Chu-yuan, *Economic Relations between Peking and Moscow*, 1949–63, New York and London, 1964, p. 91.
70. Chang and Halliday, *Mao: The Unknown Story*, p. 276n.
71. Lowell Dittmer, *Liu Shaoqi and the Chinese Cultural Revolution*, New York and London, 1998, p. 10.
72. Constantine Pleshakov, 'Nikita Khrushchev and Sino-Soviet Relations', in Westad (ed.), *Brothers in Arms*, p. 241 n.11.
73. Wingrove, 'Gao Gang and the Moscow Connection', *Journal of Communist Studies and Transition Politics*, vol. 16, no. 4, 2000, pp. 88–106.
74. Record of Stalin–Zhou meeting, 19 September 1952, appended to Westad (ed.), *Brothers in Arms*, p. 333.

75. Thomas P. Bernstein, 'Introduction: The Complexities of Learning from the Soviet Union', in Bernstein and Li (eds), *China Learns from the Soviet Union*, p. 17.
76. Quoted in Pantsov with Levine, *Mao: The Real Story*, p. 409.
77. Report on Soviet–Chinese relations of M. Zimyanin, head of Far Eastern Department of Soviet Foreign Ministry, prepared for Khrushchev, 15 September 1959, appended to Westad (ed.), *Brothers in Arms*, p. 357.
78. Quoted in Khrushchev, *Khrushchev Remembers*, p. 513.
79. Quoted in ibid., p. 246.
80. Quoted in Yang, *Mao Zedong yu Mosike*, p. 409.
81. Goldstein, 'Nationalism and Internationalism', in Robinson and Shambaugh (eds), *Chinese Foreign Policy*, p. 236. See also Bernstein, 'Introduction: The Complexities of Learning from the Soviet Union', in Bernstein and Li (eds), *China Learns from the Soviet Union*, p. 19.
82. Quoted in Khrushchev, *Khrushchev Remembers: The Last Testament*, p. 269.
83. Qian Qichen, *Ten Episodes in China's Diplomacy*, New York, 2005, p. 162. An official Soviet figure of 'over 11,000' for the number of Chinese students received in the USSR between 1951 and 1962 is given in Borisov and Koloskov, *Soviet–Chinese Relations*, pp. 161, 165.
84. Shi Zhe, *Zai lishi juren shenbian*, pp. 435–6.
85. Andrei Krushinsky, letter to mother, September 1957, in Krushinsky, 'Kartiny na "Chistom Liste" ili, Bolshoi Skachok glazami ochevidtsa', part 1, *Problemy Dal'nego Vostoka*, no. 5, 2008, pp. 152–70.
86. Quoted in Jersild, *The Sino-Soviet Alliance*, p. 40.
87. McGuire, 'Between Revolutions', in Bernstein and Li (eds), *China Learns from the Soviet Union*, p. 375.
88. Quoted in Jersild, *The Sino-Soviet Alliance*, p. 41.
89. Quoted by Deborah A. Kaple, 'Soviet Advisers in China in the 1950s', in Westad (ed.), *Brothers in Arms*, p. 129.
90. Speech of 5 July 1955 quoted in Cheng Chu-yuan, *Economic Relations*, p. 37.
91. Record of Mao conversation with Ambassador Yudin, 22 July 1958, document appended to Westad (ed.), *Brothers in Arms*, p. 355.
92. Salisbury, *To Peking – and Beyond*, pp. 96–7.
93. Qian Qichen, *Ten Episodes in China's Diplomacy*, New York, 2005, p. 161.
94. For more details see McGuire, *Red at Heart*, p. 294.
95. Valentin Ovechkin in Romanenko (ed.), *Kitai u russkikh pisatelei*, p. 430.
96. B.A. Galin in ibid., p. 439.
97. Boris Polevoi in ibid., p. 451.
98. Jersild, *The Sino-Soviet Alliance*, p. 91.
99. Polevoi in Romanenko (ed.), *Kitai u russkikh pisatelei*, p. 456.
100. Ovechkin in ibid., pp. 433–4.
101. T.A. Hsia, 'Demons in Paradise: The Chinese Image of Russia', in *Annals of the American Academy of Political and Social Science*, no. 345, September 1963, pp. 27–37.
102. He Donghui, 'Coming of Age in the Brave New World: The Changing Reception of *How the Steel was Tempered* in the People's Republic of China', in Bernstein and Li (eds), *China Learns from the Soviet Union*, p. 395.
103. Yang, *Mao Zedong yu Mosike*, p. 387.
104. Salisbury, *To Peking – and Beyond*, pp. 8–9.
105. Pantsov with Levine, *Mao: The Real Story*, p. 408.
106. Salisbury, *The Coming War between Russia and China*, pp. 113–14.
107. Pantsov with Levine, *Mao: The Real Story*, p. 410.
108. Quoted in Khrushchev, *Khrushchev Remembers: The Last Testament*, p. 285.
109. Shen Zhihua in Shen Zhihua (ed.), *Zhong Su guanxi*, p. 180.
110. Quoted in Li Hua, '1957 nian Sulian gaoceng zhengbian yu Zhonggong zhongyang de fanying', in Guan and Luan (eds), *Zhong E guanxi*, pp. 447–8.

111. Pantsov with Levine, *Mao: The Real Story*, p. 398.
112. Ibid., pp. 398–9.
113. Wingrove, 'Gao Gang and the Moscow Connection'; Dikötter, *The Tragedy of Liberation*, p. 233.
114. Mao Zedong, *Selected Works*, vol. V, Beijing, 1977, p. 162. See also Spence, *The Search for Modern China*, p. 542; Pantsov with Levine, *Mao: The Real Story*, p. 405.
115. Alexander V. Pantsov with Steven I. Levine, *Deng Xiaoping: A Revolutionary Life*, Oxford, 2015, p. 160.
116. Dikötter, *The Tragedy of Liberation*, p. 234.
117. Mao, *Selected Works*, vol. V, p. 168.
118. Zhang Baichun and Zhang Jiuchun, 'Zhong Su jishu hezuo de jingyan jiaoxun yu qishi', in Guan and Luan (eds), *Zhong E guanxi*, p. 549.
119. Li Zhisui, *The Private Life of Chairman Mao*, London, 1996, p. 68.
120. Ibid., p. 136.
121. Bernstein, 'Introduction: The Complexities of Learning from the Soviet Union', in Bernstein and Li (eds), *China Learns from the Soviet Union*, p. 18.
122. Mao, *Selected Works*, vol. V, p. 278.
123. Chang and Halliday, *Mao: The Unknown Story*, p. 429.
124. S. Goncharov and Li Danhui, 'On "Territorial Claims" and "Inequitable Treaties" in Russian–Chinese Relations: Myth and Reality', *Far Eastern Affairs*, no. 3, 2004, pp. 94–110.
125. Shi Zhe, *Zai lishi juren shenbian*, p. 511; Li Hua, '*1957 nian*', in Guan and Luan (eds), *Zhong E guanxi*, p. 447.
126. Wingrove, 'Gao Gang and the Moscow Connection'.
127. Quoted in Khrushchev, *Khrushchev Remembers: The Last Testament*, p. 252.
128. Quoted Khrushchev, *Khrushchev Remembers*, p. 466; *Khrushchev Remembers: The Last Testament*, p. 245. See also MacMillan, *Seize the Hour*, p. 125.
129. Quoted in Khrushchev, *Khrushchev Remembers*, p. 517.
130. Share, *Where Empires Collided*, p. 185; Czeslaw Tubilewicz, 'Taiwan and the Soviet Union during the Cold War: Enemies or Ambiguous Friends?', *Cold War History*, vol. 5, issue 1, February 2005, pp. 75–86.
131. Galenovich, *Pyatdesyat let s Kitaem*, p. 92.
132. Quoted in John Gittings, *The World and China, 1922–1972*, London, 1974, p. 200. See also Yahuda, *China's Role*, p. 81.
133. Zhang Zonghai, 'Miuzhong liuchuan de "huang huo" lun', in Guan and Luan (eds), *Zhong E guanxi*, pp. 113–14. See also Yahuda, *China's Role*, p. 81.
134. Salisbury, *The Coming War between Russia and China*, p. 101.
135. Deborah A. Kaple, 'Soviet Advisers in China in the 1950s', in Westad (ed.), *Brothers in Arms*, p. 129.
136. Ibid.
137. Ibid.
138. Krushinsky, *Diaries*, 17 March 1958, in Krushinsky, 'Kartiny na "Chistom Liste" ili, Bolshoi Skachok glazami ochevidtsa'.
139. Galenovich, *Pyatdesyat let s Kitaem*, p. 47.
140. Mikhail A. Klochko, trans. Andrew MacAndrew, *Soviet Scientist in Red China*, New York, 1964, p. 56.
141. McGuire, 'Between Revolutions', in Bernstein and Li (eds), *China Learns from the Soviet Union*, pp. 359–89 and *Red at Heart*, p. 287.
142. Pantsov with Levine, *Deng Xiaoping*, p. 171.
143. '*Jie gaizi*', in Chinese. In other words, he had 'exposed the problems'. See Chen and Yang, 'Chinese Politics', in Westad (ed.), *Brothers in Arms*, p. 260.
144. Li Zhisui, *The Private Life of Chairman Mao*, p. 117.
145. Mao, *Selected Works*, vol. V, p. 304; Yahuda, *China's Role*, p. 51; Goncharov, Lewis and Xue, *Uncertain Partners*, p. 122.

146. Chen Jian and Yang, 'Chinese Politics', in Westad (ed.), *Brothers in Arms*, p. 260.
147. Mao, *Selected Works*, vol. V, 'On the Ten Major Relationships', p. 304.
148. Ibid.
149. Quoted in Sergey Radchenko, *Two Suns in the Heavens*, Washington DC and Stanford, CA, 2009, p. 10. See also Mao, *Selected Works*, vol. V, p. 304; Chen Jian and Yang, 'Chinese Politics', in Westad (ed.), *Brothers in Arms*, p. 261.
150. Mao, *Selected Works*, vol. V, 'Strengthen Party Unity and Carry Forward Party Traditions', pp. 316–17.
151. Elizabeth Wishnick, *Mending Fences: The Evolution of Moscow's China Policy from Brezhnev to Yeltsin*, Seattle and London, 2014, pp. 205–6 n.87.
152. Mao, *Selected Works*, vol. V, p. 341.
153. Ibid.
154. Quoted in Li Zhisui, *The Private Life of Chairman Mao*, p. 115.
155. Lorenz Lüthi, *The Sino-Soviet Split*, Princeton, NJ, 2008, p. 55; Pantsov with Levine, *Mao: The Real Story*, p. 435; Jersild, *The Sino-Soviet Alliance*, pp. 118–19.
156. Quoted in Khrushchev, *Khrushchev Remembers*, p. 459.
157. Chen Jian and Yang, 'Chinese Politics', in Westad (ed.), *Brothers in Arms*, pp. 264–5.
158. Pantsov with Levine, *Deng Xiaoping*, p. 181.
159. See Vladislav Zubok, 'Look What Chaos in the Beautiful Socialist Camp!', *CWIHP Bulletin*, issue 10, 1998, pp. 152–62.
160. Quoted in Yahuda, *China's Role*, p. 89; Yang, *Mao Zedong yu Mosike*, pp. 403, 411; Chang and Halliday, *Mao: The Unknown Story*, p. 424. See also Pantsov with Levine, *Mao: The Real Story*, p. 439.
161. Quoted in Yang, *Mao Zedong yu Mosike*, p. 395. See also Pantsov and Levine, *Mao: The Real Story*, p. 439.
162. Mori Kazuko, 'A Brief Analysis of the Sino-Soviet Alliance: The Political Process of 1957–1959', Parallel History Project on NATO and the Warsaw Pact: The Cold War History of Sino-Soviet Relations, June 2005.
163. Mao speech to provincial leaders, 21 January 1957, quoted in Shen Zhihua (ed.), *Zhong Su guanxi*.
164. Chang and Halliday, *Mao: The Unknown Story*, p. 427.
165. Ibid., p. 429.
166. Ibid., pp. 428–9.
167. Ibid., p. 429. See also William Taubman, 'Khrushchev vs. Mao: A Preliminary Sketch of the Role of Personality in the Sino-Soviet Split', *CWIHP Bulletin*, issues 8–9, 1996–9, pp. 243–8; Shen Zhihua in Shen Zhihua (ed.), *Zhong Su guanxi*, p. 200 and *A Short History*, p. 198.
168. Quoted in Khrushchev, *Khrushchev Remembers: The Last Testament*, p. 255.
169. Quoted in Pantsov with Levine, *Mao: The Real Story*, pp. 445–6.
170. Goldstein, 'Nationalism and Internationalism', in Robinson and Shambaugh (eds), *Chinese Foreign Policy*, p. 242.
171. Li Zhisui, *The Private Life of Chairman Mao*, p. 282.
172. Shen Zhihua, in Shen Zhihua (ed.), *A Short History*, p. 212.
173. Quoted in Yang, *Mao Zedong yu Mosike*, p. 443.
174. Chang and Halliday, *Mao: The Unknown Story*, p. 426.
175. Yang, *Mao Zedong yu Mosike*, p. 434; Chang and Halliday, *Mao: The Unknown Story*, p. 430.
176. Quoted in Pleshakov, 'Nikita Khrushchev and Sino-Soviet Relations', in Westad (ed.), *Brothers in Arms*, p. 236; Radchenko, *Two Suns*, p. 13.
177. Record of Mao conversation with Ambassador Yudin, 22 July 1958, appended to Westad (ed.), *Brothers in Arms*, p. 352.
178. Li Zhisui, *The Private Life of Chairman Mao*, p. 261; see also Pleshakov, 'Nikita Khrushchev and Sino-Soviet Relations', in Westad (ed.), *Brothers in Arms*, p. 236; Taubman, 'Khrushchev vs. Mao', *CWIHP Bulletin*, issues 8–9, 1996–7, pp. 243–8; Frank Dikötter, *Mao's Great Famine*, London, 2010, p. 44.

179. Taubman, 'Khrushchev vs. Mao', *CWIHP Bulletin*, issues 8–9, 1996–7, pp. 243–8.
180. Ibid.; Dikötter, *Mao's Great Famine*, p. 44.
181. Quoted in Khrushchev, *Khrushchev Remembers*, p. 522; Lescot, *Before Mao*, p. 296. See also Henry Kissinger, *On China*, New York and London, 2011, p. 168.
182. Li Zhisui, *The Private Life of Chairman Mao*, pp. 261–2.
183. Chang and Halliday, *Mao: The Unknown Story*, p. 425.
184. Ibid.
185. Mao, *Selected Works*, vol. V, p. 363.
186. Li Zhisui, *The Private Life of Chairman Mao*, p. 262.
187. Ibid., p. 270.
188. See Priscilla Roberts (ed.), *Window on the Forbidden City: The Beijing Diaries of David Bruce, 1973–1974*, Hong Kong, 2001, diary entry 6 July 1974; Share, *Where Empires Collided*, p. 191.
189. Chang and Halliday, *Mao: The Unknown Story*, p. 424.
190. Quoted in Chen and Yang, 'Chinese Politics and the Collapse of the Sino-Soviet Alliance', in Westad (ed.), *Brothers in Arms*, p. 292 n.129.
191. Quoted in Yang, *Mao Zedong yu Mosike*, p. 395.
192. Chang and Halliday, *Mao: The Unknown Story*, p. 429.
193. Ibid.
194. Jersild, *The Sino-Soviet Alliance*, p. 145.
195. Professor Chen Jian, talk at University of Hong Kong, 17 January 2011.
196. Alexei Brezhnev, *Kitai: ternisty put' k dobrososedstvu*, Moscow, 1998, p. 40.
197. Taubman, 'Khrushchev vs. Mao', *CWIHP Bulletin*, issues 8–9, 1996–7, pp. 243–8.
198. Yang, *Mao Zedong yu Mosike*, p. 437; Pantsov with Levine, *Deng Xiaoping*, p. 193.
199. Diaries of film director Mikhail Romm quoted in Pantsov with Levine, *Mao: The Real Story*, p. 459.
200. Li Zhisui, *The Private Life of Chairman Mao*, p. 221.
201. Chang and Halliday, *Mao: The Unknown Story*, p. 430; Zubok, 'Look What Chaos in the Beautiful Socialist Camp!', *CWIHP Bulletin*, issue 10, 1998, pp. 152–62.
202. Pantsov with Levine, *Mao: The Real Story*, p. 468.
203. Taylor, *The Generalissimo's Son*, p. 215.
204. Ibid., p. 219.
205. Ibid., p. 221.
206. For the foregoing see Share, *Where Empires Collided*, pp. 195–8, 202; Tubilewicz, 'Taiwan and the Soviet Union During the Cold War', *Cold War History*, vol. 5, issue 1, February 2005, pp. 75–86.
207. Salisbury, *To Peking – and Beyond*, p. 9.
208. Ibid., pp. 9–10.
209. Snow, *Red Star over China*, p. 580.
210. Quoted in Khrushchev, *Khrushchev Remembers: The Last Testament*, p. 280.
211. See Du and Wang (eds), *Zai Sulian zhangda de*, pp. 117–20; Dittmer, *Liu Shaoqi*, p. 91. Yunbin's return to Beijing was witnessed by the Soviet scientific adviser Mikhail Klochko, who travelled out on the same plane on 8 January 1958. See Klochko, *Soviet Scientist in Red China*, pp. 24–5.
212. Goncharov, Lewis and Xue, *Uncertain Partners*, p. 224.
213. Yahuda, *China's Role*, pp. 106, 171.
214. Lüthi, *The Sino-Soviet Split*, p. 103.
215. Quoted in A. Brezhnev, *Kitai: ternisty put'*, p. 65; Chang and Halliday, *Mao: The Unknown Story*, p. 463.
216. Pantsov with Levine, *Mao: The Real Story*, p. 463.
217. Quoted in Molotov, ed. Resis, *Molotov Remembers*, pp. 16–17.
218. Georgi Arbatov quoted in Lukin, *The Bear Watches the Dragon*, p. 124.
219. Quoted in Khrushchev, *Khrushchev Remembers: The Last Testament*, p. 278.

220. Quoted in ibid., p. 525.
221. Quoted in ibid., p. 276.
222. Taubman, 'Khrushchev vs. Mao', *CWIHP Bulletin*, issues 8–9, 1996–7, pp. 243–8. See also Shen Zhihua in Shen Zhihua (ed.), *A Short History*, p. 222.
223. Sergei Khrushchev (ed.), *Memoirs of Nikita Khrushchev: Volume 3: Statesman, 1953–1964*, Philadelphia, PA, 2007, p. 468.
224. Lüthi, *The Sino-Soviet Split*, p. 149.
225. Taubman, 'Khrushchev vs. Mao', *CWIHP Bulletin*, issues 8–9, 1996–7, pp. 243–8; Shen Zhihua in Shen Zhihua (ed.), *Zhong Su guanxi*, p. 265.
226. Shen Zhihua in Shen Zhihua (ed.), *Zhong Su guanxi*, p. 265.
227. Clubb, *China and Russia*, pp. 486–7.
228. Galenovich, *Pyatdesyat let s Kitaem*, p. 43; Chen and Yang, 'Chinese Politics and the Collapse of the Sino-Soviet Alliance', in Westad (ed.), *Brothers in Arms*, p. 274.
229. Goldstein, 'Nationalism and Internationalism', in Robinson and Shambaugh (eds), *Chinese Foreign Policy*, p. 247; Taubman, 'Khrushchev vs. Mao', *CWIHP Bulletin*, issues 8–9, 1996–7, pp. 243–8.
230. Rittenberg quoted in M.A. Aldrich, *The Search for a Vanishing Beijing: A Guide to China's Capital through the Ages*, Hong Kong, 2006, p. 71.
231. Chen and Yang, 'Chinese Politics', in Westad (ed.), *Brothers in Arms*, p. 274.
232. Shen Zhihua in Shen Zhihua (ed.), *A Short History*, p. 222.
233. Suslov remarks quoted in Vladislav Zubok (ed.), 'A New "Cult of Personality": Suslov's Secret Report on Mao, Khrushchev, and Sino-Soviet Tensions', *CWIHP Bulletin*, issues 8–9, 1996–7, pp. 244–8.
234. Clubb, *China and Russia*, p. 443.
235. Khrushchev had already used this epithet to describe Mao on his return flight from Peking to Vladivostok, 4 October 1959 (see Lüthi, *The Sino-Soviet Split*, p. 149). The phrase is usually rendered politely in English as 'old boot' or 'old pair of shoes': see however Martin Page and David Burg, *Unpersoned: The Fall of Nikita Sergeyevich Khrushchev*, London, 1966, p. 19.
236. Borisov and Koloskov, *Soviet–Chinese Relations*, pp. 180–1.
237. Pantsov with Levine, *Mao: The Real Story*, p. 474; Westad in Westad (ed.), *Brothers in Arms*, p. 25; Chang and Halliday, *Mao: The Unknown Story*, p. 484.
238. Clubb, *China and Russia*, p. 406.
239. Chang and Halliday, *Mao: The Unknown Story*, p. 484.
240. Quoted in Khrushchev, *Khrushchev Remembers*, p. 514.
241. Taubman, 'Khrushchev vs Mao', *CWIHP Bulletin*, issues 8–9, 1996–7, pp. 243–8; A. Brezhnev, *Kitai: ternisty put'*, p. 67; Lüthi, *The Sino-Soviet Split*, p. 176.
242. Klochko, *Soviet Scientist in Red China*, p. 120.
243. Ibid., p. 174.
244. Ibid., pp. 172, 190.
245. Salisbury, *To Peking – and Beyond*, p. 97.
246. Klochko, *Soviet Scientist in Red China*, p. 179.
247. Ibid., p. 156.
248. Ibid., p. 165.
249. Ibid., p. 169.
250. Conversation with the late Professor Roderick MacFarquhar.
251. Yang, *Mao Zedong yu Mosike*, p. 462.

CHAPTER 7: CONFRONTATION

1. Lüthi, *The Sino-Soviet Split*, p. 191.
2. Yang, *Mao Zedong yu Mosike*, p. 469.
3. Ibid.; Lüthi, *The Sino-Soviet Split*, p. 190.

4. Yu. M. Galenovich, *Gibel' Liu Shaoqi*, Moscow, 2000, p. 130.
5. Quoted in Li Danhui, 'Zhong Su fenqi gongkaihua yu duanzhan de huanhe', in Shen Zhihua (ed.), *Zhong Su guanxi*, p. 333.
6. Ibid., p. 323; Clubb, *China and Russia*, pp. 448–9.
7. Galenovich, *Pyatdesyat let s Kitaem*, p. 78.
8. Lüthi, *The Sino-Soviet Split*, p. 206; see also Pantsov with Levine, *Mao: The Real Story*, p. 226.
9. Li Danhui, 'Zhong Su fenqi', in Shen Zhihua (ed.), *Zhong Su guanxi*, p. 338.
10. Oral tradition.
11. Lescot, *Before Mao*, p. 306.
12. Ibid.
13. Li Danhui, 'Zhong Su fenqi', in Shen Zhihua (ed.), *Zhong Su guanxi*, p. 317. See also Lüthi, *The Sino-Soviet Split*, p. 222.
14. Li Danhui, 'Zhong Su fenqi', in Shen Zhihua (ed.), *Zhong Su guanxi*, p. 356.
15. See V.N. Usov, 'Kang Sheng, China's Beria', *Far Eastern Affairs*, no. 6, 1991, pp. 184–92.
16. Zubok, 'Look What Chaos in the Beautiful Socialist Camp!", *CWIHP Bulletin*, issue 10, 1998, pp. 152–62.
17. 'Meeting of the Delegations of the Communist Party of the Soviet Union and the Chinese Communist Party, Moscow, 5–20 July 1963', 8 July 1963, History and Public Policy Program Digital Archive, SAPMO Barch JIV 2/207 698, pp. 187–330 (in Russian). Obtained by Vladislav Zubok and translated by Benjamin Aldrich-Moodie. http://digitalarchive.wilsoncenter.org/document/111237, p. 9, 13 July, accessed 29 August 2022.
18. *Peking Review*, 13 September 1963, quoted in Radchenko, *Two Suns*, p. 73.
19. Yahuda, *China's Role*, p. 152.
20. Borisov and Koloskov, *Soviet–Chinese Relations*, p. 248.
21. Khrushchev, *Khrushchev Remembers: The Last Testament*, p. 264; Borisov and Koloskov, *Soviet–Chinese Relations*, pp. 228–9.
22. AVPRF 100-53-457-24.
23. Yahuda, *China's Role*, p. 152.
24. Shifman, 'Tolstoi i Kitai', section 10, *Lev Tolstoi i Vostok*.
25. Borisov and Koloskov, *Soviet–Chinese Relations*, pp. 280–1.
26. A. Brezhnev, *Kitai: ternisty put'*, p. 85; Lüthi, *The Sino-Soviet Split*, p. 238.
27. Goldstein, 'Nationalism and Internationalism', in Robinson and Shambaugh (eds), *Chinese Foreign Policy*, p. 247.
28. Page and Burg, *Unpersoned*, p. 32; Kapitsa, *Na raznykh parallelyakh*, p. 70.
29. Li Danhui, 'Zhong Su fenqi', in Shen Zhihua (ed.), *Zhong Su guanxi*, p. 372; Lüthi, *The Sino-Soviet Split*, p. 261.
30. Pantsov with Levine, *Mao: The Real Story*, p. 536. See also Lukin, *The Bear Watches the Dragon*, pp. 127–8.
31. Borisov and Koloskov, *Soviet–Chinese Relations*, p. 230.
32. Quoted in Radchenko, *Two Suns*, p. 96.
33. George Moseley, *A Sino-Soviet Cultural Frontier: The Ili Kazakh Autonomous Chou*, Cambridge, MA, 1966, p. 110.
34. Sergey Radchenko, 'Mongolian Evidence on China's Border Policies, 1962', paper delivered at University of Hong Kong conference, February 2012.
35. Clubb, *China and Russia*, p. 458.
36. Kapitsa, *Na raznykh parallelyakh*, p. 74.
37. See e.g. Li Danhui, 'Zhong Su fenqi', in Shen Zhihua (ed.), *Zhong Su guanxi*, p. 395; Galenovich, *Pyatdesyat let s Kitaem*, p. 119; Clubb, *China and Russia*, pp. 497–8; Westad, *Restless Empire*, p. 345.
38. Quoted in Goncharov and Li Danhui, 'On "Territorial Claims" and "Inequitable Treaties"', *Far Eastern Affairs*, no. 3, 2004, pp. 94–110.
39. Khrushchev, *Khrushchev Remembers*, p. 474.
40. Clubb, *China and Russia*, p. 498.

41. Page and Burg, *Unpersoned*, p. 80.
42. Ibid., p. 46.
43. Oleg Troyanovsky, *Cherez gody i rasstoyaniya*, Moscow, 1997, p. 349; Radchenko, *Two Suns*, p. 131.
44. Khrushchev, *Khrushchev Remembers*, p. 405.
45. Chang and Halliday, *Mao: The Unknown Story*, p. 510. An alternative account of this evening is given by the former Soviet diplomats Alexei Brezhnev (no relation) and Yuri Galenovich who went with Chervonenko to bear the news of Khrushchev's resignation to the CCP leadership. According to A. Brezhnev the two men were received not by Mao personally but by Wu Xiuquan, the CCP Central Committee member de facto in charge of liaison with foreign Communist Parties; though both accounts agree that the Soviet embassy car suffered a breakdown. According to A. Brezhnev, Mao had in fact appeared some days earlier, at a farewell dinner for V.V. Grishin, a candidate member of the Soviet Praesidium, who had been attending the PRC's fifteenth anniversary festivities. The Chairman had adopted much the same attitude described by Chang and Halliday, pronouncing a general benediction while evading specifics. See A. Brezhnev, *Kitai: ternisty pyt'*, pp. 88–9; Galenovich, *Pyatdesyat let s Kitaem*, p. 139.
46. Georgi Arbatov, *The System: An Insider's Life in Soviet Politics*, New York, 1992, p. 114; Kapitsa, *Na raznykh parallelyakh*, pp. 75–6. The wording of Malinovsky's proposal varies slightly in the many different accounts of this incident. Some accounts suggest that Malinovsky addressed himself directly to Zhou; others that he first addressed his remarks to his Chinese counterpart, Marshal He Long.
47. Troyanovsky, *Cherez gody*, p. 356; Arbatov, *The System*, p. 114; Galenovich, *Pyatdesyat let s Kitaem*, p. 141; Radchenko, *Two Suns*, p. 133.
48. Li Danhui, 'Zhong Su fenqi', in Shen Zhihua (ed.), *Zhong Su guanxi*, p. 403.
49. Ibid., p. 405. See also Lüthi, *The Sino-Soviet Split*, p. 291; Arbatov, *The System*, pp. 114–15.
50. Zhou Xiaopei, *Zhong E, Zhong Su guanxi qin liji*, Beijing, 2010, p. 38; Pantsov with Levine, *Mao: The Real Story*, p. 537.
51. Chang and Halliday, *Mao: The Unknown Story*, p. 511.
52. Lukin, *The Bear Watches the Dragon*, p. 148. See also Arbatov, *The System*, p. 115; Elizabeth Wishnick, *Mending Fences*, pp. 11–12; Radchenko, *Two Suns*, p. 140; Pantsov with Levine, *Mao: The Real Story*, p. 537.
53. A. Alexandrov-Agentov quoted in Pantsov with Levine, *Mao: The Real Story*, p. 537.
54. Radchenko, *Two Suns*, p. 158.
55. Yu. M. Galenovich, 'Chzhu Lao Tszuy (k 120-letiyu so dnya rozhdeniya "Starogo Glavkoma Chzhu De")', *Problemy Dal'nego Vostoka*, no. 6, 2006, pp. 96–100.
56. A. Brezhnev quoted in Lüthi, *The Sino-Soviet Split*, p. 326.
57. Galenovich, *Gibel' Liu Shaoqi*, p. 131; Chang and Halliday, *Mao: The Unknown Story*, p. 529.
58. Yahuda, *China's Role*, p. 165.
59. Kapitsa, *Na raznykh parallelyakh*, p. 76.
60. Lüthi, *The Sino-Soviet Split*, p. 298; A. Brezhnev, *Kitai: ternisty put'*, p. 126; Pantsov with Levine, *Mao: The Real Story*, p. 499.
61. Pantsov with Levine, *Mao: The Real Story*, p. 497.
62. Chang and Halliday, *Mao: The Unknown Story*, pp. 528–9; Pantsov with Levine, *Deng Xiaoping*, p. 245.
63. See Chang and Halliday, *Mao: The Unknown Story*, p. 528; Jin Qiu, *The Culture of Power: The Lin Biao Incident in the Cultural Revolution*, Stanford, CA, 1999, pp. 57–8.
64. Radchenko, *Two Suns*, p. 175. See Frank Dikötter, *The Cultural Revolution: A People's History, 1962–1976*, London, 2017, pp. 49–50.
65. Chang and Halliday, *Mao: The Unknown Story*, p. 512.
66. Dikötter, *The Cultural Revolution*, p. 180.
67. MacMillan, *Seize the Hour*, p. 29.

68. Du and Wang, *Zai Sulian zhangda de*, pp. 127–8, 130.
69. Dittmer, *Liu Shaoqi*, p. 91.
70. Pantsov with Levine, *Deng Xiaoping*, p. 260.
71. Ibid., p. 261.
72. Ibid., p. 269.
73. Galenovich, *Pyatdesyat let s Kitaem*, pp. 167–8; Radchenko, *Two Suns*, p. 178.
74. Yu. M. Galenovich, *Istoria vzaimootnoshenii Rossii i Kitaya*, Book III, part 2, Moscow, 2011, p. 69; *Pyatdesyat let s Kitaem*, p. 172.
75. A. Brezhnev, *Kitai: ternisty put'*, p. 168.
76. Fr Dionisy Pozdnyaev, 'Istoriya pravoslavnoi Pravoslavnoi Tserkvi v Sintszyane', in Tikhvinsky et al., *Istoriya*, pp. 373–4.
77. Tess Johnston and Deke Erh, *For God and Country: Western Religious Architecture in Old China*, Hong Kong, 1996, p. 17; N.E. Ablova, 'Iz istorii Russkoi Pravoslavnoi Tserkvi v Manchzhurii (k voprosu o periodizatsii)', *Kitaisky Blagovestnik*, 1, 2001, pp. 30–1.
78. RGASPI 495-225-30.
79. See Patrick Tyler, *A Great Wall: Six Presidents and China: An Investigative History*, 2nd edn, New York, 2000, p. 48.
80. Christian F. Ostermann, 'East German Documents on the Sino-Soviet Border Conflict 1969', *CWIHP Bulletin*, issues 6–7, winter 1995–6, pp. 186–93; Tyler, *A Great Wall*, pp. 57–8.
81. Tyler, *A Great Wall*, p. 60.
82. Yang, *Mao Zedong yu Mosike*, pp. 505, 507; Dikötter, *The Cultural Revolution*, p. 207.
83. Information provided by Professor Arne Westad.
84. Yang, *Mao Zedong yu Mosike*, p. 511.
85. Tyler, *A Great Wall*, pp. 71–2.
86. Westad, *Restless Empire*, p. 362.
87. Ibid.
88. Li Zhisui, *The Private Life of Chairman Mao*, p. 514.
89. Ibid. See also p. 566.
90. Ostermann, 'East German Documents'; Wishnick, *Mending Fences*, p. 39.
91. Tyler, *A Great Wall*, p. 67.
92. Mark O'Neill, *SCMP*, 12 May 2010.
93. See Galenovich, *Pyatdesyat let s Kitaem*, pp. 212–13; Zhou Xiaopei, *Zhong E, Zhong Su*, p. 11.
94. Galenovich, *Pyatdesyat let s Kitaem*, p. 226.
95. Ibid., p. 234; Kapitsa, *Na raznykh parallelyakh*, p. 83.
96. Quoted in Kapitsa, *Na raznykh parallelyakh*, p. 90.
97. Ibid., p. 91.
98. Salisbury, *The Coming War between Russia and China*, p. 188; Quested, *Sino-Russian Relations*, p. 139.
99. Herbert J. Ellison, 'Soviet-Chinese Relations: The Experience of Two Decades', in Robert S. Ross (ed.), *China, The United States and the Soviet Union: Tripolarity and Policy Making in the Cold War*, London and New York, 1993 p. 94.
100. For the foregoing see Louis article in the *Washington Post*, 20 March 1969; Taylor, *The Generalissimo's Son*, pp. 287–9; Lukin, *The Bear Watches the Dragon*, p. 294; Share, *Where Empires Collided*, pp. 208–12.
101. Galenovich, *Pyatdesyat let s Kitaem*, p. 245.
102. Ibid.
103. Ibid., p. 257.
104. Drew Middleton, *The Duel of the Giants: China and Russia in Asia*, New York, 1978, p. 173.
105. Robert Gardner minute, 16 December 1969, FO 21/483.
106. George Walden minute, 4 November 1969, FO 21/483.
107. Galenovich, *Pyatdesyat let s Kitaem*, p. 277.

108. Pantsov with Levine, *Deng Xiaoping*, p. 266.
109. Document of CCP Central Committee, 18 September 1971, cited in Michael Y.M. Kau (ed.), *The Lin Piao Affair: Power Politics and Military Coup*, New York, 1975, p. 69.

The question naturally arises whether the Kremlin can possibly have had any involvement in the murky affair of Lin Biao. We know that Lin had a long history of contact with the Soviet Union in the earlier stages of his career. He was in Moscow for medical treatment throughout the entire period 1937–41, and again for a few months in 1951. He worked closely with Soviet officials in Manchuria during the civil war years of 1945–9. In spite of his subsequent Russophobe posture he is said by one source to have been regarded by Brezhnev as a 'healthy force' within the CCP; and one veteran scholar of Sino-Russian relations states that 'apparently' he had maintained some kind of covert contact with the Soviet Union as a kind of insurance policy. An outline of the plot by Lin Liguo and his fellow officers to topple the Chairman seems to have assumed that their coup would receive the backing of unidentified Soviet forces and the subsequent protection of the Soviet nuclear umbrella. When news of the plane crash in the MPR reached the Kremlin a team of Soviet officers were at once dispatched to the Mongolian crash site with Lin Biao's dental records with a view to identifying his corpse, and the heads of both Lin and his wife Ye Qun were severed and flown back to Moscow for forensic examination. One writer has published, without supporting evidence, a theory according to which a mole run inside the Kremlin bureaucracy by Mossad, the Israeli secret service, uncovered a Soviet scheme to help Lin seize power; the mole passed on this information to the Israeli government, which in turn relayed it to Dr Kissinger, who used it to win the goodwill of the Chairman and the rest of the Maoist leadership by tipping off Zhou Enlai during his secret visit to Peking in July 1971. (See Aldrich, *The Search for a Vanishing Beijing*, p. 129.) But here we seem to be straying on to the territory of an airport blockbuster novel.

As against all this we have the assertion of Mikhail Kapitsa of the Soviet Foreign Ministry that he and his colleagues were horrified at the thought they might have had Lin Biao on their hands, both because they saw Lin as a prominent enemy of their country and because they didn't want to antagonise Mao even more than they had done already by giving shelter to a major defector from his regime. The assumption by Lin Liguo and his confrères of Soviet support for their anti-Mao coup was very likely just that – an assumption, based on nothing more substantial than their far-fetched projects for liquidating the Chairman on his train; while the Soviet rush to inspect Lin Biao's remains, far from reflecting complicity in an abortive plot, could just as well be interpreted as further proof of the hunger for knowledge of Chinese affairs which CPSU officials exhibited so desperately at this very time. Still, it is possible that there may turn out to be a little bit more to the Lin affair than has yet come to light. During a foray into the Russian Foreign Ministry archives in 2013 I was given access to a series of year-by-year files for the Sino-Soviet relationship in the 1970s – with the notable exception of the file for 1971. Perhaps some future researcher will uncover the reason for this. Truth is the daughter of Time.

110. Henry Kissinger, *White House Years*, London, 2011, p. 1061; Tyler, *A Great Wall*, p. 131.
111. MacMillan, *Seize the Hour*, p. 196.
112. Ibid.
113. Ibid., p. 77.
114. Kissinger, *White House Years*, pp. 1058, 1059; MacMillan, *Seize the Hour*, p. 77.
115. Salisbury, *To Peking – and Beyond*, p. 17.
116. Ibid.
117. Tyler, *A Great Wall*, p. 121.
118. Henry Kissinger, *Years of Upheaval*, New York, 2011, p. 67; MacMillan, *Seize the Hour*, p. 314; Tyler, *A Great Wall*, p. 151.
119. Tyler, *A Great Wall*, p. 217.
120. Chang and Halliday, *Mao: The Unknown Story*, p. 611.

121. Roberts (ed.), *Window on the Forbidden City: Diaries of David Bruce*, 20 July 1973.
122. James Murray minute, 8 December 1969, FO 21/483.
123. Qian Qichen, *Ten Episodes*, p. 165.
124. Salisbury, *To Peking – and Beyond*, p. 11.
125. Ibid., p. 242.
126. Ibid.
127. Galenovich, *Pyatdesyat let s Kitaem*, p. 321.
128. Wishnick, *Mending Fences*, p. 30.
129. New Zealand embassy in Peking to Wellington, 25 November 1975, relayed in Australian Department of Foreign Affairs, file no. 250/10/4/3, part no. 22, p. 332, Confidential ANZED no. 762. I am grateful to Professor Priscilla Roberts for drawing this document to my attention.
130. Ibid.
131. Arkady N. Shevchenko, *Breaking with Moscow*, New York, 1985, p. 33.
132. Personally observed by me during a stint at the Nanyang University Language Centre in 1973–4.
133. MacMillan, *Seize the Hour*, p. 282.
134. Tyler, *A Great Wall*, p. 145.
135. Galenovich, *Gibel' Liu Shaoqi*, p. 30.
136. Shevchenko, *Breaking with Moscow*, pp. 167–8.
137. Joke relayed to my father, C.P. Snow, during a visit to Moscow, early 1970s.
138. Ibid.
139. Quoted in Yahuda, *China's Role*, p. 226. See also Salisbury, *The Coming War between Russia and China*, p. 35, and *To Peking – and Beyond*, pp. 240–1.
140. Alexander Solzhenitsyn, *Letter to the Soviet Leaders*, London, 1974.
141. Bezzubtsev-Kondakov and Drokanov, *Nado li Rossii boyatsya Kitaya?*, p. 48.
142. Remark addressed to myself and friends during visit to Khabarovsk, August 1971. The journalist in question was Alexander Kolesnikov.
143. Lukin, *The Bear Watches the Dragon*, p. 141; Bezzubtsev-Kondakov and Drokanov, *Nado li Rossii boyatsya Kitaya?*, pp. 37–9.
144. Qin Wenhai, *Zhong E keji hezuo zhanlüe yu duice*, Heilongjiang, 2007, p. 4.
145. Galenovich, *Pyatdesyat let s Kitaem*, p. 257.
146. Quoted in Middleton, *The Duel of the Giants*, p. 14.
147. AVPRF 100-66-289-10.
148. Galenovich, *Pyatdesyat let s Kitaem*, p. 333.
149. Statement made both to President Jimmy Carter and to former secretary of state Dr Henry Kissinger, Washington DC, 29 January 1979.
150. Cradock, Peking report to Foreign and Commonwealth Office, London, FCO 21/1696.
151. Galenovich, *Pyatdesyat let s Kitaem*, p. 294; Zhou Xiaopei, *Zhong Su, Zhong E*, p. 39.
152. Galenovich, *Gibel' Liu Shaoqi*, p. 119 and *Pyatdesyat let s Kitaem*, p. 326.
153. Pantsov with Levine, *Deng Xiaoping*, p. 371.
154. Ibid., p. 373.
155. Gamsa, *The Reading of Russian Literature*, pp. 56–7.
156. Middleton, *The Duel of the Giants*, p. 14.
157. Phrase heard by my father in the late 1970s. Brezhnev was reported as calling Deng an 'anti-Soviet dwarf'.
158. Tyler, *A Great Wall*, p. 280.
159. Galenovich, *Pyatdesyat let s Kitaem*, p. 298.
160. Quoted in Philip Short, *The Dragon and the Bear: Inside China and Russia Today*, London, 1982, p. 484.
161. Mikhail Gorbachev, *Memoirs*, London, 1997, p. 181. See also Wishnick, *Mending Fences*, p. 77; Tyler, *A Great Wall*, p. 331; Lukin, *The Bear Watches the Dragon*, p. 149.
162. Wishnick, *Mending Fences*, p. 74.
163. Lukin, *The Bear Watches the Dragon*, p. 145.

164. Qian Qichen, *Ten Episodes*, p. 16; see also Zhou Xiaopei, *Zhong E, Zhong Su*, p. 44.
165. Qian Qichen, *Ten Episodes*, p. 16; see also Zhou Xiaopei, *Zhong E, Zhong Su*, p. 44.
166. Qian Qichen, *Ten Episodes*, p. 16.
167. Troyanovsky, *Cherez gody*, p. 346; Lukin, *The Bear Watches the Dragon*, p. 151.
168. Quoted in Sergey Radchenko, *Unwanted Visionaries: The Soviet Failure in Asia at the End of the Cold War*, New York, 2014, p. 152.
169. Quoted by *New World Encyclopedia* contributors, 'Mikhail Gorbachev', https://www.newworldencyclopedia.org/p/index.php?title=Mikhail_Gorbachev&oldid=1065099, accessed 30 August 2022. An article in the *New York Times*, 18 May 1989, quotes Gorbachev as also saying on his visit to the Great Wall that the Great Wall between the Soviet Union and China had now come down.
170. Troyanovsky, *Cherez gody*, p. 364; Radchenko, *Unwanted Visionaries*, p. 166.
171. Gorbachev, *Memoirs*, p. 631.
172. Kassymzhomart Tokaev, *Meeting the Challenge: Memoirs by Kazakhstan's Foreign Minister*, Singapore, 2004, p. 58.
173. Troyanovsky, *Cherez gody*, p. 348. See also Lüthi, *The Sino-Soviet Split*, p. 1.
174. Radchenko, *Unwanted Visionaries*, p. 182.
175. Lukin, *The Bear Watches the Dragon*, p. 154; Roy Medvedev, 'Kitai i raspad SSSR', in *Problemy Dal'nego Vostoka*, no. 1, 2011, pp. 166–75.
176. Goldstein, 'Nationalism and Internationalism', in Robinson and Shambaugh (eds), *Chinese Foreign Policy*, p. 259.
177. Gorbachev, *Memoirs*, p. 633.
178. Yu. M. Galenovich, *Istoriya*, Book III, part 2, Moscow, 2011, p. 324.
179. Goldstein, 'Nationalism and Internationalism", in Robinson and Shambaugh (eds), *Chinese Foreign Policy*, p. 260.
180. Ibid.
181. Ibid., p. 259.
182. Radchenko, *Unwanted Visionaries*, p. 184.
183. Goldstein, 'Nationalism and Internationalism', in Robinson and Shambaugh (eds), *Chinese Foreign Policy*, p. 264; Radchenko, *Unwanted Visionaries*, pp. 185–6.
184. See e.g. *The Economist*, 22 October 2011, review of Ezra Vogel, *Deng Xiaoping and the Transformation of China*; Pantsov with Levine, *Deng Xiaoping*, p. 534 n.1; Radchenko, *Unwanted Visionaries*, pp. 186–7.

CHAPTER 8: EQUILIBRIUM RESTORED?

1. Quoted in Alexander Lukin, *China and Russia: The New Rapprochement*, Cambridge, 2018, p. 73.
2. Lukin, *The Bear Watches the Dragon*, p. 301.
3. Ibid., pp. 269–71. See also Michael Share, *Where Empires Collided*, p. 220; Yu. M. Galenovich, *Istoriya*, Book IV, Moscow, 2011, pp. 39–42.
4. Lukin, *China and Russia*, p. 73.
5. Schimmelpenninck van der Oye, *Russian Orientalism*, p. 3.
6. Zhao Huasheng, 'Zhong E guanxi de moshi', in Guan and Luan (eds), *Zhong E guanxi*, p. 49; Wishnick, *Mending Fences*, pp. 123–4.
7. *The Economist*, 26 April 1997; Lukin, *The Bear Watches the Dragon*, p. 304; Wishnick, *Mending Fences*, p. 154.
8. Schimmelpenninck van der Oye, *Russian Orientalism*, p. 238.
9. Lukin, *The Bear Watches the Dragon*, p. 302 and *China and Russia*, p. 154.
10. Andrei Dikarev, Institute of Oriental Studies, Moscow, quoted in *Sunday MP*, 8 June 2003.
11. Lukin, *China and Russia*, p. 45.
12. Bezzubstev-Kondakov and Drokanov, *Nado li Rossii boyatsya Kitaya?*, p. 94.
13. *SCMP*, 24 July 1998.

14. See Peter Conradi, *Who Lost Russia?*, London, 2017, p. 101.
15. Ibid., pp. 89–90.
16. Formally established September 1994. See Wishnick, *Mending Fences*, p. 126.
17. Ibid., pp. 128–9.
18. Reported in *SCMP*, 11 November 1997.
19. Galenovich, *Istoriya*, Book IV, p. 197.
20. Ibid., p. 219.
21. Galenovich, *Istoriya*, Book IV, pp. 27, 32–3.
22. Quoted in Wishnick, *Mending Fences*, p. 257 n.6.
23. Ellison, 'Soviet–China Relations', in Ross (ed.), *China, the United States and the Soviet Union*, p. 117.
24. Galenovich, *Istoriya*, Book IV, pp. 145–50.
25. Information supplied by Professor John Dolfin, June 1996.
26. Episode recorded by Zhou Xiaopei in *Zhong E, Zhong Su*, p. 101.
27. *The Economist*, 26 April 1997.
28. *SCMP*, 12 December 1999. See also Bobo Lo, *Axis of Convenience: Moscow, Beijing, and the New Geopolitics*, London, 2008, pp. 253–4.
29. Galenovich, *Istoriya*, Book IV, pp. 237–40.
30. Ibid., p. 238.
31. David Pilling in the *Financial Times*, 13 September 2012.
32. Lo, *Axis of Convenience*, p. 39.
33. *SCMP*, 7 November 2007.
34. *SCMP*, 25 November 2008.
35. Wishnick, *Mending Fences*, p. 139.
36. Ibid., p. 138.
37. *SCMP*, 7 July 2005 and 18 August 2005.
38. *The Economist*, 1 May 2004.
39. Quoted in Lo, *Axis of Convenience*, p. 132.
40. Information provided by Professor Arne Westad.
41. *SCMP*, 6 February 2014.
42. Quoted in *SCMP*, 20 January 2014.
43. *Financial Times*, 5 March 2018.
44. *The Economist*, 27 July 2019.
45. Bobo Lo and Fiona Hill, 'Putin's Pivot: Why Russia is Looking East', Brookings Institution, 31 July 2013, https://www.brookings.edu/opinions/putins-pivot-why-russia-is-looking-east/, accessed 29 August 2022. See also Lukin, *China and Russia*, pp. 55–6.
46. *The Economist*, 24 May 2014.
47. *Financial Times*, 22 May 2014.
48. Marc Julienne, European Council on Foreign Relations, *China Analysis*, October 2016.
49. *Financial Times*, 12 August 2013; *SCMP*, 26 January 2018.
50. *Financial Times*, 20 May 2014.
51. Final plenary session of the sixteenth meeting of the Valdai International Discussion Club, 3 October 2019, http://en.kremlin.ru/events/president/news/61719, accessed 30 August 2022.
52. *SCMP*, 4 November 2002.
53. *SCMP*, 17 October 2004.
54. *SCMP*, 13 March 2005.
55. *SCMP*, 28 September 2010.
56. *SCMP*, 30 December 2020.
57. Quoted in *SCMP*, 20 March 2021.
58. *Nikkei Asia*, 3 March 2022.
59. Ibid.
60. *SettimanaNews*, 13 May 2022.
61. *Nikkei Asia*, 3 March and 17 March 2022.

62. *SCMP*, 23 June 2022.
63. *SCMP*, 16 June 2022; BBC News, 21 June 2022.
64. *SCMP*, 21 October 2014.
65. BBC News, 26 June 2021.
66. A. Brezhnev, *Kitai: ternisty put'*, Preface.
67. *SCMP*, 2 December 2005.
68. *International Herald Tribune*, 3 March 2008.
69. *Financial Times*, 30 March 2022.
70. Frank Ching in *SCMP*, 20 October 2009.
71. See for example the *Astana Times*, 9 December 2019.
72. *The Economist*, 27 July 2019.
73. Quoted in Lukin, *The Bear Watches the Dragon*, p. 175.
74. *SCMP*, 28 June and 6 July 2005.
75. *International Herald Tribune*, 3 March 2008.
76. Ibid.
77. *The Economist*, 27 July 2019.
78. Lukin, *The Bear Watches the Dragon*, p. 305 and *China and Russia*, p. 77.
79. Professor Leopold Leontiev quoted in *SCMP*, 11 October 2006.
80. Quoted in *SCMP*, 25 March 2010.
81. Lukin, *China and Russia*, p. 168. The RATS headquarters was initially established in Beijing but was subsequently moved to Tashkent.
82. Reported by Charles A. Kupchan, 'The Right Way to Split China and Russia', *Foreign Affairs*, 4 August 2021.
83. An idea already current in the early 2000s. For a more recent recurrence see TASS, 26 October 2016, https://tass.com/society/908875, accessed 30 August 2022. This report observed: 'The number of unemployed people in China is more than the entire Russian population.'
84. Joke relayed by Ms Irina Ustyugova, Russian teacher and artist living in Hong Kong.
85. Lukin, *The Bear Watches the Dragon*, p. 170.
86. *SCMP*, 6 October 2005; Lo, *Axis of Convenience*, p. 59.
87. Galenovich, *Istoriya*, Book IV, pp. 401–2.
88. Ibid., p. 401.
89. Lukin, *The Bear Watches the Dragon*, p. 181.
90. Ivanov statement 18 October 2002.
91. *SCMP*, 12 December 2002.
92. *SCMP*, 13 April 2005.
93. For the foregoing see Lukin, *China and Russia*, pp. 162–5.
94. See Dominic Ziegler, *Black Dragon River: A Journey Down the Amur River between Russia and China*, New York, 2015, p. 258; Colin Thubron, *The Amur River: Between Russia and China*, London, 2021, p. 139.
95. Quoted in *Sunday Morning Post*, Hong Kong, 4 November 2007.
96. Lukin, *The Bear Watches the Dragon*, pp. 200–1.
97. *SCMP*, 24 August 2001.
98. *SCMP*, 24 July 1999.
99. *SCMP*, 12 March 2002.
100. Chinese analysis quoted in Galenovich, *Istoriya*, Book IV, p. 399. See also *Financial Times*, 22 March 2006.
101. *SCMP*, 4 December 2002.
102. *SCMP*, 9, 16 and 24 September 2004.
103. Thubron, *The Amur River*, pp. 121–2, 129.
104. Ziegler, *Black Dragon River*, p. 258.
105. *Financial Times*, 6 June 2014.
106. Quoted in Lukin, *China and Russia*, p. 54.
107. Ibid., p. 171.

108. *SCMP*, 3 March 2020.
109. *China Daily*, 14 November 2011.
110. Andrea Kendall-Taylor and David Shullman, 'China and Russia's Dangerous Convergence: How to Counter an Emerging Partnership', *Foreign Affairs*, 3 May 2021.
111. Kupchan, 'The Right Way to Split China and Russia', *Foreign Affairs*, 4 August 2021.
112. *SCMP*, 11 and 30 June 2022.
113. Danish foreign minister, Jeppe Kofod, in *SCMP*, 14 May 2022; Tom Plate in *SCMP*, 14 June 2022.
114. BBC News, 7 July 2022.
115. Kupchan, 'The Right Way to Split China and Russia', *Foreign Affairs*, 4 August 2021.
116. Kissinger interview with the *Financial Times*, 9 May 2022.
117. Sir Stephen Lovegrove, speech at Center for Strategic and International Studies, Washington DC, 27 July 2022.

SELECT BIBLIOGRAPHY

PRIMARY SOURCES

Archives

Arkhiv Vneshney Politiki Rossiiskoi Federatsii, Moscow (AVPRF)
Rossiisky Gosudarstvenny Arkhiv Sotsialno-politicheskoi Istorii, Moscow (RGASPI)
Waijiaobu dang'anguan, Beijing
Shanghai shi dang'anguan
The National Archives of the United Kingdom
– Foreign Office records (FO)
– Foreign and Commonwealth Office records (FCO)

Correspondence, diaries, memoirs, records of meetings and speeches, and published documents

Arbatov, Georgi, *The System: An Insider's Life in Soviet Politics*, Times Books, New York, 1992

Baddeley, John F., *Russia, Mongolia, China: Being Some Record of the Relations between them from the Beginning of the XVIIth Century to the Death of the Tsar Alexei Mikhailovich, 1602–1676*, Macmillan and Co. Ltd, London, 1919

Badmaev, P.A., *Rossiya i Kitai: voprosy o politico-ekonomicheskom vliyanii*, URSS, Moscow, 2011

Bell, John, of Antermony, *A Journey from St Petersburg to Pekin, 1719–22*, Edinburgh University Press, Edinburgh, 1965

Blagodatov, A.V., 'With the Chinese Revolution', in Chudodeev (ed.), *Soviet Volunteers in China*

Brand, Adam, *A Journal of the Embassy from Their Majesties John and Peter Alexeievits, Emperors of Muscovy &c., Over Land into China through Siberia, Dauria and the Great Tartary to Peking, the capital city of the Chinese Empire, by Everard Isbrand, their Ambassador in the years 1693, 1694 and 1695*, London, 1698

Braun, Otto (Li De), *A Comintern Agent in China, 1932–1939*, C. Hurst & Co., London, 1982

Brezhnev, Alexei, *Kitai: ternisty put' k dobrososedstvu: vospominaniya i razmyshleniya*, Mezhdunarodnye Otnosheniya, Moscow, 1998

Bruce, David, 'Beijing Diaries', in Priscilla Roberts (ed.), *Window on the Forbidden City: The Beijing Diaries of David Bruce, 1973–1974*, Centre of Asian Studies, University of Hong Kong, Hong Kong, 2001

Chen Yuan-tsung, *Return to the Middle Kingdom: One Family, Three Revolutionaries and the Birth of Modern China*, Union Square Press, New York, 2008
Cherepanov, A.I., 'Under Sun Yat-sen's Banner', in Chudodeev (ed.), *Soviet Volunteers in China*
Chiang Kai-shek, *Soviet Russia in China: A Summing-Up at Seventy*, Farrar, Straus and Cudahy, New York, 1957
Chiang Kai-shek, *Diaries*, vols 1 and 2 (extracts ed. Zhang Xiuzhang), Tuanjie chubanshe, Beijing, 2007
Chinese Repository, The, Canton, vols III–XX, 1834–51
Chudodeev, Y.V. (ed.), *Soviet Volunteers in China, 1925–1945*, Progress Publishers, Moscow, 1980
Chuikov, Vasilii I., *Mission to China: Memoirs of a Soviet Military Adviser to Chiang Kai-shek*, EastBridge, Norwalk, CT, 2004
Colquhoun, A.R., *The 'Overland' to China*, Harper and Brothers, London, 1900
Ehrenburg, Ilya, *Lyudi, gody, zhizn'*, in Romanenko (ed.), *Kitai u russkikh pisatelei*
Fedorenko, Nikolai, 'The Stalin–Mao summit in Moscow', *Far Eastern Affairs*, no. 2, 1989
Fleming, Peter, *News from Tartary*, Jonathan Cape, London, 1936, repr. 1995
Franck, Harry A., *Wandering in Northern China*, The Century Co., New York and London, 1923
Fu Lo-shu, *A Documentary Chronicle of Sino-Western Relations*, University of Arizona Press, Tucson, 1966
Galenovich, Yu. M., *Pyatdesyat let s Kitaem*, Vagrius, Moscow, 2011
Galin, B.A., '*Krepkaya zavyaz*" in Romanenko (ed.), *Kitai u russkikh pisatelei*
Gorbachev, Mikhail, *Memoirs*, Bantam Books, London, 1997
Goshkevich, Iosif Antonovich, 'Hong Kong: From the Notes of a Russian Traveller', *Journal of the Hong Kong Branch of the Royal Asiatic Society*, vol. 38 (1998–9)
Haney, Jack V., with Forrester, Sibelan (eds), *The Russian Garland: Being Russian Folk Tales*, New York, 1916. *The Complete Folktales of A. N. Afanas'ev*, vol. 3, University Press of Mississippi, Jackson, MS, 2021, accessed via Project Muse and Google Books
He Qiutao (ed.), *Shuofang beicheng*, Peking, 1881
Ipatova, A.S., 'Archimandrite Polycarp's Letters', *Far Eastern Affairs*, no. 3, 1991
Kalyagin, A.Y., 'Along Unfamiliar Roads', in Chudodeev (ed.), *Soviet Volunteers in China*
Kapitsa, M.S., *Na raznykh parallelyakh: zapiski diplomata*, Kniga i Biznes, Moscow 1996
Kazanin, M.I., 'At Blücher's Headquarters' in Chudodeev (ed.), *Soviet Volunteers in China*
Khrushchev, Nikita, trans. and ed. Strobe Talbott, *Khrushchev Remembers*, André Deutsch, London and Little, Brown & Co., Boston, MA, 1971
Khrushchev, Nikita, trans. and ed. Strobe Talbott, *Khrushchev Remembers: The Last Testament*, André Deutsch, London and Little, Brown & Co., Boston, MA, 1974
Klochko, Mikhail A., *Soviet Scientist in Red China*, F. Praeger, New York, 1964
Krushinsky, Andrei, letter to mother, September 1957, in Krushinsky, 'Kartiny na "chistom liste" ili, Bolshoi Skachok glazami ochevidtsa' part 1, *Problemy Dal'nego Vostoka*, no. 5, 2008
——, *Diaries*, 17 March 1958, in Krushinsky, 'Kartiny na "chistom liste" ili, Bolshoi Skachok glazami ochevidtsa' part 1, *Problemy Dal'nego Vostoka*, no. 5, 2008
Kryzhanovsky, V. (ed.), Palladius-Muraviev correspondence, *Russki Arkhiv*, no. 8, Moscow, 1914
Lange, Laurence de (Lorents Lange), *Journal of the Residence of Mr. de Lange, Agent of his Imperial Majesty of all the Russias, Peter the First, at the Court of Pekin, during the Years 1721 and 1722; Translated from the French*, in John Bell, *Travels from St. Petersburg in Russia, to Various Parts of Asia, in 1716, 1719, 1722, &c*, in John Pinkerton (ed.), *A General Collection of the Best and Most Interesting Voyages and Travels in all Parts of the World; many of which are now first translated into English; digested on a new plan*, London, 1811
Li Zhisui, *The Private Life of Chairman Mao*, Arrow Books, London, 1996

Lo Hui-min (ed.), *The Correspondence of G.E. Morrison, 1895–1912*, Cambridge University Press, Cambridge, 1976

Lu Xun, *Selected Works*, vols III and IV, Foreign Languages Press, Beijing, 1980

Maisky, Ivan, *The Maisky Diaries: The Wartime Revelations of Stalin's Ambassador in London*, Yale University Press, New Haven, CT, and London, 2015, paperback edn 2016

Mao Zedong, *Selected Works*, vol. V, Foreign Languages Press, Beijing, 1977

'Meeting of the Delegations of the Communist Party of the Soviet Union and the Chinese Communist Party, Moscow, 5–20 July 1963', 8 July 1963, History and Public Policy Program Digital Archive, SAPMO Barch JIV 2/207 698, pp. 187–330 (in Russian). Obtained by Vladislav Zubok and translated by Benjamin Aldrich-Moodie, https://digitalarchive.wilsoncenter.org/document/111237

Milescu, Nikolai Gavrilovich, *Sibir i Kitai*, Kartya Moldovenyaske, Chisinau, 1960

Molotov, Vyacheslav, ed. Albert Resis, Ivan R. Dee, *Molotov Remembers: Inside Kremlin Politics, Conversations with Felix Chuev*, Ivan R. Dee, Chicago, 1993

Myasnikov, V.S. (ed.), *Russko-kitaiskie dogovorno-pravovye akty (1689–1916)*, Pamyatniki Istoricheskoi Mysli, Moscow, 2004.

Nikitin, Afanasy, *Khozhdenie za tri morya Afanasiya Nikitina*, Akademiya Nauk SSSR, Moscow, 1958

Ovechkin, Valentin, *V dalekom I po-rodnomu blizkom Kitae*, in Romanenko (ed.), *Kitai u russkikh pisatelei*

Polevoi, Boris, extract from *30,000 li po Kitayu*, in Romanenko (ed.), *Kitai u russkikh pisatelei*

Qian, Qichen, *Ten Episodes in China's Diplomacy*, HarperCollins, New York, 2005

Qingdai Zhong E guanxi dang'an, shiliao xuabian, di san bian, vol. 1, Waijiaobu dang'anguan Zhonghua Shuju, Beijing, 1979

Record of Mao conversation with Ambassador Yudin, 22 July 1958, appended to Westad (ed.), *Brothers in Arms*

Record of Stalin–Mao meeting, 16 December 1949, appended to Westad (ed.), *Brothers in Arms*

Record of Stalin–Mao meeting, 22 January 1950, appended to Westad (ed.), *Brothers in Arms*

Report on Soviet–Chinese relations of M. Zimyanin, Head of Far Eastern Department of Soviet Foreign Ministry, prepared for Khrushchev, 15 September 1959, appended to Westad (ed.), *Brothers in Arms*

Report of Stalin–Zhou meeting, 19 September 1952, appended to Westad (ed.), *Brothers in Arms*

Romanenko, A.D. (ed.), *Kitai u russkikh pisatelei*, Algoritm, Moscow, 2008

Seaman, Louis Livingston, *From Tokyo through Manchuria with the Japanese*, D. Appleton & Co., New York, 1904

Sebes, Joseph, SJ, in *The Jesuits and the Sino-Russian Treaty of Nerchinsk (1689): The Diary of Tomas Pereira, SJ*, Institutum Historicum SI, Rome, 1961

Senkowski, Osip, extract from 'Kitai i kitaitsy', in A.D. Romanenko (ed.), *Kitai u russkikh pisatelei*

Shass, M.Y., 'A Year's Work in Revolutionary China', in Chudodeev (ed.), *Soviet Volunteers in China*

Sheng Yueh, *Sun Yat-sen University in Moscow and the Chinese Revolution: A Personal Account*, University of Kansas, Lawrence, 1971

Shevchenko, Arkady N., *Breaking with Moscow*, Knopf, New York, 1985

Shevelev, Konstantin, 'The Unknown Letters of Song Qingling and Sun Yat-sen to Mikhail Borodin', *Far Eastern Affairs*, no. 2, 2003

Shi Zhe, 'I Accompanied Chairman Mao', *Far Eastern Affairs*, no. 2, 1989

Shi Zhe, *Zai lishi juren shenbian*, Chinese Communist Party Central Party School, Beijing, 1998

Slyusarev, S.V., 'Protecting China's Airspace', in Chudodeev (ed.), *Soviet Volunteers in China*

Solzhenitsyn, Alexander, *Letter to the Soviet Leaders*, Collins, London, 1974

Steele, Robert (ed.), *The Russian Garland of Fairy Tales*, Robert M. McBride & Co., New York, 1916, https://ia802606.us.archive.org/15/items/russiangarlandof00stee/russiangarlandof00stee.pdf, accessed 6 November 2022

Timkovsky, Georgi, ed. Julius von Klaproth, *Travels of the Russian Mission through Mongolia to China and Residence in Peking in the Years 1820–1821*, London, 1827

Titarenko, M.I. (ed.-in-chief), *Perepiski I.V. Stalina i G.V. Chicherina s Polpredom SSSR v Kitae LM Karakhanom, Dokumenty avgust 1923 – 1926*, Natalis, Moscow, 2008

Tokaev, Kassymzhomart, *Meeting the Challenge: Memoirs by Kazakhstan's Foreign Minister*, Diplomatic Mission of Kazakhstan to Singapore, Singapore, 2004

Trotsky, Leon, ed. Les Evans and Russell Bloch, with Introduction by Peng Shu-tse, *Leon Trotsky on China*, Monad Press, New York, 1976

Troyanovsky, Oleg, *Cherez gody i rasstoyaniya*, Vagrius, Moscow, 1997

Tulisen, *Narrative of the Chinese Embassy to the Khan of the Tourgouth Tartars in the Years 1712, 13, 14 & 15*, London, 1821

Vishnyakova-Akimova, Vera Vladimirovna, *Two Years in Revolutionary China, 1926–1927*, Harvard University Press, Cambridge, MA, 1971

Vladimirov, Pyotr, *The Vladimirov Diaries, Yen'an, China, 1942–1945*, Robert Hale, London, 1976

Wang Zhichun, *Wang Zhichun ji*, vol. 2, Huxiang Wenku Editorial and Publishing Committee, Hunan, 2010

Weale, B.L. Putnam, *Manchu and Muscovite, Being Letters from Manchuria Written during the Autumn of 1903*, Macmillan and Co. Ltd, London, 1904

Wilbur, C. Martin, and How, Julie Lien-ying, *Documents on Communism, Nationalism and Soviet Advisers in China: Papers Seized in the 1927 Peking Raid*, Columbia University Press, New York, 1956

Witte, Count Sergei, *The Memoirs of Count Witte*, trans. and ed. Abraham Yarmolinsky, William Heinemann, London, 1921

Zhang Guotao, *The Rise of the Chinese Communist Party*, vols 1 and 2, 1921–27, University of Kansas, Lawrence, 1971, 1972

Zhang Jia'ao (Chang Kia-ngau), ed. Donald G. Gillin and Ramon H. Myers, trans. Dolores Zen, *Last Chance in Manchuria: The Diary of Chang Kia-ngau*, Hoover Institution Press, Stanford, CA, 1989

Zhou Xiaopei, *Zhong E, Zhong Su guanxi qin liji*, Shijie Zhishi Chubanshe, Beijing, 2010

Newspapers and journals

Cold War History, London

Cold War International History Project Bulletin, Woodrow Wilson International Center for Scholars, Washington DC (*CWIHP Bulletin*)

Far Eastern Affairs, Moscow

Financial Times, London

Foreign Affairs, New York

International Herald Tribune, Paris

Istoriya SSSR, Moscow

Journal of Communist Studies and Transition Politics, London

Kitaisky Blagovestnik, Moscow

Nikkei Asia, Tokyo

Novaya i Noveishaya Istoriya, Moscow

Pravoslaviye na Dal'nem Vostoke, Moscow

Problemy Dal'nego Vostoka, Moscow

Problemy Vostokovedeniya, Moscow

SettimanaNews, Bologna

Slavic Review, Urbana, IL.

Slavonic and East European Review, London

South China Morning Post, Hong Kong (*SCMP*)
Sovietskoe Kitaevedeniye, Moscow
Sunday Morning Post, Hong Kong
The Economist, London

SECONDARY SOURCES

Ablova, N.E., 'Iz istorii Russkoi Pravoslavnoi Tserkvi v Manchzhurii (k voprosu o periodizatsii)', *Kitaisky Blagovestnik*, no. 1, 2001

Adoratsky, Nikolai, hieromonk, 'Istoriya Rossiiskoi Dukhovnoi Missii v Kitae v pervy period yego deyatelnosti', in Tikhvinsky et al. (eds), *Istoriya*

Aldrich, M.A., *The Search for a Vanishing Beijing: A Guide to China's Capital through the Ages*, Hong Kong University Press, Hong Kong, 2006

Alexeev, M.P., 'Pushkin i Kitai', in *A.S. Pushkin v Sibirii*, pp. 139–45, Vostsiboblgiz, Moscow and Irkutsk, 1937

Baabar, *History of Mongolia*, The White Horse Press, Cambridge, 1999

Barmin, Valery, 'Xinjiang in the History of Soviet-Chinese relations from 1937 to 1945', *Far Eastern Affairs*, no. 1, January 2000

Barthold, V.V., *La découverte de l'Asie: Histoire de l'Orientalisme en Europe et en Russie*, Payot, Paris, 1947

Bernstein, Thomas P., and Li, Hua-yu (eds), *China Learns from the Soviet Union, 1949–Present*, Lexington Books, Lanham, MD, 2010, accessed at ProQuest Ebook Central

Bezzubtsev-Kondakov, Alexander, and Drokanov, Ilya, *Nado li Rossii boyatsya Kitaya?*, Piter, Moscow and St Petersburg, 2011

Borisov, O.B., and Koloskov, B.T., *Soviet-Chinese Relations, 1945–1970*, Indiana University Press, Bloomington, 1975

Brandt, Conrad, *Stalin's Failure in China, 1924–1927*, Harvard University Press, Cambridge, MA, 1958

Cai Hongsheng, *Cai Hongsheng shixue wenbian*, Guangdong People's Publishing House, Guangzhou, 2014

Cameron, Nigel, *Barbarians and Mandarins: Thirteen Centuries of Western Travellers in China*, Oxford University Press, Hong Kong, 1997

Chang Jung, and Halliday, Jon, *Mao: The Unknown Story*, Jonathan Cape, London, 2005

Chen Hui, 'Maxieer tiaochu shiqi Sulian dui Hua zhengce de yanbian', in Guan and Luan (eds), *Zhong E guanxi*

Chen Jian, 'Comparing Russian and Chinese Sources: A New Point of Departure for Cold War History', *CWIHP Bulletin*, issues 6–7, winter 1995–6

Chen Jian and Yang Kuisong, 'Chinese Politics and the Collapse of the Sino-Soviet Alliance', in Westad (ed.), *Brothers in Arms*

Chen Kaike, 'Eluosi guan yu Taiping Tianguo shiqi Sha E de dui Hua waijiao', in Guan and Luan (eds), *Zhong E guanxi*

Cheng Chu-yuan, *Economic Relations between Peking and Moscow*, 1949–63, Frederick A. Praeger, New York and London, 1964

Chernolutskaya, Elena, 'The Expulsion of Chinese Nationals from the Soviet Far East and their Deportation in 1938', *Far Eastern Affairs*, no. 3, 2008

Christie, Dugald, *Thirty Years in Moukden* 1883–1913, Constable & Co., London, 1914

Clubb, O. Edmund, *China and Russia: The Great Game*, Columbia University Press, New York and London, 1971

Conradi, Peter, *Who Lost Russia?*, Oneworld Publications, London, 2017

Coox, Alvin D., *Nomonhan: Japan against Russia, 1939*, Stanford University Press, Stanford, CA, 1985

Datsyshen, V.G., *Istoriya Rossiiskoi Dukhovnoi Missii v Kitae*, Brotherhood of Saints Peter and Paul, Hong Kong, 2010

Demidova, N.F., and Myasnikov, V.S., *Pervye russkie diplomaty v Kitae*, Nauka, Moscow, 1966

Dikötter, Frank, *Mao's Great Famine*, Bloomsbury, London, 2010
——, *The Tragedy of Liberation: A History of the Chinese Revolution, 1945–57*, Bloomsbury, London, 2013
Dittmer, Lowell, *Liu Shaoqi and the Chinese Cultural Revolution*, M.E. Sharpe, New York and London, 1998
Du, Weihua and Wang Yiqiu (eds), *Zai Sulian zhangda de hongse houdai*, Shijie Zhishi Chubanshe, Beijing, 1999
Ellison, Herbert J., 'Soviet–Chinese Relations: The Experience of Two Decades', in Ross (ed.), *China, The United States and the Soviet Union*
Evans, Richard, *Deng Xiaoping and the Making of Modern China*, Penguin, London, 1995
Figes, Orlando, *A People's Tragedy*, Penguin, London, 1998
——, *Natasha's Dance*, Penguin, London, 2002
Fleming, Peter, *The Siege at Peking*, Rupert Hart-Davis, London, 1959
Fokkema, Douwe W., 'Lu Xun: The Impact of Russian Literature', in Goldman (ed.), *Modern Chinese Literature in the May Fourth Era*
Foust, Clifford M., *Muscovite and Mandarin: Russia's Trade with China and Its Setting, 1727–1805*, University of North Carolina Press, Chapel Hill, 1969
Galenovich, Yu. M., *Gibel' Liu Shaotsi*, Vostochnaya Literatura/Russian Academy of Sciences, Moscow, 2000
——, 'Chzhu Lao Tszuy (k 120-letiyu so dnya rozhdeniya "Starogo Glavkoma Chzhu De")', *Problemy Dal'nego Vostoka*, no. 6, 2006
——, *Istoriya vzaimootnoshenii Rossii i Kitaya*, Books III and IV, Russkaya Panorama, Moscow, 2011
Galperin, A.L., 'Russko-kitaiskaya torgovlya v XVIII – pervoi polovine XIX veka', *Problemy Vostokovedeniya*, no. 5, 1955
Gamsa, Mark, 'California on the Amur: The Zheltuga Republic in Manchuria (1883–1886)', *The Slavonic and East European Review*, April 2003
——, *The Chinese Translation of Russian Literature: Three Studies*, Brill, Leiden and Boston, MA, 2008
——, *The Reading of Russian Literature in China: A Moral Example and a Manual of Practice*, Palgrave Macmillan, New York, 2010
Gittings, John, *The World and China, 1922–1972*, Eyre Methuen, London, 1974
Goldman, Merle (ed.), *Modern Chinese Literature in the May Fourth Era*, Harvard University Press, Cambridge, MA, 1977
Goldstein, Steven M., 'Nationalism and Internationalism: Sino-Soviet Relations', in Robinson and Shambaugh (eds), *Chinese Foreign Policy*
Goncharov, Sergei, Lewis, John W., and Xue Litai, *Uncertain Partners: Stalin, Mao and the Korean War*, Stanford University Press, Stanford, CA, 1993
Goncharov, S., and Li Danhui, 'On "Territorial Claims" and "Inequitable Treaties" in Russian-Chinese Relations: Myth and Reality', *Far Eastern Affairs*, no. 3, 2004
Goncharov, Sergei, 'Sino-Soviet Military Cooperation', in Westad (ed.), *Brothers in Arms*
Grigoriev, A.M., 'Joseph Stalin's Unpublished Speech on China', *Far Eastern Affairs*, no. 1, 2001
Guan Guihai and Luan Jinghe (eds), *Zhong E guanxi lishi yu xianshi*, Social Sciences Academic Press (China), Beijing, 2009
He Donghui, 'Coming of Age in the Brave New World: The Changing Reception of *How the Steel was Tempered* in the People's Republic of China', in Bernstein and Li (eds), *China Learns from the Soviet Union*
Hess, Christian A., 'From Colonial Jewel to Socialist Metropolis, Dalian, 1895–1955', dissertation, University of California, San Diego, 2006
Hopkirk, Peter, *The Great Game: On Secret Service in High Asia*, Oxford University Press, Oxford, 1991, reissued 2001

Hsia, T.A., 'Demons in Paradise: The Chinese Image of Russia', in *Annals of the American Academy of Political and Social Science*, 345, September 1963
Hsü, Immanuel C.Y., 'Russia's Special Position in China During the Early Qing Period', *Slavic Review*, vol. 23, December 1964
——, *The Ili Crisis: A Study of Sino-Russian Diplomacy, 1871–1881*, Clarendon Press, Oxford, 1965
Huang Dingtian in *Zhong E wenhua guanxi chugao (17 shiji – 1937)*, Changchun Chubanshe, Changchun, 2011
Ipatova, A.S.,'Rossiiskaya Dukhovnaya Missiya v Kitae: vek dvadtsaty', in Tikhvinsky et al. (eds), *Istoriya*
Ivanov, P.M., 'Pravoslavnye missionerskie stany v Kitae v nachale XX veka', in Tikhvinsky et al. (eds), *Istoriya*
Jacobs, Dan N., *Borodin: Stalin's Man in China*, Harvard University Press, Cambridge, MA, 1981
Jersild, Austin T., 'Soviet Bloc Komandirovka and its Consequences in China, 1950–1960', paper delivered at University of Hong Kong conference, 'Mao's China, Non-Communist Asia, and the Global Setting, 1949–1976', February 2012
——, *The Sino-Soviet Alliance: An International History*, University of North Carolina Press, Chapel Hill, 2014
Jiang Yongjing (Chiang Yung-ching), *Baoluoding yu Wuhan zhengquan*, Zhongguo xueshu zhuzuo jiangzhu weiyuanhui, Taipei, 1963
Jin Qiu, *The Culture of Power: The Lin Biao Incident in the Cultural Revolution*, Stanford University Press, Stanford, CA, 1999
Johnston, Tess, and Erh, Deke, *For God and Country: Western Religious Architecture in Old China*, Old China Hand Press, Hong Kong, 1996
Kaple, Deborah A., 'Soviet Advisers in China in the 1950s', in Westad (ed.), *Brothers in Arms*
Kapustin, Dmitri, 'Hong Kong: The First Port of Chekhov's Foreign Journey', *Far Eastern Affairs*, no. 3, 2009
Kartunova, A.I., 'Blücher in China', in Yu.V. Chudodeev (ed.), *Soviet Volunteers in China*
——, 'K zaversheniyu izdanii serii sbornikov dokumentov, "VKP (B) Komintern i Kitai", 1920–mai 1943 gg', *Problemy Dal'nego Vostoka*, no. 1, 2008
——, review article, 'Politichesky obraz Sun Yat-sena v perepiske I.V. Stalina I G.V. Chicherina s L.M. Karakhanom (1923–1926gg.)', *Problemy Dal'nego Vostoka*, no. 1, 2010
Kau, Michael Y.M. (ed.), *The Lin Piao Affair: Power Politics and Military Coup*, International Arts and Sciences Press, New York, 1975
Kendall-Taylor, Andrea, and Shullman, David, 'China and Russia's Dangerous Convergence: How to Counter an Emerging Partnership', *Foreign Affairs*, 3 May 2021
Kissinger, Henry, *On China*, Penguin, New York and London, 2011
——, *White House Years*, Simon & Schuster, London, 2011
——, *Years of Upheaval*, Simon & Schuster, New York, 2011
Korovyakovsky, Pyotr, 'Chinese Victims of Stalinist Repression', *Far Eastern Affairs*, no. 3, 1991
Kovalenko, Anna, 'Rol' kazachestva v ukreplenii granitsy Rossii s Mongoliei i Kitaem v XVIII-pervoi polovine XIX vv', *Problemy Dal'nego Vostoka*, no. 3, 2009
Kramer, Mark, 'The USSR Foreign Ministry's Appraisal of Sino-Soviet Relations on the Eve of the Split, September 1959', *CWIHP Bulletin*, issues 6–7, winter 1995–6
Kupchan, Charles A., 'The Right Way to Split China and Russia', *Foreign Affairs*, 4 August 2021
Kuznetsov, V.S., 'Kitai glazami russkikh pisatelei', *Problemy Dal'nego Vostoka*, no. 5, 2010
Larin, A.G., *Kitaitsy v Rossii*, Institut Dal'nego Vostoka, Moscow, 2000
Ledovsky, A.M., 'Stalin i Chan Kaishi: sekretnaya missiya syna Chan Kaishi v Moskvu, dekabr 1945–yanvar 1946', *Novaya i Noveishaya Istoriya*, no. 4, 1996
——, 'The Moscow Visit of a Delegation of the CCP in June–August 1945', *Far Eastern Affairs*, no. 4, 1996

——, 'Two Letters from Correspondence between Mao Zedong and Joseph Stalin', *Far Eastern Affairs*, no. 6, 2000

Lee, Leo Ou-fan, 'Genesis of a Writer: Notes on Lu Xun's Educational Experience, 1891–1909', in Goldman (ed.), *Modern Chinese Literature in the May Fourth Era*

Lescot, Patrick, *Before Mao: The Untold Story of Li Lisan and the Creation of Communist China*, Ecco, New York, 2004

Li Danhui, 'Zhong Su fenqi gongkaihua yu duanzhan de huanhe', in Shen (ed.), *Zhong Su guanxi*

Li Hua, '1957 nian Sulian gaoceng zhengbian yu Zhonggong zhongyang de fanying', in Guan and Luan (eds), *Zhong E guanxi*

Li Hua-yu, 'Instilling Stalinism in Chinese Party Members: Absorbing Stalin's *Short Course* in the 1950s', in Bernstein and Li (eds), *China Learns from the Soviet Union*

Li Sheng, 'Sulian yu Xinjiang San Qu geming', in Guan and Luan (eds), *Zhong E guanxi*

Lin Jun, 'Yue Fei yu Huangpu junxiao: Su E dui Zhongguo Guomindang zhengce neimu', in Guan and Luan (eds), *Zhong E guanxi*

Litvintsev, Gennady, of Voronezh, 'Manchzhurskaya Atlantida: vospominanya russkogo repatrianta', in *Rossiiskaya Gazeta – Dal'ny Vostok*, no. 3537, 29 July 2004

Liu Dexi, 'Shijiu shiji zhongye yiqian de Zhong E guanxi', in Guan and Luan (eds), *Zhong E guanxi*

Lo, Bobo, *Axis of Convenience: Moscow, Beijing, and the New Geopolitics*, Royal Institute of International Affairs (Chatham House), London, 2008

Lo, Bobo, and Hill, Fiona, *Putin's Pivot: Why Russia Is Looking East*, Brookings Institution, Washington DC, 2013

Luan Jinghe, (ed.), *History and Reality of Sino-Russian Relations*, Henan University Press, Henan, 1991

Luan Jinghe, 'Jindai yilai Eluosi dui Hua zhengce shulun', in Guan and Luan (eds), *Zhong E guanxi*

Lukin, Alexander, *The Bear Watches the Dragon: Russia's Perceptions of China and the Evolution of Russian-Chinese Relations Since the Eighteenth Century*, M.E. Sharpe Inc., New York, 2003

——, *China and Russia: The New Rapprochement*, Polity Press, Cambridge, 2018

Lundstrom, Oleg, oral reminiscences, 'Big Band from Harbin', in 'China', special issue of *Ekspert* magazine, 17 June 2000

Lüthi, Lorenz, *The Sino-Soviet Split*, Princeton University Press, Princeton, NJ, 2008

Luzyanin, S.G., and Mirovitskaya, R.A., 'SSSR i Kitai (1931–1939)', in V.V. Naumkin (ed.), *SSSR i strany vostoka nakanune i v gody vtoroi mirovoi voiny*, IV, RAN, Moscow, 2010

MacMillan, Margaret, *Seize the Hour: When Nixon Met Mao*, John Murray, London, 2006

Madariaga, Isabel de, *Catherine the Great: A Short History*, Yale University Press, New Haven, CT, and London, 2002

Maggs, Barbara Widenor, *Russia and 'le rêve chinois': China in Eighteenth-century Russian Literature*, Voltaire Foundation in association with Liverpool University Press, Oxford, 1984

Mancall, Mark, *Russia and China: Their Diplomatic Relations to 1728*, Harvard University Press, Cambridge, MA, 1971

McGuire, Elizabeth, 'Between Revolutions: Chinese Students in Soviet Institutes, 1948–1966', in Bernstein and Li (eds), *China Learns from the Soviet Union*

——, *Red at Heart: How Chinese Communists Fell in Love with the Russian Revolution*, Oxford University Press, Oxford, 2020

Medvedev, Roy, 'Kitai i raspad SSSR', *Problemy Dal'nego Vostoka*, no. 1, 2011

Melnikov, Yuri, 'Russian Fascists in Manchuria', *Far Eastern Affairs*, no. 4, 1991

Meyer, Michael, *In Manchuria*, Bloomsbury Press, New York and London, 2015

Miao Pusheng, Ma Pinyan and Li Sheng (eds), *Lishishang de Xinjiang*, Xinjiang Renmin Chubanshe, Xinjiang, 2006

Middleton, Drew, *The Duel of the Giants: China and Russia in Asia*, Charles Scribner's Sons, New York, 1978

Millward, James A., *Eurasian Crossroads: A History of Xinjiang*, C. Hurst & Co., London, 2007

Mirovitskaya, R.A., *Kitaiskaya gosudarstvennost' i sovietskaya politika v Kitae, gody tikhookean-skoi voiny, 1941–1945*, Pamiatniki Istoricheskoi Mysli, Moscow, 1999

Mirovitskaya, R.A., and Ledovsky, A.M., 'The Soviet Union and the Chinese Province of Xinjiang in the mid-1930s', *Far Eastern Affairs*, no. 4, 2007

Mitter, Rana, *China's War with Japan 1933–1945: The Struggle for Survival*, Penguin, London, 2014

Montefiore, Simon Sebag, *Stalin: The Court of the Red Tsar*, Phoenix, London, 2004

Mori Kazuko, 'A Brief Analysis of the Sino-Soviet Alliance: The Political Process of 1957–1959', Parallel History Project on NATO and the Warsaw Pact: The Cold War History of Sino-Soviet Relations, June 2005

Moseley, George, *A Sino-Soviet Cultural Frontier: The Ili Kazakh Autonomous Chou*, Harvard University Press, Cambridge, MA, 1966

Myasnikov, V.S., *The Ch'ing Empire and the Russian State in the Seventeenth Century*, Progress Publishers, Moscow, 1985

Novgorodskaya, Natalia, 'A Chinese Envoy to Russia', *Far Eastern Affairs*, no. 5, 1991

Oglechneva, E., 'Russky yazyk vostochnogo zarubezhya b pervoi polovine XX v.; k voprosu o sboeobrazii', *Problemy Dal'nego Vostoka*, no. 6, 2008

O'Neill, Mark, *From the Tsar's Railway to the Red Army: The Experience of Chinese Labourers in Russia During the First World War and Bolshevik Revolution*, Penguin Group, Australia in association with Penguin Beijing, 2014

Ostermann, Christian F., 'East German Documents on the Sino-Soviet Border Conflict 1969', *CWIHP Bulletin*, issues 6–7, winter 1995–6

Page, Martin, and Burg, David, *Unpersoned: The Fall of Nikita Sergeyevich Khrushchev*, Chapman & Hall, London, 1966

Palmer, James, *The Bloody White Baron*, Faber & Faber, London, 2008

Paludan, Ann, *Chronicle of the Chinese Emperors*, Thames & Hudson, London, 2004

Pantsov, Alexander V., with Levine, Steven I., *Mao: The Real Story*, Simon & Schuster, New York, 2012

——, *Deng Xiaoping: A Revolutionary Life*, Oxford University Press, Oxford, 2015

Perdue, Peter C., *China Marches West: The Qing Conquest of Central Eurasia*, Harvard University Press, Cambridge, MA, 2005

Pleshakov, Constantine, 'Nikita Khrushchev and Sino-Soviet Relations', in Westad (ed.), *Brothers in Arms*

Price, Don C., *Russia and the Roots of the Chinese Revolution, 1896–1911*, Harvard University Press, Cambridge, MA, 1974

Popov, Igor, *Rossiya i Kitai: 300 let na grani voiny*, Yermak Astrel, Moscow, 2004

Pozdnyaev, Fr Dionisy, 'Istoriya Pravoslavnoi Tserkvi v Sintszyane', in Tikhvinsky et al. (eds), *Istoriya*

——, 'Skazanie o muchenikakh kitaiskoi pravoslavnoi tserkvi, postradavshikh v Pekine v 1900 g', *Kitaisky Blagovestnik*, no. 1, 2000

Qin, Wenhai, *Zhong E keji hezuo zhanlüe yu duice*, Heilongjiang Daxue Chubanshe, Heilongjiang, 2007

Quested, R.K.I., *The Expansion of Russia in East Asia, 1857–1860*, University of Malaya Press, Kuala Lumpur and Singapore, 1968

——, *'Matey' Imperialists?: The Tsarist Russians in Manchuria, 1895–1917*, University of Hong Kong, Centre of Asian Studies, Hong Kong, 1982

——, *Sino-Russian Relations: A Short History*, George Allen & Unwin, Sydney, 1984

Quested, Rosemary, *The Russo-Chinese Bank*, University of Birmingham, 1977

Radchenko, Sergey, *Two Suns in the Heavens*, Woodrow Wilson Center Press, Washington DC and Stanford University Press, Stanford, CA, 2009

——, 'Mongolian Evidence on China's Border Policies, 1962', paper delivered at University of Hong Kong conference, 'Mao's China, Non-Communist Asia, and the Global Setting, 1949–1976', February 2012

——, *Unwanted Visionaries: The Soviet Failure in Asia at the End of the Cold War*, Oxford University Press, New York, 2014

Robinson, Thomas W., and Shambaugh, David (eds), *Chinese Foreign Policy: Theory and Practice*, Clarendon Press, Oxford, 1994

Romanov, B.A., *Russia in Manchuria (1892–1906)*, J.W. Edwards, Ann Arbor, MI, 1952

Ross, Robert S. (ed.), *China, The United States and the Soviet Union: Tripolarity and Policy Making in the Cold War*, M.E. Sharpe, London and New York, 1993

Rossabi, Morris, *China and Inner Asia: From 1368 to the Present Day*, Thames & Hudson, London, 1975

Salisbury, Harrison E., *The Coming War between Russia and China*, W.W. Norton & Co., New York, 1969

——, *To Peking – and Beyond: A Report on the New Asia*, Quadrangle Books/The New York Times Book Co., New York, 1973

Samoilov, Nikolai, 'Little Known Facts about Russian–Chinese Relations: Visit of the Mission of the Qing Empire to St Petersburg in 1870', *Far Eastern Affairs*, no. 1, 2009

Schimmelpenninck van der Oye, David, *Russian Orientalism: Asia in the Russian Mind from Peter the Great to the Emigration*, Yale University Press, New Haven, CT, and London, 2010

Senkowski, Osip, extract from 'Kitai i kitaitsy', in A.D. Romanenko (ed.), *Kitai u russkikh pisatelei*, Algoritm, Moscow, 2008

Sergeant, Harriet, *Shanghai*, John Murray, London, 2002

Share, Michael, *Where Empires Collided: Russian and Soviet Relations with Hong Kong, Taiwan and Macao*, Chinese University Press, Hong Kong, 2007

Shatalov, O.V., 'Arkhimandrit Pyotr (P.I. Kamensky)- nachalnik 10oi Russkoi Dukhovnoi Missii v Pekine', *Pravoslaviye na Dal'nem Vostoke*, vypusk 3, University of St Petersburg, 2001

Shen Zhihua (ed.), *Zhong Su guanxi shigang, 1917–1991*, Social Sciences Academic Press (China), Shanghai, 2016; reproduced as *A Short History of Sino-Soviet Relations, 1917–1991*, Social Sciences Academic Press (China) and Palgrave Macmillan with Springer Nature, Singapore, 2020

Shifman, A.I., *Lev Tolstoi i Vostok*, Nauka, Moscow, 1971

Short, Philip, *The Dragon and the Bear: Inside China and Russia Today*, Hodder and Stoughton, London, 1982

Sizova, Alexandra, 'Russkie konsulstva v Mongolii v rossisko-kitaisko-mongolskom politicheskom vzaimodeistvii nachala XXv', *Problemy Dal'nego Vostoka*, no. 6, 2009

Skachkov, P.E., 'Russkie vrachi pri Rossiiskoi Dukhovnoi Missii v Pekine', *Sovietskoe Kitaevedeniye*, 4, Moscow, 1958

Skrine, C.P., and Nightingale, Pamela, *Macartney at Kashgar: New Light on British, Chinese and Russian Activities in Sinkiang, 1890–1918*, Oxford University Press, Hong Kong and Oxford, 1987

Skritsky, N.V., *Pervy kavalier ordena svyatogo Andreya Admiral F.A. Golovin (1650–1706): biografichesky ocherk*, Moscow, 1995

Sladkovsky, M.I., *History of Economic Relations between Russia and China*, Israel Program for Scientific Translations, Jerusalem, 1966

——, *Znakomstvo s Kitaem i kitaitsami*, Pamyatniki Istoricheskoi Mysli, Moscow, 2006

Snow, Edgar, *Red Star over China*, Pelican, London, 1972

Snow, Philip, 'Nomonhan: The Unknown Victory', *History Today*, July 1990

Spence, Jonathan, *The Gate of Heavenly Peace: The Chinese and Their Revolution 1895–1980*, Penguin, London, 1982

——, *The Search for Modern China*, W.W. Norton, New York and London, 1990

Stephan, John J., *The Russian Far East: A History*, Stanford University Press, Stanford, CA, 1994

Stiffler, Douglas, '"Three Blows of the Shoulder Pole": Soviet Experts at Chinese People's University, 1950–1957', in Bernstein and Li (eds), *China Learns from the Soviet Union*

Sun Caishun, 'Wai Menggu duli guocheng shuping', in Guan and Luan (eds), *Zhong E guanxi*

Sun Fang, Chen Jinpeng et al., *Eluosi de Zhongguo xingxiang*, Beijing Daxue Chubanshe, Beijing, 2010

Taubman, William, 'Khrushchev vs. Mao: A Preliminary Sketch of the Role of Personality in the Sino-Soviet Split', *CWIHP Bulletin* nos 8–9, 1996–7

Taylor, Jay, *The Generalissimo's Son: Chiang Ching-kuo and the Revolutions in China and Taiwan*, Harvard University Press, Cambridge, MA, 2000

Thubron, Colin, *The Amur River: Between Russia and China*, Chatto & Windus, London, 2021

Tikhvinsky, S.L., et al. (eds), *Istoriya Rossiiskoi Dukhovnoi Missii v Kitae*, Brotherhood of Saint Vladimir, Moscow, 1997

Tikhvinsky, S.L., and Peskova, G.N., 'Vydayushchiisya russky kitaeved o. Iakinf (Bichurin) (k 220-letiyu so dnya rozhdeniya)', in Tikhvinsky et al. (eds), *Istoriya*

Treadgold, Donald, *The West in Russia and China: Volume 2, China 1582–1949*, Westview Press, Boulder, CO, 1985

Tubilewicz, Czeslaw, 'Taiwan and the Soviet Union during the Cold War: Enemies or Ambiguous Friends?', *Cold War History*, vol. 5, issue 1, February 2005

Tyler, Patrick, *A Great Wall: Six Presidents and China: An Investigative History*, 2nd edn, PublicAffairs, New York, 2000

Tyson Li, Laura, *Madame Chiang Kai-shek: China's Eternal First Lady*, Atlantic Monthly Press, New York, 2006

Urbansky, Sören, *Beyond the Steppe Frontier: A History of the Sino-Russian Border*, Princeton University Press, Princeton, NJ, 2020

Usov, V.N., 'Kang Sheng, China's Beria', *Far Eastern Affairs*, no. 6, 1991

——, *Sovietskaya razvedka v Kitae v 20e gody XX veka*, Confucius House, Moscow, 2011

Victoir, Laura, and Zatsepine, Victor (eds), *Harbin to Hanoi: The Colonial Built Environment in Asia, 1840 to 1940*, Hong Kong University Press, Hong Kong, 2013

Vilkov, O.N., 'Kitaiskie tovary na tobolskom rynke', *Istoriya SSSR* 1, January–February 1958

Wang, David D., *Under the Soviet Shadow: The Yining Incident*, Chinese University Press, Hong Kong, 1999

Wang Shicai, 'Qianxi Zhongguo Dongbei yu Eluosi de wenhua jiaoliu', in Guan and Luan (eds), *Zhong E guanxi*

Wang Zhicheng, *Shanghai Eqiao shi*, Shanghai Sanlian, Shanghai, 1993

Westad, Odd Arne, *Cold War and Revolution: Soviet–American Rivalry and the Origins of the Chinese Civil War, 1944–1946*, Columbia University Press, New York, 1993

——, *Decisive Encounters: The Chinese Civil War, 1946–1950*, Stanford University Press, Stanford, CA, 2003

——, *Restless Empire: China and the World since 1750*, The Bodley Head, London, 2012

——, (ed.), *Brothers in Arms: The Rise and Fall of the Sino-Soviet Alliance, 1945–1963*, Woodrow Wilson Press, Washington DC, and Stanford University Press, Stanford, CA, 1998

Whiting, Allen S., and Sheng Shih-ts'ai, *Sinkiang: Pawn or Pivot?*, Michigan State University Press, East Lansing, MI, 1958

Widmer, Ellen M., 'Qu Qiubai and Russian Literature', in Goldman (ed.) *Modern Chinese Literature*

Widmer, Eric, *The Russian Ecclesiastical Mission in Peking during the Eighteenth Century*, Harvard University Press, Cambridge, MA, 1976

Wingrove, Paul, 'Gao Gang and the Moscow Connection: Some Evidence from Russian Sources', *Journal of Communist Studies and Transition Politics*, vol. 16, issue 4, December 2000

Wishnick, Elizabeth, *Mending Fences: The Evolution of Moscow's China Policy from Brezhnev to Yeltsin*, University of Washington Press, Seattle, WA, and London, 2014
Wu Yuxing, 'E chuan shou hang Guangzhou maoyi fengbo zai yanjiu', in Guan and Luan (eds), *Zhong E guanxi*
Xu Wanmin, 'Gengzi Zhong E Dongbei zhi zhan fansilu', in Guan and Luan (eds), *Zhong E guanxi*
Xue Xiantian, 'Nanjing zhengfu de "geming waijiao" yu Sulian dui Dongbei de "chengfa zhanzheng"', in Guan and Luan (eds), *Zhong E guanxi*
Yahuda, Michael B., *China's Role in World Affairs*, Croom Helm, London, 1978
Yanagisawa Akira, 'Some Remarks on the Addendum to the Treaty of Kyakhta in 1768', *Memoirs of the Toyo Bunko*, 69, 2005
Yang Kuisong, *Mao Zedong yu Mosike de enen yuanyuan*, Jiangxi People's Publishing House, Nanchang, 1999
——, 'Sino-Soviet Wartime Cooperation and Conflict', in Shen (ed.), *A Short History of Sino-Soviet Relations, 1917–1991*
Ye Baichuan, *Eguo lai Hua shituan yanjiu (1618–1807)*, Shehui Kexue Wenxian Chubanshe, Beijing, 2010
——, 'Lun Eguo zaoqi dui Hua maoyi zhong tuixing de guanfang maoyi longduan zhengce', in Guan and Luan (eds), *Zhong E guanxi*
Yuan Jizhou, 'Lun Ri E si ci miyue yu Eguo de yuandong zhengce', in Luan (ed.), *History and Reality of Sino-Russian Relations*
Zatsepine, Victor, *Beyond the Amur: Frontier Encounters between China and Russia, 1850–1930*, University of British Columbia Press, Vancouver, 2017
Zhang Baichun and Zhang Jiuchun, 'Zhong Su jishu hezuo de jingyan jiaoxun yu qishi', in Guan and Luan (eds), *Zhong E guanxi*
Zhang Li, 'Eguo Weite yu Yihetuan yundong shiqi dui Hua zhengce', in Guan and Luan (eds), *Zhong E guanxi*
Zhang, Shengfa, 'The Main Causes of the Return of the Changchun Railway to China and its Impact on Sino-Soviet Relations', in Bernstein and Li (eds), *China Learns from the Soviet Union*
Zhang Xuefeng, 'Qingchao chuqi Zhong E jiaowang wenhua zhang'ai de kefu yu Eguo zongjiao chuandaotuan lai Hua', in Guan and Luan (eds), *Zhong E guanxi*
Zhang Zonghai, 'Miuzhong liuchuan de "huang huo" lun – Zhongguo ren zai Eluosi lizu de lishi genyuan', in Guan and Luan (eds), *Zhong E guanxi*
Zhao Huasheng, 'Zhong E guanxi de moshi', in Guan and Luan (eds), *Zhong E guanxi*
Ziegler, Dominic, *Black Dragon River: A Journey Down the Amur River between Russia and China*, Penguin, New York, 2015
Zubok, Vladislav, Commentary on Stalin–Mao meetings in 1949–50, *CWIHP Bulletin*, issues 6–7, winter 1995–6
——, '"Look What Chaos in the Beautiful Socialist Camp!": Deng Xiaoping and the Sino-Soviet Split, 1956–1963', *CWIHP Bulletin*, issue 10, March 1998
——, 'A New "Cult of Personality": Suslov's Secret Report on Mao, Khrushchev, and Sino-Soviet Tensions', *CWIHP Bulletin*, issues 8–9, winter 1996–7

INDEX